Praise for *The Ministry*, by Peter Hartcher

"Filled with fascinating details and explanations that shine a needed light on Pacific Rim economics." —*Publishers Weekly*

"A dazzling mix of statistics, case studies, juicy anecdotes, and analysis . . . key to understanding the recent past and future of Japan's political economy." —*Business Week*

"Peter Hartcher's new book on Japan's Ministry of Finance . . . is essential reading. . . . *The Ministry* is a must-read for all business executives who operate in global markets." —*Electronic Business*

"Hartcher's book couldn't be timelier." —*Industry Week*

"Peter Hartcher has written a fascinating account of the decline and fall of the Ministry of Finance during the years of the bubble economy in the 1980s and the great Japanese deflation of the 1990s. It is a story of Machiavellian political intrigue, incompetence, hubris, and tragedy, all culminating with Japan's most severe economic slump since the 1930s."
—David Hale, global chief economist, Zurich Group

"Hartcher has shone a torch into the dim corners of one of the world's great centres of economic power. . . . The author does not shrink from taking sides on controversial issues. Hartcher's skills as a journalist—his clear prose and eye for the interesting story—make this a good read for all who realize that Japan is important and wish to know more about how it works."
—Ross Garnaut, professor of economics, Australian National University

"By putting Japan's Ministry of Finance under a powerful microscope, Hartcher has removed the mystery surrounding this ancient institution."
—Steve H. Hanke, professor of applied economics, Johns Hopkins University

"Peter Hartcher's new book is timely and to the point. Hartcher says it is actually the Ministry of Finance (MoF) that has masterminded the 'Japan, Inc.' story—and he is right."
—Kenichi Ohmae, management consultant and Chancellor's Professor of Public Policy, University of California at Los Angeles

BUBBLE MAN

BUBBLE MAN ALAN GREENSPAN & THE MISSING 7 TRILLION DOLLARS

PETER HARTCHER

W. W. NORTON & COMPANY
NEW YORK • LONDON

Printed in the United States of America
First Edition

Manufacturing by R.R. Donnelley, Bloomsburg Division
Production manager: Julia Druskin

Library of Congress Cataloging-in-Publication Data
Hartcher, Peter.
Bubble man : Alan Greenspan and the missing 7 trillion dollars / Peter Hartcher.— 1st American ed.
p. cm.
Includes index.
ISBN-13: 978-0-393-06225-0 (hardcover)
ISBN-10: 0-393-06225-2 (hardcover)
1. Speculation—United States—History—20th century. 2. Financial crises—United States—History—20th century. 3. Finance—United States. 4. Monetary policy—United States. 5. Greenspan, Alan, 1926– 6. United States—Economic policy. I. Title.
HG4910.H36 2006
332.1'1092—dc22

2005033128

W. W. Norton & Company, Inc., 500 Fifth Avenue, New York, N.Y. 10110
www.wwnorton.com

W. W. Norton & Company Ltd., Castle House, 75/76 Wells Street, London W1T 3QT

2 3 4 5 6 7 8 9 0

Contents

To Tess, my mother, my teacher

Preface

The boardroom of the austere white-marble Federal Reserve building in Washington DC is where Winston Churchill held councils of war with Franklin Delano Roosevelt to set Allied strategy in World War II. The US Defense Department coveted the building after the war, but it was one fortress that remained impregnable to the military. Today deliberations of war and peace are made elsewhere in that city. But the decisions made in that same room set strategy for another realm of the American imperium, one upon which all others depend.

Now the men and women who meet in that room eight times a year set the price of America's money. Since the US abandoned the gold bullion standard in 1971, its dollar has not been backed by any precious metal but rests on a common faith that the greenback is something more than a piece of paper. Once lost, as we know from a barrowful of cases of hyperinflation and crisis around the world, the faith in a paper currency is desperately difficult to recover.

Preserving a shared myth that bits of coloured paper are stores of value – a kind of trance that the poet Samuel Taylor Coleridge called elsewhere "the willing suspension of disbelief" – depends in large measure on faith in the people who meet in this room. It is a faith as mysterious as any religion. It is no coincidence that the word "credit" stems from the Latin *credere* – to believe.

And, as a monetary system only a little over thirty years old, it may be considered to be still in its experimental phase. It is a system of "fiat" money, so called because its value derives from nothing more than a fiat of government. Historically such systems of paper money have been temporary affairs: there is a "monetary insanity that lurks beneath the surface of fiat money systems", according to the author of the *Encyclopedia of Money*, Professor Larry Allen. One of the fundamental tasks of the Federal Reserve is to keep it there.

The Fed, as it is commonly called, is America's central bank. It is the country's fourth attempt at a central bank, and, founded in 1913, its most enduring. But as if to emphasise the transient nature of monetary arrangements, the walls of its boardroom are decorated with framed specimens of US currency from other eras, all defunct.

It is much harder to preserve the fragile faith in money when the public can see that it is a creation of politicians, those experts in broken promises and profligacy. To combat this, the Federal Reserve, although it was begotten by the US Congress and could be struck down by it at any time, was given independence from politicians in its conduct of monetary policy.

The members of the Federal Reserve are the keepers of the faith, the high priests in what has often been called the inner temple of money. And America's money is the mainstay of the world's money. Most of the US dollars issued by the US, indeed seven out of every ten according to the US Treasury's best guess, are held abroad. This is a sincere vote of international confidence, albeit one cast principally by the world's drug dealers and other criminals, who prefer the extra furtiveness of the international cash economy over the banking system.

Surely a barrelling China and a burgeoning Asia are the driving forces of the world economy in the twenty-first century? Perhaps so, but China, whose economy was slightly smaller than Italy's and only one-seventh the size of America's in 2004, sets its currency's value by pegging it to the US dollar. And when the Federal Reserve acts, Asia responds. If, for instance, the Federal Reserve sets out on a new course of cutting interest rates in America, "Asian markets typically rise on average about 5 per cent in the three months following," reports the investment bank Goldman Sachs. Even when Asia does supply a strong growth impulse, the US remains the dominant economy, the benchmark for the world's money, the vital fount of global liquidity. Or, as Jim Grant of *Grant's Interest Rate Observer* put it, the US dollar is "the Coca-Cola of global monetary brands".

If there is a cockpit of the global economy, it is this room.

In human history, money often has been invested with mystique and even mysticism. The US Federal Reserve has some of each. The Fed's physical presence carries mystical motifs. The design of its headquarters, on Constitution Avenue facing the sane green sward of The Mall, some half-dozen blocks from the White House, is a delight to astrologers. It is in the Beaux-Arts style but shorn of the ostentatious adornment common to that school. The 1937 building is nevertheless adorned with hundreds of discreet symbols related to Virgo, the Mother Goddess, a redeemer and a teacher, and her astrological ruler, Mercury. This messenger of the gods is protector of merchants and thieves alike, both an intellectual and a trickster, a divine manipulator. His head appears on fifteen of the building's window divides, and a marble female version graces the building's north façade. The Fed also hosts two elegant glass lamp rings with the twelve signs of the zodiac etched into them. An astrologer, David Ovason, believes these to be part of a much older pattern of some twenty zodiac motifs in central Washington, crafted by Freemasons covertly establishing a cosmological relationship for the new capital in the late eighteenth century. The zodiacs in the Fed, he suggests, are a discreet twentieth-century continuation of that older pattern.

As for mystique, at the Fed it is a well-developed art form. It has had no better practitioner than its former chairman, the celebrated Alan Greenspan, chief priest at the temple from 1987 to 2006. Like many central bank chiefs around the world, he has cultivated an impenetrable linguistic style for use in public. His first technique is inaccessibility. He has never given a media interview since taking the chairmanship, or at least not since a TV faux pas in 1987. He does give journalists background briefings, where his thoughts may be reported but not directly attributed to him, but these are highly selective and keenly sought. By keeping himself scarce, he raises his value in the market of opinion and influence. His second technique is to create a sense of superiority, not through arrogance or condescension, but by preserving a formal manner and a lofty, abstract style of speech. His third is to convey depth by preserving ambiguity. He draws on obscure vocabulary, circular construction, economic jargon and the heavy use of qualifiers to achieve this. To illustrate this point, an economist, Jeremy Gluck, wrote: "When Alan Greenspan dies his headstone could read: 'I am guardedly optimistic about the next world, but remain cognisant of the downside risk.' "

He quietly rejoices in his oracular aloofness. The former chief of the Securities and Exchange Commission, Arthur Levitt, recalled bumping into him at a party and asking him how he was. Greenspan replied: "I'm not allowed to say."

Stripped of their ecclesiastical mystique and the Latin of their ceremonials, the protective jargon of economics, the sages of the Federal Reserve have a starkly simple mechanism available to them – a single great lever. Their options are few: they can choose to push it up or down or leave it untouched.

That lever is the level of official interest rates. It functions somewhat like an on–off switch of economic growth. When the Federal Reserve cheapens America's dollar by setting official interest rates at low levels, the cost of borrowing money, to spend or to invest, falls. The money flows more freely and the pace of economic activity quickens.

When the Fed decides that the economy is growing too fast, it raises interest rates. Money, now more expensive to borrow, moves more sluggishly. The economy slows. The control of this lever, this switch, is the Federal Reserve's core function and the chief source of its power.

The point of this function? Some countries' central banks have a single task handed to them – to keep inflation in check. Not America's. It has what, in central bank jargon, is called a dual mandate. In the words of its congressional charge, the Fed's job is to manage interest rates "commensurate with the economy's long-run potential to increase production, so as to promote effectively the goals of maximum employment, stable prices, and moderate long-term interest rates".

So beyond keeping the insanity at bay, it has two other tasks. It must keep interest rates so low that the country is running strongly enough to create maximum employment; on the other hand, it can't let growth run so strongly that prices become unstable or long-run interest rates get too high. And it has to do all this with just one lever.

This lever, monetary policy, is, as a former member of the

Fed's inner temple, Laurence Meyer, put it: "The story of how we stand at the helm, with our hands on the big wheel, and navigate through the storm." Or crash into one of the shoals that loom on either side of this narrow passage.

One of the problems with the Fed's lever, or big wheel, however, is that it is slow to take effect. Once the Fed moves official interest rates, it can take anywhere between six months to a year and a half before the ship responds to its wheel and the change flows through into the behaviour of the economy. So the members of the Fed's rate-setting committee, its pivotal body, the Federal Open Market Committee or FOMC, need to be fortune tellers. They are a little like the "precogs" in the Tom Cruise sci-fi thriller *Minority Report*, whose powers of prescience are used by the police to detect and prevent murders before they are committed. The twelve members of this committee need to be able to see recessions and other crises before they crash down upon the American people.

In the movie, the three precogs are kept floating in a pool of fluid to enhance their special powers of seeing the future. Alan Greenspan developed the habit of soaking in the bath in the morning while absorbing reams of reports and statistics. This may be thought to have enhanced the great man's special powers as a monetary seer, but, despite the appeal of the myth, was actually designed to ease the chronic pain in his back. He is human, after all.

Yet, despite that limitation, quite often it happens that Greenspan and the other members of the Federal Open Market Committee are allowed a startlingly vivid glimpse of the future.

As the committee convened for one of its secret sessions around the vast mahogany and granite table in the Fed's boardroom at nine o'clock on the morning of September 24, 1996, some of its members had a clear and panoramic view of what was to come. The US stockmarket had been running particularly hot. The price of shares was at an all-time high, and accelerating. Some board members were worried that prices had run so high for so long that they had created space for the mischievous sprite of speculation and the lewdly seductive slut of greed to run amok in the markets.

One of the Fed's arcane practices is that a committee member who wants to get the chairman's call to speak has to signal to the committee's deputy secretary by winking. One of the board members on that morning, Lawrence "Larry" Lindsey, a Harvard professor in his past and chief economic adviser to George W. Bush in his future, winked and, when recognised by the chairman, said: "What worries me . . . is that our luck is about to run out in the financial markets because of what I would consider a gambler's curse: 'We have won this long, let us keep the money on the table.' "

Investors, in other words, thought that the stockmarket could only go up. It had become a one-way bet. And that would only encourage more recklessness and speculation, begetting yet higher prices and an endless cycle of yet more greed and yet higher prices. He feared that America was witnessing the emergence of a "bubble" in its stockmarkets – a grotesque overextension of prices far beyond fundamental value. Financial bubbles, just like soap ones, always meet the same fate. They pop. And the bigger the bubble, the bigger the mess.

"I can attest that everyone enjoys an economic party," Lindsey continued, according to the official transcript, released, according to Fed policy, after five years. "But the long-term costs of a bubble to the economy and society are potentially great. They include a reduction in the long-term saving rate, a seemingly random redistribution of wealth, and the diversion of scarce financial human capital into the acquisition of wealth. As in the United States in the 1920s and Japan in the late 1980s, the case for a central bank ultimately to burst that bubble becomes overwhelming. I think it is far better that we do so before the bubble carries the economy to stratospheric heights."

Larry Lindsey's diagnosis was accurate and his prognosis was prescient. But the most important opinion in the room was that of the Fed chairman, the only one in the temple whose name was known to a broader public, the colossus of the world economy and oracle of the financial markets, Alan Greenspan. What did he think?

His predecessors had struggled mightily with the hydra-headed monster of inflation, that ravager of the dollar as a store of value, that agent of chaos that threatened to allow the insanity to burst to the surface. But his immediate predecessor, Paul Volcker, had tamed it with such a brutal blow – the imposition of high interest rates – that he had crushed its spirit. By the time Alan Greenspan was appointed to head the Fed in 1987, inflation, though not dead, was quiescent.

The new challenge for the world's economic managers was a different kind of inflation – not the familiar inflation in the price of goods and services, but a raging inflation in the price of assets, and especially stocks and real estate. The world had entered into a new era, post-Volcker and post-inflation. It was an era in which extreme and virulent bubbles in asset prices threatened to convulse economies and let the insanity in. Japan demonstrated this in the madness of its Bubble Economy of 1986–89. Now, even as Japan struggled seven years later to recover from the funk that had followed, the phenomenon had arrived on America's shores. A bubble had ravaged the world's second-biggest economy, and now it was about to beset the biggest. Greenspan responded: "I recognise that there is a stockmarket bubble problem at this point, and I agree with Governor Lindsey that this is a problem that we should keep an eye on."

He remarked that there was no simple solution for deflating the bubble. But he continued: "We do have the possibility of raising major concerns by increasing margin requirements," which is to demand that investors buying stock with money borrowed from their brokers increase the size of their initial down-payment. "I guarantee that if you want to get rid of the bubble, whatever it is, that will do it. My concern is that I am not sure what else it will do. But there are other ways that one can contemplate." He did not elaborate.

He plainly saw the danger. In the privacy of the Federal Reserve's magnificent boardroom, the people charged with keeping the currency sound and the economy healthy had correctly interpreted the looming problem. Alan Greenspan had even canvassed some options for dealing with it.

Over the next four years the threat they glimpsed that morning came to be realised. The US was convulsed by the mightiest mania in the four centuries of financial capitalism. The economy was indeed lifted aloft with the ascent of a vast bubble and dashed to the ground when it burst. Years later the US was still struggling with the many injuries it had suffered in the collapse. Just as it had been foreseen, so it had happened.

And the Federal Reserve? Apart from issuing a famous public warning of "irrational exuberance" in 1996, three months after that meeting in the Fed's boardroom, Greenspan and his fellow priests had attempted nothing to prevent, deflect, manage or mitigate the bubble. Greenspan spent the next three years watching it grow, and did absolutely nothing about it.

If anything, he justified it. Some argue that he actively encouraged it, became a cheerleader for the virulent madness that soon threw the US into recession, 2.3 million people out of work and cost stockholders $7.8 trillion in the three years after it burst.

So in the privacy of the Fed's boardroom he acknowledged as early as 1996 that there was a bubble and that it was a danger.

But in public he argued that it was the height of arrogance to claim to know whether a stockmarket bubble had even formed. He emphasised the wisdom of investors. In August 1999, seven months before the bubble burst, he gave a speech: "To anticipate a bubble about to burst requires the forecast of a plunge in the prices of assets previously set by the judgments of millions of investors, many of whom are highly knowledgeable about the prospects for the specific companies that make up our broad stock prices indexes."

In private he emphasised the ignorance of investors. As John Cassidy recorded in his book *Dot.con*, Greenspan "joked that he would like to introduce a law prohibiting day traders from buying a company's stock unless they could identify the product it produced".

In public he justified unprecedented stock prices. He told a committee of Congress in 1999: "I believe, at root, the remarkable generation of capital gains of recent years has resulted from the dramatic fall in inflation expectations and associated risk premiums, and broad advances in a wide variety of technologies that produced critical synergies in the 1990s."

Yet in the privacy of the inner counsels of the US Government, he shared the keen but covert concern of other top officials about the extremes in the stockmarket. The US Treasury Secretary during the bubble years, Robert Rubin, records in his 2003 memoir:

> As it seemed more and more likely that stock prices were excessive – and that the Nasdaq [index of technology stock prices] was almost manic – I became increasingly concerned that a sudden return to historical valuation levels could do harm to the economy. My considered view was never to say anything about the level of the stockmarkets, but with possible serious overvaluation posing larger risks to the economy, was there anything I could do about it? Alan [Greenspan], Larry [Summers, Deputy Secretary of the Treasury] and I talked about this issue as the Dow broke 5000, 6000, 7000, 8000 and 9000.

After that five-year succession of peaks, the Dow finally climaxed at 11,722.98 points. For half a decade Greenspan and the Treasury were privately anxious about the juggernaut of irrational exuberance, but during all that time they showed a public face of studied nonchalance.

So what went wrong? How can we account for Alan Greenspan's private concern and public complacency? What happened in between his 1996 warning of "irrational exuberance" and his 1999 rhapsodic declaration: "It is safe to say that we are witnessing this decade, in the US, history's most compelling demonstration of the productive capacity of free peoples operating in free markets"?

Is it a case of Bette Midler's lament: "I never know how much of what I say is true"? Or is there a deeper explanation for the schizophrenia in the cockpit of the world's economy and the crash-landing into which the pilots ditched the US?

Greenspan's two views outline two alternative outcomes. One is what happened – the terrible crashing end of the bubble boom of the late 1990s. The other is what might have happened. If Greenspan had acted on his concerns, if he had tried to moderate the mania, manage the bubble and calm the convulsions in the US economy, would the story have had a happier ending? This is not only a matter of historical interest. At the midpoint of the first decade of the twenty-first century, inflation remained quiescent, but bubbles swelled and gassed and blistered in stockmarkets and real estate markets around the world. And the same question that confronted Greenspan faced investors and policymakers around the world – what to do about them? Japan had not found an answer in the 1980s to the emerging monetary, financial and economic conundrum of the post-inflationary world, and, though Alan Greenspan had thought about trying in the late 1990s, he did not find one either.

The problem will not be solved by wishing it away. "There is a bit of déjà vu going on here," Laurence Meyer, a member of the Fed's FOMC from 1996 to 2002, wrote in his 2004 memoir, *A Term at the Fed*. "What is striking today, however, is that we appear to be repeating not one of the more normal periods in our economic history, but one of the most unique and remarkable . . . We have another bull market on our hands. And the policy issues facing the Fed are also remarkably similar to those faced in the second half of the 1990s . . . While we never precisely repeat the past, we certainly can learn from it."

Alan Greenspan is sometimes compared to the Wizard of Oz. As the travellers in that 1939 movie classic tremble in awe before the mighty image of the great and powerful wizard, Dorothy's dog, Toto, chances to draw aside the green curtain to expose an old man frantically pulling levers and switches. The wizard, it is revealed, is nothing more than a magical image generated by an ordinary mortal.

Exposed yet seeking to perpetuate the myth, the old man snatches back the curtain and thunders into the amplifier: "Pay no attention to that man behind the curtain . . . the . . . Great . . . er . . . Oz has spoken."

The plucky girl is not intimidated.

Dorothy (pulling aside the curtain and reprimanding him): Who are you?

The Wizard: (stuttering) I, I, I am the Great and Powerful Wizard of Oz.

Dorothy: You are! I don't believe you.

The Wizard: I'm afraid it's true. There's no other Wizard except me.

Scarecrow: You humbug.

The comparison is even more apt than it might seem. The book on which the movie is based, *The Wonderful Wizard of Oz*, published in 1900, was itself written as a monetary parable. Its author, L. Frank Baum, wrote it as an allegorical protest against the monetary system of his day, the gold standard, in favour of a more expansive one that would use both gold and silver. The moviemakers missed the point by giving Dorothy ruby slippers – in the book, Dorothy's magic footwear is silver.

If the public were allowed to enter the Fed's marble temple and pull aside the curtain, what would they find?

Chapter One

GREAT AMERICAN MADNESS

The US demonstrated the triumph of capitalism over communism in the climactic decade of the twentieth century. Then it went crazy.

The American stockmarket boom of 1996–2000 was the biggest speculative mania the world has seen. It was a dizzying display of one of the persistent problems of financial capitalism – the tendency of a rising market to move beyond all reason into hysterical excess.

The US did have a great deal to celebrate. It had vanquished the Soviet Union, built the Internet, mastered inflation and evolved something its proponents liked to call a New Economy. And for a while the stockmarket seemed to be merely a price index of the country's stunning achievements, of the limitless possibilities ahead.

But the momentum of rising share prices eventually carried the country from a well-founded optimism into collective mania.

Stock prices trebled in nine years. This was unprecedented and yet, somehow, felt natural. Indeed, the longer it ran, the more normal it seemed. The more prices gained, the more future gains seemed inevitable. "Americans came to expect rising stock prices as their right. It was extraordinary. Everything was perfect, and yet improving," remarked a Wall Street wit, James Grant, publisher of *Grant's Interest Rate Observer.*

Yet to an outside observer it was quite clear that this was not a well-founded optimism but a fevered delusion. The topmost finance official in the Japanese Government, Dr Eisuke Sakakibara, better known as Mr Yen, started referring to the US economy as "bubble.com".

The hottest spot in the fever, the part of the stockmarket with the greatest concentration of the most outlandishly speculative stocks, was the Nasdaq, an acronym that has outlived its origin, the National Association of Securities Dealers Automated Quotation System, now defunct. It is where most technology-based companies are listed. It launched a boom-time marketing slogan which captured the nation's sense that this new Elysium was a permanent condition: it called itself "The Stockmarket for the Next Hundred Years".

Five years later, the word Nasdaq had entered idiomatic American English as a synonym for a great collapse or failure, as in the *Denver Post*'s account of the travails of the fallen star of the Denver Broncos, Brian Griese: "His quarterback rating has Nasdaqed." Or when the *San Jose Mercury News* was trying to convey the depths of the unpopularity of Gary Condit, the congressman suspected of having murdered his intern: "Nasdaq is higher than his poll numbers."

The Nasdaq's slogan, though it may yet be proved technically accurate if the market can survive that long, stands with other great moments in the dismal history of hubris. The White Star Line boasted famously at the 1912 launch of the *Titanic* that the mighty ship was unsinkable. King George III confidently claimed in 1773 that the American colonies had little stomach for revolution. The US Secretary of the Navy, Frank Knox, declared on December 4, 1941: "Whatever happens, the US Navy is not going to be caught napping." The Japanese surprise attack struck the fleet at Pearl Harbor three days later.

And in the history of stockmarkets, the market for a hundred years ranks with the pronouncement by Yale University's highly regarded economist, Professor Irving Fischer, on October 16, 1929, a week before the onset of the Great Crash, that "stocks have reached what looks like a permanently high plateau."

The founders of an investment club for American children believed that the market's ever-rising trajectory was so assured that it was as inevitable as growing up: "How else can you help your child put this astounding growth into context?" asked Pat Smith and Lynn Roney, the organisers of the club StockmarKids in their book *Wow the Dow! The Complete Guide to Teaching Your Kids How to Invest in the Stockmarket*, published in the market's peak year, 2000.

Their answer: "We've come up with another one of our handy visual aids that help personalise the Dow for your child. By taking the Dow Jones Industrial Average for each of her birthdays and plotting these numbers to form a growth curve, you can see how the Dow grows along with your child . . . "

Yet it was the very opposite of a normal phenomenon. It was an aberration without precedent in the US. And, of course, because the US was and is the biggest economy the world has seen in absolute terms, the US stockmarket bubble was the largest the world has seen, too. But even if you adjust to take account of that, even if you measure it in proportion to its host economy and compare this ratio with that of other famous bubbles, it was still a breathtakingly big event. Indeed, its proportions exceeded all of the great episodes of market madness in the four centuries of financial capitalism, with only one exception.

The scale of the stock bubble was so vast that it was almost incomprehensible. Two simple comparisons show this. They give a picture, not of the price of individual stocks, but of how far a society can allow a speculation to grow beyond manageable dimensions, of how the stockmarket tail can grow so big that it can wag the national dog.

The first comparison measures recent events against overall American experience. One of the best ways to gauge the scale of the overall stockmarket is to measure it against the size of the American economy as a whole. That is, to compare the market value of all US stocks to the total annual output of the US economy, as measured by gross domestic product or GDP.

Since 1925, the value of all America's shares has averaged the equivalent of 55 per cent of GDP. So this is the historical benchmark: the total value of all stocks has averaged around half the value of the economy's output.

Sometimes the stockmarket has run up to levels well above this. Just before Wall Street's Great Crash of 1929, for example, stocks were valued at the equivalent of 81 per cent of GDP. But that was the highest the ratio reached for another 66 years. That is, until September 1995, when it hit 82 per cent.

The history of the preceding seventy years showed that this was a dangerous level, the market's historical extremity, an omen of collapse. But no, the mania was just beginning. Netscape, maker of the Netscape Navigator web browser, had listed on the stockmarket the month before. The price of its stock had vaulted by 108 per cent on its first day of trading. The company's founder, Jim Clark, had made an instant fortune of half a billion dollars. Its foundation investor, the venture capitalist firm Kleiner Perkin, had seen its $3.5 million stake transformed into a quarter-billion-dollar profit in a day. It was the first great strike of Internet gold, and the market and the media were agog. So at the point where the investor class should have been warily assessing the risks of an overextended market, it was instead awakening excitedly to the dawn of a modern alchemy. The ancient human quest for a magical transformation of base metals into gold had been achieved with the metamorphosis of copper wire and sand silicon into unimaginable riches. According to former Nixon speechwriter and techno-prophet George Gilder, America was experiencing "the final overthrow of the tyranny of matter". Alchemy indeed.

Exactly as America's stockmarket valuations returned for the first time since 1929 to the swollen proportions that preceded the Great Crash, its investors were enraptured with the advent of stunning new possibilities of great wealth. The times demanded sobriety but met euphoria.

In 1996, the ratio of the stockmarket's total value as a proportion of the economy reached 100 per cent. America's investors had put a value on listed US companies that equalled the output of the underlying economy. It was at this juncture that the chairman of America's central bank, Alan Greenspan, issued his famous and well-founded warning of the dangers of "irrational exuberance". The rise of the market was extraordinary and unprecedented, yet it had only just begun.

The next year, the market vaulted to another record to be valued at 120 per cent of the national GDP; in 1998, it hit 140 per cent; in 1999, it broke through the 170 per cent level.

Peculiar things were happening in society and the economy as a result. Children started to play the market in large numbers. "I have parents say to me, 'It's great! He sits in front of the screen five hours a day and does day trading,' " related Neale Godfrey, author of *The Ultimate Kids' Money Book.* "My God, I'd like to know what could possibly be good about that." In 1994, the Stein Roe Young Investors mutual fund had 4000 account holders. By the peak year of 2000, it had 231,000. Their average age? Eleven years old.

A survey by a Boston firm, Liberty Financial, found that 55 per cent of high-school students had bought stocks or bonds. The comparable figure in 1993 was 14 per cent.

The preferred vehicle of ordinary investors was the mutual fund. As the name implies, the fund pools clients' money and uses it to buy stock in listed companies. By the end of the bull market, there were more mutual funds offering to buy into listed companies than there were listed companies themselves. By the time of the market's peak, Americans had entrusted a cumulative total of $6 trillion to mutual funds. This was more than just an astonishing number, greater than the annual output of the Japanese economy. It was the first time in the country's history that mutual funds had more assets than the US banking system, with $5.6 trillion.

And for the first time a majority of Americans became stock-market investors. In the 1950s, 5 per cent of Americans owned equities. By the mid-1980s, it was 15 per cent. At the market's zenith in 2000, fully half of all Americans were share owners.

The famous investment strategist Barton Biggs of Morgan Stanley Dean Witter called a plumber to fix a blocked septic system. After recognising the guru, the plumber hectored him on investment strategy, urging him to be more aggressive in backing stocks. And he told Biggs that he had been so successful with his share portfolio that he had cut back his plumbing work to a part-time gig.

The sharp-eyed French social historian Alexis de Tocqueville visited the US more than 150 years ago and announced: "I know of no country, indeed, where the love of money has taken stronger hold on the affections of men." The sentiment is not new. The new development was that the stockmarket in the 1990s had become the main channel for indulging it. In 1990, Americans held one dollar in every seven of their personal wealth in the form of stocks; by 2000, it was one dollar in three. For the first time, Americans had more of their money in stocks than in the houses in which they lived, according to Federal Reserve data.

The national culture was changing under the influence of the mania. The stockmarket cable channel CNBC started to outrate the news channel CNN. A training school for butlers opened in Colorado to cater to the sudden new interest among middle-class families who could now afford to hire domestic servants. *Time* magazine's Man of the Year in 1999 was not a statesman or national leader but a man who sold books over the Internet, and not the first to do so either, but the one who had made the biggest stockmarket impact – Jeff Bezos, founder of Amazon.com.

This was a country that had sprouted more investment clubs than movie theatres. While an average of 30,000 people turned out to the games of the popular Chicago Cubs baseball team, 34,000 people were taking part in the quarterly webcasts to hear about the profits and prospects for Cisco Systems by 2001. All of this together was called "the triumph of stockmarket culture", or "equity culture".

"At no time in the post-World War II period has the economic well-being of the US and the rest of the world hinged so importantly on the performance of the American stockmarket," wrote one of Wall Street's gurus, Henry Kaufman, also known as Dr Doom, in his 2000 memoir. A leading Wall Street economist, Ed Hyman of International Strategy and Investment, put it succinctly: "The economy is the stockmarket."

The stockmarket and the sense of inevitability about its rise became one of the central realities of modern America. The market was no longer just important to the health of the US, it became central – and not just for its economy. It was a more important personal, sociological, political and geopolitical phenomenon than at any time in at least half a century.

The country's Secretary of State, Madeleine Albright, took to calling the US "the indispensable power". And the ineluctable foundation of the indispensable power was the stockmarket.

The nation's opinion of itself swelled with the market. US officials, more than usual, took to lecturing the rest of the world: "At international meetings, such as the G-7, which brought together the leaders of the advanced countries, we boasted of our success and preached to the sometimes envious economic leaders of other countries that if they would only imitate us, they too could enjoy prosperity like ours," wrote Joe Stiglitz, the chairman of the White House's Council of Economic Advisers in the Clinton Administration.

The conservative scholar Francis Fukuyama remarked: "American arrogance rises and falls with the Nasdaq."

Its zenith, reached in March 2000, was when the market hit a level equal to 183 per cent of the national economic production. This was two months after the great Wall Street stockbrokerage Merrill Lynch launched its new advertising slogan – "Be Bullish" – displayed beneath the corporate logo of an overmuscled bovine poised to charge. Bullish precisely when it should have been bearish, this captured the national sentiment of the time. Of course, Merrill Lynch very soon felt very sheepish. The slogan was withdrawn the next year. But Merrill's was not an exception but an emblem. In that year, of the thousands of stock advisories issued by the professional stock analysts employed by the Wall Street investment banks and brokerages, a mere 1 per cent carried "sell" ratings, according to Thomson First Call, a profit-monitoring firm. Just as the greatest and maddest market of modern experience came juddering to the brink of its collapse, the other 99 per cent advised Americans either to hold onto their stocks or buy more.

America's stocks were valued at almost twice the value of America's annual economy, a startling departure from historical experience that illustrates the extreme valuations that the country came to consider normal. The US market had departed so far from its historical norm that, instead of being priced at around half the value of the American economy, it distended to represent a sum equal to half the value of the economy of the entire world.

If the market had been in line with its long-run average, it would have been valued at $5.3 trillion in 2000. Instead, investors had pushed it to a peak valuation of $17.7 trillion. Three years later, $7.8 trillion of that value had evaporated as the price of stocks fell. That sum, which shareholders had considered to be theirs, documented in their 401K statements and printed in their portfolio accounts, the basis for fond spending plans and wistful retirement timetables and apparently as good as money in the bank, simply ceased to exist.

What Americans thought was the thrilling vibrancy of the

New Economy in the years to 2000 turned out to be the warning shudder of a mighty and imminent upheaval.

The second telling comparison is with the other great episodes of market mania in the four centuries of financial capitalism.

Most famous of all is the Dutch Tulip Craze of 1633 to 1637. Its name is synonymous with the madness of crowds, the wildest excesses of speculative frenzy, the very limit of how crazy humankind can be with money as the aristocracy and then the merchants and next the artisans and finally all classes were consumed by the pursuit of an inedible and economically useless underground stem. It remains the benchmark. Speaking after the American bubble had burst, the chairman of Dreman Value Management, David Dreman, said: "This was really the bubble of a generation, if not a century. It really ranks up there with tulipmania."

Yet the tulip craze was, compared to the American bubble of 1996–2000, a mere tiddler. As we have seen, the value of all America's stocks reached 183 per cent of the value of the national economic output at the zenith of the frenzy. In the Dutch craze, the equivalent ratio, the value of all tulip bulbs to the total annual output of the Netherlands economy, was a scant 0.2 per cent.

To demonstrate the extravagance of the pricing of tulip bulbs, the object of the speculation, one contemporary pamphleteer listed the goods that a Dutchman could have bought for 3000 guilders, the price of a single high-priced bulb, in December 1636:

> Eight fat pigs, four fat oxen, twelve fat sheep, 24 tons of wheat, 48 tons of rye, two hogsheads of wine, four barrels of beer, two tons of butter, a thousand pounds of cheese, a

> silver drinking cup, a pack of clothes, a bed with mattress and bedding, and a ship.

Crazy, yes?

Now consider the price of the object of speculation in the Great American Bubble of 1996–2000 – an Internet start-up – and what you could have bought with that sum. For the peak market valuation for eToys, a firm that was listed on the stock-market in 1999 proposing to sell toys over the Internet, you could have bought, in a similarly eclectic illustrative exercise:

> One thousand pounds of beef, 1000 pounds of pork, 1000 broilers, 1000 pounds of wheat, 1000 pounds of corn, 1000 pounds of soybeans, 1000 pounds of rice, 500 average-priced American houses, 100 private islands based on the price at the time of Bird Cay in the Berry Islands, the 25 most expensive apartments on Manhattan, 800 of the world's most expensive luxury sports cars, 200 luxury 64-foot yachts, 200 years of postgraduate tuition at Harvard, five famous New York skyscrapers based on the estimated 1997 sale price of the Chrysler Building, and still have enough left over to finance the entire budget of the United Nations' World Food Program, which fed some 100 million starving people a year, twice over.

You might quibble that a tulip bulb and a corporation are such inherently different items that they do not bear comparison. It doesn't really matter. The fate of both objects of speculation in booms four centuries apart was ultimately the same. After the bubble burst, eToys, which had enjoyed a peak stockmarket valuation of $10.7 billion, became, like the tulip, practically worthless.

Indeed, that was precisely the word that the company itself used in a February 2001 notice about the value of its stock – "worthless" – a month before it filed for Chapter 11 bankruptcy. The tulip resumed being the annual source of fresh blooms, which is rather more than the legacy left by eToys and its ilk.

And what of the other great speculative episodes? England's Railway Mania of 1844 to 1846 climaxed with the ratio of stock prices to the economy at 26 per cent. The Japanese Bubble of 1985 to 1989 approached the scale of America's, peaking at 147 per cent of GDP, but still fell substantially short. Of all the famous speculative episodes, only the South Sea Bubble of 1711 to 1720 eclipsed the American tech frenzy. That mania over shares in Britain's South Sea Company, which was supposedly granted a trade monopoly to exploit the riches of South America, pumped Britain's stockmarket up to the point where the total value of all shares was equal to 833 per cent of Britain's GDP, by far the most egregiously outsized bubble. The company never did establish a profitable trade with South America. This was also the bubble in which the father of modern physics and diviner of the law of gravity, Sir Isaac Newton, lost a fortune of twenty thousand pounds and received his own lesson in gravity – the inevitability of the collapse of all speculative bubbles.

Proportionately, then, in US history and across the global history of financial capitalism, America's Internet bubble of 1996–2000 was a truly outstanding episode in the scale of its speculative excess. It has been exceeded only once in four centuries in the scale of its delusion among the famous episodes, and it is without rival in its absolute size. The US stockmarket bubble at its peak placed a value on all shares of $17.7 trillion dollars.

But if that is the madness measured by its quantity, what of its quality? Surely the American mania for technology companies was sounder than a craze for tulip bulbs or a sham trading business with South America?

After all, the Great American Bubble of 1996–2000 was grounded in the well-established strength of the US economy, the reality of technological progress, and the demonstrated vitality of corporate America. Despite the caveats and cavils with which these advantages could be qualified, despite the grotesque overpricing of these strengths, surely they are more realistic generators of wealth than a tulip bulb or a confidence trick?

Apparently, but there was a terrible truth at the heart of America's stockmarket boom. Despite all the boasting and the proselytising and the hyperventilating and the CNBCing, America's overall performance as a profit dynamo did not improve during the great mania. In fact, it weakened.

This central flaw in the logic of the entire boom went unremarked except by a tiny handful of experts. It was known and widely understood that dotcoms, the Internet start-ups, would lose money initially. But the fact that the entire US private sector was suffering a decline in profitability never penetrated the public consciousness and to this day remains a little-known fact among the American investing classes. And it was hardly a fleeting oddity; it was a contradiction that persisted for three years.

It is such a clanging juxtaposition that it is difficult to credit. At the very time that stock prices surged, corporate profits slumped. From 1997 to 2000, as stock prices burgeoned by 67 per cent, corporate America's total profits actually fell by 6 per cent. As investors drove the stockmarket value of all listed US corporations up by $7.3 trillion, the aggregate profits of America Inc. retreated by $50.6 billion. According to the Commerce Department's national accounts data for non-financial companies

– the standard definition of the corporate sector – total profits fell from $868.5 billion to $817.9 billion.

This was a remarkable bout of feebleness. The country had not suffered three consecutive years of declining profits since 1956 to 1958, a recession, when earnings fell by 12 per cent. Indeed, there had only been one other instance since where profits had fallen for more than a single year, and that was during the recession of 1969 to 1970, which saw profits slump by 15 per cent. As this suggests, the profit shrinkage in the years of the Great American Bubble was the only time outside a recession when corporate America's earnings fell for more than a single year since the government started the comparable national accounts series in 1948. Yet this was supposed to be a boom.

As a share of the overall economy or GDP, corporate profits fell sharply, from 12.5 per cent to 7.1 per cent.

It is unbelievable but true that just as America was drowning in unprecedented stockmarket wealth, it was suffering an ebb of corporate profits without precedent in the post-war era.

And at the centre of the craze, the industries of the New Economy itself, there was a void. In the climactic year of the bubble, at the vortex of one of the greatest speculative frenzies the world has seen, the justification for the entire ranting, thundering, churning, wrenching $17 trillion dollar frenzy that convulsed a superpower, there was not a cent in overall profit. In the industries that make up the so-called New Economy – information, computer and electronic products, electrical equipment, appliances and components – the national accounts show an aggregate loss of $8 billion in the year 2000.

The stockmarket screamed "boom", but corporate profits squealed "bust". Perhaps that's why so much of the talk in the bubble years was about the future of the New Economy, the

New Era, the New Paradigm – because there was such an embarrassingly awkward absence of corporate profit in the present.

Money, wrote Somerset Maugham, "is like a sixth sense without which you cannot make complete use of the other five". In this case, corporate profits were the only rationale for all the other activities in the economy, the only way that all the other phenomena made any sense. Unless companies generally and New Economy companies in particular could make money, there could be no boom. So stock prices boomed, but the profits upon which they were predicated were truant.

Was this really any more solid ground for a great bull market than tulip bulbs or an imaginary trade in South American riches? Staff at the Baltimore-based funds manager and investment advisory firm T. Rowe Price didn't think so – as the bubble continued to swell, they started decorating their office doors with cut-out photos of tulips.

Both the size and the nature of the bubble of 1996–2000 qualified it as truly a Great American Madness. To invest credulity or, worse yet, money in that market was an act of faith. It was indeed, as Berkshire Hathaway's Warren Buffett said, "a Tinker Bell market – clap if you believe".

Perhaps it was the work of Loki, the Norse god of mischief, or Pan, the Greek deity of herds, but there was a hint of supernatural playfulness in the irony that the US led capitalism in a decisive triumph over rival forms of economic organisation in the last decade of the twentieth century, and then in the same decade afflicted it with a paroxysm of capitalism deranged. The same country that showed the world the power of capitalism almost immediately proceeded to demonstrate its persistent proclivity to bouts of destructive self-delusion.

Chapter Two

NEMESIS

If you had to guess the event that cost the United States more money than any other in its history, would you choose the Civil War? World War II? Or the Wall Street Great Crash of 1929? All of these are in the top five, but none even begins to approach the scale of America's most stupendously expensive event: the stockmarket collapse that the country has so recently lived through. The cost three years after the market's peak was $7.8 trillion in lost shareholder wealth. For proportion, World War II ranks second – in today's dollars, it cost the country $3.4 trillion.

The two episodes aren't comparable; wars kill people. But, in strictly monetary terms, the bursting of the bubble on Wall Street cost America twice as much as World War II. It was a stunning blow.

The ancient Greeks knew that hubris always was visited by Nemesis, and now she made her appearance on Wall Street.

When she lanced the bubble of overextended stock prices in March 2000, the imploding stockmarket dragged the economy into recession and swiftly ended the illusion of a New Era of uninterrupted growth, the delusion of a technological Utopianism, and America's self-image of a shining invincibility. After rising with an ostentatious stridency through the 1990s, it fell and fell hard in the opening years of the twenty-first century. The market's collapse and the economy's decline were already well in train before Al Qaeda's suicide pilots delivered their blows. The terrorist attacks of September 11, 2001, eighteen months after the stockmarket rout had begun and six months after the downturn in employment had started, aggravated, but did not cause, the recession.

The damage from the Wall Street collapse was not limited to the people who had decided to put their money into the market, the investors who had actively taken the risk. It turned out that the national economy had been gambled on the fate of the stockmarket. For the three years that followed the crunch, America's economy grew at an average of half the rate of the previous three – 1.9 per cent a year compared to 4.1 per cent.

More than 2.3 million people were thrown out of work.

At the epicentre, New York City, the damage from the collapse of the Great American Bubble was so intense that it eclipsed the economic cost of the terrorist attack of September 11, 2001.

Again, the events are not comparable because the stockmarket's collapse did not kill people. Yet an economist at the Federal Reserve Bank of New York, Jason Bram, published a paper estimating that, in strictly economic terms, the crash of the stockmarket and the recession that followed inflicted a greater disruption on the city of New York than the violent malice of the Al Qaeda terrorists.

"An analysis of employment and income trends suggests that the economic impact of the September 11 attack on New York City was somewhat less severe than originally thought," writes Bram in the summary of his 2003 study. "The attack created sizable job and income losses, but the city's current downturn appears to stem largely from other, cyclical factors – namely, the national economy and the financial markets." It was the bursting of the bubble, even more than the bombs, that hurt the economy of New York, he estimates.

Why survey the costs of the bust? There are four excellent reasons. One is that it is central to the story of what happened to the US and the world economy in the last decade. Another is that it helps explain the state of affairs in the world today. A third is that it sharpens the discussion about what to do to try to forestall future problems. Finally, it is a useful reminder in the face of the considerable effort under way to tell us not to worry about it.

Of course, Mr and Ms Average America do not need to be reminded of the damage to their personal finances. In one newspaper cartoon, an ordinary suburbanite finds in his mail the quarterly statement of account for his 401K retirement fund. His eyes bug out as he opens it to find it headed "4.01K statement". This is, of course, an exaggeration. Some investors lost 90 per cent of their money, but that was not typical. In aggregate, American households had shares and mutual fund investments with a market value of $12.1 trillion in 1999. By 2002 their holdings were worth $7.3 trillion. Their loss was $4.8 trillion, or $16,000 for every man, woman and child in the country.

It is not only the collapse of the Wall Street bubble that has been expensive. The cost of mitigating its effects also has been heavy and it continues to weigh on the economy years after the post-bubble recession formally ended in November 2001.

The US authorities have taken two chief measures to overcome the effects of the collapsing bubble of equity prices. They worked. The recession was relatively mild. It lasted eight months, according to the self-appointed and generally recognised arbiter of these things, the National Bureau of Economic Research. This is the same duration as the last recession, the 1990–91 downturn, and a little shorter than the average post-war recession of ten and a half months. Three years after the recession started, the unemployment rate, which had gone from a boom-time best of 3.9 per cent to a recessionary worst of 6.3 per cent, had started to work its way back down and stood at 5.7 per cent.

But each of the measures that the authorities took to achieve this softening of the recessionary blow has exacted its own cost.

First, America's central bank, the US Federal Reserve, used its control of official interest rates to stimulate the economy. Under the doleful but deliberate direction of its chairman, Alan Greenspan, it flicked the big on–off switch of American economic stimulus to "go". It cut the bank's policy interest rate, the Federal funds rate, from 6.5 per cent to 1 per cent in thirteen steps over two and a half years. This meant that it had cut official interest rates so steeply that they ended up being negative.

With an official interest rate of 1 per cent and inflation running at 2 per cent, the Fed, in effect, was subsidising borrowers to take money. Specifically, the Fed lends money at the official rate as overnight loans to banks. But when the Fed lowers these official interest rates, it indirectly brings down the cost of money in the wider market too. When the stockmarket collapse began in March 2000, the average new US home mortgage carried an interest rate of 7.95 per cent. Four years later it was 5.43 per cent.

Americans rushed to buy and build houses. This gusher of cheap money worked to stimulate the economy – housing-related spending accounted for a quarter of all consumer spending in the years 2001 to 2003 – but it was at the cost of over-exciting America's house prices.

By 2004, there was a strong case that parts of the US housing market were in their own bubble. The national average house price had gained 63 per cent between 1995 and mid-2004 according to the official numbers. The pace of the increase was quickening: up by 5.2 per cent in 1999, by 7.6 per cent in 2000, by 7.5 per cent the year after, by 7.6 per cent in 2002, 8.2 per cent in 2003, and, by the third quarter of 2004, an extraordinary 13 per cent compared to the same period a year earlier. "The growth in house prices over the past year surpasses any increase in 25 years," observed the keeper of the house price statistics, Armando Falcon, director of the Office of Federal Housing Enterprise Oversight in 2004.

America's national average house prices in 2004 were overvalued by 10 per cent according to the economists at the investment bank Goldman Sachs and as much as 20 per cent according to the ones at HSBC, a major British-owned bank based in Hong Kong.

In some parts of the market a speculative fever set in. "We are all living in Internet stocks with siding and shingles," wrote Marek Fuchs in the *New York Times* in 2002. "I own a home that has appreciated so much in value that I now consider it less shelter against the elements than a 2200-square-foot hot tip." Fuchs' home was in Westchester County in New York State, in the hinterland of the great megalopolis of New York City. His article includes a quote from a veteran real estate agent in the area, Tyra Cole of Coldwell Banker, who noted that buyers were very unhappy: "Forget the days of faxing bids or even emailing them. These days you have to get up here this afternoon and make the bid right away."

The county is home to a nuclear power plant, a prime terrorist target because of the radioactive pall that it could cast across New York City and the 21 million people within a fifty-mile radius of the reactor. The Westchester County executive, Andrew Spano, had this to say about the plant at Indian Point: "I cannot guarantee that in a fast-breaking radioactive incident such as a terrorist attack, that everyone would be protected. While our Emergency Response Plan would work effectively and efficiently in other scenarios, I remain concerned about a fast-breaking scenario. And no one can convince me that a fast-breaking scenario cannot happen." And what has happened to the price of houses in Buchanan, where the Indian Point plant is housed, since the unimaginable prospect of terrorist attack became a little more imaginable on September 11, 2001? "There have been bidding wars" for the available real estate, according to Fuchs.

And Westchester County, New York State, wasn't even on the list of the fifteen bubbliest local markets in the US. According to the Local Market Monitor, a private index that compares movements in house prices to see whether they are getting too far ahead of established ratios to incomes, almost all of the most overpriced housing markets in the US were in California – thirteen of the fifteen in late 2004. Of the other two, one was in New Jersey and the other was New York's Long Island. Houses in these areas were overpriced by between 43 and 59 per cent, the Monitor reckoned.

To fuel the fever, Americans were borrowing at a remarkable pace. Every day of the year in 2004, they were signing on for a net extra of about $2.1 billion in new mortgage debt, or some

$800 billion a year. That's not gross, but net: it is the amount in excess of mortgages that were retired or discharged. For scale, that's around the size of the total annual economic production of Canada or Spain. And it represents a rate of increase of about 11 per cent a year. One commentator, Mark Weisbrot of the progressive Center for Economic and Policy Research in Washington DC, remarked: "Since 1995, the increase in home prices has exceeded the overall inflation rate by more than 40 percentage points. This is without precedent; from 1951 to 1995, housing prices rose at the same rate as other prices. There is no way of explaining this phenomenon other than as a bubble."

The authorities denied that there was any such bubble. The authorities' credibility on this subject is, however, threadbare. We know from the documentary evidence that the authorities realised that the American stockmarket was in a dangerously distended condition of bubbledom from 1996 to 2000, but, with one notable aberration, they kept this diagnosis to themselves while showing a public face of nonchalance. We shall learn more about the reticence of officialdom later in this account.

To grasp the scale of what was happening in the US housing market, we might compare the total value of America's housing to that of the national economy, as defined by GDP. (This is akin to the comparison in the preceding chapter that so readily illustrated the enormity of the ill-fated distortion in the stockmarket.)

And what do we find? In the early post-World War II years, the national housing stock was worth only around 60 to 70 per cent of GDP, but then in the mid-1950s it moved up to be valued at around 80 per cent all the way through to the late 1970s, when it broached the 90 per cent level. In 1981, it hit 100 per cent of GDP for the first time, and stayed in the range of 100 to 115 per cent for the decade.

During the course of the 1990s, the market value of the nation's housing stayed in a steady ratio of 102 to 110 per cent. Even as the stockmarket slipped its traces and raced beyond all historical proportion to the US economy in the late 1990s, the value of the residential real estate market remained in a stable relationship with the size of the economy.

In 1999, the value of the total stock of US housing stood at 108 per cent of GDP. In the next year, the one in which the stockmarket rushed to its dizzying climax and then fell back and started its swift earthward plummet, the ratio moved to 113 per cent, about as high as it had ever been. (Only once had it been higher, in 1989, when it reached 114 per cent.)

Then, from 2001, it began a rapid run-up to entirely new heights. As Alan Greenspan's Federal Reserve started to cut interest rates decisively, the value of the nation's housing as a proportion of the economy responded dramatically. The housing market's total worth took a staccato series of swift steps into entirely new territory. In 2001 it went to 121 per cent of GDP; the year after it was 128 per cent; the next year it struck 133 per cent; and by the third quarter of 2004 it stood at 140 per cent.

This is a clear and remarkable acceleration in the run-up of the market worth of the national housing stock relative to the size of the US economy. By contrast, the post-war average is 93 per cent.

It took thirty-four years for the ratio to move from 60 per cent to 100, and another decade to go to 114 per cent. But it scaled from 120 per cent to 140 in just three years. By late 2004, the ratio stood 23 per cent higher than its previous post-war peak, reached in 1989. This movement is nowhere near as astonishing as the mushrooming of stock prices in the bubble years. But, like the stockmarket bubble, it is a clear departure from historical norms and it should serve as a clear sign of potential trouble.

Alan Greenspan assured the Congress that, although there might be some speculative activity in some parts of the housing market, the price rises overall were not a matter for concern. His reason? Although prices had risen on the tsunami of new mortgage debt, the value of homeowners' equity rose even faster as the value of properties went up. So debt might be up, but so was the value of the asset. The net effect was that household balance sheets were in good shape, with more assets than debts.

And this is entirely true – so far as it goes. But you could have made a similar case for complacency about the stockmarket bubble all the way through, until the very day it exploded. The problem with real estate is that, if a bubble forms and then bursts, the value of the house falls but the value of the debt owed on the house does not. So households are left with a depreciating asset but a fixed debt. If the prices fall far enough, the result is the extremely uncomfortable condition called "negative equity", which millions of Britons found themselves suffering in the '80s property bust. This is where you owe more to the bank than the property is worth.

If American house prices had indeed formed a bubble, this would mean that the US had overcome the effects of one burst bubble by inflating a new one. This implies serial bubble dependency, or economic management by price mania in one type of asset after another. It is a prescription for economic volatility or, if the system runs out of capacity to breed new bubbles, economic exhaustion.

Second, the Federal Government used the national Budget to stimulate the economy. It cut taxes and it spent money it didn't have. The consequence was that the Federal Budget, which had been in balance in 2001, was on course to be in deficit by almost half a trillion dollars – $478 billion or a substantial 4.2 per cent of the national output, as measured by gross domestic product, according to the Congressional Budget Office – in 2004. That means that one dollar in five spent by Washington in that year was borrowed. This passed the limit of America's political tolerance for debt. Both the President, George W. Bush, and his challenger, John Kerry, promised in the 2004 election campaign to halve the deficit in the term beginning in 2005.

So, to recover from post-bubble collapse, the US pushed both of these principal levers of economic acceleration, interest rates and government spending, fairly hard over to the "go" position. Four years after the end of the Great American Bubble, the country's national economic resources were still straining to restore America to an acceptable level of economic vigour. And the economy was recovering. But the process had left the country vulnerable to a new bubble and fiscally enfeebled.

Of the 2.3 million jobs lost during the downturn, 300,000 still had not been restored by the time of the 2004 presidential election. George W. Bush was destined to become the first president since Herbert Hoover, who was in office from 1929 to 1933 during the Great Depression, to preside over a net loss of jobs during a presidential term.

The effort of recovery also prevented American economic policy from dealing with new problems. With so much firepower concentrated on covering the economy's rear, it had very little ammunition left to blaze away at any new danger that might present itself on the horizon ahead. A shock from new terrorist attacks, an unexpected slump in demand, or any other source, would find US policy with a much-diminished power of response.

Another cost of the bubble was that in these years Americans' savings ran down to the lowest level since World War II. The reason was simple. As the market value of their stocks soared effortlessly, Americans decided that this made traditional saving redundant. Why save money and delay gratification when your wealth is piling up faster and more effortlessly than you'd ever imagined possible? Americans spent freely and threw the concept of savings into the same place they put prudence, moderation and common sense during these years.

Savings are important because they fund investment. When a country does not have enough savings to finance its investment needs, it must borrow from abroad. This shortfall is one of the two definitions of the current account deficit. (The current account has two identities. This is one. The other is the difference between everything a country sells to the world and what the world buys from it. It is a rule of national accounts that these two definitions describe the same amount – the current account deficit or surplus.)

A nation has two sources of saving – private and government. America in the early part of the twenty-first century had neither. As soon as the post-bubble downturn began, the government sector fell into deficit and became a drain on savings. And the private sector, which had been too delirious with stock-market winnings to bother with anything so Old Economy as saving, entered the recession without the habit. The personal savings rate had been 7 per cent or more of disposable income until the bubble years, when it sagged to a sad nadir in 2000 of –0.4 per cent. Three years later it was still at an uncomfortably low 3.5 per cent. With the straitened circumstances that attend a downturn, it was a bad time for Americans to start a new habit of saving. Was it just coincidence that savings collapsed as the market soared? No, according to a 2001 study by two Fed economists, Dean Maki and Michael Palumbo: "We show that the well-documented decline in the economy-wide rate of personal saving over the 1990s can be attributed almost entirely to a sharp reduction in the saving rate of families who experienced the largest capital gains." There was a direct trade-off. People making money in the stockmarket decided that they no longer needed to save. The people making the biggest stock gains were the wealthiest 20 per cent of the population, and their saving rate fell from 8.5 per cent in 1992 to –2.1 per cent in 2001. In other words, for every dollar they earned they were spending $1.02. And this collapse in savings among the rich was so severe that it damaged the national aggregates. So the current account deficit, a vulnerability in the US economy for many years, swiftly deteriorated to a new low of impoverishment.

All this also ran up the national debt. Outstanding domestic debt – the total owed by the American private sector and government sector combined – stood at $18.9 trillion in the year the stockmarket peaked, equivalent to 184 per cent of the nation's economic output as measured by gross domestic product. Four years later, it had run up to $22.7 trillion, or 195 per cent of GDP. America had spent the previous fifty years gradually increasing its indebtedness, but now its debt dependency quickened. The rate of increase in the debt ratio, the tempo of the national mortgaging, was more than double the average for the post-war period.

You might argue, quite correctly, that this is an incomplete picture. Because while the US has been getting itself more deeply indebted, it has also been buying assets overseas and lending money abroad. So what is the net position? The US net international investment position deteriorated from a negative

$458 billion when the bubble started to form in 1995 to negative $1.39 trillion by its end in 2000. As a proportion of GDP this was a worsening from 6 per cent to 14 per cent. And this corrosion quickened as the country strained to recover from the post-bubble recession. By the end of 2003, it reached $2.43 trillion or 22 per cent of GDP.

The country had enjoyed a positive balance until 1986. Now it was in hock to an extraordinary degree. A leading economic historian, Barry Eichengreen of the University of California at Berkeley, observed that there is no historical precedent for such a large economy being so heavily in debt to the rest of the world. "We are increasingly vulnerable to the kind of sudden stop, where the capital inflows dry up all at once, that's been the bane of emerging markets over the years," he said.

As Mark Twain reported a distinguished speculator exclaiming: "I wasn't worth a cent two years ago, and now I owe two millions of dollars." The illusion of permanent new wealth had been bought with the reality of permanent new debt. The wealth had vanished, but the debt obligations remained.

And the bubble did indeed have consequences for inequality in America. They were not egalitarian.

As share values surged, taxpayers reported net realised capital gains of $170 billion in 1995, $237 billion the next year, $446 billion the year after, and $507 billion in the peak year of 1999, according to the Internal Revenue Service. The great bulk of these riches were garnered by taking profits on stocks.

But surely, now that stock ownership had become democratised, with a majority of Americans investing in the market for the first time, the great mass of the people must have shared in these windfall profits? Not so. The Fed's 1998 triennial Survey of Consumer Finances found that the wealthiest 1 per cent of families owned almost half of all shares in the country and the top 5 per cent owned three-quarters. The richest 20 per cent owned an astonishing 96 per cent, which means that the other 80 per cent of the population shared a mere 4 per cent of all stock on issue.

The result? The richest 1 per cent of American families banked 42 per cent of the market's gains between 1989 and 1997, and the wealthiest 10 per cent took 86 per cent. An economist at New York University, Edward Wolff, calculated that the stock-market did deliver some benefit for the people smack in the centre of the income tree. The families in the middle of middle America – the middle fifth of the population by wealth – doubled their average stockholdings in those years from $4000 to $8000 after inflation. But these families were taking on debt even faster, so their *net* worth actually fell.

At the extreme end of the poles of wealth, the disparity, already glaring, became stark. The number of American billionaires trebled in the 1990s, and the dominant influence on this was the stockmarket. For example, the US had only two technology billionaires among its richest thirty in 1982, and they were Messrs Hewlett and Packard. But by 1999 fully half – fifteen of the top thirty – were technology billionaires. Meanwhile, the percentage of the population living in extreme poverty – defined as people living on less than half the official poverty line – rose slightly in the 1990s, from 4.9 per cent to 5.1 per cent, according to the US Census Bureau.

There was a slogan in the '90s that "a rising tide lifts all boats." It suggested that, while not everyone was winning new wealth at the same rate, the rising tide of stock wealth and national income was good for all. That these two trends could co-exist demonstrates the hollowness of that claim.

The inequalities in wealth that the bubble accentuated sat atop the long-running trend towards increasingly unequal incomes. Inequality of incomes had been becoming more pronounced for two decades, but the structure of stock ownership now aggravated it. "The larger result as the new millennium unfolded was a US long shed of its revolutionary outlook that had become home to greater economic inequality than any other major Western nation, including erstwhile aristocratic France and Britain," wrote Kevin Phillips in his 2002 work, *Wealth and Democracy.*

When the bubble burst, was this great disparity redressed? Yes, but only very marginally. For instance, the Federal Reserve estimated that while the average family's wealth fell by 14 per cent with the slump in the market and the economy in the year to October 4, 2002, the wealthiest 5 per cent of families had lost 15 per cent of their wealth in the same period. The wealthy had the advantage of disproportionately large holdings of real estate, so they could ride the secondary bubble that the Fed had inadvertently created in house prices in trying to recover from the bust in stock prices.

Or as Jay Leno posed the question: "President Bush says he has just one question for the American voters, 'Is the rich person you're working for better off now than they were four years ago?' "

The bubble, of course, brought benefits too. "Early in the decade, no one would have bet that the 1990s would prove to be the most fabulous decade since the 1960s," wrote two of the policymakers who contributed to it, Alan Blinder and Janet Yellen, in a book titled *The Fabulous Decade.* The pair had both sat on the Fed's FOMC in the early bubble years, and both worked in economic policy jobs in the Clinton Administration. They wrote:

> The unemployment rate, which reached a decade high of 7.8 per cent in June 1992, fell steadily thereafter and ended the 1990s at 4.1 per cent – the lowest level since the late 1960s. Despite this extraordinary employment performance, the inflation rate . . . which hit a decade high of 6.3 per cent in October and November, 1990, declined to 2.7 per cent by December, 1999. By the decade's end, there was even a developing consensus that America's productivity growth rate, which had languished near 1.4 per cent for more than twenty years, was perking up – perhaps substantially.

"How and why did all these wonderful things happen to the US economy?" they asked in a tone of bright wonderment. "And can we expect it to last?"

The answer was starting to emerge just as they published their work in 2001. The improvements in economy were real, but they were not sustainable. Why not? Because they were built, in part, on a bubble. Some of the employment gains remained. Inflation remained quiescent, though achieving low inflation in a recession is like getting wet when it rains – it's not hard to do and it's not the desired way of doing it. The improvement in productivity appears to have endured.

We know from the history of the last four centuries that bubbles, the grotesque overpricing of a particular type of asset in a particular place and time, or, if you prefer the textbook definition, when the price of an asset exceeds its fundamental price by a large margin, are a persistent feature of financial capitalism. The critical question is this: What lessons have been learned from this latest and extraordinarily costly event? Could the Great American Bubble have been averted, or at least better managed? Is there a better way of dealing with future bubbles?

In an appearance before Congress in July 2001, a senator put it to Alan Greenspan: "If this is the bust, the boom was sure as hell worth it. You agree with that, right?"

"Certainly," came the calm, one-word reply from the chairman of the US Federal Reserve.

If there is going to be fresh thinking about the Great American Bubble, its costs or the possibility of another such occurrence, the former chairman of the Federal Reserve evidently was not going to be the one doing it.

Chapter Three

THE BLIND MEN AND THE ELEPHANT

In an old Indian folk tale, six blind men live in a village. One day there is much excitement in the village because of an unprecedented event – an elephant is visiting. The blind men hear a great deal about the amazing beast and are curious to get a sense of it by touching it.

The first blind man happened to bring his hand up to the elephant's rough round leg and thought that the creature was very much like a tree trunk. The second blind man reached out and felt its sinuous trunk and decided that the elephant was like some great snake. The third grasped it by its thin flapping ear and received the clear impression that this animal resembled a giant fan. The fourth chanced to touch its tail and marvelled at its similarity to rope. The fifth stroked its tusk and was startled that any animal should be so like a spear. And the sixth touched its vast side and remarked that the elephant was plainly like a wall.

At this, the first man cried out in protest: "No, you fool, it's like a tree trunk." The second disagreed vehemently: "No, you are both wrong – the elephant is exactly like a snake." The third contradicted them all: "How can you say those things? I felt it myself, and it's just like a big fan." Then the fourth blind man abused the others, saying: "You are all mad – an elephant is like a piece of rope." The fifth could not contain his impatience: "How could it be? It's smooth and hard and pointed just like a spear." And the sixth continued to insist that it felt like nothing so much as a wall.

They bickered and argued, each partly right, but all wrong also, until they came to blows. A wise man passing by stopped at this spectacle and called out to them, asking them why they were fighting. The blind men told him, "We cannot agree on what the elephant is." Each stated his case. The wise man laughed. "The elephant is a mighty beast and each of you has touched just one part of it. If you put together your impressions of all the parts you will begin to get a better sense of the whole."

The story, claimed by the ancient Jainist religion as its own, is intended to illustrate the Jainist principle that the truth can be stated in seven different ways. But it can be applied to the madness that was the Great American Bubble. Blame generally falls onto six groups. Chroniclers of the time generally home in on just one and single it out as the chief culprit. Each did indeed have its own part to play, genuine but limited. And there was one wise man who comprehended the whole.

The explanations of what went wrong tend to fall into six categories. The first emphasises the role of the corporations, including the object of the speculation, the dotcom corporations, and specifically their CEOs. A second culprit is Wall Street, a rubric that emphasises the investment banks and brokerages but also often includes other parts of the financial infrastructure such as the accountants and auditors. Third is the media. Fourth is the business cycle, the routine swing from boom to bust and back to boom again. Fifth is interest rates. Sixth is government.

The investor – and sceptic of the tech mania – Warren Buffett, remarked that "it's only when the tide goes out that you learn who's been swimming naked." All these groups and institutions were shown to have been swimming naked in the ocean of bubble-era liquidity. But while the tide was high they were certainly swimming in it.

First, the corporations, which were, of course, central. They are the main moving parts in the machine of capitalism. It is the corporations that employ, invest, build, innovate, commercialise, sell, earn and re-invest to turn the raw material of the economy – capital, labour and knowledge – into the finished product of profit. The stockmarket was devised as a way for companies in need of capital to find investors who were prepared to risk some. And once investors had bought into a company, the stockmarket also allowed them to sell their share of ownership.

Five things happened to change investors' attitudes to the corporation in the late 1990s in America. First, the emergence of an apparent revolution in technology set investors afire for tech companies above traditional corporations. After the market advent of Netscape in 1995, investors put vast price premiums on companies that seemed to be connected to the tech boom. A company that seemed to be part of the boom could raise cash from stockmarket investors at an effective cost of zero per cent. Capital, for tech firms, was free. It became cool to disparage the traditional corporation. A book published in 2000, *The Cluetrain Manifesto*, the geek equivalent of a "Repent and Be Saved" placard for the world of Fortune 500 corporations, opened with a list of ninety-five "theses". Number twenty: "Companies need to realise their markets are often laughing. At them." One of the book's four authors, Christopher Locke, wrote: "Just as GM mistook the Hondas and VWs for a passing fad, most corporations today are totally misreading this invasion from Webspace. Their brand will save them. Right. Their advertising budget will save them. Uh-huh. More bandwidth will save them. Sure. Well, . . . something will save them. They're just not too sure what it is yet. But the clock is now ticking in Internet time. Maybe they should get a clue. And quick." *The Cluetrain Manifesto* likened the arrival of the Internet entrepreneurs to "an invasion from outer space: ten thousand saucers just landed and they're merely the advance wave".

Second, some existing companies tried to ride the fashion by adapting or "re-inventing" their businesses. This included the energy company Enron, the phone service provider Global Crossing and an e-commerce offshoot of the big bookseller Barnes and Noble as it tried to survive the onslaught from the new online book company, Amazon.com. In an imaginative moment the book merchants called it BarnesandNoble.com. Third, a wave of about a thousand new start-ups of a peculiar character, the so-called flying saucers, was listed on the stock-market – it was the advent of the dotcom, an expression invented by the founder of Amazon.com, Jeff Bezos. The suffix ".com" indicated that they were designed to do business in the high-growth zone of cyberspace. This wave included companies like website developer Razorfish, online rewards points clearing house Netcentives, and the online broker for business supplies b2bstores.com. Fourth, many investors came to believe that the historical experience of corporate growth and profitability no longer applied. And fifth, this allowed investors to price the shares of corporations at levels that bore no relationship to their fundamental worth – in other words, a bubble formed.

It was most exaggerated among the technology companies listed on the Nasdaq index. The share prices of the 100 biggest companies listed on the Nasdaq market are aggregated to form an index called the Nasdaq 100, and this included the established giants and standard-bearers of the American technology sector including Microsoft, Intel and Dell. At the peak of the bubble, these stocks were trading at an average price of 400 times their annual profits. This ratio is a standard valuation yardstick – the price of a stock compared to the underlying earnings that it produces in a year, the price to earnings or PE ratio. The post-war average for the 500 companies that make up the Standard and Poor's stock index is around seventeen times. That is, if you bought a share in one of those companies it would take seventeen years for that share to generate enough earnings to meet the original purchase price. For the Nasdaq in 2000 it was 400 times. That means that, if you had bought the average Nasdaq 100 stock, it would have taken you 400 years, at the existing rate of earnings, for the stock to generate earnings equal to the price you'd paid. To pay these sorts of prices an investor either had to take a very long-term view, had to believe that profits were going to accelerate exponentially, or had to think that valuation was irrelevant.

When the bubble burst, it turned out that valuation had mattered after all. The price of a share of Enron stock fell from a peak of $90.75 to 8¢ at the end of August 2001, Global Crossing's from $61 to 2¢, and BarnesandNoble.com's from $20.30 to $1.23. Entirely new dotcom businesses suffered share price collapses, like Razorfish's fall from $55 to 20¢, Netcentives from $80.63 to 9¢, and b2bstores.com from $18.38 to the place where many hundreds of dotcoms' share prices ended up – the vanishing point, worth nothing at all.

One of the few dotcom corporations to move quickly into profitability was based on a website set up to take bets on which dotcom would fail next. The site positively rejoiced in the death of the dotcom boom. It was called fuckedcompany.com, thrown together in a weekend in May 2000, the month after the Nasdaq had peaked, as a bit of sport by a remarkably crass computer programmer, Phillip J. "Pud" Kaplan. Within a year it was getting 4 million visitors a month and was declared the "Site of the Year" by Yahoo! Internet Life. It was an indicator of the anger and bitterness at the sector and its CEOs, whom Kaplan described as "twenty-something Banana-Republic-khaki-pant-wearing Gap-blue-shirt-sporting Stanford-MBA-having Boxter-driving day-trading choad-smoking secretary-ass-palming CEOs". It turned out that the crews of the flying saucers were not all entirely happy with their captains. Investors were angry at their losses, former dotcom staff like Kaplan were bitter at their abrupt joblessness, and everyone, it seemed, was retrospectively indignant, in the manner of spurned lovers, at the cavalier betrayal of their trust and credulity.

Americans reserved a special rancour for the chiefs of big companies who were exposed as the perpetrators of major fraud. The exposure usually came when their companies collapsed as the tide ran out. As they stripped their stockholders' companies, they also destroyed the livelihoods of their workers. These cases were relatively few in number, but they were vast in scale and shocking in impact. The greatest was Enron, whose CEO, Ken Lay, declared: "There is a very reasonable chance that we will become the biggest corporation in the world." A year later its collapse became the biggest outrage in America. As investors were smarting from the losses of the stockmarket's general decline, the country had no trouble empathising with the 4000 Enron staff who lost their jobs and over $1 billion in pension entitlements while simultaneously reviling Lay, who walked from Enron with over $100 million in his pocket and a smug look on his face.

Lay and top executives saw the looming iceberg and sold $1.1 billion worth of their company stock. But, wrote conservative commentator George F. Will, "employees, locked in steerage like the lower orders on the *Titanic*, were blocked from selling the Enron stock that comprised, on average, 62 per cent" of their pension plans. One worker, after twenty years' service, found her pension plan, full of Enron stock, had been reduced to a total worth of $102.

Others followed: Tyco, Global Crossing, ImClone, Adelphia, Qwest, WorldCom. Their CEOs had plundered their shareholders so wantonly and wallowed in their loot with such gluttony that they sickened many ordinary Americans. Tyco's Dennis Kozlowski, for example, had used company funds to buy himself a $13.5 million waterfront mansion in Boca Raton, Florida, a $2.5 million wharf-side cottage in Nantucket, Massachusetts, an $8.5 million spread at Bachelor Gulch, Colorado, a $2.3 million house in an exclusive coastal community at Rye, New Hampshire, another coastal cottage at Nantucket for an estimated $2.5 million, a Fifth Avenue apartment in New York City for $18 million, and yet another coastal house in Nantucket, this one a mansion plus three-bedroom guest house, for $5 million. And he appointed them all so tastefully too. The market regulator, the Securities and Exchange Commission, in preparing to charge him with fraud, conspiracy and grand larceny, discovered that he had, among other touches, bought a gold-plated wastepaper basket for $2200 and spent $6000 on a shower curtain. These were just some of the trinkets he picked up in the process of destroying the company.

In *Pigs at the Trough*, Ariana Huffington gave this assessment of the late '90s CEOs of corporate America: "They've created their own set of rules that defy logic, violate basic decency, corrupt commerce and laugh in the face of the laws and regulations established to protect the rest of us. These are the standards that comprise the Code of the Crooked CEO. It's a code of dishonour that rewards unprecedented avarice with gargantuan wealth and ensures a lifestyle of appalling excess." She concluded that the "bottom line is that the US can no longer hold its head up as the world's standard-bearer of capitalist virtue".

These highly publicised cases drew attention not only to the rapacity of the culprits but also to laxness of corporate governance, to regulatory dilatoriness, and to the permissiveness of the time. The great bulk of America's corporate leaders, neither dotcom dreamers nor raging kleptocrats, were nonetheless influenced by the times. Many flirted with e-commerce. Many followed the vogue for excess. This included the inflation of CEO salaries. In 1990, the average CEO of a major corporation was paid 85 times more than his or her average employee, already a very high ratio by international standards. By the end of the decade this ratio had blown out to such an extent that the boss was paid 531 times the wages of the average employee. And in the latter part of this decade, as we saw in the first chapter, corporate America as a whole was becoming less profitable even as its chiefs rewarded themselves more lavishly. So while not all of corporate America deserved the opprobrium that was directed at the grand thieves of the time, many of its CEOs had been making the most of the mania that had taken hold.

Fairly or not, the whole of corporate America was widely held to be guilty by association. In a poll by the *Los Angeles Times* in December 2002, Americans were asked what was to blame for the economy's poor performance. Twenty-one per cent said corporate fraud. A separate poll by *Investor's Business Daily* in January 2002 found that 22 per cent said the main cause of the recession was an excess of investment spending by business. Those polled were not given the option of differentiating between the pigs at the trough of the biggest firms in the land and the "choad-smoking secretary-ass-palming" CEOs of the dotcom sector. The corporations were essential both as the plausible objects of speculation and as contributors to the general climate of unknown possibilities and unexpected wealth. Yet they did not bestow the unprecedented levels of market valuation, nor the climate of official tolerance.

Our second culprit is Wall Street. It was here that the unprecedented levels of market capitalisation were set, and the big brokerages and investment banks of Wall Street had a great deal to do with setting them. The Wall Street firms are the deal-makers of US capitalism. They perform a service essential to modern capitalism: they provide the mechanism that allows corporations a ready market to buy other corporations in mergers and acquisitions, or to sell themselves or their divisions in divestitures.

If the company is the main moving part in a capitalist system, the Wall Street firms and stockmarket itself are the lubricant. As such, they are synonymous with greed and exploitation and often reviled. The investment banks search endlessly to create major deals that will generate fees, and they will fit the deal to the season. In some seasons there is a vogue for companies to enlarge by takeover, and in others it is fashionable for companies to get smaller – "realising value" – through break-up. Whatever the season, Wall Street will find the companies, coach them in the deal and then bring them to market for a fat fee. When the stockmarket is running hot, one of Wall Street's most profitable businesses is launching companies onto the stockmarket – launching an IPO or initial public offering in US parlance, but known as a "float" in the British and Australian markets. In America's markets during the bubble years, however, the IPO of a new tech company's stock might as well have been the acronym for an Invitation to Profit Obscenely. It did not so much float on a swell as catch a tsunami.

The debut of Netscape in 1995 was the threshold event in the tech frenzy of IPOs. After its experience, each and every one of the thousand or so tech firms to list on the stockmarket in the bubble years hoped to emulate Netscape's stunning rise as entrepreneurs, venture capitalists and investment bankers rushed to strike more of this same vein of newly discovered gold. The wildest hope of investors in an IPO is that the price of the company's stock will rise headily upon listing, and perhaps, in rare and unimaginably lucky cases, the price might even double on the first day of trading. Netscape shares were offered at $28 but the first traded price of a share in Netscape was $71, and later it peaked at $74 before finishing its first day at $58.25, a gain of 108 per cent.

How rare was that? In the whole decade of the 1980s, it had happened exactly seven times that the price of shares in new IPOs had doubled on the first day of trading, rewarding their fortunate owners with instant profits of 100 per cent or better. After Netscape it started to happen more and more frequently with tech stocks. At Home, a company offering Internet access, offered its stock to the market in July 1997 at $10.50 a share with a warning that it would lose money "for the forseeable future" and that "there can also be no assurance that the company will ever achieve profitability". Investors responded to these explicit warnings by pushing At Home's price to $25 on the first day for a profit of 138 per cent.

In the final four months of 1998, that rare and lucky lottery came up another seven times, as many times as it had in the entire 1980s. Stock in eBay, online auctioneer, surged from $18 to $47 and three-eighths on its first day, a profit of 163 per cent. In February 2000, the month before the market's peak, twenty-seven IPO stock offerings doubled on their first day, according to the University of Florida's Jay Ritter, a new record. At an average of more than one per trading day, these extraordinarily rare events had become a commonplace. TheGlobe.com, a company offering to host web pages, made even these stunning performances look feeble when it went public in November 1998. Its shares exploded from $9 to $97 on day one, a profit of 978 per cent in a day. It was by far the greatest first-day gain in the history of the US stockmarket. The great grail of a 100 per cent one-day profit had now been overtaken by the reality of a gain of nearly 1000 per cent. Yet within a year this, too, had become a regular event. In the second half of 1999, ten IPOs vaulted by at least 1000 per cent. Each of these IPOs was underwritten and arranged by an investment bank.

So, Wall Street firms brought these tech companies to investors, but how does that make them culpable for the madness?

First, the brokerages and the investment banks advised and guided the pricing of the new offerings.

Second, they systematically, deliberately underpriced the IPOs – a tactic akin to holding a balloon under water – to make sure that they would leap the moment they were released to the market. Jay Ritter studied the difference between the offering price and the closing price of a stock on its IPO. He called this gap underpricing. And he measured it over the course of twenty years. He found that the average underpricing of an IPO in the 1980s was 7 per cent. It grew to 15 per cent in 1990 to 1998. And in the peak years of 1999–2000 it jumped to 65 per cent. This underpricing meant that $66 billion was money left on the table, in Ritter's estimate – capital forgone by the issuing companies. For example, if TheGlobe.com had priced its IPO at its closing price of $97 instead of deciding to offer the stock at $9, it would have raised an additional $270 million. The whole point of an IPO is to allow a company to raise capital. Yet these firms and their advisers were content to put rapid price rises above raising of capital. The system had become seriously perverted. It no longer primarily served the need of financing firms but rather that of generating huge trading profits. And this perversion of the market was just the beginning.

Third, the Wall Street firms commonly used illicit means to guarantee these vast rises, known as "pops", in the price of an IPO. One technique is "laddering". It works like this. The stock sales staff for the investment banks and brokerages speak to their clients in allocating the number of shares each will be allowed in a forthcoming IPO. The salesman tells the eager client that the hot new stock offering is hugely oversubscribed. But, says the salesman, it just might be possible to allow the client some stock if the client is prepared to help pump up the price on the first day of trading. How can the client help escalate the price? By buying some of the new stocks at the moment when they first list on the market.

According to an investigation by the regulator, the Securities and Exchange Commission, the big investment bank of Morgan

Stanley deliberately sought to "create perception of scarcity" with an IPO. Once it had established a burning desire for the stock, Morgan then asked clients whether they intended to keep buying more stock after the IPO began trading. The company kept detailed files of customers' stated "commitments" and watched to see whether they kept their promises, according to the SEC. And Morgan Stanley let them know that if they did, it would count in their favour the next time a hot IPO offering was ready to be shared around.

At the big Wall Street investment bank Goldman Sachs, according to the SEC, one of the firm's managing directors asked a sales rep about one client's intentions once the stock started trading. The customer, replied the salesman, "will do what we say". Goldman had "deal captains" to check up and make sure. None of the firms admitted to laddering, but some of the major ones agreed to pay fines to settle the SEC's complaints that they had illegally stimulated demand by artificial means. Morgan Stanley and Goldman Sachs in 2005 agreed to pay $40 million each. JP Morgan Chase paid $25 million in 2003. And Credit Suisse First Boston paid $100 million in 2002 to settle civil charges over a number of IPO allocation practices in the bubble era.

In addition to this direct interference in the buying and selling of stocks, the Wall Street firms also deliberately, even joyously, led their customers into a false understanding of the stocks on offer. Through the investment advice to their clients, the Wall Street firms knowingly and systematically took their clients by the hand and led them through the looking glass into the mad world of the Great American Bubble.

Consider the following. When broking analysts send clients their ratings of various stocks, they have, like traffic lights, a standard set of three recommendations – buy, hold or sell, and some have shades and variations in between. But when Merrill Lynch, for instance, advised clients about the frothiest of the bubble stocks, those in the super-speculative Internet sector, that great finance house seemed to have forgotten how to spell the word "sell". The traffic lights were perpetually set on green or amber, never red. And any traffic lights that fail to flash red must eventually lure the traffic to disaster.

The Attorney General of New York State, Eliot Spitzer, filed an affidavit in the State Supreme Court in 2002 complaining that at the market's feverish peak, from the spring of 1999 through the autumn of 2001, "Merrill Lynch never published a single Reduce or Sell rating on any stock covered by the Internet group."

Among those stocks were some of the causes célèbre in Internet ignominy, shares that sold for hundreds of dollars each during the madness but crashed and burned – Pets.com, Mypoints.com, Quokka Sports, Webvan, iVillage, Buy.com, 24/7 Media, eToys, Internet Capital Group and InfoSpace. Merrill, which happened to have won the profitable work of bringing those ten firms to market in their initial public offerings, did not ever warn its clients of impending difficulty.

Internally, Merrill and its Internet stock guru, the once-feted Henry Blodget, used a more pungent rating system. As Spitzer's investigators discovered through their study of Merrill's email archive, one issue might be recommended within the firm as "pieces of shit", while another stock offering was warmly endorsed as "pieces of crap". But to the clients of Merrill Lynch, they were all presented as "buys".

The group of ten Merrill specials was offered to the market at a collective total value of $28 billion. On March 10, 2000, at the peak, they carried a collective market value of $76 billion. (For perspective, this is around the size of the annual GDP of the Philippines or Pakistan.) One and a half years later, specifically on the last day of August 2001, their market worth was $0.711 billion. That is, after the madness had passed, the market put their value at 2.5 per cent of the value of their initial offering price, and 0.9 per cent of their peak price. Another way of putting this is to say that, if you bought these stocks on the day they first went public, you would have lost 97.5 per cent of your money. But if you had been the Greatest Fool and bought them at their apogee, you would have lost 99.1 per cent of your investment. As the Merrill logo enthused, Be Bullish.

It was not that the analysts were unseeing or uncomprehending. It was that the investment banks stood to profit so much from managing the IPOs that they encouraged their analysts to boost the business with positive ratings. This is not, of course, supposed to happen. The two parts of the business are supposed to be divided by an invisible "Chinese wall" that prevents each side from knowing what the other is doing. It is supposed to keep the research honest so that the firm's clients receive sound advice, untainted by the investment banking business. And some analysts did give independent, critical advice. But they were few and they were brave. And they were punished.

A Merrill Lynch analyst, Jonathan Cohen, issued a sell recommendation on the stock of Amazon.com on September 1, 1998. He told clients that, for a company with no earnings, its share price was too expensive. The market was valuing the online book retailer at $4 billion, twice the price it accorded a competitor, Barnes and Noble, which actually made a profit. Amazon.com, he said, was "probably the single most expensive piece of equity ever, not just for Internet stocks but for any stock in the history of modern equity markets". Cohen's logic was right, but logic had fled America.

Amazon stock tripled in price in three months. At this point a then unknown analyst at a much smaller firm, Henry Blodget at CIBC Oppenheimer, made a boldly bullish prediction that the stock, now trading at $242 a share, would increase in value by a further two-thirds, to $400, within a year. Blodget was a historian and former journalist who was no expert in finance, but he knew the only thing that mattered for the time – the Merrill slogan, the national creed, "Be Bullish". Blodget's forecast was seized by the stock-promoting industry and widely hailed, and it soon became self-fulfilling. Amazon.com hit $400 three weeks later. Merrill Lynch immediately fired the unfashionably sensible Cohen and hired the lucratively excitable Blodget for $3 million, rising to $12 million a year over the next two years, according to a later New York State court filing against Merrill.

Or consider the case of a senior natural gas analyst at Merrill Lynch, John E. Olson. This thirty-year veteran refused to recommend the stock of a fashionable and fast-growing energy concern called Enron. In April 1998, two Merrill investment bankers wrote a memo to their firm's president, Herbert M. Allison, to complain that Merrill was being excluded from a $750 million offering of new Enron stock because "our research relationship with Enron has been strained for a long period of time". Olson "has not been a real supporter of the Company", the Merrill bankers wrote, in a memo later unearthed by investigators for the Senate Permanent Subcommittee on Investigations. The investment bankers asked Allison to intervene by phoning Enron's chief, Ken Lay. He did, and Merrill Lynch was allowed a piece of the deal as co-manager. The next month Merrill gave Olson the reward it felt he deserved. His boss walked into his office, shut the door, sat down and said he wanted to talk about Enron. "How could you do this?" asked the Merrill executive Andrew J. Melnick, its director of research. "You've blown this deal. We're missing this thing." He told Olson that he would lose his retirement benefits. Alternatively, if he left now, he could keep them. Olson was being forced out. His replacement upgraded the recommendation on Enron stock. According to an internal memo seven months later, Enron had awarded Merrill business worth $45 to $50 million in banking fees in the interim.

A group of 309 IPOs, most of them by high-tech firms, generated first-day trading profits of $50 billion. This is not just a vast sum – it is also more than the actual fundraising that these issues accomplished. The point of an IPO is to allow companies to raise capital from stockmarket investors. As measured by the money involved, however, this had become subordinate to the profiteering that occurred around the capital-raising.

The effect of such a climate was that the analysts virtually ceased to exercise any critical faculty when assessing stocks. Of all the recommendations issued by US stock analysts in 2000, fewer than 1 per cent were "sell" ratings, according to Thomson First Call, the profit-monitoring firm. To correct for the inherent bias in the ratings, the head of research at Thomson First Call, Chuck Hill, recommended that clients not take them literally but downgrade each level of recommendation to the one below, so that a "strong buy" would become a "buy", while a "buy" really meant a "hold", and a "hold" or "neutral" advisory was actually a recommendation to sell. "That's the only way to make sense of these things," said Hill in 2001.

It was not just the stockbrokers. All the parts of the financial infrastructure that were supposed to be dispassionate about the stockmarket joined the frenzy. By the end of the bubble, the banking system was observed to be genuflecting to the share market. The president and chairman of a bank on New York's Long Island advised customers to stop putting their money in his bank. Instead of a deposit earning 1 per cent, buy our shares, urged John Kanas of North Fork Bancorp, and earn more than twice as much. Even a bank president would not defend bank accounts in the face of the Great American Madness.

The cumulative and encompassing failure of Wall Street was exposed by the Enron collapse. It emerged that the firm concealed billions in debt by hiding it in partnerships controlled by its own executives. Profits were overstated by $600 million. And until rumours started to circulate in October 2001, Enron's chiefs got away with it. The stock price fell from $85 to 26¢ in a few weeks and it sought bankruptcy protection.

When the tide went out, it was embarrassing for Wall Street's high-priced analysts. Of the seventeen analysts who followed the company, sixteen were recommending it as a buy or strong buy as late as October, when it started to crumble.

It was excruciating for the blue-bloods of US banking, Citicorp and JP Morgan, each of which was caught with $1 billion or more in outstanding loans to Enron.

It was humiliating for the credit rating industry – on October 16, on the very cusp of the company's destruction, Standard & Poor's said it expected Enron's balance sheet to improve.

It was a disaster for the accounting and auditing profession. The big firm of Arthur Andersen approved Enron's fraudulent accounts, then destroyed thousands of documents when investigators turned their way. A venerable law firm, Vinson & Elkins, studied its accounting methods and called them "creative and aggressive" but concluded that "no-one has reason to believe that it is inappropriate".

All these parts of the financial infrastructure of US capitalism failed, their judgment skewed and the execution of their duty compromised by the mania of the time. One of the most telling quotes came from one of the era's most high-profile stock analysts, the telecommunications analyst at Salomon Smith Barney, Jack Grubman, a man who flagrantly and systematically broke all the conventions of the Chinese wall. Instead of offering clients objective investment advice at arm's length from the firm's investment banking business, he was deeply involved in the banking to the point where he even attended three board meetings of one of the companies he covered, the glorious WorldCom, later to become one of the greatest bankruptcies in US history. Asked about his conflicts of interest, the appropriately named Grubman replied: "What used to be a conflict is synergy now."

The third suspect in the story is the media. In the bubble years, America's media seems to have roughly doubled its coverage of the stockmarket, based on a sampling by the Pew Research Center. Pew monitored three mainstream news and current events outlets – *CBS Evening News*, *Newsweek* and *The NewsHour with Jim Lehrer* – and found that from 1990 to 1996 they ran a combined average of 100 stories a year on the stockmarket, excluding the regular nightly updates. From 1997 to 2002, this rose to more than 200 stories annually. The increase was broadly in line with the spread in stock ownership among the population. The *New York Times* and the *Wall Street Journal* each added a new weekly technology section. *Forbes*, *Business Week* and *Fortune* increased their tech coverage. Even *Entertainment Weekly* added an Internet section. Among business media the upsurge in coverage was steeper yet as a bundle of new business magazines thudded onto the national doorstep. Among them were *eCompany Now*, *Business 2.0*, *The Industry Standard*, *Wired*, and *Fast Company*. The most striking new outlet, however, was a cable TV channel devoted to business and market news, CNBC, which stood for Consumer News and Business Channel. It was a 1989 offshoot of NBC, and it was not initially well supported within NBC nor by its corporate master, General Electric. "There was a lot of scepticism," recalled NBC chairman Robert C. Wright. "Quite frankly, at NBC they thought it was the worst idea in the world." The chief executive of GE, the storied Jack Welch, also resisted the proposal. "I had to convince Jack Welch this was a good idea." By 2000, it was generating an estimated $300 million a year in revenues.

Through the medium of CNBC, the ever-rising share prices of the 1990s delivered Americans the dual satisfaction of bread and circuses in a single venue – Colosseum and marketplace, all in one. As they made money they could watch the spectacle on TV at the same time. At the market's peak, 418,000 Americans watched CNBC daily. The prominent Chicago-based economist David Hale called it "Bubble Vision". As it started to outrate CNN, its popularity surprised even its own staff. "The idea that we would be the most-watched cable news channel, that's not normal," said presenter Joe Kernen in a 2002 retrospective. "We were beating CNN. It's weird for business news to be in a position where global events and political events are on the back burner. It shows you how far things were out of whack." When the bubble burst, the vision was lost. Audience numbers halved.

In fact the problem was not so much the quantity of the media's coverage of the bubble as its quality. Although there was a healthy dose of initial scepticism, as the years went by the tone of the media coverage became more credulous. As the sceptics were proved wrong time and again, they seemed to become less credible. Only the bulls seemed to have a plausible explanation for what was happening to America, so they came to dominate the coverage and the commentary. Like the rest of the country, the media generally, but not uniformly, fell into the national swoon. "The news media are fundamental propagators of speculative price movements," wrote Robert Shiller in his 2000 analysis of the bubble, *Irrational Exuberance*.

And when the stockmarket sceptics were granted some public airspace, they sometimes came to feel the unpopularity of their position. "Once, just before going on national television, the anchor looked me squarely in the eye and told me that what I said could conceivably have an impact on the market, and that people can get upset if they perceive prognosticators as disrupting the market," recalled Shiller.

In October 1997, *Time* magazine carried a piece so fervid that it seemed it must be ironic. The piece, titled "Married to the Market", opened: "Worried about retirement? Don't be. Little Biff and Betsy are just a few years from college? No sweat. Vacation house? Go ahead. Heck, chuck all your financial concerns . . . Omnipresent and omnipotent, the stockmarket god will take care of all." Two-thirds through, the essayist paused, and posed the obvious question: "Is it all misguided devotion?" But no, *Time* was deadly serious: "Hardly", it answered itself. It concluded by arguing that the only real risk for investors was to lose the faith and divest.

In the 1920s, the New York governor and national chairman of the Democratic party, John J. Raskob, also the financier who helped create General Motors and Du Pont, published a notorious article in the *Ladies' Home Journal* headed "Everyone Ought to Be Rich". It was notorious because it preceded by two months the Great Crash of 1929. But now, in December 1999, the business magazine *Forbes* ran the same exhortation as its cover: "Everyone Ought to Be Rich". It argued that Raskob's ill-timed argument had been, finally, vindicated. *Forbes*' timing was almost as good as Raskob's. The market began its fall three months later.

At CNBC, the spirit of the times was in evidence too, under the channel's slogan "Profit From It" and amid an onscreen riot of moving tickers, tapes and graphs. The programming was thick with stock shills – analysts and chief executives coming on for interviews in which they talked up their products. A high point came when the chief executive of a software firm, Mark Breier of Beyond.com, appeared in an interview wearing only his underpants. How cool was that? It was plain that all the old rules were no longer applicable. Well, for a while at least. Beyond.com filed for bankruptcy in 2002.

The president of CNBC, Bill Bolster, when confronted with the suggestion that the channel had been cheerleading for the stockmarket during a 1997 market downturn, replied: "That is an observation that I am very comfortable with."

Even when CNBC tried to apply the old rules, they didn't seem to work any more. After Henry Blodget's brazen forecast that the price of Amazon.com's stock would increase by two-thirds within a year to an outlandish $400 a share had been handsomely rewarded, there was an outbreak of would-be imitators. So in the same week that *Forbes* published its ill-timed cover story, an obscure analyst at brokerage Paine Webber, Walter Piecyk, predicted that an overpriced wireless technology stock, Qualcomm Inc., was about to soar. It had already got giddily airborne, moving from $26 a share to $503 within a year. Now Piecyk foresaw it reaching $1000 within twelve months. CNBC's morning program, *Squawk Box*, thought that this was too far-fetched, and derided it. One presenter, David Faber, remarked that "analysts don't know much of anything", and amplified the point with sound effects. But the *Washington Post* reported that this attempt to ridicule the forecast only gave it the exposure to generate a price rise – the "Squawk bounce", it was called – and Qualcomm shares immediately shot up by 14 per cent to $575. The man whose credibility the CNBC presenters had questioned in the morning was invited to appear on the channel to be interviewed in all seriousness later in the day. Walter Piecyk, twenty-eight years old, also was interviewed by the CNN channel specialising in financial news, CNNfn, and the *Wall Street Journal.* A year later the stock was trading at $82 and a year later again, at the end of 2001, it was back at $26.

After issuing his famous forecast for Amazon.com, and before he was barred for life from the securities industry, Henry Blodget was interviewed on TV on hundreds of occasions. Even he, it later emerged, had been taken aback at the effect of his pronouncement: "It was like touching a match to a bucket of gasoline. I was shocked," he recalled in an interview in 2000. If the dotcom sector supplied the fuel, and analysts like Blodget lit the match, and the stockmarket shot up in flames, the media supplied the oxygen of public exposure and popular excitement to keep it flaring brightly.

The fourth suspect is the business cycle. A poll of 1000 adults in December 2001 by Fabrizio, McLaughlin & Associates, a firm with solid Republican credentials, found that 56.5 per cent blamed "normal fluctuations in the business cycle" for the country's recession. The business cycle is the rhythm of economic activity through a familiar sequence of growth and contraction. The US has ridden thirty-two of these cycles since 1854, according to the National Bureau of Economic Research, and ten since World War II. There is irony in this readiness to blame the business cycle. The so-called New Economy that the US was supposed to be pioneering in the 1996–2000 boom was supposed to have banished the business cycle. According to some of the advocates of the New Economy or New Era, the US was now on a permanent and elevated growth track.

In February 2000, the US economic expansion became the longest unbroken run of growth in the country's history. In a time of great optimism, this produced a further surge in excitability. "The business cycle – a creation of the industrial age – may well become an anachronism," wrote the award-winning journalist and author Thomas Petzinger Jr in the *Wall Street Journal* on December 31, 1999. He cited experts such as Mark McElroy, a principal in IBM's Global Knowledge Management Practice: "Conventional economics is dead. Deal with it!"

The theory ran like this. In agrarian economies the harvest set the business cycle. The advent of the Industrial Revolution changed this. From the middle of the nineteenth century it was the great waves of investment that established the new ebb and flow of boom and bust. As businesses saw opportunities, they would invest money in plant and equipment to exploit them. But the planned investment would not exactly match the future demand. There would be a groundswell of optimism, a number of firms would rush the same opportunities, and inevitably the investment would prove to be too much. New investment would halt while the existing over-investment was worked off. This rush to invest, followed by a period of retrenchment, was the cause of the business cycle in the industrial age.

Now, by the time of the late 1990s, the New Economy had made this redundant, for three main reasons. First, because the fuel for growth was suddenly unlimited. "In a knowledge-based economy, there are no constraints to growth," claimed Michael

Mauboussin, CS First Boston's managing director of equity research. "Man alive! That's not something new?" Second, even in the traditional physical economy, information technology now allowed firms to track their inventory so accurately in "real time" that there were no longer big clunky orders and backlogs and bottlenecks and industries moving in fits and starts, but only a smooth and finely tuned flow where production meshed perfectly with demand. And third, globalisation had changed the way the economy worked in at least three ways. It had increased competitive pressure on US wages, keeping the cost of labour in check. This, in turn, would help keep inflation down. Next, globalisation was enlarging the market available to US firms and therefore promised almost limitless sales growth. Finally, the greater mobility of capital in a globalised world meant that the US's voracious hunger for foreign capital could be sated without risk of interruption.

The notion that this added up to a New Economy was not only entertained by a few over-caffeinated consultants. "It became an article of faith for many economists that, especially in the industrialised economies of the West, the business cycle had been banished," wrote Anirvan Banerji of the Economic Cycle Research Institute in 2002. And it was formally entertained by the US Government at the highest levels. The Economic Report of the President, 2001, began: "Over the last eight years the American economy has transformed itself so radically that many believe we have witnessed the creation of a New Economy." In English-language newspapers in 1992, there were six articles that referred to an "old economy" and a "new economy". The next year there were seven; the year after fourteen; in 1995, there were eight. The number didn't change much in succeeding years – four, five, nine. It was not until 1999 that the concept entered popular discourse with thirty-one stories on the subject, before an almighty explosion of theorising in 2000 – 1012 articles.

But all of this theorising peaked with the stockmarket and the economy itself. Thirteen months after the US celebrated its longest boom in history, it came to an end. The onset of recession put a swift and brutal end to all the talk of a New Economy. The Great American Bubble was not a stockmarket manifestation of a new Utopia of uninterrupted high-speed growth. It was just a mania ballooning out of a classic bout of over-investment.

Investment usually amounts to one-sixth of the US GDP, but during the final three years of the bubble it surged to make up one-third. When new investment came to a stop in the usual shuddering halt, recession followed. "The defining characteristic of the 2001–2002 US global recession has been the collapse of business investment spending," remarked Citibank Asset Management economists in a research note of December 2001. "To find precedents we have to go back to the second industrial revolution in the late 1800s and early 1900s, where boom-bust economic cycles were commonly caused by capital investment and stockmarket bubbles in the then 'new economy' industries" of railroads, electric utilities, motor vehicles, telephones, electric motors, radio and aircraft. Far from being some new and unique phenomenon, the so-called New Economy departure from the business cycle was nothing but a reversion to old and very familiar patterns of boom and bust.

In the four years to mid-2000, investment spending added 1.5 percentage points a year to America's annual economic growth rate. That is, it accounted for more than a third of all growth in the US economy in those boom years. Then from mid-2000, the halt in new investment was so precipitous that it cut 1.8 percentage points from economic growth in the following twelve months.

So was the downturn in the business cycle responsible for the end of the bubble and the boom? No. The stockmarket turned down first, as it almost always does. Of the forty-two recessions the US has suffered since 1802, the stockmarket fell by at least 8 per cent before thirty-nine of them, or 93 per cent of the time.

Often, however, a downturn in the stockmarket is an indicator of what is to come, a warning of recession, a flag waving to signal a new direction in the wind. In this case, however, the stockmarket actually dragged the economy down; it was not a flag in the wind but the wind itself. "The deflation of the global technology stock bubble has already had discernible real consequences," reported the Bank for International Settlements, the world's club of central banks, often described as the central bank for central banks, in its annual report dated May 2001. And it gave a succinct explanation of how this had occurred:

> In particular, the effect on investment through the cost of capital was immediately apparent. Technology start-ups, which had relied particularly heavily on initial public offerings (IPOs) for raising capital, were especially hard hit . . .
>
> The stockmarket decline has also had consequences for the reported incomes and cash flows of US companies through their defined benefit pension plans and stock option grants. In 1998 and 1999, profits had been boosted by the fact that gains in the stockmarket had resulted in an overfunding of defined benefit plans, which companies could report as income. The decline in the market in 2000

> deprived many companies of that income . . . At the same time, technology firms had increasingly tended to issue stock options to employees as a form of compensation. In the US, the exercise of these options allowed companies to reduce their taxes and thus add to their cash flows . . . For some of the larger technology companies, these benefits accounted for as much as 60 per cent of cash flows from operations. At current stock prices, however, a substantial amount of stock options will not be exercised. These companies are now finding themselves with increased tax bills even as their sales slow and their inventory costs rise.

The stockmarket reached its apex in March 2000. Total domestic investment spending in the US peaked in the months that followed, the second quarter of 2001. And within that overall investment, the category that drove the rise and then accounted for the bulk of the fall – equipment and software – hit its all-time high in the second and third quarters of the year, when it was $926 billion and $924 billion respectively, before it started a serious slide in the following quarter. So the stockmarket, which had led the boom in investment on the economy's way up, also led the business cycle down. The stockmarket, in an important sense, had become the business cycle. So the downturn in the business cycle did lead to recession, but it was the stockmarket that had most directly led the business itself.

All the rhapsodising and theorising of an end to the business cycle was utter bunkum. The National Bureau of Economic Research dates the expansion as running from March 1991 to March 2001, an unusually long growth cycle of 120 months compared to the post-war average of fifty-seven months, but part of a cycle nonetheless. The recession that followed is dated from March 2001 to November 2001, a duration of eight months, a little shorter than the post-war average of ten months, but a recession nevertheless.

The fifth suspect in the drama is interest rates. The *Investor's Business Daily*'s search for a culprit in its poll in January 2002 found that 24 per cent of its 906 respondents agreed that "high interest rates" were to blame for the recession. And this is an entirely reasonable accusation. For four years, the US Federal Reserve had pursued a policy of keeping money cheap. From July 1995 to June 1999, the Fed had cut official interest rates for the entire duration of the boom, with only a single exception – in March 1997, it made a minuscule upward adjustment from 5.25 to 5.5 per cent in the key policy rate, the Federal funds rate – before it resumed cutting rates once more. This attitude was only reversed when, in eleven months from June 1999 to May 2000, the Fed raised its key policy rate in six steps from 4.75 per cent to 6.5 per cent.

The Fed was worried that the economy was growing faster than its potential, with demand exceeding supply at a clip that seemed sure to generate inflation. It intended the rate increases to slow the economy, and that was exactly what happened. The twelve members of the Fed's policy group, the Federal Open Market Committee (FOMC), gathered in the Fed's magnificent boardroom on March 21, 2000, under the baleful gaze of its chairman, Alan Greenspan. The meeting was about to administer what was to be the second-last increase in interest rates of the era. The committee already had lifted interest rates four times in the preceding eight months, and was concerned that this was not going to be enough. The view around the table was summarised in the minutes of the meeting:

> The growth in aggregate demand continued to display remarkable vigour, evidently driven by high levels of consumer and business confidence and accommodative financial markets . . .
>
> Of key importance was the prospective performance of the stockmarket, whose robust gains in recent years had undoubtedly boosted consumer confidence and spending. The members noted that equity prices generally had posted further gains during the inter-meeting period [since the FOMC's last session six weeks earlier], but in their view the large increases of recent years were not likely to be repeated, and an absence of such gains would have a restraining effect on consumer expenditures over time. Even so, further increases in household incomes along with the lagged wealth effects of the sharp earlier advances in stockmarket prices seemed likely to sustain relatively strong consumer spending for some period of time.

In other words, the economy was still running hot, and even if the stockmarket had already started to fall this was not good enough. The market, the FOMC believed, had generated so much momentum in the economy that it was likely to keep propelling the economy forward even if stock prices themselves no longer rose. To contain these pressures, the committee decided to increase official interest rates a fifth time, from 5.75 per cent to 6 per cent. This appears to have been the tipping point for the markets. The stockmarket reached its very apex three days later and began its long and costly three-year crunch. These higher interest rates first bit into stock prices, and this in turn bit into business investment, household consumption and corporate borrowing. The committee members walked from the Fed's boardroom that day thinking that their work probably was not quite finished:

> Looking ahead, the committee would continue to assess the need for further tightening [raising interest rates] to contain inflation. Even after taking account of the lagged effects of the considerable tightening that already had been implemented since mid-1999, additional tightening might well be needed to ensure that financial conditions would adjust sufficiently to bring aggregate demand into better balance with potential supply.

And that's exactly what they came back to do two months later, when they jacked up official rates from 6 per cent to 6.5. The Fed specifically used higher interest rates to slow the economy. It did not intend to pitch the economy into recession. In hindsight, the FOMC's members would no doubt prefer that they had not imposed that final increase in the cost of money. Nevertheless, they fully intended to use higher interest rates to slow the economy, and that's precisely what they did. Guilty as charged. The means by which the higher rates took effect, however, was chiefly the stockmarket.

The sixth key culprit commonly blamed for the bubble and its ugly aftermath is the government. In popular culture this took the form of blaming Bill Clinton or George W. Bush or the US Congress. It is difficult to have too much sympathy for politicians who are unfairly blamed when things go wrong, if only for the fact that they are invariably the first to make unfair claims for credit when things go right. Still, consider the opinion polling. In December 2001, with the market bust a year and a half old, the recession well under way and the Bush Administration approaching its first birthday, a Gallup poll asked a sample of 1019 Americans "whether you think each of the following deserves a great deal of blame, some blame, not much blame, or no blame at all for the country's current economic recession". Forty-four per cent said that the Bush Administration carried a great deal or some blame; 62 per cent said blame rested with Clinton; 75 per cent said Congress was to blame.

There are three chief points to be made about this verdict of His Honour Justice Gallup and his jury. First, those polled apportioned blame on a bipartisan basis, and were happy to hold the executive and the legislative branches of government responsible. There is a sense that everyone in the elected organs carried some blame, that "The Government" was culpable. Second, as time passed, Clinton's share of the blame shrank and Bush's grew. In another poll a year later conducted by the *Los Angeles Times*, given a list of potential culprits for the economy's performance that ranged beyond politics, 22 per cent of people polled fingered Bush and a scant 6 per cent blamed Clinton. This suggests that the incumbent tended to get a larger share of blame the longer he had been in power, and the part of the former administration had faded in memory. We cannot know, but it seems plausible that respondents were holding Bush responsible not so much for causing the downturn as for failing to quickly reverse it. Third, it must be said that it is completely nonsensical to blame the Bush Administration for events that happened years and months before Bush was anything other than governor of the great state of Texas. The stockmarket began its three-year slide on March 24, 2000. The bust was well advanced by the time of the election in November 2000, and the market had lost one-tenth of its value by the time George W. Bush put his hand on the inaugural bible in January 2001. The recession was judged formally to have started in March 2001, according to the self-appointed and independent arbiter of these things, the National Bureau of Economic Research. The Great American Bubble inflated during Clinton's time in the White House, and it burst during Clinton's time in the White House, setting in train the downturn that led to the recession that formally commenced six weeks after Bush had moved into the executive mansion. George W. Bush can be held accountable for a great deal. He cannot be held accountable for the bubble or its bust.

Did the Clinton Administration and the Congress deserve blame for the bubble? Apart from monetary policy, which is the sole prerogative of the Federal Reserve, the national government has only one other macroeconomic function, and that is its control of fiscal policy, otherwise known as the budget. A government can add to demand in the economy by spending more than it collects in taxes, and if the US Government had done this during the bubble years it would indeed have been guilty of adding fuel to the fire. But in the bubble years the US Government – the Clinton Administration and the Congress – were exceptionally disciplined. Rather than add to demand, the government sector as a whole actually subtracted demand by spending less than it collected in tax, that is, by running budget surpluses. It was taking fuel from the fire, and exerting a cooling influence on the economy.

From its outset, the Clinton Administration, with the coaching of Alan Greenspan, cut the Federal deficit. By 1997, this was negligible at $22 billion, and then in 1998 a minor miracle was achieved when it moved into a surplus of $69 billion, the first surplus since 1969, rising to a peak surplus in 2000 of $236 billion. But, you may say, wasn't Federal revenue bloated by all the extra taxes streaming into the Treasury as a result of all the bubble-era capital gains? Yes, it was, but even after adjusting to take account of the cyclical windfall the government was still admirably restrained. According to the non-partisan Congressional Budget Office, after stripping out the effects of the boom the Federal deficit was still only a relatively modest $78 billion in 1997, falling to $34 billion in 1998 and then moving into a small surplus of $8 billion in 1999 and a peak surplus in 2000 of $116 billion. So in its sole macroeconomic function, the Clinton Administration and the Congress behaved responsibly.

Beyond the crudeness of the debate by opinion poll, which is like trying to discuss philosophy through the expressive subtlety of pillow fight, there is a more sophisticated critique of the role of government in this episode. There is a case that government failed not through its macroeconomic function – its control of the budget – but in its regulatory function.

One of the economic officials in the Clinton Administration, Joe Stiglitz, chairman of the White House's Council of Economic Advisers from 1993 to 1997 and winner of the 2001 Nobel Prize for economics, argued after the event that "we were too trapped into the mantra of deregulation, mindlessly stripping back on regulation." He had four core areas in mind in his 2003 book, *The Roaring Nineties*:

> Deregulation of the telecommunications sector paved the way for the over-investment bubble, which then burst so resoundingly in 2001. Deregulation of the electricity market led to the market manipulation that hurt the California economy, the heart of so much of America's innovation. Deregulation of banking – notably the repeal of the Glass-Steagall Act – opened up new opportunities for conflicts of interest, when what was needed was stronger regulations

> to address extant and growing conflicts of interest which would eventually do so much to undermine confidence in our securities markets. Lax regulation of the accounting sector provided opportunities and incentives to proffer misleading or wrong information.

Stiglitz was right about each of these four areas where deregulation did, indeed, produce some ugly unintended consequences. The Telecommunications Reform Act of 1996 was an important part of the story of the 1990s. It was designed to open the long-distance telecoms sector to open competition. This would unleash the dynamism of the technological and economic possibilities of telecommunications. And the common understanding was that this would be vital to build the networks to carry the great burgeoning volumes of expected Internet traffic.

The Telecommunications Reform Act of 1996 was the invitation to an orgy of corporate investment. By the end of the process of deregulating long-distance telecommunications, a sector once shared by just three phone companies was now open to seventeen. By 2000, six of these companies were racing to build new, nation-wide underground networks of fibre-optics cables. The roads and pavements of America's inner cities looked like excavation zones as one company would dig up pavement to lay cable, only to be followed weeks later by another company which would dig up the same pavement and lay another cable for a separate network. By 2002, America's telecoms companies had borrowed $1.6 trillion from banks and raised an additional $600 billion by selling corporate bonds through the Wall Street investment banks. They raised billions more on the stockmarket.

"From coast to coast, the digital age has arrived in America – in the form of workers digging up streets in the blazing summer sun," wrote *Washington Post* reporters Justin Gillis and Jackie Spinner in 1999:

> Dozens of communications companies are in the midst of an unprecedented building boom. They're spending billions, block by painful block, to install thin glass fibers that can carry extraordinary amounts of information on waves of light. Freed by Congress three years ago from burdensome regulation, heartened by the explosion of Internet use, these companies are part of a digital gold rush.

The net result of this frenetic activity was too much cable, not enough users, falling profits and a vast misallocation of capital. The return on equity in the telecommunications sector fell from 14 per cent in the year the act was passed with strong bipartisan support in Congress to 6 per cent in 2000. Capacity utilisation was just 2.5 per cent in 2001.

Yet there were great splurges in other sectors that were not affected by deregulation. For instance, manufacturers of semiconductors and computers, together with communications makers, expanded their productive capacity by a stunning 50 per cent in a single year, 2000, according to Federal Reserve data. This was excessive, and so it was followed, naturally, by a severe downturn. But these investment decisions had been neither held up by earlier regulation nor were they galvanised by deregulation. So deregulation is neither a sufficient nor a necessary condition for excess investment across the economy, although it certainly exacerbated the problem in telecoms.

Likewise, Stiglitz appears to be right that banking liberalisation

– and specifically the repeal of the Glass-Steagall Act – aggravated the bubble. This law stemmed from 1933, a direct response to the banking collapses that followed the Great Crash of 1929. Glass-Steagall put a firewall between the banking system and the stockmarket. It barred commercial banks – the type of bank familiar to the bulk of the people, banks that take deposits and make loans – from entering the business of investment banks, the deal-making institutions that offer stocks and bonds for sale. And vice versa. Why? Because if a bank is promoting the stock of, say, Enron, that bank will always be inclined to lend money to Enron whenever it asks. Even if Enron were to fail the normal requirements of creditworthiness, the bank might still be tempted to support the firm in pursuit of the fees it might earn from helping Enron with a forthcoming issue of stocks or bonds. This would be a conflict of interest, and Senator Carter Glass and Representative Henry Bascom Steagall decided to resolve it by a legislative act.

The US banks did not like this constraint, however, and lobbied for its repeal. In 1999, they were successful. Joe Stiglitz blamed, in part, his colleague, the Treasury Secretary, Robert Rubin: "Rubin was a banker himself – the former co-chair of Goldman Sachs – and he actively supported the repeal effort." The result: "In the succession of corporate and financial scandals that followed Enron, numerous other cases came to light in which the banks continued to lend almost to the day of bankruptcy; they knew, or should have known, of the risk, but the lure of the mega-profits from new deals, should the firm weather the storm, made the lending attractive nevertheless."

A post-mortem in the *Wall Street Journal* on January 14, 2002, laid bare some of the detail of the consequences of allowing banks to become giant financial supermarkets:

> Enron's decline shows how these multi-faceted institutions are often on many sides of big deals in arrangements bristling with potential conflicts. Consider the many hats worn by J.P. Morgan as one of Enron's main lenders. (J.P. Morgan says its lending exposure to Enron is more than $2.6 billion.) It has arranged billions of dollars in loans to Enron, keeping chunks of that financing on its own books. It also has underwritten bonds for Enron. Less visible are other roles. J.P. Morgan trades currencies, bonds and derivative contracts, both with Enron and with other institutions that trade the debts and obligations issued by Enron. It has a research analyst covering Enron who until last fall had recommended investors buy Enron stock. J.P. Morgan also sold Enron credit derivatives, among other things, even as its asset-management arm managed a stock fund for the Employee Retirement System of Texas that held Enron stock. (The Enron stock was liquidated from the portfolio at the end of November, a spokeswoman for the Texas system says – more than a month after Enron's troubles were well known.) A spokeswoman at J.P. Morgan says the asset-management arm is likely to join some of the shareholder suits against Enron even though teams from other areas of the bank were advising Enron on the same decisions that are now being called into question by lawsuits.

This is a fitting punchline to the riot of conflicts of interest – that one part of J.P. Morgan was planning to sue its former client for something it did at the urging of another part of J.P. Morgan.

When the boom finally went bust in 2000, Citibank staff hastily wrote reassuring messages on whiteboards to tell customers in bank branches that for every year the stockmarket suffered a loss, it enjoyed three years of gains. This was historically accurate but practically useless information: the market not only stayed down in 2000, it fell further the next year, and further still the year after. The banks had become apologists and PR agents for the stockmarket.

But even Stiglitz concedes in a footnote that the repeal of the Glass-Steagall Act "was not at the centre of the story, but it did make a bad situation even worse". It did not require the repeal of Glass-Steagall to create a stockmarket frenzy, but it helped. Again, deregulation was neither a sufficient nor a necessary reason for the bubble and its consequences. But it did exacerbate the situation by broadening the scope for rash behaviour and unethical practices.

Another regulatory failure occurred with the supervisors of the markets. From 1993 to 2000, the number of complaints by investors rose by an average of 13 per cent a year. By contrast, the staffing at the agency responsible for investigating them, the Securities and Exchange Commission (SEC), grew by an average of 1 per cent a year. The SEC chairman during those years, Arthur Levitt, proposed a raft of regulatory changes to police what he called the "dysfunctional relationships" on Wall Street. He had little success. It was an unpopular cause. The mood in Washington was distinctly laissez faire. In the words of the then leader of the Republicans in the House of Representatives, Dick Armey: "The market is rational, and the government is dumb." Those who held this view were fondly and regularly stroked by companies and industries that stood to gain from it. For instance, Enron, which pressed for deregulation in everything from derivatives trading to electricity, donated money to almost half the 435 members of House of Representatives and three-quarters of the 100-member Senate in pursuit of its agenda. It contributed a total of $2.5 million to politicians in the 2000 presidential election cycle. Enron's chief, Ken Lay, bought his way to first-rate political access. He played golf with Bill Clinton and was the biggest single financier of the political career of George W. Bush. So the SEC, starved of funds and of the power it sought, was forced to retreat just as fraud and abuse advanced. Where once it had reviewed the accounts of corporations every three years, it was now obliged to extend this to six. Enron, last subjected to an SEC review in 1997 and not due for another until 2003, collapsed a year before the regulator was due to examine its affairs. Alan Greenspan, incidentally, was a leading champion of deregulation and a reliable opponent of any new proposals for regulatory measures.

The Federal Government, in addition to its budget function and its regulatory role, also has a broad responsibility for economic and financial stability. The US Secretary of the Treasury has been quite prepared to act on this responsibility. For instance, on October 27, 1997, the stockmarket had a rough day. The Dow Jones Industrial Average, an index of the price of thirty leading firms' stocks, fell 554 points or 7 per cent. The reason was edginess about the effects of the unfolding Asian financial crisis. The Treasury Secretary of the day was Robert Rubin. After conferring with his deputy, Larry Summers, the Fed's Alan Greenspan, and Gene Sperling from the White House's National Economic Council, Rubin made an appearance on the steps of the Treasury building in Washington DC in an effort to calm the market: "It is important to remember that the fundamentals of the US economy are strong and have been for the past several years," he told a battery of TV cameras. He added that the economic outlook was good. This was treated as a major news event. The market recovered somewhat the next day. And when Larry Summers succeeded him, he took the same approach. In mid-April

2000, as the bubble was bursting, the Nasdaq plunged 10 per cent in a day. Summers, now the Secretary of the Treasury, appeared on CNN and appealed for calm. The market did not respond on this occasion.

The peculiar aspect of these rare public comments on the markets is that these two treasury secretaries only ever intervened publicly when the stockmarket was falling precipitously. They never intervened publicly when the market was rising precipitously. Even though they knew that there was a major bubble under way, even though they knew that it was creating dangerous imbalances and growing risks, even though they spent years fretting about it in private, they never saw fit to utter a peep publicly. Rubin wrote in his memoir:

> As it seemed more and more likely that stock prices were excessive – and that the Nasdaq was almost manic – I became increasingly concerned that a sudden return to historical valuation levels could do harm to the economy. My considered view was never to say anything about the level of the stockmarkets, but with possible serious overvaluation posing larger risks to the economy, was there anything I could do about it? Alan [Greenspan], Larry [Summers] and I talked about this issue as the Dow broke 5000, 6000, 7000, 8000 and 9000. Warning off the investing public might have seemed tempting, but I thought, and still think, that public officials ought not to comment on the level of the stockmarket.

Rubin was prepared to break his rule to help support the stockmarket, to throw the weight of the US Government behind the cause of holding stock prices up. But, no matter how obvious the mania in the markets or how dangerous the imbalances, he never broke his silence to contain madly skyrocketing stock prices. Summers did exactly the same. In other words, it was the policy of the US Government to calm a potential panic, but not a potential mania. The government was concerned about instability that could flow from falling prices, but not the instability that might flow from rising ones, no matter how clear the danger. Plainly, the government, or specifically the Clinton Administration, was prepared to give tactic approval to the mania. This is entirely understandable from a political viewpoint. Which politician wants to be seen to be cheating the investing public of stock profits? However, there was one agency of the government with a mandate for financial and economic stability, one that also had independence from politics – the Federal Reserve. How did it use its power and independence? We shall see in the chapters that follow.

A word on Al Qaeda. It does not qualify as one of the six principal suspects for the bubble and the recession that followed. Opinion polling showed that anywhere between 13 and 79 per cent of Americans attributed some or all the blame for America's recession to the terrorist attacks on New York and Washington DC on September 11, 2001, depending on the poll. And the attacks did worsen the recession. But by the time they occurred, the stockmarket had been falling for a year and a half and the economy had been in recession for six months. The recession ended only two months after the attack. The recession was principally a result of what had gone before – it was the aftermath of the bubble. Osama bin Laden cannot take any credit for causing the bubble, the boom or the bust, and can only be held responsible for exacerbating an existing economic downturn.

And so each of the six suspects is blamed for its part in the Great American Madness and its aftermath. And each accuser, stressing the contribution of just one of the six, does indeed have a case. Each of the six was an indispensable part of the drama, but only a part.

The dotcoms and the other New Economy companies made the technological progress, or at least gave the impression of doing so. Their CEOs cut bold figures, marketed their firms to the media and cut the deals with the Wall Street firms. The Wall Street firms helped them raise cash from a credulous public, but raised more for themselves in the process. They knowingly misled some clients and manipulated others to whip the market into a state of high excitement to keep the profits coming. The media suspended its critical faculties and validated the excitement. It served as a vital marketing outlet to entice an ever-growing pool of investors into the game. The combined effect of all this was to feed capital, cost-free, to companies that seemed to be part of the New Economy. This gusher of free cash, in turn, galvanised companies into investing more money in New Economy-related projects, creating an old-fashioned investment-driven business cycle. All of this was accommodated by Greenspan's Federal Reserve, which allowed interest rates to move lower the longer the frenzy ran. The other arms of government aggravated the situation by declining to regulate or discourage the excesses and the chicanery of the time, and by dismantling existing regulatory constraints. When the Fed finally raised rates in 1999 and 2000, it brought the whole episode to a messy end.

Like the six blind men who each had a claim to part of the truth, those who put emphasis on any one of these six suspects for the Great American Bubble have a part of the story, but only a part. They are all true, but none has the whole truth. Then there was the wise man.

Chapter Four

THE WISE MAN

Alan Greenspan was the chairman of the US Federal Reserve, America's central bank. He is a consummate politician who remained at the head of a powerful and prestigious Federal agency for nearly nineteen years and was appointed or re-appointed by four Presidents. When Bill Clinton asked him in 2000 if he would like to be appointed to a fourth term as chairman or whether he'd prefer to "go out now on top", the seventy-three-year-old replied: "Oh, no. This is the greatest job in the world. It's like eating peanuts. You keep doing it, keep doing it, and you never get tired."

His age has been no barrier. "I'm not senile yet," the chairman said in 1999. "Of course, I may not be able to remember the name of someone I just met. But when it comes to numbers and statistics, it just sticks." Anyone who spoke with him, or saw him perform in congressional hearings, could attest that his mind was both subtle and sharp. Even the world's smartest woman gushed over the great man. Marilyn vos Savant, listed in the *Guinness Book of Records* Hall of Fame as owner of the world's highest recorded IQ, upon being told that smart students should become doctors so they could help people, replied: "Yes, but doctors help people one at a time, while an Alan Greenspan can help millions of people at a time."

He was not in it for the money. To enter government service he left behind an annual income of some $300,000 for a government salary of $42,500 to take the chairmanship of the Council of Economic Advisers in the Nixon White House. When he decided to stay on as Fed chief after 2000 for another term, he accepted an income of about $165,000 a year. He could have charged this much for a couple of speeches, and multiples of this sum for a single, well-chosen consultancy. His investments were valued at between $4.2 million and $12.1 million in 2002, a legacy of his consulting firm on Wall Street. His wife, Andrea Mitchell, a star reporter at NBC, earned multiples of his salary as Fed chairman. "Money does not motivate him," she attested. "He couldn't care less. I drag him kicking and screaming to buy a new suit. He just doesn't care about money."

"I bet he'll stay there until they carry him out," Clinton had quipped to his staff, out of Greenspan's hearing. But no. The great man has yielded neither to infirmity nor death. It took a law, the legislative limit to the time one may serve on the Federal Reserve Board, to bring his tenure to an end, in January 2006, aged seventy-nine. Among the heads of government agencies in Washington, only J. Edgar Hoover, the ferocious power vampire who ran the FBI, has surpassed Alan Greenspan's facility in establishing a durable, personal power base that transcends politics and time.

He was a unique commodity, this modern American hero, and almost a paradox: a gravely serious central banker who was also a celebrity. He spoke in impenetrable monetary riddles, but he was enough of a pop figure that he once made a cameo appearance on *The Simpsons*. Bart tried to high-five the great man, who was much too aloof even to notice. The prominent conservative commentator George F. Will called him "the fourth arm of government", yet he managed to win widespread popular trust, despite his intimate association with the suspect institution of America's Federal bureaucracy.

He was important enough for the *Washington Post* to publish profiles of him, and socially sexy enough for the same newspaper to publish a profile of his barber. A ridiculous 0.2 per cent of Americans could explain what he did, according to one of his biographers, Justin Martin – ridiculous because what he did was vital yet so stunningly simple: he operated the money supply, the giant on–off switch of American economic growth. But nine Americans out of ten reportedly recognised his name. He was sufficiently élite to win an honorary knighthood from the Queen of England, yet familiar enough that a greeting-card company put his face on the front of a birthday card – promising to keep you young with another cut in your interest rate.

The paradox of being, at once, unapproachably serious yet rock-star racy may be resolved by the observation of a reporter for America's ABC TV, Betsy Stark: "He's so square, he's cool." The only debate about the extent of his influence was whether he was the world's second most powerful man, or whether he actually surpassed the President. *Newsweek* years ago put his picture on its cover with the caption "The World's Second Most Powerful Man". Yet, before Greenspan stepped down, as soon as his name was spoken to the leading Washington political analyst Charlie Cook, he shot back his unequivocal ranking: "The most powerful man in the world".

Christopher Hitchens wrote in the magazine *Vanity Fair*, just as the great American boom was climaxing: "He probably does possess more power than any President. A nod from him about the interest rate and global markets quiver along every nerve and ganglion . . . He can't, on his own initiative, reach for the thermonuclear button, but then, outside the realm of Hollywood, neither can the President. He doesn't have to waste time at any ceremonial events. He is obliged to report to Congress only twice a year, and at formal occasions, where he is received with the deference that was once accorded the Emperor of Japan."

A newspaper cartoonist, Sandy Campbell, sketched five figures in 2000 under the heading "Enduring National Monuments". Four were famous buildings – the Washington Monument, the Capitol Dome, the Lincoln Memorial and the Jefferson Memorial – and the fifth was labelled "The Alan Greenspan".

Greenspan's public image is one of dour dryness. His one-time idol, the libertarian proselytiser Ayn Rand, author of *Atlas Shrugged*, nicknamed Greenspan, then her gangly young clarinet-playing acolyte, "the undertaker" for the lugubriousness of his looks. George F. Will thinks he nurses some "secret sadness", and wonders whether he has lost the ability to smile. He has been described as Woody Allen with math skills. Bush's no-nonsense Vice-President, Dick Cheney, who has described himself as "serious, secretive and uncommunicative", said at a journalists' dinner: "Reporters often wonder what I am really like. Actually, I am a lot like Alan Greenspan, but not as zany."

But there is a private side to Greenspan, too, and it's not so dry. Jim Wolfensohn, one-time Australian, was president of the World Bank and long-standing friend of the Fed chairman. Every year, the Wolfensohns host the Greenspans at their magnificent retreat amid the national parkland at Jackson Hole, Wyoming.

"We have a guest book at the house," Wolfensohn related, "and one time, some years ago, I looked in it and I was amazed to find that Alan had signed it, and forecast accurately the departure of Boris Yeltsin, the exact closing level of the Dow Jones index for the year, the exact closing value of the dollar, and, I think, a fire in Chicago." This might suggest an eerie power of prescience. But no; it is just an eye for a prank: "It was only my son who noticed how he did it. He left his entry blank, and then the next year he came back and filled it in – he filled it in for the previous year, having guarded the page. He has a fantastic sense of humour."

J. Edgar Hoover stayed atop the FBI for an astonishing forty-eight years, until his death in 1972 at the age of seventy-seven. No-one else has begun to approach this record. Greenspan's only rival when it comes to longevity is one of his predecessors, William McChesney Martin, Fed chairman for almost nineteen years. To take a moment for pedantry, he actually served for four months longer than Greenspan – eighteen years and nine months, compared to eighteen years and five months. Martin, however, was forced out by Nixon in an act of political vindictiveness. Greenspan, a much better politician, has not been under political pressure to resign and is only obliged to relinquish office because of a law that stipulates that a Fed chairman may only serve one full term as a governor of the Fed, which is fourteen years, plus the unexpired portion of any unfinished term he might have inherited when first appointed, which, in Greenspan's case, was almost five years.

The Fed chief probably would resent the comparison with J. Edgar Hoover. Hoover notoriously abused his position to enhance his power – he avidly squirrelled away compromising information on congressmen, officials, even Presidents. To ensure secrecy, he deliberately mislabelled these files; his dossier on Richard Nixon was tagged "Obscene Matters". Greenspan himself may have been a target of Hoover tactics at one point.

In 1974, when a pair of FBI agents turned up to question Greenspan's first wife, Joan Mitchell (by a curious coincidence Greenspan's first and second wives were both named Mitchell), about her ex-husband, she did not realise at first exactly what they were probing for. Joan Mitchell, now Joan Mitchell Blumenthal, recounted the scene later to Justin Martin.

The agents kept repeating a phrase: "When you want to know the negatives about a person, you ask the ex-wife." Blumenthal would reply: "Yes, I understand that's why you're here, but I don't know what you want." Their obtuseness led to an increasingly frustrating 45-minute interview, until a light went on in Blumenthal's mind: "Oh, you're trying to find out if he's gay!" She went on to assure them: "Absolutely not. There's no question."

"It was incredible how he always had a beautiful woman at his side," said Barbara Branden, an acolyte of Ayn Rand and a member of what was ironically called her Collective, the circle around which the youthful Greenspan moved, though never fully entered, in the 1950s. "I think it was the attraction of his intellectual power and probably his reserve. You couldn't knock him over by batting your eyelashes at him. He certainly had a profound effect on women." Greenspan had a habit of dating female staff who worked for him. He started a small economic consulting firm in New York, at 52 Wall Street, in 1954. It was called Townsend-Greenspan. He carried on a relationship for several years with Kathryn Eickoff, a female economist he had hired, described by another of his biographers, Jerome Tuccille, as an attractive blonde. And he had a long romance with another employee, Marjorie Scheffler, described as a stunning redhead.

Another explanation for his powers of attraction came from Joan Mitchell: "He is very clever, he knows a lot about a million things, and he has a wonderful sense of humour. Alan is charming and always interesting." But the most revealing and extraordinary of her remarks on her ex-husband is this: "I've never seen him angry. That's an interesting kind of person." Indeed.

Alan Greenspan's cultivation of power relied on very different techniques to Hoover's. First and most obvious was his direct and formal power as Chairman of the Board of Governors of the Federal Reserve System. The Fed is an extraordinary institution. It has political independence. And it has financial independence. This gives it a unique status among the institutions of the American state. It needs seek no-one's permission to make decisions, and it needs seek no-one's largesse to fund its budget. Alone among government agencies in the US, it does not need to prostrate itself on Capitol Hill and beg the Congress for its annual budget. The Fed funds its annual budget of about $3 billion, from which it pays for all its needs including its 25,000 staff and its own fleet of aircraft, from the enormous income it earns chiefly from interest payments on the Treasury securities it holds. How big is its income? It is typically between $20 billion and $30 billion a year. This makes it about as profitable as the biggest private sector banks in the US. In 2002, for instance, while Citigroup reported net income of $20.5 billion, the Fed disclosed net income of $26 billion. After looking to its own budget needs, the Fed pays the great bulk of this money, around 95 per cent on average, to the US Treasury. The Fed also enjoys other privileges, including an exemption from audits by the US General Accounting Office and exemption from the Federal Labor Relations Act so that none of its employees has ever been covered by a collective bargaining agreement.

The Fed, created by an act of Congress in 1913, has not always been independent. During the two world wars it agreed to subordinate sound monetary policy to the need to finance the war effort, and effectively financed US Treasury borrowing at very low rates. Having prostrated itself during the emergency, the Fed found it difficult to stand up again afterwards. Until it negotiated a division of labour with the US Treasury in 1951, it was essentially an agent of the Treasury. The break occurred when Harry Truman's Administration was demanding that the Fed keep monetary conditions easy; the Fed flexed its muscles, determined to stamp out rising inflation by restricting money. Finally, in an extraordinary application of political pressure, President Truman called the Fed's entire Federal Open Market Committee into the Oval Office for a fireside chat to impress his will on its members, who listened to him in silence. When they left, Truman issued a press statement claiming that the Fed had capitulated and that interest rates would stay low. Still the Fed stood its ground. The negotiated settlement from that episode gave the Fed de facto independence from the Treasury, and hence from the administration.

Presidents appoint Fed chairmen, but they also live in fear of them. Presidents have simple and invariable desires on the question of monetary policy: they always want interest rates to be lower in the approach to re-election. They want a tide of prosperity to carry them effortlessly back into power. Or, if the President is nearing the end of his time, he wants to leave the legacy of a fast-growing economy and a favourable inheritance to his endorsed successor, often his Vice-President. The needs of the economy do not naturally align with the President's timetable, however. This is precisely the reason the Fed has independence – so that the national economy is not run at the electoral convenience of the President.

In the best-known line about the purpose of the Fed, its chairman from 1951 to 1970, William McChesney Martin, said that its job was "to take away the punchbowl just when the party gets going". In other words, the Fed has to remove the intoxicant of easy money to keep economic activity sober and orderly. For most of the post-war era the risk of an excessively rowdy party has been the inflation that it can generate. In the post-Volcker years inflation remains active but quiescent, and the more likely and virulent danger of an economic bacchanalia comes from the other form of inflation – sharp run-ups in asset prices, especially stocks and real estate, otherwise known as bubbles. No politician would want to spoil a party. That's why the job falls to the Fed. And that's why it has the independence to pursue sustainable growth free of political interference.

Through its control of the money supply and hence the speed of economic growth, the Fed can make or break the President's prospects for re-election. Successive chairmen have had to wage a constant vigil to protect its prerogatives against pushy politicians.

A former Fed governor, Andrew Brimmer, wrote that there was a state of almost "continuous and at least public and vigorous conflicts" between Presidents and the Federal Reserve. Of the fourteen Presidents to hold power from the time of the creation of the Fed to the time in which he was writing, 1989, twelve – from Woodrow Wilson to George Bush – had "some kind of public debate, conflict, or criticism of Federal Reserve monetary policy".

Congress, from time to time, has tried to intimidate the Fed too. Members often present bills that propose some attack on the Fed's powers, although they rarely pass. In 1933, a bill was proposed to abolish the Fed altogether. And on two occasions, once in 1975 and again in 1982, both times of economic downturn, the House of Representatives passed resolutions specifically instructing the Fed to lower interest rates to boost the economy.

The Congress did give the Fed its mandate: it is tasked with managing interest rates "commensurate with the economy's long run potential to increase production, so as to promote effectively the goals of maximum employment, stable prices, and moderate long-term interest rates". So although the Fed has freedom in how it pursues its goals, the goals themselves are set out by Congress in its charter.

In international comparisons, the Fed has never been judged to be the world's most independent central bank. That honour always went to Germany's Bundesbank and the central bank of Switzerland, but these have been overtaken by the new European Central Bank, which even a Fed governor publicly conceded was now the most independent central bank in the world. But in academic rankings the independence of the US Federal Reserve has been consistently placed at the very top of the second tier of central banks around the world.

The vice-chairman of the Fed from 1994 to 1996 and former Clinton adviser, Alan Blinder, once defined the Fed's independence this way. The "hallmark of independence is near irreversibility. In the American system of government, for example, neither the President nor the Supreme Court can countermand the decisions of the Federal Open Market Committee," the committee charged with controlling the money supply and therefore official interest rates, the Fed's key power. "This makes FOMC decisions, for all practical purposes, immune from reversal. Without this immunity, the Fed would not really be independent, for its decisions would hold only so long as they did not displease someone more powerful."

A president can, and does, try to control a Fed chief. President Lyndon Johnson called William McChesney Martin to his ranch in Texas to try to bully him into reversing a decision to increase interest rates in December 1965. Martin stood his ground.

Richard Nixon believed that the Fed had cost him the 1960 election, and he took vengeance on its chairman, again Martin, by replacing him with Arthur Burns as soon as he had the chance, which happened to be in 1970. It was a ten-year grudge.

The tough and towering Fed chairman from 1979 to 1987, Paul Volcker, crushed inflation with high interest rates and proved his courage and independence, which was exactly why the Reagan Administration stacked the Fed's board to outnumber and outvote him, halfway through Reagan's second term, in February 1986. The majority of the board demanded an immediate cut in rates. Volcker refused and was formally voted down. His authority denied, Volcker resigned immediately. He reconsidered later in the day when the majority of the board backed down and the administration, realising that the public destruction of the Fed chairman could have far worse consequences than an unchanged interest rate, kept the event quiet and no rate cut was announced. Reagan was pleased, however, to see him leave at the end of his second term. Volcker was prepared to stay for a third term if he could be sure that he had the strong and enthusiastic support of the President. He did not get it. "We got the son of a bitch," rejoiced James A. Baker III, Secretary of the Treasury in the Reagan Administration and a key political strategist, when he heard the news.

Baker, a mainstay of the Republican Administration who went on to become a key figure in George W. Bush's 2000 election victory, had often disparaged Volcker as a "known Democrat", according to Bob Woodward's book on Greenspan,

Maestro. Baker told Ronald Reagan that "it's time to have your own Fed chairman," and "to my mind there's only one person we can turn to." That person was Alan Greenspan, a friend of Baker's and a confirmed Republican.

Even so, the Republicans did not get everything they wanted from Greenspan. In 1988, an undersecretary of the Treasury wrote a letter to the Fed urging it to cut interest rates. Alan Greenspan publicly rebuked the official.

And Reagan's Republican successor, George H. W. Bush, the forty-first President, held Alan Greenspan directly responsible for his loss of the 1992 election. By raising interest rates to contain inflation, the Fed had produced the 1990–91 recession. It was this recession that Bill Clinton swooped upon as his great opportunity for the presidency, summed up by the catchphrase: "It's the economy, stupid." The recession destroyed George Bush senior's re-election prospects only eighteen months after his victory in the first Gulf War, and he blamed Greenspan. Said Bush: "I re-appointed him, and he disappointed me."

You might have noticed a pattern: politicians generally press for interest rates to be lower, rarely higher. Hence the wisdom of removing monetary policy from their grasp and giving it to an independent agency to protect it from political date-rape. Consistently cheap money could produce rampant inflation, major bubbles in stocks or real estate, dramatic losses of value in the dollar, and the economic crises that can flow from any of these. When the Fed decides to cut rates, it can be certain that it will win popularity in Washington. When it raises them, it can be confident of odium. That is why the real test of a central banker is an equal readiness to raise as to lower, depending not on the political condition but the economic need. And that's why, when Greenspan made his very first decision to raise rates, on September 4, 1987, he found his predecessor, Paul Volcker, on the line: "Congratulations. Now that you've raised the discount rate, you're a central banker."

Does political pressure on the Fed work? Looking beyond the individual episodes and considering the evidence over a long time-frame, some academics hold the view that the Fed is robustly independent. Others have found that the Fed is indeed influenced by political pressure in setting monetary policy. One notable 1993 study, by Thomas Havrilesky of Duke University in North Carolina, counted the number of articles in the *Wall Street Journal* in which administration officials were quoted as expressing a desire for a change in monetary policy. Havrilesky called this "signalling". Then he related it to the way that the Fed moved official interest rates in the weeks that followed. He did this for the years 1964 to 1991. And he found that there was indeed a measurable relationship: "This corroborates the emerging belief in the monetary policy literature that the administration systematically can influence monetary policy."

Curiously, though, he found that this administration pressure on the Fed didn't always work. It only seemed to work when there was a second condition in place – when the Fed was also under threat from the Congress. When the Congress was angry at the Fed, threatening to attack its budgetary authority or its regulatory powers or its control over monetary policy, "it forces the [Federal Reserve] System to seek administration support for the institutional status quo. One way for the central bank to win this backing is to be responsive to administration desires with regard to monetary policy," Havrilesky wrote.

In other words, the Fed can withstand an assault from the administration, but it won't stand against the administration and the Congress combined. It will seek shelter from the congressional storm under the wing of the President, and to do so it is prepared to do the bidding of the President. "The history of monetary policy, as analysed in these pages," concludes Havrilesky, "suggests that the chairman as anti-inflationary hero is an inadequate institutional defence against both branches of government bent on monetary excess." One more interesting point: in a separate study using economic modelling and co-authored with two other scholars, Havrilesky also found that the strongest channel of influence for the President to sway official interest rates was through his power to appoint governors to the Fed's board.

The Fed chairmanship bestows other formal powers, too, in addition to its main role in managing the economy. The Fed has overarching responsibility for all of America's financial services industries, including the banking system and the financial markets.

But Greenspan developed three other vital sources of power, sources that cannot be encompassed or explained by his formal, legal power alone.

One is the management of his own institution. His predecessor, Paul Volcker, learned to his cost that a Fed chairman can be surrounded and outnumbered by his own board. He was outvoted and humiliated when the Reagan Administration stacked the Fed against him.

Greenspan himself had a salutary near-death experience in 1991 when he came very close to suffering a humiliating defeat at the hands of the FOMC. He was approaching the end of his fourth year as Fed chairman. This has a particular significance. A chairman's term is four years, so re-appointment was a looming question for Greenspan at the time. His term was to expire in August. He convened a conference call of the FOMC members on April 12. His relationship with the first Bush Administration was strained. The economy was just emerging from recession, although that was not yet entirely clear. As usual, the administration wanted the Fed to cut interest rates. And as re-appointment was on Greenspan's mind, re-election was on George H. W. Bush's. A story in the *Wall Street Journal* on April 10 said that the White House had not decided on whether to re-appoint Greenspan, and that the administration wanted lower interest rates.

When the Fed chairman convened the impromptu conference call of the Federal Open Market Committee that April, it surprised the other members. The transcript plainly showed that Greenspan proposed an immediate cut in the key policy interest rate, the Federal funds rate, of half a percentage point. He argued that he was acting in anticipation of an unexpectedly benign inflation report due out later the same morning. He said that the markets were expecting a rate cut and that if the Fed did not provide one, "the markets could break". He met resistance. There was opposition to the idea that the Fed should act merely to satisfy market expectations.

After some discussion it seemed that the chairman had a maximum of five votes on his side and it seemed likely that he would lose a vote. In the face of the revolt, Greenspan did not bring the call to a vote but suspended the conference call. Six days later the *Washington Post* ran a story wondering at the meaning of what had happened in the secret conference call, and quoted three members of the FOMC denying that Greenspan's authority was under challenge.

Eighteen days after the call Greenspan unilaterally cut the rate anyway. It was a cut only half as big as the one he had proposed – a reduction of one-quarter of a percentage point – but it was nevertheless a cut made on his own authority. He then organised a phone hook-up to inform the rest of the FOMC of his decision. He met no challenge. He had recovered from a potential rout to reclaim his authority.

But after this near-disaster he took care to caucus with other members before a meeting of the FOMC.

The committee has twelve members. These are drawn from two groups. All the seven governors from the Board of Governors, people appointed to fourteen-year terms by the President and based in Washington DC, are automatic and permanent voting members of the FOMC. The other five are drawn in rotation from among the presidents of the twelve district reserve banks that constitute the rest of the Federal Reserve System. The presidents of these district banks are elected by the boards of their own local institutions and live in their various regions. The reason for this design is to balance the top-down political appointments against the grass-roots representation of America's regions. The president of one of the twelve district banks has a permanent seat at the FOMC table – the Federal Reserve Bank of New York, because of its unique importance as seat of the main financial centre of the United States.

Greenspan made a practice of consulting closely with the seven members of the Board of Governors in an effort to keep them united as a solid core of support. "To ensure he has the votes to support his policy recommendation, the chairman visits with the members of the board in advance of FOMC meetings," wrote a governor from 1996 to 2002, Laurence Meyer. "When I began my term, the chairman would meet individually with the other governors during the week before FOMC meetings. His assistant would call to make an appointment" – incidentally, these men worked in offices along the same corridor in the Fed's headquarters, only a few paces from each other – "and he would then come to the office of each of the governors during the week. He would sit down and explain his views on the outlook and his 'leaning' with respect to the policy decision that would be considered by the committee at the upcoming meeting. Some governors found this rather off-putting. They interpreted the chairman's visit as his way of informing them in advance of the outcome of the FOMC meeting . . . I was just happy to have the opportunity to visit one-on-one with the chairman and to talk economics and monetary policy."

Later, Greenspan did away with the one-on-one sessions. Instead, he caucused with the other governors at the meeting that the Board of Governors would hold on the Monday immediately preceding the Tuesday meetings of the full FOMC. These were a free-flowing exchange of ideas, in contrast to what Meyer described as the "pre-packaged presentations" of the full FOMC. Regardless of the free play at the governors' meeting, however, the result was always the same: "At the end of the pre-FOMC Monday board meetings, there was, in my view, an implicit commitment to support the chairman the next day," wrote Meyer. "Thus, by the time the chairman enters the FOMC meeting, he is virtually guaranteed the support of the members of the board, who are, in turn, the majority of the voting members of the committee."

Greenspan was sufficiently confident of his position that he would not wait for the FOMC actually to meet before drafting the statement to be issued publicly at the end of the FOMC meeting. These statements are vital. They are short, terse and minutely scrutinised by the markets. They announce any decision to change official interest rates, and they set out the FOMC's future leaning – whether it is inclined to raise or lower rates in the future, or whether it is inclined to the status quo – and why. Yet Greenspan, by drafting the statement before the meeting, usually in conjunction with one or two of the Fed's staff but no other FOMC member, was allowing no scope for the FOMC meetings to make even a glancing effect on the announcement of Fed policy. He had mastered the Federal Reserve's pivotal policymaking body in part by hollowing it out, removing the decision-making power from the FOMC and making it his own preserve.

The FOMC's minutes and transcripts record that there is quite often debate and dissent. Occasionally a member will disagree with the chairman's recommendation so forcefully that he or she will formally vote against the chairman's recommendation, and these votes are noted in the FOMC's minutes. These are rare events, however. Even the most active of the dissenters, the president of the Kansas Federal Reserve, Thomas Hoenig, cast only three dissenting votes out of his total tally of thirty-two votes cast in FOMC meetings from 1991 to 2003, according to a count by the Financial Markets Center, a non-profit Fed-watching think tank. The next most rebellious member, the president of the Reserve Bank of St Louis, William Poole, cast two dissenting votes out of twenty-three votes since he took office in 1998. As one former governor, Henry Wallich, explained: "It is not a pleasant thing to have to keep dissenting. One dissents less frequently than you would think. After all, you are a member of a group and you want to get along with the other members." Even central bankers, it seems, are human.

Larry Meyer argued in 2004 that two dissenting votes in any FOMC meeting was the limit. "A third, however, would be viewed as a sign that the FOMC was in open revolt with the chairman's leadership," according to Meyer. "Because of this, I came to think of the voting process as a game of musical chairs. There were two imaginary red chairs around the table – the 'dissent chairs'. The first two FOMC members who sat in those chairs were able to dissent. After that, no-one else could follow the same course." In fact, there have been more. In June 1988, there were three dissenting votes to the chairman's majority vote of eight, and in 1990 there were four dissenters against Greenspan's seven, yet this precipitated no major crisis in the Fed or its credibility. It is striking, however, that the number of dissenting votes subsided markedly during Greenspan's term, and that Meyer's perception in 2004 could be so different from actual practice in 1988 and 1990.

Like a parliament in a communist state or a court in a dictatorship, Greenspan had kept the trappings of due process but gutted their substance.

Greenspan also spent his eighteen and a half years at the Fed without cultivating or grooming an obvious successor. When his vice-chairman from 1994 to 1996 and former Clinton adviser, Alan Blinder, appeared to be shaping up as a potential future chairman, he suspects that Greenspan worked covertly to frustrate and undercut him until finally he felt obliged to resign. And Greenspan reportedly connived secretly to destroy the candidacy of another vice-chairman perceived to be a credible potential successor, the former investment banker Felix Rohatyn, before he could even be appointed to the Fed's board. He preferred non-threatening technicians like his deputy after 1999, Roger Ferguson.

But it would be wrong to believe that Greenspan's dominance of the Fed relied on manoeuvring alone. He also won the admiration of many of the other FOMC members with his prodigious knowledge and command of detail.

For example, Larry Lindsey, a Fed governor from 1991 to 1997, is a man not easily awed. He is a former Harvard economics professor who went on to become economic adviser to George W. Bush. But he seemed to be in awe of Greenspan. Lindsey said that the chairman's grasp of detail can be overwhelming for his fellow board members. Lindsey recalled a time when the Mississippi was in flood: "At the time of the weekly board of governors' meeting, the US economy was literally linked together by a single bridge. Greenspan not only knew the location of the bridge, but also the various re-routing that could be used to get merchandise there. Those type of facts fit naturally into the mind of a man who studies statistics on boxcar loadings at all the major terminals in the country."

Lindsey made no secret of his adulation. In his 1999 book, *Economic Puppetmasters*, Lindsey depicted himself fawning all over the chairman: "When I mention to Greenspan that he is probably considered the best Fed chairman in history, he shifts uncomfortably in his chair and puts on the customary grimace that signals that he doesn't like the way the conversation is going."

The great man's answer: "I was just in the right place at the right time."

So Greenspan won all the votes? Largely, but not quite. In matters other than the central one of monetary policy, in other committees of the Fed, he was quite prepared to change his mind and alter his position. His vice-chairman from 1996 to 1999, another former Clinton adviser, Alice Rivlin, made this telling remark: "Greenspan doesn't like to lose, and if he thinks he'll lose, he switches sides." She hastened to add, however, that "when it came to monetary policy, the votes were never close," and Greenspan's proposals invariably carried the day.

The second informal source of Greenspan's power is his astute management of the principal power centres in Washington, the White House, the Congress and the media. He is a masterful cultivator of other powerful people.

Consider this tale from Brian Wesbury, chief economist at a Chicago investment bank, Griffin, Kubik, Stephens & Thompson. In the mid-1990s, Wesbury worked as an aide on Capitol Hill. When he started work in the Congress, one of his duties was to prepare for the Joint Economic Committee of Congress to exercise its oversight function of the Fed. He recalled his first meeting with the aides to the Republican senators who would be questioning the Fed chairman at a forthcoming session of the committee.

"Before the meeting started, one of the staffers came to me and said, 'Hey, before we get started, my boss wants you to know that he's best buddies with Alan Greenspan – they play tennis together – and he doesn't want to do anything to upset him,' " testified Wesbury. "Then another staffer came in and said, 'Hey, I think you should know that my boss has his birthday in the same week as Greenspan and they celebrate it together every year, and they're best buddies.' By the time the meeting started, almost every one of them had explained how his senator was best buddies with Greenspan. It was amazing. The guy is just an incredible politician. He's everywhere and he knows everyone. So he's got an extremely friendly environment to operate in. There are very few Congress members who truly understand monetary policy, and even if they spend the time and get to know something about it, they get flustered in front of him. And these are tough politicians – people who'd happily drive a nail through your eyeball."

This helps explain why the members of Congress and the

senators to whom he must give account twice a year often seemed more like his fan club than his inquisitors.

"It's always great to get the insights of the chairman of the Federal Reserve, who has done such an outstanding job," gushed Jon Corzine, a senator who was a former chief of the investment bank Goldman Sachs, at a hearing in 2002. It seemed that the one-time colossus of Wall Street might at any moment fall to his knees and ask the great man for his autograph.

Even on occasions when a member of Congress struck an adversarial pose, Greenspan displayed the same extraordinary calm that his first wife remarked upon. He never raised his voice or showed a hint of impatience. He handled every question with tremendous diplomacy. Clinton's first Treasury Secretary, Robert Rubin, described Greenspan as the master of the art of handling congressional questions: "Alan would doff his cap in the direction of a question, even if, on occasion, it was somewhat off the mark. 'That's an interesting observation you make, Senator, about the earth being flat,' he'd say. 'If I might, let me rephrase the question.' "

Another of his techniques for handling Congress was laid bare in January 1998, with the Asian economic crisis still unfolding, when Greenspan appeared before the House Banking Committee together with Rubin and Rubin's then deputy, Larry Summers. They were there to argue for an unpopular cause – to increase US funding to the International Monetary Fund to strengthen its ability to support countries in economic crisis. A member of Congress, Maxine Waters, a Democrat from Los Angeles, began her remarks by saying: "I will just cut this short by saying a few months ago, I would have been an unequivocal 'no' in opposition. Today I have an open mind, and one of the reasons I have an open mind is because of something as simple and fundamental as Chairman Greenspan being willing to listen to what I am concerned about, and taking that trip to South Central Los Angeles and walking along a block that can be developed, that can be invested in. And because of that, my mind is open, and I hope we can fashion a solution that works."

Greenspan had taken the time and trouble to accompany the congresswoman to a poor area of her constituency and to listen to her concerns about economic rehabilitation of a neighbourhood. Now, in turn, she was open to a proposal to provide funds to countries on the other side of the world. When members of congressional committees raised problems with Greenspan in public, he frequently invited them to discuss their concerns with him at a later date in private, drawing off the antagonist and seeking to turn a potential opponent into an ally.

Greenspan also makes a great effort to cultivate the executive branch of government. For example, he courted Bill Clinton. First, he deferred to the President-elect by travelling from Washington DC to Little Rock, Arkansas, for an audience. He conferred intimately with the incoming President's economics team. He coached the new administration in how and why it should cut the Federal deficit. He told incoming officials that in his estimate, based on a Fed exercise in economic modelling, long-term interest rates would fall by one-tenth of a percentage point for every $10 billion the Clinton team could cut from the deficit.

The implicit deal here was clear: if the administration shrank the deficit, Greenspan would let interest rates fall. Or, as Robert Rubin later observed, "knowing Greenspan's views helped us gauge his likely reaction to our fiscal choices".

Their understanding worked. Clinton did indeed cut the deficit, and Greenspan did indeed cut interest rates accordingly.

Bill Clinton remained wary of Greenspan, however, and decided to try to stack the Fed's board with reliable Democrats as a way of riding shotgun on the chairman. We shall explore the success of this stratagem later in this tale.

The Fed chairman had an even more intimate relationship with the next administration, that of George W. Bush. The Vice-President, Dick Cheney, a major power in the Bush Administration, had been a close friend since 1968. "They are very close, to the point where I think they speak to each other almost daily," said a former Republican official, Harald Malmgren. Indeed, when Cheney planned a trip to Japan and China in 2003, postponed because of the Iraq war, Greenspan was set to go along as companion on an unofficial program.

Greenspan even got involved in the second Bush Administration's recruitment efforts. He helped Bush and Cheney sign up their first Treasury Secretary, the Alcoa chief executive Paul O'Neill. After the President-elect had pressed a reluctant O'Neill over a hamburger lunch to take the job, Greenspan phoned O'Neill: "Paul, I'll be blunt," the Fed chief said, according to O'Neill, in a pitch that verged on the romantic. "We really need you down here. There is a real chance to make some lasting changes. We could be a team at the key moment, to do the things we've always talked about," specifically reform Social Security and Medicare. O'Neill signed up, but they achieved neither.

One vow that Greenspan and O'Neill took together in the earliest days of the Bush Administration was to work to prevent any return to Federal budget deficits, which had been ground down from a peak of $340 billion in 1992 and transformed into a surplus of $86 billion by 2000. Through the medium of O'Neill's storyteller, reporter Ron Suskind, we have this account of the two men's conversation of January 5, 2001, over a standard

Greenspan breakfast of oatmeal with raisins and grapefruit and decaffeinated coffee. "We're not going back into the red, Greenspan said. Paul nodded solemnly. For these two, it was a blood oath." They would support Bush's proposed tax cut only to the point where the budget remained in the black. They would insist that the tax law contain "triggers" that automatically cancelled any tax cuts the moment the surplus was in danger.

It might have been a blood oath for Paul O'Neill, who argued valiantly against Bush's second round of tax cuts on the ground that they would indeed push the budget back into deficit. And O'Neill shed blood on its account. He was drummed out of the administration for his stance, although it must be said he was also a singularly hamfisted Treasury Secretary in any event. His final confrontation with Dick Cheney produced one of the great lines in modern political economy. As O'Neill insisted that the US was "moving toward a fiscal crisis", Cheney cut him off: "Reagan proved deficits don't matter. We won the midterms. This is our due." The next month Cheney phoned O'Neill to tell him he'd been fired: "Paul, the President has decided to make some changes in the economic team." Pause. "And you're part of the change."

But it was not an oath for which Greenspan was prepared to raise a sweat, let alone shed blood. Although he had pressed the Democrats in the Clinton Administration to cut the deficit, Greenspan soon proved ready to endorse policies that would allow the Republicans in the Bush Administration to run the deficit back up again. Greenspan endorsed publicly the first wave of Bush tax cuts in 2001, and did not call for any reconsideration when the budget surplus disappeared. Nor did he resist the next wave of Bush tax cuts in 2003 even though it was clear that they would plunge the budget deep into deficit.

There were bitter recriminations among Democrats. A Clinton labour secretary, Robert Reich, told the *Washington Post*: "He risks politicising his office by venturing so far into the political realm, putting the prestige of his office at the service of a particular set of political judgments and values." A Democratic candidate for the presidency in 2004 and former governor of Vermont, Howard Dean, said that he would not re-appoint Greenspan as a result: "If he lacks the political courage to criticise the deficits, if he was foolish enough – and he's not a foolish man – to support the outrageous tax cuts that George Bush put through, then he has become too political and we need a new chairman of the Federal Reserve." The Democrat economist Paul Krugman in his column in the *New York Times* fulminated: "By using his office to promote a partisan agenda, he has betrayed his institution, and the nation."

While O'Neill was working to confront the President and his agenda, Alan Greenspan reached an understanding with him, subtle but perceptible. In essence, the accommodation involved the new President changing his initial approach of publicly pronouncing on Greenspan's every move. Bush backed off. In exchange for this, Greenspan endorsed Bush's tax cuts in 2001 and 2003.

Bush had begun his presidency issuing public assessments of the Fed chairman's every decision. Like a schoolmaster grading a pupil, he endorsed Greenspan's cut in interest rates on January 3, 2001. Soon afterwards he commended the central bank chief on his Senate testimony. Then, in the same month, a reporter asked Bush whether he thought Greenspan should again cut interest rates. The cut was already a fait accompli, but Bush replied: "That's the last time I'm going to comment about the actions Greenspan takes. He's an independent voice and needs to be an independent voice."

From that moment, Greenspan was able to have confidence that the President would allow him, in public at least, the freedom and the dignity and the apparent independence to do his work unimpeded. The price? Greenspan reversed his longstanding position and endorsed Bush's plan to hand out $1.6 trillion worth of tax cuts over ten years. Anna Schwartz, an economist at the US National Bureau of Economic Research and co-chair of a private body that scrutinises the Fed, the Shadow Open Market Committee, observed: "There is a new administration and Greenspan wants to be part of the team. And he has responded accordingly."

This left the Democrats feeling stunned and betrayed. When he delivered his bombshell to the Senate Budget Committee in January 2001, you could hear the indignation in the Democrats' voices. "Mr Chairman, I'm your friend," said a Democratic senator from South Carolina, Ernest Hollings. "I voted for you four times [in Senate confirmation votes]. But in all candour, you shocked me with this statement [calling for a tax cut]."

The Democrats had good reason to feel shocked. Greenspan had long held that the US Government should use surplus revenues to pay down government debt, not to give away tax cuts. He had said this repeatedly and at length. Indeed, Greenspan has always championed fiscal rectitude and reconstruction. As we have seen, he talked Clinton into it.

Clinton once remarked that the most important single decision of his presidency was one of his earliest – his 1993 decision to cut spending and ultimately pursue a balanced budget. And who was, in large measure, responsible for this policy? Alan Greenspan. So now to hear Greenspan embrace Bush's tax cuts over Clintonesque fiscal reconstruction, the Democrats understandably sensed a deep political betrayal.

Of course, Greenspan had a good explanation for his change of mind. The estimated size of the surpluses the Government was expecting to collect over the decade had burgeoned. The Government should be able to pay off all its outstanding debt by 2010, Greenspan said, "a prospect that did not seem likely a year or even six months ago". The expected surpluses – likely to be as big as $3.1 trillion over and above Social Security needs in the ten years to follow, according to the Congressional Budget Office – would be so big that the Government would not only pay off the debt but would soon start piling up treasure. And it would need to put this treasure somewhere. It would be obliged, said Greenspan, to invest it in private asset markets, creating all sorts of potential distortions in the markets. Better to hand it out as tax cuts.

Instead of being diametrically opposed to the new President's program, Greenspan was now in full support. This was clever but implausible. Even his former deputy at the Fed, Alice Rivlin, dismissed this as "a weak argument for cutting taxes". The projected surpluses were just that – projected, and therefore uncertain. And any likely stockpile of treasure was many years distant. It could be handed out as tax cuts if and when it emerged from the fogs of phantasm. Of course, those surpluses never did materialise.

The President had agreed to leave the Fed chairman alone to do his work, and the Fed chief had agreed to let the President deliver his promised tax cuts unopposed.

How much time does Greenspan spend on cultivating politicians? Because it is usually done in private, it is impossible to see. The Fed chairman cultivates the image of the aloof, independent central banker, but one researcher decided to unearth the extent of Greenspan's subterranean political contacts by filing requests under the Freedom of Information Act to get access to the chairman's daily diary.

The researcher, a lecturer in finance at the Wharton School, Ken Thomas, made a number of interesting discoveries from the summaries of the Fed chairman's diaries to which he was allowed access, covering the period from 1996 to the first half of 2004. First, he found that Greenspan had been increasingly busy with political meetings. In 1996, he was averaging a total of ninety-five private meetings a year with members of Congress and the administration combined, or an average of 1.8 meetings a week. That increased steadily to 170 in 2003, and in 2004 was running at an annual pace of 202, or 3.9 a week. So Greenspan's number of scheduled political appointments had doubled. In rough terms he was holding a formal meeting with a politician on four weekdays out of every five.

Second, it emerged that Greenspan's contact with members of Congress waxed and waned, but his number of meetings with White House officials exploded. From 1996 to 2000, the Clinton years, the pattern was roughly one meeting per month at the White House for an annual total of between 11 and 13. Then in 2001, when George W. Bush took over, this escalated to 37, then 55 the next year, and 68 in 2003. In 2004 he was running at an annual pace of 52 White House meetings. Far from being aloof and apolitical, concluded Thomas, "he's one of the most political people in Washington."

The media is another powerful force and, after some initial stumbles, he made it work to his advantage too. The essence of his approach to the media was to apply to himself a principle which comes naturally to a man responsible for issuing a currency – to make it valued, keep it scarce. And he applied a second principle in public appearances – to preserve maximum flexibility, avoid clarity at all costs. So his two main lines of approach were to be rarely seen, and to be little understood.

This did not mean that he refused to deal with the media. On the contrary, he had regular contact with selected journalists. It's just that he was very careful to be unobtrusive about it. He preferred to guide serious newspaper commentary, speaking on a non-attributable background basis, than to put himself out in front for the TV cameras. In short, he sought to manipulate rather than to star, an approach which may sum up his overall modus operandi as chairman.

On the way to his present mastery of the media, he received two early, painful lessons in public presentation that formed his thinking.

Greenspan's life had been shaped from birth by the stockmarket. He was born into the family of a Wall Street stockbroker on March 6, 1926, as one of the great bull markets of American experience was becoming fevered with speculation. It collapsed, as all bubbles must, in the Great Crash of 1929. Brokers' incomes rise and fall with the level of activity in the stockmarket. After 1929, the US market fell into an extended stasis, stressing the family finances and contributing to the failing marriage of Greenspan's parents, Herbert and Rose. They divorced when Alan was five years old.

The experience apparently was a powerful one. Alan Greenspan seems to have kept some sense of empathy for stockbrokers even in his later life. He committed his first major gaffe by expressing sympathy for brokers over and above poor folks. On September 19, 1974, Greenspan was serving as the head of President Gerald Ford's Council of Economic Advisers, and appeared at an economic summit as a representative of the President. America was in dire economic circumstances. Inflation was rampant and unemployment punishing. The summit sought solutions.

A union leader complained that the Ford Administration's policies favoured rich bankers over poor citizens. Greenspan responded in part: "If you really wanted to examine who percentage-wise is hurt the most in their incomes, it is the Wall Street brokers. I mean, their incomes have gone down the most. So if you want to get statistical, let's look at what the facts are."

Boos rang out. A participant jumped up and shouted: "That's the whole trouble with the administration!"

A group of house-builders in Oregon lampooned Greenspan by setting up a charity with the name "Save Our Brokers". This group of concerned builders mailed handkerchiefs and paper cups to the suffering stockbrokers – the handkerchiefs for them to weep into, the paper cups to drink their champagne from in these tough times. The union movement's umbrella body, the AFL-CIO, nominated Greenspan for its annual "dubious distinction" award. He apologised in a congressional appearance: "Obviously the poor are suffering more."

The lessons? Don't be too visible, and don't be too revealing about your honest opinions.

He committed his second notable faux pas in a TV interview. It was in his first weeks as the head of the Federal Reserve. The stockmarket had been troubled but the mighty slump of Black Monday, October 19, 1987, was still two weeks away. Appearing on *This Week with David Brinkley* in an effort to calm the market, he was asked about the prospects for higher inflation. Greenspan answered that there was no evidence of a pick-up in inflation, but "if everyone gets it into his head that inflation is inevitable, they will start taking actions that will create inflation." The Fed is the guardian, and the only guardian, against inflation. For the Fed chairman to speak like this implied a certain helplessness, a certain resignation to an inflationary outbreak. It was a mistake.

Bond yields rose and stock prices fell. Greenspan vowed never to grant another interview on the record. When Brinkley died sixteen years later, Greenspan made an exception and appeared on *This Week*. He remarked that Brinkley had a knack for making his interview subjects say more than they intended: "I must admit I made some inadvertent news as a consequence . . . And to this day, David Brinkley's show is the last Sunday show I've appeared on, until today, in memory of David." And he made another exception when he granted newspaper interviews to explain himself when he was personally embroiled in the savings and loan (S & L) crisis. The notorious swindler and head of Lincoln Savings and Loan, Charles Keating, had been a client of Greenspan's economic consulting business. At that time, in 1985, Greenspan had written a letter of recommendation for Keating, attesting that his business was "vibrant and healthy". When it collapsed amid scandal in 1989, Greenspan was chairman of the Fed. He needed to plead *mea culpa* on the record, and he did: "Of course, I'm extremely embarrassed by my failure to foresee what eventually transpired," Greenspan told the *New York Times*. "I was wrong about Lincoln."

Other than these exceptions, Greenspan would meet influential journalists only in private for conversations whose content could neither be quoted nor attributed to him – no fingerprints. He used these opportunities to shape expectations about the direction of Fed policy. Reporters known to have access to him, such as Greg Ip of the *Wall Street Journal* or John Berry at the *Washington Post*, were keenly read in the financial markets and in the policy community because this was often as close as it got to a clear indication of what Greenspan was really thinking.

When he spoke in public, Greenspan was a master obfuscator. In a candid moment, he admitted in a 1995 speech: "I spend a substantial amount of my time endeavouring to fend off questions, and worry terribly that I might end up being too clear." He needn't have worried. He was deliberately ambiguous, and it worked. Reporting his testimony to Congress on June 7, 1995, the *New York Times* headline ran: "Greenspan Sees Chance of Recession". Reporting on the same testimony, the *Wall Street Journal* ran this headline: "Fed Chairman Doesn't See Recession on the Horizon".

He sowed confusion very deliberately as a tactic for dealing with the media. As he once remarked to a fellow official, the Clinton Administration's Gene Sperling, in another context: "I'll just say a little bit this way, and a little bit that way, and I'll completely confuse them so there'll be no story." In private conversation he was utterly clear, even blunt, when it suited him. The fog of words he generated, the shroud he drew over himself in public, was not a natural condition but a studied art.

The social sphere carries its own significance, provides another playing field for politics, in any capital, and here, too, Greenspan was an active participant. He and his second wife, Andrea Mitchell, diplomatic correspondent for NBC, are one of the prime Washington A-list power couples. Charlie Cook, publisher of the non-partisan *Cook Political Report*, spoke with Greenspan at social events and testified that "Greenspan is completely knowledgeable about politics and can hold a detailed conversation with you about the electoral prospects for some particular senator – previous Fed chairmen wouldn't know who half the members of the Senate were."

Stranded in Zurich airport after his flight home had been turned back, Greenspan phoned Andrea Mitchell on September 11, 2001. He had only scant information on what had happened in the US and was desperate to know the full situation, and knew that his wife would be fully informed. But his call came through just as she was about to go on air. Mitchell told Greenspan that she had to go on camera immediately, but that she would keep the phone line open and by her side as she gave a seven-minute account of the morning's terrorist attacks on New York and Washington DC. "And so it was", concluded the *Financial Times*, "that a man who usually has more information at his fingertips than most people will ever need, first learned the details of the events that turned the world upside down that September day."

In addition to his talent for internal and external machinations, the third and most significant reason for Greenspan's standing and the most important source of his power has been his monetary judgment, particularly in moments of acute crisis just like that September day. His philosophy in such conditions can be summarised succinctly: in a crisis, cut interest rates hard, and cut fast. He established this approach, and with it his credentials, almost as soon as he first assumed the chairmanship. Just sixty-nine days after Greenspan took office, he confronted one of the worst financial panics in the post-war world. Wall Street was assailed by a great wave of panic selling that drove the Dow Jones index of thirty leading companies' stock prices down by a record number of points lost on any single day, 508. This equated to a stunning one-day loss of 22.6 per cent of the Dow's value, a fall exceeded on only one other occasion, in 1914. It reverberated around the world and markets fell everywhere. The scale of the setback was so vast that when Greenspan, who knew that the stockmarket had started the day badly, later asked a staff member how the market had finished and received the reply, "It was down five-oh-eight," Greenspan could not comprehend it. "Wow, what a terrific rally!" he replied, thinking the man had meant that the Dow was down by 5.08 points from a morning opening of 2246 points. It did not occur to him that it could have fallen by 508 points.

It was Black Monday, October 19, 1987. The day was named in a conscious association with the infamous Black Thursday, October 24, 1929, the first day of the Great Wall Street Crash, which was followed by Black Monday and Black Tuesday. The crash was the event that presaged the Great Depression. In 1987, there were dire fears that history would repeat: a major stockmarket collapse would once more lead to a severe downturn. But the 1929 crash did not have to lead directly to the Great Depression. It was not an inevitability. The vast loss of stockmarket wealth, the systemic shock, translated into an economic disaster only if it were not offset by some other source of liquidity. The stockmarket crash of 1929 only became a disaster in the real economy because of the inaction of the US authorities, and especially the US Federal Reserve, in trying to offset the shock. This was one of the key lessons of the twentieth century for central bankers.

Greenspan took the lesson. The Fed stepped in and offset the carnage in the markets by injecting massive amounts of liquidity into the financial system. After the markets closed on October 19, 1987, the Fed started buying large volumes of Treasury bills. The money it paid for the bills flowed directly into the hands of the bankers receiving it, putting instant liquidity into a strained banking system. The Fed's Open Market Desk supplied $17 billion to the banking system, an extraordinary sum, equivalent to more than 25 per cent of bank reserves and 7 per cent of the national money supply. The next morning, at 8.41, just before the markets re-opened, Greenspan issued a one-line statement: "The Federal Reserve, consistent with its responsibilities as the nation's central bank, affirmed today its readiness to serve as a source of liquidity to support the economic and financial system." This was a critical point of reassurance and comfort for the markets. But it was still not enough. The stockmarket was on the brink of seizing up altogether. The traders with the unique function of guaranteeing continuous buying and selling of stocks on the floor of the New York Stock Exchange, the so-called specialists because each trades only a handful of companies' stocks, were about to run out of cash. They started Black Monday with combined capital of $2.3 billion. The morning after they were down to $852 million. With the loss of nearly 60 per cent of their capital, they would soon run out of liquidity to continue trading. If there were no trades, prices could fall even more steeply still. So on the Tuesday morning, the president of the New York Federal Reserve Bank, E. Gerald Corrigan, applied pressure directly to the chief executives of major banks to supply money to participants in the markets. Martin Mayer, in his book *The Fed*, described the scene in the chief executive's suite at Bankers Trust in New York, a bank which was refusing to lend to the specialists: "E. Gerald Corrigan, large and muscular, walked over the three blocks from the Fed to Bankers Trust and entered the office of Charles Sanford, chairman and CEO, a smooth, slight, southern gentleman, and remained with him until Sanford issued orders that all the cash the Fed had flowed into his bank should flow out to support the operations of the market makers in New York."

Other central banks around the world did likewise, and the enormous infusion of liquidity into the financial systems around the world provided the shock absorber that interrupted the transformation of a stockmarket crash into an economic downturn. After the Great Crash of 1929, the Dow ended up losing an eventual 89 per cent by 1932 and the industrialised world went into depression. After Black Monday, 1987, the Dow finished the year up by 2 per cent and chalked up a further 12 per cent the next year and 27 per cent the year after. The economy sailed on, unaffected. It was a mighty triumph, and Greenspan was hailed as a hero. As Roger Lowenstein wrote in the *Wall Street Journal*: "The crash marked the hour of his arrival, the beginning of his status as near-deity on Wall Street."

It was the template for handling other crises, including the terrorist attacks on the US in 2001. While the markets in New York were in disarray and the financial system in chaos, and as the Fed's staff was evacuated from the headquarters building, the only Fed governor who happened to be in Washington DC at the time was the vice-chairman, Roger Ferguson. He stayed on in the office and soon issued a statement which read, in full: "The Federal Reserve System is open and operating. The discount window is open to meet liquidity needs." The Fed's operations followed through on the promise. Through the discount window where banks can borrow from the Fed, the central bank provided the commercial banking system with $45 billion, a 200-fold increase on the previous week. And through the Open Markets Desk where the Fed bought large volumes of Treasury paper, the Fed injected an enormous $80 billion in liquidity into the financial system on that day. Greenspan had been in contact by phone, but by the time he was able to get a military flight back to the US the immediate liquidity crisis was already passing. But the attacks were still a mighty assault on the national confidence and Greenspan's Fed followed through with a succession of deep cuts in the Federal funds interest rate, the key policy rate. In four steps in the following four months the FOMC halved the rate, down by 1.75 percentage points to leave it at just 1.75 per cent. Again, Greenspan was a hero.

Not only had Greenspan brought the US economy unharmed through the terrifying ordeal of the stockmarket crash of 1987 and stabilised the system after the stunning blow of September 11, he also worked to keep the US recession of 1991–92 to a historically brief eight months' duration, he promptly eased the liquidity crunch of 1998, and, in all, presided over the greatest bull market that America had ever seen with a policy of keeping money easy.

So here is the hero. Carefully manoeuvring within the Federal Reserve to keep a firm grip on his own institution; patiently cultivating the key people in the other power centres of Washington DC to keep his job and enhance his power; obfuscating publicly to preserve maximum freedom of movement; and cutting interest rates decisively in crisis. This formula for holding and wielding power could be summed up this way: manipulate, cultivate, obfuscate and liquidate.

It seemed that he had found the elusive balance between his own quest for power and good public policy. In late 1999, with the economy running strongly and the stockmarket booming, the leading candidates for the presidency in the 2000 election were avid to associate themselves with the Great Man. The Democrat candidate and Clinton's Vice-President, Al Gore, declared: "I am his biggest fan." A Republican candidate, George W. Bush, bit back dynastic bitterness to commend him: "He has done a great job." And his rival for the Republican candidacy, Senator John McCain, captured his indispensability: "I would not only re-appoint Alan Greenspan, if he would happen to die, God forbid, I would do like they did in the movie *Weekend at Bernie's*. I would prop him up and put a pair of dark glasses on him."

So what went wrong? How was it that this canny manipulator, this Machiavelli of monetary policy, this supreme judge of economic conditions, ended up presiding over the most exaggerated bubble, the most pronounced mania in centuries? And, at the end of it, losing a third of the nation's retirement assets while dumping the economy into recession? And, worse yet, after the national effort to recover, this experience left the superpower seriously strained, its government in record deficit, and a new bubble emerging in its housing market.

There was nothing inevitable about the Great American Bubble of 1996–2000. It was a man-made phenomenon, and therefore it was subject to human control. Alone among all the many participants and enablers and bystanders and regulators in and around the Great American Bubble, Alan Greenspan had all five of the elements necessary to try to manage it in the national interest. He had the comprehension, the credibility, the power, the mandate and the determination to mitigate the risk and contain the damage while it was still in its formative phase.

Some, including some economists and historians and analysts, had the comprehension to grasp that the country was in a bubble, but had neither the power nor the mandate to do anything about it. Others, like Clinton's Treasury Secretary, Robert Rubin, had the comprehension and the credibility and even the mandate, but, equipped only with a jawbone to talk at the market, lacked the power to act in any meaningful way. Besides, as a political creature serving a president, Rubin had a divided loyalty – he had an interest in keeping the market and the economy running hot to assist the administration and the Democratic Party's election prospects. Only Alan Greenspan had all the requisite elements.

How do we know? From everything we already know about the Fed and about Alan Greenspan, he plainly had the credibility, the power and the mandate to act against any threat to sustainable economic growth. How do we know he had the comprehension and the determination? The transcript of the Federal Open Market Committee meeting on September 24, 1996, tells us so.

One of the twelve members of the committee was particularly gripped with anxiety over the state of the stockmarket. That member was Lawrence Lindsey. "Everyone enjoys an economic party," Lindsey told the committee. "But the long-term costs of a bubble to the economy and society are potentially great . . . As in the US in the late 1920s, and Japan in the late 1980s, the case for a central bank ultimately to burst that bubble becomes overwhelming. I think it is far better that we do so while the bubble still resembles surface froth, and before the bubble carries the economy to stratospheric heights. Whenever we do it, it is going to be painful, however."

Alan Greenspan responded: "I recognise that there is a stockmarket bubble problem at this point, and I agree with Governor Lindsey that this is a problem that we should keep an eye on." The chairman ruminated that it would be tricky to use the money supply to deflate the bubble – raising interest rates. But he canvassed other options: "We do have the possibility of raising major concerns by increasing margin requirements [forcing stockmarket investors to pay for their shares with more cash and less debt]. I guarantee that if you want to get rid of the bubble, whatever it is, that will do it. My concern is that I am not sure what else it will do. But there are other ways that one can contemplate." He did not elaborate.

So there was no failure of comprehension. He was indeed the wise man. As the wise man in the Jainist parable saw all the parts of the elephant, all real but none explaining the whole beast, so Alan Greenspan saw all the individual parts of the systemic failure called a bubble, and understood how all the parts composed a whole. And just as all the parts of the elephant are connected through the being of the animal, so Greenspan knew that the many and various phenomena that operated in the bubble were all connected through the medium of money. And it was Greenspan who ultimately had control of the ebb and flow of the American money supply. He could either expand the bubble by allowing the money supply to flow, or he could constrict it by engineering an ebb. Five years ahead of the bust, the Fed chairman had correctly diagnosed the bubble. He saw it bloating and distending, and he was already canvassing options for what to do about it. He further explored the problem. He convened a hearing on the state of the stockmarket at the Fed's headquarters on December 3, 1996. Among those invited were one of the stockmarket's most consistently upbeat cheerleaders, Abbey Joseph Cohen of Goldman Sachs, and one of the foremost sceptics, Professor Robert Shiller, a Yale University economist. The bearish case evidently proved more persuasive than the bullish. The in-house seminar confirmed for Greenspan his existing view: that a dangerous bubble had formed in the stockmarket, and that something needed to be done about it. Two days later he took the first step into public view to do something about it. All his power, his skill and, crucially, his courage were about to be put to the test.

Chapter Five

THE MOMENT OF TRUTH

It did not feel like it to the 1300 dinner guests who had to suffer through it, but the speech that Alan Greenspan gave on the evening of December 5, 1996, was about to create the biggest test he had ever faced. To those who were at the black-tie dinner, the speech was interminable, an excruciating survey of two centuries of economic policy. The delivery was every bit as electrifying as the title: "The Challenge of Central Banking in a Democratic Society". Midnight approached, eyelids drooped. It was the annual dinner of the American Enterprise Institute, a conservative think tank in Washington DC and incubator for some thirty officials who went on to serve the Bush Administration. "These occasions are usually very entertaining and lively," said one regular guest, Owen Harries, then editor of *The National Interest*, a journal of foreign policy. "They usually have star performers, and there is a lot of laughter and applause. Greenspan was the dullest I can remember, and I went to eight or nine. It was a most unsuitable lecture – heavy, boring and long. It was an evening of yawns and raised eyebrows."

As Greenspan ground through all 5000 words of the lecture in his raspy monotone, very few even noticed the two words that were about to reverberate around the world, move trillions of dollars and enter the English language as a new expression, a new mantra, and, eight years later, recur 19,300 times in the Factiva database of English-language newspaper articles and 96,000 times in a Google search of the web. The newswire reporters picked up the key words instantly and sent them worldwide in minutes. The news: the chairman of the US Federal Reserve had publicly questioned whether the stockmarket was in the grip of "irrational exuberance". These words have gone down as some of the most memorable and best-known in the lexicon of twentieth-century markets.

As Greenspan stooped his way back to his seat and the grateful guests revived, his wife, Andrea Mitchell, asked the dignitaries at the head table whether they had noticed anything newsworthy in the great man's remarks. None had been struck by the words that Greenspan had deliberately calibrated to jolt the markets. Even as the diners revived from their somnolence in Washington DC, investors in Tokyo noticed. Like investors everywhere, they were thunderstruck. The Nikkei stock average fell by 3 per cent on the day, its biggest loss of the year. Investors in Hong Kong noticed. Stock prices fell by nearly 3 per cent. And they noticed in Australia, down 3 per cent, and Germany, down 4 per cent, and London, down 2 per cent. And when the markets opened in New York the next morning, the Dow Jones Industrial Average of thirty leading companies' stock prices fell by 2 per cent, 144.6 points, in the first half-hour of trading and ended the day down by 55 points.

Most of the guests at the dinner would not realise that they had been present at a major news event until they picked up their newspapers the next morning. Watching the event on TV, a stockmarket pundit, Jim Bianco of Bianco Research LLC, offered this observation: "I bet that 97 per cent of the crowd who heard him say it did not appreciate it. There was no gasp in the crowd. People didn't say to each other, 'Did he just say the market was overvalued?' " A comprehension rate of 3 per cent may have been a bit generous. Owen Harries recalled: "I am sure 99 per cent of the audience sat through it without registering that something terribly important and shocking had been said. No-one talked about it on the night. It wasn't till we read it in the *Washington Post* the next morning that we realised its importance."

Even a Fed governor who had read the speech the previous day had failed to see the key words and their meaning – it was the first shot in a campaign to challenge the mania that had taken hold in America's stockmarkets. Laurence Meyer later wrote that he should have been more alert: "I came to understand", he wrote in his memoir *A Term at the Fed*, "that the chairman would circulate his speeches in advance when they offered an important new opinion." Meyer insisted that he really did read the speech, but that "somewhere along the way, maybe as the story crossed into the 1970s, I must have let my concentration lapse. I don't know why! In any case, on page 6, and seemingly out of the blue, the chairman dropped a bombshell."

Well, not quite out of the blue. First he reminded his audience that the Fed's task was to keep prices stable, while pursuing the maximum sustainable economic growth. Then he prepared the ground by asking this question – which prices, exactly, should we be keeping stable? This, he said, was not a simple question.

He was working up to the point where he would suggest a big conceptual shift. He was about to suggest that the Fed might have to consider not just the price of traditional items – food, clothing, shelter, energy, a haircut – but the price of assets too, including stock prices. It might have to broaden its ambit to include consumer price inflation and asset price inflation.

This would be a major conceptual shift for a central bank. It was thoroughly at odds with the prevailing orthodoxy. The orthodoxy said that central banks should only target the price of goods and services, and never target the price of assets. The reason? Traditional inflation would cause distortions in economic behaviour that would punish investment and destroy long-run growth, but asset prices didn't matter to the so-called real economy, where businesses invest and produce and people shop and work. Greenspan could see that the risks to the economy had shifted away from traditional inflation to asset price inflation.

Years earlier Greenspan had ventured his own definition of inflation, articulated in congressional testimony in 1989. He said that the Fed aimed to achieve price stability. And he defined it this way: "For all practical purposes, price stability means that expected changes in the average price level are small enough and gradual enough that they do not materially enter business and household financial decisions." It was now plain that while this definition of price stability did apply in consumer price inflation, it should be ringing alarms when it came to asset price inflation.

The price inflation on the stockmarket had become the dominant influence on consumer spending and on business investment, making it the single biggest force in the economy. In the words of a respected economist at the New York consultancy ISI Group, Ed Hyman, "the stockmarket is the economy." It was generating vast distortions. By Greenspan's own definition, this was a dangerous inflation that needed to be contained.

The bubble in the stockmarket was a clear and present danger. And he realised that a new intellectual framework was needed to confront it. He was about to present one. This was Greenspan at his best. He was alert to a new danger, and he was about to demonstrate intellectual and institutional leadership in confronting it. In his history of the first half of the Federal Reserve's life, from 1913 to 1951, Professor Allan Meltzer wrote: "Individuals matter most when they are able to lead others to act in ways that do not fit comfortably within the prevailing orthodoxy." He cited important acts of leadership by the Fed's early chairmen, and concluded: "These and other episodes show that leadership was important at times. Events of this kind are rare. Most policy decisions and actions apply a framework or theory based on prevailing beliefs." He continued: "Theories, or beliefs, go a long way toward explaining why the Federal Reserve did not avoid crises in 1920–21, 1929–33, and 1937–38. The beliefs that officials used to interpret events, and the interpretations they reached, were conventional at the time." Now Greenspan was to challenge the conventional wisdom to prevent a crisis in the final years of the twentieth century. This is how Greenspan approached it, but reduced from the original 5000 words to the essential three hundred:

> When industrial product was the centrepiece of the economy during the first two-thirds of this century, our overall price indexes served us well. Pricing a pound of electrolytic copper presented few definitional problems. The price of a ton of cold rolled steel sheet, or a linear yard of cotton broad woven fabrics, could be reasonably compared over a period of years.

> But as the century draws to a close, the simple notion of price has turned decidedly ambiguous. What is the price of a unit of software or a legal opinion? How does one evaluate the price change of a cataract operation over a ten-year period when the nature of the procedure and its impact on the patient changes so radically?
>
> Indeed, how will we measure inflation, and the associated financial and real implications, in the twenty-first century when our data – using current techniques – could become increasingly less adequate to trace price trends over time?

This brought him to the threshold of his redefinition of which prices matter:

> But where do we draw the line on what prices matter? Certainly prices of goods and services now being produced – our basic measure of inflation – matter. But what about futures prices, or, *more importantly, prices of claims on future goods and services, like equities, real estate, or other earning assets? Are stability of these prices essential to the stability of the economy?* [Emphasis added]

He then acknowledged one of the contemporary arguments used to justify the bubble – that because the US was enjoying sustained low inflation, this implied a more certain future and could therefore justify a higher valuation for shares. Then came the bombshell:

> *But how do we know when irrational exuberance has unduly escalated asset values which then become the subject of unexpected and prolonged contractions, as they have in Japan over the past*

> *decade? And how do we factor that assessment into monetary policy?*
>
> We as central bankers need not be concerned if a collapsing financial asset bubble does not threaten to impair the real economy, its production, jobs, and price stability. Indeed, the sharp stockmarket break of 1987 had few negative consequences for the economy. *But we should not underestimate or become complacent about the complexity of the interactions of asset markets and the economy.* [Emphases added]

Although he had posed it as a question, it was a clear warning. Decoded, he had said that Wall Street could well be in the grip of irrational exuberance, and the Fed was thinking about the possibility of raising interest rates to interrupt the proceedings, taking the punchbowl away.

Did Greenspan really know what he was doing? Was it really so deliberate? Or was it just a little late-night hypothesising, and had he just miscalculated the market response?

Before the speech, indeed two and a half months before the speech, the FOMC had debated the matter in secret, and Greenspan, as we have seen, bluntly stated his opinion: "I recognise that there is a stockmarket bubble problem at this point." He had not rushed, but had bided his time until the presidential election in November was safely out of the way and Bill Clinton had been re-elected. Clinton would have been angered by any Fed decision to raise interest rates or prick the stockmarket bubble before the election, but now that he was safely restored to the White House, there was a clearer political space for any difficult decisions by the Fed. At the next FOMC meeting, one of the other governors, Larry Lindsey again, returned to the state of the overvalued stockmarket. This time, four of the other committee members also expressed concern about the bubble in stock prices, which continued to increase in size. Lindsey said the Fed needed to consider "injecting a little risk" into the stock-market to check rampant speculation. "And frankly, I think that call is going to be our toughest decision in the years ahead." Next, Greenspan had convened the in-house seminar at the Fed to hear all the cases for and against the proposition that the market was in the midst of a bubble. He had then crafted his speech and circulated it in advance to other Fed governors in a clear signal that he was about to make an important new pronouncement. At least one of the other governors, Alice Rivlin, had seized upon the phrase "irrational exuberance", and went to talk to the chairman about it, so that he could have had no doubt about its weight by the time he took the podium at the American Enterprise Institute dinner. "It was not a shot-from-the-hip," he later told a Senate committee. "We thought long and in detail that any such statement could very well have immediate market effects."

And as soon as he had delivered his oration, he chatted to one of the few guests who had actually followed it, Joe Stiglitz, a member of the Clinton Administration's Council of Economic Advisers: "When I approached him after his speech to discuss several of the ideas that he had thrown out, it was clear that he was fixated on the 'irrational exuberance' remark," reported Stiglitz. "He knew that the pundits would know that it was the US rather than Japan that he had in mind. He was worried about the stockmarket, which was having a blow-out year – or so it seemed as the Dow climbed from 5000 to 6500," although "when it reached 12,000 a little more than three years later, the gains of '96 would no longer be remembered as such a big deal." On the day that Greenspan gave the speech, the Dow had closed at 6437.10 points, up by 25 per cent so far that year.

So there can be no doubt. Greenspan was deliberately and consciously launching an effort to manage the risks inherent in a major bubble. But Joe Stiglitz was puzzled about what came next. "And then . . . nothing happened," he wrote in his 2003 retrospective, *The Roaring Nineties*. "What exactly had Greenspan been up to? If he thought share prices were heading out of control – if he feared the wider effects of a bubble – why didn't he go ahead and *act*?" It's a good question. The answer lies in the political reaction to his declaration of "irrational exuberance". The market shockwave had been powerful, but the political response to the speech was poisonous.

The hit to share prices was precisely the effect that Greenspan had been seeking. He had indeed injected an element of risk. Note that he very deliberately followed the question of "irrational exuberance" with the question about how to use monetary policy. Speculators now had to worry – the one-way bet of ever-rising stock prices was suddenly in doubt.

But the political reaction was something else entirely. Some of the most powerful men in Washington were furious. The angriest public reaction came from the most senior Republican in the Congress, the majority leader in the Senate, Senator Trent Lott. Three days after the speech, Lott appeared on *Fox News Sunday* and was asked, "Does it scare you that one man has that much power?"

Lott replied: "You know I've always been a little nervous about the Fed, quite frankly. I try not to be a Fed-basher, but I sometimes think they focus too much on one side of the equation, rather than the broader basket of things. And I'm a little nervous about the degree of [their] independence." This was a plain, public threat against the Fed's independence. The Federal Reserve is a creation of the US Congress, he was reminding

Greenspan, and it had the power to redraw the boundaries of Fed freedom. "And I think probably the chairman would say, 'I wish I had chosen some other words,' " Lott concluded. He added that "interest rates should be lower, even than what they are, certainly." Greenspan hastened to meet Lott privately on Capitol Hill the next day, presumably to mollify him, for Lott then fell silent on the subject.

On the other side of American politics, there was a clear sign of displeasure from the Clinton Administration. It came from the Treasury Secretary, Robert Rubin, Greenspan's primary point of contact with the administration. It was even more significant because Rubin had been protecting Greenspan's Fed for years. As a matter of policy, Rubin had prohibited any comment by any administration official on the Fed or its chairman. The Fed should be seen to be independent of the administration. Rubin had, on one occasion, gone public to chastise the White House Chief of Staff, Leon Panetta, for daring to ventilate a view on interest rates. On several occasions Rubin even had to restrain the President himself.

So it was significant that Rubin now allowed himself this remark in a TV interview: "The chairman was simply raising a question, not suggesting an answer. He was just seeking to widen the intellectual debate over the level of the markets."

Greenspan had made a point of injecting risk into the stockmarket. Now Rubin was taking it out again. It was safe for irrational exuberance, he seemed to be saying – Greenspan is just waffling, there's no chance that he'll actually do anything.

The chief of the Federal Reserve was politically surrounded. The Republicans in Congress were angry at him, and the Democrats in the administration were no longer prepared to protect him. Those two words had put him in a cursed circle, standing alone. No politician would stand with an official whose policy, even if it were in the national interest, could anger their constituents. The situation recalled a rebuke that a Texas Baptist pastor, Kent York, once made of his congressman, Bill Sarpalius, in 1993: "We didn't send you to Washington to make intelligent decisions. We sent you to represent us."

At his next appearance before the Congress, in a hearing of the Senate Banking Committee in January 1997, a Republican, a member of Greenspan's own tribe, made the Fed chairman listen while he read out a letter from a constituent. Senator Chuck Grassley told Greenspan: "On December 9, after your comments were made, I received this letter from a person in Des Moines, Iowa. 'I'm writing to you to voice my concern about the recent comments made by Chairman Greenspan,' " Grassley read aloud. " 'I feel very strongly that he was completely out of line for the comments that he made. I'm a retired person who uses my variable annuity to supplement my retirement and lost over $400 the day after his comments. The bottom line is that it will take a week of normal stockmarket activity for me to be just at the level I was on December 5. You can see what his shooting from the hip did to millions of small investors and retired investors. I would ask you to pass this message on. This matter is very serious and cannot be overlooked.' "

The senator pressed his attack: "Specifically, what did you intend by the comment 'irrational exuberance'? Were you successful in achieving that end?"

Greenspan ducked. He did not defend the core idea of his speech. He did not want to admit that he had been deliberately trying to alter the psychology of the stockmarket, that the electric shock that the constituent was complaining of was exactly the jolt that Greenspan had sought to administer. He would not defend his case. He weaved: ". . . if we are endeavouring to explain, as I was in that speech, the full structure of policy-making as the Federal Open Market Committee implements it, then it would be important to make certain that everybody knows what we look at. Were we successful in indicating that, in fact, we do that sort of thing? Yes and no. The yes part is everyone noticed what I was saying. [Laughter.] The no part is that they didn't read as much of the context in which that was being stated, as I would have preferred."

As one-time US presidential candidate Paul Tsongas said in 1992: "That's a good question. Let me try to evade you."

The truth is that the constituent's letter demonstrated exactly the sort of psychology that Greenspan had tried to attack. This retiree, if he were a typical investor, had lost about 0.8 per cent of the value of his stocks on that day. Now he fully expected to win this back in a week, implying that he expected to earn a return of over 40 per cent a year on his stock portfolio. And this was what he described as "normal". He treated it as if it were some sort of right or entitlement that would continue in perpetuity, and he complained to his senator when this happy expectation was disturbed. This is the very essence of a mania. But Greenspan kept his counsel.

Another vital feature of the political landscape that Greenspan now looked out upon had also darkened. Bill Clinton was trying to surround him inside his own stronghold, the Federal Open Market Committee, where official interest rates are set. Much as Reagan had stacked the board of governors so as to create a revolt against Paul Volcker, Clinton now tried to alter the balance of forces on the FOMC to put Greenspan in check.

Every ship in the Soviet navy, every unit in the Soviet army carried at least one officer who had nothing to do with combat or military affairs. This officer was a trusted member of the Communist Party, planted solely to monitor the political and ideological reliability of the unit. He was known as a "political officer". As it had been with one superpower's greatest organisation, so it was with the surviving superpower's most revered institution. But now the US President had installed not just one but two "political officers" at the Fed.

In his book *Maestro*, Bob Woodward told the tale of how Bill Clinton went about appointing his political officers to the Fed's board. It was mid-1996, an election was due in November, and the post of deputy chairman at the Fed was open. The President wanted the director of his Budget Office, Alice Rivlin, to take the job. She was reluctant. Woodward described this scene: "Clinton asked for a second meeting. He was up for re-election . . . a year not to be taken lightly. He indicated that what would happen at the Fed with interest rates could be as important as anything. He needed a package – Greenspan and two Democrats."

Though Clinton had excellent relations with Alan Greenspan, the head of the central bank was a lifelong Republican. The President plainly didn't trust him. Greenspan's stature was so great that Clinton simply had to re-appoint him as chairman, but he wanted to keep him in check by appointing two politically reliable Democrats to the board at the same time.

"The loss of the Congress in the 1994 elections had been devastating," continued Woodward in relating Clinton's pitch to Rivlin. "The party could not afford to lose the presidency in 1996." And if Greenspan decided to raise rates, an economic slowdown, perhaps even a recession, could be in prospect – a political disaster. Rivlin took the job and held it for three years.

The account in *Maestro* was completely unsourced, so it was important to ask Rivlin on the record whether the motivation for her appointment was really so blatant. Rivlin replied: "It was 1996. It wasn't entirely clear that Greenspan was as pro-growth as it turns out he was. There may have been some of that notion in my appointment." In short, it really was that blatant. The other member of the "package" was Laurence Meyer, a noted economic forecaster and a committed Democrat. He has said that he was at no point asked directly to ride shotgun on Greenspan, but he knew the reason he was being appointed ahead of a dozen other candidates: "The President seemed partial to the view that the obsession of the Fed (and specifically of its chairman, Alan Greenspan) with inflation was resulting in a tighter monetary policy than was appropriate and slower growth than would otherwise have been possible. In order to make monetary policy more accommodative and growth oriented, Clinton wanted to appoint governors to the board who shared his convictions and would challenge the chairman." But of course. The pair took their places on the Fed's Board of Governors in June 1996, five months before the presidential election. In a curious twist, however, Meyer seems to have upset the President's expectation. Meyer developed a concern that nascent inflationary pressures needed to be headed off, and, just before the FOMC's September meeting, he went to see Greenspan privately. Meyer urged Greenspan to consider raising interest rates at the forthcoming meeting, which was less than two months before the election on November 5, 1996. In one sense it would not have made any difference to the election if Greenspan had taken this advice. Changes in official rates take anywhere from six to eighteen months to translate into any change in economic conditions in the so-called real economy – in other words, the economy as it is experienced by people through investment, inflation, unemployment. Still, it would have been politically inconvenient and might have been used against

Clinton by his rivals. In the event, Greenspan rebuffed the idea. He was thinking about a larger idea, and he was content to wait until after the election.

Now that the presidential election was past, the implicit pressure on Greenspan must have been partly relaxed. And no doubt this was a factor in his decision to launch his campaign against "irrational exuberance" in December, after the election. But Clinton still had another four years in the White House, and the Democrats could still have been expected to resist any serious tightening of the money supply unless they thought there was an irresistible case for moving to contain an inflationary surge. There was not, at that point, any such case. This moment was not about traditional inflation but about inflation in asset prices, and specifically the stockmarket. So if Greenspan was going to raise interest rates to deflate the bubble, he was going to have to do it in the face of likely opposition inside the Fed, opposition from the Congress, opposition from the Clinton Administration.

Interestingly, this put the Fed chief in the most politically vulnerable position, as defined by Thomas Havrilesky's 1993 work on the political pressures on the Fed – under threat from the Congress, unsupported by the administration, and facing the prospect of pressure within the FOMC through the President's power of appointment.

The FOMC met again twelve days after the celebrated speech. The chairman had nothing to say on the subject. He did not propose to raise interest rates, reconsider margin lending requirements, or take any other action. In fact, Greenspan's only remark on the subject of his speech was a jocular aside. Larry Lindsey, again, had touched on the subject. The official transcript shows that he foresaw some positive forces for economic growth in the year ahead, 1997, "but in each case it is going to be creating bigger problems for us to solve down the road. So, 1998 looks like the year in which irrational exuberance will meet its match."

Greenspan: I will make another speech. [Laughter.]

Lindsey: Don't wait a whole year.

The market never looked back. And though Greenspan made a few more references to possible overvaluations in the stockmarket, and though the FOMC made a single small increase in official interest rates in March 1997, it was evident that Wall Street was right – Greenspan was not serious. For instance, in the FOMC statement announcing and explaining the interest rate increase in March 1997 from 5.25 per cent to 5.5 per cent, the Fed made no reference whatsoever to the stockmarket or asset prices. It also happened to be the only time the Fed raised interest rates in the entire period of four years and four months stretching from February 1995 to June 1999, almost exactly the period of the bubble's reign.

And it was not just that the Fed made only this one feeble effort at raising rates. During that same stretch in which it raised rates by a total of 0.25 of a percentage point, it made six cuts to official rates totalling 1.5 percentage points. So Greenspan's Fed made a net change to official rates of –1.25 percentage points during the bubble years. The Fed, in short, was feeding cheap money into the bubble. Far from restraining the bubble, the Fed was its most important accomplice.

Easy money is the handmaiden of any great mania. It is the supply of punch which intoxicates the party. As the economic historian Charles Kindleberger wrote in his classic study *Manias, Panics and Crashes*, "speculative manias gather speed through expansion of money and credit or perhaps, in some cases, get started because of an initial expansion of money and credit." In the five years to 1994, the annual growth in US money supply, as measured by the broad definition of money known as M3, averaged only 1.3 per cent. And then it surged to an average growth rate of 8.6 per cent for the rest of the decade – a sixfold quickening. One of the greatest speculative frenzies in history was under way, fully diagnosed but completely unchecked.

Looking back, the Fed governor who had pressed Greenspan to act on the bubble explained the events of the time this way: "People said, 'How dare you take our bubble away!' " Larry Lindsey says. "The political reaction was extremely hostile. Greenspan decided that he didn't have a mandate. The lesson from the irrational exuberance speech was that you have a democratic society in which the vast majority of people benefit enormously from something that may be hazardous in the long run."

But that's supposed to be the whole point of the Fed. Congress gave control of monetary policy to an independent central bank so that the technocrats could make difficult, but necessary, decisions on managing the economy. If it just wanted popular economic decisions, Congress could abolish the Fed and run the economy itself. Greenspan had set out on a course of what he judged to be wise policy, but then had allowed himself to be intimidated by the political difficulty involved. Curiously, a full reading of his "irrational exuberance" speech shows that he actually seemed to anticipate the political uproar that the speech was about to create: "Our monetary policy independence is conditional on pursuing policies that are broadly acceptable to the American people and their representatives in the Congress." Hey look, he seemed to be saying, we can only do this if you'll let us.

During a committee meeting of Congress in 2002, a congressman told him that he was "the best politician I have ever seen in Washington". Greenspan took it as a compliment: "Thank you" was his only response.

Jim Grant, publisher of *Grant's Interest Rate Observer*, believes that this has been more of a professional liability than an asset: "What makes Greenspan such a good politician is what makes him such a bad central banker." He put such a priority on politicking, and was so adroit in the art, that he chose what he knew to be smart politics rather than what he believed to be wise policy.

Larry Lindsey argued in retrospect that the time of the "irrational exuberance" speech – the tail-end of late 1996 and then early 1997 – was the Fed's last chance to have tempered the mania. Crises followed that demanded low interest rates – the Asian crisis, the collapse of Long-Term Capital Management, the panic over Y2K – and the Fed met all of these events with a fresh gusher of liquidity that further bloated the bubble on Wall Street.

Greenspan seemed to have intended that the tiny, tentative increase in official interest rates of 0.25 of a percentage point in March 1997 was to be the first of a series. "I think the odds are better than 50:50 that the move we are considering will not be our last tightening move," he told the FOMC just before they voted in favour of the increase. This was the only time in Greenspan's entire chairmanship of almost two decades that the Fed made a one-off hike in interest rates. All the others formed part of a series. He was in no haste: "We have a lot of time to take various actions as we perceive the need to take them." He was wrong. The Asian financial and economic crisis erupted in July 1997. He had missed his best and last opportunity to temper the madness by raising interest rates.

It was eight months after the "irrational exuberance" speech before any of the FOMC members raised the issue with their chairman again: "What do we do with monetary policy when there is no inflation but asset prices are booming?" asked Cathy Minehan, the president of the Boston Federal Reserve Bank, in August 1997. This cut to a central dilemma for the Fed and for central banks everywhere. Inflation was the Fed's traditional target, the reason it might need to raise interest rates. But it was now tame, and did not need to be suppressed. Indeed, raising rates could even slow the economy unnecessarily. Yet the stockmarket was raging and Greenspan's speech had raised the prospect that it might need to be given a calming dose of monetary medicine – higher interest rates. One indicator said, "Don't do it," while the other said, "Maybe you should."

Greenspan: We have not been able to address that issue because I don't think we know how to handle a problem where we have one instrument and conflicting goals. What do we do? What should the Japanese have done when confronted with a very benign product price environment and rapidly escalating asset prices?

Minehan: Hindsight tells us to prick the bubble sooner, but how does foresight tell us we have a bubble?

Greenspan: That was the context of that speech, and the state of my knowledge, at least, has not gone beyond that. I do not know what to do.

She attempted to continue the discussion, but the chairman cut her off.

There are three points to make about this exchange. First is that the dilemma outlined was, and remains, a hotly debated one, to which we will return later in this tale. Second, Greenspan appears to have completely forgotten his earlier conclusion, voiced in the FOMC in September 1996, that there was indeed "a stockmarket problem". It was this conviction that led him to the "irrational exuberance" speech. And since then, the market had continued to roar. Third, he seems to have forgotten the other main point he had made in that earlier FOMC discussion: "We do have the possibility of raising major concerns by increasing margin requirements [forcing stockmarket investors who buy shares with money borrowed from their brokers to pay for their shares with more cash and less debt]. I guarantee that if you want to get rid of the bubble, whatever it is, that will do it." That was a second "instrument" that the Fed had available to it. Even if he decided that it was unwise to use interest rates to influence share prices – that the big stick of monetary policy was too crude an instrument – he still had a second instrument to hand that more narrowly targetted the stockmarket and would not influence the broader economy.

Margin lending requirements were put in place in the 1930s to curb speculation in stocks. Since 1974, the margin required to be deposited up front has been unchanged at 50 per cent of the value of the investment. As Greenspan had himself told the FOMC, he had the power to raise this margin.

Raising the requirement had been used to good effect in the past. Between 1934 and 1974, the Fed raised the requirement on thirteen occasions. On eight of those, the stockmarket slowed. The pace of share-price appreciation eased in the following three, six and twelve-month periods, according to a study by the Financial Markets Center. On four of these occasions the Fed was raising interest rates too, but in the other four there was no such move, and yet raising the margin requirement worked regardless. And when the Fed lowered the requirement, prices tended to take off again.

One advocate of the use of this tool was a prominent economist at the New York investment bank of Morgan Stanley, Stephen Roach. He argued that it would burn many speculators and send them a powerful message: "Speculate at your own risk." He made the case that "it's hardly a coincidence, in my view, that the recent explosive surge of margin indebtedness – with year-over-year growth peaking at 87 per cent in February 2000 [the month before the market's apogee] – traced the contours of the recent Nasdaq bubble with great precision." Margin debt reached a high of $278 billion at the market's peak. The Fed may also have had other options available to it, to change market psychology perhaps, but Greenspan raised none, in public or in the privacy of the Fed's boardroom, again.

It is hard to avoid the conclusion that Lindsey offered: Greenspan had been persuaded that the politics of the situation were too difficult. He appeared to have lost all interest in addressing the bubble. Instead of acting to mitigate it, the Fed started to brace for the crash that it knew was to come when the bubble collapsed. From 1996 onwards, the economic forecasts routinely prepared by its staff started to incorporate an expectation of a stockmarket fall of around 20 per cent. Of course, for the next four years the market did not crash but only continued to boom. The Federal Government's stockmarket disaster emergency squad, which the *Washington Post* christened the "plunge protection team", chaired by the Treasury Secretary, Robert Rubin, and including the Fed chairman and other top officials, continued to meet regularly to review contingency plans for a crash, but with a mounting sense of apprehension.

In 1998, a Nobel prize-winning economist at the Massachusetts Institute of Technology, Paul Samuelson, observed of Greenspan that by failing to raise interest rates to remove money from circulation, by failing to starve the bubble, by keeping the giant money spigot open for the preceding two years, "he is now dealing with the physics of avalanches."

In the FOMC's last meeting for 1996, the one immediately after Greenspan's most famous pronouncement, Larry Lindsey foresaw what was to come. He remarked to the chairman: "I think that in spite of your best efforts, 1997 is going to be a very good year for irrational exuberance." *Pace* Lindsey, Greenspan had not made his best efforts; he had surrendered in the face of political difficulty. Greenspan had failed the test. And for that reason 1997, as well as 1998, 1999 and the first quarter of 2000, were indeed the very best of years for irrational exuberance.

Chapter Six

PUNCH-DRUNK

The last years of the twentieth century in America were stamped with two distinctive socio-economic characteristics. One was the popularisation of the Internet, and the other was the great boom in the stockmarket. In a personal sense, Alan Greenspan stood aloof from both. He did not use email. He did not buy shares. And in an intellectual sense, as we know, he was profoundly sceptical of the fusion of these two phenomena in the form of the technology-driven stockmarket surge. As early as September 1996, he had come to the conclusion that it was not a New Era but just a dangerous bubble. Yet he now engaged in an extraordinary three-year embrace of what he had privately recognised as "a stockmarket bubble problem".

Abandoning his efforts to contain the bubble once he'd encountered stiff political resistance, the chairman of the US Federal Reserve now became its most important accomplice. He did not take a middle course. He changed direction completely, and clasped the whole madness to his aged breast with the zeal of a convert. He supplied three essential commodities to bloat and blister the Great American Bubble beyond all American historical experience. First, he went to great lengths to continue supplying the cheap money that all bubbles need to feed upon. Second, he endorsed the mania and dignified it by his patronage, affirming the sense that the market was correctly recognising a great historical transformation. Third, he lent an air of assurance to investors, a notion that the Fed would protect investors against disaster.

The man who was supposed to be the guardian of economic stability and financial prudence now became the charismatic leader of a manic cult. The last line of defence for sanity and good policy had become the front line of advance for delusion and cupidity. The seer who had challenged irrational exuberance now became its cheerleader. Greenspan became so closely identified with the tech frenzy that the then President, Bill Clinton, light-heartedly likened him to the object of the speculative mania of the time – a dotcom. He poked gentle fun at the chairman's enthusiasm: "His devotion to new technologies has been so significant, I've been thinking of taking Alan.com public; then we can pay the debt off even before 2015."

Clinton's investment banking instincts were sound. The mere act of changing a company's name to add the magic rubric "dotcom" had the effect of increasing its stockmarket valuation by an average of 74 per cent in 1999. Of course, relabelling a company increases its profitability no more than an idiot might raise his intelligence by declaring himself a genius. It was a time of madness, yet this was the euphoria that Greenspan now supported and legitimised. Greenspan's conversion recalled the observation of his former deputy, Alice Rivlin: "Greenspan doesn't like to lose, and if he thinks he'll lose, he switches sides."

On July 22, 1997, Greenspan rhapsodised to a Senate committee that the economy's recent performance had been "exceptional", so much so that it might represent a "once or twice in a century phenomenon that will carry productivity trends nationally and globally to a new higher track". This was music to the market's ears. The Dow Jones Industrial Average, which had lost 144 points in trepidation at Greenspan's warning of irrational exuberance, now jumped for joy with a rise of near-identical proportions. It rose by 150 points. The Dow finished the day above 8000 points for the first time. Since the Fed chairman's famous warning of seven months earlier, investors had bid up the overall value of US shares by 24 per cent – the creation of an extra $1.9 trillion in shareholder wealth on top of what Greenspan had already considered to be a bubble.

When the crash came, every dollar of these gains would be vaporised. Indeed, on precisely the fifth anniversary of this bullish testimony, July 22, 2002, the average American retail investor, the so-called Mom and Pop investor, would lose the last dollar of profit that he or she had made in the entire course of the bull market, dating from 1990, according to Jim Bianco of Bianco Research, a firm that tracks stock profits.

The Fed had thought about taking the punchbowl away, but now Greenspan was indicating that it would leave it on the table so that all could have some, and have as much as they wanted. Indeed, listening to the chairman, investors grasped that he had started to drink from the same bowl. Alan Greenspan had joined the party. The intoxication, the euphoria, had already seemed extraordinary. Now it was going to become breathtaking. At the beginning of 1984, the Dow stood at 1258 points. It had taken eighty-eight years to reach that level. Now, beginning in 1996, investors were bidding it up by at least that many points every year. In 1996, the Dow jumped by 1331 points, 1460 the next year, 1273 the year after, and then blew out completely, by 2316 points, in 1999. To the political reaction to his "irrational exuberance" warning – which was, in Larry Lindsey's words, "How dare you take our bubble away?" – Greenspan now almost seemed to be saying, "You want a bubble, I'll give you a bubble all right." And so he did.

It moved beyond the markets and the economists to establish a firm grip on the popular culture.

In a TV ad for a money management firm in 2000, a pair of lovers at twilight are sharing a drink on a cliff-top terrace overlooking the Mediterranean. But something is deeply wrong. The camera takes us closer. She turns to him, beautiful but angry. "If you don't understand asset allocation, you don't understand me," she cries in an American accent. Frustrated beyond words, she throws her drink in her lover's face and flounces off. Too late, her darkly handsome man calls after her in a Mediterranean lilt: "But wait – I love you." It makes no difference. He watches, uncomprehending, as she leaves him forever.

The man, a European, was quite out of touch with America at the turn of the millennium. As Jim Grant of *Grant's Interest Rate Observer* understood: " 'Buy and hold' have replaced 'I love you' as the three most popular words in the English language."

David Hale, a prominent Chicago-based economist, found himself in a taxi in New York in March 2000, the market's apex. The experience frightened him. Whenever the cab stopped at a red light, the driver busied himself with a small computer. "The guy was trading his stock portfolio," says Hale, the global economist at the Zurich Group. "It's unbelievable. We have a whole subculture feeding on itself. It's the bell-hop syndrome. That's the scariest thing in the US now." The bell-hop syndrome? "When

Joe Kennedy was asked how he managed to sell in time to avoid the Great Crash of 1929, he said the sign was that bell-hops were giving stock tips."

Francis Fukuyama, the conservative philosopher and author of *The End of History*, was disturbed by the effect of the bubble on the character of America: "Tom Wolfe wrote *The Bonfire of the Vanities* to describe the bond traders of the 1980s, and he touched a nerve because there was a really unpleasant side to the materialism and ambition," Fukuyama said in 2000. "I think it's just moved over to this other sector. It's not the bond traders now that are the masters of the universe, because the bond market has been stagnant for a decade, it's all the self-congratulatory people in the IT sector. They think they walk on water. Their arrogance is summed up in this phrase, it's one of my favourites: 'You just don't get it.' "

Though a pro-market, pro-capital conservative, Fukuyama was troubled by the influence of the new prosperity.

> There are all these things going on in the class structure now that people are only dimly comprehending. One of the more revealing ones was a story in the *New York Times* about a year ago about a butler school in Colorado . . . because so many Americans are wealthy enough to have servants now. You see all these people who got rich on the stockmarket building these enormous houses with ten bedrooms and eleven bathrooms. It's disgusting.
>
> All I can say is, it's not the America I thought I understood. I read about these kids at Palo Alto high school [in California]. One of them is driving a Mercedes and another one is in a Lexus and they have an accident in the school parking lot. But when it gets to court their parents are too

busy making money in their dotcom start-ups to make an appearance for their kids.

While all this was going on, many social problems remained unsolved. While millions of children played the market, one in five American children lived in poverty. Inequalities had become aggravated, and affluence was not necessarily a matter of deserved personal reward.

Whereas Americans held one dollar in every seven of their wealth in the stockmarket in 1990, by decade's end it was one dollar in three, a larger share than they had invested in their homes. The weight of that stock wealth, like the moon exerting a gravitational pull on the tides, came to exert an important influence on the spending and confidence of the American people. They took to calculating the size of their stockmarket profits, counting them as money in the bank, and spending accordingly. The US Federal Reserve did a lot of work on this so-called wealth effect; it estimated that of every dollar in stockmarket profits Americans clocked up each year, they spent three to four cents on consumer outlays, buying clothes, eating out, replacing their cars. Greenspan observed: "The so-called wealth effect has been a very prominent factor in the major expansion in economic activity, especially since 1995."

An economic consultancy in New York, the ISI Group, found a close correlation between the Nasdaq and the spending patterns of American households since about 1996. "The Nasdaq has become almost four times more important than disposable personal income in explaining swings in consumer spending," the firm's researchers concluded as the bubble approached its peak. "This is a crazy way to have to think about forecasting gross domestic product, but that's the way it is."

Yet while the American public had so much riding on the market, and while they grew to pride themselves on understanding market arcana like PE ratios and stock splits, they were in general deeply ignorant of equity markets, their workings and their history – and therefore highly vulnerable as a class of investors. Jim Bianco of Bianco Research found that from the beginning of the bull market in October 1990 until mid-2002, Americans put $1.3 trillion in net new cash into US shares through their mutual funds, the vehicle of choice for Americans investing in shares. As the market rose, the total profit on this investment peaked at $750 billion in March 2000, he said. But as Wall Street started to crumple from March 2000, so did these profits until, by July 22, 2002, they were reduced finally to zero. "Why are we back to zero profit even though the Dow Jones index is still above 7000 points [a level it didn't reach until 1997]?" Bianco asked. "The reason is that the public's such a lousy market timer. They didn't buy much stock when the Dow was at 3000 and 4000. They were putting money into the market at the rate of $5 billion to $10 billion in 1991, '92 and '93. But then when it was peaking around 10,000 and 11,000, they were buying much more heavily; they were investing $50 billion a month when the Dow was at 11,000."

And the last ones to arrive were the most wildly bullish. A Gallup poll in 1999 found that investors who'd been in the market for twenty years or more expected annual stockmarket returns of 13 per cent. People who had arrived in the past five years were counting on gains of 23 per cent.

In diagnosing the psychology of market manias, an expert on financial frenzies and failures, the late Charles Kindleberger, wrote that it is a case of "monkey see, monkey do".

"In my talks about financial crisis," he wrote in his classic work, *Manias, Panics and Crashes*, "I have polished one line that always gets a nervous laugh: 'There is nothing so disturbing to one's well-being and judgment as to see a friend get rich.' When the number of firms and households indulging in these practices grows large, bringing in segments of the population that are normally aloof from such ventures, speculation for profit leads away from normal, rational behaviour to what has been described as manias or bubbles."

This was precisely what was happening. The broad mass of the American public was drawn into stock investing by Wall Street marketing hype amplified in the echo chamber of a credulous media. It was a group of people agog at the gains of friends and acquaintances, ignorant, greedy and unwittingly putting its money into a bubble in its final and most unstable phase. The money of these people, their confidence as consumers and their national economy were all increasingly hostage to a mass hysteria masquerading as a smart path to great wealth. Thinking that they were aboard a great rocketship delivering them to an exciting new world of endless profits and easy living, the ordinary American investor was actually strapping himself onto a mighty firework arcing skyward, where it was destined to explode and fall, burnt and blackened, back to earth.

Alan Greenspan had tried to warn the country in December 1996. Now, rebuffed, he turned to helping them strap themselves on for the ride. The first essential commodity that Greenspan made sure to supply was easy money. Apart from the lone increase in interest rates, by one-quarter of a percentage point in March 1997, the only movements in official interest rates were downwards, until mid-1999. It must be said that these easings were not some personal indulgence of Alan Greenspan but were responses to major contingencies. Three important dangers between 1997 and 2000 demanded lower rates and a buffer of liquidity to protect against harm – the Asian economic crisis, the collapse of Long-Term Capital Management and the alarm at the risks of the so-called Y2K or millennium bug. The first was a serious threat to economic growth, the second a serious threat to the financial system, and the third turned out to be a serious threat only to the credibility of the consultants and other experts who had proved to be the Chicken Littles of forecasting. Still, the Fed needed to take all these events seriously. And it did, and handled them judiciously and well.

The problem is that the Greenspan Fed proved lightning-fast at cutting rates, and extraordinarily dilatory about raising them. The effect was that the Fed made a net change to official rates of –1.25 percentage points during the boom years, a 21 per cent overall reduction in the rate. Greenspan was a hare when it came to the popular work of cutting rates and letting the money flow, and a tortoise when the more politically difficult task of raising rates beckoned. Quite apart from the question of whether the central bank should take stock prices into account in setting rates, Greenspan resisted raising rates even in the face of conventional concerns about traditional inflation. Even when there was a sound case for raising rates, even when the bulk of the other members of the Federal Open Market Committee thought that they should, and even when the consensus of economists favoured such a move, Greenspan resisted. He needed a sound intellectual basis for this, however, and he found one.

Greenspan developed a suspicion that the changes in the economy had created a new, higher speed limit for economic growth. Economists have a theory, derived from an idea of the US monetarist Milton Friedman, that an economy has a "natural rate of unemployment". The economy will start to develop the friction burns of inflation whenever it grows fast enough to reduce unemployment beyond that threshold. At this point, a shortage of skilled labour would mean that employers would have to bid up wages, generating inflation. This threshold, which economists have infelicitously dubbed the non-accelerating-inflation rate of unemployment or NAIRU, was estimated by the Fed's economists, and most others, to be around 6 per cent in the mid-1990s. So when unemployment fell below that point, inflation would start to accelerate. The response of a central bank should be to slow the economy by raising interest rates. But now that the level was being tested as America's expansion continued, Greenspan did not want to raise rates. He challenged the estimate. In August 1994, unemployment hit this theoretical danger zone of 6 per cent and continued to fall. By the end of the year it had hit 5.5 per cent. But there was no sign of an acceleration in inflation. The longer the boom ran, the further the jobless rate fell, and the more anxious economists and FOMC members grew. Greenspan stood his ground. Larry Meyer described how this developed into a ritual at committee meetings during the spring and summer of 1997: "The staff forecast would suggest the need for a tightening [raising rates], and the FOMC members would part into hawks and doves," standard classification for those who took a hard anti-inflationary line and those who did not, respectively. "And then the chairman would come in, as always, speaking like a hawk and walking like a dove. This seemed to fall into a pattern: the chairman would ask for no change in the funds rate, suggest that the time was approaching for action, and indicate that there was a high probability of a move at the next meeting. At the next meeting, he would explain that the data did not yet provide a credible basis for tightening, and in any case, that the markets didn't expect a move. However, he would conclude that he expected the committee would be forced to move at the next meeting."

Alice Rivlin, sent to the Fed as one of Clinton's "political officers" to restrain Greenspan from raising interest rates, found, to her surprise, that she didn't need to – he was on her side: "As it turned out, he and I were the leaders of the pro-growth faction, together with Bill McDonough [president of the New York Federal Reserve Bank]. Greenspan gets a lot of the credit for allowing the economy to grow faster in 1996–99 on the grounds that he believed, as I do, that there was something really fundamental going on in technology" that permitted the economy to break the conventional speed limits. "The right thing to do in monetary policy from 1996 to mid-1999 was nothing, and that's basically what we did." Meyer, the other "political officer", marvelled at the role reversal. Instead of having to hold Greenspan back from raising interest rates, he found himself worried that Easy Al, as some monetarists nicknamed him, was not keeping rates high enough. "The chairman and I actually traded places on the issues."

Greenspan stood firm until finally, by the end of the boom, unemployment was at 3.8 per cent. There had been no inflationary breakout. Greenspan had been right. And the explanation? In two words, higher productivity. Productivity is the measure of how much economic output you can achieve with any given stock of workers or capital or both. Greenspan saw that labour productivity – the amount of output you can squeeze from the country's workforce – was growing at a faster rate than the official statistics showed. He suspected that technological change was lifting productivity growth at a clip faster than the one the statisticians could discover. He was right. Later, upgraded figures would show that US labour productivity had risen at an annual rate of about 3 per cent from 1995 to 2003, double the average from 1973 to 1995. This made the old NAIRU speed limit redundant. Greenspan was credited, justly, for recognising that the economy had changed. This allowed it to grow faster and longer, and to generate more jobs, than it would have been permitted to do under a more conventional Fed chairman. But there is limited value in creating these conditions if you know they are unsustainable and dependent on a bubble which will soon burst. And it is striking to note that Greenspan was much bolder and more insistent in advancing an unorthodox approach when it was politically popular, as it was in this instance, than he was when it came to a politically unpalatable cause, as in the short-lived stand against irrational exuberance.

The change that came over Greenspan was so marked it was as if "we have two Alan Greenspans, not one," wrote Clive Crook, deputy editor of the British magazine *The Economist* and a columnist for America's *National Journal*. He argued that the first Greenspan ran the Fed from 1987 to 1996, and "he was steady, predictable, and judicious." The second Greenspan, after 1996, "likes a bet, springs surprises now and then, and works by instinct". How did he measure this bifurcation? By using a formula called the Taylor rule, famed among monetary types, named after an economist and Treasury undersecretary in George W. Bush's administration, John Taylor. This rule seeks to prescribe American monetary policy by use of a couple of simple and consistent guide-rails. It seeks to smooth the economic cycle by preventing booms from getting out of control. It responds to accelerations in output by raising interest rates. Alan Greenspan once employed the younger John Taylor at his consulting firm, Townsend-Greenspan, but utterly rejected his rule as a way to set monetary policy. Greenspan always resisted any measure that might restrict the scope of his freedom to move rates at his own discretion. The funny thing is that the first

Greenspan set interest rates as if he were following the Taylor rule for his nine years, so closely did his actions fit the formula, but the second Greenspan abandoned the Taylor rule. Clive Crook wrote: "Growth in output accelerated after 1996. The Taylor rule called for higher interest rates. They mostly stayed down . . . The second Greenspan has gambled on an optimistic view of the economy."

All experience as well as theory tells us that official monetary policy has a strong influence over the market, and this is supported by all the evidence from within the Fed itself. For instance, the Fed's research covering 1989 to 2002 found that any given surprise move in the Federal funds rate will produce an effect three to six times as big in stock prices. So a cut of 1 percentage point in the Fed's policy rate would push stock prices up by 3 to 6 per cent. And it works in reverse too – so that if the Fed puts its rate up, stock prices fall by three to six times the size of the change. Presenting this research in 2003, a Fed governor, Ben Bernanke, described this as "an effect of moderate size", but "not one of the major influences on equity prices".

It can be a critical influence, however. In early 1994, the market had been running hot. The Federal Open Market Committee raised rates by one-quarter of a percentage point on February 4. The total market's value immediately slumped by 2.27 per cent. The market's response was nine times the size of the Fed's move. And the market was still flat three weeks later when Alan Greenspan convened a conference call to review the situation.

> Let me say that looking back at our action, it strikes me that we had a far greater impact than we anticipated. I think we partially broke the back of an emerging speculation in

> equities . . . In retrospect, we may have done the same thing inadvertently in the bond market . . . I suspect that there was a significant overshoot in the markets. We pricked that bubble as well, I think. We also have created a degree of uncertainty; if we were looking at the emergence of speculative forces, which clearly were evident in the very early stages, then I think we had a desirable effect.

The Fed had not been taking aim at the markets. It was moving in anticipation of an overheating in the economy. The episode demonstrates that changes in official rates can have a very powerful effect, depending on the circumstances. And one of the key reasons, as Greenspan mentioned, is that such changes introduce uncertainty. The Fed continued to raise rates during the year and into early 1995, by a total of 2.75 percentage points, and the markets remained subdued. When Greenspan decided to reverse course and started to cut rates from mid-1995, the markets roared again. The economy had continued to grow but any overheating had been damped down. And a speculative bubble had been pricked. It had been a successful episode in monetary management – it had kept the expansion running smoothly, prolonging the growth without creating dangerous imbalances. It was also conducted by the first Alan Greenspan.

The second vital commodity that Greenspan supplied to the bubble in its later years was a certificate of sanity to the stockmarket, an endorsement of the underlying rationale for the bubble – the idea that a historic technological revolution validated the soaring prices.

Although there was a major technological change afoot, that was never the issue. The question was how to price it in the stockmarket. And, as if to prove that nobody really had the least idea of how to value an Internet stock, their market value gyrated ridiculously. In an eight-month period in late 1998 and early 1999, in the midst of the boom, the total market value of the biggest seven stocks in the Bloomberg Internet index – a group including Amazon.com, America Online and Yahoo! – soared as high as $425 billion and plunged as low as $42 billion, a difference of ten times.

The promoters of the New Era were saying foolish things to justify increasingly foolish prices. The market was working itself into a delusional fever that profits no longer mattered. Nonsense could only be admitted as truth if our concept of reality had itself been revolutionised. And so promoters promised: "Within ten or twenty years the world will be completely transformed," rhapsodised the creator of *Wired* magazine, Louis Rossetto. "Everything we know will be different. Not just a change from L. B. J. to Nixon, but whether there will be a president at all. I think Alvin Toffler's basically right: we're in a phase change of civilisations."

Or, as management consultant Ron Nicol explained the changed reality in 1999: "It's just not cool to make things anymore." What was virtual had become real, and what was concrete had become immaterial. It was a shrewd mix of the fevered evangelism of believers with the commercial cynicism of the profiteers, neatly paired in this reflection by the founder of the web browsing firm Netscape, Jim Clark: "I continued to preach the Gospel, assuring the unsaved that the Internet was their salvation. But we needed something else to get the world's attention. More marketing bullshit!" It worked for him. When Netscape shares were first listed on the stock exchange on August 9, 1995, an investor frenzy made Clark's share of the company worth over half a billion dollars on day one.

The Internet and IT revolutions were, and are, important, but they could no more immunise the stockmarket against downturn than the "hot" technologies of 1929, the automobile and the wireless, could prevent the Great Crash. In his 1999 history of bubbles, *Devil Take the Hindmost*, the British banker Edward Chancellor pointed out:

> The 1990s bull market was accompanied by the reappearance of a new era ideology similar to that of the 1920s. Known as the "new paradigm" or the "Goldilocks economy", the theory suggested that the control of inflation by the Federal Reserve, the decline in the Federal deficit, the opening of global markets, the restructuring of corporate America, and the widespread use of information technology to control inventory stock levels had combined to do away with the business cycle. Point for point, this was a reiteration of the new era philosophy (of the 1920s).

The New Era of the 1990s was the third to be pronounced in twentieth-century America. The first New Era was in the 1920s, and ended with the Great Wall Street Crash of 1929, followed by the Great Depression. The second was 1955–66, and ended in a crash, from which it took the market twenty-six years to recover, in real terms, to its peak of 1966. Strikingly, each wave of euphoria followed the end of a major war, and each was attended by enormous optimism for the future amid a technological revolution. The 1920s, of course, followed the end of World War I, and the technological revolution was centred on the popularisation of the automobile and the radio. "In fact, a new age is taking form throughout the entire civilised world; civilisation is taking on new aspects," wrote the head of the

Moody's Investors Service, John Moody, in 1928. "We are only now beginning to realise, perhaps, that this modern, mechanistic civilisation in which we live is now in the process of perfecting itself." The 1955–66 New Era followed World War II and was enraptured with the transforming possibilities of television. "Once again the feel of a 'new era' is in the air," reported *US News and World Report* in 1955: "Confidence is high, optimism almost universal, worry largely absent." The bubble of the 1990s followed the end of the Cold War in 1989, and the technological revolution revolved around the Internet. "Everything is perfect," said the chief of the business advisory house Alliance Capital, David Williams, in 1997.

Historically, America's technical experts, as opposed to the marketers, consider the Internet to be rather ordinary as far as twentieth-century technological revolutions go. The US National Academy of Engineering in 1999 ranked the greatest technological innovations of the twentieth century according to how much each had improved the quality of life. This was their ranking: electrification, the automobile, the aeroplane, water supply and distribution, electronics, radio and television, agricultural mechanisation, computers, the telephone, airconditioning and refrigeration, highways, spacecraft, the Internet, imaging, household appliances, health technologies, petroleum and petroleum technologies, laser and fibre optics, nuclear technologies, and high-performance materials.

One of the lessons of technological innovation is that while companies will capture some of the benefit, most goes to the public in the form of better and cheaper living conditions. In one great new technology sector, the telegraph, there were fifty companies in 1851, yet only one, Western Union, survived. It was the same story with the telephone. There were thousands of companies in the industry in the US, yet all died off except for those in the Bell System. One of the twentieth century's most successful investors, Warren Buffett, described the difficulty that the private sector has found in trying to profit from innovation: "I thought it would be instructive to go back and look at a couple of industries that transformed this country much earlier in the century: automobiles and aviation. If you had foreseen in the early days of cars how this industry would develop, you would have said, 'Here is the road to riches.' " He discovered that in its early phase, the US car industry boasted 2000 makes: "After corporate carnage that never let up, we came down to three US car companies – themselves no lollapaloozas for investors." Buffett suggested that it would have been smarter to short the market for horses than to invest in cars. As for the aeroplane manufacturing industry, Buffett counted about 300 participants in the years 1919–39, "of which only a handful are still breathing today". What about airlines? "As of 1992," says Buffett, "the money that had been made since the dawn of aviation by all of this country's airline companies was zero. Absolutely zero. I'd like to think that if I'd been at Kitty Hawk in 1903 when Orville Wright took off, I would have been farsighted enough, and public-spirited enough – I owed this to future capitalists – to shoot him down."

The founder of Amazon.com, Jeff Bezos, was amazed to hear Buffett's analysis: "I noticed that decades ago, it was de rigueur to use 'motors' in the name, just as everybody uses 'dotcom' today. I thought, wow, the parallel is interesting. We still have the opportunity to be a footnote in the e-commerce industry." But if all of this was news to Bezos, the man who invented the appellation "dotcom", none of it was to Alan Greenspan. He was familiar, in a personal and professional sense, with the patterns of boom and bust, or New Era delusion and the bitter return to reality. As we have seen, his own childhood had been a victim of the Great Crash of 1929, when his stockbroker father had been damaged by the bust and his family broke up. This made his enthusiastic embrace of the late-bubble madness even more outlandish.

But embrace it he did. He gave his stamp of approval to the fashionability of the virtual over the concrete, the idea that "it's just not cool to make things anymore." This, incidentally, was the core insight, too, of Enron's Ken Lay. His plan was to sell assets – he called them "old iron" – and for Enron to become a virtual company that traded everything from financial derivatives and Internet bandwidth to advertising space and memory chips. More investment bank than power utility, at its zenith Enron was making 80 per cent of its revenue from trading activities. It had been voted America's Most Innovative Company five years in a row by readers of *Fortune* magazine. *The Economist* called him the "messiah" of an evangelical cult disguised as a company. Greenspan, too, might have been called the leader of an evangelical cult, one disguised as a country. "Over the past century, by far the smallest part of the growth in America's real GDP reflects increased physical product measured in bulk or weight," Greenspan said in September 1997. "Most of our gains have been the result of new insights into how to re-arrange physical reality to achieve ever-higher standards of living." And next month he again warmed the hearts of the techno-fantasists: "We are witnessing the substitution of ideas for physical matter in the creation of economic value – a shift from hardware to software, as it were." Note that while this was quite true, it was also the wrong time in American life for the head of the central bank to be emphasising one of the main themes that was used to gull a credulous public into supporting a bubble.

Greenspan said, time and again, that a "virtuous cycle" had been set up. The technological achievements of the New Economy had created a productivity revolution. This justified the expectation that "the extraordinary growth of profits . . . extended into the distant future". This excited stock prices to yet higher levels. And the buoyant stockmarket, in turn, "provided impetus to productivity-enhancing capital investment". This further galvanised productivity, setting the whole cycle off once more.

He was generally careful to hedge or qualify his visionary pronouncements. For instance, he is also on the record as telling a conference of newspaper editors in 1998 that "as a central banker, I always have great scepticism about new eras and changing structures of how the world functions." He, more than anyone, knew that it must one day end badly. He would always be able to point to the qualifications that he would routinely attach to his speeches, like this one, delivered in 1998: "There is one important caveat to the notion that we live in a new economy, and that is human psychology." Yet there was always enough optimism in his speeches for the stock-promoters and the speculators and the giant marketing machine called Wall Street to be able to quote him as their gospel and claim him as their patron saint. And occasionally he would allow the rhetoric to soar, as in this millennial moment in September 1999: "It is safe to say that we are witnessing this decade, in the US, history's most compelling demonstration of the productive capacity of free peoples operating in free markets."

The Fed chairman's timing was particularly dismal for his address to the Boston College Conference on the New Economy on March 6, 2000:

> When historians look back at the latter half of the 1990s a decade or two hence, I suspect they will conclude we are now living through a pivotal period in American history . . . It is the growing use of information technology throughout the economy that makes the current period unique. However, until the mid-1990s, the billions of dollars that businesses had poured into information technology seemed to leave little imprint on the overall economy. The investment in new technology arguably had not yet cumulated to be a sizeable part of the U.S. capital stock, and computers were still being used largely on a stand-alone basis. The full value of computing power could be realised only after ways had been devised to link computers into large-scale networks. As we all know, that day has arrived.

Having declared that the day had arrived for the final realisation of technology's potential, he then sketched a limitless horizon of growth and profit:

> Technological synergies have enlarged the set of productive capital investments, while lofty equity values and declining prices of high-tech equipment have reduced the cost of capital. The result has been a veritable explosion of spending on high-tech equipment and software, which has raised the growth of the capital stock dramatically over the past five years. The fact that the capital spending boom is still going strong indicates that businesses continue to find a wide array of potential high-rate-of-return, productivity-enhancing investments. And I see nothing to suggest that these opportunities will peter out any time soon.

The Nasdaq index reached its apogee ninety-six hours later. Then it began the crash which wiped out 80 per cent of its value. It brought the broader stockmarket and then the capital spending boom down with it. And with that came the entire economy.

And although Greenspan certainly did not invent the term "new era economy", he did popularise it. The term had no general currency until *Business Week* published its July 14, 1997, cover story attributing the term to Greenspan, according to research published by Robert Shiller in his book *Irrational Exuberance*. The cover line: "Alan Greenspan's Brave New World". A fellow Fed governor, Laurence Meyer, wrote: "By the beginning of 1998, the chairman had become the poster boy of the New Economy."

While the bubble was still expanding, it gave rise to increasingly outlandish visions and forecasts. A pair of economists, James Glassman and Kevin Hassett, wrote a book with the title *Dow 36,000*. The Dow Jones Industrial Average took ninety-nine years to achieve its first 5000 points, and just four years to achieve its next 5000. It closed above 10,000 points for the first time in March 1999. As it did, Glassman and Hassett wrote that "a perfectly reasonable level for the Dow would be 36,000 – tomorrow, not ten or twenty years from now". They employed the madman's defence: it was not they who were insane but the rest of the world. Their theory passed quickly into vogue and was much discussed for the next year. And it is simply this: investors are gradually realising that putting their money into leading US stocks is not as risky as they had long thought. And they are re-evaluating the stockmarket as a result. From 1926 until the 1980s, investors had demanded returns from the US stockmarket an average 7 per cent higher than the return they could get from a risk-free investment – which is always taken to be a US government bond. The reason, of course, is that the US Government guarantees the return on the bond, but nobody guarantees anything when it comes to stocks. This 7 per cent difference is the traditional "risk premium" on stocks. But guess what? Glassman and Hassett wrote that "since 1982, and especially during the past four years . . . investors have become calmer and smarter. They are requiring a much smaller extra return, or risk premium, from stocks to compensate for their fear."

That premium was around 3 per cent in 1999. "We believe it is headed for its proper level: zero. That means stock prices should rise accordingly."

The catch? The risk premium is not the product of some scientific or inexorable natural force. It is a measure of the collective confidence or fear of the investor community. And that is a feature of human psychology. If the risk premium were to continue falling, it could only happen if the preponderance of investors became continuously more bullish and less fearful. But the wild bullishness of the time dissipated when the bubble burst. At that time in 1999, with the Dow hitting 10,000, the Federal Reserve's own model for valuing it indicated that the index was already overheated by 31 per cent.

But even the *Dow 36,000* guys were outdone by Lawrence Kudlow, co-host of a TV show, *Kudlow & Kramer*, and a columnist in the *Washington Times*. For Kudlow,

> the dominant event of the late 20th century is the bull-market prosperity of the 1980s and 1990s. This was caused largely by a shift back to free-market economics, a reduction in the role of the state and an expansion of personal liberty. At the turn of the new century, taking the right road

> will extend the long cycle of wealth creation and technological advance for decades to come. By 2020 the Dow index will reach 50,000, and the 10,000 benchmark will be reduced to a small blip on a large screen.

The further the market drew away from reality, the more extreme the theories needed to sustain it. The Internet sector, in particular, laboured under the disadvantage that it was making no profits, only losses. Gratefully, theories were supplied to explain away this awkwardness.

A central one was the belief that growth in the new sectors was to be exponential, and hence a company's prospects could not be captured by conventional yardsticks of stock price valuation. The statistic that established itself as the conventional wisdom was that Internet traffic was doubling every hundred days, an extraordinary growth rate of over 1300 per cent a year. While this was correct in the early days of the Internet, it had slowed so that by 1997 traffic was doubling not every hundred days but every year. The rate of increase was not more than 1300 per cent a year but a much more moderate 200 per cent. So as the bubble was taking off, this core assumption was already outmoded and unreliable. Yet it became entrenched and unchallengeable and in 1998 the US Government dignified it by publishing it as fact in a report by the Commerce Department.

Roger Lowenstein, in his book *Origins of the Crash*, explained how this falsehood became a mainstay of the market's belief system. It started in a new Virginia-based business called UUNet Technologies, which provided Internet services to companies. An engineer at the firm, Tom Stluka, was tasked with building a model for projecting demand for the company's services. He developed his estimates, then sent them to the company's chief operating officer, Kevin Boyne. But Boyne consistently rejected Stluka's figures as being too low. The engineer eventually realised that the boss already had a preconceived figure in mind. Boyne insisted that traffic had to be doubling every hundred days, even though the company's figures did not support that. Boyne was deliberately exaggerating the numbers in what Stluka understood to be nothing more than a marketing ruse. But Boyne insisted, and doubling every hundred days was adopted as the company's baseline assumption of demand.

Then UUNet was taken over by WorldCom, which, after the boom had turned to bust, was later to become the biggest bankruptcy case in American history. The new bosses, including WorldCom's chief, Bernie Ebbers, whose name was later to become a byword for fraud and corruption, started to quote the inflated growth statistic as fact. So the dutiful Tom Stluka told his superiors that this was not accurate. "He would say, 'If traffic is growing at 2x, why are we increasing capacity at 10x?' " wrote Lowenstein. "By now, though, people were using 10x to justify their budgets. They didn't want to hear carping from the guy who had built the model." From here, like something heard in a game of Chinese whispers, it was taken up by the chairman of the phone industry's dominant company, AT&T, Michael Armstrong. The growth formula did not apply to AT&T's Internet traffic either, and the formula had been specifically repudiated by an AT&T researcher, Andrew Odlyzko. But the formula had taken on a life of its own. When the US Commerce Department published it as fact in April 1998 – Internet traffic "doubles every hundred days" – it had relied on WorldCom as its only source. Yet this marketing mirage could be now cited as firm fact.

Alan Greenspan neither endorsed nor repudiated this formula, but he did lend credibility to some of the airiest of the most insubstantial forecasts issued in the course of the mania. For instance, the research firm The Gartner Group had forecast in February 2000 that the value of commerce conducted on business-to-business websites – B2B in the shorthand of those in the know – would surpass $7.29 trillion in 2004. It had been estimated at $145 billion for 1999, so this assumes, again, exponential growth. Greenspan, in March 2000, said: "It appears to be only a matter of time before the Internet becomes the prime venue for the trillions of dollars of business-to-business commerce conducted every year."

These sorts of empty assertions, euphoric visions and sheer fallacies helped to whip up the feverish reception for the increasingly tatty parade of dotcoms brought before the investing public in the climactic days of the Great American Bubble. A 2004 study by the Federal Reserve Bank of New York looked at IPOs brought to US markets from 1980 and 2002 and discovered that "offering firms show a marked deterioration in profitability in the 1990s . . . Indeed, a look at the financial strength of technology and Internet IPOs over the entire period reveals an unambiguous pattern of deterioration." Internet and other tech companies offering stock in IPOs in the first half of the 1980s were earning a healthy 77 cents a share in profit when they were brought to the market, the study reported. In the second half of the '80s, that fell to 59 cents a share – a lesser amount, but still in profit. In the years 1990–94, the average company on offer was losing 1 cent per share. From 1995 to 2000, companies offering IPOs were losing $1.17 per share on average. "Within this group, the Internet firms performed particularly poorly, averaging a loss of $3 per share before going public," reported the New York Fed's economists. It was not just a question of profitability, either. On every financial ratio, there was a steady worsening in the quality of the companies. There was a conspicuously sharp deterioration from 1998 till the bust in 2000.

The theory of the New Era said that the absence of profits didn't matter. The old rules no longer applied. Because there was going to be unparalleled growth, all that mattered in this early phase of the New Era was establishing market share or, as the Internet sector counted it, "eyeballs" seeing your product. After the untold growth there would be plenty of time for the unimaginable profit. However, it was not to be. The Fed's study shows that the companies that listed in the bubble years were the ones most likely to disappear, to be delisted by their host stock exchanges for poor performance:

> Delistings climbed gradually over the sample period, reaching a high in 2001 when an unprecedented 600 IPO firms – accounting for 3.8 per cent of all publicly traded stocks – were dropped by the major stock exchanges. Driving this result were delistings by firms that had gone public in the five preceding years: indeed, this group of relatively recent issuers accounted for an average 68 per cent of the delistings.

Yet the worse the condition of the companies, the more excitedly they were sought by investors. And they generated increasingly large first-day price gains, so big that even the US Government seemed to be stunned. The 2001 annual report of the White House Council of Economic Advisers observed that "the average first day return on IPO securities (calculated as the percentage by which the price at the end of the first day of trading exceeds the offering price) was an amazing 69 per cent." It reported that this was "three times higher than the average first day return in any year between 1975 and 1999". We have already seen the role that Wall Street chicanery played in achieving these "bounces", and how the main purport of the exercise – to help firms raise capital – had been subverted to become secondary to the "bounce" profits that the company's executives and underwriters could harvest for themselves. But the whole enterprise also was supported by fallacious theories of Internet wonders and by the aura of credibility lent by the ultimate authority on all monetary matters, the chairman of the US Federal Reserve.

Dotcoms would readily confess their pathetic condition to prospective investors. "We Are Not Profitable and Expect to Continue to Incur Losses" read a bold headline on page three of the prospectus for Priceline.com, a company offering a website where customers could bid for airline tickets. Some of the other headlines in the prospectus: "We May Be Unable to Meet Our Future Capital Requirements". And: "Our Brand May Not Achieve the Broad Recognition Necessary to Succeed". And: "Our Business Model Is Novel and Unproven". As the journalist John Cassidy remarked: "Short of printing a warning from the Surgeon General, it is hard to see what else could have been done to alert the public to the dangers of investing in Priceline.com." And when it went public on March 30, 1999? The stock was issued at $16 a share, but the market price went immediately to $85, and by the end of the day stood at $68. It had jumped 325 per cent on the day and was now valued by the market at nearly $10 billion. You could have bought three major US airlines themselves for this sum – United, Continental and Northwest had a collective market capitalisation smaller than that of a new and loss-making Internet firm that offered nothing more than the chance to buy cheap tickets on these very airlines. Priceline's share price reached an apex of $96 to value the company at $14 billion before collapsing. Three years later it was trading at $5 a share, giving it a value of half a billion dollars.

The dotcoms were the most egregious part of the market, but, as we have seen, the entire corporate sector of the US was suffering from falling profits. While stock prices boomed by 67 per cent in 1997 to 2000, the total profits of corporate America fell by 6 per cent, according to the national accounts. It was a retrenchment unmatched by anything since 1958. Very few companies generated profits that matched the performance of the stockmarket. Of the 10,000 publicly traded companies in the US, the number that produced growth in earnings per share of 20 per cent or higher in each of the five years of the bubble was exactly eleven (yes, eleven – this is not a misprint), according to the Bank Credit Analyst research group. Many stock prices performed as well, or better than this, but only because of the volumes of money bidding their prices up, not because their prices accurately reflected their underlying earnings. So the market's stunning performance had a great deal more to do with easy money and a buying craze than it did with actual corporate earnings.

While the private sector was in this crisis of profitability, Lawrence Kudlow celebrated the Dow's impending ascension to 50,000 and bragged of the gleaming state of that same sector and prepared to celebrate a "shift back to free-market economics, a reduction in the role of the state and an expansion of personal liberty without precedent". And Alan Greenspan congratulated his countrymen on "history's most compelling demonstration of the productive capacity of free peoples operating in free markets" even while the very foundation of that system, its wealth-generating corporations, exhibited a persistent feebleness that they had not experienced in two generations. Greenspan spoke as if he were standing atop the summit of a mighty mountain of millennial achievement, when he knew full well that he was sitting on a seething volcano of madness, hubris and cupidity.

Many market professionals understood that they were in the midst of a bubble. The investment weekly *Barron's* conducted a so-called Big Money Poll in April 1999. It asked professional money managers: "Is the stockmarket in a speculative bubble?" Seventy-two per cent of the replies were "yes", and only 28 per cent "no". The real victims of the episode were the ordinary people, drawn in by the hype and the excitement, who made their personal funds and their national economy hostage to a bubble.

And these ordinary investors were disastrously misinformed about the risks they faced in the stockmarket. In a survey of 933 stockmarket investors conducted for the Securities Investor Protection Corporation in 2001, five out of six investors said that they believed that there was, or that there might be, some kind of government insurance for any losses they may suffer in the stockmarket.

How could they have formed this preposterous notion? This is the third essential commodity that the chairman of the Federal Reserve brought to sustain and enlarge the bubble. The then strategist for the Wall Street investment bank Morgan Stanley Dean Witter, Byron Wien, told the *New York Times* in 2002 that "more investors got hoodwinked on Fed easing than on any other single concept." That is, investors believed the Fed would cut interest rates to protect them from losses, and this belief was more potent than even the most fervid theories of technological revolution.

Alan Greenspan had gone from critic to cheerleader. In the years after the bubble had come to its inevitable and costly end,

Greenspan worried about his responsibility for it, though he never hinted at this in public. His friend Allan Meltzer, professor of political economy at Carnegie Mellon University and author of a well-regarded history of the Federal Reserve, remarked of Greenspan's record: "The Reagan-Volcker expansion and the Clinton-Greenspan expansion are the two greatest expansions in US history; so he bears some of the praise for that big, long expansion. But on the negative side, it clearly worries him to what extent was he responsible for the rise in stock prices."

A group of economists has tried to calculate exactly that – the extent of Greenspan's responsibility for the rise in stock prices. Citing surveys taken in the bubble's peak year of 2000, the economists pointed out that Greenspan had created the impression in the minds of many investors that he would offer some protection, or insurance, against the risk of a fall in stock prices. Investors believed that Greenspan's Fed could be relied upon to cut interest rates if the stockmarket were in trouble, but that it would not raise rates to constrain a bubble. In short, Greenspan had created the idea that the stockmarket had no downside, only upside.

"We argue that the asymmetric behaviour of the monetary authorities has played a key role as investors came to believe that there was a floor to market prices, but no ceiling," wrote Marcus Miller and Lei Zhang from England's University of Warwick and Paul Weller of the University of Iowa in a paper presented on September 7, 2001.

Specifically, these economists, in a computer modelling exercise, arrived at the conclusion that investors perceived that Greenspan's Federal Reserve had reduced the riskiness of investing in stocks by up to 40 per cent. There is an amusing coincidence here. Greenspan once said that a rise in equity prices constitutes a bubble if they later fall by 40 per cent or more. Was the presence of Greenspan himself enough to constitute a bubble?

"What we describe is not so much 'irrational exuberance' as exaggerated faith in the stabilising power of Mr Greenspan and the Fed," the economists concluded.

These economists were not expressing an eccentric or uncommon view. They were merely trying to put a specific value on a phenomenon widely recognised in the market during the bubble years. Call it Greenspanism.

The American economics columnist Robert J. Samuelson wrote in the *New Republic* in 2002 that "trust in Greenspan became, in the late 1990s, almost a religion. The economy might have bad moments, but Alan would find a way out. He was a magician."

Even Bill Clinton's second Treasury Secretary, Robert Rubin, was unsettled by the cult of Greenspanism. He wrote in his memoir that, after stepping down from his Cabinet post and moving back to New York in 1999, "what had struck me after returning to New York was the pervasive assumption that everything would always be well and that any interruptions in the advance of prosperity would be temporary and mild – solvable, in any case, by the Federal Reserve Board."

"Under Greenspan, the Fed has evolved into a kind of national financial fire department," wrote Jim Grant in his *Interest Rate Observer*. "The more dependably the Fed fends off disaster, the bolder and more leveraged investors become. The bolder investors become, the higher the markets go. And the higher the prices and the greater the degree of leverage, the more likely does a financial accident become. In response to which, of course, the Fed would intervene." The interest rate on Fed funds of 1 per cent, a rate that prevailed for the year to June 30, 2004, was the natural legacy of this approach. The exhaustion of the Fed's policy tool was the natural consequence of an endless cycle of interventions.

And London's *Financial Times* pithily declared in January 2001, two months before share prices reached their frenzied climax: "It's official. There is a Greenspan put option." That is, investors believed that Greenspan had given them, in effect, a contractual right to sell their shares at an agreed price at a future date – a "put option" – guarding against potential loss.

Was Greenspan aware of the madness being committed in his name? Did Greenspan know of Greenspanism? One of the Fed's top officials, the director of research and statistics at the Federal Reserve Board in Washington DC, Michael Prell, gave a speech in January 1999 that indicated that the Fed not only knew exactly what was going on, but explicitly recognised it as a source of instability in the US financial system. Prell spoke of the notion:

> that the Fed has learned how to eradicate the business cycle and how to ensure eternal bull markets in stocks and bonds. I hope that I shall not be viewed as disloyal if I express a little scepticism that my bosses really have achieved quite that degree of insight and power.
>
> But, given that one hears something akin to that thought being expressed by people with some frequency these days, might one not ask, in all seriousness, whether a new sort of moral hazard hasn't been introduced into the macroeconomic scene? Might people – business managers, consumers, investors – be taking risks that they would not have taken were it not for an exaggerated confidence in the

> ability of the Fed to cushion the economy and financial markets against any and all shocks? If so, there conceivably could be a greater potential instability in the system than is readily apparent at this time.

So Greenspan's head of research publicly articulated the fear that Greenspanism might be a source of latent instability in the national financial system – "a new sort of moral hazard", leading investors to cast aside normal prudence and trust in the saving power of the authorities.

A similar concern was raised with Greenspan privately within the Fed. The great man's standing had attained such exaggerated heights that it started to trouble his then vice-chairman, Alice Rivlin. Alan, she told him, it's important that you reinforce the notion that you do not run the world, that you demonstrate that the Fed is an institution rather than an individual. She was worried that confidence in the US economy had become dependent on Greenspan's well-being, and vulnerable to any mishap that might befall him. The chairman agreed with his deputy, but changed nothing and continued to monopolise all the headline appearances, according to Bob Woodward's book on Greenspan, *Maestro*.

That book, a starstruck account of Greenspan's brilliance by a writer who was supposed to be an investigative reporter, was itself a part of the closely entwined twin phenomena of bubblemania and Greenspan worship. It appeared in 2000, at the precise peak of the Great American Bubble.

Once again, as in the December 1996 recognition of "irrational exuberance", there was no failure of comprehension inside the Fed. It was a failure of policy, not of understanding. A few years after the event, a Fed governor during those years,

Laurence Meyer, a member of the Federal Open Markets Committee, wrote ruefully, "I can see that in protecting the market against downside risks, we might have inadvertently lowered the equity premium" – that is, the perceived level of risk in investing in stocks. But there has been no such admission from the chair of that committee, Alan Greenspan.

The sign on Greenspan's desk reads: "The buck starts here." This is a little central bankers' humour. President Harry S. Truman had a famous sign on his desk that read: "The buck stops here." This was taken to mean that he bore the ultimate responsibility for making decisions, and for their consequences. Greenspan's sign is a pun on the Fed's control of the money supply, but it carries the Trumanesque connotation of high office and ultimate responsibility. Will the buck also stop on his desk?

He is making every effort to make sure that blame passes him by. Greenspan repeatedly has defended his record. In speeches, he has argued that bubbles can only be identified with certainty after the fact; that dealing with a bubble through use of margin lending rules would have been ineffectual; and that to raise interest rates to have dealt with the problem would have crunched the overall economy, not just the bubble. In private conversation, he has claimed that it would have taken an increase in official interest rates of 10 percentage points to have deflated the bubble at any earlier phase. This would have meant a tripling of the rate, surely a disaster for the economy. Instead, he said, the Fed had focused on policies "to mitigate the fallout when it occurs and, hopefully, ease the transition to the next expansion". In short, don't try to reduce the risk of inevitable disaster, but wait for it and clean up afterwards.

Let's take those defences point for point and then consider them as a whole. First, his argument that bubbles can be identified only after the event is exposed as false by FOMC transcripts that reveal his confident and accurate diagnosis of "a stockmarket bubble problem" as early as 1996. Some of his defenders have claimed that the Fed could not possibly be asked to see into the future in gauging the consequences of a bubble. This is spurious. Every action that the FOMC takes is an act in divining the future, anticipating inflation or recession. Monetary policy works with a lag of six months to eighteen months. So the Fed, of necessity, is a constant and long-standing practitioner of futurology.

Second, Greenspan's claim that raising margin lending requirements is ineffective is undermined by his own private view on the subject, as recorded in the FOMC's transcripts, that it is a highly effective tool. It is also undermined by the research of the Financial Markets Center, as cited earlier, which shows that although this is not a wholly dependable tool, it has proved to be effective most of the time that the Fed has used it to cool stock speculation.

Third, the claim that using the "big stick" of monetary policy to contain the bubble would have crushed the economy, and not just the bubble, is at odds with experience. As we have seen, Greenspan himself noted that he "partially broke the back of an emerging speculation in equities" in 1994 by raising official rates just one-quarter of a percentage point. With the right timing and tactics, even a small adjustment can be used to good effect. And the research by the Fed's own economists is also at odds with the chairman's contention. By demonstrating that surprise changes in official interest rates have a "multiplier" effect on stock prices of between three and six times, their work simply affirms what market strategists already knew – the Fed can make a powerful difference. And a tightening would certainly introduce an element of risk for speculators and interrupt the one-way bet that generates speculative momentum.

These point-by-point counters to Greenspan's defence should also be considered all together – if he truly thought none of these measures could work in isolation, then why did he not consider applying more than one in concert? For we know from the official transcripts that he never seriously proposed to the FOMC any form of action using any of the elements at his disposal – rhetorical, regulatory or monetary – at any time after his warning of irrational exuberance met a hostile political response.

Finally, if, as we have seen, the market was driven to its final frenzy in good part by false notions, then Greenspan could certainly have tried to confront those fallacies. But instead of challenging the fantasises of techno-utopia, a New Era and a Greenspan guarantee against stockmarket losses, the chairman, at best, tacitly endorsed them or, at worst, aided and abetted them. We are left with the conclusion that, because of acts of omission as well as acts of commission, Alan Greenspan was not prepared to contain or manage in any way one of the most deluded and dangerous market manias in four centuries of financial capitalism until it had assumed such vast proportions that recession was inevitable.

When the bubble collapsed and the economy fell into recession, there were, of course, recriminations. Some blamed Greenspan for allowing the bubble to run so long and so large from 1996. Others, in the mistaken belief that the bubble was sustainable, the norm rather than the aberration, attacked him for the increase in official interest rates of 1.5 percentage points from mid-1999 that finally precipitated the bubble's collapse in March 2000. He starred in *Newsweek*'s 2004 issue about America's most powerful people, but for the wrong reason. He was the main figure in a piece headlined: "Twilight of the Gurus". The article said: "It sure looks as if Greenspan, who could have left in triumph several years ago, has stayed in the job too long. When he used to speak, everyone listened. Now many just tune him out."

Greenspan did not want to offer his critics a chink, and refused to concede any error: "The notion that a well-timed incremental tightening could have been calibrated to prevent the late 1990s bubble is almost surely an illusion," he said in a speech on August 30, 2001. He also defended his lack of any other action and claimed that it was impossible to recognise a bubble until after it had exploded. His detractors pounced on his lack of contrition: "It reminds me of my kids," said Paul Kasriel, head of research at the Northern Trust Company in Chicago and a former Fed economist. "I have two perfect kids – nothing is ever their fault."

Yet, in the public mind, Greenspan remained a great guru. Polled on their feelings towards their central-banker-in-chief, Americans' regard for him remained undimmed. During the bubble and afterwards, the proportion of respondents who said they had "very positive" or "somewhat positive" feelings towards Greenspan remained steady at a little over 50 per cent, and another 20 per cent or so reported feeling neutral. The proportion feeling negative towards him was 10 per cent in 2000, and 11 per cent in 2003, despite all that had happened in between. And, asked in an NBC-*Wall Street Journal* poll in 2002 to pick the greatest cause of the recession and downturn, 12 per cent of Americans were happy to blame the Clinton Administration and another 12 nominated Bush, while the "effects of the September

11 terrorist attacks and the war on terrorism" rated 34 per cent and the normal business cycle 16 per cent. And what of the man who controls the money supply? "Policies of Alan Greenspan and the Federal Reserve" attracted a mere 3 per cent of the blame, and in another poll a year later even two-thirds of these respondents had found it in themselves to forgive the old man. His share of the blame had fallen to just 1 per cent. Essentially, among the public at large, Alan Greenspan was blameless.

If Alan Greenspan bore so much responsibility for stock-market boom and bust, and the recession and losses that followed, why was he still held in such high public regard? It is logical that, if only 0.2 per cent of Americans know what Greenspan does, only a tiny fraction could possibly hold him responsible for failing to do it well. But it still represents an impressive evasion of blame by the Fed chairman. The true brilliance of his escape from responsibility, however, is that the pollsters conducting most of the other opinion polls on the subject of the economic downturn didn't even think to list Greenspan or the Fed as one of the potential culprits.

This must make him the envy of every politician, of every public officeholder, of every chief executive everywhere – he has achieved real power without real responsibility.

Greenspan may have been protected from calls for retribution from the investing masses of America by his aura of unapproachable gravitas, his deliberately impenetrable language, and the mysteriousness of his work. But he has enjoyed protection from most of the economics profession because when he erred, at least part of his error fell within the prevailing orthodoxy. The economic orthodoxy said that a central bank should leave bubbles alone. The US was not suffering an inflationary outbreak in the conventional sense, so, according to the conventional wisdom, there was no need to act. Greenspan continued to enjoy the protection of this conventional wisdom, even as it was being rethought in other nations.

The ultimate expression of Greenspan's ability to crash the economy and walk away unscathed from the most costly event in the history of the US is the fact that President George W. Bush re-appointed him in 2004 for a final nineteen months as chairman, up to the limit that his term as a member of the Board of Governors would allow. This guaranteed that, until he retired in January 2006 at the age of seventy-nine, he was perfectly positioned to defend his legacy and deny the US the ability to learn from it. And even after the trauma of a punishing, three-year-long stockmarket downturn and a recession, vestiges of a wistful Greenspanism lived on. Five years on, US stocks were once again trading at prices far above the historical averages of reasonable valuation and a bubble was apparent in the housing market.

Why did Bush re-appoint him? There are at least three reasons. First, Greenspan had reached an accommodation with the Bush Administration and they had a close working relationship, although it was far too close for the tastes of the Democratic Party. Second, there was an absence of clear alternatives. In George W. Bush's first term he had asked his chief economic adviser, Larry Lindsey, the same man who, as a Fed governor, had urged Greenspan to act against the bubble in 1996, to draw up a list of possible replacements for Greenspan. Lindsey later remarked that there were no strong alternatives. Greenspan's manoeuvrings to prevent the emergence of a clear successor from within the Fed had, no doubt, helped to produce this outcome. And third, because Greenspan still enjoyed solid public regard it was a riskless decision for Bush.

Yet the writers on *Late Night with Conan O'Brien* could clearly see the irony that most of the economics profession, the markets and the President have not. Said O'Brien: "It was reported today that Alan Greenspan has agreed to serve another term as chairman of the Federal Reserve. As he said, 'Where else could I get a job in this economy?' "

Chapter Seven

THE ENRON AWARD

The entertainer Heidi Joyce once railed against a great American institution: "I can't believe we still have the Miss America pageant. This is America! Where we're not supposed to judge people based on how they look; we're supposed to judge people based on how much money they make." Is this stand-up comic offering us the secret to the phenomenon of the Great American Bubble? That it tapped a peculiarly American passion for money, a national attribute noted by Alexis de Tocqueville more than 150 years earlier? Was the US uniquely vulnerable to the Utopian idea of an ever-rising stockmarket based on a dazzlingly optimistic outlook?

There was a sense at the time that the bubble was a specifically American event. And the annual report on the world's millionaires by Cap Gemini, Ernst & Young and Merrill Lynch seems to offer some support to that notion. European millionaires were more defensive and sought confidentiality, discretion and stability, while "the behaviour of North American [millionaires] is shaped more by confidence in 'the American dream'." And this was a report issued in June 2002. American optimism seemed to be intact despite the crash and the recession.

We know that the US is prone to Utopianism, that America, alone among nations, ranks the "pursuit of happiness" as a fundamental human right in one of the founding documents of nationhood. Zachary Karabell in his history of American Utopianism, *A Visionary Nation*, wrote: "Running through the currents of our history is a presumption that it is possible to have it all. And not just that a few people can have it all, but that all of us can." And belief in the New Era seemed to be a modern iteration of this 400-year-old dream: "The Internet is new. But the vision is not. The magical fusion of the Web, the computer and the stockmarket is a unique product of our cultural moment; the presence of visionaries who believe that they are fundamentally transforming culture is not. The New Economy is simply the latest in a series of Utopian dreams that have defined American society since the time of the Puritans."

Karabell argued that the US has cycled through six manifestations of Utopianism. First was the Puritan vision for a City on a Hill in the seventeenth century; second was the ideal of individualism, freedom and liberty that took hold during the American Revolution in the eighteenth century; third was the drive to national union from the promulgation of the Constitution through to the Civil War in 1863; fourth was the impulse to territorial and economic expansion in the late nineteenth century; fifth was the belief in the transforming potential of government through the New Deal in the 1930s and the Great Society of the 1960s; and the sixth, of course, was the Internet revolution, the New Economy and the New Era.

If the New Era and its financial handmaiden, the ever-rising stockmarket, appealed to an American Utopian impulse in general, it also catered to some American articles of faith in specific.

One is the belief in capitalism. Another is the idea of the free market. A third is trust in democracy. A fourth is the synthesis of these three – a belief in the possibility of democratic free-market capitalism, in the idea of a people's market. The co-founder in 1940 of that great stockbrokerage Merrill Lynch, Charles Merrill, called it "bringing Main Street to Wall Street". And the fifth, and the clincher in the New Era, is faith in technological solutions.

Surely, then, the Great American Madness at the climax of the twentieth century was a result of the historical convergence of factors that appealed to a unique American predisposition to believe? Tinker Bell turned up and enraptured Americans clapped?

It is a tempting explanation, but only a partial one. Speculative manias are not an American phenomenon, nor a recent invention, nor necessarily limited to stocks. Dispelling all three ideas is the simple fact that the most famous early financial bubble was the Dutch tulip craze of 1636, where the object of speculation was tulip bulbs. And there have been dozens of others in more than a score of countries since.

Indeed, a vast bubble had built and burst only a few scant years before the one on Wall Street. Tokyo's stockmarket bubble had destroyed itself with shattering consequences in 1989, a mere six years before the Netscape debut, six years before the US definitively entered the bubble phase, and eleven years before it, too, collapsed. The world's second-biggest economy had been convulsed by a stockmarket mania, then the world's biggest economy proceeded to do the same almost immediately.

The events were alike in broad design as well as in some of the smallest details. Much as the Japanese bubble threw up a fad for putting fine shavings of gold leaf atop sushi, in the American bubble the *Wall Street Journal* carried ads for $14,000 men's suits with tiny flecks of real gold stitched into them. Both bubbles were justified by fallacious theories that proved irresistibly useful. Both were accompanied by surges in national hubris. While Joe Stiglitz had noted the propensity of American officials to lecture the rest of the world even more insufferably than usual – "we boasted of our success and preached to the sometimes envious economic leaders of other countries" – one of Japan's economic princes, a top official of Nomura Securities, went so far as to propose turning California into a joint US–Japanese economic zone so that he could pay his taxi fares in yen. In the 1980s, the world came to depend on Japanese growth. Japan's financial system was so dependent on land values as the core collateral for its banks that *Euromoney* magazine declared that the world had moved on to a "Japanese real estate standard". In the late 1990s, it could be said that the world had become so reliant on US growth, and the US system so heavily dependent on the stockmarket, that the world had moved onto a Nasdaq standard.

So the event that so gripped the US in the last decade of the twentieth century, like the one that convulsed it in the third decade before collapsing famously in the Great Crash of 1929, was an American experience with its own circumstances and characters and based on American beliefs. But it was also one of a long series of similar events that began before the US existed and that erupts periodically across the far reaches of the planet. It is American, but also beyond American, because bubbles are an outgrowth of not just the American psyche, but of human behaviour. They can occur wherever people gather to trade.

The Great American Madness was sung to a very familiar tune, four centuries old, widely known around the world, fitted with contemporary American lyrics. The economic historian Charles Kindleberger catalogued thirty-five major speculative bubbles ranging across 400 years, a score of countries and dozens of speculative objects including coins, cotton, land, coffee, ships, canals, wheat, housing, British exports to Brazil, silver, railroads, eurodollars, oil and banks. The details always differ, but the pattern is always the same.

"Speculative excess", wrote Kindleberger, "referred to concisely as a mania, and revulsion from such excess in the form of a crisis, crash or panic can be shown to be, if not inevitable, at least historically common."

The International Monetary Fund published a 2003 study that looked more narrowly, seeking only bubbles in stockmarkets and housing markets, and only in the years from 1959 to 2002. It surveyed only the countries that qualified as industrialised for the whole period, nineteen countries in all. Despite the narrower lens of IMF scrutiny, it found many more bubbles in the post-war experience of the rich countries than Kindleberger had discovered worldwide in 400 years. The reason seems to be that Kindleberger took an anecdotal approach, attracted by colour and movement, while the IMF was more thorough, in the interests of science.

The IMF's conclusions, first on stockmarkets only: To qualify, a nation's equity market had to suffer a crunch of over 37 per cent, but the IMF's experts still identified fifty-two such busts across nineteen countries: "This is equivalent to roughly one crash a country every thirteen years," reported the study, titled *When Bubbles Burst*. Every country had suffered at least one bust. On average, stock prices fell by 45 per cent, unfolding over two and a half years. And, on average, a stockmarket bust cost a country 4 per cent of GDP in foregone output. In housing markets, the IMF studied a shorter segment of the century, from 1970 to 2000, and a smaller number of countries because of data difficulty. To qualify as a crash, real house prices had to fall by 14 per cent. The study found twenty crashes across fourteen countries – "this corresponds to roughly one bust a country every twenty years." The average price fall in a housing market downturn was 30 per cent, and unfolded over an average of four years. The cost to GDP averaged 8 per cent.

In a different sampling of bubbles, Jeremy Grantham, co-founder and chief strategist of the Boston-based funds management firm Grantham Mayo Van Oterloo, researched twenty-eight bubbles of the last century or so. He cast his research net beyond stocks and land to include currencies and commodities including oil, gold, nickel and cocoa. He came to an interesting conclusion about the fate of the prices of all of these items once the bubble had burst: "We found that in every case, in every market, the market returns to where it was before the bubble began. It happened in commodity markets, it happened in currencies, it happened in stockmarkets." Grantham presented this finding to audiences totalling 2400 professional investors and analysts and wanted to know if any of them knew of any exceptions to this rule. "I asked them to find me an exception just one exception. Put up your hand, send me an email, maybe I missed Kuwait in the '70s or something. Not one of these guys can find an example. If you believe in a new era, you carry a terrible burden of proof. History is full of bubbles where everyone believed they were in a new era, but they all turned out to be just bubbles."

The history of bubbles, the problem of bubbles, was well known to the US authorities when Wall Street started to bloat in

1996. The man tasked by law to keep the US economy healthy, Alan Greenspan, was fully alert to the problems that speculative bubbles can create. Indeed, in a speech in August 1999, he spoke of the recurring problem of manias and crashes. He described the tipping point where a great frenzy turns to become a great panic overnight: "It is almost as though, like a dam under mounting water pressure, confidence appears normal until the moment it is breached . . . History tells us that sharp reversals in confidence happen abruptly, most often with little advance notice . . .

"What is so intriguing is that this type of behaviour has characterised human interaction with little appreciable difference over the generations. Whether Dutch tulip bulbs or Russian equities, the market price patterns remain much the same." Greenspan did not explicitly include American Internet stocks in the list of overpriced assets vulnerable to instant collapse, but that was the implicit point of his speech. He knew that what had happened before was about to happen again.

Nor was the disaster that followed the end of the matter. In 2004 and early 2005, there appeared to be a bubble in the US housing market and a reviving one in the stockmarket. And a study of thirty-eight bubbles since 1970 by economists at the European Central Bank in 2003 found that bubbles were lasting longer – while they ran for an average of one and a half years in the 1970s, they were averaging a duration of just over five years in the late 1990s. This is not a problem that shows any sign of going away. Traditional inflation has been broadly suppressed; although it remains active, it is quiescent and the methods for dealing with it familiar and tested. But asset price inflation is the new inflation for central banks, one that is becoming more virulent, not less, and one for which there is not yet an agreed treatment.

One of the wise heads of Wall Street, Albert Wojnilower, a friend and contemporary of Alan Greenspan's and senior economic adviser to the Clipper Group, explained the emerging pattern: "The experience of the US in the 1920s and Japan in the 1980s was that if you have easy money and it's not reflected in the cost of living – that is, it doesn't cause price inflation – then it flows into asset prices." And it happened again in the late 1990s. "We've certainly had easy money this time round, and it's flowed into asset prices."

One of the critical drivers of inflation is inflationary expectations – the broad social expectation of where inflation is headed. All the evidence of the last twenty years is that these expectations have been beaten back by repeated cudgellings by central bankers armed with the "big stick" of higher interest rates. Today the public in the rich countries does not expect inflation to get much beyond 3 per cent where they once expected 10 per cent or more. So guess what? They behave accordingly. Everyone in the system has arrived at a consensus that inflation is highly undesirable, and they make decisions on wages and purchasing and pricing that reflect that consensus. But while this re-education has been going on about inflation, the broad social expectation of inflation in asset prices has gone in precisely the opposite direction. It has become broadly fixed in the public mind that investors can earn an easy 10 to 20 per cent in stock profits annually. As Jeremy Grantham said: "People won't throw in the towel readily. They will return to the market because they have been brainwashed for years. Even though the long-run earnings per share growth on the S&P 500 is an average of 1.8 per cent, they still expect 10 or 15 per cent." This appears to be occurring in the market for housing too.

The core difficulties in dealing with bubbles are matters of doctrine and politics.

One obstacle is the school of rational expectations or rational markets. Some academics, and even some policymakers, argue that these bubbles are not irrational at all, that as long as a seller finds a buyer at an agreed price the transaction is perfectly rational – at any price. The argument goes that a market synthesises all available knowledge about the object of the transaction and that all of this is captured in the price, which is, therefore, inherently rational. Considering this argument from inside the craters left by the Japanese and American bubbles, it does not pass the laugh test. That is, if you say it out loud, it's so silly that it makes you laugh. The price of an Internet share during the bubble captured some knowledge about the stock, no doubt. But it also was informed in varying degrees by fallacies of exponential growth, euphoria about a techno-utopia, expectations of a Federal Government guarantee against loss, and knowledge that the investment banks were rigging the IPO market to get maximum bounce. And colouring all of this was the simple and historically persistent mania that grips crowds during bubbles.

The former chief economist of the International Monetary Fund, Michael Mussa, expressed his scepticism of the "rational markets" theory this way: "In my observation, everyone is at least a little bit crazy about something, and it would be an amazing triumph of hope over experience to believe that averaging out the craziness of many people leads inevitably to collective rationality." He suggested that the supporters of the "rational markets" view were themselves irrational: "I find that academic economists are irrationally attached to the theoretical assumption that economic agents are perfectly rational."

This argument, the "rational markets" hypothesis, is the economics equivalent of an apologia for Armin Meiwes. He is the German computer programmer who advertised on the Internet for "well-built young men for slaughter" in the notorious cannibalism case. His ad was answered by a software designer, Bernd-Jurgen Brandes, who replied that to be dismembered would be "the highest point of my life". So they agreed to meet. Meiwes took him to his purpose-built "slaughter room" and began, by mutual consent, by cutting off Brandes' penis while he was still alive. The two men in a spirit of shared endeavour tried to eat the organ before discovering that it was too tough and needed cooking. Meiwes ultimately butchered Brandes and cooked and ate some twenty kilograms of his flesh. Because the two participants entered into the transaction willingly – indeed, as the court heard, enthusiastically – on agreed terms, this would be a perfectly rational act, according to the "rational markets" hypothesis. Such a finding would even have the support of the psychological evaluations tendered to the court, which found Meiwes to be disturbed, but not insane. The "rational markets" theory can be used as a rationale for even the most absurd and destructive behaviour, which is one more reason that it is not a practical guidepost for policy in the real world.

A second doctrinal difficulty lies in persuading central bankers that they have a legitimate role in dealing with bubbles. Bubbles can be dangerous to the stability of national economies, as we have seen. But the orthodoxy among the central banks and other financial authorities of the world has been, until now, that bubbles are none of their business. It was a strict doctrine of "hands off". Even as the Japanese bubble economy of the 1980s demonstrated the destructive power of a modern financial mania, sending the country into a craze for a few years and a funk for a decade, the keepers of the West's economic orthodoxy remained unimpressed and the doctrine immutable. In the Japanese aphorism, the Western countries considered Japan to be "a fire across the water", a conflagration in a distant land, something that could not happen here.

A deeply rooted orthodoxy has tremendous powers of resistance to raging reality. "To see what is in front of one's nose needs a constant struggle," George Orwell reminded us. The world's second biggest economy had suffered a terrible self-inflicted wound, but it was only when the world's biggest economy blew itself up in a similar fashion ten years later that the economics profession started to reconsider.

For the developed countries outside the US, this rethinking has started to take hold in the official establishment. In Britain, in the European Union, in Canada, in Australia, in Norway, in New Zealand and in the Swiss-based organisation known as the central bankers' central bank, the Bank for International Settlements, a conceptual breakthrough has occurred: an acknowledgment that the authorities do have a legitimate role in managing bubbles to minimise the damage they can inflict. The orthodox thinking would permit a central bank to adjust interest rates to take into account any traditional inflationary ripples from a bubble, but not to consider the bubble itself. The governor of the Bank of England, Mervyn King, suggested that the two goals can be reconciled. Those who set interest rates could take into account not only traditional inflation but also the potentially disastrous effects of a bubble simply by adopting a longer view: "In normal circumstances, monetary policy should focus on meeting the inflation target eighteen months to two years ahead, in practice it may be necessary to look even further ahead about the consequences of present actions."

A pair of economists at the Bank for International Settlements, Claudio Borio and Philip Lowe, suggested a slightly different tack. They suggested that the truly disruptive bubbles were the ones that involved a big run-up in debt, as the US and Japanese bubbles did. This blow-out in credit, rather than in the price of stock or real estate itself, should be directly considered by central banks as a danger to stability, they argued. This would not require any central bank to clearly define a bubble – it would only require that the authorities observe a big credit increase to be an increase in risk in itself. And the governor of New Zealand's central bank, Alan Bollard, drew a conclusion that seems to be framed with Alan Greenspan expressly in mind: "There's an old adage that a popular central banker is seldom a good central banker . . . A central banker trying to constrain an asset bubble would certainly not be flavour of the month because everyone loves a bubble on the way up. Still, central bankers are required to think long-term and sometimes that means taking decisions that won't be welcomed at the time but, in the longer run, are in the public interest."

And this raises the third difficulty of addressing the problem of bubbles, the political one. This was ultimately the one that Greenspan baulked at. It cannot be easy to step in front of a great mania and declare oneself to be its nemesis, a destroyer of wealth, which is the way that a central banker can be expected to be portrayed in expressly confronting a bubble. The world's central bankers have reached a difficult juncture indeed: today they need to work with politics and the public to define a new approach to a new danger, or at the very least to an old danger that has renewed its virulent and persistent assault on national economies.

In the United States, the scene of the latest disaster, the lesson has not been learned. There, the orthodoxy is vigorously defended. Without a rethinking of its past, America will be fated to replay it in future. Indeed, a survey of its housing market suggests that it may be already on course for a replay. It has been a learning experience for others, but, quixotically, not for the country that paid the price. The Great American Bubble has been a turning point in the modern world's understanding of how to manage an economy; the US has missed the turn.

The country's leading monetary guru has dismissed bubbles as an unfortunate inevitability. He is not alone. A number of America's leading officials, academics and financiers give every indication of being similarly unconcerned. Alan Greenspan is able to take shelter from blame in this orthodoxy, and in turn he uses his position and prestige to protect the conventional wisdom from a serious re-examination.

Yet the argument that bubbles are inevitable, that nothing can be done but brace for the next one, is defeatist, or fatalist. If other branches of human endeavour were so ready to resign themselves to their failings we would have no electricity or high-rise buildings but we would certainly have leper colonies and religious persecution.

In a capitalist system, the allocation of capital is central to the organisation of the economy and the society. One of the main lessons of the twentieth century is that the market is the best mechanism to do the allocating. One of the main lessons of the last 400 years of financial capitalism is that this mechanism can sometimes be pushed far out of balance when a mania develops. So it is of central importance to examine epic misallocations in an effort to comprehend what went wrong and what might be done about it. This is the challenge of the times, and it is the challenge that Alan Greenspan prepared to meet in 1996 before retreating timidly in the face of political difficulty. Instead of fulfilling his mandate even in the face of opposition, he sought to hide himself in the orthodoxy of the day and the madness of the crowd. Despite his many accomplishments, he failed this vital test. He has gone into retirement a national hero, and yet with the uneasy knowledge of this failure weighing on his mind. He is a brilliant man, a powerful man, a successful man, yet he lacked the leadership and the boldness to be remembered as a great man. He has won many awards and accolades, and the Federal Reserve proudly listed many of them on its website. But there is one honour he was granted, and which he travelled to Houston, Texas, to receive, that his official biographical notes do not record. It was the Enron Award for Public Service. It was a tribute for which the times had suited him. This is what we find, entering the Fed's marble temple and pulling aside the curtain. It turns out that the wizard, in Jim Grant's phrase, "is just a fellow in a business suit trying not to lose his job".

In his classic *The Great Crash: 1929*, first published in 1954, John Kenneth Galbraith foresaw Greenspan's dilemma, and his failure, on the occasion of the Great American Bubble, without knowing when it might occur or who might be in charge: "Inaction will be advocated in the present even though it means deep trouble in the future. Here, at least equally with communism, lies the threat to capitalism. It is what causes men who know that things are going quite wrong to say that things are fundamentally sound."

Epilogue

OLD BULL, YOUNG BULL

The valedictory tributes gushed. Alan Greenspan was "a legend" according to George W. Bush. Princeton University's Professor Alan Blinder, formerly Greenspan's deputy at the US Federal Reserve, pronounced him the "greatest central banker who ever lived". Yet Greenspan was not dead, merely retiring, a legend in his own lifetime.

At the age of seventy-nine, after nearly nineteen years at the big wheel of American monetary policy, he had improved his rating as the world's second most powerful man to widespread recognition as the first. With all the mainstream presidential candidates at successive elections vying to kiss his feet and find his favour, his position evoked the line written by a great eighteenth-century German composer: "There are and will be thousands of princes. There is only one Beethoven." The title of Bob Woodward's 2000 book did proclaim him "Maestro".

Of all the praise, it was perhaps the acclaim from an obscure congressman from New Mexico, the Republicans' Steve Pearce, that was most revealing. In the search for an original compliment during Greenspan's penultimate congressional hearing, he described the Fed chairman as "a handsome man".

Greenspan's looks have been compared to those of Woody Allen and the *San Francisco Chronicle* said he had the face of a basset hound. The prophet of libertarianism, Ayn Rand, had called him the Undertaker. But handsome? This tells us nothing about Greenspan but everything about the feverish climate of adulation surrounding the man. A sycophant, according to *The Devil's Dictionary*, the indispensable 1915 reference work by Ambrose Bierce, is "one who approaches Greatness on his belly so that he may not be commanded to turn and be kicked". Under the apprehension that Greenspan was the father of national prosperity, America approached him on its belly.

Of course, there were some critics in the twilight of his tenure. Harry Reid, the Senate Democratic leader, had been unfeeling enough to call him "a political hack" for endorsing Bush's program of tax cuts, enlarging the Federal deficit. An economics professor from Southern Methodist University, Ravi Batra, wrote an angry tirade titled "Greenspan's Fraud," an ideological rant that held him responsible for most of the world's economic ills, including poverty in Europe.

These critics assailed him for positions he took in areas outside his own immediate domain, not for policies he actually enacted in his field of responsibility. How did the evidence stand at the end of his term in January, 2006, if he's held to account for the Fed's actions, for his manoeuvring of the big wheel?

The line about his good looks should, in market jargon, trade at a steep discount to face value.

Alan Blinder's glorification of him as the "greatest central banker who ever lived" should also be subjected to a reality check. Here is one: As Greenspan's retirement approached, an Australian newspaper columnist proposed someone as a candidate to replace him whose name would have drawn only blank looks in New York or Washington – Ian Macfarlane.

Ian who? Macfarlane was the governor of the Reserve Bank of Australia for a decade. The suggestion was tongue in cheek, but the *Wall Street Journal* took the point and followed up with an article of its own: "As Mr Greenspan's retirement approaches in January [2006], anxious investors wonder: Can anyone reproduce his record? A glance at Australia and elsewhere suggests that the answer is yes."

The paper published a comparison by Global Insight Inc. of Lexington, Massachusetts, of the US economy's performance in the Greenspan era with that of eight other developed countries and found that half of them – Australia, Canada, the UK and Spain–had done as well as or better than the US in reducing inflation and unemployment. Two of those four – Australia and Spain – had also enjoyed faster overall economic growth than America. If other countries' economic performances across the same nineteen years are as good or better, then it's hard to sustain the claim that Greenspan's performance is somehow unique. "Very similar results have been attained elsewhere," observed the head of Israel's central bank and former Citigroup executive, Stanley Fischer. And the other countries did not suffer a 2001 post-bubble recession, a discretionary US event.

Nevertheless, the main measures of economic performance in the US at the close of the long Greenspan chapter did look solid. At the opening of 2006, the US economy was growing at a respectable 3 to 4 per cent a year, consistent with its post-war compound annual average of 3.4 per cent. After the bubble and the recession that attended its bursting, American growth was back on historical track.

Unemployment was 5 per cent – not as low as its boomtime best of 4 per cent but a recovery from a recessionary worst of 6 per cent. Inflation, though temporarily swollen by a worldwide surge in oil prices, appeared to be well in hand. Long-term interest rates, measured by the ten-year Treasury bond, were moderate, at around 4.5 per cent.

Surely the Greenspan Fed had met its congressional mandate to manage interest rates "commensurate with the economy's long-run potential to increase production, so as to promote effectively the goals of maximum employment, stable prices, and moderate long-term interest rates." On the face of it, then, Greenspan did deserve accolades. It seemed like a clear case of what George W. Bush might once have been tempted to call "Mission Accomplished".

As a bonus, by the beginning of 2006 the stockmarket had recovered about nine dollars of every ten lost from the peak of the Great American Bubble to the low point of the bust. The missing $7 trillion had been carried out on the ebb tide for a few years, but now nearly all of it had flowed back as share prices rose again. And though the market did not return to its 2000 peaks of exuberance, there was certainly effervescence in stock prices. Consider two ready reckonings. One measures the price of a stock against the underlying corporate earnings that it represents, the price-to-earnings ratio or PE. For the five hundred stocks in the Standard & Poor's index of share prices, the average from the end of World War Two to the beginning of the bubble in 1996 was 14. That is, at their current rate of earnings, it would take 14 years for these stocks to repay the price of buying them. At the peak of the bubble this shot up to 30 times. At the end of 2005 the ratio stood at 19 times – not as extreme as the bubble-era valuations, but still well above the long-run average of American experience.

Another useful reckoning is the value of all listed stocks measured against the national economic output, as measured by GDP. The stockmarket's total value had a long-run average of 55 per cent of America's GDP, as explained in chapter one. By the peak of the bubble in March 2000, this had inflated to an all-time high of 183 per cent before crumpling as the market crashed. By the end of 2005, it had recovered to 135 per cent. Again, this is not as crazy as the bubble mania at its worst, but it is where prices stood mid-madness, in 1998, and remains way out of line with American historical experience. The ratio stood at 81 per cent immediately before the Great Crash of 1929, for instance. Naturally, even though these indicators suggest that the US stockmarket is once again overpriced, the shareholders were not complaining. "Wealth," said the philosopher Arthur Schopenhauer, "is like sea-water; the more we drink, the thirstier we become." Stockmarket investors at the end of 2005 had been drinking well and were thirsty for more.

Is this the happy inheritance of Greenspan's successor, Ben Bernanke? The first career academic ever named to run America's central bank, Bernanke was a childhood spelling champ who was knocked out of the national final on the word "edelweiss," a natural scholar whose mother said he liked to do his homework twice.

George W. Bush announced his choice of Bernanke on October 24, 2005, and it was generally acclaimed as an excellent one. The most sincere compliment was the one paid with money – stockmarket investors greeted the news by pushing US stock prices up by an average 1.6 per cent that day.

Bernanke is like Greenspan in that both men came to the chairmanship of the Federal Reserve after serving Republican presidents. Bernanke served five months in 2005 as the chairman of the Council of Economic Advisers in the Bush White House in what was, apparently, a very protracted job interview. According to a member of the White House staff, the candidate impressed the President and his other advisers with vows and affirmations of the primacy of market forces. This attitude, too, he has in common with his predecessor. And he continues in the Greenspan tradition of cultivating in private the politicians who are supposed to hold him to account in public. At his confirmation hearing, one of the senators said that Bernanke had been calling on the senators in their offices in what he called a "charm offensive on the US Senate".

Bernanke strikes a contrast with Greenspan in almost every other way. One is his sense of humour. It's impossible to imagine the dourly formal Greenspan at his desk in Hawaiian shirt and Bermuda shorts, Bernanke's suggested attire for the top office bearers at the Fed. But that's no doubt why it was funny. It's not that Greenspan doesn't have a sense of humour, it's just that it's under deep cover. Bernanke also distinguished himself with the tan socks incident. The President chided his economic adviser for turning up at a meeting in the Oval Office wearing tan socks that clashed with his dark suit. Bernanke's response was to arrive early to another meeting with Bush the next day. He handed pairs of the offending item around to all the participants so that, when the President arrived, everyone else in the room, including Dick Cheney, was wearing tan socks.

Another is his generation. At 51, he is fully 28 years junior to Alan Greenspan. Third is background. Greenspan came to Washington from Wall Street. Bernanke's special field was the business of central banking – monetary policy, with a particular interest in the history of the Great Depression. He had some practical experience too, serving three years as a governor on the board of the Greenspan Fed, from August 2002 to June 2005.

Fourth is his promise not to issue public advice to Congress on how to tax and spend. "I think that's outside my realm of authority," he said in his Senate confirmation hearing, "and I think I would leave that . . . to Congress to make up their own minds." Senator Harry Reed responded archly: "Your predecessor was not equally inhibited."

Fifth is his professed intention to speak plainly, something Greenspan spent his career avoiding.

So did Bernanke take delivery of a well-balanced economy with an outlook as smooth as a millpond?

Dr Bernanke seemed to think so. He has listed three long-term potential problems for the US – funding Social Security and Medicare in the next few decades, improving the lifelong education of Americans, and maintaining technological leadership.

But he has said that "the near-term situation is strong". And in his very first public utterance after being nominated, Bernanke said, "My first priority will be to maintain continuity with the policies and policy strategies established during the Greenspan years."

With the former and current Fed chairmen pleased with the status of the US economy, with both Greenspan and Bernanke as one on the fundamentals of how to run the world's principal economy, who could possibly challenge them?

Perhaps the only person alive who commands greater authority than the combined weight of Greenspan and Bernanke is the man who laid the foundation for them, the central banker who broke the back of inflation in the twentieth century, Paul Volcker. As chairman of the Federal Reserve from 1979 to 1987, Volcker single-handedly tamed the inflationary dragon, solving the greatest economic problem of the post-war industrialised world. It was under Volcker that US inflation peaked, in 1982, five years before the dawn of the Greenspan era. It was Volcker who made possible the long, low-inflation expansions that followed. Doing so did not win him much popularity at the time. The cure for runaway inflation was a painful application of high interest rates, and Ronald Reagan's Treasury Secretary, James Baker III, was elated when Volcker ultimately retired: "We got the son of a bitch" was his response to the news.

But it was Volcker who established the brand of US inflation credibility; Greenspan, followed by Bernanke, managed the franchise.

So what does Paul Volcker think? In a speech in February, 2005, he surveyed the mirrorlike surface of the US economic millpond. He noted that "the US expansion appears on track". He acknowledged the "vast, really unprecedented accumulation of wealth, real and paper and, certainly in California and elsewhere, housing. So, what's not to like?"

He had a suggestion. Volcker invited his audience at the Stanford Institute for Economic Policy Research to look a little deeper: "Under the placid surface, there are disturbing trends: huge imbalances, disequilibria, risks – call them what you will." The "heart of the problem" was that "as a nation we are consuming and investing – that is, we are spending – about 6 per cent more than we are producing" each year. He continued: "Altogether the circumstances seem to me as dangerous and intractable as any I can remember, and I can remember quite a lot." (Volcker was born in 1927.)

Six per cent does not sound like terribly much. But it is 6 per cent of the entire US economy. In 2005 this 6 per cent represented around $800 billion. This was America's current account deficit, the bottom line balance of all the country's dealings with the rest of the world. It encompasses every transaction that crosses a country's borders–its trade in goods, its traffic in services, its flows of capital. To keep financing it, America needs foreigners to inject a fresh net $3 billion every working day of the year. This is not charity. For their $3 billion a day, foreigners get ownership of American land or stocks or Treasury bonds or businesses. And with ownership of an asset comes the income that the asset yields–rent and dividends, interest and profits.

The US has run a current account deficit for 24 of the last 27 years, so in itself this is nothing new. The problem is threefold. First, the scale of this current account deficit has burgeoned as a proportion of the US economy. It has more than quadrupled, from 1.3 per cent in 1995 to today's 6 per cent, a record.

Second, foreigners' claims on US assets pile up, year in and year out. The result is that foreigners had claims on a net $2.48 trillion in US assets by the end of 2004, equivalent to a quarter of the US total economic output, or GDP. This, too, was a record.

Third, the US is now hooked on habit of ever-expanding debt. At its current rate, America's net indebtedness will double in proportion to reach 50 per cent of the nation's GDP within five years, and it will eventually hit 100 per cent, according to economists at the Organisation for Economic Co-operation and Development. Until 1986, the US was a net creditor to the world. Today, it is the biggest debtor that the world has ever known. Lawrence Summers, a former US Treasury Secretary, mused that "there is something odd about the world's greatest power being the world's greatest debtor". It's odd because indebtedness on this scale is a surrender of power, an erosion of sovereignty. Foreigners now own 40 per cent of US Treasury bonds. The biggest buyers are the central banks of China and Japan. As the Northern Trust Company's head of research, Paul Kasriel, put it, "What happens if the Chinese decide they no longer want to lend us the money for us to buy our SUVs and so we can buy the missiles that we might one day be aiming back at them?"

Volcker commented on this issue: "I don't know of any country that has managed to consume and invest 6 percent more than it produces for long . . . As things stand, it is more likely than not that it will be financial crises rather than policy foresight that will force the change."

It is quite possible for a country to live beyond its means indefinitely as long as it can control its appetites. In America's situation, it could run an annual current account deficit of a maximum of about 1.3 per cent of GDP without increasing its indebtedness, according to Michael Kouparitsas, an economist at the Federal Reserve Bank of Chicago. But at 6 per cent, America's taste for other people's money has developed to the point of becoming self-destructive. The country crossed the threshold from sustainable appetites to self-cannibalistic ones in the last few years.

How did this happen? The US current account deficit worsened sharply as the Great American Bubble expanded. It doubled from about 2 per cent to 4 per cent of GDP by the time the bubble reached its zenith. As we saw in chapter two, this happened because Americans thought that the fabulous wealth they were earning on the stockmarket meant that they didn't need to save money in the traditional way, and the rate of personal savings fell to a record low.

When the Great American Bubble finally burst in 2000 and sent the economy into recession in 2001, American officialdom took two main actions to restore the economy to growth. The Greenspan Fed cut interest rates radically, and the Federal Government went into deficit.

These are textbook responses to recession. And they worked.

Americans took advantage of low interest rates to go on a borrowing binge, and they used the money to go into a frenzy of house buying. This created a bubble in house prices. As homeowners watched the value of their houses rise, they felt richer and saved even less than they were already saving. The personal savings rate in the US went into negative territory – a new record low. At the same time, the Federal Government fell from surplus into heavy deficit. This is an automatic response to recession, but in this case it was aggravated by an expensive foreign war and a program of tax cuts.

All of this extra spending by homeowners and the Government drove national consumption higher, and national saving lower. As America spent more but saved less, its call on the savings of the rest of the word increased to its annual rate of 6 per cent of GDP.

In other words, the US recovered from its recession by aggravating its current account deficit. It bought an immediate growth hit by selling an unsustainably large share of its assets to the rest of the world each year, a Faustain bargain indeed.

Paul Volcker sees it ending in a crisis. Alan Greenspan and Ben Bernanke have given speeches on the subject of the current account shortfall, but where Volcker sees crisis, they see a much more benign outcome of gradual re-adjustment. And Bernanke doesn't see that it's something the Fed needs to worry about. "I do believe the current account deficit needs to come down over a period of time," he has said, but the Fed should look to employment and inflation and "allow other factors to be predominant in curing the current account situation". In short, it's not my problem.

Indeed, a glance around the landscape of US officialdom shows that nobody seems to think it's his problem, and this worries Volcker most of all: "What really concerns me is that there seems to be so little willingness or capacity to do much about it."

Bernanke does have a new idea for the Fed, a reform that Alan Greenspan always refused, but it has nothing to do with the problem of how America can find a sustainable way to continue to finance its growth. The incoming Fed chairman committed his honeymoon period, and all the goodwill and latitude that come with it, to imposing this one reform: to give the Fed an explicit, public target for the inflation rate.

Is this a good idea? Publicly announced inflation targets are considered among central bankers to be "best practice". Demonstrating that even central bankers are followers of fashion, this policy ensemble was first modelled by New Zealand in 1989 and has since been taken up by a total of 22 countries. Greenspan resisted it because he feared a loss of flexibility. It has been valuable in many countries as a way of establishing anti-inflation credentials.

For the US to introduce one today, however, would be like creating a monetary Maginot Line. An inflation target for the US, like the famous line of French defences in World War 2, would do no real harm. But, like the fixed defensive artillery that was supposed to keep the Germans out of France, it would not be very useful either. Ultimately, the Maginot Line became a metaphor for futility when Hitler's forces simply went around it. However, the line itself did not fail. It was a splendid irrelevancy.

And so it is with Bernanke's campaign to introduce an inflation target, which he had earlier suggested should be set at 1 to 2 per cent. The Fed already has one, although it is undeclared, or "covert". By studying the Fed's actions over the past quarter of a century, Richard Dennis, an economist at the Federal Reserve Bank of San Francisco, inferred that the Fed has been aiming for an inflation rate of 1.4 per cent. (The inflation rate, for the purpose of this discussion, is measured by the Fed's favourite yardstick, the rate of inflation in personal consumer expenditures, minus food and gasoline).

We already know that members of the Fed's monetary policy committee in 1996 discussed how they should define their congressional mandate to achieve "price stability". The transcript of the meeting shows Greenspan summarising the debate: "We have now all agreed on 2 per cent [inflation]."

Now Bernanke has arrived proposing the Fed publicly disclose its inflation target. He wants to state openly – adopting as an avowed target – pretty much what the Fed has been doing, quietly and effectively, for a quarter century. As Bill Dudley, chief US economist for Goldman Sachs, put it: "So it's not like crossing the Rubicon. If he does this, it would be crossing a small stream."

This idea has been a long-standing favourite of Bernanke's, but otherwise it's hard to see why he is devoting all his initial political capital to this issue. Like the Maginot Line, it is all about the last war. Other countries adopted inflation targets to achieve the anti-inflation credibility that Volcker had already established for the US. For America today, the pursuit of targeting would be a tail-chasing exercise.

The clue to what is driving Bernanke may be found in a speech he gave in March 2003: "Credibility is not a permanent characteristic of a central bank; it must be continuously earned." In effect, an untested Fed chairman is seeking to establish through a formal arrangement the credibility that his two legendary predecessors won through action.

If Bernanke's proposal is a splendid irrelevancy, what does Volcker suggest to deal with the problem of American indebtedness? "I'm not suggesting anything unorthodox or arcane. What is required is a willingness to act now . . . and to act even when, on the surface, everything seems so placid and favourable. What I am talking about really boils down to the oldest lesson of economic policy: a strong sense of monetary and fiscal discipline."

Fiscal discipline is the domain of the Congress and the President. But monetary discipline is squarely Bernanke's responsibility. In generating a recovery, Greenspan's Fed had cut official interest rates to 1 per cent, a level that, because it was below the inflation rate, was effectively a negative rate of interest. The Fed was, in effect, subsidising the banks to take money, a super-stimulatory stance.

In his last year at the Fed, Greenspan very gingerly started to remove the stimulus. Although it is the subject of much debate, there is a general consensus that a neutral rate for Fed funds is 4 to 5 per cent – that is, a rate that neither stimulates economic growth nor restrains it. Greenspan ended his 19 years at the Fed with official interest rates in this neutral range. Volcker evidently wanted the rate to go higher in pursuit of monetary discipline. This would start to slow the economy, and that would act to suppress America's appetite for funds from the rest of the world. From Bernanke's remarks, we can conclude that he does not consider this to be part of his brief. He would increase rates only in response to the threat of higher inflation. But what of bubbles? Greenspan's cautious tightening of interest rates in his last year showed some sign that of starting to constrain the bubble in the US housing market. This was a happy coincidence. The housing bubble would one day burst, and the longer it ran, the messier and more costly the consequences. Although the Fed was raising rates in 2005 to pre-empt a possible outbreak of inflation in the future, it was simultaneously and fortuitously constraining a potentially dangerous housing bubble.

But what will happen when there is no such happy coincidence? What will happen in the future when, as it inevitably must, some new bubble arises, yet there is no inflationary threat to justify raising interest rates?

The experience of Japan in the 1980s, and the US in the 1990s until today, is that easy money no longer flows so much into traditional inflation, but into asset price inflation, or bubbles. By contrast, as long as consumer price inflation stayed low, American money was easy. The country blew up its economy with vast speculative asset price bubbles. After watching the US stockmarket bubble burst and drag the economy into recession, other central bankers around the world showed intellectual flexibility in trying to figure bubbles into their thinking.

The US central bank, under Alan Greenspan, avoided focusing on it. Greenspan was determined to defend his decisions rather than to reflect on them. The enemy reformed, but the Fed's threat perception did not. Yet, as we have seen, the stockmarket bubble convulsed the economy, led to recession when it burst, and then, as the country struggled to recover, created the sharp deterioration in America's current account deficit which now threatens its economic sovereignty.

Greenspan had no answer. The key question today is: What does Ben Bernanke think about bubbles?

His position is similar to that of Greenspan's, or, rather, the position that Greenspan assumed after the political rebuff to his declaration of "irrational exuberance". That is, Bernanke believes it is a mistake to try to manage bubbles with the big stick of interest rates: "Certainly there is no way to direct the effects of monetary policy at a single class of assets while leaving other financial markets and the broader economy untouched. One might as well try to perform brain surgery with a sledgehammer."

Yet Bernanke also differs from Greenspan in that he thinks that more precise surgical implements might well be useful in dealing with bubbles. As he put it in a 2002 speech: "My suggested framework for Fed policy regarding asset-market instability can be summarized by the adage Use the right tool for the job."

Rather than wield the blunt macroeconomic instrument of interest rates, Bernanke continued, "a far better approach, I believe, is to use micro-level policies to reduce the incidence of bubbles and to protect the financial system against their effects." These could include, he said, bank supervision, more rigorous scrutiny of the investment portfolios of the biggest investors, increased transparency in the accounting and disclosure practices of institutional investors, and improved financial literacy. He concluded: "Although eliminating volatility from the economy and the financial markets will never be possible, we should be able to moderate it without sacrificing the enormous strengths of our free-market system."

Greenspan's mishandling of the Great American Bubble had dreadful consequences for the US at the time in the form of a shattering stockmarket collapse, the most financially expensive event in the history of the US, and the recession that followed.

And six years after the bubble burst, the consequences continued. The American recovery was built on self-destructive levels of indebtedness. To feed itself, America was cannibalising itself. This is Greenspan's legacy and Bernanke's inheritance. The new chairman of the US Federal Reserve will face problems and crises. His monetary Maginot Line will not do him much good. But he will have the benefit of some clear ideas about how to manage bubbles. And that is progress.

Acknowledgments

I've become convinced that the author of a book is not the one who suffers most for his work. It's the people around him, who make a thousand sacrifices without the satisfaction of getting to write the words. So to Helen, my wife, go my thanks for your inexhaustible forbearance and faith. To Kate, Dylan and Nina, my apologies for the times when I was unavailable, preoccupied, grumpy, when you would have preferred your dad to be more fun.

I've been fortunate to have had the support of my employers at two of the great daily newspapers while I worked on this project. At the *Australian Financial Review*, Michael Gill as publisher of the paper and Colleen Ryan and then Glenn Burge as editor, sent me to Washington as correspondent and were staunch supporters. And since my return to Australia, *The Sydney Morning Herald*'s editor, Robert Whitehead, has been an important source of strength during the task of writing. Newspapers are vital parts of a nation's intellectual life. But it takes wise and farsighted editors to allow them to make their fullest contribution.

I'm grateful for the trust and support of two of Australia's most important entrepreneurs in the world of ideas – Allan Gyngell, executive director of the Lowy Institute for International Policy, and Morry Schwartz, publisher of Black Inc. books. The Lowy Institute provided a very welcome place for me to work and to test my ideas as a visiting fellow, and also the services of the indefatigable intern Lena Siara, who did valuable and original historical research for this book. Black Inc. has been a wonderful publisher, supportive, trusting, efficient and, above all, patient. I thank Chris Feik for his deft and thoughtful editing. Both these institutions are marvellous new assets in Australian affairs, stimulants to the national life of the mind, courtesy of Frank Lowy and Morry Schwartz, respectively. We are lucky to have them.

Index

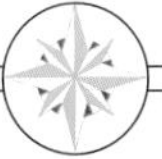

EYEWITNESS TRAVEL

PHILADELPHIA

AND THE PENNSYLVANIA DUTCH COUNTRY

EYEWITNESS TRAVEL

PHILADELPHIA

AND THE PENNSYLVANIA DUTCH COUNTRY

MAIN CONTRIBUTOR: RICHARD VARR

LONDON, NEW YORK,
MELBOURNE, MUNICH AND DELHI
www.dk.com

MANAGING EDITOR Aruna Ghose
ART EDITOR Benu Joshi
EDITORS Ankita Awasthi, Bhavna Seth Ranjan
DESIGNERS Mathew Kurien, Divya Saxena, Shruti Singhi
SENIOR CARTOGRAPHER Uma Bhattacharya
CARTOGRAPHIC RESEARCHER Suresh Kumar
PICTURE RESEARCHER Taiyaba Khatoon
DTP COORDINATOR Shailesh Sharma
DTP DESIGNER Vinod Harish

MAIN CONTRIBUTOR
Richard Varr

PHOTOGRAPHER
Demetrio Carrasco

ILLUSTRATORS
Arun Pottirayil, T. Gautam Trivedi, Mark Warner

Printed and bound in Malaysia by Vivar Printing Sdn. Bhd.

First published in Great Britain in 2005
by Dorling Kindersley Limited
80 Strand, London WC2R 0RL

13 14 15 16 10 9 8 7 6 5 4 3 2 1

Reprinted with revisions 2007, 2009, 2011, 2013

A CIP catalogue record is available from the British Library.

ISBN: 978-1-40938-640-7

THROUGHOUT THIS BOOK, FLOORS ARE REFERRED TO IN ACCORDANCE WITH AMERICAN USAGE, IE THE "FIRST FLOOR" IS AT GROUND LEVEL, UNLESS STATED OTHERWISE.

Front cover main image: Independence Hall, Philadelphia

The information in this
DK Eyewitness Travel Guide is checked regularly.

Every effort has been made to ensure that this book is as up-to-date as possible at the time of going to press. Some details, however, such as telephone numbers, opening hours, prices, gallery hanging arrangements and travel information are liable to change. The publishers cannot accept responsibility for any consequences arising from the use of this book, nor for any material on third party websites, and cannot guarantee that any website address in this book will be a suitable source of travel information. We value the views and suggestions of our readers very highly. Please write to: Publisher, DK Eyewitness Travel Guides, Dorling Kindersley, 80 Strand, London, WC2R 0RL, Great Britain, or email: travelguides@dk.com.

◁ **Philadelphia's skyscrapers towering over the Schuylkill River**

CONTENTS

The Liberty Bell, one of the world's greatest symbols of freedom

INTRODUCING PHILADELPHIA AND THE PENNSYLVANIA DUTCH COUNTRY

The relaxing environs of tree-shaded Rittenhouse Square

A panoramic view of the Camden waterfront at dusk

PHILADELPHIA AREA BY AREA

Delicate bloom at the Magnolia Garden in Society Hill

TRAVELERS' NEEDS

SURVIVAL GUIDE

Trademark horse and buggy in the Pennsylvania Dutch Country

The 18th-century Independence Hall

HOW TO USE THIS GUIDE

This Dorling Kindersley travel guide helps you get the most from your visit to Philadelphia. It provides detailed practical information and expert recommendations. *Introducing Philadelphia* maps the city and the region, sets it in its historical and cultural context, and describes events through the entire year. *Philadelphia at a Glance* is an overview of the city's main attractions. The main sightseeing section of the book is *Philadelphia Area by Area*, which covers all the important sights, with photographs, maps, and illustrations. *Farther Afield* suggests sights just outside the city core, while *Beyond Philadelphia* describes Dutch Country and historic Gettysburg among other areas. Information about hotels, restaurants, shopping, entertainment, and sports is found in *Travelers' Needs*. The *Survival Guide* has practical advice on everything from using Philadelphia's medical services and transport system to public telephones and post offices.

FINDING YOUR WAY AROUND THE SIGHTSEEING SECTION

Each of the four sightseeing areas in Philadelphia is color-coded for easy reference. Every chapter opens with an introduction to the area of the city it covers, describing its history and character, and has a *Street-by-Street* map illustrating an interesting part of that area. Finding your way around the chapter is made simple by the numbering system used throughout. Sights outside Philadelphia have a regional map.

Each area has color-coded thumb tabs.

1 Introduction to the Area

For easy reference, the sights in each area are numbered and plotted on an area map. This map also shows SEPTA subway stops and regional rail stations, as well as indicating the area covered by the Street-by-Street map. The area's key sights are listed by category.

Locator map

A locator map shows where you are in relation to other areas in the city.

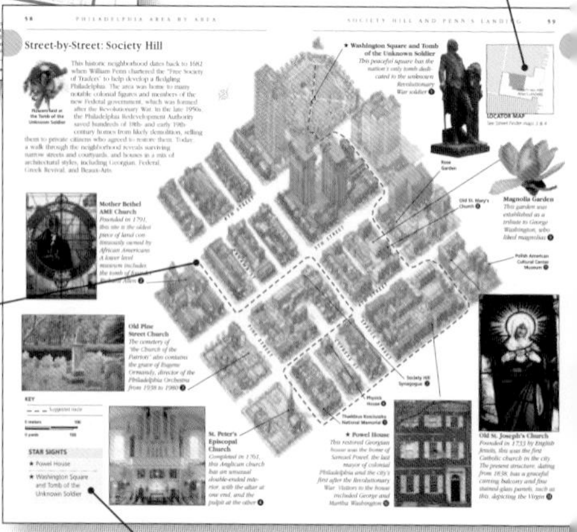

A suggested route takes in some of the most interesting and attractive streets in the area.

2 Street-by-Street Map

This gives a bird's-eye view of the most interesting and important parts of each sightseeing area. The numbering of the sights ties in with the preceding area map and with the fuller descriptions of the entries on the pages that follow.

The list of star sights indicates the places that no visitor should miss.

PHILADELPHIA AREA MAP
The colored areas shown on this map *(see inside front cover)* are the four main sightseeing districts used in this guide. Each area is covered in detail in *Philadelphia Area by Area (see pp36–109)*, as are sights located outside the city center and the walks. These areas are also highlighted on other maps throughout the book. In *Philadelphia at a Glance (see pp24–31)*, for example, they help locate the top sights.

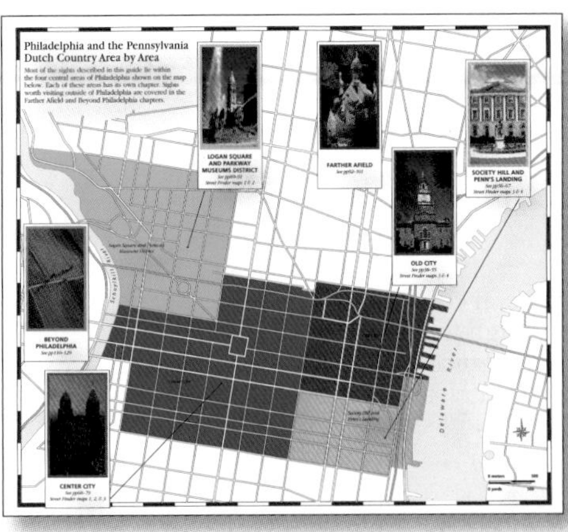

Numbers refer to each sight's position on the area map and its place in the chapter.

Practical information provides everything you need to know to visit each sight. Map references pinpoint the sight's location on the *Street Finder* maps *(see pp190–97)*.

3 Detailed Information
All the important sights in Philadelphia are described individually. They are listed in order, following the numbering on the area map at the start of the section. Practical information includes telephone numbers, opening hours, and map reference. The key to the symbols used is on the back flap.

The visitors' checklist provides all the practical information needed to plan your visit.

Story boxes provide information about historical or cultural topics relating to the sights.

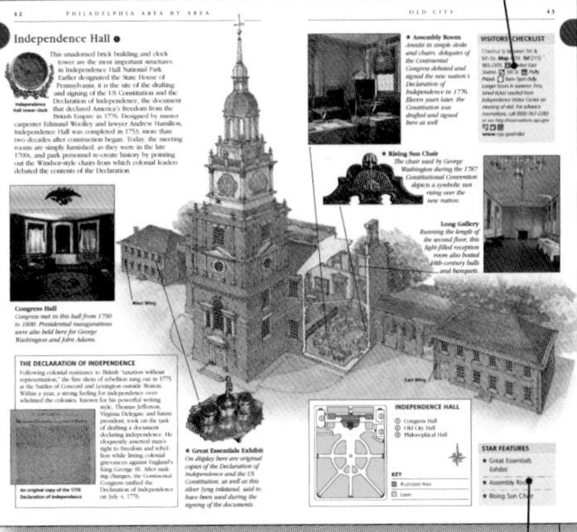

4 Philadelphia's Major Sights
These are given two or more full pages in the sightseeing area where they are found. Historic buildings are dissected to reveal their interiors; color-coded floor plans in museums and galleries help you find important exhibits.

Stars recommend the features that no visitor should miss.

INTRODUCING PHILADELPHIA
AND THE PENNSYLVANIA DUTCH COUNTRY

FOUR GREAT DAYS IN PHILADELPHIA

You could easily spend a few weeks enjoying all the historic sights and attractions in Philadelphia, not to mention separate excursions to the Pennsylvania Dutch Country and Gettysburg. Most visitors, however, only have a few days and will want to make the most of their time. Outlined here are ideas for four separate days of sightseeing and enjoyment – three of them in Philadelphia and one in the Pennsylvania Dutch Country. They include suggestions on what to see, where to eat, and what to do for entertainment. Of course, the suggestions are just that, and can be modified to suit your requirements. The prices are indicative of the cost of transport and admission (if any) for two adults or a family of four.

Grave, Christ Church Burial Ground

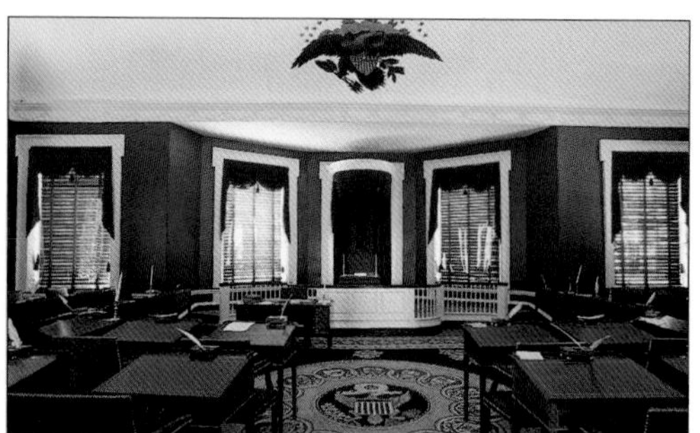

Interior of Congress Hall, adjacent to Independence Hall

HISTORIC PHILADELPHIA

- **Tour Independence Hall and National Constitution Center**
- **Lunch at Bourse Building**
- **Tour historic Old City**
- **Watch the Lights of Liberty Show**

TWO ADULTS allow at least $60

Morning

It is best to arrive at the **Independence Visitor Center** *(see p45)* when it opens at 8:30am to pick up your free, timed tickets to **Independence Hall** *(see pp42–3)*. The earlier you arrive, the better the chances of being admitted quickly. Note that tickets are usually gone by noon. Once you have your tickets the day can be planned accordingly. Visitors are first guided through the **Liberty Bell Center** *(see p44)*, and should spend the remainder of the morning visiting the **National Constitution Center** *(see pp48–9)*. Stop for lunch at the satisfying food court in **The Bourse** *(see p145)* in Independence Mall East.

Afternoon

Start off by visiting the **Christ Church Burial Ground** *(see p46)* where Benjamin Franklin is buried. Allow 15 to 30 minutes here, and then go on to take a half-hour tour of the **Betsy Ross House** *(see p52)*. Visit the Colonial portrait gallery at the **Second Bank of the US** *(see p47)* and pass by the imposing façades of the **First Bank of the US** *(see p53)* and the **Philadelphia Merchants' Exchange** *(see p54)*. The **City Tavern** *(see p55)* is a good place to stop for some refreshment.

In the evening, take in the one-hour **Lights of Liberty Show** *(see p175)*, the premier nighttime 3D experience. It features spectacular images flashed onto historic buildings, taking visitors on a starlit journey through Independence National Historical Park. Reservations required.

A SHOPPING DAY

- **Browse boutiques along Rittenhouse Row**
- **Lunch at Rittenhouse Square**
- **Visit King of Prussia Mall**

TWO ADULTS allow at least $80

Morning

Start by browsing through the elegant boutiques on **Rittenhouse Row** *(see p156)*, which has such high-fashion names as Jones New York and Ann Taylor. Also visit the nearby **Shops at Liberty Place** *(see p156)*. As noon approaches, check out the specialty shops at the **Bellevue Building** *(see p156)*

Mural at Italian Market, famous for specialty foods and eateries

◁ Artist's impression of street life near the former State House (now known as Independence Hall) c.1800

and then have a quick bite at the building's upbeat food court. For restaurants with outdoor seating, head toward **Rittenhouse Square** *(see p78)*. **Devon Seafood Grill**, **Smith & Wollensky** steakhouse, and **Parc** are good choices *(see p149)*.

Afternoon

Visit **The Gallery at Market East** mall *(see p156)* for some more shopping. Do not miss the nearby **Reading Terminal Market** *(see p73)*, and if you have time left over, head to the **Italian Market** *(see p99)* for coffee and Italian pastries. End your spree by taking a SEPTA bus to visit the colossal **King of Prussia Mall** *(see p156)*.

The Franklin Institute in the Parkway Museums District

A FAMILY DAY

- **Visit museums around Logan Square**
- **Walk along Penn's Landing**
- **Take the RiverLink Ferry**
- **Visit the Adventure Aquarium**

FAMILY OF FOUR allow at least $175

Morning

Depending on time and budget, visit one or more of the four museums along the Benjamin Franklin Parkway – **The Franklin Institute** *(see p85)*, the **Academy of Natural Sciences** *(see p85)*, **The Barnes Foundation** *(see pp86–87)*, or the **Philadelphia Museum of Art** *(see pp90–93)*. Break for lunch at one of the museum cafeterias before heading to the interactive **Please Touch Museum** *(see p170)* for children up to the age of seven.

Afternoon

Head over to **Penn's Landing** *(see p66)* and visit the **Independence Seaport Museum** *(see pp64–5)*. Later, take the RiverLink Ferry to the **Camden Waterfront** *(see p101)*. The ferry runs from April through mid-November. Make it a point to head to the **Adventure Aquarium** *(see p171)*, as the kids will love the aquatic life there. In the warmer months, the **Ghost Tour of Philadelphia** *(see p175)* is a great option for an evening activity. In winter, ice skate on one of the city's many rinks such as the **Blue Cross RiverRink** *(see pp168–9)*.

PENNSYLVANIA DUTCH COUNTRY

- **Tour Landis Valley Museum**
- **Have an Amish-style lunch**
- **Visit the Amish Experience**
- **Hop on board the Strasburg Railroad**

FAMILY OF FOUR allow at least $130

Morning

Arrive at **Lancaster Central Market** *(see p114)* by 8am to eat a hearty country breakfast. Only steps away are the **Lancaster Heritage Center Museum** and the **Lancaster**

The Blacksmith Shop at the Landis Valley Museum

Quilt & Textile Museum *(see p114)*. Go on to the **Landis Valley Museum** *(see pp116–17)* off Route 272 and spend some time exploring this living history village that provides an insight into the region's early farming communities. Head east on Route 340 through Bird-in-Hand and stop for a family-style lunch at the **Plain and Fancy Farm Restaurant** *(see p153)* next to the **Amish Experience** *(see p118)*.

Afternoon

Visit the Amish Experience and wander through the Country Homestead, a typical Amish home. Then watch the multimedia cultural presentation, *Jacob's Choice*, at the Amish Experience Theater. Spend the second part of the afternoon at Kitchen Kettle Village in **Intercourse** *(see p118)*, shopping for crafts and jarred foods. During the summer months, you can extend the day by hopping onto the 7pm train on the **Strasburg Railroad** *(see p119)* for the last ride through miles of farmland.

Tourists shopping for art and antiques in Lancaster

Putting Philadelphia on the Map

Located in the northeast region of the United States, Philadelphia sits on the southeastern edge of Pennsylvania along the Delaware River, which separates Pennsylvania from New Jersey. Founded by William Penn in the late 17th century, Philadelphia is now the nation's fifth largest city and the second largest on the East Coast. More than 1.5 million people live within the city's 135-sq-mile (350-sq-km) area.

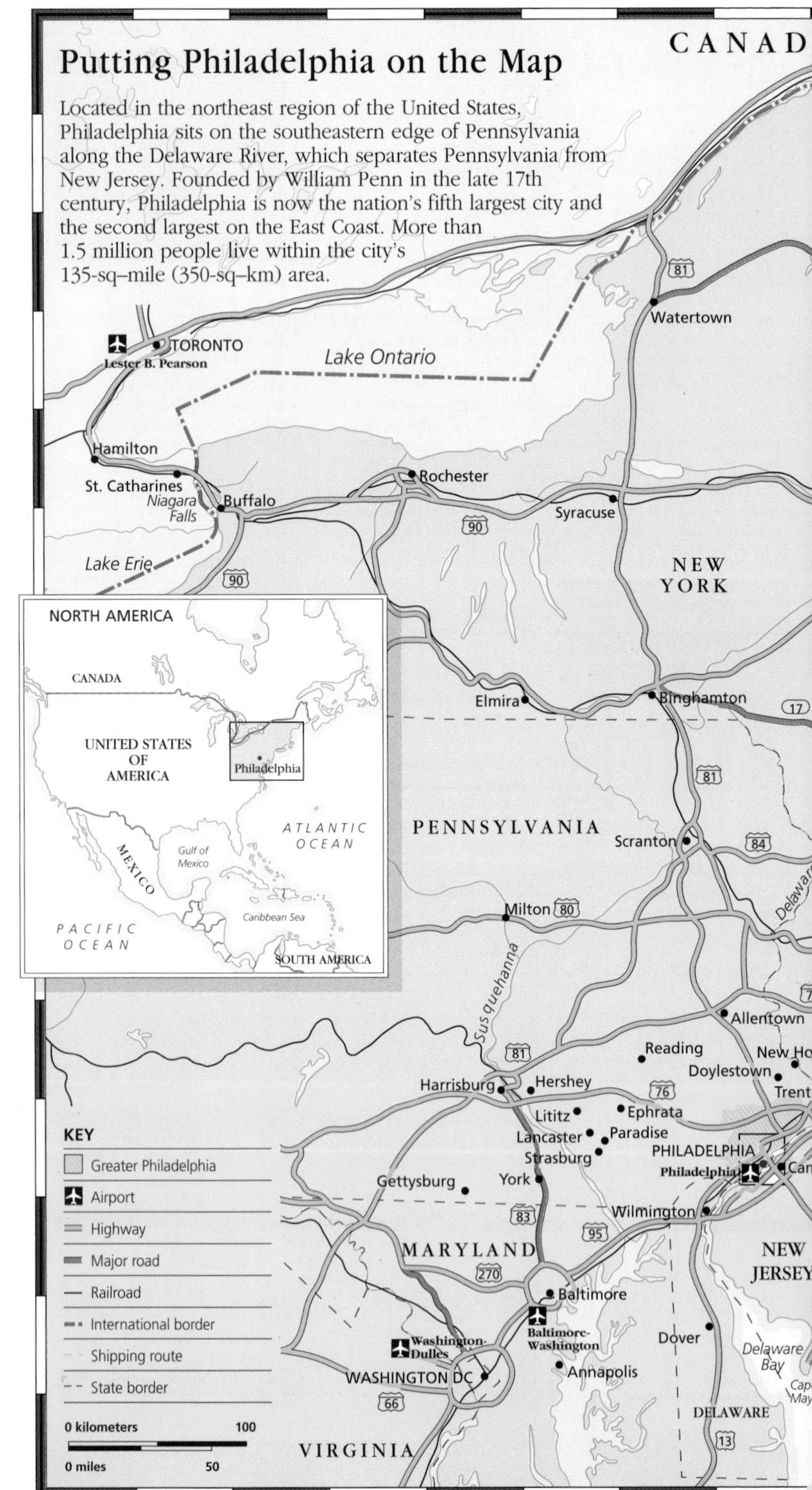

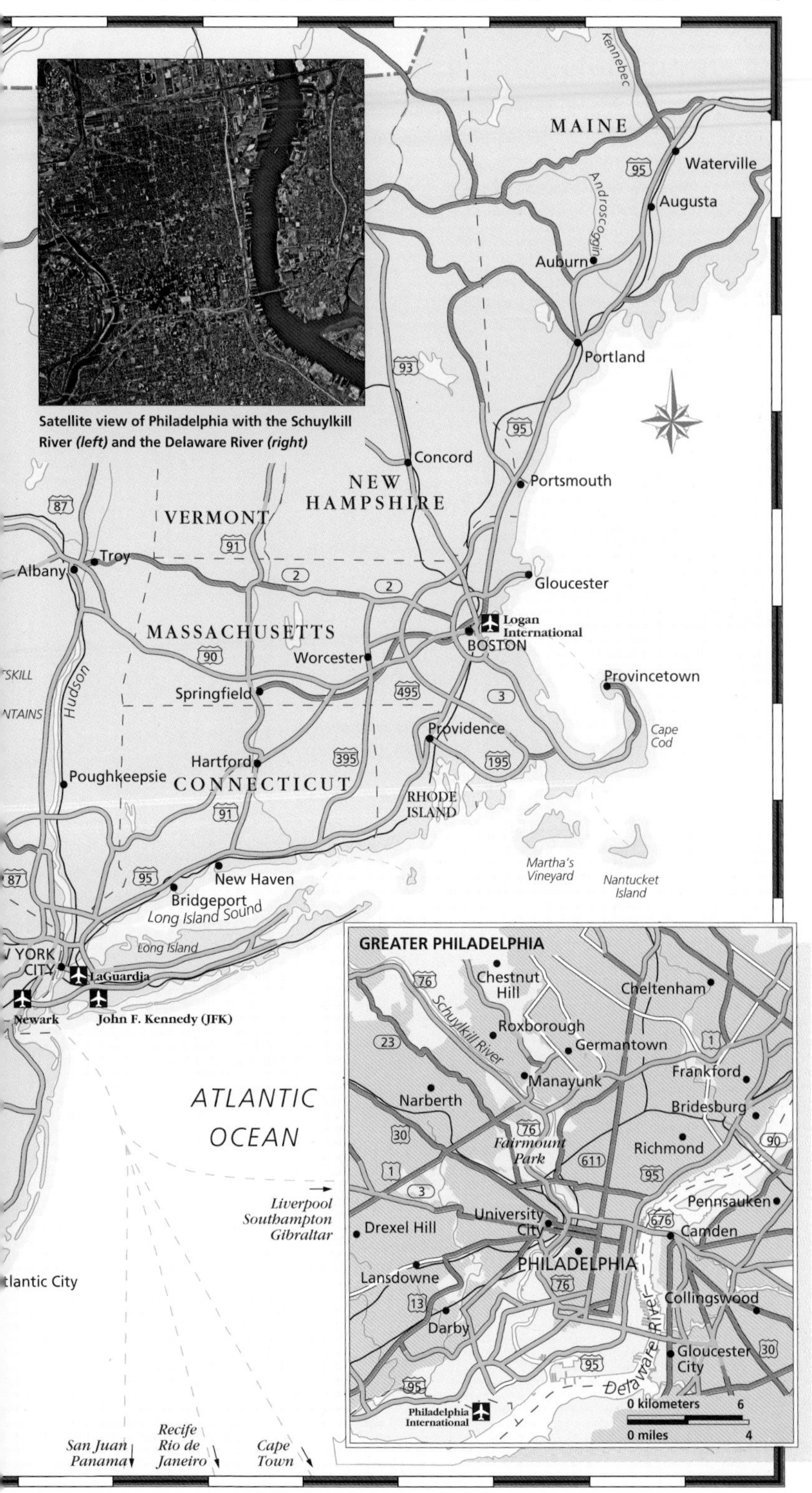

Satellite view of Philadelphia with the Schuylkill River *(left)* and the Delaware River *(right)*

Central Philadelphia

Flanked by the Delaware and Schuylkill Rivers, central Philadelphia comprises several distinct neighborhoods, which together span more than three centuries of development. Much of the modern-day layout is based on city founder William Penn's original grid pattern – a crisscross of streets with five green squares. Four of these squares remain as pleasant, shaded parks today. The fifth, Penn's original Center Square, contains City Hall. The oldest districts are Old City and Society Hill.

Central Philadelphia
Center City (see pp68–79) *skyscrapers can be seen along the Schuylkill River.*

Statue of George Washington at Eakins Oval
A prominent equestrian statue pays tribute to America's founding father and first president against the backdrop of the imposing temple-like façade of the Philadelphia Museum of Art (see pp90–93).

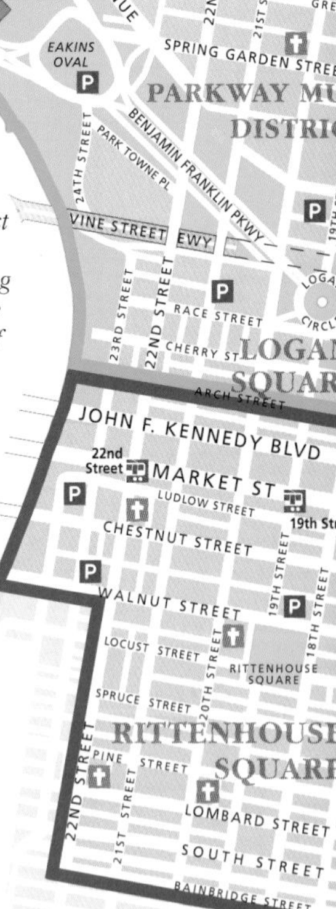

Rittenhouse Square
One of William Penn's original five squares, this Center City park (see p78) *is popular with downtown workers and residents. Extravagant high-rise buildings and upscale restaurants surround the square.*

KEY

- Star sight
- SEPTA subway stop
- SEPTA regional rail station
- PATCO rail station
- SEPTA trolley stop
- Greyhound bus terminal
- Police station
- Parking
- Hospital
- Visitor information
- Church
- Synagogue

Old City Hall
Located next to Independence Hall (see pp42–3) *in the heart of Old City, where a new nation was born in 1776, Philadelphia's Old City Hall was home to the US Supreme Court from 1791 to 1800.*

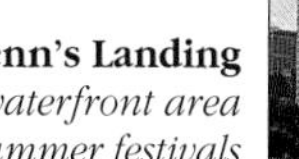

Penn's Landing
This waterfront area hosts summer festivals and is home to the city's tall ships, the submarine Becuna *and the USS* Olympia. *Also located here is the Independence Seaport Museum* (see pp64–5).

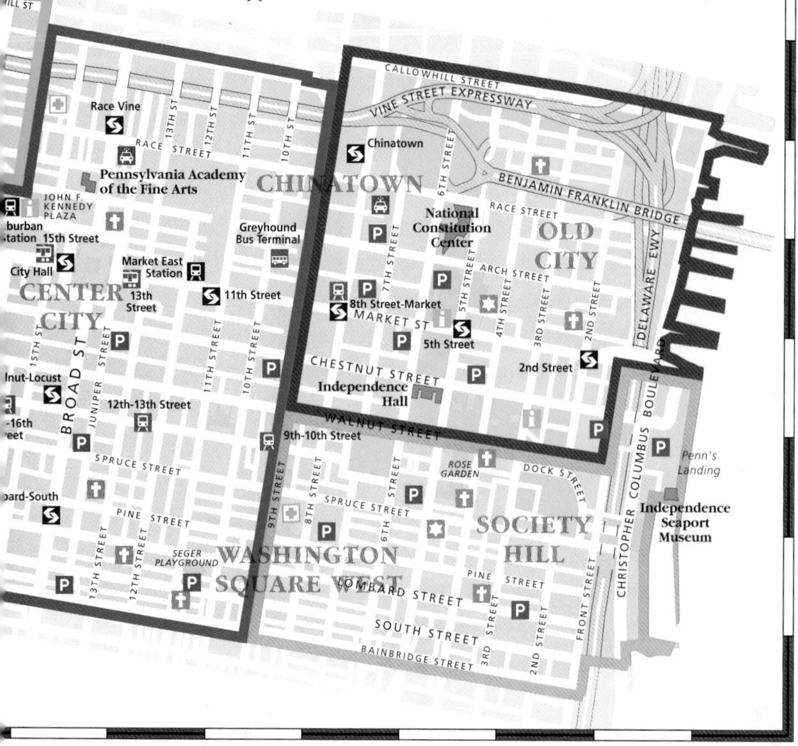

RING
RDEN
17TH STREET
ILL ST
Race Vine
RACE STREET
13TH ST
12TH ST
11TH ST
10TH ST
Pennsylvania Academy of the Fine Arts
JOHN F. KENNEDY PLAZA
burban Station
15th Street
City Hall
CENTER CITY
Greyhound Bus Terminal
Market East Station
13th Street
11th Street
15TH ST
BROAD ST
JUNIPER STREET
11TH STREET
10TH STREET
lnut-Locust
12th-13th Street
-16th eet
SPRUCE STREET
9th-10th Street
oard-South
PINE STREET
13TH STREET
12TH STREET
SEGER PLAYGROUND
CHINATOWN
CALLOWHILL STREET
VINE STREET EXPRESSWAY
Chinatown
6TH STREET
BENJAMIN FRANKLIN BRIDGE
National Constitution Center
RACE STREET
OLD CITY
7TH STREET
5TH STREET
ARCH STREET
4TH STREET
3RD STREET
2ND STREET
DELAWARE EWY
8th Street-Market
MARKET ST
5th Street
2nd Street
CHESTNUT STREET
Independence Hall
WALNUT STREET
9TH STREET
8TH STREET
6TH STREET
SPRUCE STREET
ROSE GARDEN
DOCK STREET
CHRISTOPHER COLUMBUS BOULEVARD
Penn's Landing
Independence Seaport Museum
SOCIETY HILL
WASHINGTON SQUARE WEST
LOMBARD STREET
PINE STREET
SOUTH STREET
BAINBRIDGE STREET
3RD STREET
2ND STREET
FRONT STREET

THE HISTORY OF PHILADELPHIA

William Penn first landed in the New World in 1682. Armed with a land charter, he founded a colony based on religious freedom that just a century later, would give birth to a new nation. Penn named the new city Philadelphia, derived from Greek words meaning "City of Brotherly Love."

Before William Penn's arrival, the Delaware River basin and the Schuylkill River watershed were inhabited by Algonquian-speaking Native Americans known as Lenni-Lenape. They were mostly peaceful hunters and gatherers, and many lived along the Delaware River and its tributaries. They were named "Delawares" for that reason by the first European settlers.

Chief Tammany, Delaware Indian chief

FIRST EUROPEAN EXPLORERS AND SETTLERS

Chartered by the Dutch East India Company, Englishman Henry Hudson's ship, the *Half Moon*, sailed into Delaware Bay in 1609 and claimed it for Holland. Dutch navigators followed shortly after: Captain Cornelius Hendricksen sailed up the Delaware in 1616 to where it meets the Schuylkill River; and in 1623, Cornelius Jacobsen explored the region further, leading to the establishment of a number of trading posts, including one on the Schuylkill in 1633.

The first settlement in what is now Pennsylvania, however, did not occur until 1643, when Swedish Lutheran settlers – who had first settled in Wilmington, Delaware, in 1638 – established their capital of New Sweden on Tinicum Island, near present-day Philadelphia. Eight years later, the Dutch, whose previous colonial efforts had been directed elsewhere, seized control and annexed the region as part of the Dutch Colony. From 1655 to 1664, the Dutch controlled the area until the English captured the Dutch colonies, calling them New York, after the Duke of York.

THE FOUNDING OF PENNSYLVANIA AND PHILADELPHIA

The son of a wealthy British admiral, William Penn was born in 1644. While attending Oxford University, Penn joined the Religious Society of Friends, the Quakers, a group who worshipped, without dogma or clergy, silently in unadorned meetinghouses. The faith was based on

TIMELINE

1600 | **1615** | **1630** | **1645** | **1660** | **1675**

1609 Explorer Henry Hudson sails into Delaware Bay

Henry Hudson, English navigator

1616 Dutch Captain Cornelius Hendricksen sails up the Delaware to the Schuylkill River

1623 Dutchman Cornelius Jacobsen explores the region further

1638 Swedish Lutheran settlers arrive in Wilmington, Delaware

1643 Swedes establish capital on Tinicum Island near present-day Philadelphia

1644 Birth of William Penn

1655 Dutch seize control of New Sweden

1664 England takes control of the Dutch colonies

◁ **Detail from *Penn's Treaty with the Indians* by Edward Hicks, 1830–1840**

William Penn receiving the Charter for Pennsylvania from King Charles II of England

pacifism and equality. Expelled from university, Penn was later harassed and even imprisoned for his devotion to Quakerism. However, his wealth and social position allowed him to retain influence in the King's court.

The Charter for Pennsylvania was founded in 1681 as a result of a debt owed by King Charles II to Penn's father. The king repaid the £16,000 debt by granting the younger Penn land between Maryland and New York. In October 1682, Penn's ship, the *Welcome*, landed at New Castle in Delaware with many Quaker passengers. A few days later, Penn sailed up the Delaware to the capital of his new colony: Philadelphia.

As a Quaker, Penn espoused nonviolence, and one of his first initiatives was to reach an agreement with the Delawares, thus forming treaties and enduring friendships with the Native Americans. The new colony also promised religious freedom, and was seen as a "Holy Experiment." More settlers followed, including both English and Dutch Quakers, German Mennonites, and the Amish, who settled in what is now called Pennsylvania Dutch Country.

Penn and surveyor Thomas Holmes designed Philadelphia in a grid pattern between the Delaware and Schuylkill Rivers. Their plan included five public spaces, as Penn and Holmes wanted to create a "green countrie towne." These tree-lined areas – Washington, Rittenhouse, Logan, and Franklin Squares – still remain today. City Hall now occupies the original "Center Square" at the junction of Market and Broad Streets.

Detail from *Peaceable Kingdom* by Edward Hicks (1780–1849), painted in 1826

TIMELINE

1683 Penn signs treaty with Delawares

1684 Penn leaves Philadelphia and returns to England

1699 Penn returns to Philadelphia

1701 Penn grants charter to City of Philadelphia

1718 Death of Penn in England

1680 | **1690** | **1700** | **1710**

Gloria Dei Church

1677 Swedes establish Gloria Dei church

1682 Penn arrives in Pennsylvania and establishes Philadelphia

1701 Penn leaves America for good and returns to England

1710 Christ Church built at 2nd Street

COLONIAL EXPANSION

At the beginning of the 18th century, Philadelphia was already witnessing rapid growth. Penn had left Philadelphia in 1684 but returned in 1699 to find the population at more than 7,000. In October 1701, he granted a charter to the City of Philadelphia and left for England, never to return. As a port city, Philadelphia soon became an important center of commerce, with imports of sugar, rum, and molasses from the Caribbean. As trade flourished, so did manufacturing and shipbuilding. An increase in the number of homes led to a burgeoning community of craftsmen. The city also boasted a paper mill, furnaces, distilleries, tanneries, and a glass factory. One of its most famous residents, Benjamin Franklin *(see p53)*, arrived from Boston in 1723. His achievements as a scientist, inventor, printer, publisher, and statesman turned Philadelphia into a cultural center. In 1751, along with physician Thomas Bond, Franklin founded Pennsylvania Hospital, America's first public hospital.

Franklin, famous Philadelphia resident

The mid-1700s saw a clash between pacifist Quaker beliefs and the need to establish defenses for the colony. Pennsylvania was part of the British Empire and was involved in skirmishes against the French over land in North America. The conflicts climaxed with the French and Indian War, fought between the French and the British from 1754 to 1763, where a 21-year-old native of Virginia named George Washington received his first command. Britain was eventually victorious, but the war's end signaled a turning point for colonists, who now craved independence from Britain.

NEW NATION TAKES SHAPE

On July 4, 1776, independence from Britain was declared in Philadelphia, and in 1789, George Washington was elected the first president of the fledgling nation. The city remained the political heart of the country for a decade, serving as the capital from 1790 until 1800. During this time, America's first bank was chartered in 1791 to unify the nation's currency and to pay off war debts. The US Mint was established the following year.

In 1793, Philadelphia suffered a yellow fever epidemic, resulting in a large loss of life. Despite this, immigrants continued to flock to the city, increasing its population to nearly 70,000 by 1800, making it America's largest city at the time.

Yellow fever epidemic in Philadelphia, 1793

1723 Benjamin Franklin arrives from Boston

1743 Franklin founds American Philosophical Society

1754 Start of the French and Indian War

1763 French and Indian War ends

1720 | 1730 | 1740 | 1750 | 1760

1724 Carpenters' Company founded

Journal published by Franklin in 1741

1751 Pennsylvania Hospital founded

Pennsylvania Hospital

Colonial Philadelphia and the American Revolution

Gunpowder casket, 1800s

The years leading up to, including, and after the American Revolutionary War are arguably the most important years of the history of Philadelphia. Rebellion against British rule began as early as 1765 with opposition to taxation without representation in Parliament. A decade later, the colonists elected Washington to lead their army – the Continental Army – in the war for independence. In 1776, the Declaration of Independence was signed in Philadelphia, though by 1777 the city was again occupied by British forces. Freedom was gained in 1781, and Britain at last recognized the colonies' independence with the 1783 Treaty of Paris. Five years later, the US Constitution *(see pp48–9)* was ratified at Independence Hall, Philadelphia.

George Washington
The Second Continental Congress elected Washington to lead the Continental Army against the British in 1775.

Drafting the Declaration
Thomas Jefferson wrote the first draft of the Declaration of Independence. Leaders of 13 North American colonies later ratified it at Independence Hall.

DECLARATION OF INDEPENDENCE (1776)
Delegates of the Continental Congress ratified the Declaration of Independence on July 4, 1776. This 1817 John Trumbull painting shows the presentation of the Declaration by the drafting committee. The signing of the Declaration was completed that August.

TIMELINE

1774 First Continental Congress held

1775 Second Continental Congress in Philadelphia

1776 Signing of the Declaration of Independence

1776 Washington's army crosses Delaware River and defeats hired Hessian soldiers at Trenton

1777 Continental Army retreats after losing battles at Brandywine and Germantown

1781 British surrender at Yorktown, Virginia

1783 Signing of the Treaty of Paris

Postcard depicting George Washington

1788 US Constitution ratified

1789 George Washington elected nation's first president

1775 | 1780 | 1785

Crossing the Delaware River
Washington's army crossed the Delaware River on Christmas Day in 1776, as depicted in this 1851 Emmanuel Leutze painting. They later defeated British troops at Princeton.

The Battle of Germantown (1777)
British troops barricaded themselves behind the stone walls of Cliveden, a Germantown mansion, forcing the Continental army to retreat.

Valley Forge, 1777–78
After losing the battles of Brandywine and Germantown in 1777, Washington's army lost over 2,500 men to exposure and disease during the winter encampment here.

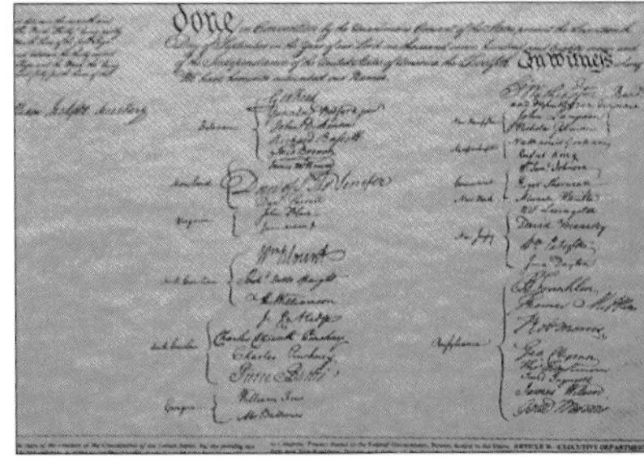

Adoption of the Constitution (1787)
In 1787, delegates from all 13 original states, except Rhode Island, gathered at the Constitutional Convention in Philadelphia to draft and adopt a Constitution for the new nation.

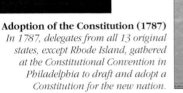

1790 Death of Benjamin Franklin

1793 Yellow fever epidemic kills 4,000

1800 Capital moves to Washington DC

White House, Washington DC

1790	1795	1800

1791 First Bank of the US chartered

1790 Philadelphia becomes the nation's capital

The First Bank of the United States

1799 Death of George Washington

The City & Port of Philadelphia (1800), engraving with watercolor by William Russell Birch

INDUSTRIALIZATION

By the 1830s, the city's financial and political prominence had begun to wane, as Washington DC, due to its location midway between the north and the south, became the nation's capital. Commercial activity and trade also diminished, as it could not compete with the more accessible port of New York City. Instead, Philadelphia turned to industry and manufacturing, becoming a regional center for textiles, iron and steel, and the shipping of coal. Shipbuilding continued along the Delaware. The city kept growing, with row houses built within the city limits and in surrounding boroughs and districts, including Germantown and Chestnut Hill. These areas soon became new neighborhoods by way of the city consolidation bill of 1854, under which they were incorporated within the city limits.

Growth also brought social clashes. For instance, there were rebellions against anti-slavery movements, and Pennsylvania Hall, the meeting place of the abolitionists, was set on fire in 1838. The 1840s saw violence against Catholics and immigrants, especially the Irish, with angry mobs burning down St. Augustine's Church, across from St. George's Church, in 1844.

POST CIVIL WAR PHILADELPHIA

The need for weapons, munitions, uniforms, and warships for the Union forces bolstered Philadelphia's economy during the Civil War years (1861–65). During the nation's centennial celebrations in 1876, the city held one of the first World Fairs and dedicated grand new buildings, some of which can be seen even today. These include Memorial Hall, a Beaux-Arts structure in Fairmount

Centennial Exhibition in 1876 at Fairmount Park, one of the oldest municipal parks in America

TIMELINE

Burning of St. Augustine

1838 Anti-abolitionists burn Pennsylvania Hall

1840

1844 Anti-Catholic rioters burn churches

1854 Surrounding boroughs incorporated

1856 Completion of Pennsylvania Railroad to Pittsburgh

1860

1861 Civil War begins

Wagons from the Civil War era

1876 City celebrates centennial with nation's first World Fair

1880

1890s Electric trolleys introduced

1900

1907 First underground rail line commences

1914 World War I begins

1920

1920s Broad Street Subway completed

Park, and the Victorian-style Pennsylvania Academy of the Fine Arts. Politically, however, this was a time of corruption as Republican leaders controlled city contracts and thousands of jobs. Their influence only waned in the 1930s and 40s when voter support was lost due to allegations of corruption and financial mismanagement in city government.

Streetcar on 9th Street, Philadelphia, 1921

THE EARLY 20TH CENTURY

The city's infrastructure was well-established by the end of the 19th century. For instance, its streetcar system was run by electric power as early as the 1890s. There were further improvements in mass transit with the completion of its first underground rail line, the Market Street Subway, in 1907. Economic and industrial activity in Philadelphia remained brisk during World War I (1914–18), though it registered a dip during the Great Depression of the 1920s and 30s. World War II (1939–45) revived steel, chemical, and petroleum production, but Philadelphia gradually lost most of its manufacturing sector to other regions of the US.

MODERN PHILADELPHIA

After World War II, the city lost jobs and population to the suburbs, and then underwent political restructuring in 1951, with a new city charter that called for a stronger mayor and new city departments. It was also a time of urban preservation efforts downtown, but some neighborhoods in the city's north and west deteriorated. Racial tensions mounted in the 1960s and through the mayoral terms of Frank Rizzo and W. Wilson Goode, the city's first African-American mayor, before stabilizing in the late 1980s. In 1985, during Goode's term as mayor, the controversial bombing of the headquarters of the black radical group MOVE took place, resulting in the deaths of 11 persons.

Today, Philadelphia's economy is diversified. While some manufacturing units remain, corporate business has gained ground. Companies here specialize in technology, banking, pharmaceuticals, and insurance. Tourism is also key to the local economy. The city has more than 80 universities, colleges, medical schools, and world-class hospitals. In 2000, it hosted the Republican National Convention, which nominated George W. Bush for president, and in 2008 the city bolstered its global presence by hosting two Olympic trials ahead of the Beijing games.

Celebrations at the Republican National Convention in 2000 in Philadelphia

1941 World War II

1976 Bicentennial celebrations in Philadelphia

1985 Bombing of MOVE headquarters

2000 City hosts Republican National Convention

2005 Philadelphia is the only US city to host a Live 8 concert, a global campaign to end poverty

1940 | 1960 | 1980 | 2000 | 2020

1929 Great Depression begins

1951 New city charter provides strong mayoral leadership

Wilson Goode, Philadelphia's first African-American mayor

1990s Philadelphia becomes a model for urban renewal despite a declining population

2008 Philadelphia is the only US city to host two Olympic trial events – table tennis and gymnastics

PHILADELPHIA AT A GLANCE

Many of Philadelphia's most popular sights are to be found in Old City, within what's called "America's most historic square mile." They include Independence Hall *(see pp42–3)* and the iconic Liberty Bell *(see p44)*. Outstanding museums, including the Pennsylvania Academy of the Fine Arts *(see pp74–5)*, the Philadelphia Museum of Art *(see pp90-93)* and The Barnes Foundation *(see pp86–7)*, are located in the city center. More than 100 places of interest are described in the *Area by Area* and *Beyond Philadelphia* sections of this book. To help you make the most of your stay, the following six pages are a guide to the best of Philadelphia, with a selection featured below.

PHILADELPHIA'S TOP TEN SIGHTS

Independence Hall
(see pp42–3)

Liberty Bell Center
(see p44)

The Barnes Foundation
(see pp86–7)

Fairmount Park
(see p97)

Pennsylvania Academy of the Fine Arts
(see pp74–5)

Philadelphia Museum of Art
(see pp90–93)

National Constitution Center
(see pp48–9)

Reading Terminal Market *(see p73)*

Penn's Landing
(see p66)

Liberty Place
(see p79)

◁ **Staircase and Grand Foyer of the Pennsylvania Academy of the Fine Arts** ***(see pp74–5)***

Philadelphia's Best: Museums

Philadelphia has several world-famous museums that reflect its cultural diversity, as well as its maritime and colonial past. Many are along the Benjamin Franklin Parkway, including The Franklin Institute, the Academy of Natural Sciences, and the Philadelphia Museum of Art, which is the third-largest fine arts museum in the country. The Rodin Museum near Logan Square houses the largest collection of sculptor Auguste Rodin's works outside Paris, while the University of Pennsylvania Museum of Archaeology and Anthropology, across the Schuylkill River, has an excellent collection of artifacts from civilizations past and present. In 2012, the Barnes Foundation moved to the Benjamin Franklin Parkway. The foundation has an extraordinary collection of early French-modern and Postimpressionist art *(see pp86–7).*

Philadelphia Museum of Art
This museum houses over 300,000 objects, including a 12th-century stone portal from a French Augustinian abbey (see pp90–93).

Rodin Museum
The Shade *is just one of nearly 130 plaster, bronze, and marble sculptures housed in an impressive temple-like structure along the Benjamin Franklin Parkway* (see p88).

Logan Square and Parkway Museums District

Center City

The Franklin Institute
The Giant Walk-Through Heart *is a key exhibit of this children-friendly science museum named after statesman and inventor Benjamin Franklin* (see p85).

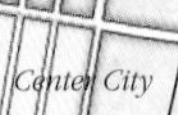

The Barnes Foundation
The foundation contains one of the world's leading collections of Impressionist, Postimpressionist, and early modern art, as well as African sculpture and much more (see pp86–7).

Academy of Natural Sciences
A favorite exhibit at Philadelphia's natural history museum is Dinosaur Hall, *home to fossil constructions of the largest carnivores to ever walk the earth* (see p85).

Pennsylvania Academy of the Fine Arts
An ornate, arched foyer is the entrance to the country's oldest fine art school and museum. It was founded in 1805 with a collection of American paintings by artists such as Benjamin West and Impressionist Mary Cassatt (see pp74–5).

The African American Museum in Philadelphia
This museum celebrates important aspects of African-American history through permanent and changing exhibitions (see p51).

Philadelphia History Museum at Atwater Kent
On display here are more than 100,000 objects, including Norman Rockwell's Saturday Evening Post *covers depicting "vignettes of daily life"* (see p50).

Old City

National Museum of American Jewish History
Housed in an impressive five-story building overlooking Independence Square, this museum explores over 350 years of American Jewish history (see p46).

Society Hill and Penn's Landing

Independence Seaport Museum
A prominent seafaring museum, showcasing the submarine Becuna *and the cruiser* Olympia. *This view* (right) *is of the interior of the submarine* Becuna (see pp64–5).

0 meters 500

0 yards 500

Philadelphia's Architecture

Early architectural styles, derived from the colonists' native Britain, can still be seen in the older areas of Philadelphia. Colonial buildings incorporated simple Georgian and Palladian designs, which evolved into a bolder Federal style, with touches of Roman and Greek classical styles. The 19th century brought grander designs fueled by the Victorian era and the French-influenced Beaux-Arts style, which inspired many of the city's architectural wonders along the Benjamin Franklin Parkway. While modernist buildings crowd parts of Center City, it is the scattering of postmodernist skyscrapers that enliven the city skyline.

Philadelphia Merchants' Exchange, an example of the Greek Revival style

Betsy Ross House, a simple Georgian-style structure

GEORGIAN

Named after three British kings called George, this architectural style proliferated in early 18th-century Britain and soon became popular in colonial Philadelphia. Developed from the Roman Palladian style and often with columned façades, many of the early Georgian-style designs in the colonies were less elaborate than their English counterparts.

Independence Hall *(see pp42–3)* is a Georgian structure influenced by the style of English master architect Christopher Wren, while Christ Church *(see p52)* is a bold example of Georgian ecclesiastical architecture. colonial Georgian-style homes include the Deshler-Morris House, which was George Washington's summer retreat, and Cliveden, both in Germantown *(see pp106–107)*. Both houses have columned doorways and nine front windows. A more simple home is the Betsy Ross House *(see p52)*.

FEDERAL

In Colonial America, the-Georgian style quickly evolved into a more sophisticated Federal style, often with classical Greek and Roman influences. Particularly popular after the American Revolution until about 1820, this architectural style is characterized by oval and circular rooms, classical entryway detailing, rounded fanlights over doors, and Palladian windows. Also typical of this style are free-standing mansions and town houses with symmetrical brick façades and shuttered windows. Entrances are often cut from granite slabs and feature gently fluted columns. The largest and most elegant rooms of Federal houses are usually found on the second floor. Some stately examples of such architecture are Old City Hall, Congress Hall, and the east and west wings of Independence Hall. Idyllic Fairmount Park, next to the Schuylkill River, has several mansions built with this architectural style, including Sweetbriar, Strawberry Mansion, and Lemon Hill, which has oval rooms on all three floors *(see pp108–109)*.

GREEK REVIVAL

Philadelphia's merchants' Exchange *(see p54)*, with a four-columned Corinthian portico at one end and an unusual, semi-circular portico at the other, testifies to the nation's infatuation with Greek Revival architecture in the 1830s. It was designed by the up-and-coming architect William Strickland, already noted for designing the steeple atop Indepen dence Hall. He also drafted

Strawberry Mansion, a Federal-style house in Fairmount Park

Parlor of the Victorian-style Ebenezer Maxwell House

the architectural plan for another prominent Greek Revival structure, the imposing Second Bank of the US *(see p47)*, with sturdy stone columns on its Greek temple-like façade.

A smaller Greek Revival structure, now housing the Philadelphia History Museum at Atwater Kent *(see p50)*, was designed by John Haviland, a contemporary of Strickland. This was the first home of the Franklin Institute *(see p85)*, where Strickland and other architects taught the nation's first architecture classes.

Detail of Philadelphia Museum of Art façade

VICTORIAN

Ornate, Victorian-style façades were designed for Philadelphia buildings from the 1850s onwards.

Victorian-era architecture is influenced by various styles, such as Second Empire, Italianate, and Gothic Revival. For example, City Hall *(see p72)*, with its colonnades and mansard roof, is a French Second Empire design. The Academy of Music *(see p76)*, designed by prominent 19th-century architect and Philadelphia native Napoleon LeBrun, is Italianate in style, with period gas lamps on its high-windowed façade and lavish interiors. The Italianate Revival Athenaeum also has gas lamps on its walls. The city's only authentically restored Victorian home is the Ebenezer Maxwell House in Germantown *(see pp106–107)*, which is capped with a high tower, a mansard, and gable roof design.

Colonnaded entrance of the Beaux-Arts style Philadelphia Museum of Art

BEAUX-ARTS

American architects trained at the École des Beaux-Arts in France brought home this Greek- and Roman-influenced style of architecture, with elaborate detailing, balustrades, and prominent columns. Due to the grandiosity and size of these structures, Beaux-Arts became the favored style for court houses, government buildings, museums, and railroad terminals, and was used in many late 19th- and early 20th-century buildings. The 1876 centennial celebration in Philadelphia ushered in Fairmount Park's Memorial Hall *(see p109)*, dotted with bronze sculptures and topped by a glass and iron dome creating a spacious atrium.

With one of the city's most splendid Corinthian porticos, 30th Street Station *(see p184)* is an example of this grand style, as is the Philadelphia Museum of Art *(see pp90–93)*. Displaying much of the same grandeur is the Free Library of Philadelphia *(see p84)*, and the similar structure next to it, both with porticos sheltering imposing colonnaded façades. On a smaller scale, the nearby temple-like Rodin Museum *(see p88)* features columns and a portico topped with a balustrade.

Philadelphia's skyscrapers, Liberty One *(left)* and Mellon Bank Center

POSTMODERNIST

The late 20th century witnessed a rebellion against the box-like glass and steel structures built after World War II. Thus was born the postmodern era in architecture, which featured sleek modernism tempered by conservative and historical design. This is evident in the twin towers of Liberty Place *(see p79)* with their pointed apexes. Also in the same style are the top floors of the Bell Atlantic Tower, while the Mellon Bank Center building is crowned with a pyramid-like dome. The latest addition to the city's skyline is the cutting edge Comcast Center.

Philadelphia's Best: Parks and Gardens

William Penn wanted his city to be "a green countrie towne" and included five squares in his original city grid. Today, four of these, Logan, Rittenhouse, Franklin, and Washington Squares, are pleasant areas with trees and park benches. Along the Schuylkill River on the outskirts of Center City is Fairmount Park. Its 9,200 acres (3,700 ha) of parkland and gardens make it America's largest urban park. The area has biking and walking paths along the river and one of its tributaries, Wissahickon Creek, which runs within a gorge. Fairmount Park includes the peaceful Shofuso Japanese House and Garden and restored historic houses that were once the homes of the colonial elite. Beyond Philadelphia, near the Delaware state border, are the exquisite Longwood Gardens.

Morris Arboretum of the University of Pennsylvania
Located in the Chestnut Hill neighborhood, this scenic tract of land includes ponds, greenhouses, meadows, and gardens with thousands of rare plants and "trees-of-record" (see p97).

↙ Longwood Gardens
22 miles (35 km)

Longwood Gardens
Industrialist Pierre S. du Pont designed this extravagant horticultural wonderland filled with spectacular choreographed fountains, whimsical topiaries, conservatories with exotic plants, and meadows and gardens replete with more than 11,000 varieties of indoor and outdoor plants (see p128).

Fairmount Park
This extensive greenbelt along the Schuylkill River and Wissahickon Creek is dotted with statues and features miles of running and biking paths (see p97).

0 kilometers 2

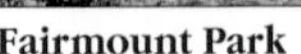

0 miles 2

Wissahickon Gorge
The country's only covered bridge within a major city is sited on a biking trail in this gorge, whose forests and creek are home to over 100 bird species.

Logan Square
This grand square was once used as a burial ground and pastureland. Its centerpiece is the majestic, multi-spouted Swann Memorial fountain designed by sculptor Alexander Stirling Calder (see p84).

Washington Square and Tomb of the Unknown Soldier
Named in honor of George Washington, the first president of the US, the centerpiece of this peaceful park is his statue, and the tomb of the unknown soldier of the Revolutionary War (see p60).

Rittenhouse Square
Center City's most popular park often fills with downtown workers who lunch under the trees. Reminiscent of New York's Central Park, it is flanked by upscale restaurants (see p78).

Welcome Park
Named after Penn's ship, this park was completed in 1982, three centuries after the founding of Philadelphia. Marble slabs depicting the city's original grid crisscross the park (see p55).

PHILADELPHIA THROUGH THE YEAR

Moderating mid-Atlantic coastal waters often temper the effects of extreme heat and harsh cold, making Philadelphia's summers enjoyable and the winters bearable. Spring flowers and warmer temperatures breathe new life into the city, with restaurants and cafés setting up tables outdoors, while city residents head to parks and riverfronts, anticipating summer festivals and excursions to beaches and lakes. Activities continue outdoors in fall, which heralds a rush of cool air and colorful foliage to Philadelphia's forested greenbelts. After Thanksgiving, activities tend to move indoors with a rush of Christmas shoppers to quaint boutiques and shopping malls. Sports and cultural activities are in full swing during the winter months, right through to spring.

Phillies logo

School and college track teams compete at the Penn Relays

SPRING

Cherry blossoms bloom along the Schuylkill River in early spring, as Philadelphians flock to the Schuylkill river walk to enjoy the warmer weather. April also signals the start of the Philadelphia Phillies' baseball season.

MARCH

Philadelphia Flower Show *(early Mar)*, Pennsylvania Convention Center. Largest indoor flower show in the United States.

St. Patrick's Day Parade *(mid-Mar)*, Center City. A parade celebrating Philadelphia's strong Irish heritage.

APRIL

Cherry Blossom Festival *(early Apr)*. Features performances of traditional Japanese arts and culture at various locations throughout the city.

Philadelphia Antiques Show *(late Apr)*, 33rd Street Armory. Dealers from across the United States gather to display their unique finds.

Philadelphia Cinefest *(mid-Apr)*. Showcases the best in independent and foreign cinema.

Fairmount Arts Crawl *(late Apr)*, Fairmount Area. During this festival, bars, restaurants, and shops turn into galleries with installations, exhibits, live demonstrations, music, and activities for kids.

Penn Relays *(late Apr)*, Franklin Field. High school and college track stars compete in the longest uninterrupted collegiate track meet in the nation.

Equality Forum *(late Apr)*. Begun in the 1960s, this week-long gathering celebrates the cultural and political legacy of the gay, lesbian, bisexual, and transgender communities.

International Children's Festival *(late Apr–early May)*, Annenberg Center for the Performing Arts. Jugglers, folk singers, puppeteers, and dancers delight young audiences.

Juggler in action

Philadelphia Phillies Baseball *(Apr–Oct)*, Citizens Bank Park. The season starts with many home games at the 43,500-capacity park.

Blooms at the Philadelphia Flower Show, a spring-time celebration

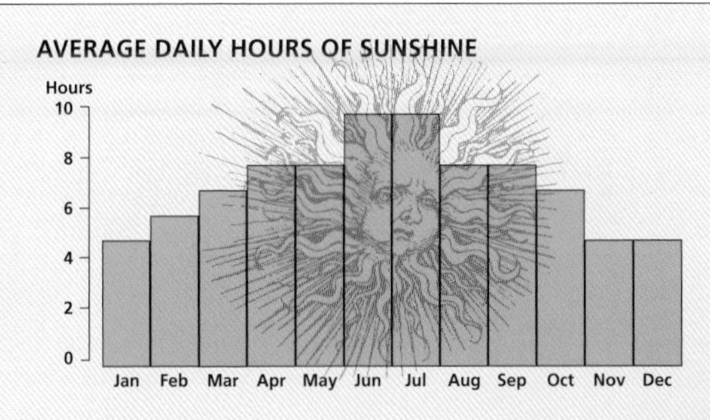

Sunshine Chart
This chart shows the average daily number of hours of sunshine in Philadelphia each month. June, July, and August have long days with lots of sunshine. Spring and fall have lesser hours of sunshine, with the shortest days in winter, which can still have ample hours of bright sun on clear, cold days.

MAY

Broad Street Avenue Run *(early May)*, Olney to south Philadelphia. This 10-mile (16-km) run raises funds for the American Cancer Society.
Rittenhouse Row Spring Festival *(early May)*. A spring festival that draws 50,000 visitors to enjoy the best of living, dining, shopping, and entertainment this classy neighborhood has to offer.
Dad Vail Regatta *(second weekend)*, Schuylkill River at Kelly Drive. Largest collegiate regatta in the United States with more than 100 colleges and universities participating.
Devon Horse Show and Country Fair *(late May and early Jun)*, Devon Fair Grounds. Equestrian talents on display at the country's oldest and largest event of its kind.
The Mann Center *(May–Sep)*, Fairmount Park. Performances through the summer by the Philadelphia Orchestra, Philly Pops, and others.
Penn's Landing Festivals *(May–Sep)*. Concerts along with ethnic events for families.
Annual Student Exhibition *(May/Jun)*, Pennsylvania Academy of the Fine Arts. This century-old tradition displays the works of award-winning students.

SUMMER

Summer ushers in a variety of festivals and live music on Penn's Landing. Fairmount Park fills with picnickers and thousands jam roadways to the New Jersey shore. Philadelphians celebrate the nation's birth, which took place in their own city, on the Fourth of July with remembrances, concerts, parades, and a massive display of fireworks above the Philadelphia Museum of Art.

JUNE

TD Bank Philadelphia International Championship *(first week)*. Philadelphia Museum of Art to Manayunk. The country's largest one-day professional cycling race.
Bloomsday *(Jun 16)*, Rosenbach Museum & Library. James Joyce fans celebrate the day on which Leopold Bloom, the protagonist of Joyce's *Ulysses*, made his "odyssey" through Dublin.
Odunde Afrikan American Street Festival *(mid-Jun)*, South Street. Celebrates the Yoruba New Year, beginning with a procession to the Schuylkill River and ending with a lively street fair.
Manayunk Arts Festival *(late Jun)*, Main Street. The region's largest outdoor arts and craft festival.

TD Bank Philadelphia International Championship professional bike race

Fourth of July fireworks over the Philadelphia Museum of Art

JULY

Wawa Welcome America! (week leading up to Jul 4). A week-long celebration with a concert and free events.
Fourth of July Parade *(Jul 4)*, Center City. Parade followed by fireworks.
Let Freedom Ring *(Jul 4)*, Liberty Bell Center. Descendants of those who signed the Declaration of Independence tap the Normandy Bell, an exact cast of the Liberty Bell.
Philadelphia International Gay & Lesbian Film Festival *(mid–late Jul)*. Showcases gay and lesbian films.

AUGUST

Philadelphia Folk Festival *(late Aug)*, Schwenksville. Music, dance, and crafts fair.
Philadelphia Eagles Football *(Aug–Dec)*, Lincoln Financial Field. The season features several home games.
Philadelphia Fringe Festival *(late Aug–early Sep)*. Citywide. Avant-garde theater.

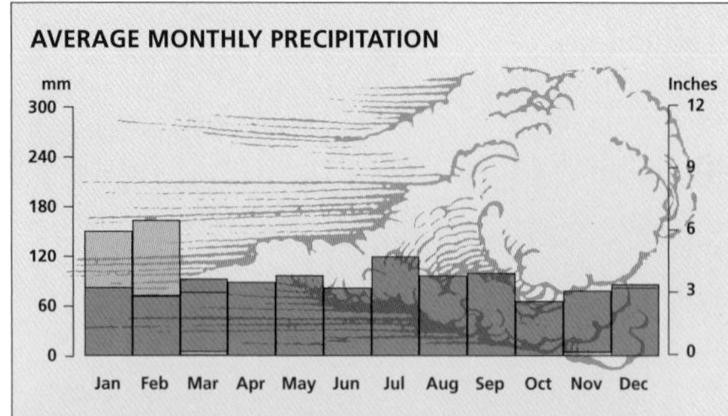

Rainfall Chart
This chart shows the average monthly rainfall and snowfall. The heaviest rain is in July and August, with a yearly average of 41 inches. Considerable snow falls in January and February. The annual snowfall average is 21 inches.

Rainfall (from baseline)

Snow (from baseline)

Rowers in Lancaster County in the fall

FALL

Summer gradually gives way to cooler temperatures by mid-September, as thousands of students flock to the city's more than 80 colleges and universities. The bright reds and yellows of fall foliage begin to make an appearance by the end of September, with dramatic colors in October and early November. Football season gets into high gear, as fans head out to watch the Philadelphia Eagles. Autumn also kicks off many cultural activities, signaling a new season for the city's world-class performing arts, opera, and symphony companies.

SEPTEMBER

Von Steuben Day Gala and Parade *(late Sep)*, Center City. Celebrates the city's German heritage and pays tribute to Baron Friedrich von Steuben, a general in the Revolutionary War.

Puerto Rican Day Parade *(last Sun)*, Center City. Celebrating Puerto Rican heritage with a festival and parade.

Philadelphia College Festival *(late Sep or early Oct)*. College Day concert in the Benjamin Franklin Parkway, plus various career fairs and cultural events.

OCTOBER

Pulaski Day Parade *(first Sun)*, Center City. Pays tribute to the Polish Revolutionary War hero, General Casimir Pulaski.

Columbus Day Parade *(second Sun)*, South Broad Street. The parade honors explorer Christopher Columbus and the Italian American community.

Philadelphia Open Studio Tours *(mid-Oct)*. Local artists throughout the city open their workshops for two weekends.

Philadelphia 76ers Basketball *(Oct–Apr)*, Wachovia Center. NBA basketball season begins with a number of home games.

Philadelphia Flyers Hockey *(Oct–May)*, Wachovia Center. The NHL hockey season kicks off with home games.

Terror Behind the Walls *(mid-Oct through Oct 31)*, Eastern State Penitentiary. A "haunted" house in the former prison celebrates Halloween.

NOVEMBER

Philadelphia Museum of Art Craft Show *(early Nov)*, Pennsylvania Convention Center. Features handmade textiles, jewelry, household wares, and more.

Philadelphia Marathon *(third Sun)*. A 26-mile (42-km) run through the city starts and ends at the Philadelphia Museum of Art.

Thanksgiving Day Parade *(fourth Thu)*. Benjamin Franklin Parkway. The oldest such parade in the country.

Colorful floats and giant balloons at the Thanksgiving Day Parade

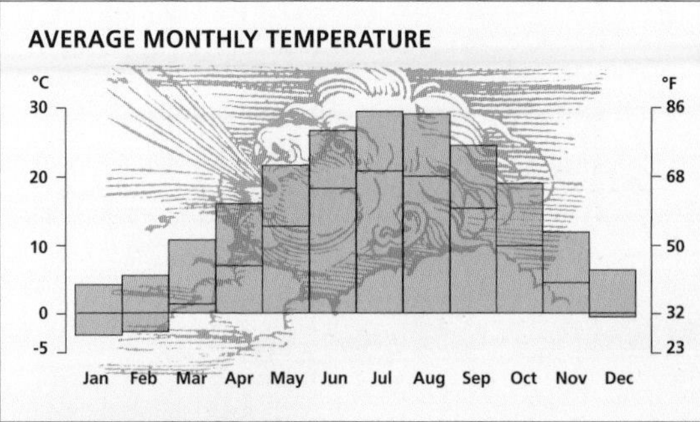

Temperature Chart
Spring is usually mild with some brisk days. Summer can be hot and muggy on certain days, although most days are comfortable. Fall brings clear and colder days. In winter, wind chills sometimes drop temperatures to below freezing, but many days are refreshingly chilly and bright.

Christmas lights at the Wanamaker Building

WINTER

Strings of sparkling lights illuminate streets, buildings, and trees throughout Center City and beyond, as Christmas shoppers throng the city's main shopping districts. New Year's Day brings the Mummers Day Parade, one of Philadelphia's most honored traditions, in which costumed revelers and string bands march down the street. Sports enthusiasts spend the winter months attending Philadelphia 76ers basketball and Flyers hockey games.

DECEMBER

Christmas Tree Lighting *(Wed after Thanksgiving)*, City Hall. Signals the start of the holiday season.
Philadelphia Holiday Festival *(dates vary)*. Citywide performances by Mummers string bands, festivities, lighting events, and even tax-free shopping for shoes and clothing.
Washington Crossing the Delaware River Reenactment *(Dec 25)*, Washington Crossing. Reenactment of this historic turning point in the American Revolutionary War.
New Year's Eve *(Dec 31)*, Penn's Landing. A night of celebrations with fireworks along the Delaware River.
The Nutcracker *(dates vary)*, Academy of Music. Part of Pennsylvania Ballet's season, productions of this ballet are put on before Christmas.

JANUARY

Mummers Day Parade *(Jan 1)*, Center City. A Philadelphia tradition, where up to 20,000 people in decorative costumes parade to the music of string bands.
Chinese New Year Celebrations *(dates vary)*, Chinatown. Parades and festivities for two weeks.
Welcome Spring *(mid-Jan through Mar)*, Longwood Gardens. Indoor displays of bulbs, trees, and flowers create the illusion of spring during the winter months.

FEBRUARY

Philadelphia International Auto Show *(first week)*, Pennsylvania Convention Center. Highlights the latest in classic and luxury cars.
Mardi Gras *(Fat Tuesday before Ash Wednesday)*, South Street. Day-long revelry and celebration.
African American History Month *(all month)*. Various events throughout the city.

PUBLIC HOLIDAYS

New Year's Day (Jan 1)
Martin Luther King Day (3rd Mon in Jan)
Presidents' Day (3rd Mon in Feb)
Memorial Day (Last Mon in May)
Independence Day (Jul 4)
Labor Day (1st Mon in Sep)
Columbus Day (2nd Mon in Oct)
Veterans Day (Nov 11)
Thanksgiving Day (4th Thu in Nov)
Christmas Day (Dec 25)

Mummers Day Parade, a Philadelphia New Year's Day tradition

Georgian-style houses on Elfreth's Alley *(see p52)*, the oldest continuously-occupied street in the US ▷

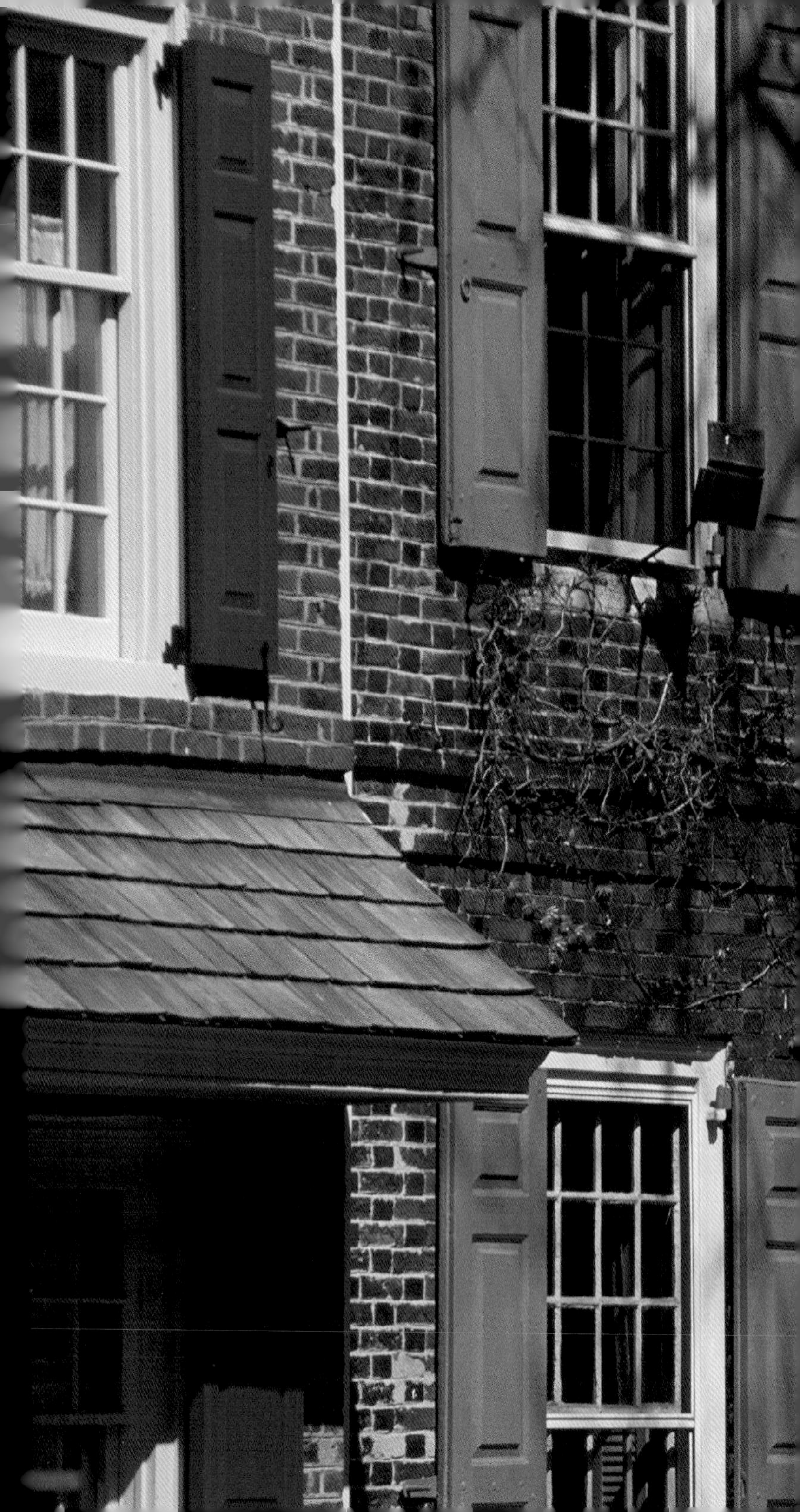

PHILADELPHIA AREA BY AREA

OLD CITY

The foundations of Philadelphia, and all of the United States, are rooted in the neighborhood of Old City, which includes the Liberty Bell and Independence Hall, both of which form part of Independence National Historical Park. This area was settled by city founder William Penn and his fellow Quakers in the late 16th century. It later served as the seat of government for rebellious colonial patriots during the American Revolution in the 1770s. Today, well-preserved historical structures, buildings, and homes that date back to the 18th and 19th centuries, some still situated on narrow cobblestoned streets, stand alongside modern buildings and high-rises.

Plaque at Independence Hall

SIGHTS AT A GLANCE

Historical Buildings and Districts

Arch Street Friends Meeting House 8
Betsy Ross House 21
Bishop White House 28
Carpenters' Hall 26
Christ Church Burial Ground 9
City Tavern 30
Curtis Center and Dream Garden Mosaic 14
Declaration House 16
Elfreth's Alley 20
First Bank of the US 25
Franklin Court and B. Free Franklin Post Office 23
Free Quaker Meeting House 5
Independence Hall pp42–3 1
Philadelphia Merchants' Exchange 29
Philosophical Hall & Library 13
President's House: Freedom and Slavery in the Making of a New Nation 3
Second Bank of the US 12
Todd House 27
US Mint 7

Museums and Galleries

The African American Museum in Philadelphia 17
Fireman's Hall Museum 19
Independence Visitor Center 4
Liberty Bell Center p44 2
National Constitution Center pp48–9 6
National Liberty Museum 24
National Museum of American Jewish History 10
Philadelphia History Museum 15

Places of Worship

Christ Church 22
Congregation Mikveh Israel 11
St. George's United Methodist Church 18

Parks and Gardens

Welcome Park 31

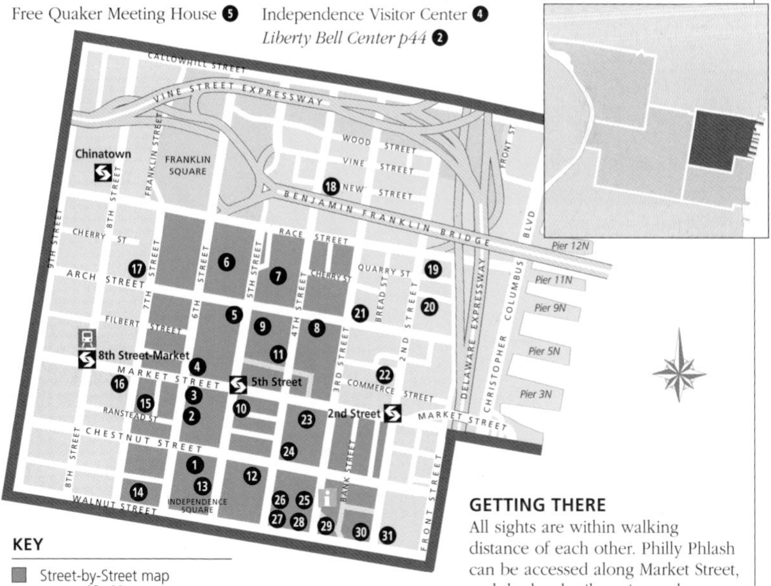

KEY

- Street-by-Street map *see pp40–41*
- SEPTA subway stop
- PATCO rail station
- Visitor information

0 meters 500
0 yards 500

GETTING THERE

All sights are within walking distance of each other. Philly Phlash can be accessed along Market Street, and the local rail service makes stops at the Market East Station. The Market-Frankford line has two stops in Old City, at 2nd and Market, and 5th and Market. SEPTA buses 21, 38, and 42 also have stops in Old City.

◁ **The south face of Georgian-style Independence Hall, formerly known as the State House** ***(see pp42–3)***

Street-by-Street: Independence National Historical Park

Known locally as Independence Mall, this urban park encompasses several well-preserved 18th-century structures associated with the American Revolution. The Declaration of Independence that heralded the birth of a new nation was written and signed in this historic area. Dominated by the tall brick tower of Independence Hall, the park includes the US Mint and several special-interest museums that explore Philadelphia's colonial and seafaring past, as well as its ethnic heritage. At least 20 of the buildings are open to the public.

Plaque commemorating Independence Hall

US Mint
This mint, the oldest in the country, struck its first coins in 1793. It also mints commemorative coins such as the Eisenhower dollar ❼

Christ Church Burial Ground ❾

★ National Constitution Center
This museum features interactive exhibits explaining the US Constitution. Visitors can walk among life-sized statues of the delegates who were present when this document was adopted in 1787 ❻

Free Quaker Meeting House ❺

Philadelphia History Museum at Atwater Kent ⓯

KEY

— — — Suggested route

STAR SIGHTS

- ★ National Constitution Center
- ★ Liberty Bell Center
- ★ Independence Hall

Independence Visitor Center
Located in what is called "America's most historic square mile," the Independence Visitor Center provides visitors with practical information and a cultural and historical orientation. Timed tickets for Independence Hall are available here ❹

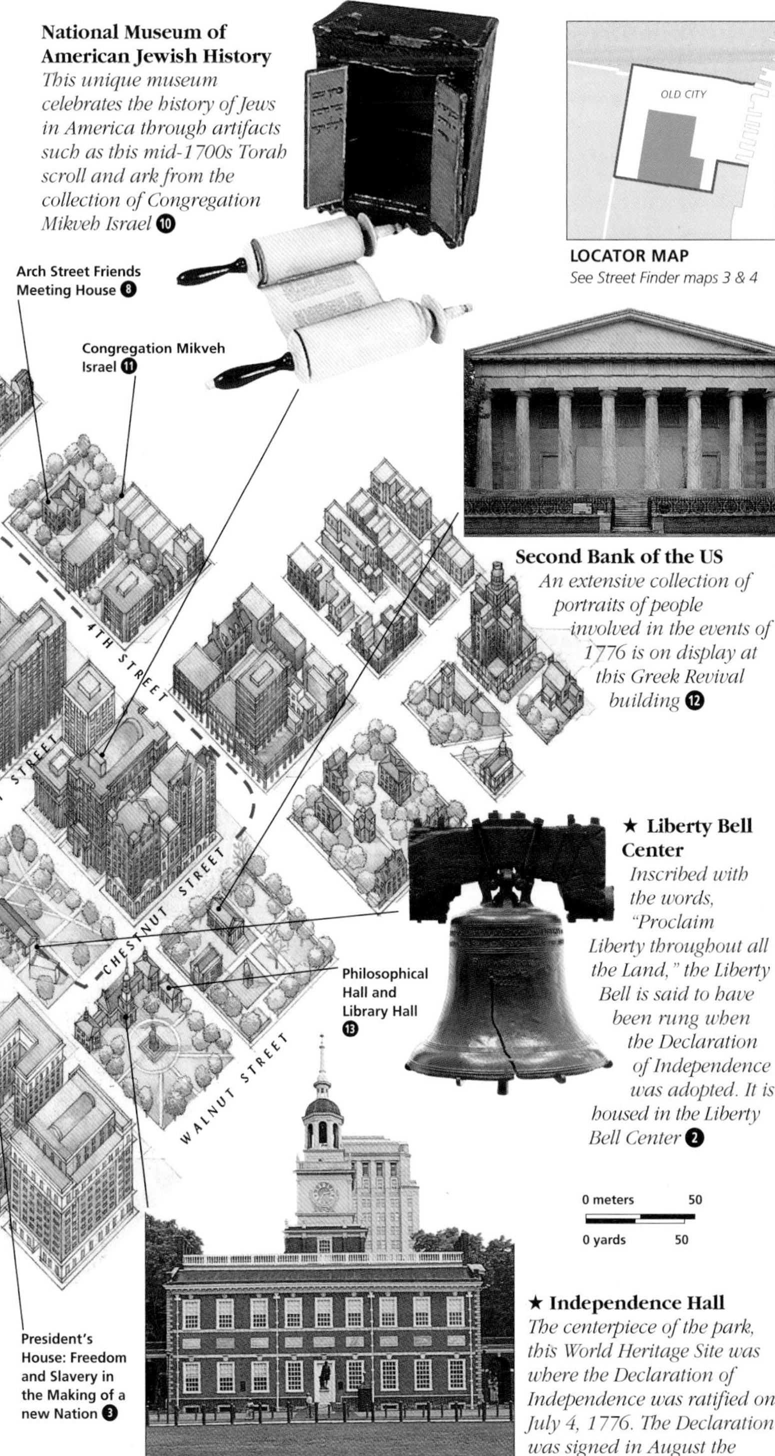

National Museum of American Jewish History
This unique museum celebrates the history of Jews in America through artifacts such as this mid-1700s Torah scroll and ark from the collection of Congregation Mikveh Israel 10

LOCATOR MAP
See Street Finder maps 3 & 4

Second Bank of the US
An extensive collection of portraits of people involved in the events of 1776 is on display at this Greek Revival building 12

★ Liberty Bell Center
Inscribed with the words, "Proclaim Liberty throughout all the Land," the Liberty Bell is said to have been rung when the Declaration of Independence was adopted. It is housed in the Liberty Bell Center 2

★ Independence Hall
The centerpiece of the park, this World Heritage Site was where the Declaration of Independence was ratified on July 4, 1776. The Declaration was signed in August the same year 1

Independence Hall ❶

Independence Hall tower clock

This unadorned brick building and clock tower are the most important structures in Independence Hall National Park. Earlier designated the State House of Pennsylvania, it is the site of the drafting and signing of the US Constitution and the Declaration of Independence, the document that declared America's freedom from the British Empire in 1776. Designed by master carpenter Edmund Woolley and lawyer Andrew Hamilton, Independence Hall was completed in 1753, more than two decades after construction began. Today, the meeting rooms are simply furnished, as they were in the late 1700s, and park personnel re-create history by pointing out the Windsor-style chairs from which colonial leaders debated the contents of the Declaration.

Congress Hall
Congress met in this hall from 1790 to 1800. Presidential inaugurations were also held here for George Washington and John Adams.

West Wing

THE DECLARATION OF INDEPENDENCE

Following colonial resistance to British "taxation without representation," the first shots of rebellion rang out in 1775 at the battles of Concord and Lexington outside Boston. Within a year, a strong feeling for independence overwhelmed the colonies. Known for his powerful writing style, Thomas Jefferson, Virginia Delegate and future president, took on the task of drafting a document declaring independence. He eloquently asserted man's right to freedom and rebellion while listing colonial grievances against England's King George III. After making changes, the Continental Congress ratified the Declaration of Independence on July 4, 1776.

IN CONGRESS, July 4, 1776.

An original copy of the 1776 Declaration of Independence

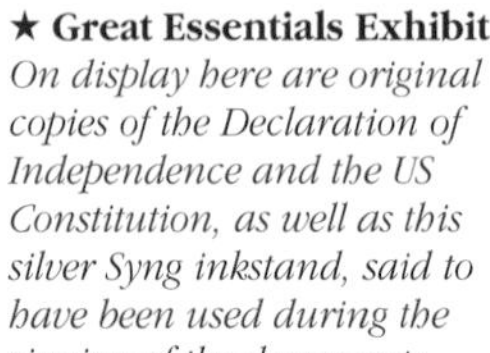
★ Great Essentials Exhibit
On display here are original copies of the Declaration of Independence and the US Constitution, as well as this silver Syng inkstand, said to have been used during the signing of the documents.

★ Assembly Room
Amidst its simple desks and chairs, delegates of the Continental Congress debated and signed the new nation's Declaration of Independence in 1776. Eleven years later, the Constitution was drafted and signed here as well.

VISITORS' CHECKLIST

Chestnut St between 5th & 6th Sts. **Map** 4 D3. ***Tel*** *(215) 965-2305.* *Market East Station.* *5th St.* *Philly Phlash.* *9am–5pm daily. Longer hours in summer. Free, timed ticket needed from Independence Visitor Center on morning of visit. For advance reservations, call (877) 444-6777 or see http://reservations.nps.gov*
www.nps.gov/inde/

★ Rising Sun Chair
The chair used by George Washington during the 1787 Constitutional Convention depicts a symbolic sun rising over the new nation.

Long Gallery
Running the length of the second floor, this light-filled reception room also hosted 18th-century balls and banquets.

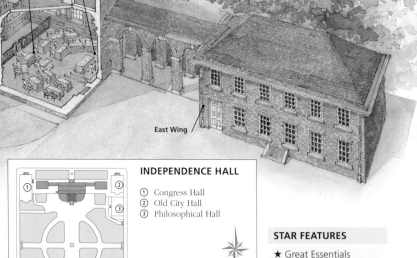

East Wing

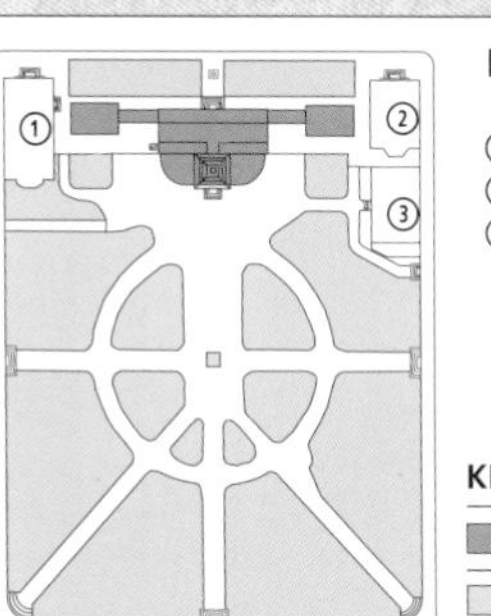

INDEPENDENCE HALL

① Congress Hall
② Old City Hall
③ Philosophical Hall

KEY

Illustrated Area

Lawn

STAR FEATURES

★ Great Essentials Exhibit

★ Assembly Room

★ Rising Sun Chair

Liberty Bell Center ❷

Originally rung to signal Pennsylvania Assembly meetings in the State House (now Independence Hall) in the mid-18th century, the Liberty Bell is one of the world's greatest symbols of freedom, bearing the inscription "Proclaim Liberty throughout all the Land unto all the Inhabitants thereof." Famous for its irreparable crack, the 2,080-lb (940-kg) bell was moved to its current home in the Liberty Bell Center in 2003. The center details the bell's history and significance, and how it became an icon for other freedom struggles. Clearly visible on the bell is the unsuccessful "stop drilling" repair, where, in 1846, the edges of the fracture were filed down to reduce friction and stress in an effort to slow the growth of the crack.

VISITORS' CHECKLIST

Market St between 5th & 6th Sts. **Map** 4 D3. ***Tel*** *(215) 965-2305.* *Market East Station.* *5th St.* *Philly Phlash.* *9am–5pm.* **www**.nps.gov/inde

Multimedia Display Gallery
This gallery displays old newspaper reports, videos, and photographs of people who have fought for liberty, such as the Dalai Lama and Nelson Mandela.

The Liberty Bell
The bell cracked the first time it was rung in 1753. Recast twice by Philadelphia's Pass and Stow Foundry, it was placed in the steeple of the State House (now called Independence Hall). It is said to have been first referenced as "Bell of Liberty" by 19th-century abolitionists.

Curved wall

Entrance

Liberty Bell Center
The center is an elongated building where visitors first walk through a multimedia display gallery. This leads to the bell itself, set next to a large window with an excellent view of Independence Hall. A commemorative installation, "The President's House: Freedom and Slavery in the Making of a New Nation", is next to the Liberty Bell. This was the official residence of the President before the White House.

LIBERTY BELL TIMELINE

1750 | 1800 | 1850 | 1900 | 1950 | 2000

- **1752** Pennsylvania Assembly orders the bell from Whitechapel Foundry in England
- **1753** It cracks when first rung, and is recast twice
- **1776** Possibly rung on July 8 after first public reading of the Declaration of Independence
- **1835** Termed "Bell of Liberty" by abolitionists
- **1841–45** Cracks again in this period
- **1915** Tapped when transcontinental telephone service started
- **1944** Tapped during Normandy Invasion on June 6
- **1976** Moved from Independence Hall to outside pavilion for country's bicentennial
- **1988** Liberty Bell Medal created
- **2003** Bell moved to Liberty Bell Center

President's House: Freedom and Slavery in the Making of a New Nation ❸

6th & Market Sts. **Map** 4 D3. *Market East Station.* *5th St.* *Philly Phlash.* *24 hrs a day.*

Focusing on the untold stories of slavery in Philadelphia, the President's House brings to light the people and events that shaped the history of the slave trade in America. The outdoor installation sits on the site where America's first president, George Washington, resided. At the time he owned nine slaves, whose stories are told here. America's second president, abolitionist John Adams, also resided here.

This outdoor installation allows guests to walk through the house's footprint and examine important artifacts. Visitors can learn about the political climate of the time by looking at exhibits that show the dynamics of the abolitionist movement in Philadelphia and the relationship between free blacks and slaves, as well as the laws signed by Washington and Adams and how they defined the American Presidency.

The site's location is one of the most significant features of the attraction. The Liberty Bell, a nation's symbol of freedom, sits atop the land where the slave quarters were located. Though Philadelphia was the epicenter of the fight for freedom in the 18th century, it was still a place where not all men were free.

Independence Visitor Center ❹

6th & Market Sts. **Map** 4 D2. ***Tel*** *(215) 965-7676.* *Market East Station.* *5th St.* *Philly Phlash.* *8:30am–6pm daily (until 7pm Memorial Day–Labor Day).* *Jan 1, Thanksgiving, Dec 25.* **www.** independencevisitorcenter.com

One of the first stops for any visitor to Philadelphia should be the Independence Visitor Center. This expansive center offers information on more than 4,000 attractions in the city and the region. Apart from screening historical and orientation films, such as the short film *Independence* directed by John Huston, it has maps and brochures, touch-screen information kiosks, daily listings of events, and trip-planning services. Both National Park Service rangers and experienced City of Philadelphia tourism specialists provide assistance and advice about historical sights, attractions, shopping, and dining. A large gift shop has all manner of souvenirs themed around Philadelphia. Café Independence and Independence Al Fresco Café offer refreshments.

Of particular interest is a rotating exhibition of original engravings of colonial Philadelphia by William Russell Birch, which were first published in 1800. Prints of these line the Market Street entrance corridor.

The Visitor Center is also the place to obtain timed-entry tickets for Independence Hall. These are available on a first-come-first-served basis.

The Independence Visitor Center in "America's most historic square mile"

Plain brick façade of the 18th-century Free Quaker Meeting House

Free Quaker Meeting House ❺

Arch & 5th Sts. **Map** 4 D2. *Market East Station.* *5th St.* *Philly Phlash.* *11am–4pm Wed– Sun.*

This simple Georgian brick building was built in 1783 for Quakers who were compelled to bear arms in the American Revolution. Bearing arms meant defying the pacifist beliefs of the order, which led to expulsion from the main Quaker community. About 200 such people called themselves the "Free Quakers" and founded their own meetinghouse. However, in the years that followed, attendance dropped to just a few dozen, and by 1834, only two Free Quakers, Betsy Ross and John Price Wetherill, still attended meetings. Shortly thereafter, the meetinghouse was permanently closed. Since then, the building has served as a school, a library, and a warehouse.

Today, the building contains two benches and a window from colonial times. Also on display is Betsy Ross's five-pointed star tissue pattern, which she is said to have used to shape stars to make the colonial-era American flag. Today, the descendants of the original Free Quakers hold annual meetings here to decide how to distribute funds generated by rental of the hall and how best to invest income for charitable purposes. Actors dressed in colonial garb give lectures on the building's history, and guides demonstrate how to cut a five-pointed star in one snip.

National Constitution Center 6

See pp48–9.

US Mint 7

5th & Arch Sts. **Map** 4 D2. ***Tel*** *(215) 408-0140.* *Market East Station.* *5th St.* *Philly Phlash.* *9am–4:30pm Mon–Fri.* *group tours by prior arrangement.* **www**.usmint.gov
Federal Reserve Bank of Philadelphia 6th & Arch Sts. ***Tel*** *(215) 574-6000.* *photo ID required to enter.*

The Philadelphia mint, the oldest in the US, produces gold bullion coins and medals, and also makes most of the coins that Americans use everyday. The first US coins, minted in 1793, were copper pennies intended solely for commerce in the colonies. Today, 24 hours a day, five days a week, hundreds of machines and operators, in a room the size of a football field, blank, anneal, count, and bag millions of dollars worth of pennies, dimes, and quarters. The gift shop, open on a limited basis, sells commemorative coins and numismatic collectables.

A related exhibit, Money in Motion, is on display at the **Federal Reserve Bank of Philadelphia**, which is located one block west of the US Mint. It explains US monetary policy and history with the help of interactive computer screens and impressive exhibits.

Philadelphia's oldest Quaker meetinghouse, on Arch Street

Arch Street Friends Meeting House 8

4th & Arch Sts. **Map** 4 E2. ***Tel*** *(215) 627-0627.* *Market East Station.* *2nd St.* *Philly Phlash.* *10am–4pm Mon–Sat.* *10:30am Sun; 7pm Wed.* **www**.archstreetfriends.org

This brick structure is the oldest Quaker meeting house still in use in Philadelphia. Built in 1804, the site first served as a Quaker burial ground, but later accommodated victims of the yellow fever epidemic in the 1790s. Today, the house has a central hall and two adjacent meeting rooms. The East Room features Quaker artifacts and six dioramas depicting William Penn's life as a Quaker. The West Room contains worn wooden benches and now serves as the main meeting and worship hall.

Inspecting coins at the US Mint

Christ Church Burial Ground 9

5th & Arch Sts. **Map** 4 D2. ***Tel*** *(215) 922-1695.* *Market East Station.* *5th St.* *Philly Phlash.* *10am–4pm Mon–Sat, noon–4pm Sun (burial ground); 9am–5pm Mon–Sat, noon–5pm Sun (church).* **www**.oldchristchurch.org

This crammed cemetery dates back to 1719, and is an expansion of the church's original graveyard. More than 5,000 people are buried here, most from colonial times. The burial ground is the final resting place of Benjamin Franklin, his wife Deborah, and their daughter and son-in-law Sarah Franklin and Richard Bache. Four other signers of the Declaration of Independence – Dr. Benjamin Rush, Francis Hopkinson, George Ross, and Joseph Hewes – are also buried here. Franklin's grave is on the perimeter of the grounds, and is visible through an iron grating. Passers-by toss pennies on the grave, both to show respect and to bring good luck. With headstones already deteriorating by the mid-19th century, all gravestone inscriptions were copied and published in 1864 in order to preserve records of people interred in this graveyard.

Headstone, Christ Church Burial Ground

National Museum of American Jewish History 10

101 South Independence Mall East. **Map** 4 D2. ***Tel*** *(215) 923-3811.* *Market East Station.* *5th St.* *Philly Phlash.* *10am–5pm Tue–Fri, 10am–5:30pm Sat & Sun.* *Mon, Jewish holidays.* **www**.nmajh.org

This is the only institution in the nation dedicated solely to the story of the American Jewish experience. The core exhibition traces the lives of American Jews from 1654 to the present, exploring how they created a new home in a free land and examining how this country shaped their lives, communities, and livelihoods.

The museum includes nearly 1,100 artifacts, films, and state-of-the-art technology that provide a powerful testament to what free people can accomplish for themselves and for society at large.

Exhibits devoted to everyday relationships and popular culture make the collection accessible to both Jewish and non-Jewish audiences. The *Only in America Gallery/Hall of Fame* illustrates the accomplishments of prominent American Jews.

Federal-style façade of Library Hall, a reproduction of the 1789 original

Congregation Mikveh Israel ⓫

44 N 4th St. **Map** 4 E2. ***Tel*** *(215) 922-5446. Market East Station. 5th St. Philly Phlash. 10am–5pm daily. 7:15am daily; Fri evening; 9am Sat.* **www**.mikvehisrael.org

Philadelphia's oldest Jewish congregation, Mikveh Israel, dates to before the 1740s. The congregation built its first synagogue in 1782, and moved into its current building in 1976.

Mikveh Israel's archival collection includes two pairs of Torah finials crafted by silversmith Myer Myers in 1772 and letters written by US Presidents George Washington and Abraham Lincoln. Past congregation members included colonial patriot and financier Haym Salomon; Nathan Levy, whose ship brought the Liberty Bell to America; and Rebecca Gratz, who founded educational and social institutions. The synagogue still holds a traditional service, which has remained virtually unchanged since the colonial era.

Redbrick exterior of Congregation Mikveh Israel

Second Bank of the United States ⓬

420 Chestnut St. **Map** 4 D3. ***Tel*** *(215) 965-7676, (800) 537-7676. Market East Station. 5th St. Philly Phlash. 11am–4pm Wed–Sun.* **www**.nps.gov/inde

Built between 1819 and 1824, this is one of America's finest examples of Greek Revival architecture. Once a repository that provided credit for federal government agencies and private businesses, it now houses a collection of 185 paintings from the late 18th and early 19th centuries. On view are portraits of colonial and federal leaders, military officers, explorers, scientists, and founding fathers.

Many of the portraits are by Charles Willson Peale (1741–1827), his brother James, and their respective children, who together form America's most distinguished family of artists. Peale began collecting portraits after the Revolutionary War. Today, 94 of his paintings, including likenesses of George Washington, Thomas Jefferson, and the Marquis de LaFayette, the Continental Army's French ally, are on display, along with portraits by other artists.

Philosophical Hall and Library Hall ⓭

105 S 5th St. **Map** 4 D3. ***Tel*** *(215) 440-3400. Market East Station. 5th St. Philly Phlash. American Philosophical Museum: Apr–Oct: 10am–4pm Thu–Sun (to 8pm first Fri of month); Nov–Dec: 10am–4pm Fri–Sun. public hols.* **www**.amphilsoc.org

A Colonial-era "think tank," the American Philosophical Society was founded in 1743 by Benjamin Franklin to promote the study of government, nature, science, and industry. Built in 1789, the Federal-style Philosophical Hall was a meeting place for doctors, clergymen, and the founding fathers of the nation. Reopened in 2001 for the first time since the early 19th century, the hall today hosts art, history, and science exhibitions.

The society also owns Library Hall, once the home of the Library Company founded by Franklin in 1731. The company's vast collections served as the Library of Congress until 1800. The current building, a reconstruction of the 1789 original, stores some of the society's most precious works, including the title page of an 1859 manuscript of Darwin's *Origin of Species,* the journals of explorers Lewis and Clark, and Jefferson's handwritten Declaration of Independence.

National Constitution Center ❻

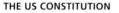

Washington's statue in Signers' Hall

The inscription "We the People" is boldly engraved on the massive Indiana limestone façade of this sprawling center, which was opened on July 4, 2003. It explains the US Constitution through more than 100 interactive and multimedia exhibits, including artifacts, sculptures, photographs, video, and film. Visitors can listen to President Franklin Delano Roosevelt's speeches or to actual arguments from Supreme Court cases at a replica of the Supreme Court Bench, or walk through a re-creation of the 19th-century Senate floor. The circular main hall also contains displays that illuminate the text of the Constitution and highlight the themes of liberty and freedom.

Engraved Façade
"We the People," part of the opening words of the US Constitution, engraved on the façade of the center.

THE US CONSTITUTION

After the Revolutionary War, delegates from the original 13 states, except Rhode Island, gathered in Philadelphia for the Constitutional Convention in 1787. It took them nearly four months to draft a document creating a strong centralized government for the new nation. Adopted on September 17, the Constitution ensures individual liberties and defines distinct powers for Congress, the president, and the federal courts, while also establishing a system of "Checks and Balances" so that no branch of government can dominate the others.

We the People

A copy of the Constitution of the United States

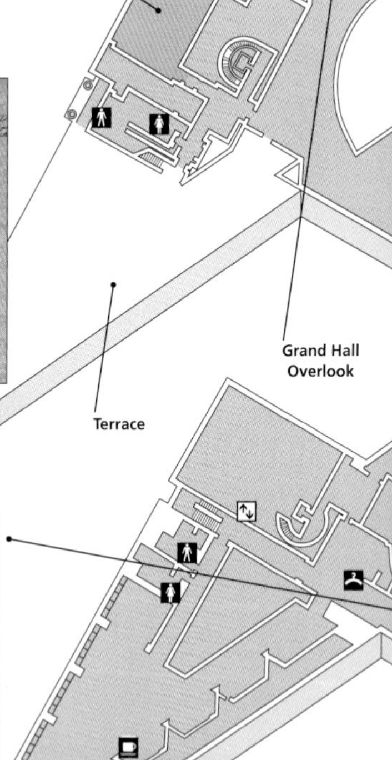

Grand Hall Lobby
Flags of US states hang from the Grand Hall's second floor overlook, from where the lobby's two-story glass windowpanes provide a stunning view of Independence National Historical Park.

STAR EXHIBITS

- ★ "Freedom Rising"
- ★ American National Tree
- ★ Signers' Hall

VISITORS' CHECKLIST

525 Arch St. **Map** 4 D2. ***Tel*** *(215) 409-6600. Market East Station. 5th St. Philly Phlash. 9:30am–5pm Mon–Fri, 9:30am–6pm Sat, noon–5pm Sun. Thanksgiving, Dec 25.* **www**.constitutioncenter.org

★ "Freedom Rising"
The circular, 350-seat Kimmel Theater features "Freedom Rising," a multimedia production that narrates the story of the US Constitution. This 17-minute show is projected on a 360-degree screen.

★ American National Tree
With the "We the People" wall in the foreground, the circular American National Tree features stories of more than 100 Americans who have influenced the Constitution. Each story exemplifies tolerance, diversity, and opportunity.

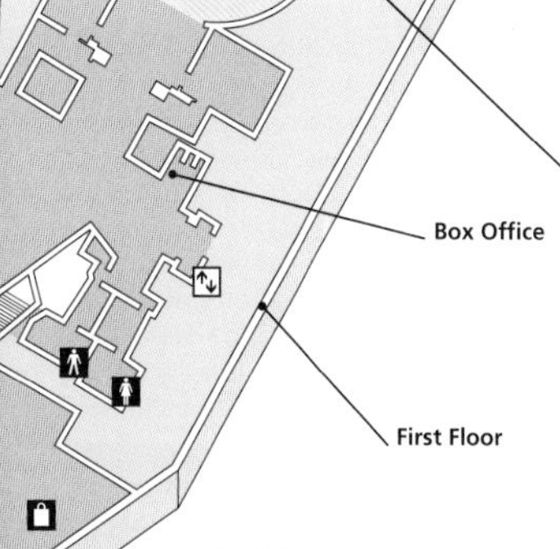

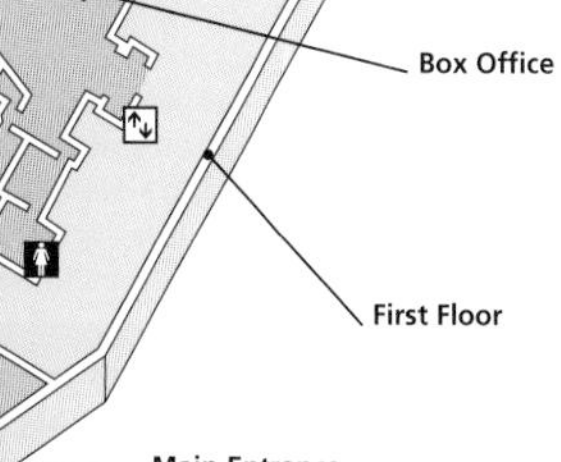

★ Signers' Hall
Walk among life-sized bronze statues of the 39 men who signed the Constitution (including that of Benjamin Franklin, seated in the front), and the three who dissented.

KEY

- Richard and Helen DeVos Exhibit Hall
- Kimmel Theater
- Posterity Hall
- Signers' Hall
- F.M. Kirby Auditorium and Theater
- First Public Printing of the Constitution
- Non-exhibition space

CENTER GUIDE

The Grand Hall Lobby and Kimmel Theater are on the ground floor. Permanent displays and interactive exhibits are situated on the second floor in the circular DeVos Hall.

Curtis Center and Dream Garden Mosaic ⓮

6th & Walnut Sts. **Map** 4 D3. ***Tel*** *(215) 238-6450. Market East Station. 5th St. Philly Phlash. 8am–6pm Mon–Fri, 10am–1pm Sat.*

This Beaux-Arts building is where Cyrus Curtis kicked off his publishing empire in 1883 with the founding of the *Ladies Home Journal*. His publishing company also breathed new life into the *Saturday Evening Post*, and created popular magazines such as *American Home*, *Jack and Jill*, *Holiday*, and *Country Gentleman*.

Inside the building is the enormous *Dream Garden Mosaic*, a 49ft x 15ft (15m x 4.5m) glasswork that dominates the lobby. Designed by Maxfield Parrish, the mosaic was completed in 1916 by Louis Comfort Tiffany and Tiffany Studios. The artwork, depicting a garden with trees and streams, has more than 100,000 pieces of hand-fired favrile glass. In 1998, it was sold to a Las Vegas casino owner, but the people of Philadelphia resisted the move. Local artists and historians helped in raising $3.5 million for the Pennsylvania Academy of the Fine Arts *(see pp74–5)* to buy back the mosaic. It later underwent painstaking restoration.

Philadelphia History Museum at Atwater Kent ⓯

15 S 7th St. **Map** 4 D3. ***Tel*** *(215) 685-4830. Market East Station. 8th St. Philly Phlash. 11am–4pm Wed–Sat. Jan 1, Thanksgiving, Dec 25.*
www.philadelphiahistory.org

Philadelphia's official history museum since 1938, the former Atwater Kent Museum was refurbished and rebranded (to its current name) in 2010. Its collection of 100,000 objects and images spanning over 300 years remains the museum's foundation. Designed by John Haviland in Greek Revival style and completed in 1826, this was the original home of The Franklin Institute. The nation's first architecture classes were taught here. The building was saved from demolition in 1935 when A. Atwater Kent purchased it for a museum.

A colorful walk-on map of the city covers the first floor gallery. Past exhibitions have included furniture used by President George Washington while living in Philadelphia and Benjamin Franklin's wine glass. The museum has an expansive collection of *Saturday Evening Post* covers showing "vignettes of daily life" in America by Norman Rockwell, who created 322 images for the Philadelphia-based magazine between 1916 and 1963.

Atwater Kent exterior detail

Declaration House, reconstructed in 1975 by National Park Service

Declaration House ⓰

7th & Market Sts. **Map** 4 D2. ***Tel*** *(215) 965-7676, (800) 537-7676. Market East Station. 8th St. Philly Phlash. hours vary, call to confirm.*

The current brick structure of Declaration House is a 1975 reconstruction of the Georgian-style home where Thomas Jefferson drafted the Declaration of Independence *(see p42)* from June 11 to 28, 1776. He had rented two upstairs rooms from bricklayer Jacob Graff, who had built the house in 1775. Although only a few blocks from Independence Hall, the house faced a field and stable, and offered Jefferson a quieter setting to write the Declaration.

Today, along with a bust of the famous American statesman and third president, the house includes copies of Jefferson's rough drafts of the Declaration. The two

***Dream Garden Mosaic*, an enormous glass artwork gracing the Curtis Center lobby**

rooms upstairs contain period furnishings, and include recreations of Jefferson's bedroom and parlor, where he wrote the document.

The African American Museum in Philadelphia ⓱

701 Arch St. **Map** 4 D2. ***Tel*** *(215) 574-0380. Market East Station. 5th St. Philly Phlash. 10am–5pm Tue–Sat; noon–5pm Sun; Martin Luther King Day. Mon, public hols.* **www**.aampmuseum.org

A Smithsonian affiliate, this museum is one of several founded in Philadelphia during the nation's bicentennial year. The museum is dedicated to "collecting, preserving, and interpreting the material and intellectual culture of African Americans" in the local area and the Americas. Since opening in 1976, the collection has swelled to more than 500,000 artifacts, including photographs, documents, fine and folk art, costumes, books, periodicals, and a number of other memorabilia.

Permanent and changing exhibitions celebrate important aspects of African-American life and history, including the Civil Rights movement, and contributions in the arts, entertainment, sports, medicine, politics, religion, law, and technology. The permanent exhibit, "Audacious Freedom: African Americans in Philadelphia in 1776–1876", uses interactive displays to recount the stories and contributions made by people of African descent in Philadelphia. Previous exhibitions have showcased African woodcarvings and textile designs while interpreting the traditions and ceremonies of several African countries. Others have focused on struggles against slavery and oppression, including the Haitian Revolution, which resulted in Haiti establishing the world's first Black republic in 1804. The museum also organizes regular workshops and demonstrations.

L'Ouverture **by Ulrick Jean-Pierre, African American Museum**

Exhibit at the African American Museum

St. George's United Methodist Church ⓲

235 N 4th St. **Map** 4 E2. ***Tel*** *(215) 925-7788. Market East Station. 5th St. Philly Phlash. 10am–3pm Mon–Fri; Sun morning after worship; Sat by appt.*

The American Methodist movement began in St. George's United Methodist Church in 1769, making it the country's oldest Methodist church in continuous use. This simple brick structure, its inside walls adorned with a muted blue tint, has not changed much since it was remodeled in 1792. Colonial-era wooden pews and floorboards remain, as do the wrought iron candle chandeliers and candelabra, although now wired with electric lights. A two-room museum has 18th- and 19th-century artifacts, hymnals, bibles, and other important church keepsakes. They include a 1785 silver chalice from John Wesley, the founder of the movement, the original handwritten journals of Joseph Pilmoor, the first pastor of the church, and a bible from Francis Asbury, considered the father of the American United Methodist Church.

St. Augustine's Church across the street dates back to 1796. Burned down in 1844 by anti-Catholic rioters, the current building was designed by architect Napoleon LeBrun and rebuilt in 1847.

Fireman's Hall Museum ⓳

147 N 2nd St. **Map** 4 E2. ***Tel*** *(215) 923-1438. Market East Station. 2nd St. Philly Phlash. 10am–4:30pm Tue–Sat (until 9pm 1st Fri of month).* **www**.firemanshall.org

Housed in an old firehouse that was operational between 1902 and 1952, this unique museum narrates the history of firefighting in Philadelphia, back to colonial times. The building still contains the original brass sliding pole used for quick access to fire trucks. Several pieces of old equipment are on display, including an 1896 hook-and-ladder, a 1903 high-pressure Cannon Wagon, and a 1907 steam-powered pumper. Of special note are two well-preserved hand-pumpers, one from 1815, and the other from 1730, six years before Benjamin Franklin founded the nation's first fire department. Also on display are axes, saws, nozzles, old fire plaques indicating insured buildings, and leather fire hats from the early 19th century. A large stained-glass window memorializes fallen firefighters.

Façade of the Fireman's Hall Museum

Elfreth's Alley ⑳

N 2nd St between Arch & Race Sts. **Map** 4 E2. *Elfreth's Alley Museum, 126 Elfreth's Alley, (215) 574-0560.* *Market East Station.* *2nd St.* *Philly Phlash.* *11am–4pm Tue, 10am–5pm Wed–Sun.* **www**.elfrethsalley.org

The oldest continuously occupied residential street in the country, this narrow cobblestoned lane is lined with 33 historic homes, most in simple Georgian style. Named after Jeremiah Elfreth, a blacksmith who built and rented out some of the first homes, the alley dates back to 1702, when it was a path used by carts hauling goods from the Delaware River docks. Its early occupants were tradespeople, artisans, and sea captains, while the industrial boom later brought in laborers and tailors.

The oldest homes are at 120 and 122, built between 1724 and 1728. The street's Mantua Maker's Museum House, at 126, has been restored to resemble the period between 1762 and 1794, when it was owned by sisters-in-law Mary Smith and Sarah Milton, makers of mantuas and dresses. The home at 124 is now a gift shop.

Halfway down the street is another smaller alley, Bladen Court, which includes three houses and a courtyard. Visitors can take a guided or self-guided audio tour. Twice a year, in June and December, many Elfreth Alley residents open their homes for tours during Fete Days celebrations.

Betsy Ross House, where the first American flag was sewn

Betsy Ross House ㉑

239 Arch St. **Map** 4 E2. ***Tel*** *(215) 686-1252.* *Market East Station.* *2nd St.* *Philly Phlash.* *Apr–Sep: 10am–5pm; Oct–Mar: 10am–5pm Tue–Sun.* *Jan 1, Thanksgiving, Dec 25.* *limited access.* **www**.betsyrosshouse.org

One of Philadelphia's most visited historic sites, this simple colonial home was where Quaker seamstress and upholsterer Betsy Ross is said to have sewn the first American flag – although no official documentation exists to prove it. Instead, the story was handed down through generations of her family. Nonetheless, the 1740 row house has been restored to around 1777, when Ross was supposedly commissioned by George Washington to create the "Stars and Stripes" for the struggling new nation. The home, with narrow stairwells and low ceilings, is decorated with period antiques and reproduction pieces, but also has a few original items that once belonged to Ross, including her eyeglasses, a family bible, and an American Chippendale walnut chest-on-chest.

Elfreth's Alley, dating to the early 18th century

Christ Church ㉒

2nd St above Market St. **Map** 4 E2. ***Tel*** *(215) 922-1695.* *Market East Station.* *2nd St.* *Philly Phlash.* *9am–5pm Mon–Sat; 12:30pm–5pm Sun.* *Jan & Feb: Mon & Tue.* *9am & 11am Sun, noon Wed.* **www**.oldchristchurch.org

Founded in 1695, Christ Church was Philadelphia's only Church of England parish for 66 years. The existing structure, built in 1754 in Georgian style, after Wren's London churches, was the town's tallest building at the time. Often called the "Nation's Church," it was where revolutionary leaders, including Benjamin Franklin, Betsy Ross, and George and Martha Washington, once worshipped. Plaques mark some pews used by the colonial elite.

Inside is the baptismal font in which William Penn was baptized, dating from the 14th century and donated by London's All Hallows Church in 1697. Bishop William White *(see p54)*, parish rector for 57 years, is buried in the chancel of the church.

Franklin Court and B. Free Franklin Post Office ㉓

Between 3rd & 4th Sts and Chestnut & Market Sts. **Map** 4 E3. ***Tel*** *(215) 965-7676, (800) 537-7676.* *Market East Station.* *2nd St.* *Philly Phlash.* *court: hours vary; post office: 9am–5pm Mon–Sat.*

This expansive court, which cuts through an entire city block, is where Benjamin Franklin's home once stood. Although razed in 1812, a "Ghost House" frame depicts the exact positions of the house and adjacent print shop, while excavations underneath reveal the original foundations. An impressive, underground museum has exhibits explaining Franklin's life. On the court grounds are several former residences once owned by Franklin, which now house artifacts, replicas and demonstrations of colonial printing and book-binding operations, and the B. Free Franklin Post Office and Museum, which has an active post office. Another building houses the restored offices of *The Aurora*, the newspaper published by Franklin's grandson, Benjamin Franklin Bache.

Tribute to valor – the National Liberty Museum

National Liberty Museum ㉔

321 Chestnut St. **Map** 4 E3. ***Tel*** *(215) 925-2800.* *Market East Station.* *2nd St.* *Philly Phlash.* *10am–5pm Tue–Sat, noon–4pm Sun.* *Mon (first Mon in Sep–last Mon in May), Jan 1, Thanksgiving, Dec 25.* *for adults.* **www**.libertymuseum.org

Through exhibits heralding freedom and diversity, the National Liberty Museum takes an unconventional approach to its mission of defusing violence and bigotry. The museum honors 1,000 people worldwide who have stood up against repression. On display are life-sized dioramas of South Africa's Nelson Mandela in his jail cell, and concentration camp victim Anne Frank's Amsterdam bedroom, in which she hid from the Nazis. Another display has photographs of every rescue worker who died in the September 11, 2001 attacks. With more than 100 glass artworks, the museum is the only one in the world to use glass as a symbol for freedom, and has a two-story structure, the *Flame of Liberty*, by Dale Chihuly, as its centerpiece.

Classical façade of the First Bank, designed by Samuel Blodgett

First Bank of the United States ㉕

116 S 3rd St between Chestnut & Walnut Sts. **Map** 4 E3. ***Tel*** *(215) 965-7676.* *Market East Station.* *2nd St.* *Philly Phlash.* *closed to the public.*

The dispute over building the First Bank instigated the new nation's first debate on the interpretation of the US Constitution *(see pp48–9)*, which neither allowed nor prohibited the building of a federal bank. Alexander Hamilton, treasury secretary from 1789 to 1795, led the charge to provide the nation with a firm financial footing and a means to pay off the Revolutionary War debt. Chartered by President Washington and Congress in 1791, the bank building was completed six years later, with its classical design signifying culture and political maturity.

In 1811, Congress voted to withdraw the charter. The building was then occupied by Girard Bank through the 1920s, and finally taken over by the National Park Service in 1955. Original brick rooms and sheet iron vault doors still remain in the building, which now houses the Civil War and Underground Museum of Philadelphia.

BENJAMIN FRANKLIN

Benjamin Franklin (1706–90)

One of America's finest statesmen, Benjamin Franklin wore many hats as a printer, inventor, author, philosopher, postmaster, and diplomat. Born in Boston in 1706, Franklin moved to Philadelphia in 1723. He established the first library and fire department in the city, and upgraded its postal services. Franklin also founded the University of Pennsylvania and the Pennsylvania Hospital. In the Revolutionary War, he presided over the 1776 Constitutional Convention and helped draft the Declaration of Independence *(see p42)*. He won favor with the French who would come to America's aid against the British. In 1787, he signed the US Constitution, and died in Philadelphia three years later. In 2006, the city honored Franklin with a year-long celebration of his 300th birthday.

Carpenters' Hall 26

320 Chestnut St. **Map** 4 E3. **Tel** *(215) 925-0167.* *Market East Station.* *5th St.* *Philly Phlash.* *Jan–Feb: 10am–4pm Wed–Sun; Mar–Dec: 10am–4pm Tue–Sun.* *Jan 1, Thanksgiving, Dec 25.* **www**.carpentershall.org

This two-story structure was built for the Carpenters' Company, the country's oldest trade guild, established in 1724. It played an important role in the Revolutionary War, secretly hosting the First Continental Congress in 1774.

Today, the Carpenters' Hall houses displays of original Windsor chairs, used during the Congress, and colonial-era carpenters' tools. Two rebuilt structures share the grounds – Pemberton House, named after a Quaker merchant, is now a gift shop, while the New Hall Military Museum displays weapons of the colonial army and navy. The original 1791 building housed War Department offices.

Georgian-style Carpenters' Hall, designed by Robert Smith in 1770

Todd House 27

4th & Walnut Sts. **Map** 4 D3. **Tel** *(215) 965-7676.* *Market East Station.* *5th St.* *Philly Phlash.* *compulsory; free tickets available at Independence Visitor Center on first-come, first-served basis.*

This Georgian-style home reflects the way the middle class lived in late 18th-century Philadelphia. What makes Todd House particularly interesting is its famous resident, Dolley Payne, who later married James Madison, the fourth president of the US. Built in 1775, the home was occupied by Dolley and her first husband, lawyer John Todd, both Quakers, from 1791 to 1793. Dolley lost Todd and their infant son in 1793 during the city's yellow fever epidemic. The following year, she met Madison during an arranged meeting.

Today, the three-story home has been restored to when John and Dolley Todd lived here, with furnishings that reflect subtle Quaker conservatism. Period items include replicas of Dolley's dressing table, and John Todd's first-floor law library, which contained more than 300 volumes.

Reconstructed dining room of Bishop White House

Bishop White House 28

309 Walnut St. **Map** 4 E3. **Tel** *(215) 965-7676.* *Market East Station.* *5th St.* *Philly Phlash.* *compulsory; free tickets available at Independence Visitor Center on first-come, first-served basis.*

The residence of Bishop William White for nearly 50 years, this three-story Federal structure, built in 1786, is an excellent example of a late 18th-century upper-class Philadelphia home. Dr. White, the first Episcopal Bishop of Pennsylvania and rector of Christ Church *(see p52)* and St. Peter's Episcopal Church *(see p61)*, often entertained the colonial elite here, including George Washington and Benjamin Franklin. The house has been restored, and period and original family pieces decorate the rooms, including whale oil lamps on the fireplace mantel and an assortment of silver pieces in the dining room. Chair placement and bookcases in Dr. White's upstairs study have been accurately reconstructed, thanks to a painting of the room commissioned after his death. An inside privy, which remains today, is indicative of the home's upper-class status.

Philadelphia Merchants' Exchange, designed in Greek Revival style

Philadelphia Merchants' Exchange 29

143 S 3rd St at Walnut St. **Map** 4 E3. **Tel** *(215) 965-2305.* *Market East Station.* *2nd St.* *Philly Phlash.* *8:30am–4:30pm (lobby exhibit).*

The oldest stock exchange building in the country, this

imposing edifice is one of Old City's finest architectural gems. Completed in 1834, it was designed in Greek Revival style by the up-and-coming architect William Strickland, already noted for designing the new steeple atop Independence Hall *(see pp42–3)* and for his work on the Second Bank of the US *(see p47)*. Strickland's admiration of classical Greek design is reflected by the columned Corinthian portico at one end and the unusual, semicircular portico at the other.

With the financial district shifting to Center City in the late 19th century, the building soon became neglected. The National Park Service took it over in 1952, making it a part of Independence National Historical Park. Today, the Park Service maintains offices in the building. Although the exchange is closed to the public, visitors are permitted to enter the lobby and view a small exhibit that details the history and architecture of the exchange.

City Tavern ㉚

138 S 2nd St between Walnut & Chestnut Sts. **Map** 4 E3. ***Tel*** *(215) 413-1443.* *Market East Station.* *2nd St.* *Philly Phlash.* *from 11:30am; reservations taken until 8:30pm.* **www**.citytavern.com

Recalling the atmosphere of an authentic London tavern, the City Tavern also boasted the second largest ballroom in the colonies when it first opened in 1773.

City Tavern, still a popular dining spot in Philadelphia

Welcome Park, dedicated to city founder William Penn

However, just a year later, with the Revolutionary War in the offing, the three-story building was used by members of the First Continental Congress as an unofficial gathering place. Later, in 1777, when he became the leader of the Continental Army, Washington used the tavern as his headquarters.

After the Revolutionary War, the Constitutional Convention held its closing banquet here in 1787. Frequented by the likes of George Washington, Thomas Jefferson, and other colonial notables, it was once called "the most genteel tavern in America," by John Adams, the second president of the United States.

However, by the 1790s, the City Tavern had lost its prominence and served as a merchants' exchange until 1834, when it was partially destroyed by fire. The original structure was finally demolished in 1854 to make way for new brownstone buildings.

After careful research, the National Park Service reconstructed the tavern in 1975. Today, the inn is almost identical to the original, with serving staff in period dress and colonial-style dishes on the menu. These include such delicacies as sweet potato biscuits, said to be a favorite of Jefferson, turkey pot pie based on Martha Washington's recipe, West Indies pepperpot soup, and ales brewed according to Washington's and Jefferson's original recipes.

Welcome Park ㉛

S 2nd St at Walnut St (2nd St & Sansom St Alley). **Map** 4 E3. *Market East Station.* *2nd St.* *Philly Phlash.*

Named after the ship that ferried Penn and the first Quakers from England to the New World, the *Welcome*, this open city square is dedicated to the city's founder, William Penn. It was constructed in 1982 to commemorate the 300th anniversary of the founding of the colony of Pennsylvania. The centerpiece of the park is a smaller version of Penn's statue from City Hall *(see p72)*. Emblazoned along the south wall of the park is a timeline of Penn's life and the events leading to the creation of the new colony. The park is located where the Slate Roof House – Penn's home and the Pennsylvania Seat of Government from 1700 to 1701 – once stood. This postmodernist square is made of concrete crisscrossed by marble slabs, depicting the main streets of the original city grid planned by William Penn and his surveyor Thomas Holmes.

Statue of William Penn

At the park's north end sits the Thomas Bond House, named after the surgeon who, in 1751, along with Benjamin Franklin and others, founded Pennsylvania Hospital, the nation's first public hospital *(see p67)*. The restored 1769 Georgian-style home is now a bed-and-breakfast *(see p134)*.

SOCIETY HILL AND PENN'S LANDING

William Penn first stepped ashore on the banks of the Delaware River at what is today known as Penn's Landing, the eastern edge of this neighborhood. An elongated and tree-lined promenade, Penn's Landing includes a plaza for concerts, historic ships and dinner boats along the piers, and the Independence Seaport Museum.

Detail, Old St. Mary's Church

Heading west, several walkways lead to Society Hill, a well-preserved area with churches, synagogues, and 18th-century homes. The area's southern border, South Street, contrasts with the more serene Society Hill, indulging in the excitement derived from a trendy and eclectic mix of cafés, restaurants, shops, nightclubs, and bars.

SIGHTS AT A GLANCE

Historical Buildings and Districts

New Market and Head House Square 15
Penn's Landing 14
Pennsylvania Hospital 17
Physick House 6
Powel House 12
South Street and Walkway 16

Parks and Gardens

Rose Garden and Magnolia Garden 9
Washington Square 1

Places of Worship

Mikveh Israel Cemetery 18
Mother Bethel AME Church 2
Old Pine Street Church 3
Old St. Joseph's Church 10
Old St. Mary's Church 8
Society Hill Synagogue 7
St. Peter's Episcopal Church 4

Museums and Galleries

Independence Seaport Museum pp64–5 13
Polish American Cultural Center Museum 11
Thaddeus Kosciuszko National Memorial 5

GETTING THERE

Most sights here are a 5- to 15-minute walk from Independence Mall. Philly Phlash buses run May–Oct and are accessible on Market Street, while the Market-Frankford line has stops at 2nd and Market, 5th and Market, and 8th and Market. SEPTA bus 42 runs along Spruce and Walnut Streets.

KEY

Street-by-Street map *see pp58–9*

SEPTA subway stop

◁ **Penn's statue outside Pennsylvania Hospital, founded in 1751 *(see p67)***

Street-by-Street: Society Hill

Flowers laid at the Tomb of the Unknown Soldier

This historic neighborhood dates back to 1682 when William Penn chartered the "Free Society of Traders" to help develop a fledgling Philadelphia. The area was home to many notable colonial figures and members of the new Federal government, which was formed after the Revolutionary War. In the late 1950s, the Philadelphia Redevelopment Authority saved hundreds of 18th- and early 19th-century homes from likely demolition, selling them to private citizens who agreed to restore them. Today, a walk through the neighborhood reveals surviving narrow streets and courtyards, and houses in a mix of architectural styles, including Georgian, Federal, Greek Revival, and Beaux-Arts.

Mother Bethel AME Church
Founded in 1791, this site is the oldest piece of land continuously owned by African Americans. A lower level museum includes the tomb of founder Richard Allen ❷

Old Pine Street Church
The cemetery of "the Church of the Patriots" also contains the grave of Eugene Ormandy, director of the Philadelphia Orchestra from 1938 to 1980 ❸

KEY

— — — Suggested route

0 meters 100

0 yards 100

STAR SIGHTS

★ Powel House

★ Washington Square and Tomb of the Unknown Soldier

St. Peter's Episcopal Church
Completed in 1761, this Anglican church has an unusual double-ended interior, with the altar at one end, and the pulpit at the other ❹

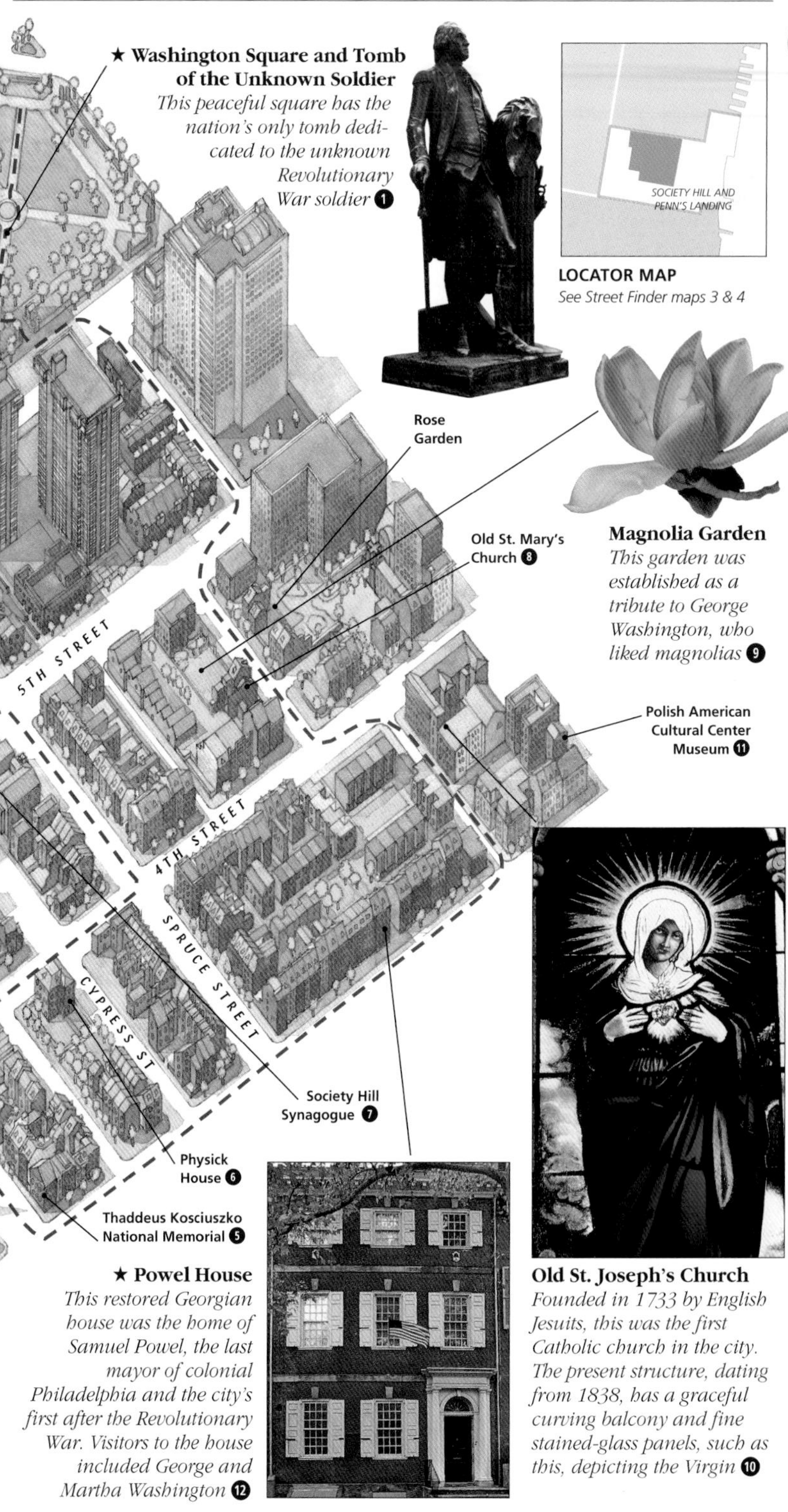

★ Washington Square and Tomb of the Unknown Soldier
This peaceful square has the nation's only tomb dedicated to the unknown Revolutionary War soldier 1

Magnolia Garden
This garden was established as a tribute to George Washington, who liked magnolias 9

★ Powel House
This restored Georgian house was the home of Samuel Powel, the last mayor of colonial Philadelphia and the city's first after the Revolutionary War. Visitors to the house included George and Martha Washington 12

Old St. Joseph's Church
Founded in 1733 by English Jesuits, this was the first Catholic church in the city. The present structure, dating from 1838, has a graceful curving balcony and fine stained-glass panels, such as this, depicting the Virgin 10

Washington Square, one of the five original squares in Penn's grid

Washington Square and Tomb of the Unknown Soldier ❶

Walnut St between 6th & 7th Sts. **Map** 4 D3. *Market East Station.* *5th, 8th, 9th-10th Sts.* *42, Philly Phlash.*

One of the five original squares in Penn's city grid, Washington Square, named after the nation's first president, is a pleasant park with benches and towering trees. This quiet space is also hallowed ground, having served as a cemetery for 90 years until the late 18th century. More than 2,000 Revolutionary War soldiers and prisoners of war were buried in massive pits here. Congressman John Adams described the pathos in a letter to his wife Abigail in 1777, writing that he spent an hour "in the Congregation of the dead" and that "I never in my whole life was affected with so much melancholy." In 1793, mass graves were again dug for victims of the city's yellow fever epidemic. Today, the park's centerpiece is the Tomb of the Unknown Soldier, with a statue of Washington, which was erected in the 1950s as a tribute to those who fought in the Revolutionary War. The tomb includes the remains of a revolutionary soldier who was buried on the site.

Washington's statue at Washington Square

Mother Bethel AME Church ❷

419 S 6th St. **Map** 4 D4. ***Tel*** *(215) 925-0616.* *Market East Station.* *5th St.* *42, Philly Phlash.* *10am–3pm Mon only by appt.* **www**.motherbethel.org

Standing on the oldest piece of land to be continuously owned by African Americans in the US, Mother Bethel traces its roots to former slave Richard Allen (1760–1831), the first Bishop of the African Methodist Episcopal Church. Allen began preaching in 1786 at St. George's United Methodist Church *(see p51)*, where he successfully built up a black parish. He founded his own church in 1794, by buying and moving a blacksmith's shop to the current site, and using the anvil as his pulpit. The current structure was built in 1889 and still contains the original curved pews and stained-glass windows.

In 1830, the church hosted the first national convention for African Americans, and for years was a stop along the Underground Railroad, the system set up by abolitionists to transport fugitive slaves to Canada and the free states. Today, a museum in the lower level houses the tomb of Allen and his wife Sarah, along with historic church artifacts, including the original pews from the blacksmith shop.

Old Pine Street Church ❸

412 Pine St. **Map** 4 D4. ***Tel*** *(215) 925-8051.* *Market East Station.* *2nd, 5th Sts.* *42, Philly Phlash.* *10am–3pm Mon–Sat, call in advance.* *9:30am Sun.* *limited access.* **www**.oldpine.org

The only remaining colonial Presbyterian place of worship in Philadelphia today, Old Pine Street Church was founded in 1768. Designed in Georgian style by Robert Smith, it was later remodeled into an imposing columned Greek Revival building. George Duffield, the church's first pastor, served as chaplain to the Continental Congress of 1774 and second US President John Adams and Dr. Benjamin Rush, the "Father of American Psychiatry," were parishioners here, earning it the moniker "Church of the Patriots."

In 1777, occupying British forces used the church as a hospital and stable, also burying 100 Hessian soldiers in a mass grave outside the church wall. Today, there are more than 3,000 tombs in the surrounding cemetery, including that of Eugene Ormandy, conductor of the Philadelphia Orchestra from 1938 to 1985.

Detail of a gravestone from the Old Pine Street Church graveyard

Interior and altar of St. Peter's Episcopal Church

St. Peter's Episcopal Church ❹

313 Pine St. **Map** 4 D4. ***Tel*** *(215) 925-5968.* *Market East Station.* *2nd, 5th Sts.* *42, Philly Phlash.* *8am–4pm Mon–Fri; 11am–5pm Sat; 1–3pm Sun.* *9am, 10am & 11am Sun.* **www**.stpetersphila.org

Opened for worship in 1761, St. Peter's was founded by Society Hill Anglicans who were members of a then overcrowded Christ Church *(see p52)*, and who wanted a church closer to their homes. Christ Church and St. Peter's functioned as one parish until 1832, with Bishop White *(see p54)* serving as rector of both churches.

St. Peter's, built in Georgian style by Robert Smith, has a unique design. The placement of the wine-glass pulpit and altar at opposite ends of the building, and the seats in boxed pews facing either way, give the church no definitive front or back. In 1842, well-known architect William Strickland designed the landmark tower and spire that still house bells from London's Whitechapel Foundry, which had forged the first Liberty Bell in 1753 *(see p44)*.

Buried in the graveyard are several important colonial Americans, including portrait painter Charles Willson Peale, naval hero Stephen Decatur, and George M. Dallas, vice president of the US from 1845 to 1849, after whom counties were named in Texas, Iowa, Arkansas, and Missouri.

Thaddeus Kosciuszko National Memorial ❺

301 Pine St. **Map** 4 D4. ***Tel*** *(215) 597-9618.* *Market East Station.* *2nd St.* *42, Philly Phlash.* *limited access.* *noon–4pm Wed–Sun.* **www**.nps.gov/thko

Remembered as the "Hero of Two Continents," General Thaddeus Kosciuszko fought for freedom in both his native Poland and colonial America. During the Revolutionary War, he designed and built fortifications at Saratoga and West Point that proved critical to American victories over the British troops.

After the war, Kosciuszko returned to Poland in 1784 and took part in its fight for independence from Russia, but he was wounded and imprisoned by the Russians. He was released only upon the condition that he leave Poland. He then returned to Philadelphia to recuperate from his war wounds for nine months in this Society Hill house. His upstairs room has been restored and furnished with period pieces similar to those he owned. It also contains his medals, walking crutch, and a sable fur given to him on his release by Russia's Tsar Paul I. While nursing his injuries, Kosciuszko spent most of his time reading, sketching, and receiving guests, including his close friend and then US Vice President, Thomas Jefferson.

Physick House ❻

321 S 4th St. **Map** 4 D4. ***Tel*** *(215) 925-7866.* *Market East Station.* *2nd, 5th Sts.* *42, Philly Phlash.* *Feb 25–Dec 31: noon–4pm Thu–Sat; 1–4pm Sun; Jan 1–Feb 24: by appt only* **www**.philaland marks.org

Named after Dr. Philip Syng Physick, the "Father of American Surgery" and grandson of silversmith Philip Syng, who designed the inkwell used during the signing of the Declaration of Independence *(see p42)*, this is one of the few free-standing colonial homes that remain today. Built in 1786 by wine importer Henry Hill, this Federal-style house has what was believed to be the largest fanlight in colonial Philadelphia over its door. After acquiring the home in 1815, Physick set up his medical practice, treating such prominent patients as Dolley Madison *(see p54)* and President Andrew Jackson.

Physick lived there until his death in 1837, and the house has been restored to that period. Original, locally quarried Pennsylvania Blue Marble can be seen in the hall. Family pieces, such as a mid-18th-century oval wooden case that belonged to William Penn's grandson, a British Wagstaff grandfather clock, and original silver items are also displayed. Physick's medical instruments can be seen in an upstairs room, and include surgical tools and medicine chests with bottles.

Physick House entrance fanlight

Interior of Physick House, containing original colonial-era furnishings

Society Hill Synagogue 7

418 Spruce St. **Map** 4 D4. ***Tel*** *(215) 922-6590.* *Market East Station.* *5th St.* *42, Philly Phlash.* *9am–4pm Mon–Thu; call in advance.* *Fri night & Sat morning.* **www**.societyhillsynagogue.org

Originally built as a Baptist church, this impressive structure was designed by 19th-century architect Thomas Ustick Walter, who was most noted for his design of the dome and House and Senate wings of the US Capitol in Washington DC. The original structure was built in Greek Revival style in 1830, but two decades later, Walter was again commissioned to design a new Italianate façade, much of which remains today. The building was home to Baptist worshippers for more than 80 years, until a group of Romanian Jews acquired it in 1912.

By 1916, the building was known as the Great Romanian Synagogue. The name, written in Yiddish, is still visible over the entrance. In the mid-1960s, it became the new home of Society Hill Synagogue, which is an active congregation rooted in the texts and practices of conservative Judaism.

Italianate façade of Society Hill Synagogue

Old St. Mary's Church 8

252 S 4th St. **Map** 4 D4. ***Tel*** *(215) 923-7930.* *Market East Station.* *5th St.* *42, Philly Phlash.* *9am–5pm Mon–Fri.* *Sun.* **www**.ushistory.org/tour/tour_stmary.htm

Founded to take on parishioners from an overcrowded Old St. Joseph's Church, this redbrick church was built in 1763. Together, the two houses of worship served the city's Catholic population as one parish until the 1820s. Old St. Mary's witnessed several significant events in the years leading up to the birth of the nation. During the American Revolutionary War, members of the Continental Congress attended services here. The first public religious commemoration of the Declaration of Independence took place here in 1779, on the third anniversary of its adoption. Following the British surrender at Yorktown in 1781, the church held a Thanksgiving service, with the flags of the conquered army laid on the altar steps. In 1810, Old St. Mary's was enlarged to its present size and became the first Catholic cathedral of the new diocese of Philadelphia. Its graveyard, dating to 1759, contains the tombs of Commodore John Barry, "Father of the American Navy," and the first to capture a British ship during the Revolutionary War, Thomas Fitzsimons, one of the signers of the Constitution, Mathew Carey, 18th-century American publisher and bookseller, and Michael Bouvier, the great-great-grandfather of first lady Jacqueline Kennedy Onassis.

Detail from Old St. Mary's Church

Roses in full bloom in Society Hill's Rose Garden

Rose Garden and Magnolia Garden 9

Locust St between 4th & 5th Sts. **Map** 4 D3. *Market East Station.* *5th St.* *42, Philly Phlash.*

These two public gardens, directly across each other on Locust Street, are nestled within shaded and quiet courtyards, characteristic of Society Hill's charm. The Rose Garden stretches through the center of the entire block, all the way up to Walnut Street. It commemorates the signers of both the Declaration of Independence and the US Constitution. The funding to plant roses, which flower during spring and summer, is povided by The Daughters of the American Revolution, an organization whose members are drawn from the direct descendants of those who fought in the Revolutionary War. Inside the garden is a section of a cobblestoned street dating back to 1800.

The Magnolia Garden was established as a tribute to George Washington, who had often expressed an interest in horticulture and, in particular, magnolia trees. Different varieties of magnolias are planted around the restful garden, whose centerpiece is a small fountain.

Interior of Old St. Joseph's Church with its unusual curving balcony

Old St. Joseph's Church ⑩

321 Willings Alley. **Map** 4 D3. ***Tel*** *(215) 923-1733.* *Market East Station.* *5th St.* *42, Philly Phlash.* *9:30am–4pm Mon–Fri (to 6:30pm Sat), 7:30am–2pm Sun.* *noon Mon–Sat, 7:30am & 9:30am Sun.* **www**.oldstjoseph.org

Located in a narrow alleyway, Old St. Joseph's was Philadelphia's first Catholic church. Reverend Joseph Greaton, an English Jesuit, founded it in 1733. In 1734, efforts were made to thwart Roman Catholic church services, but these were unsuccessful, with religious freedom for all assured by Penn's 1701 Charter of Privileges.

The old chapel was replaced by a larger building in 1757, and six years later, Old St. Mary's was built a block away to handle the growing number of members. St. Joseph's current structure dates from 1838 and features a grand columned altar and a curved balcony at the sanctuary's front end. On the ceiling is the fresco, *The Exaltation of Saint Joseph into Heaven*, painted by 19th-century Italian artist Filippo Costaggini, whose work can also be seen in the US Capitol in Washington DC.

Portrait of General Pulaski, Polish American Cultural Center Museum

Polish American Cultural Center Museum ⑪

308 Walnut St. **Map** 4 E3. ***Tel*** *(215) 922-1700.* *Market East Station.* *2nd, 5th Sts.* *42, Philly Phlash.* *10am–4pm Mon–Fri.* *public hols.* **www**. polishamericancenter.org

Through portraits and memorabilia from Poland, this small museum's mission is to promote awareness and appreciation of Polish culture and history. It honors Poles who have made significant contributions to history, ranging from figures such as Nicholas Copernicus, the astronomer, and composer Frédéric Chopin, to such modern-day luminaries as the late Pope John Paul II and politician and Nobel Peace Prize winner Lech Walesa. Of particular note are displays on the heroes of the American Revolutionary War, Thaddeus Kosciuszko and General Casimir Pulaski, the namesake of an annual city parade that celebrates Polish heritage *(see p34)*. Also on display is traditional Polish folk art – festive garb, Easter eggs, decorative paper cutouts, and wooden plates.

Powel House ⑫

244 S 3rd St. **Map** 4 E4. ***Tel*** *(215) 627-0364.* *Market East Station.* *2nd St.* *42, Philly Phlash.* *noon–5pm Thu–Sat, 1–5pm Sun.* *compulsory.* **www**.philalandmarks.org

This grand Georgian home built in 1765 is an exquisite example of how the colonial elite lived. Samuel Powel, one of the wealthiest men in colonial America, was its second owner, purchasing it in 1769 when he was about to marry Elizabeth Willing. Powel was Philadelphia's last mayor before the Revolutionary War and the first after the nation's birth. He died in 1793, a victim of the city's yellow fever epidemic.

The Powels used their lavish home to entertain the country's most important citizens, including Benjamin Franklin, George Washington, and John Adams, the second president of the US. Original features that remain today include a Pennsylvania Blue Marble fireplace on the first floor, the stairwell of Santo Domingo mahogany, and the cypress front door. Noteworthy furnishings include a small scale from Benjamin Franklin, original china and a sewing cabinet gifted to Mrs. Powel by the Washingtons, Gilbert Stuart portraits, and original silhouettes of Washington cut on cobalt blue paper by Samuel Powel at a social event. Outside the house is a peaceful garden dating back to the late 1700s.

Powel House, an elegant upper-class colonial-era residence

Independence Seaport Museum ⓭

Olympia exhibit

Located on Penn's Landing waterfront, the mission of this museum is to preserve US maritime history and traditions with a special focus on Delaware Bay and the Delaware River and its tributaries. Displays combine artifacts and paintings of naval encounters, along with computer games, large-scale ship models, and audiovisuals that include sounds of ship horns and accounts by sailors and shipbuilders. The museum re-creates the Benjamin Franklin Bridge as a three-story replica that spans a carpeted Delaware River. Exhibits include a replica of the bridge of the destroyer USS *Lawrence*, and of steerage compartments in which many immigrants traveled to America. There is an active boatbuilding workshop, and berthed nearby are the World War II submarine *Becuna*, commissioned in 1944, and the cruiser *Olympia*, Admiral George Dewey's flagship in the 1898 Spanish-American War.

Waterfront Museum
This expansive facility is the centerpiece of Penn's Landing.

J. Welles Henderson Library & Archives

Submarine Becuna
This World War II vessel with torpedo launching tubes was the submarine flagship of the Southwest Pacific Fleet, which was under the command of General Douglas MacArthur.

First Floor

★ Workshop on the Water
Craftspeople build and restore traditional boats of the 19th century at this workshop dedicated to the skills and traditions of wooden boatbuilding and sailing in the Delaware River Valley and the New Jersey shore.

MUSEUM GUIDE

The first floor houses most of the exhibits, the museum shop, and visitor information. The second floor includes the Community Gallery featuring rotating exhibits, the Olympia Gallery, What Floats Your Boat exhibit, a concert hall, and the J. Welles Henderson Library & Archives.

KEY

- Workshop on the Water
- Home Port Philadelphia
- Divers of the Deep
- Disasters on the Delaware
- Olympia Gallery
- On the Rivers, On the Shores
- Non-exhibition space

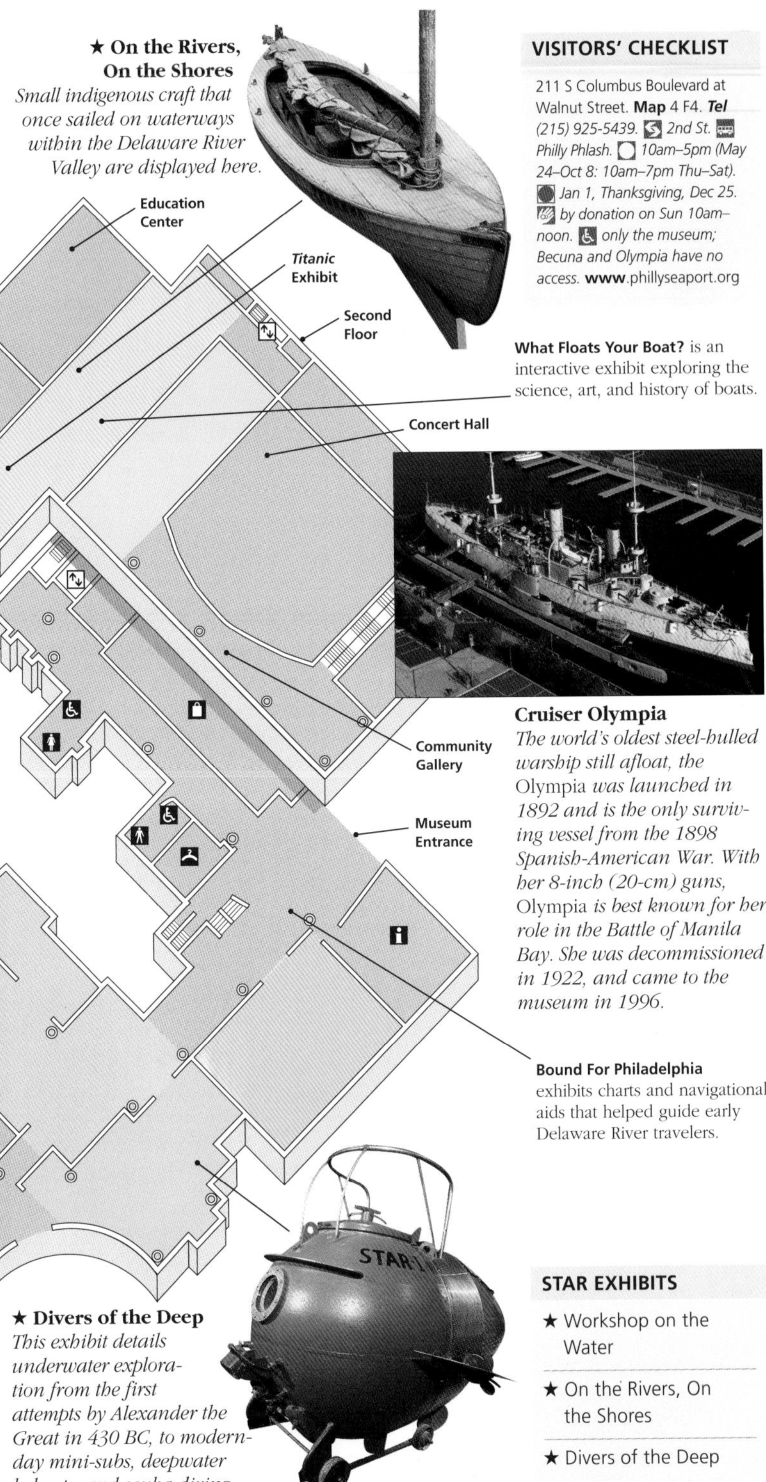

★ On the Rivers, On the Shores
Small indigenous craft that once sailed on waterways within the Delaware River Valley are displayed here.

What Floats Your Boat? is an interactive exhibit exploring the science, art, and history of boats.

Cruiser Olympia
The world's oldest steel-hulled warship still afloat, the Olympia *was launched in 1892 and is the only surviving vessel from the 1898 Spanish-American War. With her 8-inch (20-cm) guns,* Olympia *is best known for her role in the Battle of Manila Bay. She was decommissioned in 1922, and came to the museum in 1996.*

Bound For Philadelphia exhibits charts and navigational aids that helped guide early Delaware River travelers.

★ Divers of the Deep
This exhibit details underwater exploration from the first attempts by Alexander the Great in 430 BC, to modern-day mini-subs, deepwater helmets, and scuba diving.

VISITORS' CHECKLIST

211 S Columbus Boulevard at Walnut Street. **Map** 4 F4. ***Tel*** *(215) 925-5439.* *2nd St.* *Philly Phlash.* *10am–5pm (May 24–Oct 8: 10am–7pm Thu–Sat).* *Jan 1, Thanksgiving, Dec 25.* *by donation on Sun 10am–noon.* *only the museum; Becuna and Olympia have no access.* **www**.phillyseaport.org

STAR EXHIBITS

★ Workshop on the Water

★ On the Rivers, On the Shores

★ Divers of the Deep

Small boats at Penn's Landing marina with the Benjamin Franklin Bridge in the background

Penn's Landing ⓮

Western shore of the Delaware River between Market & South Sts. **Map** 4 F3. *Market East Station.* *2nd St.* *21, Philly Phlash.* **www.**delawareriverwaterfrontcorp.com

A popular waterfront on the Delaware River, Penn's Landing is where city founder William Penn first stepped onto his new colony in 1682 *(see p18)*. Development of the docks seen today began in 1967, before which it was an unappealing stretch of land. Among its attractions are grassy areas with trees, walkways, and an amphitheater where summer festivals and concerts are held.

The Race Street Pier is a park on the waterfront with unique architectural landscaping and spectacular waterfront views. Several vessels are anchored here, including the century-old sailing ship *Moshulu (see p148)*, the dinner cruise boat *Spirit of Philadelphia*, the 1883 three-masted barkentine *Gazela*, once a Portuguese fishing boat, and the paddle-boat charter *Liberty Belle*.

Nearby is the Independence Seaport Museum *(see pp64–5)* with its two historic vessels – the cruiser *Olympia* and the submarine *Becuna* – docked in a small harbor.

Along the Chestnut Street overpass is the impressive Irish Memorial, a bronze sculpture with 35 life-sized figures, which honors the more than one million people who died and the others who fled Ireland during the Great Hunger of the 1840s.

New Market and Head House Square ⓯

2nd St between Pine & Lombard Sts. **Map** 4 E4. *Market East Station.* *2nd St.* *42, Philly Phlash.*

One of the oldest in America, this covered marketplace was established in 1745. Called the "Shambles," meaning butcher shop, it was the second public marketplace in colonial Philadelphia – the first was located at the eastern end of High Street, now called Market Street. It was where vendors sold fresh produce, meat, poultry, and fish two days a week. The original New Market stretched two blocks from Pine Street to South Street and was flanked by two firehouses, known as head houses. The two firehouses once contained fire gear and apparatus for three volunteer fire companies.

Today, only the firehouse at 2nd and Pine Streets remains. Built in 1805, it is thought to be the country's oldest existing firehouse. New Market was restored in the 1960s, and has since housed the Crafts and Fine Arts Fair on summer weekends.

South Street and Walkway ⓰

South St. **Map** 4 E5. *Market East Station.* *2nd St.* *42, Philly Phlash.*

Known as Cedar Street in colonial times, and bordering on what was then New Market and Head House Square, South Street remains a marketplace of sorts today, but with an emphasis on pop culture and counterculture.

South Street, promising revelry and an exciting atmosphere

The South Street Head House District, which stretches from Front to 11th Streets and includes some surrounding streets, is an eclectic melting pot of more than 300 shops, galleries, cafés, restaurants, bars, and more. Eateries range from pizzerias and sushi bars to vegetarian cafés and fine-dining restaurants, while shops sell everything from jewelry and fine art to funk culture items and grunge-style clothing. There are also body piercing and tattoo parlors, jazz clubs, and rocking nightclubs. The strip often overflows with younger revelers on weekend nights that usually extend into the early hours of the morning. A walkway over I-95 (also called the Delaware Expressway) links Columbus Boulevard to South Street, offering fine views of Penn's Landing, and *Battleship New Jersey* across the Delaware River.

Exterior of Pennsylvania Hospital with a statue of William Penn

Pennsylvania Hospital ⓱

800 Spruce St. **Map** 3 C4. ***Tel*** *(215) 829-3370 (call to book a tour). Market East Station. 8th St. 42, Philly Phlash. book in advance.*
www.pennmedicine.org/pahosp

Founded by surgeon Thomas Bond and Benjamin Franklin in 1751 to care for the "sick-poor and insane," Pennsylvania Hospital was the nation's first public hospital. The old section, the Pine Building, was built in stages. The wings are

Pennsylvania Hospital's surgical amphitheater

Georgian, the east wing being completed in 1755, and the west in 1796. The Federal center section was built in 1804 and includes the Great Court, the area open for self-guided tours.

Inside the center section is artist Benjamin West's masterpiece, *Christ Healing the Sick in the Temple*, which was delivered to the hospital in 1817, along with portraits of colonial physicians, including Dr. Philip Syng Physick *(see p61)* and Benjamin Rush, well-known for his contributions to the field of psychiatry. In the Great Court are the hospital's early fire pumper, purchased in 1803, and the musical planetarium clock constructed by colonial clockmaker and astronomer, David Rittenhouse, in 1780.

On the second floor is a medical library founded in 1762 with a collection of more than 13,000 volumes, some dating back to the 15th century. The library, located in this room since 1807, houses the country's most complete collection of medical books published between 1750 and 1850. Under a skylight on the top floor is the nation's first surgical amphitheater, called the "dreaded circular room," which was used for operations from 1804 to 1868. Outside, an 18th-century statue of William Penn stands over a peaceful courtyard overflowing with wisteria shrubbery.

Mikveh Israel Cemetery ⓲

44 N 4th St. **Map** 3 C3. ***Tel*** *(215) 922-5446. Market East Station. 8th St. 42, Philly Phlash. 10am–5pm Tue–Sat, and by appt.*
www.mikvehisrael.org

This burial ground, the oldest Jewish cemetery in the city and one of the oldest in America, was founded in 1740 after shipper and merchant Nathan Levy sought a place to bury one of his children according to Jewish law. Governor Thomas Penn, son of William Penn, granted land here and deemed it a Jewish graveyard. Levy, whose ship brought the Liberty Bell to Philadelphia, is also buried here. Other notables include members of the prominent Gratz family, including philanthropist Rebecca Gratz, the inspiration for the eponymous character in Sir Walter Scott's novel *Ivanhoe*, fur trader Aaron Levy, founder of Aaronsburg, Pennsylvania, rabbis of the congregation, and financier Haym Salomon. His grave is unmarked, only noted by a memorial at the entrance. Jewish soldiers of the Revolutionary War, the War of 1812, and the Civil War are also buried here. The cemetery was walled in the late 18th century to protect it from people "setting marks and firing shots."

Marker at Mikveh Israel cemetery

CENTER CITY

This sprawling, modern downtown district is Philadelphia's financial and business center. The city's tallest skyscraper, Comcast Center, is situated west of City Hall, on 17th Street and JFK Boulevard. At the neighborhood's eastern end is Chinatown, flanking the Pennsylvania Convention Center and adjacent Reading Terminal Market, with Center City's major department store, Macy's, nearby. Along Broad Street, the central north-south artery, are 19th-century buildings that house the Masonic Temple and the Pennsylvania Academy of the Fine Arts in the north, while the theater district is located in the south. In Rittenhouse Square, some of the city's most lavish apartment buildings and hotels tower over town homes that line quiet streets.

Classical urn at Rittenhouse Square

SIGHTS AT A GLANCE

Historical Buildings and Districts
Chinatown 7
City Hall 4
Liberty Place 15
Library Company of Philadelphia 8
Masonic Temple 3
Reading Terminal Market 5
Rittenhouse Square 13

Places of Worship
Arch Street United Methodist Church 2
St. Mark's Episcopal Church 14

Museums and Galleries
College of Physicians of Philadelphia/Mütter Museum 16
Rosenbach Museum and Library 12

Cultural Venues
Academy of Music 9
Kimmel Center for the Performing Arts 10
Pennsylvania Academy of the Fine Arts pp74–5 1
Pennsylvania Convention Center 6
Suzanne Roberts Theatre 11

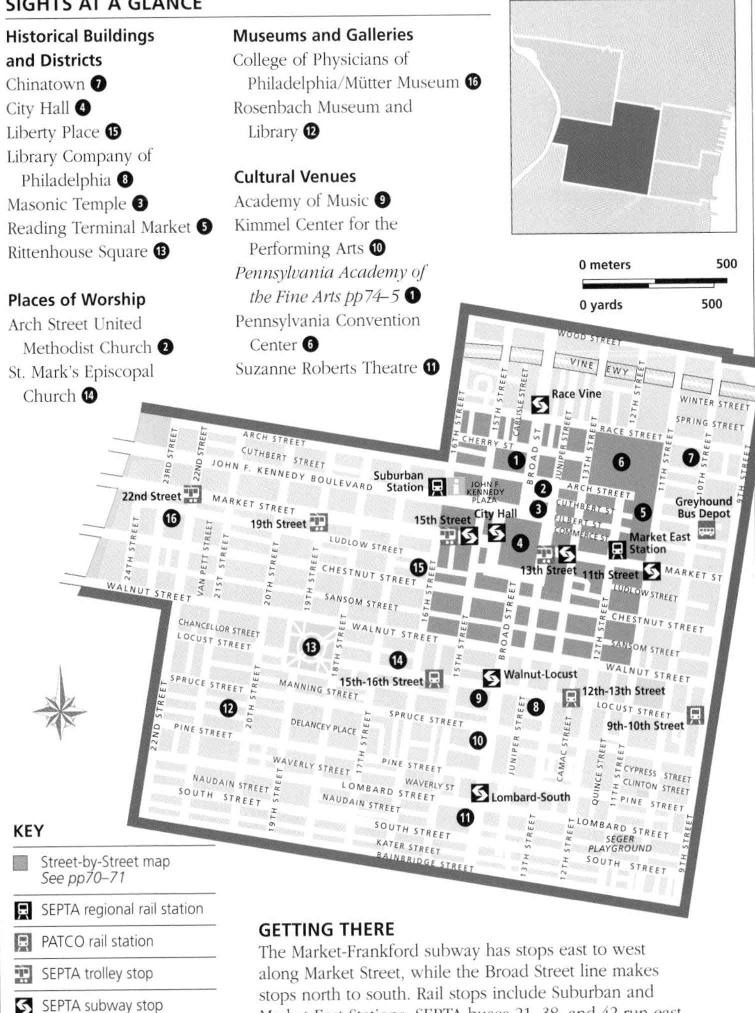

KEY

- Street-by-Street map *See pp70–71*
- SEPTA regional rail station
- PATCO rail station
- SEPTA trolley stop
- SEPTA subway stop
- Visitor information

GETTING THERE

The Market-Frankford subway has stops east to west along Market Street, while the Broad Street line makes stops north to south. Rail stops include Suburban and Market East Stations. SEPTA buses 21, 38, and 42 run east to west along Market, Chestnut, and Walnut Streets.

◁ **High-rise office buildings dominating the skyline in Center City, Philadelphia's business district**

Street-by-Street: Center City

City Hall sits in the heart of Center City, where Market Street and Broad Street – the city's main east-west and north-south arteries – converge. Most of this area, dominated by 19th- and 20th-century architecture, was developed well after the American Revolutionary War. Diagonally across from City Hall is JFK Plaza, where Philadelphia's famous LOVE statue stands next to a pool and fountain, providing respite from the area's heavy commercial activity. Just a block north of City Hall are the landmark Masonic Temple and the Pennsylvania Academy of the Fine Arts.

The Union League of Philadelphia on Broad Street, is a classic French Renaissance-styled building.

★ **City Hall**
A 37-ft (11-m) high statue of William Penn stands atop this Beaux-Arts building, one of the largest and most elaborate city halls in the country ❹

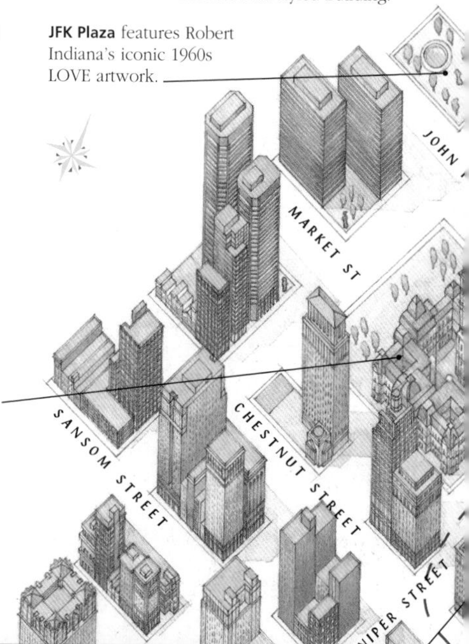

JFK Plaza features Robert Indiana's iconic 1960s LOVE artwork.

JOHN
MARKET ST
SANSOM STREET
CHESTNUT STREET
JUNIPER STREET
WALNUT STREET

0 meters 250
0 yards 250

KEY

– – – Suggested route

STAR SIGHTS

- ★ City Hall
- ★ Pennsylvania Academy of the Fine Arts
- ★ Reading Terminal Market

The Wanamaker Building is designed in Beaux-Arts style with a restrained Renaissance exterior. It is built around a soaring central atrium, which houses an enormous pipe organ. The building hosts an annual holiday light-and-sound show and is home to Macy's department store.

★ Pennsylvania Academy of the Fine Arts
America's oldest fine art museum was founded in 1805 by portrait artist Charles Willson Peale. Its collection spans three centuries 1

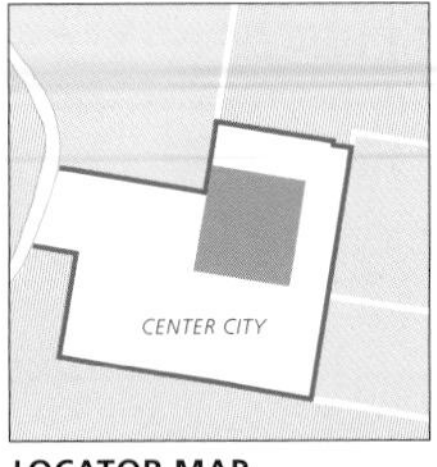

LOCATOR MAP
See Street Finder maps 1, 2, & 3

Arch Street United Methodist Church
This Gothic Revival church is the square's oldest structure 2

Pennsylvania Convention Center
Opened in 1993, the center has since undergone extensive expansion to increase the amount of space to a massive 1 million square feet (92,900 square meters) for exhibitions, trade shows, and conventions 6

Masonic Temple
Home to the Grand Lodge of Freemasons, the impressive interiors and architecture of this temple feature Spanish, Italian, and Egyptian influences. It is also revered for its ornate Romanesque Revival façade 3

★ Reading Terminal Market
Once the largest arched-roof train shed in the world, this is now one of the best farmers' markets in the country 5

Pennsylvania Academy of the Fine Arts ❶

See pp74–5.

Arch Street United Methodist Church ❷

55 N Broad St. **Map** 2 F4. ***Tel*** *(215) 568-6250.* *Suburban Station.* *15th St, City Hall.* *Philly Phlash.* *10am–3pm Mon–Fri.* *8:30am & 11am Sun.* **www**.archstreetumc.org

This Gothic Revival marble building, constructed in two sections between 1864 and 1870, is the oldest structure on William Penn's original Center Square. The church was founded in 1862 during the American Civil War and was still being built when the funeral procession of President Abraham Lincoln passed by it in 1865. It was designed by Quaker Addison Hutton, whose architectural plan called for a radical change from the unadorned and plain Quaker meetinghouses of the 18th and 19th centuries.

The original construction included the installation of a 2,322-pipe organ by J.C.B. Standbridge, Philadelphia's leading builder of organs. The organ has been restored twice, once in 1916 and again in 1959. The sanctuary's spacious

Philadelphia's Masonic Temple, an architectural masterpiece

atrium is detailed with a Victorian stenciling pattern and stained glass. Today, a diverse congregation from the Center City neighborhood worships at the church.

Masonic Temple ❸

1 N Broad St. **Map** 2 F4. ***Tel*** *(215) 988-1900.* *Suburban Station.* *15th St, City Hall.* *Philly Phlash.* *Jul–Aug: Sat; Mon, public hols.* *by donation.* *11am, 2pm, & 3pm Tue–Fri, 10am & 11am Sat (call to verify times).* **www**.pagrandlodge.org

An architectural jewel, dedicated as the Grand Lodge of Free and Accepted Masons of Pennsylvania in 1873, this remarkable building contains a number of ornate meeting halls in various styles. Among them, the Oriental Hall's (1896) ornamentation and coloring have been copied from the Alhambra in Granada, Spain; the Renaissance Hall (1908) follows an Italian Renaissance motif; while the Egyptian Hall (1889) takes its inspiration from the temples of Luxor, Karnak, and Philae. High arches, pinnacles, and spires form the Gothic Hall, and the cross-and-crown emblem of Sir Knights – "Under this sign you will conquer" – hangs over a replica of the Archbishop's throne in Canterbury Cathedral, England.

The halls were created to honor the building trades, and much of the stone and tilework are imperceptibly faux finished – an attestation to the skill of the men who made them. President George Washington, a Freemason, wore his Masonic apron when he laid the cornerstone of the US Capitol in Washington DC. The apron is on display, along with other Masonic rarities, in a museum on the first floor.

City Hall ❹

Broad & Market Sts. **Map** 2 F4. ***Tel*** *(215) 686-2840.* *Suburban Station.* *15th St, City Hall.* *38, Philly Phlash.* *building and tower:12:30pm Mon–Fri; tower: every 15 mins from 9:30am–4:30pm Mon–Fri.* **www**.phila.gov

Built on Penn's original Center Square, this imposing marble, granite, and limestone landmark is the largest and perhaps the nation's most ornate city hall. The building, which took 30 years to build and was completed only in 1901, is designed in French Second Empire style with a mansard roof and prominent 548-ft (167-m) high tower. City Hall was the nation's tallest occupied building until 1909. The tower, with four clocks and a 37-ft (11-m) tall statue of Penn, was the city's highest structure until 1987 *(see box)*.

Philadelphia artist Alexander Milne Calder designed the 60,000-lb (27-ton) statue, the largest atop any building in the world. Calder also designed

NO BUILDING HIGHER THAN WILLIAM PENN'S STATUE

While skyscrapers sprang up across America in the 20th century, Philadelphia maintained a "gentlemen's agreement" not to build higher than 491 ft (150 m) – lower than the statue of William Penn on top of City Hall. Honoring Penn and the city's colonial heritage, the rule remained unchallenged for almost a century. But lured by new revenues and jobs, the agreement was broken in 1987 when the 61-story One Liberty Place *(see p79)* was built. It towers over City Hall by more than 400 ft (122 m). Within just five years, several other skyscrapers followed, including Two Liberty Place, the Mellon Bank Center, the Bell Atlantic Tower, and, in 2008, the city's tallest skyscraper, the Comcast Center.

City Hall with Penn's statue

Ornamental, French-influenced City Hall in the midst of Center City

more than 250 other sculptures in the building, including the tower's bronze eagles, and the bronze figures of Native American and Swedish settlers.

Inside, rooms not to be missed include the Mayor's Reception Room, and Conversation Hall, which has statues of George Washington and other colonial notables. The Council Caucus Room, with its grand domed ceiling, features carvings representing the four seasons as stages in life. An elevator takes visitors to a deck on the tower that offers spectacular city views while on the ground level the visitor center stocks maps and brochures of the city's sights.

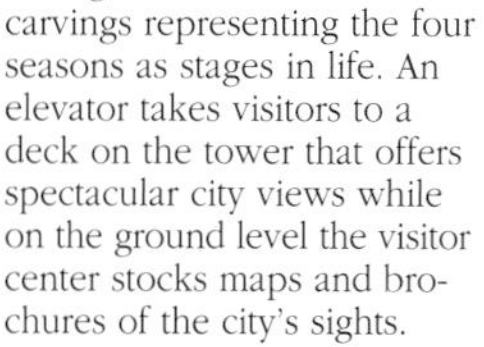
Jars of preserves at Reading Terminal Market

Reading Terminal Market ❺

12th & Arch Sts. **Map** 3 B2. ***Tel*** *(215) 922-2317.* *Market East Station.* *11th St.* *Philly Phlash.* *8am–6pm Mon–Sat.* *Jan 1, Easter, Jul 4, Memorial Day, Thanksgiving, Dec 25.* **www**.readingterminalmarket.org

Once a Center City railroad terminal and marketplace, Reading Terminal Market is now considered by many to be one of the finest farmers' markets in the United States. It was created in 1892, after two farmers' markets on this site were leveled to make space for a new train terminal. These markets were relocated beneath the new train shed. So modern was the market for its time that people came from as far off as the New Jersey shore to buy fresh Lancaster County produce. Over the years, the market gradually declined and was nearly destroyed in the 1970s. New construction routed the city's trains around the old terminal in the 1980s, and the market was refurbished in the early 1990s.

Today, the revitalized Reading Terminal Market houses more than 80 vendors, 6 days a week, selling an extensive variety of free-range meats and poultry, seafood, country vegetables, pastas, Amish specialties, and baked goods, as well as other items such as books, clothing, flowers, jewelry, crafts, unique spices, and hard-to-find specialties and ethnic foods. Several stands also offer freshly-made and prepared foods, ranging from Pennsylvania Dutch country breakfasts to soul food.

Pennsylvania Convention Center ❻

Between Market & Race Sts and 11th & 13th Sts. **Map** 2 F3. ***Tel*** *(215) 418-4700, (800) 428-9000.* *Market East Station.* *11th St, 13th Sts.* *38, Philly Phlash.* *for conventions; Head House entrance open 24 hrs.* **www**.paconvention.com

A sprawling 1 million sq ft (92,900 sq m) of meeting and exhibition space make up one of the country's most unique convention centers. The building's Grand Hall, above Reading Terminal Market, was once a bustling train terminal for the Reading Railroad. Reopened in 1994, the hall retains its Victorian features, including the majestic ceiling that had once made it the largest single-arch train shed in the world. Much of the original wooden roof and milk-glass windows remain, now casting natural light onto the terrazzo marble floor with simulated tracks where commuter trains once awaited passengers. Visitors can enter through the old railroad headhouse (now part of the Philadelphia Downtown Marriott) on the Market Street side for a peek at the Grand Hall, where a storyboard outlines its history. A second entrance on North Broad Street is part of a striking floor-to-ceiling glass façade.

Scattered throughout the multiblock complex is a collection of contemporary works of art by nearly 60 artists.

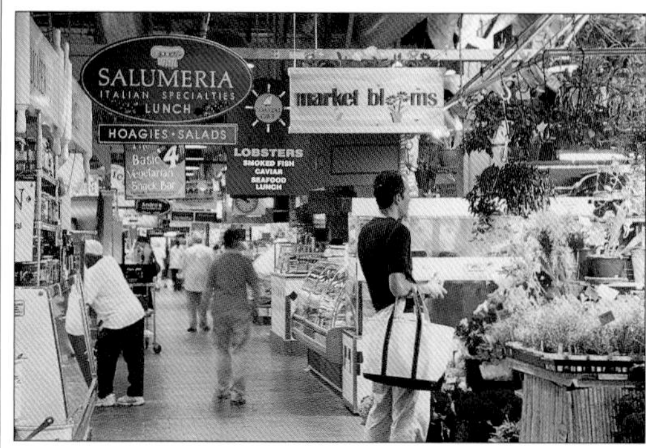

Colorful wares for sale at Reading Terminal Market

Pennsylvania Academy of the Fine Arts ❶

Founded by Colonial painter and scientist Charles Willson Peale and sculptor William Rush in 1805, the Pennsylvania Academy of the Fine Arts is America's oldest art museum and fine arts school. Its galleries display works by some of the world's best-known artists. One of them, the classical stylist Benjamin West (1738–1820), a Quaker from Pennsylvania, helped organize the British Royal Academy in 1768. Former student, the Impressionist Mary Cassatt (1844–1926), and modern abstractionist Richard Diebenkorn (1922–93), among others, share its wall space. The academy's main building, the distinctive National Historic Landmark Building, with its ornate arched foyer, is considered one of the finest examples of Victorian architecture in America. The contemporary Samuel M.V. Hamilton Building, with new galleries, opened in 2005 as part of the museum's 200th anniversary celebrations.

National Historic Landmark Building
Designed by Furness and Hewitt, the academy's main building opened during the nation's centennial in 1876.

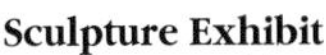

Sculpture Exhibit
The 1873 marble sculpture Semiramis, *by William Wetmore Story (1819–95).*

★ The Cello Player
One of America's greatest painters, Thomas Eakins (1844–1916) taught at the academy from 1876 to 1886. This penetrating study of a cello player, capturing a moment of intense concentration, was painted in 1896. Rudolph Hennig, a leading musician, posed for it.

National Historic Landmark Building Second Floor

★ The Fox Hunt
This 1893 masterpiece by naturalist painter Winslow Homer (1836–1910), considered one of the greatest American artists of the 19th century, is among the academy's vast collections.

Lenfest Plaza

STAR EXHIBITS

- ★ The Cello Player
- ★ The Fox Hunt
- ★ Pantocrator

★ Pantocrator

Vincent Desiderio's monumental 2002 oil-on-linen triptych, 8 ft (2.5 m) tall and 17 ft (5 m) wide, is part of the Academy's collection of contemporary American art.

Samuel M.V. Hamilton Building Second Floor

Upper Foyer Gallery

Samuel M.V. Hamilton Building First Floor

Entrance

Lower Foyer Gallery

VISITORS' CHECKLIST

118 N Broad St at Cherry St. **Map** 2 F3. ***Tel*** *(215) 972-7600.* *Suburban Station.* *City Hall.* *Philly Phlash.* *10am–5pm Tue–Sat, 11am–5pm Sun.* *Mon, public hols.* *Morris Gallery free.* *11:30am & 12:30pm Tue, Thu, Fri; 1 & 2pm Wed, Sat, Sun.* **www**.pafa.org

Samuel M.V. Hamilton Building

Adjacent to the National Historic Landmark Building, this contemporary structure doubles the academy's available display space, and includes a sculpture study center and a painting deck.

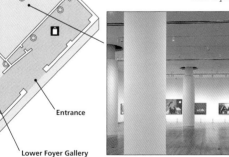

Fisher Brooks Gallery

This expansive new space on the first floor of the Samuel M.V. Hamilton Building houses the academy's post-World War II collection and also holds special exhibitions.

KEY

- Fisher Brooks Gallery
- Foyer Galleries
- 18th–20th century art
- Exhibit gallery
- Tuttleman Sculpture Gallery
- Non-exhibition space

GALLERY GUIDE

The grand staircase of the National Historic Landmark Building leads up to the gallery level on the second floor, which displays sculpture and 18th- to early 20th-century works, including portraiture, Impressionist, American genre, and landscape paintings. The Samuel M.V. Hamilton building houses contemporary artworks after 1945.

Ornamental gate at the entrance of Chinatown

Chinatown ❼

North of Arch St at 10th St. **Map** 3 C1. *Market East Station.* *11th St.* *Philly Phlash.*

This thriving neighborhood spans an area nearly four blocks wide and includes more than 50 restaurants, a score of grocery stores, and other shops and boutiques. Chinatown's origin dates to the 1860s when the first Chinese laundry was established in the area. It witnessed rapid growth after World War II owing to a huge influx of immigrants.

In the US's fourth largest Chinatown, behind those in New York, San Francisco, and Washington, D.C. visitors can still find a variety of Asian fare including traditional eel, squid, and duck dishes, and Chinese cultural gifts such as porcelain, wooden Buddhas, and dragons. The colorful Friendship Gate, with ornate dragons and Chinese art, is at 10th and Arch Streets and should not be missed.

Library Company of Philadelphia ❽

1314 Locust St. **Map** 2 F5. ***Tel*** *(215) 546-3181.* *Suburban Station.* *Walnut-Locust.* *21, 42.* *9am–4:45pm Mon–Fri.* **www**.librarycompany.org

Founded as the country's first lending library by Benjamin Franklin in 1731, the Library Company has the distinction of being America's oldest cultural institution. Its extraordinary collection of historic books, papers and images – numbering more than 500,000 books, 75,000 graphics, and 160,000 manuscripts – documents American culture from the colonial era through the 19th century.

The **Historical Society of Pennsylvania**, housed on the same block as Library Company, was founded in 1824 and is one of the oldest historical societies in the US. Its stockpile has 600,000 printed items, and more than 19 million manuscripts and graphic materials from the 17th century onwards.

Dragon figurine in a Chinatown shop

Historical Society of Pennsylvania
1300 Locust St. ***Tel*** *(215) 732-6200.* *12:30–5:30pm Tue & Thu, 12:30–8:30pm Wed; 10am–5:30pm Fri (last admittance at 4:45pm).* *public hols.* **www**.hsp.org

Academy of Music ❾

S Broad & Locust Sts (1420 Locust St). **Map** 2 E5. ***Tel*** *(215) 893-1935.* *Suburban Station.* *Walnut-Locust.* *21, 42, Philly Phlash.* *for performances.* *tickets sold one hour before a performance & until half-an-hour after the last performance begins; tickets also sold at the Kimmel Center 10am–6pm.* *by appt; call (215) 893-1935.* **www**.academyofmusic.org

Often referred to as the "Grand Old Lady of Locust Street," the Academy of Music was the city's foremost performing arts venue before the construction of the Kimmel Center in 2001. It remains the country's oldest grand opera house still in use.

Designed by Philadelphia architects Napoleon LeBrun and Gustavus Runge, the Victorian Italianate style structure took two years to build and was completed in 1857. The interior's horseshoe design offers greater visibility to the audience seated on both sides of the balconies, which are supported by Corinthian-style columns. While the façade has ornate gas lamps, the main hall still has a glittering, 5,000-lb (2,300-kg) crystal chandelier, originally with 240 gas burners, and later wired for electricity. Statues representing Poetry and Music crown the proscenium arch. The former home of the Philadelphia Orchestra – which now performs in the Kimmel Center – the academy today hosts the Pennsylvania Ballet and the Opera Company of Philadelphia *(see p164)*.

The Academy of Music, home to Philadelphia's opera and ballet

The Kimmel Center's glittering, modern façade

Kimmel Center for the Performing Arts ⑩

260 S Broad St. **Map** 2 E5. ***Tel*** *(215) 790-5800, (215) 893-1999 (tickets).* *Suburban Station.* *Walnut-Locust.* *21, 42, Philly Phlash.* *10am–6pm; later for performances.* **www**.kimmelcenter.org

The centerpiece of the city's performing arts district, this modern complex includes two venues in a spacious atrium under a barrel-vaulted glass roof. The center is named after philanthropist and businessman Sidney Kimmel, who made the single-largest private donation towards the complex.

The cello-shaped Verizon Hall, whose acoustics have been designed specifically for the Philadelphia Orchestra, seats more than 2,500 people. The Perelman Theater seats 650 people and has a rotating stage for chamber music, dance, and theatrical shows.

Other highlights include an expansive lobby with a stage for separate functions, an education center for performing arts classes, and a smaller studio and theater. The center's glass-enclosed roof garden offers great city views.

The center is the inspiration for the Philadelphia International Festival of the Arts that took place in spring in 2011 and 2013, featuring more than 100 performances across the city.

Suzanne Roberts Theatre ⑪

480 S Broad St. **Map** 3 A4. ***Tel*** *(215) 982-0420.* *Suburban Station.* *Lombard-South.* *21, 42.* **www**.philadelphiatheatrecompany.org

The Suzanne Roberts Theatre, is home to the Philadelphia Theatre Company. The theater is named after former actress, playwright, director, and philanthropist Suzanne Roberts, who, for more than 40 years, has devoted her energy and talent to the city's theater community. It is housed in a modern facility that boasts a dramatic glass façade, two-story lobby, mezzanine level reception areas, and a 365-seat auditorium with state-of-the-art lighting and sound facilities. A second, 100-seat flexible stage is used for more intimate performances.

Rosenbach Museum and Library ⑫

2008-2010 DeLancy Pl at 20th St. **Map** 2 D5. ***Tel*** *(215) 732-1600.* *Suburban Station.* *Lombard-South.* *21, 42.* *noon–5pm Tue & Fri, noon–8pm Wed & Thu, noon–6pm Sat & Sun.* *Mon, public hols.* **www**.rosenbach.org

Home to Dr. Rosenbach, one of America's most prominent rare book and manuscript dealers, this 1865 townhouse with a museum and research library sits on a quiet and shaded Rittenhouse street. Dr. Abraham Simon Wolf Rosenbach (1876–1952) and his brother Philip ran their company during the first half of the 20th century, combining great scholarship and business acumen. Apart from books, they also bought and sold 18th- and 19th-century artifacts such as silver, furniture, sculptures, drawings, and paintings.

So precious were many of their acquisitions that the brothers kept them for their own collection, which includes 30,000 books and 300,000 manuscripts and letters. Some of these are displayed today, including manuscript pages of James Joyce's *Ulysses*, over 100 personal letters of George Washington, and three of President Lincoln's speeches in manuscript form. In the house are the brothers' original possessions, including Chippendale furniture, gold-plated silver, and portraits by American artist Thomas Sully.

The museum's Maurice Sendak Gallery showcases the works and personal collections of the celebrated children's author, Maurice Sendak, best known for his 1963 classic *Where the Wild Things Are.*

Suzanne Roberts Theatre, Avenue of the Arts

Shaded walkway and benches at Rittenhouse Square, a favored outdoor park

Rittenhouse Square ⓭

Walnut St between 18th & 19th Sts. Map 2 D5. *Suburban Station.* *Walnut-Locust.* *21, 38, 42, Philly Phlash.*

One of Center City's most popular outdoor parks, on any sunny day shaded Rittenhouse Square teems with local residents and downtown workers relaxing under the trees. One of the five public areas planned by Penn in his 1682 city grid, it was originally known as Southwest Square. It was renamed in 1825 in honor of David Rittenhouse (1732–96), first director of the US Mint, astronomer, clockmaker, and a descendant of Wilhelm Rittenhouse, who established the nation's first papermill near Wissahickon Creek in 1690.

In the mid-19th century, the first house was built opposite the square, which soon became a prominent public garden. The park was given its present-day appearance in 1913 by French American Beaux-Arts architect Paul Cret, who also designed the Barnes Foundation's gallery building and the Valley Forge memorial arch. Benches line the many walkways that crisscross the park and lead to the small fountain and reflecting pool at its center. Flowers add color in spring and summer.

Since its development, the square has been a desirable address in town. Extravagant high-rise apartments and hotels, and upscale restaurants and cafés surround the square, reminiscent of a New York City park scene.

St. Mark's Episcopal Church ⓮

1625 Locust St. **Map** 2 E5. ***Tel*** *(215) 735-1416.* *Suburban Station.* *Walnut-Locust.* *21, 38, 42, Philly Phlash.* *daily.* *only by appointment.* **www.** saintmarksphiladelphia.org

Founded by a local group of Anglican worshippers in 1847, St. Mark's Episcopal Church is one of the nation's best examples of Gothic Revival architecture. The parishioners raised $30,000 and hired John Notman, a prominent Philadelphia architect, to design and build a new church in the medieval designs of the 14th- and 15th-century high Gothic period. The church was opened in 1849 during the early development of the Rittenhouse Square neighborhood.

Inside is a baptistry made of inlaid Italian marble and colorful panels in a spacious sanctuary that is reminiscent of an old English church.

Not to be missed is the adjoining structure, the spectacular Lady Chapel. It was donated by Rodman Wanamaker as a memorial to his wife, who died in 1900 and is buried in the chapel's crypt. The 12 panels in this chapel have ornate carvings depicting scenes from the life of St. Mary the Virgin. Its ornate and beautiful marble altar, encased in silver, was made by Carl Krall and is one of only three such in the world. Still used for mass, it is the most well-known of St. Mark's ecclesiastical treasures. In 1937, the organ, considered to be one of the best examples of tonal construction in the nation, was dedicated to the church.

Downtown Philadelphia's Gothic-style St. Mark's Episcopal Church

Liberty Place ⑮

16th & Chestnut Sts. **Map** 2 E4. ***Tel*** *(215) 851-9055. Suburban Station. Broad St. Philly Phlash. 9:30am–7pm Mon–Sat; noon–6pm Sun.* **www**.shopsatliberty.com

This gleaming, modern office complex, which sprawls over a vast area, is built on two city blocks and anchors what were once Philadelphia's tallest skyscrapers. Designed by Murphy and Jahn Associates and built by Rouse & Associates, the two steel towers with sapphire blue glass sheathing have a postmodern architectural aesthetic. Built in 1987 with pyramidal tops and spires reminiscent of New York's Chrysler Building, the 945-ft (288-m) One Liberty Place tower was the first structure to break the 86-year gentlemen's agreement not to build higher than the height of the hat on Penn's statue on top of City Hall *(see p72)*. The 61-story One Liberty Place stretches almost 100 ft (30 m) higher than its 58-story companion tower Two Liberty Place, which houses the national headquarters of the CIGNA Insurance Corporation, luxury condominiums, and R2L Restaurant, located on the 37th Floor, offering panoramic views of the city. The mall complex that connects the two towers houses 60 stores that cover the needs and fashion desires of Center City office workers, running the gamut from specialty food shops, chic boutiques, and trendy shoe shops to more practical outlets. A food court has several vendors.

One Liberty Place, with Two Liberty Place behind it

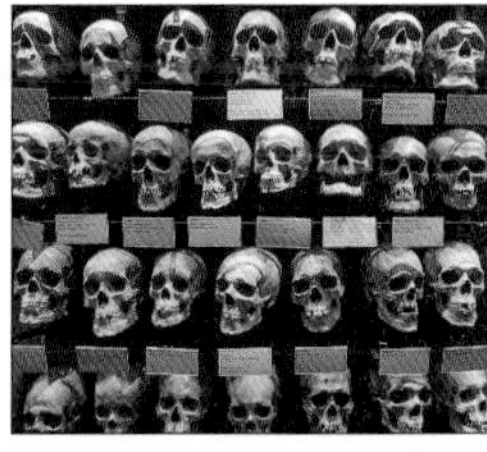

Joseph Hyrtl's collection of 139 skulls, Mütter Museum

College of Physicians of Philadelphia/Mütter Museum ⑯

19 S 22nd St. **Map** 1 C4. ***Tel*** *(215) 563-3737. Suburban Station. 15th St. 21, 38, 42. 10am– 5pm. Jan 1, Thanksgiving, Dec 25.* **www**.collphyphil.org

A non-profit society founded in 1787 "to advance the Science of Medicine," the College of Physicians provides health education to medical professionals and the public through the C. Everett Koop Community Health Information Center, the Historical Medical Library, the Free Library, and computerized databases.

For a visitor, the college's most fascinating resource is the Mütter Museum. Named after professor of surgery Thomas Mütter, who in 1858 donated 2,000 specimens he had used for teaching, the museum displays some curious and unusual items, including preserved specimens and wax anatomical and pathological models. These were used for educational purposes in the mid-1800s, when diseases and genetic defects were identifiable only by their physical manifestations.

Key exhibits include the skull collection of Joseph Hyrtl, a 19th-century Viennese anatomist, a plaster cast of the original Siamese twins, Chang and Eng, who died in 1874, and When the President is the Patient, one of the only major exhibitions in the US to focus on the long, hidden history of illness in the White House. Memorabilia from famous scientists and physicians is also on display.

LOGAN SQUARE AND PARKWAY MUSEUMS DISTRICT

Logan Square, with its multispouted Swann Memorial Fountain, is the centerpiece of Parkway Museums District, bordered by the Schuylkill River on the west and the Cathedral of Saints Peter and Paul on the east. Benjamin Franklin Parkway, often referred to as the Champs Elysées of Philadelphia, is the route for most parades held in the city. It runs through the heart of this area and is flanked by buildings with imposing architectural styles, reminiscent of the ancient temples of Greece and Rome. To the north is the Eastern State Penitentiary, a fortress-turned-museum that once housed some of the country's most notorious criminals.

Detail, Philadelphia Museum of Art façade

SIGHTS AT A GLANCE

Historical Buildings and Districts

Eakins Oval 9
Fairmount Water Works Interpretive Center 11
Free Library of Philadelphia 2
Logan Square 3
Thomas Eakins House 13

Museums and Galleries

Academy of Natural Sciences 5
The Barnes Foundation pp86–7 1
Eastern State Penitentiary 12
The Franklin Institute 7
Moore College of Art and Design 6
Philadelphia Museum of Art pp90–93 10
Rodin Museum 8

Places of Worship

Cathedral of Saints Peter and Paul 4

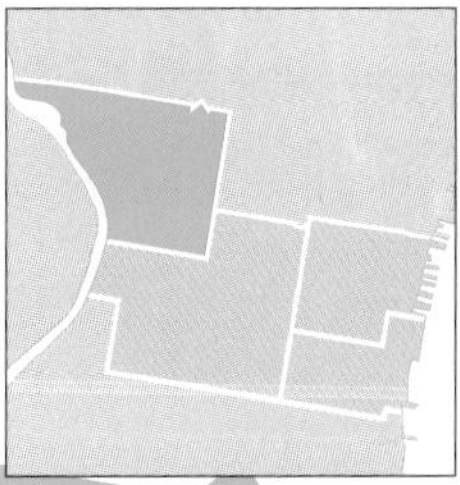

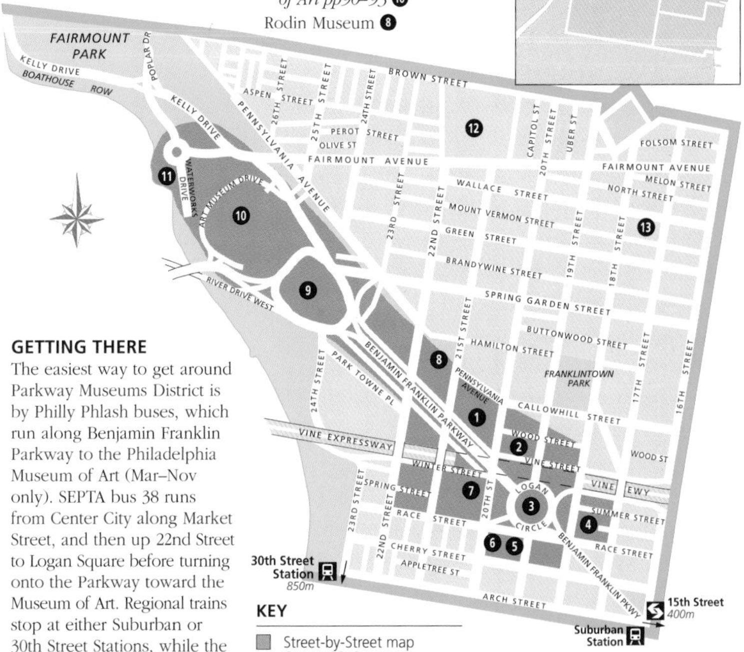

GETTING THERE

The easiest way to get around Parkway Museums District is by Philly Phlash buses, which run along Benjamin Franklin Parkway to the Philadelphia Museum of Art (Mar–Nov only). SEPTA bus 38 runs from Center City along Market Street, and then up 22nd Street to Logan Square before turning onto the Parkway toward the Museum of Art. Regional trains stop at either Suburban or 30th Street Stations, while the subway stops are at 15th and 30th Streets. Once at Logan Square, most of the sights are within walking distance.

KEY

Street-by-Street map *See pp82–3*

SEPTA regional rail station

SEPTA subway stop

0 meters 500

0 yards 500

◁ **The Swann Memorial Fountain located in the center of Logan Square**

Street-by-Street: Logan Square and Parkway Museums District

Central to this neighborhood is the Benjamin Franklin Parkway – a grand boulevard lined with trees and grassy areas stretching from Center City to the Philadelphia Museum of Art. Statues and sculptures around the museum add to the area's European flair. Imposing structures housing many of the city's other key museums were built along the Parkway and around Logan Square in the 19th and early 20th centuries. Today, they hold some of the world's most prized antiquities, artworks, and natural history collections. Among them are the Rodin Museum, The Franklin Institute, and the Barnes Foundation.

Fairmount Water Works Interpretive Center
Stately temple-like façades that once housed the nation's first municipal water-pumping station now serve as home to a diving, entertainment, and education center, as well as an excellent restaurant ⓫

Eakins Oval
Ornate fountains and statues are the centerpieces of this traffic circle named after the 19th-century Philadelphia artist Thomas Eakins ❾

★ The Franklin Institute
A massive statue of Benjamin Franklin sits in the atrium of this popular interactive science museum. The museum highlights Franklin's discoveries in technology and also houses a planetarium and IMAX theater ❼

WINTER

RACE

STAR SIGHTS

- ★ The Barnes Foundation
- ★ The Franklin Institute
- ★ Philadelphia Museum of Art
- ★ Rodin Museum

Academy of Natural Sciences
The oldest continuously operating natural history museum in the Western hemisphere has dinosaur fossils among its more than 17 million specimens ❺

Moore College Art and Design

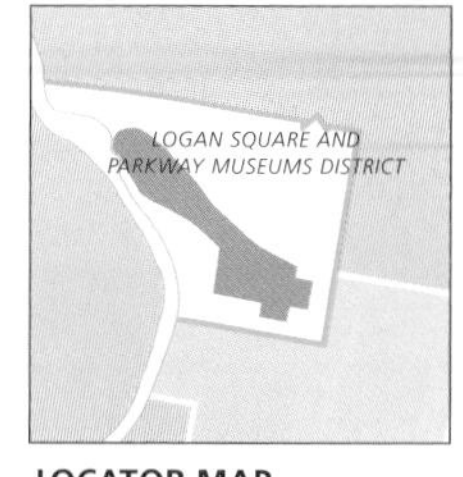

LOCATOR MAP
See Street Finder maps 1 & 2

★ Philadelphia Museum of Art
The country's third largest fine art museum, sited in a landmark building, has vast collections of paintings, sculptures, and decorative arts showcasing more than 2,000 years of human creativity ⑩

★ Rodin Museum
This small museum has more than 130 sculptures by Auguste Rodin, including The Thinker. *This is the largest collection of his works outside France* ⑧

★ The Barnes Foundation
The gallery is famed for Impressionist and Modernist works such as Roger de La Fresnaye's, Married Life *(1913). The collection is revered for its depth and quality.* ①

Logan Square
Originally called Northwest Square, Logan Square is now centered by the Swann Memorial Fountain and flanked by the Free Library of Philadelphia ③

STREET
FRANKLIN
STREET
21ST
PARKWAY
20TH STREET
19TH STREET
VINE STREET
18TH STREET

Cathedral of Saints Peter and Paul ④

KEY

Suggested route

0 meters 200
0 yards 200

The Barnes Foundation ❶

See pp86–7.

The Beaux-Arts façade of the Free Library of Philadelphia

Free Library of Philadelphia ❷

1901 Vine St. **Map** 2 E2. ***Tel*** *(215) 686-5322. Suburban Station. Race-Vine. 38, Philly Phlash. 9am–9pm Mon–Wed, 9am–4pm Thu–Fri, 9am–5pm Sat, 1–5pm Sun. Sun in summer, public hols. tour starts at Rare Book Dept at 11am.* **www**.freelibrary.org

Opened in 1894, this library first occupied rooms in City Hall. It relocated a few times before moving into its current Beaux-Arts building in 1927.

Today, the library has up to 1.75 million volumes, and its key collections include maps, children's books, social sciences and history books, and the largest public library chamber music collection in the eastern US. The Rare Book Department is also one of the nation's largest, with holdings that span 4,000 years and include Sumerian cuneiform tablets, medieval manuscripts, incunabula, early American children's books, and letters and manuscripts from authors such as Charles Dickens and Edgar Allen Poe *(see p96).*

Logan Square ❸

19th St at Benjamin Franklin Parkway. **Map** 2 D3. *Suburban Station. Race-Vine. 38, Philly Phlash.*

Part of William Penn's original grid plan, Logan Square (then known as Northwest Square) was initially used as a burial ground, then for pastureland, and later for public executions. It was renamed Logan Square in 1825 in honor of Penn's secretary James Logan. The square changed dramatically during the 1920s, when the construction of the Benjamin Franklin Parkway turned it into a traffic circle, which is why it is today also referred to as Logan Circle.

At its center is the Swann Memorial Fountain, designed by Alexander Stirling Calder in 1924. It features three statues, meant to represent the city's three main waterways – the Delaware and Schuylkill Rivers, and Wissahickon Creek. The Sister Cities Park is also located here. This public park has many activities for kids. There is also a milk and honey café that serves locally grown and produced food.

Window of the Cathedral of Saints Peter and Paul

Cathedral of Saints Peter and Paul ❹

18th St at Benjamin Franklin Parkway. **Map** 2 E3. ***Tel*** *(215) 561-1313. Suburban Station. Race-Vine. 38, Philly Phlash. 7am–4:30pm Mon–Sat. daily.*

This grand cathedral, with a copper dome more than 60 ft (18 m) high, is a prominent city landmark. Designed by architects John Notman and Napoleon LeBrun, the Victorian Italianate basilica with Renaissance features was modeled after the Lombard Church of St. Charles in Rome and completed in 1864. The sanctuary is shaped in the form of a cross with a white marble floor, a marble altar, and six marble columns rising more than 40 ft (12 m) along the curved walls of the apse. Stained-glass windows add a touch of beauty to the main altar area, side altars, and the eight side chapels. Of particular note is the organ, one of the largest in the city, with 75 pipes and four manuals. The cathedral is now the seat of Philadelphia's Roman Catholic Archdiocese.

Logan Square's Swann Memorial Fountain, named after the founder of the Philadelphia Fountain Society

Exhibit at Dinosaur Hall, Academy of Natural Sciences

Academy of Natural Sciences ❺

1900 Benjamin Franklin Parkway. **Map** 2 D3. ***Tel*** *(215) 299-1000.* *Suburban Station.* *Race-Vine.* *38, Philly Phlash.* *10am–4:30pm Mon–Fri, 10am–5pm Sat & Sun.* *Jan 1, Thanksgiving, Dec 25.* **www**.ansp.org

A natural history museum and research library, the Academy of Natural Sciences was founded in 1812 by seven naturalists, who pooled their fossils and specimens to foster education and research about the earth's diverse species. Its collection has since swelled to 17 million specimens. Exhibits are housed on four levels, and include mounted animals, ranging from birds native to Pennsylvania to bison from North America and cape buffalo from Africa. Dinosaur Hall is a favorite with children, while the live butterfly exhibit is a reproduction of a tropical rainforest. The animals in the Live Animal Center cannot survive in the wild and are thus used for teaching purposes.

Moore College of Art and Design ❻

20th St & Benjamin Franklin Parkway. **Map** 2 D3. ***Tel*** *(215) 965-4000.* *Suburban Station.* *Race-Vine.* *38, Philly Phlash.* *galleries: 10am–5pm Tue–Fri, noon–4pm Sat & Sun.* *Mon, public hols.* **www**.moore.edu

This school is the first and only women's art and design college in the United States, and one of only two in the world. It was founded as the Philadelphia School of Design for Women in 1848 by Sarah Worthington Peter (1800–77). Her aim was to educate women for careers that would lead to financial independence, and in accordance with that, the original curriculum provided training in the new fields spawned by the Industrial Revolution, such as textile design. Today, the college offers nine undergraduate degree programs in fine arts and design.

Two galleries of the college are open to the public. Rotating exhibitions highlight the works of alumnae and women artists. The Paley Gallery exhibits national and international artists, while the Levy Gallery showcases local artists and provides a center for exploration and experimentation for emerging and established talent. Past shows have featured work by Mary Cassatt, Karen Kilimnik, and Jacqueline Matisse.

Franklin's statue in the museum atrium

The Franklin Institute ❼

222 N 20th St at Benjamin Franklin Pkwy. **Map** 2 D3. ***Tel*** *(215) 448-1200.* *Suburban Station.* *Race-Vine.* *38, Philly Phlash.* *museum: 9:30am–5pm daily; IMAX theater: 10am–6pm daily (to 9pm Fri & Sat).* **www**.fi.edu

The oldest science and technology institution in continuous use in North America, this museum was founded in 1824. Named after Benjamin Franklin *(see p53)*, the institute's first location was in the building that now houses the Philadelphia History Museum at Atwater Kent *(see p50)*. The current building opened in the 1930s and contains a spacious rotunda with a 21-ft (6-m) tall marble statue of Franklin. Exhibits highlight Franklin's accomplishments in medicine, astronomy, meteorology, and optics. Among the museum's attractions are Electricity Hall, which showcases his discovery of electricity, the Giant Walk-Through Heart with interactive devices *(see p26)*, and the Train Factory, which has an original Baldwin steam locomotive.

The KidScience exhibit, for five to eight year olds, is designed to teach basic principles of science. Children are taken on a fictional journey across *The Island of the Elements* where they learn about Light, Water, Earth, and Air.

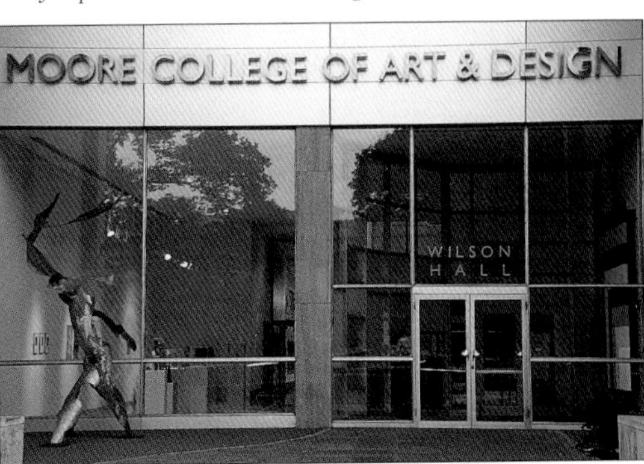

Moore College of Art and Design, housed in a modern building

The Barnes Foundation ❶

Floral motif, chest detail

Established in 1922 by pharmaceutical magnate Albert C. Barnes and originally located on his estate in the Philadelphia suburb of Merion, the Barnes Foundation has one of the world's best displays of Impressionist, French Modern, and Post-impressionist paintings. There are more than 800 works, including pieces by Renoir, Cezanne, and Matisse. It also has ancient Egyptian and Greek art, American furniture, and African sculpture. Now located on the Benjamin Franklin Parkway, the collection is grouped into 96 ensembles, displayed without labels and with little regard for chronology, so as to highlight artistic affinities between diverse works. The collection is in keeping with the foundation's aim of promoting "the advancement of education and the appreciation of the fine arts." The original Merion site is now home to the arboretum and archives.

★ The Postman
Painted by Vincent van Gogh in 1889 in Arles, France, this is a portrait of postman Joseph Roulin. The foundation is home to seven van Gogh paintings.

Group of Dancers
Over half of the Impressionist Edgar Degas's pieces depict dancers; this painting, completed c1900, is just one of the many fine examples of his work on view at the Barnes Foundation.

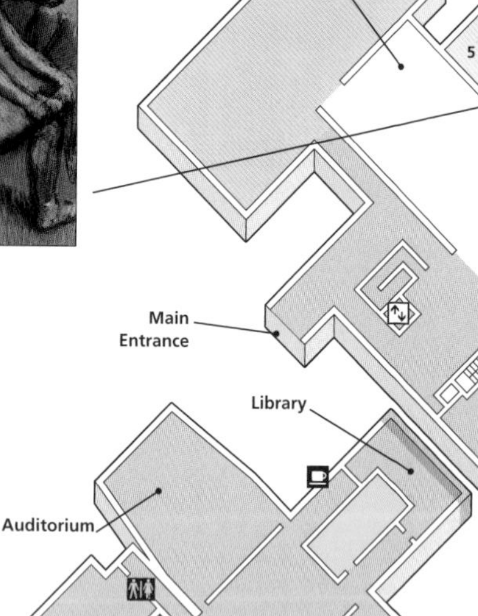

Gardanne
Paul Cezanne, the renowned French artist, painted this scenic landscape of the town of Gardanne in the mid-1880s. It is located in Room 1. Sixty-nine of Cezanne's works are at the Barnes, helping to make it one of the finest Impressionist collections in the world.

STAR EXHIBITS

- ★ The Postman
- ★ Leaving the Conservatory
- ★ Card Players and Girl

GALLERY GUIDE

Artworks can be viewed on both the first and second floors. Galleries in the foundation display various paintings and sculptures that highlight different themes. An artist's oeuvre is not necessarily displayed together.

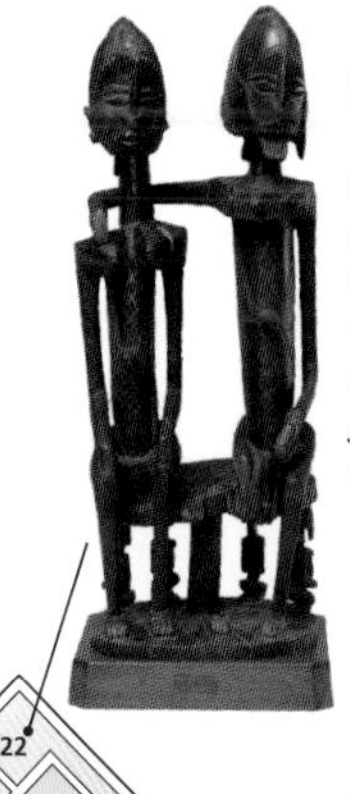

Dogone Couple
While many of his contemporaries viewed African art as "primitive" artifacts, Albert C. Barnes was an early and active collector of it. As a result, in addition to modern American and European art, the foundation holds a distinguished collection of African art.

VISITORS' CHECKLIST

2025 Benjamin Franklin Parkway. **Tel** *(215) 278-7000.* *Suburban Station.* *Spring Garden.* *38, Philly Phlash.* *9:30am–6pm Mon, Wed, Thu, Sat & Sun; 9:30am–10pm Fri.* *Tue, public hols.* **www**.barnesfoundation.org

22

Second Floor

23

19

18

14

17

16

15

Mezzanine

2

1

13

8

9

12

11

10

Terrace

First Floor

★ Leaving the Conservatory
The Barnes has over 180 works by Pierre-Auguste Renoir, including this one, which was completed by the famous French Impressionist in 1877. Renoir painted several thousand works over 60 years, even while suffering from severe arthritis toward the end of his life.

★ Card Players and Girl
Often referred to as the father of modern art, Paul Cezanne completed this painting in 1892. Cezanne's compositions and use of color greatly influenced 20th-century art.

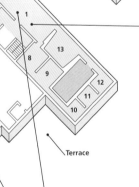

Models
(1886-1888)
Georges Seurat was a pioneer of Pointilism, an Impressionist technique in which paintings are made from colored dots, as this piece shows.

KEY

- Joy of Life gallery
- Permanent exhibition
- Temporary exhibition
- Non-exhibition space
- Interior garden

Rodin's sculpture, *The Thinker*, outside the Rodin Museum

Rodin Museum 8

22nd St at Benjamin Franklin Parkway. **Map** 2 D2. ***Tel*** *(215) 763-8100.* *Suburban Station.* *Spring Garden.* *38, Philly Phlash.* *10am–5pm Wed–Mon.* *Tue, public hols.* **www**.rodinmuseum.org

French sculptor Auguste Rodin's (1840–1917) most famous artwork, *The Thinker*, sits outside the columned façade that leads into the courtyard of this small, temple-like museum. With nearly 130 sculptures, it contains the largest collection of Rodin's work outside of Paris.

Opened in 1929, the Rodin Museum's entrance showcases the impressive, 20-ft (6-m) high *The Gates of Hell*, which Rodin worked on for 37 years until his death. Outside, in the garden to the east of the building, is the lifesized sculpture of six heroes of the Middle Ages, known as *The Burghers of Calais*. Other notable works include *Apotheosis of Victor Hugo* and sculptures of kissing lovers, known as *Eternal Springtime*.

Eakins Oval 9

Benjamin Franklin Parkway. **Map** 1 C1. *30th St Station.* *Spring Garden.* *38, Philly Phlash.*

Named after prominent Philadelphia artist Thomas Eakins, this oval was part of the Benjamin Franklin Parkway project in the 1920s. Located opposite the entrance to the Philadelphia Museum of Art, Eakins Oval has a prominent equestrian statue of President George Washington at its center. The center also features a fountain, which has figurines of wild animals surrounding four statues that symbolize four of the country's major rivers – the Delaware, Mississippi, Hudson, and Potomac. Two smaller fountains flank the large central one – the Ericsson fountain, named for the engineer who designed the USS *Monitor*, a Union naval vessel of the Civil War, and another named after Fairmount Park Commission chairman Eli Kirk Price (1797–1884) who led efforts to build the parkway. Today, the oval is at the center of a traffic circle and includes a shaded green area with park benches and a parking lot.

Washington's statue at Eakins Oval

Philadelphia Museum of Art 10

See pp90–93.

Fairmount Water Works Interpretive Center 11

640 Waterworks Dr. **Map** 1 B1. ***Tel*** *(215) 685-0723.* *30th St Station.* *Spring Garden.* *38, Philly Phlash.* *10am–5pm Tue–Sat, 1–5pm Sun.* *Mon, public hols.* **www**.fairmountwaterworks.org

Situated on the elevated banks of the Schuylkill River, these impressive Greek Revival buildings were constructed between 1812 and 1871 to supply drinking water to Philadelphia – the first American city to take on providing water as a municipal responsibility. When it opened in 1822, its huge water wheels, turbines, and pumps and the beauty of the site made it a destination for engineers and visitors from the US and Europe.

Water pumping ended in 1909, and today the restored buildings house old pumping apparatuses and an interpretive center with a number of fascinating interactive exhibits. All the exhibits here are based on the theme "Water Is Our World" and challenge children and adults alike to learn about water resources. Other exhibits include a real-time fish migration up the river, a virtual helicopter tour of the watershed, and a computer simulation of historic technology. The on-site restaurant offers beautiful city views.

Fairmount Water Works Interpretive Center, now a National Historic Landmark

Reconstruction of Al Capone's cell at the Eastern State Penitentiary

Eastern State Penitentiary ⓬

22nd St at Fairmount Ave. **Map** 2 D1. ***Tel*** *(215) 236-5111.* *Spring Garden.* *38, Philly Phlash.* *10am–5pm daily.* *children under 7 not allowed.* **www**.easternstate.org

Named the "House" by inmates and guards, the Eastern State Penitentiary was a revolutionary concept in criminal justice. Prior to its opening, convicts lived in despicable conditions and suffered brutal physical punishments. The Philadelphia Quakers proposed an alternative in the form of a facility where a lawbreaker could be alone to ponder and seek penitence for his misdeeds. This led to the opening of the penitentiary in 1829. During incarceration, with sentences seldom less than five years, prisoners were hooded when outside their cells to prevent interaction with others.

The prison, with its fortress-like Gothic Revival façade, had a single entrance and 30-ft (9-m) high boundary walls. Inside, seven cellblocks extended from a central rotunda, and each solitary cell had a skylight and private outdoor exercise yard. In the early 20th century, the isolation form of imprisonment was abandoned, and more cellblocks were added. Over the years, the prison has housed several infamous personalities including the gangster Al Capone.

Officially closed in 1971, it is now a National Historic Landmark and museum. Today, the structure's chipped walls and aging cellblocks host changing exhibitions from its collections of old artifacts and photographs. The prison also conducts tours, with audio excerpts from former guards and inmates, and each Halloween it hosts *Terror Behind the Walls*, a "haunted" house experience *(see p34).*

Thomas Eakins House ⓭

1729 Mt Vernon St. **Map** 2 E1. ***Tel*** *(215) 685-0750.* *Spring Garden.* *38, Philly Phlash.* *hours vary.*

This brick row house was home to the artist Thomas Eakins for most of his life, with the exception of the time he spent abroad: first in Paris studying art at the École des Beaux-Arts from 1866 to 1868, and then traveling to Spain in 1869 before returning home in 1870. One of the country's most renowned Realist painters of the late 19th and early 20th centuries, Eakins' works often reflected life in Philadelphia through portraits and family paintings, as well as through his popular city and nature paintings, which included sculling and sailing scenes on the Schuylkill and Delaware Rivers.

Today, the Thomas Eakins House is home to the city's Mural Arts Program. Changing exhibitions in the building's galleries highlight artwork created by Philadelphia's youth participating in the Mural Arts and other outreach programs.

Façade of Thomas Eakins House, home to the Mural Arts Program

MURAL ARTS PROGRAM

Philadelphia has America's largest collection of colorful, outdoor and indoor murals, which are emblazoned on walls all across the city. Through artists' visions and the sheer manpower of inspired local youth, more than 3,000 variegated and vibrant murals have been painted since the Mural Art Program's inception in 1984 as an anti-graffiti initiative. With extensive preparation including scaffolding and undercoating, a typical mural is completed within two months and can cost as much as $20,000. The murals often highlight famous community leaders, role models, artistic cityscapes, and themes of culture, history, diversity, and anti-drug messages.

Murals on city walls, a tradition in the city of Philadelphia

Philadelphia Museum of Art ⑩

Beaux-Arts roof detail

Founded in the country's centennial year of 1876, Philadelphia's most prominent museum attracts major exhibitions to supplement its superlative permanent collections. More than 200 galleries showcase works of art spanning more than 2,000 years, with some Asian exhibits dating from the third millennium BC. The medieval cloister courtyard and fountain on the second floor is very popular, as are the French Gothic chapel and the pillared temple from Madurai, India. In addition to outstanding collections of Old Master, Impressionist, and Postimpressionist paintings, Pennsylvania Dutch and American decorative arts are also featured with American art. Scattered throughout the museum are computerized stations with information on the exhibits.

Mask of Shiva
A 9th-century copper alloy artifact from India.

★ Sunflowers
Impressionist painter Vincent van Gogh (1853–90) is perhaps best known for his series of sunflower paintings. This version was painted just 18 months before his death.

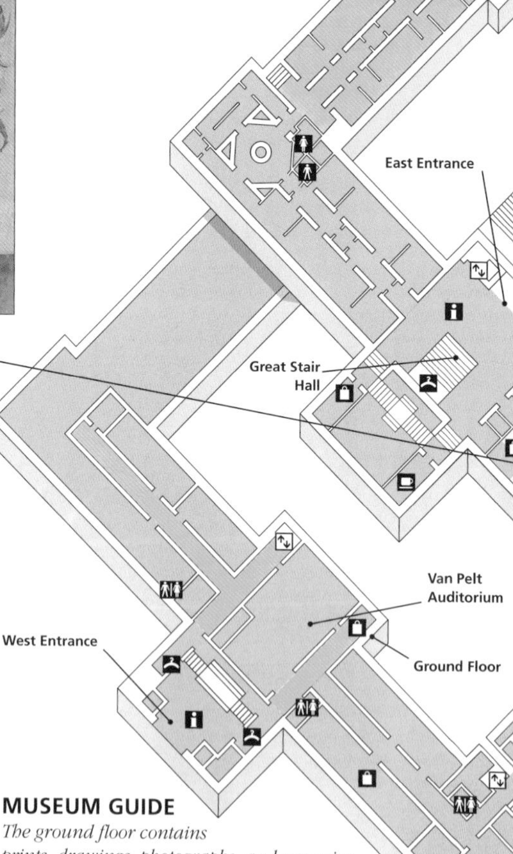

KEY

- Modern and Contemporary Art Galleries 48–50, 166–188
- European Art 1100–1500 Galleries 200-219
- European Art 1500–1850 Galleries 250-299
- European Art 1850–1900 Galleries 150–164
- Special Exhibition Galleries
- American Art Galleries 110–119, 285–287, 289
- Arms and Armor Galleries 245–249
- Asian Art Galleries 220–244
- Non-exhibition space

MUSEUM GUIDE
The ground floor contains prints, drawings, photographs, and ceramics, while the first floor displays Impressionist, Post-impressionist, American, and contemporary art. The second floor has collections of European and Asian art. First Floor refers to the floor above ground level.

The West Entrance of the Philadelphia Museum of Art

VISITORS' CHECKLIST

26th St & Benjamin Franklin Parkway. **Map** 1 C1. ***Tel*** *(215) 763-8100.* *30th St Station.* *Philly Phlash.* *10am–5pm Tue–Sun; 10am–8:45pm Fri.* *Mon, public hols.* *pay what you wish on Sundays.* **www**.philamuseum.org

★ East Asian Art

Delicate ceramics, figurines and other objects of the Tang Dynasty (618–907) are on display here, including this gilded bronze statue of the Seated Bodhisattva.

Second Floor

First Floor

Cloister with Elements from the Abbey of Saint-Genis-des-Fontaines

Surrounded by marble arcaded walkways and centered by a rare fountain, this cloister is based on medieval French design.

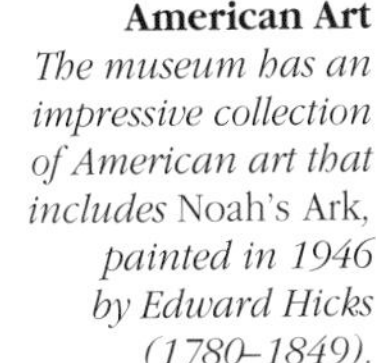

American Art

The museum has an impressive collection of American art that includes Noah's Ark, *painted in 1946 by Edward Hicks (1780–1849).*

★ Thomas Eakins Collection

Several pieces from acclaimed Philadelphia artist Thomas Eakins, such as Portrait of Dr. Samuel D. Gross (The Gross Clinic) *(1875) are on display in the American Art gallery.*

STAR EXHIBITS

- ★ Sunflowers
- ★ East Asian Art
- ★ Thomas Eakins Collection

Exploring the Philadelphia Museum of Art

Stained glass roundel, France (1246–48)

The Museum of Art is home to over 300,000 objects from Europe, Asia, and the Americas, spanning more than 4,000 years. Its key exhibits include European paintings, from medieval and Renaissance to Impressionist and Postimpressionist pieces. Modern art collections feature works by Pablo Picasso and Henri Matisse, while Asian art includes furniture and ceramics. American art sections contain extensive works by Philadelphia artists Thomas Eakins and Charles Willson Peale, and the museum's collections of prints, drawings, and photographs feature works by 19th- and 20th-century US and European artists. It also has one of the oldest and largest collections of costumes and textiles in America.

Fra Angelico's *Dormition of the Virgin* (c. 1427)

EUROPEAN PAINTINGS, SCULPTURE, DECORATIVE ARTS, AND ARCHITECTURE

Most of the museum's second floor is devoted to European art from 1500 to 1850. In addition, it has rooms with sculpture, furniture, descriptive interiors, and original façades that highlight periods of European history from 1100 to 1800. The Portal from the Abbey Church of Saint-Laurent dates to 1125. Its imposing stone arched walls were once the main entrance to the Augustinian abbey church of Saint-Laurent in France.

The Cloister with Elements from the Abbey of Saint-Genis-des-Fontaines is based on one in a late 13th-century abbey in Roussillon in southwestern France.

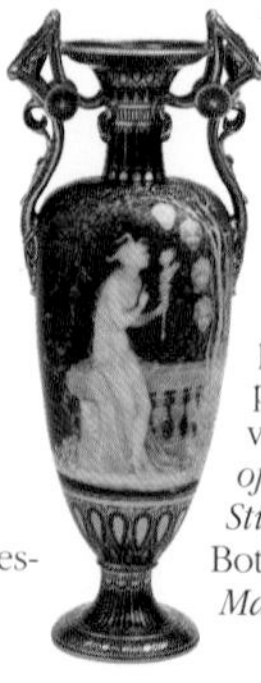

Jester Vase (1894) by Marc-Louis-Emmanuel Solon

Other decorative arts include ceramic vases, stained and painted glass, stone sculptures, and metal and wooden objects ranging from candelabra to mahogany furniture and glass goblets. Key European paintings include masterpieces by Fra Angelico, Sandro Botticelli, Rogier van der Weyden, Peter Paul Rubens, and Nicolas Poussin, as well as classic European views and land- and cityscapes from 18th-century verdute artists Canaletto, his nephew and pupil Bernardo Bellotto, and Francesco Guardi. Renaissance portraits and religious paintings include Jan van Eyck's *Saint Francis of Assisi Receiving the Stigmata* (1428–30), Botticelli's *Saint Mary Magdalene Listening to Christ Preach* (c.1484–91) and Edouard Manet's *Basket of Fruit* (c. 1864). Ruben's *Prometheus Bound* (1618) is a centerpiece painting combining historical and mythological subjects.

The first floor has some excellent Impressionist and Postimpressionist paintings by artists such as Renoir, Monet, Cezanne, Pissarro, and van Gogh. Works include Renoir's *The Large Bathers* (1884–87), van Gogh's *Sunflowers* (1889), Cezanne's *Group of Bathers* (1895), and Monet's *Poplars* (1891), to name just a few.

AMERICAN ART

One of the finest public holdings of American art, this collection is sourced from the Philadelphia area. Decorative arts, paintings, and sculptures include 18th- and 19th-century silver, ceramics, and porcelain, as well as Pennsylvania German items including toys, textiles, furniture, and illuminated folk art called fraktur. Bookcases, desks, chairs, and chests made in colonial Philadelphia, along with other decorative arts, demonstrate the cultural links between European and

The Staircase Group (1795) by Charles Willson Peale

Japanese ceremonial teahouse, surrounded by a bamboo garden

early American lifestyles and designs. Key paintings include Charles Willson Peale's *Rachel Weeping* (1772) and *The Staircase Group* (1795), in which he painted his sons ascending a staircase. Thomas Eakins' works, including *The Gross Clinic* (1875), are the most significant part of the museum's collection of 19th-century paintings. However, *The Gross Clinic* rotates ownership with the Pennsylvania Academy of Fine Arts. Sculptures by the renowned artist are also housed here. Other paintings include Sanford Gifford's *A Coming Storm* (1863) and Edward Hick's *Noah's Ark* (1846).

Bird Tree, Pennsylvania (1800–1830)

MIDDLE EAST AND ASIAN ART

Within the second-floor galleries of Asian Art are exquisite carpets, delicate jade carvings, porcelains, ink paintings, and sculptures forming part of the museum's collections of Southeast Asian, Korean, Chinese, Japanese, Persian, and Turkish art.

The Chinese Ming Dynasty (1368–1644) is represented by a room brought from China, the imposing Reception Hall from a Nobleman's Palace, and paintings and hardwood furniture. Works by Japanese artists from the 12th to 20th centuries include exquisitely painted scrolls and screens, decorative arts, and fine modern designs. A centerpiece exhibit is *Evanescent Joys*, a ceremonial teahouse acquired from Japan in 1928. Korean art includes ceramics, lacquer, and sculpture, of which an example is a rare 15th-century cast-iron tiger. Also on display are outstanding Persian and Turkish carpets, including the showpiece 16th- to 17th-century *Tree Carpet*. The carpets were gifted by collectors Joseph L. Williams and John D. McIlhenny in the 1940s and 50s. The museum's Indian art collection includes *Nandi, the Sacred Bull of Shiva*, a 13th-century schist carving from Mysore, and the impressive Pillared Hall from Madurai. Reconstructed from the ruins of three temples, its granite pillars are the only examples of stone architecture from India in an American museum.

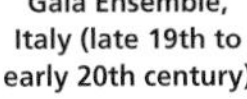

Gala Ensemble, Italy (late 19th to early 20th century)

MODERN AND CONTEMPORARY ART

The museum's modern art collection began with acquisitions of works by Pablo Picasso and Constantin Brancusi in the 1930s.

Today key holdings include Picasso's *Self-Portrait with Palette* (1906) and *Three Musicians* (1921), encompassing his decade-long study of Synthetic Cubism. Works by Marcel Duchamp include the *The Large Glass* (1915–23), applied on two planes of glass with lead foil, fuse wire and dust, and the 1912 *Nude Descending a Staircase (No. 2)*, a mechanical portrayal of a subject with Cubist qualities.

The museum's growing contemporary collection includes works by artists such as Cy Twombly, Jasper Johns, and Sol LeWitt.

COSTUMES AND TEXTILES

Acquisitions from the 1876 Centennial Exposition initiated the museum's costume and textile collections. The first textiles showcased designs and techniques used in India, Europe, and the Middle East. The collections grew in the early 20th century with the addition of 18th- and 19th-century French textiles, and today number over 20,000 objects, including fashionable Philadelphia apparel, Pennsylvania Dutch quilts, weaving pattern books, and colonial-era clothing. One of the most famous costumes is the wedding dress worn by Princess Grace of Monaco, a Philadelphian. Other items include African-American quilts, 20th-century hats, 19th-century needlework, church embroideries and vestments, and three-century old Japanese Noh robes, dating from between 1615 and 1867.

FARTHER AFIELD

The growth of neighborhoods away from the historic center of Philadelphia only began in the 19th century, with the exception of areas such as Germantown and Fairmount Park, which were distinct areas even as far back as colonial times. These are home to some of the city's most renowned sights, including the University of Pennsylvania just beyond the Schuylkill River. Fairmount Park runs along the river, leading to the chic neighborhoods of Manayunk and Chestnut Hill. Sights to the south include the Italian Market and the Mummers Museum, while to the east, just across the Delaware River in the bordering state of New Jersey, are the varied attractions of the Camden Waterfront.

Statue at Fairmount Park

SIGHTS AT A GLANCE

Historical Buildings and Districts

Boathouse Row and Kelly Drive 6
Camden Waterfront 14
Chestnut Hill 3
Edgar Allen Poe National Historic Site 1
Fort Mifflen 13
Germantown 2
Italian Market 10
Main Street Manayunk 4
University of Pennsylvania and University City 8
Walt Whitman House 15

Parks, Gardens, and Zoos

Fairmount Park 5
Philadelphia Zoo 7

Museums and Galleries

Mario Lanza Institute and Museum 11
Mummers Museum 12
University of Pennsylvania Museum of Archaeology and Anthropology 9

KEY

- Main sightseeing area
- Urban area
- Airport
- Highway
- Major road
- Minor road
- Railway
- State border

0 kilometers 4

0 miles 4

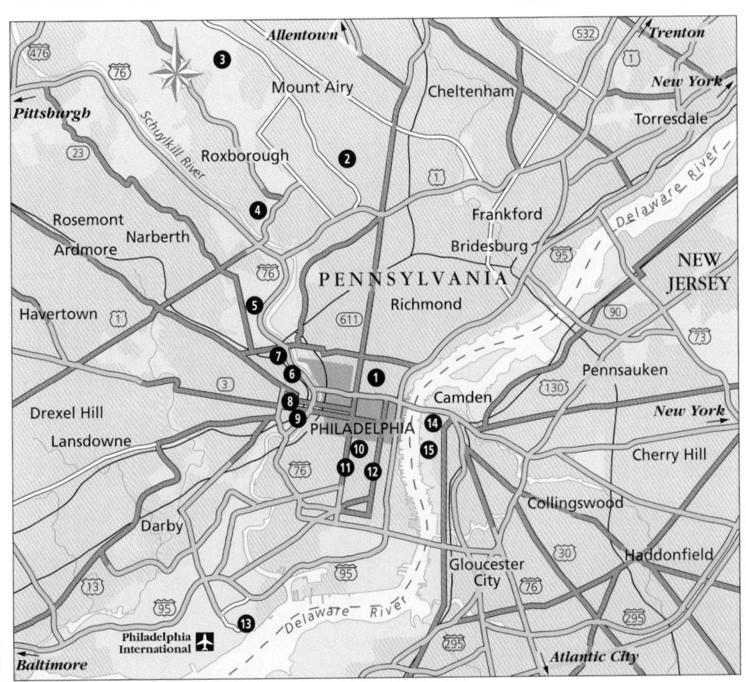

◁ Turrets punctuate the roofline of Rosemont College, near Philadelphia

Three-story brick house rented by Edgar Allan Poe in the mid-1840s

Edgar Allan Poe National Historic Site ❶

532 N 7th St. ***Tel*** *(215) 597-8780.* *Spring Garden.* *47.* *9am–5pm Wed–Sun.* *Mon, Tue; Jan 1, Veterans Day, Thanksgiving, Dec 25.* *limited.* **www**.nps.gov/edal

The great American writer Edgar Allan Poe (1809–49) lived in Philadelphia for six years from 1838 to 1844 in several residences. This three-story brick house was his rented residence for about a year between 1843 and 1844, and his only home that remains today in the city.

The inside, with original walls and creaking wooden floors, is empty as there are no accurate descriptions of what the house looked like during Poe's time, and none of his personal belongings have survived. The visitor area, though, has exhibits and a video highlighting his life and a room decorated as depicted in his essay "The Philosophy of Furniture."

In fact, Poe's years in the city were some of his most productive with the publishing of "The Murders in the Rue Morgue," "The Gold Bug," and "The Tell-Tale Heart." Poe fans seem to think that the house's basement may have inspired him to write "The Black Cat." One wall has brick columns similar to where, in the story, the murderer had entombed his victim. The raven statue outside is a tribute to one of his poems, "The Raven."

Germantown ❷

Centered by Germantown Avenue at Chelten Ave. *Chestnut Hill West SEPTA regional rail to Chelten Ave station.* *23.*

A few miles northwest of Philadelphia, this neighborhood was first inhabited in 1683 by German settlers wooed by Penn's promise of religious freedom. Its most prominent historical period was during and after the American Revolutionary War. It was the site of the Battle of Germantown in 1777, when British troops withstood an attack by the Continental Army, forcing the Americans to retreat to Valley Forge for the winter *(see pp20–21)*. In 1793, President Washington and his family moved here to escape the yellow fever epidemic in the city. Several historic homes in this now urban neighborhood have been preserved and are open to visitors *(see pp106–107)*.

At its center is Market Square, a busy marketplace in colonial times and now a small park dominated by a Civil War memorial. Flanking the square are the Deshler-Morris House, and the **Germantown Historical Society Museum and Library**. The center's museum features rotating exhibitions chosen from among its 20,000 historical artifacts and documents, some of which date back to the 1600s. To its north is the **Awbury Arboretum**, a landscaped area with gardens, ponds, and a Victorian estate originally owned by a Quaker family. This neighborhood is safer to visit during the day.

Germantown Historical Society Museum and Library
5501 Germantown Ave. ***Tel*** *(215) 844-1683.* *9am–1pm Tue, 1–5pm Thu; call for Sun hours.*

Awbury Arboretum
1, Awbury Rd. ***Tel*** *(215) 849-2855.* *dawn–dusk.* *limited access.*

Chestnut Hill ❸

Centered by Germantown Ave at Chestnut Hill Ave. *Chestnut Hill East or Chestnut Hill West SEPTA regional rail to Chestnut Hill stations.*

What began as a settlement of farmhouses and taverns in the mid-1700s is now one of Philadelphia's most upscale neighborhoods. Located on the city's northern border, Chestnut Hill is an urban village bisected by Germantown Avenue. Its shaded, cobblestoned streets

Boutiques and cafés line the sidewalks of Chestnut Hill

are lined with boutiques, fine-food restaurants, cafés, and galleries. Within its hilly terrain are the Wissahickon Gorge greenbelt and the **Morris Arboretum of the University of Pennsylvania**, an immense area that includes thousands of rare plants and "trees-of-record," greenhouses, ponds, and meadows. Some of the other attractions in this area include the **Woodmere Art Museum**, which is housed in a Victorian mansion and features a collection of more than 300 paintings and sculptures. The **Chestnut Hill Historical Society** has a collection of more than 15,000 items that date from the 1680s to the present, including artifacts, documents, and photographs.

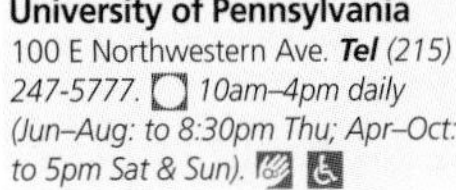

Rose at Morris Arboretum

Morris Arboretum of the University of Pennsylvania
100 E Northwestern Ave. ***Tel*** *(215) 247-5777.* *10am–4pm daily (Jun–Aug: to 8:30pm Thu; Apr–Oct: to 5pm Sat & Sun).*
www.morrisarboretum.org

Woodmere Art Museum
9201 Germantown Ave.
Tel *(215) 247-0476.* *10am–5pm Tue–Thu & Sun, 10am–8:45pm Fri, 10am–6pm Sat.*
www.woodmereartmuseum.org

Chestnut Hill Historical Society
8708 Germantown Ave. ***Tel*** *(215) 247-0417.* *9:30am–2:30pm Tue–Fri, 10am–4pm most Saturdays; appointments preferred.*
www.chhist.org

Main Street Manayunk ❹

Main St, Manayunk. ***Tel*** *(215) 482-9565.* *Manayunk/Norristown SEPTA regional rail Manayunk Station.* *61.* **www**.manayunk.com

Once an industrial urban village, this neighborhood has been revitalized, with trendy stores, galleries, restaurants, and cafés lining the fashionable Main Street. In 1824, it changed its name to Manayunk, from the Lenape word *manaiung*, which means, "Where we go to drink." With the completion of the Manayunk Canal, the early 19th-century town grew into a thriving mill and industrial town. Today, the old mills are home to upscale apartments and an eclectic mix of store-fronted shops. Main Street comes to life especially on weekends when sidewalk café tables fill up. The pedestrian walk along the canal is also popular with walkers.

Fairmount Park ❺

On both sides of the Schuylkill River & along Wissahickon Creek. ***Tel*** *(215) 683-0200.* *30th St Station.* *Spring Garden.*
www.fairmountpark.org

Stretching along the shores of the Schuylkill River and Wissahickon Creek, Fairmount Park forms part of an extensive greenbelt. Its grassy fields and dense wooded areas are dotted with statues and crisscrossed by miles of hiking paths. The most popular path runs parallel to Kelly and Martin Luther King Jr. drives and stretches 8 miles (13 km) along both sides of the river.

West of the Schuylkill River is The Mann Center, an outdoor amphitheater and summer home of the Philadelphia Orchestra *(see p164)*. The nearby **Horticulture Center** has elongated ponds with fountains, while the **Shofuso Japanese House and Garden** is a 17th-century-style Shoin mansion that has a koi pond. The grand Memorial Hall, a centerpiece during the country's centennial celebration, was formerly the city's art museum. It was dedicated by President Ulysses S. Grant, but is now home to the **Please Touch Museum** for children *(see p170)*.

Other key attractions include 18th- and early 19th-century mansions that were once the rural homes of prominent colonial families *(see pp108–109)*.

Outdoor seating at a café along Manayunk's Main Street

Horticulture Center
Tel *(215) 685-0096.* *Apr–Oct: 8am–6pm; Nov–Mar: 8am–5pm.*

Shofuso Japanese House and Garden
Tel *(215) 878-5097.* *Apr & Oct: 11am–5pm Sat & Sun; May–Sep: 10am–4pm Wed–Fri, 10am–5pm Sat & Sun.* *Nov–Apr.*
www.shofuso.com

Please Touch Museum
Tel *(215) 581-3181.* *9am–5pm Mon–Sat, 11am–5pm Sun.*
www.pleasetouchmuseum.org

Geese at Fairmount Park, part of Philadelphia's greenbelt

Boathouse Row and Kelly Drive 6

West of Philadelphia Museum of Art along Kelly Drive. *30th St Station.* *38, Philly Phlash.*

This row of quaint stone and brick boathouses is home to what's affectionately known as the "Schuylkill Navy," namely rowing and sculling clubs patronized by area universities and high schools. Situated on the river's eastern shore, some feature Victorian Gothic architecture and date back to the 19th century. These boathouses, and others farther upstream, host the country's largest intercollegiate sculling contest in May, the annual Dad Vail Regatta *(see p33)*.

At one end of Boathouse Row is the Azalea Garden, where people picnic under the magnolias and large oaks. At the other end is the small 1887 lighthouse that once flashed beacons to warn barges and steamboats of the nearby Fairmount dam. Also close to Boathouse Row is Icelandic sculptor Einar Jonsson's 1918 statue of Thorfinn Karlsefni, the Viking explorer who is said to have landed in America a millennium ago. At night, strings of lights illuminating the boathouses reflect off the river, creating an idyllic scene often highlighted on calendars and postcards. A popular path along Kelly Drive offers miles of walking and biking on both sides of the Schuylkill River.

Philadelphia Zoo 7

3400 Girard Ave. ***Tel** (215) 243-1100.* *30th St Station.* *34th St.* *38.* *Mar–Oct: 9:30am–5pm daily (to 4pm Dec–Feb).* *Jan 1, Thanksgiving, Dec 24, 25, & 31.* **www**.philadelphiazoo.org

Boasting Victorian gardens and historic architecture, including the country home of William Penn's grandson John, the Philadelphia Zoo was opened in 1874. The zoo is the country's oldest and is home to more than 1,600 exotic animals from around the world.

The zoo houses several rare species such as naked mole rats and blue-eyed lemurs. A walk-through giant otter habitat shows these animals at their playful best. The magnificent big cats – clouded leopards, lions, tigers (including rare white tigers), and jaguars – are kept in near-natural habitats or inside the Bank of America Big Cat Falls exhibit, in weather-protected cages that provide a close-up view. Other features are an open birdhouse with uncaged finches and hummingbirds; the Reptile and Amphibian House with venomous king cobras, giant tortoises, and alligators basking in a tropical paradise; and a large reserve area for ten primate species. The Zooballoon takes passengers aloft for panoramic views of the city.

Hummingbird at Philadelphia Zoo

University of Pennsylvania and University City 8

Main Campus between Chestnut St & University Ave and between 32nd & 40th Sts. ***Tel** (215) 898-5000.* *SEPTA Airport, Warminster, or Media/Elwyn line regional rail to University City Station.* *34th St.* *42.* **www**.upenn.edu

This highly regarded Ivy League school has the honor of being America's first university. Founded by Benjamin Franklin in 1749, the University of Pennsylvania started classes two years later, beginning what would become the nation's first liberal arts curriculum. The university is also home to the country's first medical school, student union, and the oldest collegiate football field still in use.

Today, with more than 20,000 students enrolled in undergraduate, graduate, and professional school programs, it is often listed among America's top ten universities.

Scenic Boathouse Row along Schyulkill River, to the west of the city

Shaded walkway at the University of Pennsylvania campus

Its vast urban campus features 19th-century buildings along grassy areas and shaded walkways, including Locust Walk, its main pedestrian street. Among the notable sculptures on the campus are two of Franklin along Locust Walk, one with the statesman and inventor seated on a bench.

The Penn campus is located within University City, a revitalized neighborhood with one of the Philadelphia area's most ethnically diverse and educated populations. It has Victorian-era homes, as well as its own brand of galleries, cafés, and restaurants. Within University City are also several medical centers and other institutions of higher learning, including Drexel University.

University of Pennsylvania Museum of Archaeology and Anthropology ❾

3260 South St. ***Tel*** *(215) 898-4000.* *Airport, Warminster, or Media/Elwyn lines to University City Station.* *34th St.* *42.* *10am–5pm Tue–Sun (to 8pm Wed).* *Mon, public hols.*
www.penn.museum

A world-class museum with nearly one million artifacts, this institute is one of Philadelphia's best. The museum's expansive 90 ft (27 m) rotunda is the largest unsupported masonry dome in the country, and features Chinese art and early Buddhist sculpture. The museum's collections have been gathered since its founding in 1887 through more than 400 archaeological digs and research expeditions around the world. More than 30 galleries spread over three floors house impressive remnants of civilizations past and present spanning the earth, including a 13-ton (28,650-lb) granite Sphinx of Rameses II from 1200 BC, well-preserved mummies, an Etruscan warrior helmet from the 7th century BC, Zapotec figures from Mexico, African stringed musical instruments, and an Alaskan Umiak, a whaling boat with a skin hull.

Italian Market ❿

Along 9th St between Christian & Wharton Sts. *Ellsworth-Federal.* *47.* *9am–5pm Tue–Sat, 9am–2pm Sun.* *Mon.*
www.phillyitalianmarket.com

Under numerous awnings and corrugated tin roofs, this open-air market is the largest and oldest of its kind in the country. The market dates to the late 1800s, when Italian immigrants sold meats and produce, and Jewish merchants sold clothing. Although still predominantly Italian, today it comprises a mix of nationalities. The sights and sounds of the market, however, have not changed much from a century ago. Several stalls offer fresh fruit and vegetables, butcher shops sell prime cuts, poultry and game meats, while seafood vendors stack fish and shellfish on ice. Other specialties include pastas, cheeses from all over the world, spices, coffees, and teas. Bakeries have pastries ranging from ricotta-filled Italian cannolies to Amish baked goods. Food stands and cafés dish up Philly cheesesteaks, pizzas, and traditional Italian dishes.

A flower stall at the Italian Market

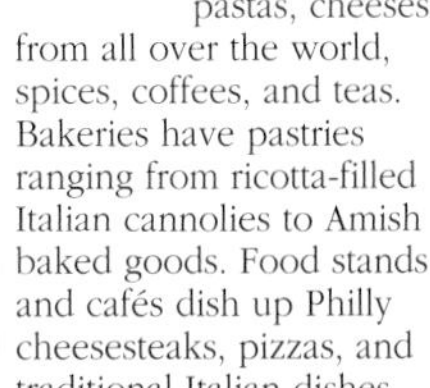

Mural depicting the Italian Market and Frank Rizzo, 1970s city mayor

Art Deco façade of the three-story Mummers Museum

Mario Lanza Institute and Museum ⓫

Columbus House, 712 Montrose St. *Tel (215) 238-9691.* *Ellsworth-Federal.* 47. *10am–3pm Mon–Wed, Fri & Sat.* *Sun, public hols.* **www**.mariolanzainstitute.org

Housed in a former church rectory, the museum honors the world-famous Philadelphia tenor and movie star, Mario Lanza (1921–59). Lanza developed an interest in opera as he grew up, and his talents were soon recognized. His career flourished with best-selling recordings and starring roles in several major films of the 1940s and 50s, such as *The Great Caruso* and *For The First Time.*

Mario Lanza bust

Through posters, newspaper clippings, photographs, and other memorabilia, the museum charts his life from his childhood to his death in Rome from a heart attack. The museum shop sells many of the 460 songs Lanza recorded during his career.

Mummers Museum ⓬

1100 S 2nd St. *Tel (215) 336-3050.* 57. *9:30am–4:30pm Wed–Sat.* *Sun–Tue public hols.* **www**.mummersmuseum.com

Opened during the nation's bicentennial year in 1976, this museum celebrates the city's Mummers tradition and annual New Year's day Mummers Parade where thousands of people strut to the rhythm of marching string bands *(see p35).* Permanent and rotating exhibits showcase the museum's extensive collections. Artifacts from past parades are displayed to re-create the excitement of the event. They include floats, musical instruments used in the parades, and plumed and sequinned costumes. The museum's library has newspaper clippings dating back to the late 19th century, and more than 6,000 manuscripts, photographs, works of art, and films that highlight the parade's history and tradition.

Every Thursday, May through September, string bands perform a free concert at 8pm so that visitors can sample the sounds of the Mummers celebrations.

Fort Mifflin ⓭

Fort Mifflin Rd near Island Ave. *Tel (215) 685-4168.* *Mar–mid-Dec: 10am–4pm (by appt).* *public hols; mid-Dec–Mar, except for groups.* **www**.fortmifflin.us

Historic Fort Mifflin, with its well-preserved ramparts and soldiers' barracks, is the only fort in Philadelphia. Surrounded by a moat, it overlooks the Delaware River and offers views of the city skyline, and the nearby and often noisy Philadelphia airport.

Construction of the fort began with the installation of sturdy granite walls in 1771 – the only remnants of the original fortification that remain today – and the fort stayed in continuous use through the Korean War in the 1950s.

Its most prominent moment, however, was during the Revolutionary War, when the Continental troops in the fort managed to keep the British at bay for seven weeks. This allowed Washington to retreat to Valley Forge and thwarted British efforts to open a supply route along the Delaware River for their troops who had occupied Philadelphia.

Today, Fort Mifflin is a popular tourist attraction. The former soldiers' barracks now

MUMMERS TRADITION AND PARADE

The Mummers tradition dates to the late 1600s when Swedish and Finnish settlers ushered in the new year with parades and masquerades. Others soon joined in with the use of costumes based on Greek celebrations of King Momus, the Italian feast of Saturnalia, and the British Mummery Play. Today, the parade features the Comics, who dress as hobos and clowns and poke fun at the crowds; the Fancies, who dazzle in sequined outfits; the Fancy Brigades, who perform themed shows; and the String Bands, where marchers play banjos, drums, and glockenspiels. The parade is followed by the Fancy Brigade Finale, held at the Pennsylvania Convention Center.

Costumed revelers at a Mummers Day parade

Moat around 18th-century Fort Mifflin, Philadelphia's lone fort

house a small museum and a diorama depicting the siege of 1777. On display are tools, cannonballs, and grapeshot from the Revolutionary War, as well as items from the American Civil War, when Confederate soldiers, Union deserters, and civilian lawbreakers were imprisoned at the fort.

Camden Waterfront ⓮

Delaware River, NJ. ***Tel*** *(856) 757-9154.* *PATCO Speedline from Center City, New Jersey Transit.* *New Jersey Transit.* *RiverLink Ferry.* **www**.camdenwaterfront.com

This spacious riverfront area in New Jersey, opposite Penn's Landing, has gardens, a music venue, a minor league baseball stadium, art galleries, a theater, and other attractions.

One of the biggest draws is the **Adventure Aquarium**. It boasts one of the largest tanks in North America and contains over 5,000 aquatic creatures, such as sharks, seals, and stingrays. Nearby is the floating museum, the **Battleship New Jersey**, with nine 16-inch (40-cm) guns in three triple turrets. One of the nation's most decorated battleships, she served in World War II and the Vietnam War. The waterfront is also home to the 6,500-seat Campbell's Field, which hosts the Camden Riversharks baseball team. For concerts, head to the 7,000-seat Susquehanna Bank Center, an indoor and outdoor amphitheater. The **RiverLink Ferry** *(see p186)* offers a scenic ride across the Delaware River to and from Penn's Landing.

Adventure Aquarium, exterior detail

Adventure Aquarium
1 Aquarium Dr. ***Tel*** *(856) 365-3300.* *10am–5pm daily (Jul 7–Aug 26: 10am–7pm daily).*
www.adventureaquarium.com

Battleship New Jersey
42 Battleship Place, Clinton Street at the waterfront. ***Tel*** *(856) 966-1652.* *Feb 4–Mar 31, Nov & Dec: 9:30am–3pm Sat & Sun; Apr & Sep 4–Oct 31: 9:30am–3pm daily; May 1–Sep 3: 9:30am–5pm daily.*
www.battleshipnewjersey.org

RiverLink Ferry
Tel *(215) 925-5465.* *Memorial Day–Labor Day: 9:30am–4pm Mon–Thu, 9:30am–7pm Fri–Sun.*
www.riverlinkferry.org

Walt Whitman House ⓯

330 Mickle Boulevard, NJ. ***Tel*** *(856) 964-5383.* *PATCO Speedline, New Jersey Transit.* *New Jersey Transit.* *RiverLink Ferry.* *only by appointment: 10am–noon, 1–4pm Wed–Sun.*

This modest, two-story house two blocks east of the Camden Waterfront is the only home that renowned American poet Walt Whitman (1819–92) ever owned. He lived here from 1884 until his death in 1892.

Whitman left Washington DC after suffering a stroke in 1873, coming to live with his brother George in Camden. When his brother decided to move to a nearby rural area, Whitman opted to stay on here. With the surprising success of the 1882 edition of his most famous volume of poetry, *Leaves of Grass*, he was able to purchase this home. Already a prominent poet, Whitman was visited in Camden by famous writers, such as Charles Dickens and Oscar Wilde, and Philadelphia artist and friend Thomas Eakins *(see p89)*, who photographed and painted the aging poet.

Today, the house, a National Historic Landmark, contains some of Whitman's personal belongings, letters, and old photographs, including the earliest known image of the poet from 1848.

USS New Jersey, berthed at the dock adjacent to the Susquehanna Bank Center at Camden Waterfront

TWO GUIDED WALKS AND A DRIVE

Philadelphia's colonial history around Society Hill and Independence National Historical Park, also called "America's most historic square mile," is best explored on foot. However, for those who wish to explore other historical areas, this section introduces some neighborhoods that can be explored through a guided walk or drives.

Maritime painting in the Seaport Museum

The first is a walking tour around the Penn's Landing area along the scenic Delaware River. This tour includes stops at Gloria Dei (Old Swedes') Church, the oldest church in Pennsylvania, and the Irish, Korean, and Vietnam memorials. The second walk explores colonial-era homes along Germantown, which was settled in 1683. This 90-minute walk includes the "White House," where the first president of the US, George Washington, and his family stayed to escape the city's 1793 yellow fever epidemic. The third is a drive through Fairmount Park, close to the Philadelphia Museum of Art on the banks of the Schyulkill River. This tour also highlights historic homes, many of which were once the summer retreats of the colonial elite. This drive includes splendid panoramic views of the city skyline at Belmont Plateau.

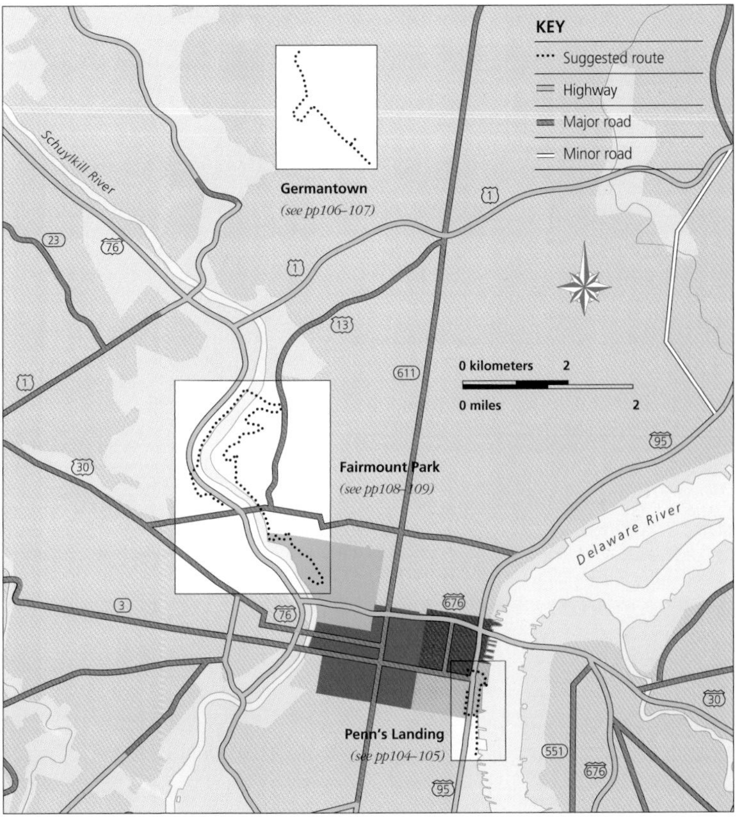

◁ **One of the rowing teams of the "Schuylkill Navy" brings its boat ashore at Boathouse Row *(see p98)***

A Two-Hour Walk Along Penn's Landing

Penn's Landing's plaza, walkways, marina, and Christopher Columbus Park provide the setting for a scenic walk along the Delaware River, the natural boundary between the states of Pennsylvania and New Jersey. Docked along the riverside are some of Philadelphia's historic ships and popular dinner cruise boats, as this area is now a commercial and entertainment zone. The walk, which starts in the neighborhood of Old City and includes historic sights, stretches south along the river to the Gloria Dei Church and then doubles back to include the city's monuments to the Vietnam War and Korean War.

Penn's statue at Welcome Park ①

Independence Seaport Museum ⑥, showcasing US maritime heritage

Corn Exchange National Bank, with a unique domed clock tower ②

Welcome Park to Irish Memorial

The walk begins in Welcome Park ① *(see p55)* at 2nd Street and the Sansom Street alley. Dedicated to William Penn, the park is located where his home, the Slate Roof House, once stood. Pass by the historic Thomas Bond House Bed and Breakfast *(see p134)* along 2nd Street to Chestnut Street, where the Corn Exchange National Bank building ② sits across the street. Designed in Colonial Revival style, the structure dates back to the mid-19th century and now contains a bank, restaurants, and a newspaper office.

Turn right onto Chestnut Street and stop in front of 126 Chestnut ③. A time capsule is buried at the site and a plaque on the sidewalk reads: "From the people of the Bicentennial to the Tricentennial – our mementos to be opened by the Mayor of Philadelphia on July 4, 2076."

Cross Front Street to the Irish Memorial ④, a memorial to those who suffered during the Irish Potato Famine (1845–50).

Irish Memorial to Christopher Columbus Park

Pass over I-95 and enter Penn's Landing ⑤ *(see p66)*. Head down the curving walkway toward the river for great views of the Benjamin Franklin Bridge and the Camden Waterfront *(see p101)*, home to the Adventure Aquarium and the *Battleship New Jersey*.

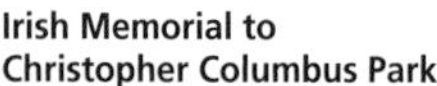

Detail of Irish Memorial Sculpture ④

Walk past the RiverLink Ferry port and the Independence Seaport Museum ⑥ *(see pp64–5)*, where the museum's cruiser *Olympia* and submarine *Becuna* are berthed. A dead-end walkway stretches out into the Delaware River offering splendid views of the river and the Benjamin Franklin Bridge. Continue around the marina to Christopher Columbus Park ⑦, which has as its centerpiece a tribute dedicated in 1992 to the 500th anniversary of the explorer's voyage to America. Across from the *Olympia* and *Becuna* is the Penn's Landing Visitor Center.

Christopher Columbus Park to Korean War Memorial

Continue south along the waterfront to the *Moshulu* ⑧, a 1904 four-masted sailing ship that is now a floating restaurant *(see p148)*. The *Spirit of Philadelphia*, a dinner cruise ship, is also berthed here. Then walk along Columbus

Camden Waterfront, across Penn's Landing and along the scenic Delaware River ⑤

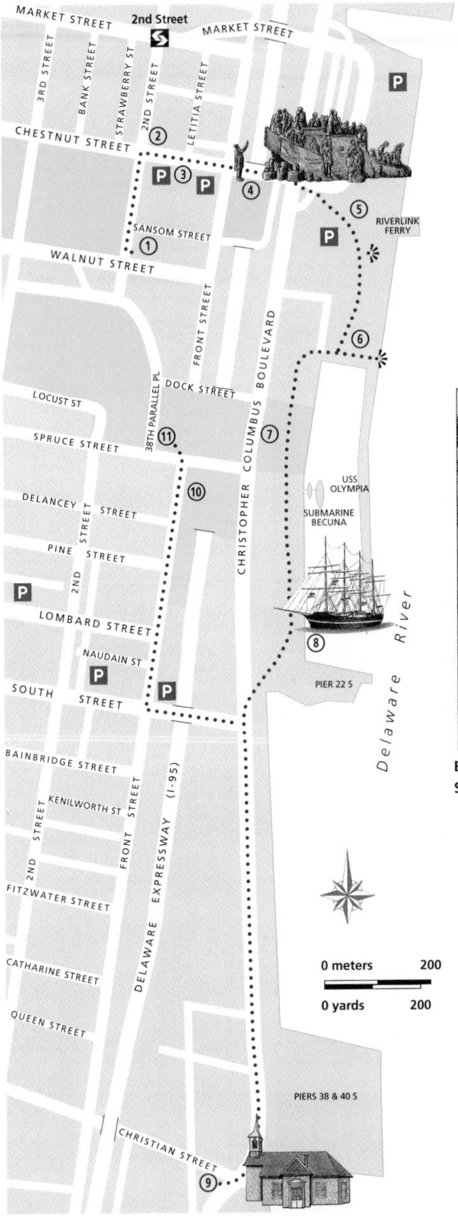

TIPS FOR WALKERS

Starting point: *Welcome Park on 2nd St between Chestnut and Walnut Sts.*
Length: *2 miles (3 km).*
Getting there: *Philly Phlash.*
Stopping-off points: *Stop at the Irish Memorial, take in the views along the river at Penn's Landing, and relax under the trees at Christopher Columbus Park. Take time to explore the Gloria Dei Church and a few moments to reflect at the Vietnam War and Korean War memorials.*

Exterior of the restored Gloria Dei (Old Swedes') church, founded in 1677 ⑨

KEY

- Suggested route
- Viewpoint
- SEPTA subway stop
- Parking

0 meters 200
0 yards 200

Boulevard past the old Municipal Piers 38 and 40. Cross the boulevard at Christian Street to reach the Gloria Dei (Old Swedes') Church ⑨, the oldest in the state. Swedish Lutherans, who settled here in 1643, founded the church in 1677, before the arrival of William Penn. The brick building standing today was completed in 1700, with the steeple added in 1703. Now an Episcopal parish, the church still contains the original marble baptismal font and carved wooden cherubim holding a bible, which were brought to the New World by the Swedish colonists. Among those buried in the church cemetery are soldiers of the Revolutionary War.

Head back up Columbus Boulevard and cross back over I-95 using the South Street overpass. Turn right on Front Street and continue to the Vietnam War Memorial ⑩. It pays tribute to the city's 80,000 veterans who served in the Vietnam War (1960–75), and has the names of more than 600 of those killed etched in stone. Cross Spruce Street and enter Foglietta Plaza, whose centerpiece is the Korean War Memorial ⑪ with the names of 603 local veterans killed or declared missing in action during the Korean War (1950–53).

A 90-Minute Walk of Historic Homes in Germantown

Once a small country town a few miles northwest of Old City, Germantown *(see p96)* is now one of Philadelphia's oldest neighborhoods. It was settled in 1683 by immigrants from the Rhine Valley in Germany, who were attracted by Penn's promise of religious freedom. Within a century it evolved into a retreat for wealthy Philadelphia families. The homes on this walk, along cobblestoned Germantown Avenue, have been well preserved by the active Germantown Historical Society and are National Historic Landmarks. The stop-offs should be made during the day, as the area is best avoided at night. The route can be easily driven through, and tourism markers make the homes easy to find.

Germantown Historical Society and Visitor Center ①

Germantown Historical Society Museum and Library to Deshler-Morris House

The walk starts at the Germantown Historical Society Museum and Library ①. This museum traces Germantown's history, in addition to selling maps of the region. The museum's rotating exhibits are culled from the society's 20,000-artifact collection of paintings, kitchenware, toys, and period clothing. Exit the center, turn left on Germantown Avenue, and walk a few blocks to Grumblethorpe ②, built in 1744 and home of wine merchant John Wister. Sally, his daughter, lived here during the American Revolution and kept a diary recording her impressions of the turbulent times. British General James Agnew died here after being mortally wounded in the fierce Battle of Germantown in 1777 *(see p21)* and a bloodstain remains on the first floor. The Georgian Grumblethorpe displays items that belonged to the family and the gardens outside still retain their 19th-century appearance.

Head back up Germantown Avenue to one of the community's most famous homes, the Deshler-Morris House ③. The house is situated opposite the Visitor Center and Market Square, which has a Civil War monument as its centerpiece. Built in the mid-1700s by Quaker David Deshler, the home served as the headquarters of British General William Howe during the Battle of Germantown. After the Revolutionary War, the building became known as the Germantown "White House" when President Washington and his family lived here to escape the 1793 yellow fever epidemic. Today, the house exhibits period furnishings and original paintings by colonial artists Gilbert Stuart and Charles W. Peale.

Grumblethorpe, home to one family for 160 years ②

The Deshler-Morris House, now a National Park Service property ③

Back parlor of the Wyck House and Garden ④

TIPS FOR WALKERS

Starting point: *Germantown Historical Society Museum and Library.* ***Tel*** *(215) 844-1683.*
Length: *1.5 miles (2.5 km).*
Getting there: *Take the Chestnut Hill West SEPTA regional rail line to Chelten Avenue station.*
Stop-off points: *Visits to all homes are recommended, though these would be dependent on opening hours.*

Deshler-Morris House to Ebenezer Maxwell Mansion

Continue up Germantown Avenue several blocks to the Wyck House and Garden ④, owned for three centuries by nine generations of the same Quaker family. It contains the family's belongings, collected from 1689 until 1973, including antiques, books, and manuscripts that highlight the family's history and its devotion to the Quaker faith.

Turning left on Walnut Lane, walk two blocks to turn right on Greene Street to the Ebenezer Maxwell Mansion ⑤. Built in 1859, it is the city's only authentically restored Victorian residence. It features original 19th-century stenciled designs in the upstairs rooms, Rococo furniture in the dining room and parlor, and various other period items that reflect life in the 1860s.

Ebenezer Maxwell Mansion to Cliveden

Turn right on Tulpehocken Street back to Germantown Avenue and turn left for the Johnson House ⑥, built in 1768. This stone house was owned by three generations of an abolitionist Quaker family, who made it into the city's only stop on the Underground Railroad that led slaves to freedom in Canada and the northern states *(see p60)*.

Continuing up Germantown Avenue, the next home on the walk is Upsala ⑦. Built around 1740 and expanded in 1800, the home is an outstanding example of Federal architecture, with wooden and marble mantels inside *(see p28)*. This house is where the Continental Army made its stand during the Battle of Germantown on October 4, 1777. Across the street is Cliveden ⑧. Built in 1767, it is one of the finest surviving colonial homes in the city. During the Battle of Germantown, British troops occupied the Georgian-style Cliveden and repulsed the colonial army. Chipped bricks from rifle shots are still evident on the home's façade, and one room has an original musket ball hole from the battle that raged in the street outside. Reenactments of the battle are held on the grounds on the first Saturday of every October.

Ebenezer Maxwell Mansion ⑤, a 19th-century Victorian house

BAYNTON ST
Germantown
PRICE STREET
CHELTEN AVENUE
LENA STREET
KENYON STREET
AVENUE
CHURCH LANE
COULTER STREET
WAKEFIELD STREET
PENN STREET
BRINGHURST STREET
ASHMEAD STREET
MAPLEWOOD
SCHOOL HOUSE LANE
① ② ③

KEY
••• Suggested route
SEPTA subway stop

0 meters 400
0 yards 400

The study at Cliveden, an example of a colonial-era house ⑧

A Three-Hour Drive Around Fairmount Park Historic Mansions

Prominent colonial Philadelphia families took note of the trees and rolling hills in the landscape just west of the city along the Schuylkill River, and built mansions in what is today Fairmount Park *(see p97)*. Some of the homes had working farms with grazing lands and orchards, while others were upscale summer retreats. The park was established when the city began purchasing these properties in the mid-19th century, thus preserving scenic land and the homes in their architectural splendor. They are open for tours and are best seen as part of a driving tour. Those without vehicles can take a trolley tour during the Christmas holiday season.

Boathouse Row along Kelly Drive

Lemon Hill to Laurel Hill

Begin the drive from the parking lot at the Philadelphia Museum of Art's West Entrance ①. Turn left at the traffic light onto Kelly Drive, then drive straight on. At the seated statue of President Lincoln ②, take the fork to the right, and then make a sharp left to reach Lemon Hill ③. The house was named after the lemon trees that once grew here when Revolutionary War financier and signer of the Declaration of Independence Robert Morris owned the land. A later owner, Henry Pratt, built the mansion in 1800. The oval rooms, with curved doors, fanlights, and fireplaces on all three levels, are Federal elements, while the Palladian windows are Georgian remnants. Return to the Lincoln statue, and turning right, continue up Kelly Drive past Boathouse Row. At the statue of Ulysses S. Grant turn right onto Fountain Green Drive and then left for Mount Pleasant ④. Once described by President John Adams as "the most elegant seat in Pennsylvania," this Georgian house has ornate woodwork and classical motifs in the entrance hall and stairway. Returning to Fountain Green Drive, which merges with Reservoir Drive, continue to Ormiston ⑤. Built in the 1790s in Georgian style, the house has an original Scottish oven and an open fireplace. Events and rotating exhibits at Ormiston highlight the area's British heritage.

Drive down Reservoir Drive and turn left onto Randolph Drive. Continue to Edgeley Drive for Laurel Hill ⑥, a 1767 Georgian-style country house with a two-story octagonal wing, perched on a prominent bluff overlooking the river.

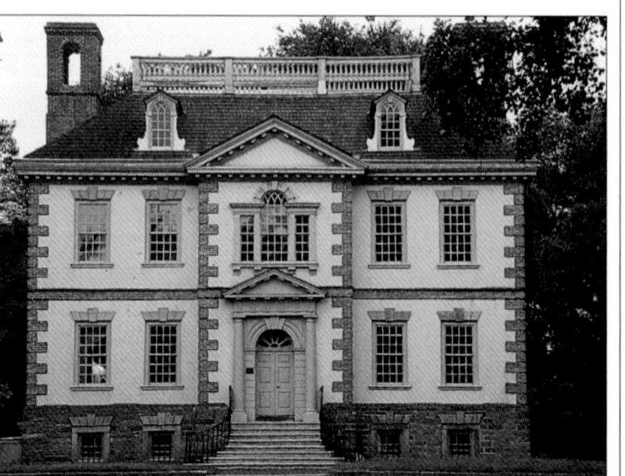

Mount Pleasant, built between 1762 and 1765 ④

Woodford, a National Historic Landmark ⑦

Laurel Hill to Memorial Hall

Continue through an intersection that has an equestrian statue of an American Indian, and onto Dauphin Drive. Turn left before 33rd Street onto Greenland Drive to reach Woodford ⑦, built in 1758 by William Coleman, a merchant and friend of Benjamin Franklin. The Georgian house has an array of exquisite colonial decorative arts and furniture, donated by Naomi Wood, a Philadelphian collector. Continue up Greenland Drive a short distance to Strawberry Mansion ⑧, with its Federal-style center wing built by Judge William Lewis in 1789. Two large wings, in Greek Revival style, were added later. The house displays Empire and Federal period furnishings. Key exhibits include a doll collection and a well-preserved Victorian doll-house. Drive down Strawberry Mansion Drive, turn right at Woodford Drive, and cross the Strawberry Mansion Bridge. Make a quick left onto West River Drive, continue for about a mile (1.6 km) and turn right onto Black Road toward the Smith Civil War Memorial ⑨. Turn right at the Memorial onto North Concourse Drive to reach Memorial Hall ⑩. Built in Beaux-Arts style, it was the city's first art museum and now houses the Please Touch Museum for children *(see p170)*. Guided tours of Memorial Hall allow visitors to view the building behind the scenes.

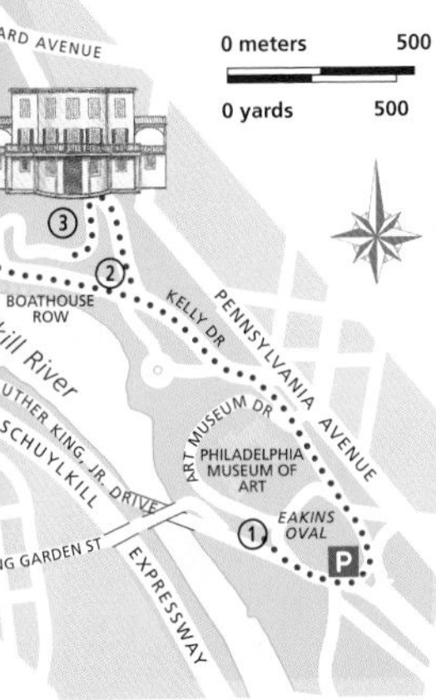

KEY

••• Suggested route

P Parking

Memorial Hall to Sweetbriar

Returning to the Smith Civil War Memorial, turn left, and then make a quick right onto Cedar Grove Drive and head to Cedar Grove ⑪, a house that was built elsewhere and reassembled in Fairmount Park. This Georgian house has an unusual two-sided wall of closets on the second floor, and much of its original, early Pennsylvania furniture. It is now maintained by the Philadelphia Museum of Art. For the last stop, turn right after Cedar Grove towards the Federal-style Sweetbriar ⑫, the home of merchant Samuel Breck, built in 1797. The Etruscan Room is decorated in keeping with Breck's interest in classical forms and ancient Etruscan wall painting.

TIPS FOR DRIVERS

Starting point: *Philadelphia Museum of Art, West Entrance parking lot.*
Length: *5 miles (8 km) to visit homes, then another 2 miles (3 km) back to the museum.*
Stop-off points: *Homes open to the public can be visited, depending on opening hours and time.*
Trolley tour: *Tours during the Christmas holiday season leave from the Philadelphia Museum of Art and the Independence Visitor Center (6th & Market Sts).* ***Tel*** *(215) 925-8687. May–Dec 15: 10:30am & 1:45pm Wed–Sun.*

Sweetbriar, a three-story house built in Federal style ⑫

Cedar Grove, built as a summer home in 1750 ⑪

BEYOND PHILADELPHIA

Exploring Beyond Philadelphia

To the west of Philadelphia, the area encompassing Lancaster County is known as the Pennsylvania Dutch Country, and is made up of bucolic hills and farmland as far as the eye can see. The region is home to the Amish *(see p115)* who wear traditional clothing and are often seen riding in horse-drawn buggies. Farther west is the town of Hershey, home of the chocolates, and Gettysburg, site of the American Civil War's bloodiest battle. To the east, the glitzy casinos of Atlantic City are just over an hour's drive away, and a little farther is the idyllic beach resort of Cape May.

Statue, Gettysburg

Fountains at Longwood Gardens

SIGHTS AT A GLANCE

- Atlantic City, NJ 19
- Bird-in-Hand, PA 6
- Brandywine Battlefield State Park 24
- Brandywine River Museum 25
- Cape May, NJ 20
- Ephrata, PA 4
- Doylestown, PA 14
- Gettysburg, PA 9
- Hagley Museum 21
- Hershey, PA 12
- Harrisburg, PA 11
- Intercourse, PA 5
- Lancaster, PA 1
- *Landis Valley Museum pp116–17* 2
- Lititz, PA 3
- Longwood Gardens 23
- New Hope, PA 15
- Paradise, PA 7
- Pennsbury Manor 18
- Reading, PA 13
- Strasburg, PA 8
- Trenton, NJ 17
- Valley Forge National Historic Park 26
- Washington Crossing Historic Park 16
- Winterthur Museum 22
- York, PA 10

SEE ALSO

- ***Where to Stay*** pp139–41
- ***Restaurants and Cafés*** pp151–3

Boy outside a candy and ice cream store in Strasburg

KEY

- Highway
- Major road
- Other roads
- Major rail
- Minor rail
- State boundary

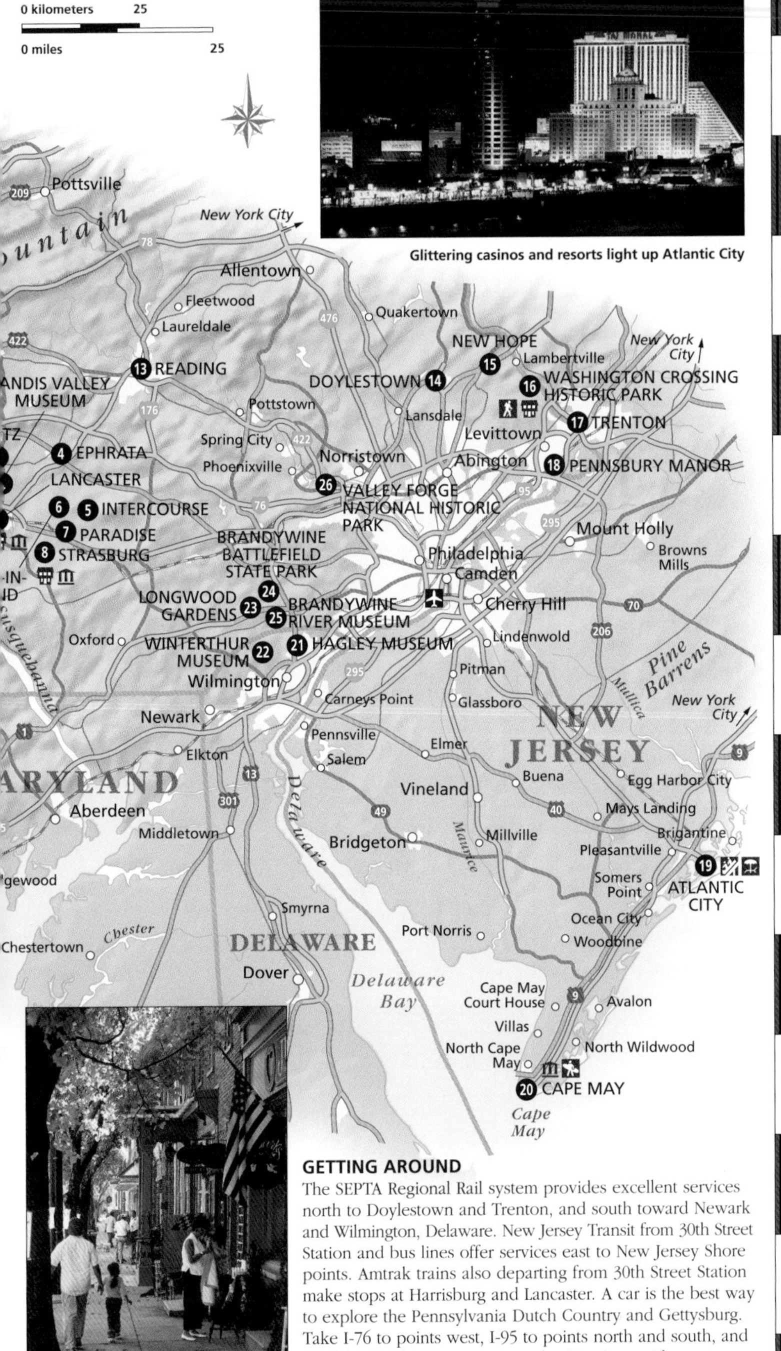

Glittering casinos and resorts light up Atlantic City

GETTING AROUND

The SEPTA Regional Rail system provides excellent services north to Doylestown and Trenton, and south toward Newark and Wilmington, Delaware. New Jersey Transit from 30th Street Station and bus lines offer services east to New Jersey Shore points. Amtrak trains also departing from 30th Street Station make stops at Harrisburg and Lancaster. A car is the best way to explore the Pennsylvania Dutch Country and Gettysburg. Take I-76 to points west, I-95 to points north and south, and the Atlantic City Expressway to the New Jersey Shore.

Shoppers at Main Street, Lititz

For additional map symbols *see back flap*

Soldiers and Sailors Monument in Penn Square, Lancaster

Lancaster ❶

Lancaster County, PA. 55,000. Pennsylvania Dutch Country Visitors Center: Route 30 at Greenfield Exit, 501 Greenfield Rd; 1-800-PA-DUTCH. **www**.padutchcountry.com

Founded by John Wright in 1730 and named after his birthplace in England, today Lancaster is the county seat. Its tree-shaded streets are still lined with 18th- and 19th-century buildings. In the heart of downtown is Penn Square with its centerpiece Soldiers and Sailors Monument, dedicated in 1874 to local men who fought in the American Civil War between 1861 and 1865. On the square's northwest corner, three adjoining buildings dating from the 1790s house the **Lancaster Heritage Center Museum**. Its collection includes striking colonial grandfather clocks. A Renaissance-style mural adorns the vaulted ceiling of one of the buildings.

At the **Lancaster Central Market**, next to the museum, vendors and Amish farmers sell cheeses, meats, flowers, fresh produce, and treats such as homemade cider. Nearby, in a Beaux Arts-style building modeled after New York's Penn Station, is the **Lancaster Quilt & Textile Museum** with a collection of 82 Amish and Mennonite quilts.

Located west of downtown is **Wheatland**, the estate of the 15th president of the US, James Buchanan, who served during the tumultuous years leading up to the Civil War. The house, named for the wheat fields it once overlooked, features most of Buchanan's original belongings, and has a beautiful 19th-century garden.

An old-fashioned pretzel

Lancaster Heritage Center Museum
5 W King St. ***Tel*** *(717) 299-6440.* *9am–5pm Mon–Sat; first Fri of month: 5–9pm; Dec: noon–4pm Sun.*

Lancaster Quilt & Textile Museum
37 Market St. ***Tel*** *(717) 397-2970.* *10am–5pm Mon, Wed & Thu, 9am–5pm Tue, Fri & Sat, 5–9pm first Fri of month.*

Wheatland
1120 Marietta Ave. ***Tel*** *(717) 392-4633.* *Apr–Oct: 10am–4:30pm Mon–Sat, noon–4pm Sun; Nov & Dec: 10am–4:30pm Fri & Sat.* *Jan–Mar, Thanksgiving, Dec 25.*

Landis Valley Museum ❷

See pp116–17.

Lititz ❸

Lancaster County, PA. 9,000. *Lititz Welcome Center: 18 N Broad St, (717) 626-7960.* **www**.lititzpa.com

Named after a town in Bohemia, Lititz was founded by Moravians in 1756 and remained a closed settlement for nearly a century. The town boasts 18th-century buildings, a quaint Main Street, and the Lititz Springs Park, which has a natural spring-fed creek. Moravian Church Square today includes the centerpiece church. Nearby is the **Lititz Historical Museum** with its star exhibit, the Johannes Mueller House, a restored 1792 Moravian stone house named for a local tanner and dyer. A room in the museum is dedicated to General John Sutter, founder of Sacramento and a Lititz resident. It was the discovery of gold on his land that led to the 1849 California Gold Rush.

The **Sturgis Pretzel House**, dating from 1861, offers pretzel tours. The **Wilbur Chocolate Candy Store and Museum** displays 19th-century chocolate molds that highlight the company's history since 1884.

Lititz Historical Museum
137–145 East Main St. ***Tel*** *(717) 627-4636.* *Memorial Day–Oct: 10am–4pm Mon–Sat; special weekends in May, Nov, & Dec.*

Sturgis Pretzel House
219 East Main St. ***Tel*** *(717) 626-4354.* *Martin Luther King Day–Mar 15: 10:30am–3:30pm (tours), 10am–4pm (store); Mar 16–Dec 31: 9:30am–4pm (tours), 9am–5pm (store).*

Wilbur Chocolate Candy Store and Museum
48 N Broad St. ***Tel*** *(717) 626-3249.* *10am–5pm Mon–Sat.* **www**.wilburbuds.com

Lititz's historic Main Street shopping district

The Amish, Mennonites, and Brethren

The Mennonites and the Amish trace their roots to the Swiss Anabaptist ("New Birth") movement of 1525, an offshoot of the Protestant Reformation, whose creed rejected the formality of the established churches. Lured by the promise of religious freedom held out to them by William Penn, the Mennonites were the first to arrive in Germantown in the late 17th century. They were soon followed by the Amish who settled in what is now Lancaster County in the early 18th century. However, not all Pennsylvania Dutch are Amish or Mennonites; Brethren and other sub-groups are also part of the community. The mostly German heritage of these groups has given rise to a popular myth about the name "Pennsylvania Dutch" – it is thought that it came from other early colonists mispronouncing "Pennsylvania Deutsch."

Detail from an Amish quilt

Amish farms *have changed little since the 17th century. Farming is usually done with horsedrawn equipment with bare metal wheels.*

AMISH

The Amish sect began in the 1690s when Jacob Amman, a Swiss bishop, split from the Mennonites. The conservative Old Order Amish disdain any device that would connect them to the larger world, including electricity, cars, modern farm tools, and telephones.

Amish families *dress in plain, dark attire, with women in white caps and men in straw hats.*

Buggies are used even today

MENNONITES

Taking their name from Menno Simons, a young Dutch priest who advocated adult baptism by faith in the 1530s, Mennonites are pacifists and believe in simple living. However, they do not segregate themselves from society, and in recent years, urbanization has lured many to the cities.

Mennonites in traditional dress

Old Order Brethren at a Pennsylvania Dutch Country covered bridge

BRETHREN

Alexander Mack founded this movement in 1708, breaking away from the established and reformed faiths of the time and following the German Pietists in espousing worship on a more personal level. The pacifist Brethren migrated to America in the late 1720s. They believe in adult baptism and adhere only to the teachings of the New Testament.

The Brethren church *is where the community worships and baptizes adults by "dunking" them thrice in the name of the Holy Trinity.*

Landis Valley Museum ❷

Wares at the Country Store

The descendents of German settlers, brothers George and Henry Landis, started the Landis Valley Museum in the 1920s. At that time, it included more than 75,000 objects from the 18th and 19th centuries, featuring the traditions and farming culture of the Pennsylvania German community. Now supported and run by the state Historical and Museum Commission, Landis Valley is a living history village of Pennsylvania German life and home to nearly 100,000 artifacts such as quilts, rugs, leather goods, carriages, kitchen utensils, baskets, and lace. More than 30 homes, barns, sheds, shops, and other structures highlight the trades and crafts of earlier generations, complemented by regular demonstrations by craftspeople.

Maple Grove School
This late 1800s school features authentic wooden desks.

★ Landis Collections Gallery
Items like this silver lamp are displayed in the museum's historic collection, which dates from 1740 to 1940.

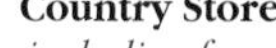

Country Store
A wide range of items, including farm tools, saddles, phonograph records, and glass-jarred licorice, stock the shelves of this reconstructed store.

STAR SIGHTS

- ★ Landis Collections Gallery
- ★ Transportation Building
- ★ Landis House and Stable
- ★ Gun Shop

Firehouse and Surveyor Shop
The larger firehouse, which has original pumpers inside, resembles a late 19th-century fire company.

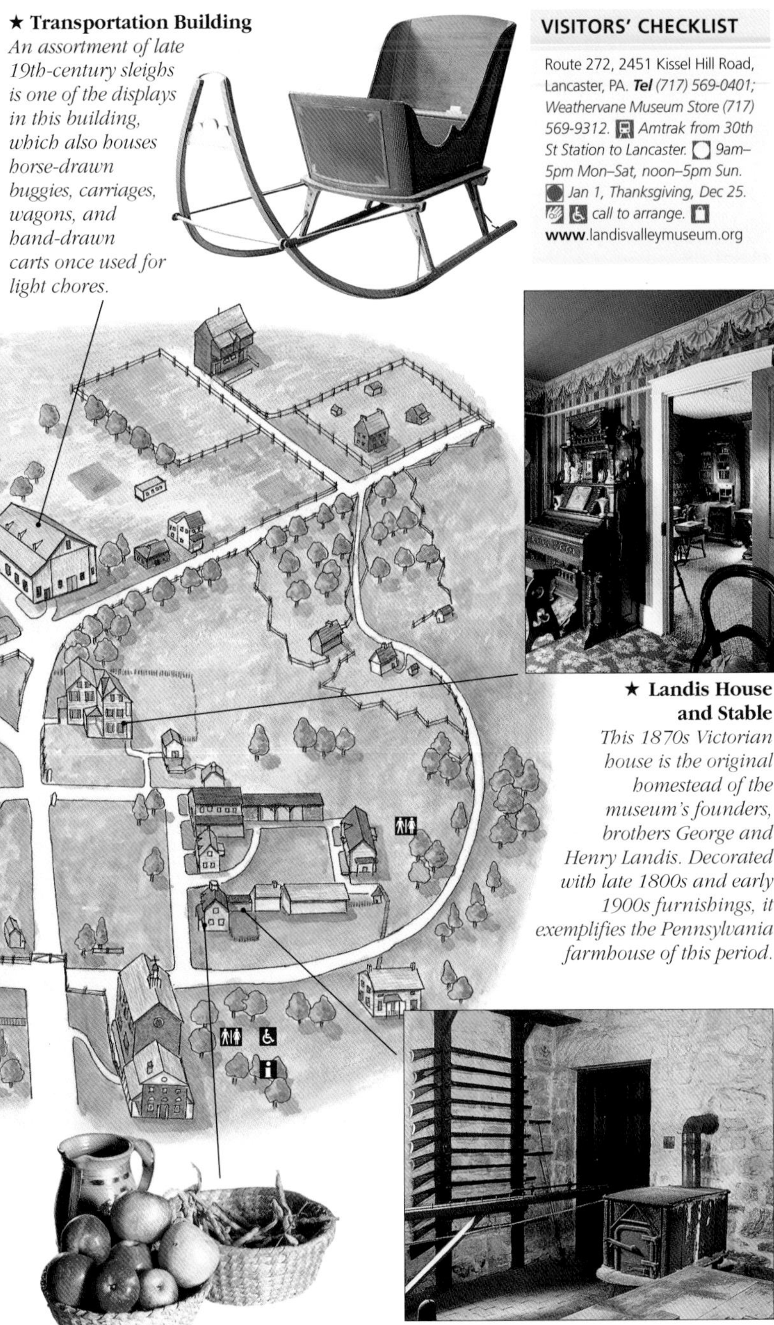

★ Transportation Building
An assortment of late 19th-century sleighs is one of the displays in this building, which also houses horse-drawn buggies, carriages, wagons, and hand-drawn carts once used for light chores.

VISITORS' CHECKLIST

Route 272, 2451 Kissel Hill Road, Lancaster, PA. ***Tel*** *(717) 569-0401; Weathervane Museum Store (717) 569-9312.* *Amtrak from 30th St Station to Lancaster.* *9am–5pm Mon–Sat, noon–5pm Sun.* *Jan 1, Thanksgiving, Dec 25.* *call to arrange.* **www**.landisvalleymuseum.org

★ Landis House and Stable
This 1870s Victorian house is the original homestead of the museum's founders, brothers George and Henry Landis. Decorated with late 1800s and early 1900s furnishings, it exemplifies the Pennsylvania farmhouse of this period.

Tavern
The spacious brick-paved kitchen of the inn, with its enormous walk-in fireplace and displays of baskets, utensils, and stoneware jugs, reflects 18th-century cooking methods.

★ Gun Shop
An elaborate exhibit of Pennsylvania long rifles, powder horns, and gunsmithing tools sits within this stone structure. Early settlers used such shops to perfect the accuracy of their weapons.

Austere interior of the Saal, the meetinghouse in Ephrata Cloister

Ephrata ❹

Lancaster County, PA. 13,000. 16 E Main St, Suite 1; (717) 738-9010. **www**.ephrata-area.org

This northern Lancaster County community was settled in 1732 by a German religious order led by Conrad Beissel, who founded one of America's earliest communal societies. The order built the medieval-style buildings that make up the **Ephrata Cloister**. Today, nine structures from the mid-1700s remain. The Sisters' House, next to the meetinghouse, has rows of windows for each small chamber where members slept on narrow benches. Other buildings include a schoolhouse, bakery, woodshop, and print shop. The visitor center displays artifacts, such as the Mennonites' 1,500-page *Martyrs' Mirror*. Just north of town, vendors at the Green Dragon Farmers' Market sell antiques, Pennsylvania Dutch treats, and crafts every Friday.

Ephrata Cloister
632 W Main St. ***Tel*** *(717) 733-6600.* *9am–5pm Mon–Sat, noon–5pm Sun.*
www.ephratacloister.org

Intercourse ❺

Lancaster County, PA. *900.* *3551 Old Philadelphia Pike; (717) 768-3231.* **www**.intercoursevillage.com

Theories abound on how the village acquired its interesting name, including it coming from the intersection of the two main roads, from an old racecourse, or even from Intercourse being a center for social interaction. Founded in 1754, the village is one of the main centers for Amish business. Key to its success are the extensive gift shops and stores that lure tourists by the busloads. For instance, Kitchen Kettle Village, a mini-shopping center, has over 30 restaurants and country shops selling everything from quilts and baskets to woodcraft. One store delights customers with homemade jellies and relishes bottled on the spot by Amish women. In the center of town, along Old Philadelphia Pike, is the **People's Place Quilt Museum**. Opened in 1988, the museum displays antique Mennonite and Amish quilts through rotating exhibitions.

Exhibit detail at the People's Place Quilt Museum

West of the town center is the **Amish Experience at Plain & Fancy Farm**, where visitors can tour a modern Amish home and view the multi-media show, *Jacob's Choice*, which chronicles an Amish family's efforts to preserve its lifestyle.

People's Place Quilt Museum
3510 Old Philadelphia Pike. ***Tel*** *(800) 828-8218.* *9am–5pm Mon–Sat.*
www.ocsquiltmuseum.com

Amish Experience at Plain & Fancy Farm
3121 Old Philadelphia Pike, Route 340, Bird-In-Hand. ***Tel*** *(717) 768-8400, ext 210.* *Times vary by tour type. Visit the website or call for details.*
www.amishexperience.com

Bird-In-Hand ❻

Lancaster County, PA. *300.* *2727 Old Philadelphia Pike; (800) 665-8780.* **www**.bird-in-hand.com

This village is said to have received its unusual name from a historic 1734 inn *(see p141)* that once dangled a tavern sign depicting a man with a perched bird in his hand. The village contains a cluster of restaurants, stores, hotels, and quaint farmhouses.

The **Farmers' Market** bustles with stalls packed with foods ranging from farm vegetables to fresh bacon and sausage. Across the street, the **Americana Museum** displays antiques from 1890 through 1930, which depict important professions and trades, and include an early 20th-century toy store, apothecary, print shop, wheelwright shop, and milliner's. Set up in 1877, the Weavertown One-Room School showcases a typical

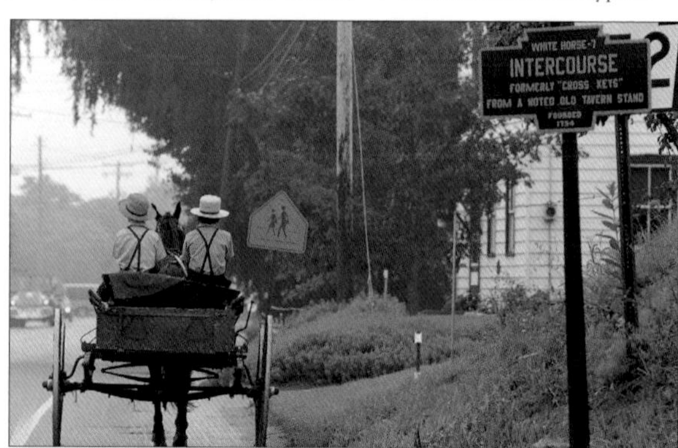

Amish boys ride a buggy into the village of Intercourse

schoolhouse still attended by Amish children today.

Farmers' Market
2710 Old Philadelphia Pike. **Tel** *(717) 393-9674.* *Apr–Jun & Nov: 8:30am–5:30pm Wed, Fri, & Sat; Jul–Oct: 8:30am–5:30pm Wed–Sat; Dec–Mar: 8:30am–5:30pm Fri & Sat.*

Americana Museum
2709 Old Philadelphia Pike. **Tel** *(717) 391-9780.* *Apr–Nov: 10am–5pm Tue–Sat; winter tours by request.*

Paradise ❼

Lancaster County, PA. *1,000.* *Pennsylvania Dutch Country Visitors Center: 501 Greenfield Rd; (717) 299-8901.* **www**.800padutch.com

The origins of this small village along Route 30 date from colonial times when the road served as a link between Lancaster and Philadelphia. Paradise grew as the number of inns and taverns increased along Route 30. One of them, the Historic Revere Tavern, was built in 1740 and is still a working restaurant *(see p153)*. President James Buchanan purchased it in 1841 as a home for his brother, a reverend, whose wife was the sister of songsmith Stephen Foster, writer of such American favorites as "Oh! Susanna" and "My Olde Kentucky Home".

A short drive east is the one-of-a-kind **National Christmas Center**, where the spirit of Yuletide is always in the air. Spread over 20,000 sq ft (1,860 sq m) are life-sized scenes depicting Christmas feasts and snowy villages, toy train and nativity displays, and several versions of St. Nicholas from around the globe.

Signage at the National Christmas Center

National Christmas Center
3427 Lincoln Hwy East. **Tel** *(717) 442-7950.* *May 1–Jan 1: 10am–6pm daily; Mar & Apr: 10am–6pm Sat & Sun.* *Jan–Feb, Thanksgiving, Dec 25.* **www**.nationalchristmascenter.com

An Amish house and buggy in Strasburg

Strasburg ❽

Lancaster County, PA. *2,800.* *Pennsylvania Dutch Country Visitors Center: 501 Greenfield Rd; (717) 687-0405.* **www**.strasburgpa.com

Initially settled by French Huguenots in the early 18th century, Strasburg is named after the cathedral city of Strasbourg in France. The first structures, built in 1733, are now part of the historical district along with numerous colonial stone and log homes. The town developed as an educational and cultural center as followers of different faiths chose to settle here. But by the mid-19th century, it had become home to the railroads that are today its most popular attraction. Set up in 1832, the **Strasburg Railroad** offers 45-minute rides in refurbished railcars pulled by early 20th-century coal-fired, smoke-belching locomotives. Directly across the highway is the **Railroad Museum of Pennsylvania**, with spacious hangars housing one of the nation's largest collections of classic railroad cars, locomotives, and colorful cabooses. The **National Toy Train Museum** has exhibitions of collector-item locomotives and exquisite model train layouts. The **Choo Choo Barn**, meanwhile, has one of the most unique model railroads in the world, with 22 trains running through scenes of Lancaster County.

North of town is the **Amish Village** with an 1840s Amish house, smokehouse, blacksmith shop, and operational water wheel. The majestic Millennium Theater nearby is home to inspirational, Biblical-themed stage productions.

Strasburg Railroad
301 Gap Rd Ronks, Rte 741, E of Strasburg. **Tel** *(717) 687-7522.* *Feb–Dec; check website or call for times.* *Jan.* **www**.strasburgrailroad.com

Railroad Museum of Pennsylvania
300 Gap Rd. **Tel** *(717) 687-8628.* *Apr–Oct: 9am–5pm Mon–Sat, noon–5pm Sun; Nov–Mar: 9am–5pm Tue–Sat, noon–5pm Sun.* *Jan 1, Easter, Nov 11, Thanksgiving, Dec 24, 25, & 31.*

National Toy Train Museum
300 Paradise Lane, off Rte 741, E of Strasburg. **Tel** *(717) 687-8976.* *check website or call for times.* *Jan–Mar.* **www**.nttmuseum.org

Choo Choo Barn
Rte 471, E of Strasburg. **Tel** *(717) 687-7911.* *Jan 13–16 & Mar 10–Dec 31: 10am–5pm daily.* *Jan 1–12 & Jan 17–Mar 9, Easter, Thanksgiving, Dec 25.* **www**.choochoobarn.com

Amish Village
Rte 896, N of Strasburg. **Tel** *(717) 687-8511.* *spring, summer & fall: 9am–5pm Mon–Sat, 10am–5pm Sun.* **www**.theamishvillage.net

Gettysburg ⓽

Lincoln's chair at Wills House

This south-central Pennsylvania town amidst gently sloping hills is home to the greatest military encounter ever fought in North America, the Battle of Gettysburg in 1863, during the Civil War (1861–65). Shaded streets are lined with well-preserved Civil War-era buildings, which served as makeshift hospitals during the conflict. Many of these have today been converted into museums, restaurants, and hotels. Shops sell Civil War souvenirs and artifacts, including authentic rifles and a seemingly unending supply of cannon balls and bullets unearthed from the battleground. Other attractions include museums with dioramas – some with waxwork figures – depicting events of the Gettysburg battle and the Civil War.

The *Gettysburg Cyclorama*, a 360-degree painting of Pickett's Charge

Gettysburg Museum and Visitor Center

1195 Baltimore Pike. ***Tel*** *(717) 338-1243.* *Apr–Oct: 8am–6pm daily; Nov–Mar: 8am–5pm daily.* *Jan 1, Thanksgiving, Dec 25.* **www**.gettysburgfoundation.org

The Gettysburg Museum and Visitor Center opened in 2008 at the Gettysburg National Military Park. The 139,000 sq ft (12,900 sq m), awe-inspiring facility houses a modern visitor center that serves to navigate visitors around the park. A 20-minute film, introducing the Battle of Gettysburg, is repeated here every 30 minutes throughout the day. The facility also houses the Museum of Civil War where wide-ranging military artifacts, including an impressive display of artillery shells and fuses, are on display. Also on view is the *Gettysburg Cyclorama*. First exhibited in Boston in 1883, this colossal panoramic painting depicts Pickett's Charge, the conflict's climactic moment *(see pp122–3)*.

Dobbin House Tavern

89 Steinwehr Ave. ***Tel*** *(717) 334-2100.* *11:30am onward.* **www**.dobbinhouse.com

Built in 1776, this stone house is Gettysburg's oldest standing structure. An upstairs museum displays a secret crawl space that once hid runaway slaves as part of the Underground Railroad *(see p60)*. Now a restaurant, the building has original fireplaces, hand-carved woodwork, and a colonial wooden bar in the downstairs tavern *(see p152)*.

Eisenhower National Historic Site

250 Eisenhower Farm Drive. ***Tel*** *(717) 338-9114.* *check website or call for times.* *Jan 1, Thanksgiving, Dec 25.* *tickets available at Gettysburg Visitor Center.* *mandatory.* **www**.nps.gov/eise

Before being elected president in 1952, Dwight D. Eisenhower had served as Supreme Commander of the Allied Forces during World War II. While president, he and his wife Mamie owned this farm on the outskirts of Gettysburg and used it for weekend retreats. Inside are original furnishings and exhibits highlighting his career as president.

Farnsworth House Inn

401 Baltimore St. ***Tel*** *(717) 334-8838.* *hours vary.* **www**.farnsworthhouseinn.com

Dating from 1810, this historic home sheltered Confederate sharpshooters, one of whom is thought to have shot Jennie Wade. Most impressive are the more than 100 bullet piercings still evident on the house's brick façade from Union soldiers returning fire. Now an inn *(see p152)*, the house offers ghost tours and a Mourning Theatre in the cellar with Civil War-related ghost tales told around a coffin by candlelight.

General Lee's Headquarters Museum

401 Buford Ave. ***Tel*** *(717) 334-3141.* *mid-Feb–Nov: 9am–5pm, longer summer hours (call for details).* *Dec–mid-Feb.*

Confederate General Robert E. Lee spent the night of July 1, 1863, at this house so he could see the Union line with his fieldglasses. Inside are war artifacts and the wooden table on which he dined.

General Lee's Headquarters, today a museum

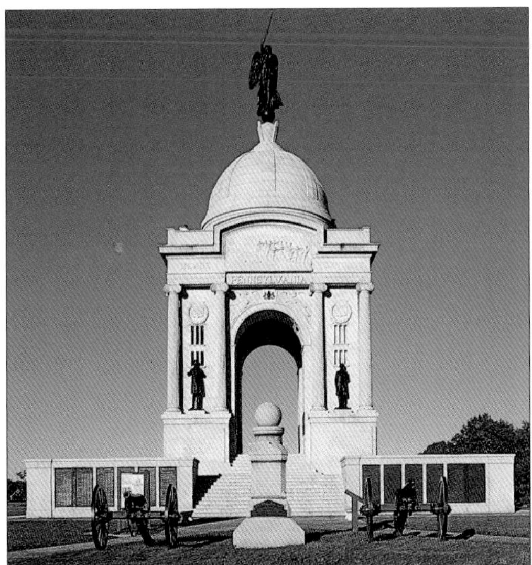

Entrance to the Pennsylvania Memorial in Gettysburg

Jennie Wade House

528 Baltimore St. **Tel** *(717) 334-4100.* *Mar–Sep: 9am–5pm.*
www.jennie-wade-house.com

Twenty-year-old Jennie Wade was the only civilian killed during the Battle of Gettysburg. A sharpshooter's bullet pierced two doors and struck her while she baked bread for Union soldiers. The home contains original furnishings, and a statue of her stands outside.

Lincoln Railroad Station

35 Carlisle St. *10am–5pm; extended hours in summer.*

This 1858 Italianate-styled railroad depot is where President Lincoln stepped off the train from Washington, a day before delivering the Gettysburg Address. Inside is an interpretive center, with exhibits about the train station and town history, and information on sights, attractions, and tours.

Soldiers' National Cemetery

Taneytown Rd, across Visitor Center.
www.nps.gov/gett/gncem.htm

This peaceful and shaded cemetery contains the graves of 6,000 US servicemen killed in various conflicts in America's history, from the Civil War to the Vietnam War. More than 3,500 are Union soldiers killed at the three-day Battle of Gettysburg. They are buried in a semi-circle around the Soldiers' National Monument, which marks the spot where President Lincoln delivered his moving Gettysburg Address. The now-famous address is commemorated by the nearby Lincoln Speech Memorial, which contains an inscription of his speech and his bust.

Soldiers' National Monument

VISITORS' CHECKLIST

Gettysburg Convention & Visitors Bureau: 35 Carlisle St.
Tel *(717) 334-6274.*
9am–5pm Mon–Fri.
Apple Blossom Festival (May), Gettysburg Anniversary Civil War Battle Reenactments (Jul), Apple Harvest Festival (Oct), Remembrance Day (Nov).
www.gettysburg.travel

Shriver House Museum

309 Baltimore St. **Tel** *(717) 337-2800.* *Mar: 10am–5pm Sat, 10am–3pm Sun; Apr–Oct: 10am–5pm Mon–Sat, noon–5pm Sun.* *Feb.*

This 19th-century home portrays the life of a family under the three-day Confederate occupation. The third-floor attic has original holes in the brick wall where rebel sharpshooters stood poised. A small museum displays artifacts, including three unfired bullets discovered during restoration.

Wills House and Lincoln Room Museum

8 Lincoln Square. **Tel** *(877) 874-2478.* *Mar: 9am–5pm Thu–Mon; Apr & Sep–Nov: 9am–5pm Wed–Mon; May–Aug: 9am–6pm daily; Dec–Feb: 10am–5pm Fri–Sun.*

President Abraham Lincoln slept in this corner house on the town's center square the night before he delivered the Gettysburg Address. His bedroom, where he made revisions to his speech, is part of the Lincoln Room Museum. It has copies of the letter sent by attorney David Wills inviting Lincoln to visit the town.

LINCOLN'S GETTYSBURG ADDRESS

Four months after the battle, President Abraham Lincoln visited Gettysburg to dedicate a cemetery for Union soldiers. Although not the main speaker, and asked only to make "a few appropriate remarks," Lincoln's 272-words, two-minute speech on November 19, 1863 not only gave new meaning to the war's losses, but was an inspiration to preserve a nation divided. His words conferred significance on the sacrifice of the thousands who died during the battle, urging for the "resolve that these dead shall not have died in vain."

Lincoln's bust at Soldiers' National Cemetery

A Tour of Gettysburg National Military Park

The Battle of Gettysburg was fought on the first three days of July 1863. Not only was it the turning point of the American Civil War between the North and South, it was also the war's largest battle, leaving more than 51,000 Union and Confederate soldiers killed, wounded, captured, or missing. Although the Union army won this critical battle, it took a further two years for them to decisively win the Civil War on April 26, 1865. This self-guided tour traces the course of the three-day battle.

Eternal Light Peace Memorial ②
From Oak Hill, Confederates attacked Union forces on the first day. This memorial to "Peace Eternal in a Nation United" was built in 1938.

McPherson's Ridge ①
This quiet farm with McPherson's barn is where the Battle of Gettysburg began early in the morning on July 1, 1863. Confederate infantry advanced eastward and engaged in heavy fire with Union Cavalry.

Oak Ridge ③
Union troops held this ridge but retreated to Cemetery Hill on July 1 as their defenses collapsed.

North Carolina Memorial ④
On the second day, the Confederates stood on Seminary Ridge. Union troops held Culp's and Cemetery Hills.

Virginia Memorial ⑤
This monument on Seminary Ridge overlooks the field where, on July 3, 12,000 Confederates launched their last major assault, known as "Pickett's Charge." In less than an hour, 10,000 of them were dead or wounded.

Pitzer Woods ⑥
Confederates occupied these woods on the second day. An observation tower offers grand views of the "Pickett's Charge" battlefield.

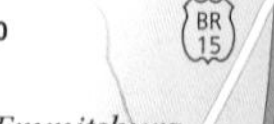

KEY

- Suggested route
- Other roads
- Visitor information
- Parking

Warfield Ridge ⑦
On the battle's second day, Confederates charged Union troops at Devil's Den and Little and Big Round Tops.

High Water Mark ⑮
On the last day, Union troops held off "Pickett's Charge" here, forcing the Confederates to retreat. The spot is marked by memorials and old cannon.

TIPS FOR DRIVERS

Tour length: *18 miles (29 km).*
Duration of tour: *About 3 hours.*
Distance from Philadelphia: *118 miles (189 km). This is usually a 2-hour drive.*
Starting point: *Gettysburg National Military Park and Visitor Center.*
Stop-off points: *The tour has 16 stops, all of which have plaques explaining historical significance. Some stops have a scattering of monuments.*
When to go: *Mar–Dec.*
Tourist information: *Gettysburg Convention and Visitors Bureau, 35 Carlisle St.* ***Tel*** *(800) 337-5015.* **www**.gettysburg.travel

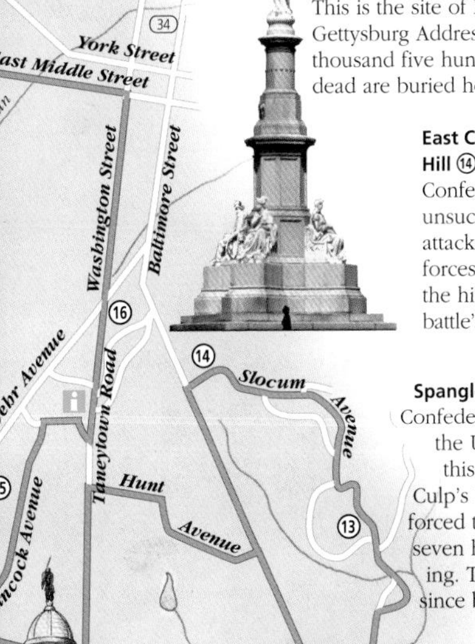

National Cemetery ⑯
This is the site of Lincoln's Gettysburg Address. Three thousand five hundred Civil War dead are buried here.

East Cemetery Hill ⑭
Confederates unsuccessfully attacked Union forces occupying the hill, ending the battle's second day.

Spangler's Spring ⑬
Confederates attacked the Union army at this spring below Culp's Hill, but were forced to retreat after seven hours of fighting. The spring has since been covered.

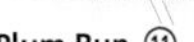

Plum Run ⑪
Union forces crossed this area as they retreated from Peach Orchard to Cemetery Ridge.

Pennsylvania Memorial ⑫
An ornate, stately memorial marks the Union position along Cemetery Ridge.

Peach Orchard ⑩
On the second day, Confederate soldiers overran this position despite heavy Union cannon fire.

The Wheatfield ⑨
Charges and countercharges here on the second day left over 4,000 men dead and wounded.

Little Round Top ⑧
At first undefended on the second day, this position was reinforced when an alert Union general called for help. Monuments, such as this one to the 155th Pennsylvania Volunteer Infantry, dot the hill.

The Golden Plough Tavern, one of York's historic establishments

York ⑩

York County, PA. *40,500.* *1425 Eden Rd, (717) 852-9675.* **www**.yorkpa.org

The first Pennsylvania town west of the Susquehanna River, York was laid out in 1741, with inhabitants that were mainly tavern-keepers and craftspeople catering to pioneers heading west. Since then, manufacturing has been the town's economic strength.

East of York is the **Harley-Davidson Final Assembly Plant**, noisy, colorful, and the size of two football fields. Its giant presses mold steel while motorcycles fly overhead. A small museum depicts Harley Davidson's history from its 1903 inception as a motorized bike company to the present.

Harley-Davidson Final Assembly Plant
1425 Eden Rd. ***Tel*** *(717) 852-6590.* *9am–2pm Mon–Fri.* *9am–2pm Mon–Fri; some Saturdays in summer; under 12 not allowed.*

Harrisburg ⑪

Dauphin County, PA. *47,000.* *Hershey Harrisburg Regional Visitors Bureau: (877) 727-8573.* **www**.visithersheyharrisburg.org

First settled in the early 18th century by Englishman John Harris, Harrisburg is situated along the Susquehanna River. The city was not planned until the 1780s and became the capital of Pennsylvania in 1812. Today, the state government is the biggest employer in the city, which has the impressive **State Capitol** as a focal point. The Renaissance-style building was dedicated in 1906 by President Theodore Roosevelt.

The **National Civil War Museum** tells the story of the war through permanent displays of artifacts, photographs, manuscripts, and documents from its 24,000-item collection. City Island, located in the middle of the Susquehanna, offers panoramic views of the city. It includes marinas, parks and nature areas, riverboat rides and dinner cruises, and a replica of John Harris's 18th-century trading post.

Hershey's Chocolate World signage

State Capitol
3rd & State Sts. ***Tel*** *(717) 787-6810.* *8:30am–4:30pm Mon–Fri.* *8:30am–4:30pm Mon–Fri, 9am, 11am, 1pm, 3pm Sat–Sun & hols.* *Jan 1, Easter, Thanksgiving, Dec 25.*

National Civil War Museum
Lincoln Circle (Reservoir Pk). ***Tel*** *(717) 260-1861.* *10am–5pm Mon, Tue, Thu & Sat, noon–5pm Wed.* *Mon, Jan–Mar.* **www**.nationalcivilwarmuseum.org

Hershey ⑫

Dauphin County, PA. *12,800.* **www**.hersheypa.com

This factory town, now a tourist destination, revolves around chocolate, so much so that even its streetlights are shaped like silver-foil-wrapped Hershey Kisses. The town's main attraction is **Hershey Park**, an amusement park that has 80 rides on offer, and a fine, four-row carousel. There are also two resort hotels in the park. Nearby is Chocolate World, which features a 15-minute ride through animated tableaux that reveal Hershey's chocolate-making process. A free sample awaits at the end of the tour.

Hershey Park
100 W Hersheypark Drive. ***Tel*** *1-800-HERSHEY.* *May 21–Sep 1: 10am–8pm daily (for other times check website).* **www**.hersheypark.com

State Capitol complex in Harrisburg, the seat of Pennsylvania's government

The towers and parapets of Mercer Castle, Doylestown

Reading ⓭

Berks County, PA. 80,000. *Greater Reading Convention & Visitors Bureau, 2525 N 12th St, (610) 375-4085.* **www**.readingberkspa.com

Once a center of industry, Reading has reinvented itself as a discount-store capital *(see p157)*, with more than 80 name-brand stores, from Brooks Brothers to Mikasa and Wedgewood. The Reading Pagoda, on the outskirts of the town, is the main attraction here. Built in the early 20th century, it is modeled after a Shogun structure.

The **Mid-Atlantic Air Museum**, located at Reading Regional Airport, includes a selection of over 60 different military and civilian aircraft.

Mid-Atlantic Air Museum
11 Museum Drive. ***Tel*** *(610) 372-7333.* *9:30am–4pm.* **www**.maam.org

Doylestown ⓮

Bucks County, PA. *9,200.* *Bucks County Visitors Center: 3207 Street Road, Bensalem, (800) 836-2825.*

Doylestown's origins date to 1745, when William Doyle built a tavern here. The town later developed as a cultural and commercial center, and today it is also the Bucks County seat.

The biggest attractions in town are the castle-like museums that tower over shaded grassy areas close to the town center. The **Mercer Museum**, built by archaeologist Henry Mercer in 1916, displays his collection of folk art, woodwork, textiles, and furnishings. After his death in 1930, his 44-room home, **Fonthill**, was turned into a tile museum.

Named after a famous writer from this area, the **James A. Michener Art Museum**, inside a 19th-century county jail, has a superb collection of Pennsylvania Impressionist paintings.

Mercer Museum
84 S Pine St. ***Tel*** *(215) 345-0210.* *10am–5pm Mon–Sat, noon–5pm Sun.* **www**.mercermuseum.org

Fonthill Museum
E Court St and Rt 313. ***Tel*** *(215) 348-9461.* *mandatory; reservations advised.* **www**.mercermuseum.org

James A. Michener Art Museum
138 S Pine St. ***Tel*** *(215) 340-9800.* *10am–4:30pm Tue–Fri (to 5pm Sat), noon–5pm Sun.* **www**.michenerartmuseum.org

New Hope ⓯

Bucks County, PA. *2000.* *Visitor Center: Main & Mechanic Sts, (215) 862-5030.* **www**.newhopepa.com

This delightful waterfront village and shoppers' paradise teems with upscale boutiques and restaurants. Tracing its roots to the early 18th century, it gained its name when Benjamin Parry's gristmill, which ground grain, burned down in 1790. He rebuilt it and named it "New Hope Mills" with a promise of prosperity for the town.

Today, that prosperity is evident with more than 200 art galleries, boutiques, and craft and antiques shops, including a branch of the **James A. Michener Art Museum**. Train rides aboard restored 1920 passenger cars, horse-drawn carriages, and mule-drawn barge trips down the scenic 19th-century canal add to the town's ambience.

Parry, who also helped finance the first bridge across the Delaware, built a house in 1784 that was occupied by successive generations of his family until 1966. Today, the **Parry Mansion Museum** showcases its separate rooms, decorated according to different periods of its history.

Parry Mansion Museum
45 S Main St. ***Tel*** *(215) 862-5652.* *late Apr–early Dec: 1–5pm Sat & Sun.* *by appointment.*

James A. Michener Art Museum – New Hope
500 Union Square Dr, New Hope. ***Tel*** *(215) 862-7633.* **www**.michenerartmuseum.org

Storefronts line New Hope's old-world, picturesque streets

Delaware River at Washington Crossing Historic Park

Washington Crossing Historic Park 16

Washington Crossing, PA. **Tel** *(215) 493-4076.* *public hols except Jul 4, Memorial Day, Labor Day, Dec 25.* *10am–4pm Thu–Sun (seasonally).*

This waterfront park, set up in 1917 to commemorate Washington's historic crossing of the Delaware River, is divided into two sections. The McConkey's Ferry section, named after a local 18th-century inn, includes the riverbank from which Washington and his army departed in Durham boats. A monument marks this area outside the visitor center. Nearby is a 19th-century boathouse containing replicas of the boats, which are now used for the annual Christmas Day crossing reenactment.

About 4 miles (6 km) upstream is the Thompson's Mill section, which includes historic buildings, a gristmill, an observation tower, and a cemetery along the peaceful Delaware Canal containing the graves of Revolutionary War soldiers.

On the New Jersey side of the river, Washington Crossing State Park marks the site where Washington landed. This forested area includes historic homes, a visitor center and museum, and miles of hiking, riding, and biking trails.

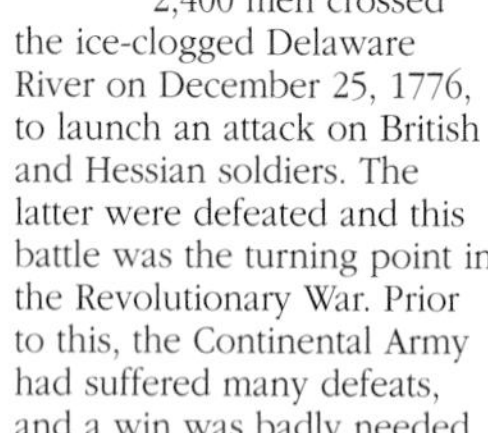

Plaque marking the river crossing

Trenton 17

Mercer County, NJ. *85,000.* *Lafayette at Barrack St, (609) 777-1770.* **www**.trentonnj.com

The capital of New Jersey, Trenton's origin dates to 1679 when Quaker Mahlon Stacy built a gristmill along the Delaware. In 1714, his son sold land to merchant William Trent who laid out a new city called "Trent's Town" in 1721. Today, a big attraction is the Trenton Battle Monument. It pays tribute to the Battle of Trenton, in which General Washington and 2,400 men crossed the ice-clogged Delaware River on December 25, 1776, to launch an attack on British and Hessian soldiers. The latter were defeated and this battle was the turning point in the Revolutionary War. Prior to this, the Continental Army had suffered many defeats, and a win was badly needed to boost morale in the fight for independence. The Old Barracks, dating to 1758, were occupied by Hessian soldiers during the encounter, and now house a museum.

Old Barracks Museum
Barrack St. **Tel** *(609) 396-1776.* *10am–5pm.* *Jan 1, Easter, Thanksgiving, Dec 24–25.* **www**.barracks.org

Pennsbury Manor 18

400 Pennsbury Memorial Rd, Morrisville, PA. **Tel** *(215) 946-0400.* *Jan 1–Feb 29: by appt only; Mar 1–Dec 31: 9am–5pm Tue–Sat, noon–5pm Sun.* *Mon.* **www**.pennsburymanor.org

An elegant brick Georgian house 26 miles (42 km) north of Philadelphia, this manor is a re-creation of William Penn's country home and estate from the 1680s. The plantation sits on the site chosen by Penn, and this manor was built in 1939 on original foundations, where some 17th-century bricks are the only remnants of Penn's initial home. Inside, a hall served as a waiting room between the family's quarters and governor's parlor, while the second floor had three bedrooms and a nursery.

The estate today includes farm animals similar to those owned by Penn. Other recreated structures include a blacksmith shop, brew house, smokehouse, and horse shelter. The visitor center offers activities for schools, a gallery, office space, an auditorium and facilities for video conferencing.

Gardens at Pennsbury Manor, Penn's country estate

Atlantic City's glamorous resorts by night – lighting up the Jersey coast

Atlantic City ⓳

Atlantic County, NJ. 40,000. *Atlantic City Convention & Visitors Authority: 2314 Pacific Ave.* ***Tel** (609) 348-7100, (888) 222-4748.* **www**.atlanticcitynj.com

Called the "Queen of the Coast" by generations of beachgoers, Atlantic City has been a favored vacation spot since the mid-1800s. The first casino opened on the famous Boardwalk in 1978, and since then the town has become one of the most popular destinations on the eastern seaboard. All gambling – referred to as "gaming" – takes place in the large, ostentatious casino hotels that lie within a block of the beach and Boardwalk, which is lined with shops and amusement arcades.

More than a dozen casino resorts – with their towers shooting up along the Boardwalk – make up the dazzling city skyline. They include Caesars, Bally's, Harrah's, Showboat, Resorts, Tropicana, and the properties owned by billionaire developer Donald Trump, such as the 51-story Trump Taj Mahal *(see p139)*. Among the flashier hotels are the Borgata Hotel Casino and Spa, a 2,000-room hotel, and its companion property, The Water Club. The city's most luxurious hotel, Revel, hosts headlining concerts and has 13 restaurants. Many resorts include spas, several restaurants each, convention facilities, nightclubs, and concert halls with popular comedy and musical acts. Visitors not enchanted by the casinos instead head for the lively local attractions. Amusement parks jut out over the ocean on the Central Pier Arcade and Speedway, and the Steel Pier. Another attraction is the Absecon Lighthouse, the tallest lighthouse in New Jersey, which offers views of the city and waterfront. Atlantic City also hosts the annual Miss America Pageant, held here since 1928. Shopping is also a big draw, with the arrival of Atlantic City Outlet – The Walk – housing stores like Banana Republic and Coach.

Playing cards used in gaming

In nearby Margate City, **Lucy the Elephant** stands tall in celebration of American marketing ingenuity. Built by a real estate developer in 1881 to draw prospective buyers to his holdings, "Lucy" has served as a residence and a tavern over the years. Today, guided tours take visitors into the structure that has become instantly recognizable as part of the Jersey shoreline.

Lucy the Elephant
3200 Atlantic Ave, Margate. ***Tel** (609) 823-6473. mid-Jun–Labor Day: 10am–8pm Mon–Sat, 10am–5pm Sun; weekends in spring and fall; Nov–Dec: hours vary.* **www**.lucytheelephant.org

Cape May ⓴

Cape May County, NJ. 4,000. *Cape May Welcome Center: 609 Lafayette St, (609) 884-5508.*

First explored by Cornelius Mey for the Dutch West India Company in 1621, Cape May is one of the oldest resorts on the Atlantic coast. Popular with Philadelphia socialites during the late 1800s, it has, since then, continued to enjoy a fine reputation among beach lovers. The building boom of the Victorian era characterizes Cape May today. **Historic Cold Spring Village** is a living history museum showcasing 25 restored buildings, with costumed actors portraying 19th-century lifestyles.

Historic Cold Spring Village
720 US 9. ***Tel** (609) 898-2300. mid-Jun–Labor Day: 10am–4:30pm Tue–Sun; only weekends Labor Day–mid-Sep & Memorial Day–mid-Jun.*

Brightly painted façade of a house at Cape May, America's largest Victorian district

Hagley Museum ㉑

200 Hagley Rd, Rte 141, Wilmington, DE. **Tel** *(302) 658-2400.* *9:30am–4:30pm daily.* *Thanksgiving, Dec 25 & 31.* *call or check website for times.* **www**.hagley.org

Not a museum in the conventional sense, this forested site along the rocky Brandywine River is where the DuPont Company was founded. In 1802, French immigrant Eleuthere Irenee du Pont built a factory to manufacture gunpowder and "black powder" used in explosives. The earliest buildings included the first du Pont family home, gardens, and company office. Through its 119-year-history, overseen by five generations of du Ponts, the mill expanded downriver, with waterwheels powering production facilities that sifted, mixed, and crushed raw materials into fine powder.

Today, only the façades of the original buildings remain. Some have working exhibitions, such as a rolling mill using safe charcoal. Staff members demonstrate the workings of a steam engine and the operations in a machine shop, but most impressive is the ignition of a powder sample. Some buildings house artifacts, original furniture, and rare du Pont cars, including a 1911 electric car and a 1928 Phaeton.

View of the Brandywine River at Hagley Museum

Interior of the conservatory at Longwood Gardens

Winterthur Museum ㉒

5105 Kennett Pike, Rte 52, Winterthur, DE. **Tel** *(302) 888-4600.* *10am–5pm Tue–Sun.* *Mon (except hols), Jan 1, Thanksgiving, Dec 25.* **www**.winterthur.org

Once the home of Henry Francis du Pont, great-grandson of Eleuthere Irenee du Pont, this vast estate contains an extraordinary 175-room mansion. The original home, the core of the current mansion, dates to 1839. It was built by J.A. Bidermann and his wife, Evelina, Eleuthere du Pont's daughter. Henry Francis inherited the estate in 1926, expanding it during the two-decade-long conversion of his home into a museum. Today, it houses 85,000 items from the 17th to the 19th centuries, including paintings, textiles, furniture, ceramics, and Chinese porcelain. The main dining room features original silver tankards crafted by Paul Revere, and works of art by Gilbert Stuart and Benjamin West. The parlor features a unique oval Mont Morency staircase and is elegantly decorated with Chippendale furniture. The estate contains meadows, streams, and woods, including a tulip-poplar tree, which has been around since William Penn's days, and the fairy-filled Enchanted Woods.

Longwood Gardens ㉓

Rte 1, Kennett Square, PA. **Tel** *(800) 737-5500, (610) 388-1000.* *Apr–Oct: 9am–6pm; Nov–Mar: 9am–5pm.* *Mon (except hols), Jan 1, Thanksgiving, Dec 25.* **www**.longwoodgardens.org

This well-manicured horticultural wonderland consists of colorful gardens, woodlands, lush meadows, greenhouses, and spectacular fountains amid idyllic bucolic scenery. Settler George Pierce acquired the land in 1700, and in 1798, his descendants established an arboretum that, by the mid-19th century was one the nation's finest.

Industrialist Pierre S. du Pont bought it in 1906 and it is his design that remains today. It includes over 11,000 plant varieties in both indoor and outdoor displays, whimsical topiaries, and a children's garden. The massive main greenhouse and conservatory are engineering marvels that shelter an array of exotic plant life. But the most breathtaking sights are the fabulous fountains with choreographed eruptions highlighted at night by colored lights, which create dazzling displays that are often the backdrop of musical events.

Brandywine Battlefield State Park ㉔

878 Baltimore Pike, Rte 1, Chadds Ford, PA. **Tel** *(610) 459-3342.*
9am–5pm Tue–Sat, noon–5pm Sun. *Mon.*

The Battle of Brandywine, fought on these rolling hills on September 11, 1777, was the biggest engagement of the American Revolution. General Washington stationed his troops atop this high ground at Chadds Ford along the Brandywine River in an attempt to stop the advancing British. The Americans were outmaneuvered as the British crossed the Brandywine River at an unguarded ford to the north of Washington's troops, forcing them to retreat.

Today, the battlefield is a state park with a visitor center and two historic houses, both restored to the way they were in 1777. The Benjamin Ring House was owned by a Quaker farmer and served as Washington's headquarters on the eve of the battle. The French patriot and American Revolution hero, Marquis de La Fayette, stayed in the farmhouse of Quaker Gideon Gilpin. The visitor center includes a small museum.

Revolutionary War hero La Fayette's quarters at Brandywine Park

Brandywine River Museum ㉕

1 Hoffman's Mill Road, Chadds Ford, PA. **Tel** *(610) 388-2700.*
9:30am– 4:30pm. *Dec 25.*
Apr–mid-Nov: timed tours of N.C. Wyeth House & Studio, and Kuerner Farm Wed–Sun.
www.brandywinemuseum.org

Located in a Civil War-era gristmill along Brandywine River, this museum is best known for housing artworks by three generations of the Wyeths – N.C., Andrew, and Jamie. Galleries showcase landscapes inspired by the Brandywine River Valley, and paintings and illustrations by the Wyeths and other artists.

N.C. Wyeth (1882–1945) was a famous illustrator of the early 20th century, completing more than 1,000 illustrations, including some for classics such as *Treasure Island* and *Robin Hood*. N.C.'s son Andrew is known for mastering dry-brush watercolor and egg tempura mediums. His son Jamie painted portraits of figures such as President John F. Kennedy and artist Andy Warhol.

Tours are organized to the N.C. Wyeth House and Studio, and the Kuerner Farm, which inspired Andrew for over 70 years. A farmhouse and barn display his works related to the farm.

National Memorial Arch at Valley Forge

George Washington's restored headquarters at Valley Forge

Valley Forge National Historic Park ㉖

1400 N Outer Line Drive, Valley Forge, PA. **Tel** *(610) 783-1077.*
Visitor Center: 9am–5pm daily (Jun 17–Sep 3: to 4pm daily).
Jan 1, Thanksgiving, Dec 25.
www.nps.gov/vafo

George Washington and his soldiers spent the harsh winter of 1777–78 at Valley Forge, retreating to these hills after losing to British forces at Brandywine and Germantown *(see p107)*. No battles were fought here, but nearly 2,000 soldiers died of typhus, typhoid, pneumonia, and dysentery. Today, reconstructed cabins, statues, and cannon are scattered through the park. Key exhibits are the National Memorial Arch, designed by Paul Cret, and built in 1917 in the memory of those who died in the winter of 1777–78, and stone farmhouses that once served as officers' quarters. The park has miles of fields and woods crisscrossed by hiking paths, and a visitor center with artifacts such as muskets and powder horns.

The American Revolution Center is the country's first museum dedicated to that conflict. Built within a quarry bluff, it will showcase the largest collection of Revolutionary artifacts, information, and experiences ever assembled.

JAKE & AMOS
TOMATO RELISH
Zucchini Relish
ONION RELISH
DUTCH GOLD
PURE HONEY
PURE NATURAL HONEY
RAW HONEY
Cloth Angels
Handmade by
an Amish girl
12.00 plus tx.

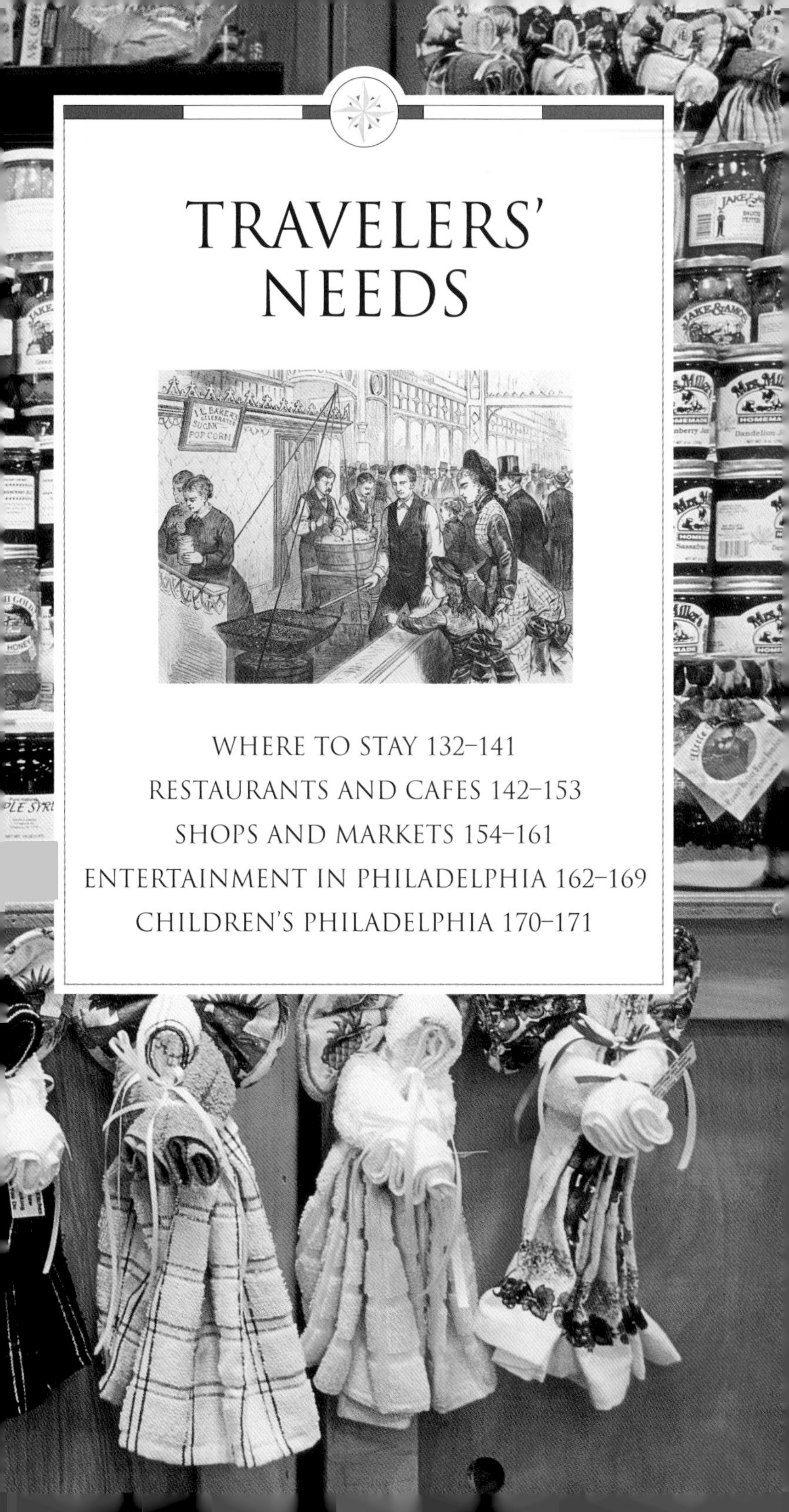

TRAVELERS' NEEDS

WHERE TO STAY

The Philadelphia area offers a wide selection of hotel rooms to fit every style and budget. More expensive hotels include towers overlooking scenic Center City and riverfront views, boutique hotels, upscale chain hotels, and smaller but luxurious bed-and-breakfasts – some with colonial themes. The more budget-conscious traveler will find a wide range of comfortable chain hotels, motels, inns, and bed-and-breakfasts within the city and beyond. Hotel rates are quite reasonable, though they tend to be higher in the more popular business district and tourist areas.

Doorman at Westin

LOCATIONS

The Center City district has the highest concentration of hotel rooms in the Philadelphia metropolitan area with over 10,000 rooms available. Business travelers prefer to stay in one of the many Center City properties, which include high-end names, such as the Four Seasons Hotel and the Ritz Carlton. In particular, hotels are clustered near Logan Square and on Market, Chestnut, and Walnut Streets, with many in and around Rittenhouse Square, the Pennsylvania Convention Center, and along the Avenue of the Arts in the theater district.

A few hotels can be found in Old City and Society Hill, while some are also located along the Delaware River waterfront. Quality hotels are also concentrated in University City, along City Line Avenue on the city's northwestern edge, at the airport, and in the suburbs of Valley Forge and King of Prussia.

FACILITIES AND AMENITIES

All hotels in Philadelphia have standard air conditioning, cable TV, and other conveniences. Upscale properties and some chain hotels have in-room business services and centers, including computer and fax facilities, though only a few smaller hotels or bed-and-breakfasts offer Internet access to guests.

Chain hotels, in particular, offer fitness facilities and some of the larger hotels have pools. Sometimes, hotels make arrangements with nearby health clubs for the use of their facilities by hotel guests. Additional charges may apply for certain amenities, and some may be costly. It is best to call and clarify when booking accommodation.

View of the First Bank of the US from a Ritz-Carlton Hotel room *(see p137)*

RESERVATIONS

Most larger chain hotels have toll-free reservation numbers, or visitors can make reservations through their Internet sites, with some offering discounts for online bookings. Prices quoted are often for double occupancy and do not include taxes or parking charges. Online hotel reservation service companies offer reduced rates for rooms, but often add hidden fees and taxes. A good resource is the website of the **Greater Philadelphia Tourism and Marketing Corporation**, with current hotel packages that may include tours, show performance tickets, and other offers.

HIDDEN COSTS

If you are traveling solo, always make sure you are quoted the rate for one person, as hotels usually quote room rates assuming double occupancy. Room taxes in Philadelphia amount to around 14 percent, while parking rates range anywhere from $10 to $30 per day. Rooms with a view can also cost more – the splendid panoramas of the waterfront, skyline, and neighborhoods can be seen from the higher floors of many hotels in the city.

◁ **Jars of traditional Amish jams, jellies, preserves, and pickles at Reading Terminal Market**

Entrance to the Radisson Plaza-Warwick Hotel Philadelphia *(see p136)*

DISCOUNTS

Discounts are often available when booking packages. The "Philly's More Fun When You Sleep Over" promotion runs at different times in the year and offers free parking, gifts, and other discounts on two weekend hotel nights for two. It is also available through the website of the **Greater Philadelphia Tourism and Marketing Corporation**.

BED-AND-BREAKFASTS

Accommodations at places offering bed-and-breakfast (B&Bs) are found within quiet and shaded neighborhoods, with some housed in quaint 18th- and 19th-century buildings and Victorian homes. Prices vary depending on services, amenities, and location. B&Bs include breakfast, but tend not to have restaurants, business facilities or exercise areas. Most B&Bs in the city are located in the neighborhoods of University City, Chestnut Hill, Center City, and near City Line Avenue. To find out more and make reservations, contact **A Bed and Breakfast Connection of Philadelphia**.

HOSTELS

Younger travelers and students often stay in hostels, which offer much cheaper accommodation than hotel rooms. Some good hostels are: the **Bank Street Hostel**, in a renovated 19th-century building, has modern amenities and is located near Independence Mall; and the **Hosteling International Chamounix Mansion**, which is situated in one of Fairmount Park's historic homes.

TRAVELING WITH CHILDREN

With Philadelphia's many historic attractions and science-oriented museums, children are warmly welcomed at most city hotels. Younger children can usually stay for free in their parents' rooms, but it is best to check when making reservations. Ask about family rates and suites that might better accommodate kids. Hotels often supply cots at an additional cost. Family hotel packages are available through the **Greater Philadelphia Tourism and Marketing Corporation** website. These may include accommodations, meals, tickets for different historic tours, or free child meals and free parking.

Bedroom at Rittenhouse 1715, a boutique hotel *(see p136)*

DISABLED TRAVELERS

Most of the larger hotels accommodate wheelchairs, while smaller establishments, such as B&Bs, may not have full amenities for the disabled as they are housed in 18th- and 19th-century homes. For more information, contact the hotels or call the **Mayor's Commission on People with Disabilities**.

DIRECTORY

ONLINE BOOKING SERVICES

Hotels.com
www.hotels.com

Lodging.com
www.lodging.com

HOTEL PACKAGES AND PROMOTIONS

Greater Philadelphia Tourism and Marketing Corporation
www.visitphilly.com

Philadelphia Convention Visitors Bureau
www.PhiladelphiaUSA.travel

BED-AND-BREAKFAST BOOKING

A Bed and Breakfast Connection of Philadelphia
Tel *(800) 448-3619, (610) 687-3565.*
www.bnbphiladelphia.com

HOSTELS

Bank Street Hostel
32 S Bank St. **Map** 4 E3.
Tel *(215) 922-0222.*
www.bankstreethostel.com

Hosteling International Chamounix Mansion
3250 Chamounix Drive, W Fairmount Park.
Tel *(800) 379-0017, (215) 878-3676.*
www.philahostel.org

DISABLED TRAVELERS

Mayor's Commission on People with Disabilities
1401 JFK Blvd. **Map** 2 F4.
Tel *(215) 686-3480.*
www.phila.gov/aco/index.html

Choosing a Hotel

Hotels have been selected across a wide price range for facilities, good value, and location. All rooms have private bath, TV, air conditioning, and have disabled access unless otherwise indicated. Most have Internet access, and in some cases, fitness facilities may be offsite. The hotels are listed by area. For map references, *see pp194–7.*

PRICE CATEGORIES
The price ranges are for a standard double room per night, including tax, during the high season. Breakfast is not included, unless specified.
($) $60–$105
($)($) $106–$145
($)($)($) $146–$185
($)($)($)($) $186–$240
($)($)($)($)($) Over $240

OLD CITY

Comfort Inn Downtown/Historic Area ($)($)

100 N Columbus Blvd, Philadelphia **Tel** *(215) 627-7900* **Fax** *(215) 238-0809* **Rooms** *185* **Map** *4 E2*

This budget-priced, high-rise hotel has no frills but is in a great location within walking distance of historic sites. It offers clean, comfortable rooms, as well as a free Continental breakfast. In addition, children under 18 stay free with parents. It offers easy access to the I-95 and good views of the Delaware River. **www.choicehotels.com**

Best Western Independence Park Hotel ($)($)($)

235 Chestnut St, Philadelphia **Tel** *(215) 922-4443* **Fax** *(215) 922-4487* **Rooms** *36* **Map** *4 E3*

Small, historic hotel dating back to 1856 with exquisitely decorated rooms, located within the heart of Old City and just a few blocks from Independence Mall and Penn's Landing. The hotel offers complimentary breafast and free wired or wireless high-speed Internet access. **www.independenceparkhotel.com**

Holiday Inn Historic District ($)($)($)

400 Arch St, Philadelphia **Tel** *(215) 923-8660* **Fax** *(215) 829-1796* **Rooms** *364* **Map** *4 E2*

Comfortable chain hotel with reasonably priced rooms. Its excellent and convenient location – one block from Independence Mall and within walking distance of the Market Street shopping area – make it a popular destination for tourists. Children love the rooftop pool during the warmer months. **www.phillydowntownhotel.com**

Morris House Hotel ($)($)($)

225 S 8th St, Philadelphia **Tel** *(215) 922-2446* **Fax** *(215) 922-2466* **Rooms** *15* **Map** *3 C3*

This 1787 home is now a luxury boutique hotel and is one of the city's best hotels to experience colonial ambience. It has the coziness of a B&B and unique features such as a private garden, colonial-style reading room, two dining rooms with fireplaces, and rooms with hardwood floors. **www.morrishousehotel.com**

Omni Hotel ($)($)($)($)

401 Chestnut St, Philadelphia **Tel** *(215) 925-0000* **Fax** *(215) 925-1263* **Rooms** *150* **Map** *4 D3*

This four-star, four-diamond hotel has large-sized rooms with marble bathrooms. It is just a few blocks from key restaurants and nightlife spots, and within walking distance of shopping stores and Jewelers' Row. The rooms offer views of the Independence Mall area. **www.omnihotels.com**

Penn's View Hotel ($)($)($)($)

14 N Front & Market Sts, Philadelphia **Tel** *(215) 922-7600* **Fax** *(215) 922-7642* **Rooms** *52* **Map** *4 E3*

Cozy and family owned, this European-style hotel features murals and marble throughout the property. Its superb Italian "Ristorante Panorama" and the unique "Il Bar" offers over 120 wines by the glass *(see p147)*. Situated across from Penn's Landing, it is just a block away from excellent restaurants and nightlife. **www.pennsviewhotel.com**

Hotel Monaco Philadelphia ($)($)($)($)($)

433 Chestnut St, Philadelphia **Tel** *(215) 925-2111* **Rooms** *268* **Map** *4 D3*

Housed in the historic 1907 Lafayette Building, this luxurious boutique hotel is located near the iconic Liberty Bell. The comfortable rooms are decorated with early-period design features and include all modern amenities. The adjoining restaurant, Red Owl Tavern, has a rooftop lounge. **www.monaco-philadelphia.com**

SOCIETY HILL AND PENN'S LANDING

Sheraton Society Hill ($)($)($)

1 Dock St, Philadelphia **Tel** *(215) 238-6000* **Fax** *(215) 238-6652* **Rooms** *365* **Map** *4 E4*

The Sheraton Society Hill is another excellent hotel for the business traveler. There is a 24-hour business center, computer rentals, and a secretarial service. Situated on cobblestoned Dock Street, the hotel is also ideal for tourists as it is just a block or two from Penn's Landing. **www.sheraton.com/societyhill**

Key to Symbols *see back cover flap*

Hyatt Regency Philadelphia at Penn's Landing $$$$

201 S Columbus Blvd, Philadelphia ***Tel*** *(215) 928-1234* ***Fax*** *(215) 521-6543* ***Rooms*** *350* ***Map*** *4 F3*

This upscale property on Penn's Landing is Philadelphia's only waterfront hotel. Twenty-two stories overlook the Delaware River, and also offer superb views of Society Hill and Center City. Elegant rooms with a full range of amenities make it ideal for the business traveler. **www.hyattregencyphiladelphia.com**

CENTER CITY

Alexander Inn $$

12th & Spruce Sts, Philadelphia ***Tel*** *(215) 923-3535* ***Fax*** *(215) 923-1004* ***Rooms*** *48* ***Map*** *3 B3*

This boutique hotel has modern decor that adds a touch of European charm. It has an excellent Center City location, just a couple of blocks from the theater district. The restaurant only serves a breakfast buffet, and the business center allows guests to access emails. **www.alexanderinn.com**

Hampton Inn Convention Center $$

1301 Race St, Philadelphia ***Tel*** *(215) 665-9100* ***Fax*** *(215) 665-9200* ***Rooms*** *250* ***Map*** *3 B1*

Located right next to the Convention Center, this property is ideal for people attending conventions. It is situated a few blocks from Chinatown and the Market Street shopping area and within walking distance of historic sights. The rooms have modern amenities, including high-speed Internet access. **www.hershahotels.com**

Hilton Garden Inn Philadelphia Center City $$

1100 Arch St, Philadelphia ***Tel*** *(215) 923-0100* ***Fax*** *(215) 925-0800* ***Rooms*** *279* ***Map*** *3 C2*

This popular and fashionable chain hotel is located near the Pennsylvania Convention Center, a block or two from Chinatown. All rooms are outfitted with a kitchenette. The rooftop restaurant and lounge offer city views. **www.philadelphiacentercity.stayhgi.com**

Holiday Inn Express Midtown $$

1305 Walnut St, Philadelphia ***Tel*** *(215) 735-9300* ***Fax*** *(215) 732-2593* ***Rooms*** *166* ***Map*** *3 B3*

A comfortable budget chain hotel, this Holiday Inn has a convenient location just a few blocks from the theater district and the Market Street shopping area. Complimentary Continental breakfast is served and the hotel gives passes for a nearby fitness center to those guests who wish to keep in shape. **www.himidtown.com**

La Reserve Center City Bed and Breakfast $$

1804 Pine St, Philadelphia ***Tel*** *(215) 735-1137* ***Fax*** *(215) 735-0582* ***Rooms*** *7* ***Map*** *2 D5*

A luxurious and cozy B&B in a Philadelphia townhouse, La Reserve has elegant rooms with antiques and beautiful lamps. The establishment has an all-you-can-eat gourmet breakfast and free wireless Internet access. Parking is available at nearby lots. **www.lareservebandb.com**

Travelodge $$

1227 Race St, Philadelphia ***Tel*** *(215) 564-2888* ***Fax*** *(215) 564-2700* ***Rooms*** *50* ***Map*** *3 B1*

This budget chain hotel has clean rooms and serves a complimentary Continental breakfast. Located directly across from the Pennsylvania Convention Center and just one block from Chinatown, it is within walking distance of historic sights and the Market Street shopping district. **www.travelodge.com**

Courtyard by Marriott Philadelphia Downtown $$$

21 N Juniper St, Philadelphia ***Tel*** *(215) 496-3200* ***Fax*** *(215) 496-3696* ***Rooms*** *498* ***Map*** *2 F4*

This is a comfortable Marriott-brand hotel housed in the historic, former City Hall Annex building. Located across the street from the Masonic Temple and the Pennsylvania Academy of the Fine Arts, it is just a few blocks from the Convention Center. Lobby and lounge areas are expansive. **www.philadelphiadowntowncourtyard.com**

Doubletree by Hilton Philadelphia $$$

237 S Broad St, Philadelphia ***Tel*** *(215) 893-1600* ***Fax*** *(215) 893-1664* ***Rooms*** *427* ***Map*** *2 F5*

A high-rise hotel in the heart of Philadelphia on the Avenue of the Arts, this property is across from the Kimmel Center, the Academy of Music, and the Merriam Theater. The lobby has a comfortable lounge area and sports bar and bistro, and the roof garden sports a jogging track. **www.philadelphia.doubletree.com**

The Independent Hotel $$$

1234 Locust St, Philadelphia ***Tel*** *(215) 772-1440* ***Fax*** *(215) 772-1022* ***Rooms*** *24* ***Map*** *3 B3*

This sophisticated boutique hotel is housed in a restored Georgian Revival building in Center City's hip, midtown village district. The rooms are stylish and well equipped; single and double rooms have queen size beds while the executive room beds are king size. A complimentary breakfast is served in the hotel's fireside lounge. **www.theindependenthotel.com**

Latham Hotel $$$

135 S 17th St, Philadelphia ***Tel*** *(215) 563-7474* ***Fax*** *(215) 563-4034* ***Rooms*** *139* ***Map*** *2 D4*

This small, European-style boutique hotel is in the heart of the fashionable Rittenhouse Row shopping district. Rooms are modern and contemporary in style. The hotel offers all modern amenities, including free wireless Internet access in all rooms. It also boasts a hip bar and restaurant. **www.lathamhotel.com**

Rodeway Inn Center City $$$

1208 Walnut St, 19107 ***Tel*** *(215) 546-7000* ***Fax*** *(215) 546-7573* ***Rooms*** *32* ***Map*** *3 B3*

No-frills accommodations, but shortcomings in luxury are compensated for by the location, blocks from City Hall, theaters, and an exciting restaurant and bar scene along 13th Street. Rooms are small, and parking is at an independent lot across the street. **www.rodewayinn.com**

Crowne Plaza Philadelphia Center City $$$$

1800 Market St, Philadelphia ***Tel*** *(215) 561-7500* ***Fax*** *(215) 561-7500* ***Rooms*** *445* ***Map*** *2 E4*

Located within the city's cluster of skyscrapers, this chain hotel is ideal for business travelers. It offers modern, comfortable rooms. Just a few blocks from Rittenhouse Square with its many fine restaurants and boutiques, it is within walking distance of the theater and museum districts. **www.cpphiladelphia.com**

Hotel Palomar $$$$

117 S 17th St, 19103 ***Tel*** *(215) 563-5006* ***Fax*** *(215) 563-5007* ***Rooms*** *230* ***Map*** *2 E4*

A modernist renovation of a historical building has resulted in an eye-catching, stylish, and eco-friendly boutique hotel. A well-regarded restaurant and hip lobby bar add to the appeal. The location is only steps away from Center City shopping areas, the upscale Rittenhouse Park, and an array of dining choices. **www.hotelpalomar-philadelphia.com**

Hyatt at the Bellevue $$$$

200 S Broad St,,Philadelphia ***Tel*** *(215) 893-1234* ***Fax*** *(215) 732-8518* ***Rooms*** *172* ***Map*** *2 E5*

A residential-style hotel with international flair, the Hyatt is perched on the upper floors of the 1904 Bellevue Building, which was once nicknamed the "Grand Dame of Broad Street." Marble staircases and chandeliers highlight the old world elegance. The property has upscale shops on its premises. **www.philadelphia.bellevue.hyatt.com**

Loews Philadelphia $$$$

1200 Market St, Philadelphia ***Tel*** *(215) 627-1200* ***Fax*** *(215) 231-7205* ***Rooms*** *581* ***Map*** *3 B2*

This high-rise luxury hotel is housed in the landmark PSFS building, a 1932 former bank office. It has been renovated with elegant decor and Art Deco accents, including exotic woods and carved glass. Rooms offer astounding views. A spa and fitness center encompass the entire fifth floor of the hotel. **www.loewsphiladelphia.com**

Philadelphia Marriott Downtown $$$$

1201 Market St, Philadelphia ***Tel*** *(215) 625-2900* ***Fax*** *(215) 625-6000* ***Rooms*** *1,408* ***Map*** *3 B2*

A world-class convention hotel connected to the Convention Center and Reading Terminal Market, the Philadelphia Downtown Marriott offers upgraded amenities on concierge-level floors. Located in the heart of the Market Street shopping area and within walking distance of historic sights and the theater district. **www.philadelphiamarriott.com**

Radisson Plaza-Warwick Hotel Philadelphia $$$$

1701 Locust St, Philadelphia ***Tel*** *(215) 735-6000* ***Fax*** *(215) 790-7788* ***Rooms*** *300* ***Map*** *2 E5*

One block from fashionable Rittenhouse Square, this is a prestigious hotel whose guests have included celebrities and presidents. Built in 1926 in English Renaissance style, it has a majestic two-story lobby with a sweeping staircase, and an upscale steakhouse, The Prime Rib *(see p149)*. **www.radisson.com/philadelphiapa**

Sofitel Philadelphia $$$$

120 S 17th St, Philadelphia ***Tel*** *(215) 569-8300* ***Fax*** *(215) 569-1492* ***Rooms*** *306* ***Map*** *2 E4*

An elegant, four-diamond hotel with a distinctive French flair in design and embellishments, the Sofitel houses a chic French restaurant, and the lobby has a bar with dramatic floor-to-ceiling windows. The spacious rooms have elegant and modern decor. Rittenhouse Row shopping areas and restaurants are only a block away. **www.sofitel-philadelphia.com**

The Westin Philadelphia $$$$

99 S 17th St, Philadelphia ***Tel*** *(215) 563-1600* ***Fax*** *(215) 564-9559* ***Rooms*** *294* ***Map*** *2 E4*

This is an elegant chain hotel with luxuriously decorated lobby, lounge areas, and restaurants. The hotel is connected to Liberty Place, which has trendy shops and boutiques. It has a great location just a few blocks from the Rittenhouse Row shopping hub, and the theater and museum districts. **www.westin.com/philadelphia**

AKA Rittenhouse Square $$$$$

135 S 18th St, Philadelphia ***Tel*** *(215) 825-7000* ***Fax*** *(215) 563-8486* ***Rooms*** *80* ***Map*** *2 D5*

This luxury development, overlooking Rittenhouse Square, is one of a new generation of extended stay hotel residences that offer the comfort of a furnished apartment with the amenities of a hotel. Accommodations comprise contemporary studios, one and two bedroom apartments, and penthouse suites. Minimum one week stay. **www.hotelaka.com**

Le Meridien Philadelphia $$$$$

1421 Arch St, 19102 ***Tel*** *(215) 422-8200* ***Fax*** *(215) 422-8277* ***Rooms*** *202* ***Map*** *2 F3*

A classic stone Georgian-revival building, this hotel features a striking atrium lobby and a mix of antiques and contemporary style. Overlooking City Hall, it is centrally located near the Convention Center, museums, and major business headquarters. Off-site valet parking means planning ahead to retrieve your car. **www.lemeridien.com/philadelphia**

Rittenhouse 1715 $$$$$

1715 Rittenhouse Sq, Philadelphia ***Tel*** *(215) 546-6500* ***Fax*** *(215) 546-8787* ***Rooms*** *23* ***Map*** *2 D5*

This 16-room boutique hotel offers posh accommodation in a refurbished 1900s Philadelphia carriage house. It boasts a private, elegant, and luxurious lobby, serves a complimentary Continental breakfast in a Parisian-like breakfast room, and has a 24-hour concierge service. Parking is available at nearby lots. **www.rittenhouse1715.com**

The Rittenhouse Hotel & Condominiums $$$$$

210 W Rittenhouse Sq, Philadelphia **Tel** *(215) 546-9000* **Fax** *(215) 732-3364* **Rooms** *98* **Map** *2 D5*

This top-of-the-line luxury hotel is one of the city's finest and boasts two award-winning restaurants, the Lacroix and the Smith & Wollensky steakhouse *(see p149)*. A five-diamond property with lavishly decorated rooms and marble bathrooms, the hotel also has an upscale spa and salon. **www.rittenhousehotel.com**

The Ritz-Carlton Hotel Philadelphia $$$$$

10 S Broad St, Philadelphia **Tel** *(215) 523-8000* **Fax** *(215) 568-0942* **Rooms** *273* **Map** *2 F4*

This exquisite, five-diamond luxury hotel sits directly across from City Hall in the former Girard/Mellon Bank Building. It has an impressive columned façade entrance and the lobby is situated in the expansive rotunda. The rooms are lavishly decorated and have superb city views. **www.ritzcarlton.com/philadelphia**

LOGAN SQUARE AND PARKWAY MUSEUMS DISTRICT

Best Western Center City Hotel $$$

501 N 22nd St, Philadelphia **Tel** *(215) 568-8300* **Fax** *(215) 557-0259* **Rooms** *183* **Map** *2 D1*

A four-story budget hotel, this Best Western has the advantage of a good location within walking distance of the museum district. Some rooms offer excellent views of the Philadelphia skyline. Children who are 18 and younger can stay free with a paying adult. **www.bestwestern.com/centercityhotel**

Embassy Suites Hotel Philadelphia Center City $$$

1776 Benjamin Franklin Pkwy, Philadelphia **Tel** *(215) 561-1776* **Fax** *(215) 561-1850* **Rooms** *288* **Map** *2 E3*

Popular hotel in a landmark cylindrical building opposite Logan Square. This chain features only suites – every room has an adjacent living room and a balcony. Situated in the museum district and close to the Museum of Art and Rittenhouse Square. The fitness room has a jogging track. **www.philadelphiacentercity.embsuites.com**

Sheraton Philadelphia Downtown $$$

201 N 17th St, Philadelphia **Tel** *(215) 448-2000* **Fax** *(215) 448-2853* **Rooms** *757* **Map** *2 E3*

This upscale, high-rise hotel is ideal for both the business and vacation traveler. Located four blocks from the Convention Center, it has a fabulous seafood restaurant and an impressive modern design with a four-story high lobby atrium. The comfortable and gracious rooms have all the modern amenities. **www.sheratonphiladelphiadowntown.com**

The Windsor Suites $$$$

1700 Benjamin Franklin Pkwy, Philadelphia **Tel** *(215) 981-5678* **Fax** *(215) 981-5609* **Rooms** *148* **Map** *2 E3*

Specialty hotel that offers furnished suites and unfurnished apartments. All rooms have complimentary high-speed Internet access and kitchens. Some suites have living rooms, separate sleeping areas, and private balconies. The hotel has two restaurants on its premises. **www.thewindsorsuites.com**

Four Seasons Hotel $$$$$

1 Logan Sq, Philadelphia **Tel** *(215) 963-1500* **Fax** *(215) 963-9507* **Rooms** *364* **Map** *2 E3*

One of Philadelphia's most elegant hotels, the Four Seasons is luxuriously decorated with Federal-style furnishings. It features one of the city's best restaurants *(see p150)*, as well as a courtyard café with decorative water fountains. It is located close to the financial, commercial, and museum districts. **www.fourseasons.com/philadelphia**

FARTHER AFIELD

The Hotel ML $

915 Rt 73, Mount Laurel, NJ, 08054 **Tel** *(856) 234-7300* **Fax** *(856) 802-3912* **Rooms** *281*

This pleasant suburban hotel is excellent for both business travelers and tourists. The hotel features a premier restaurant and bar and a heated pool. Concierge-level rooms have upgraded amenities and balconies. There is also a game room for children, tennis courts, and a water park, which is connected to the hotel. **www.thehotelml.com**

Howard Johnson Inn and Conference Center $

2389 Rt 70 W, Cherry Hill, NJ, 08002 **Tel** *(877) 851-6763* **Fax** *(856) 317-0800* **Rooms** *90*

This budget hotel is located within 5 miles (8 km) of Center City in Philadelphia. It is also well-placed to visit other sights, such as the Adventure Aquarium and the Camden Waterfront. The hotel offers a complimentary Continental breakfast and there is an Indian restaurant on the premises. **www.hojo.com**

Ramada Inn Philadelphia Airport $

76 Industrial Hwy, Essington, PA, 19029 **Tel** *(610) 521-9600* **Fax** *(610) 521-9388* **Rooms** *292*

Located 3 miles (5 km) south of Philadelphia Airport, this comfortable hotel has a complimentary, 24-hour shuttle service to the airport. Each room has its own balcony. Special discounts are available for groups of ten or more people. **http://ramadaphl.com**

Chestnut Hill Hotel $$

8229 Germantown Ave, Philadelphia, PA, 19118 **Tel** *(215) 242-4900* **Fax** *(215) 242-8778* **Rooms** *36*

Built in 1891, this historic hotel is situated along the cobblestoned streets of Germantown Avenue. Although furnished with 18th-century decor, it offers all modern amenities. Within walking distance of Fairmount Park's Wissahickon Gorge and a short drive from historic Germantown. **www.chestnuthillhotel.com**

Conwell Inn at Temple University $$

1331 Polett Walk, Philadelphia, PA, 19122 **Tel** *(215) 235-6200* **Fax** *(215) 235-6235* **Rooms** *22*

A small hotel, Conwell Inn lies within the heart of the Temple University campus. A deluxe historic landmark hotel, it has cozy and comfortable rooms and suites that have been decorated very tastefully. The hotel provides a complimentary European breakfast. **www.conwellinn.com**

Fairfield Inn Philadelphia Airport $$

8800 Bartram Ave, Philadelphia, PA, 19153 **Tel** *(215) 365-2254* **Fax** *(215) 365-2254* **Rooms** *109*

Located just half a mile away from the airport, this comfortable, high-end budget property by Marriott offers full amenities and conveniences at superior value for the dollar. Complimentary Continental breakfast. 3 miles (5 km) from professional sports venues in south Philadelphia. **www.marriott.com**

Hampton Inn Philadelphia Airport $$

8600 Bartram Ave, Philadelphia, PA, 19158 **Tel** *(215) 966-1300* **Fax** *(215) 966-1313* **Rooms** *152*

The Hampton Inn is a quality budget hotel with clean and comfortable rooms. The hotel offers a shuttle service to the airport, which is about 2 miles (3 km) away. A short drive away are professional sports stadiums and south Philadelphia sights, including the Italian Market. **www.hamptoninn.com**

Quality Inn & Conference Center $$

531 Rt 38 W, Maple Shade, NJ, 08052 **Tel** *(856) 235-6400* **Fax** *(856) 727-1027* **Rooms** *109*

This three-diamond hotel and conference center is ideal for both the business and leisure traveler and features Jacuzzi suites. The bar by the poolside is open only on the weekends. About 10 miles (16 km) from central Philadelphia, it is also close to a number of entertainment areas. **www.qualityinn.com/hotel/nj129**

Cornerstone Bed & Breakfast $$$

3300 Baring St, Philadelphia, PA, 19104 **Tel** *(215) 387-6065* **Fax** *(215) 387-0590* **Rooms** *6* **Map** *1 A2*

This intimate urban inn sits in a restored 1870s church-stone mansion, and has a wrap-around porch and stained glass windows. Its lavishly decorated rooms and lounge areas have original wood floors and high ceilings. The inn is situated close to the Philadelphia Zoo and the Museum of Art. **www.cornerstonebandb.com**

Crowne Plaza Hotel Philadelphia – Cherry Hill $$$

2349 W Marlton Pike, Cherry Hill, NJ, 08002 **Tel** *(856) 382-6179* **Fax** *(856) 662-1414* **Rooms** *408*

Located in suburban Cherry Hill, this upscale and full-service Hilton property features modern rooms with full amenities, dark oak furniture, and marble countertops. It is convenient for visiting the Adventure Aquarium and the Camden Waterfront, while the Atlantic City beaches and casinos are just an hour away. **www.crowneplaza.com/cherryhillnj**

Embassy Suites Hotel – Philadelphia International Airport $$$

9000 Bartram Ave, Philadelphia, PA, 19153 **Tel** *(215) 365-4500* **Fax** *(215) 365-4803* **Rooms** *263*

This three-diamond, modern chain hotel is an all-suites establishment. It has a unique tropical atrium lobby, which is filled with ducks and fishponds. The hotel offers a complimentary cook-to-order breakfast. Just one mile (1.6 km) from the Philadelphia Airport. Free airport shuttle. **www.philadelphiaairport.embsuites.com**

Hilton Inn at Penn $$$

3600 Sansom St, Philadelphia, PA, 19104 **Tel** *(215) 222-0200* **Fax** *(215) 222-4600* **Rooms** *238*

Just across the Schuylkill River from Center City, this upscale Hilton hotel sits in the heart of the University of Pennsylvania campus. Also close to the Drexel University, Philadelphia Zoo, 30th Street Amtrak Station, and the University of Pennsylvania's Museum of Archaeology and Anthropology. **www.theinnatpenn.com**

Hilton Philadelphia Airport $$$

4509 Island Ave, Philadelphia, PA, 19153 **Tel** *(215) 365-4150* **Fax** *(215) 937-6382* **Rooms** *331*

The Hilton chain offers comfort and a touch of elegance with this full-service hotel, located just one mile (1.6 km) from the airport. The Landing Restaurant and Grill is highly recommended, as are its bar and indoor pool. A complimentary 24-hour airport shuttle service is offered. Close to the city's sports stadiums. **www.hilton.com**

Hilton Philadelphia City Avenue $$$

4200 City Ave, Philadelphia, PA, 19131 **Tel** *(215) 879-4000* **Fax** *(215) 879-9020* **Rooms** *209*

An upscale chain hotel on the outskirts of the city, this Hilton hotel is a short drive from Fairmount Park and the Barnes Foundation. It has comfortable and elegantly furnished rooms. Guests can indulge in plenty of shopping and culinary delights in the shops and restaurants on City Avenue. **www.philadelphiacityavenue.hilton.com**

Holiday Inn Philadelphia Stadium $$$

900 Packer Ave, Philadelphia, PA, 19148 **Tel** *(215) 755-9500* **Fax** *(215) 339-0842* **Rooms** *238*

This hotel is ideal for fans taking in a game at one of the nearby professional sports venues in south Philadelphia. The rooms are comfortable, with a full range of amenities for leisure and business travelers. There is a sports bar and restaurant on the premises. **www.ichotelsgroup.com**

Key to Price Guide *see p134* **Key to Symbols** *see back cover flap*

Residence Inn Cherry Hill Philadelphia $$$

1821 Old Cuthbert Rd, Cherry Hill, NJ, 08034 ***Tel*** *(856) 429-6111* ***Rooms*** *96*

Located just 12 miles (20 km) from Philadelphia, this hotel offers spacious and comfortable studio and two-bedroom suites that include a kitchenette, a living space, and a large work area for extended stays. The hotel also provides a shuttle service to the Philadelphia International Airport. **www.residenceinncherryhill.com**

Sheraton University City Hotel $$$

3549 Chestnut St, Philadelphia, PA, 19104 ***Tel*** *(215) 387-8000* ***Fax*** *(215) 387-7920* ***Rooms*** *332*

This is a large and efficient full-service chain hotel on the University of Pennsylvania campus. Rooms have modern decor with plush beds and oversized chairs. Ideal for visiting Philadelphia Zoo and the Museum of Archaeology and Anthropology. The lobby features complimentary, wireless Internet access. **www.philadelphiasheraton.com**

Renaissance Hotel Philadelphia Airport $$$$

500 Stevens Dr, Philadelphia, PA, 19113 ***Tel*** *(610) 521-5900* ***Fax*** *(610) 521-8954* ***Rooms*** *350*

This four-diamond, modern, and upscale chain hotel is on I-95, close to the airport. It is tastefully decorated with the Renaissance's signature European flair. There is an expansive lobby atrium and the rooms have high-speed Internet access. It is in a convenient location for a quick drive into the city on the interstate. **www.renaissancehotels.com**

Philadelphia Airport Marriott $$$$$

Arrivals Rd, Philadelphia, PA, 19153 ***Tel*** *(215) 492-9000* ***Fax*** *(215) 492-4799* ***Rooms*** *419*

This upscale and full-service Marriott Hotel is the only one in Philadelphia connected to the airport via a skybridge to Terminal B. Nearby is the convenient R1 commuter train linking the airport with Center City. Terrific in-hotel dining and lounge at Riverbend Bar and Grille. **www.philadelphiaairportmarriott.com**

BEYOND PHILADELPHIA

ATLANTIC CITY Bally's Atlantic City Hotel & Casino $$$$

1900 Pacific Ave, Atlantic City, NJ, 08401 ***Tel*** *(609) 340-2000* ***Fax*** *(609) 340-4713* ***Rooms*** *1,246*

One of the few remnants of historic Atlantic City, the 1860s Dennis Hotel has been restored as part of this mega-resort complex, which also includes a modern 45-story tower. Fans of the board game Monopoly will know that the hotel stands on the city's most valuable corner. The hotel's casino features a Wild West theme. **www.ballysAC.com**

ATLANTIC CITY Caesars Atlantic City Hotel Casino $$$$

2100 Pacific Ave, Atlantic City, NJ, 08401 ***Tel*** *(609) 348-4411* ***Fax*** *(609) 343-2405* ***Rooms*** *1,144*

A premier destination on the New Jersey shore, Caesars is a luxurious hotel and casino on the Boardwalk with an "Ancient Rome" theme. The hotel's lobby is done up to look like a Roman temple, and there are 11 restaurants and 3 lounges. The 1,100-seat Circus Maximus Theater offers the best in entertainment. **www.caesarsac.com**

ATLANTIC CITY Trump Taj Mahal Hotel Casino and Resort $$$$$

1000 Boardwalk at Virginia Ave, Atlantic City, NJ, 08401 ***Tel*** *(609) 449-1000* ***Rooms*** *1,250*

One of Atlantic City's landmark casinos, this luxury five-diamond resort has all the opulence that lives up to the Trump name. A 51-story tower hovers over the Boardwalk, and the themed hotel and casino has 9 in-house restaurants *(see p152)* and a 5,000-seat arena for concerts and sports events. **www.trumptaj.com**

BRANDYWINE VALLEY Brandywine River Hotel $$

1609 Baltimore Pike, Chadds Ford, PA, 19317 ***Tel*** *(610) 388-1200* ***Rooms*** *40*

A Victorian-style country B&B, the Brandywine River Hotel has elegantly decorated rooms with fireplaces and Jacuzzis. It is a short drive from Longwood Gardens, Brandywine Battlefield, Brandywine River Museum, Chadds Ford, and Winterthur. The hotel is surrounded by several award-winning restaurants. **www.brandywineriverhotel.com**

CAPE MAY The Chalfonte Hotel $$

301 Howard St, Cape May, NJ, 08204 ***Tel*** *(609) 884-8409* ***Fax*** *(609) 884-4588* ***Rooms*** *70*

This whitewashed Victorian-era hotel was built in 1874 and offers old-fashioned charm with rocking chairs on the wrap-around front porch. Chalfonte has always been unconventional – rooms have no televisions or phones, and the hotel is just two blocks from the beach. **www.chalfonte.com**

CAPE MAY Queen Victoria Bed and Breakfast $$$$

102 Ocean St, Cape May, NJ, 08204 ***Tel*** *(609) 884-8720* ***Rooms*** *32*

Built in the 1870s and fully restored in 1995, this mansard-roofed Victorian inn is located in the heart of Cape May, just a block from the beach, antiques shops, gourmet dining, and historic tours. Bicycles to tour the area are available for free, and the hotel provides a complimentary European breakfast buffet. **www.queenvictoria.com**

DELEWARE Hotel du Pont $$$$$

11th & Market Sts, Wilmington, DE, 19801 ***Tel*** *(302) 594-3100* ***Fax*** *(302) 594-3108* ***Rooms*** *217*

Dating back to 1913, this four-diamond, four-star hotel is the ultimate in luxury in Delaware. Each room is lavishly furnished with mahogany furniture and brass bathroom fixtures. Close to most of the region's attractions, including the Brandywine River Museum, Winterthur, Hagley Museum, and Longwood Gardens. **www.hoteldupont.com**

DOYLESTOWN Hargrave House $$$

50 S Main St, Doylestown, PA, 18901 **Tel** *(215) 340-1814* **Fax** *(215) 340-2234* **Rooms** *7*

This historic inn is within walking distance of the Mercer Museum and the James A. Michener Art Museum. Many rooms overlook Doylestown Historical Society Park. The rooms are decorated with 19th-century furnishings, but have all modern conveniences. A full country breakfast is offered on weekends. **http://hargravehouse.net**

GETTYSBURG Quality Inn at General Lee's Headquarters $

401 Buford Ave, Gettysburg, PA, 17325 **Tel** *(717) 334-3141* **Fax** *(717) 334-1813* **Rooms** *45*

Quaint inn with renovated rooms next to Confederate General Robert E. Lee's former headquarters. The three-diamond inn has spacious, bright, and clean rooms with antique furniture. Two-story suites are also available. Free Continental breakfast and admission to General Lee's Headquarters Museum. **www.thegettysburgaddress.com**

GETTYSBURG Farnsworth House Inn $$

401 Baltimore St, Gettysburg, PA, 17325 **Tel** *(717) 334-8838* **Fax** *(717) 334-5862* **Rooms** *16*

This B&B is housed in one of Gettysburg's most historic buildings, with walls that still have bullet holes from the Civil War, and a small open-air garden. The lavish rooms have period decor, and the B&B conducts ghost tours of some of the "haunted" rooms. It also has quaint dining rooms *(see p152)*. **www.farnsworthhouseinn.com**

GETTYSBURG Gettystown Inn $$

89 Steinwehr Ave, Gettysburg, PA, 17325 **Tel** *(717) 334-2100* **Fax** *(717) 334-6905* **Rooms** *9*

Victorian B&B consisting of three separate Civil War-era houses near where President Lincoln delivered his famous Gettysburg Address *(see p121)*. Rooms are lavishly decorated with 19th-century antiques and furnishings. A complimentary breakfast is served at the adjacent Dobbin House Tavern *(see p152)*. **www.dobbinhouse.com**

GETTYSBURG The Brafferton Inn $$$

44 York St, Gettysburg, PA, 17325 **Tel** *(717) 337-3423, (866) 337-3423* **Rooms** *17*

This elegant and lovely B&B is located in a 1786 fieldstone house – the oldest residence in Gettysburg. All rooms are furnished with 18th- and 19th-century family antiques, elaborate stencils, and family portraits. A two-night stay is the minimum on weekends from April to November. **www.brafferton.com**

GETTYSBURG Hilton Garden Inn Gettysburg $$$

1061 York St, Gettysburg, PA, 17325 **Tel** *(717) 334-2040* **Fax** *(717) 334-2073* **Rooms** *88*

A pleasant hotel focused on both business and leisure travelers. All the rooms are beautifully appointed, with a refrigerator, microwave, and complimentary Internet access. The hotel is located a short distance away from the historic battlefield, museums, and the town center. **www.hiltongardeninn.com**

HARRISBURG Hilton Harrisburg $$$

1 N 2nd St, Harrisburg, PA, 17101 **Tel** *(717) 233-6000* **Fax** *(717) 233-6830* **Rooms** *341*

This upscale, full-service Hilton hotel is just three blocks from the State Capitol. It has elegant rooms; "Tower Level" guest rooms are accorded enhanced amenities, including a complimentary Continental breakfast and evening hors d'ouevres. The hotel has four restaurants on its premises. **www.harrisburg.hilton.com**

HERSHEY Hampton Inn & Suites Hershey $$$$

749 East Chocolate Ave, Hershey, PA, 17033 **Tel** *(717) 533-8400* **Fax** *(717) 520-1892* **Rooms** *110*

A comfortable chain hotel in downtown Hershey, the Hampton Inn & Suites is only 1 mile (1.6 km) from the renowned attractions of the area, including Hershey Chocolate World and Hershey Park. The hotel offers a complimentary Continental breakfast and high-speed Internet access. **www.hamptoninn.com**

HERSHEY The Hotel Hershey $$$$$

100 Hotel Rd, Hershey, PA, 17033 **Tel** *(717) 533-2171* **Fax** *(717) 534-8887* **Rooms** *232*

This grand hotel with its majestic gardens and fountains sits atop a hill overlooking the town. Luxurious and lavishly decorated rooms and common areas have old-world charm, and historic photographs and original artworks line the walls. Turndown service at night with Hershey's "Kisses" chocolates. **www.thehotelhershey.com**

PENNSYLVANIA DUTCH COUNTRY General Sutter Inn $

14 E Main St, Lititz, PA, 17543 **Tel** *(717) 626-2115* **Fax** *(717) 626-0992* **Rooms** *15*

The General Sutter Inn is one of the oldest in Pennsylvania, dating back to 1764. Spacious rooms and suites are decorated with antiques in Victorian style. It is home to two fine restaurants and a lively bar, and has a delightful courtyard that is used for outdoor dining and cocktails. **www.generalsutterinn.com**

PENNSYLVANIA DUTCH COUNTRY Revere Inn & Suites $

3063 Lincoln Hwy, Paradise, PA, 17562 **Tel** *(717) 687-8601* **Fax** *(717) 687-6141* **Rooms** *95*

This unique hotel has comfortable and tastefully decorated rooms and suites in three different buildings, including the 18th-century Revere House. All rooms have modern amenities and the historic Revere Tavern restaurant is situated on the property. Located on Route 30 in the heart of the Pennsylvania Dutch Country. **www.reveretavern.com**

PENNSYLVANIA DUTCH COUNTRY Bird-In-Hand Family Inn $$

2740 Old Philadelphia Pike, Bird-In-Hand, PA, 17505 **Tel** *(800) 665-8780* **Fax** *(717) 768-1117* **Rooms** *125*

This large, three-diamond property is an ideal getaway for a family holiday. Facilities such as tennis courts, mini-golf, a playground, game room, and even a petting zoo keep the kids busy. It has a family restaurant with an all-you-can-eat buffet. **www.bird-in-hand.com/familyinn**

Key to Price Guide *see p134* **Key to Symbols** *see back cover flap*

PENNSYLVANIA DUTCH COUNTRY Bird-In-Hand Village Inn & Suites $$

2695 Old Philadelphia Pike, Bird-In-Hand, PA, 17505 ***Tel*** *(717) 293-8369* ***Fax*** *(717) 768-1117* ***Rooms*** *24*

This 1734 inn is responsible for the unique naming of this small town. Four well-preserved historic buildings house rooms and suites. The complimentary Continental breakfast includes local freshly baked treats. Guests can take a 2-hour complimentary bus tour of the area. **www.bird-in-hand.com/villageinn**

PENNSYLVANIA DUTCH COUNTRY Fulton Steamboat Inn $$

Rt 30 at Rt 896, Lancaster, PA, 17602 ***Tel*** *(717) 299-9999* ***Fax*** *(717) 299-9992* ***Rooms*** *97*

This unique hotel is shaped like a 19th-century steamboat in honor of inventor Robert Fulton, who was born nearby in 1765. Family-oriented, with three "decks" of spacious guest rooms and"cabins" with bunk beds for kids, the inn is not far from the Strasburg Railroad and the Amish Village. Two-night minimum stay. **www.fultonsteamboatinn.com**

PENNSYLVANIA DUTCH COUNTRY The Inn at Kitchen Kettle Village $$

3529 Old Philadelphia Pike, Intercourse, PA, 17534 ***Tel*** *(717) 768-8261* ***Rooms*** *11*

Located among Pennsylvania Dutch Country farms, 11 tastefully decorated rooms and suites are tucked amidst the specialty shops at Kitchen Kettle Village, which comprises 32 shops, restaurants, and lodging. The rooms are comfortable and offer all modern amenities. **www.kitchenkettle.com**

PENNSYLVANIA DUTCH COUNTRY Strasburg Village Inn $$

1 W Main St, Strasburg, PA, 17579 ***Tel*** *(717) 687-0900* ***Fax*** *(717) 687-3650* ***Rooms*** *10*

Dating back to the late 1780s, this historic inn is situated on one corner of Strasburg's center square. Ten rooms in "Williamsburg" style are warmly furnished in Victorian-style decor with canopy beds and antiques. The inn sits next door to the old-style Strasburg Creamery, an ice cream and sandwich shop. **www.strasburg.com**

PENNSYLVANIA DUTCH COUNTRY Amishview Inns & Suites $$$

Rt 340, 3125 Old Philadelphia Pike, Bird-In-Hand, PA, 17505 ***Tel*** *(717) 768-1162* ***Rooms*** *50*

This country inn has scenic views of cornfields and silos. It is located halfway between Intercourse and Bird-In-Hand on the Plain and Fancy Farm, which is also home to Lancaster's first family-style restaurant *(see p153)*. Adjacent to the Amish Experience Theater and the Amish Homestead. **www.amishviewinn.com**

PENNSYLVANIA DUTCH COUNTRY Historic Strasburg Inn $$$

1400 Historic Dr, Strasburg, PA, 17579 ***Tel*** *(717) 687-7691* ***Fax*** *(717) 687-5290* ***Rooms*** *102*

The Historic Strasburg Inn sits on 18 acres (7 ha) of beautifully landscaped grounds with views of Amish farmland and is just a short walk from popular shops and restaurants. The accommodation ranges from traditional doubles to multi-room family options to luxury Jacuzzi suites. **www.clarioninnstrasburg.com**

PENNSYLVANIA DUTCH COUNTRY The Inn & Spa at Intercourse Village $$$

Rt 340, Main St, Intercourse, PA, 17534 ***Tel*** *(800) 801-2219* ***Rooms*** *12*

This 1909, Victorian-style B&B is a four-diamond facility with traditional fireplaces in suites with beamed ceilings and private baths with Jacuzzis. Enjoy candlelit gourmet breakfasts in the ornate dining room. The B&B is located close to antiques and craft shops in the heart of Intercourse's main shopping street. **www.inn-spa.com**

TRENTON Trenton Marriott at Lafayette Yard $$

1 W Lafayette St, Trenton, NJ, 08608 ***Tel*** *(609) 421-4000* ***Fax*** *(609) 421-4002* ***Rooms*** *197*

An upscale and modern three-diamond hotel in downtown Trenton, the hotel has elegant guest rooms. It is adjacent to the Trenton War Memorial, and is just one block from the tourist information center and Old Barracks Museum. A short drive away are Washington Crossing State Park and New Hope. **www.marriott.com**

VALLEY FORGE Dolce Valley Forge $$

301 West Dekalb Pike, King of Prussia, PA, 19406 ***Tel*** *(610) 337-1200* ***Fax*** *(610) 337-1959* ***Rooms*** *348*

This hotel provides lodging just minutes from Valley Forge National Historic Park and the King of Prussia Mall. Each guest room artfully combines traditional touches with modern facilities and amenities. The hotel's executive and luxury suites are ideal for extended stays. **www.dolcevalleyforge.com**

VALLEY FORGE Crowne Plaza Valley Forge $$$

260 Mall Blvd, King of Prussia, PA, 19406 ***Tel*** *(610) 265-7500* ***Fax*** *(610) 265-4076* ***Rooms*** *225*

This upscale hotel is walking distance from the colossal King of Prussia Mall. The property has tastefully decorated rooms with many amenities, including Jacuzzis. It also offers complete business facilities. The hotel is 2 miles (3 km) from the Valley Forge National Historic Park. **www.cpvalleyforge.com**

VALLEY FORGE Homewood Suites Valley Forge $$$

681 Shannondell Blvd, Audubon, PA, 19403 ***Tel*** *(610) 539-7300* ***Fax*** *(610) 539-2970* ***Rooms*** *123*

This spacious, all-suite hotel is located near Valley Forge National Historic Park and the King of Prussia Mall. Suites are available for short and extended stays; all have fully equipped kitchens and free Internet access. Breakfast (daily) and light evening meals (Monday through Thursday) are complimentary. **www.homewoodsuitesvalleyforge.com**

VALLEY FORGE Wayne Hotel $$$

139 E Lancaster Ave, Wayne, PA, 19087 ***Tel*** *(610) 687-5000* ***Fax*** *(610) 687-8387* ***Rooms*** *40*

Dating back to 1906, this hotel along Philadelphia's fashionable Main Line has been restored to its former Victorian elegance. Tudor Revival-style architecture adds to the old-world charm. It is a just a few miles from the King of Prussia Mall. Fitness facilities and pool can be used at nearby establishments. **www.waynehotel.com**

RESTAURANTS AND CAFES

Though the city is perhaps traditionally best known for the Philadelphia cheesesteak, its culinary repertoire has expanded widely and is today home to some of the country's top-rated restaurants. In addition to superb American fare, some of the city's best dining rooms specialize in international cuisine, including French, Italian, Thai, Moroccan, Chinese, and more. Excellent bistros, seafood restaurants, and steakhouses that feature cooking styles from Southern home cooking and colonial fare to Pennsylvania Dutch can be found in Center City. Modest restaurants and eateries, many serving traditional cheesesteak sandwiches, can be found in every city neighborhood and beyond.

Typical Dutch Country pretzel

Park-side alfresco dining at Rouge in Rittenhouse Square *(see p149)*

PHILLY FARE

For breakfast, the locals love to order grilled pork rolls along with their eggs and hash brown potatoes. At noon, cheesesteaks and lunchmeat-filled "hoagies" or "grinders" are favorites, and these can be found at the many food courts, pizzerias, and sandwich shops dotted around the city. Hoagies are Italian rolls filled with fresh meats and cheeses, as well as lettuce, tomatoes, and onions, topped off with a dash of oregano. Philly cheesesteaks consist of finely-sliced grilled beef along with onions, which are topped off with thick cheese sauce served up in a foot-long roll.

In Pennsylvania Dutch Country, meals are influenced by the traditional cooking of the Amish and Mennonites *(see p115)*. Family-style restaurants usually offer a good selection of this distinctive food, while staple and favorite treats are readily available at local farmers' markets scattered throughout the area *(see p144)*.

RESTAURANTS, BISTROS, AND CAFES

Many of Philadelphia's best restaurants are in Center City. Fine dining rooms can also be found in Center City hotels and near the theater district, home to the Kimmel Center and other performing arts venues. In Old City, head to the area around Market and Chestnut Streets, between Front and 4th Streets, where some popular establishments can be found. Chinatown is home to several excellent restaurants, while some of the best family-owned trattorias are located in the Italian Market in south Philadelphia.

Numerous restaurants in the city's popular outdoor areas, such as Rittenhouse Square, Manayunk, and Chestnut Hill are stylish with upscale bistros and cafés. There are more than 200 restaurants here offering outdoor dining. Many are small, cozy establishments serving cocktails and trendsetting dishes in an ambience reminiscent of a Parisian café. Several restaurants and comfortable neighborhood bars are also located along Fairmount Avenue, close to the Museum of Art.

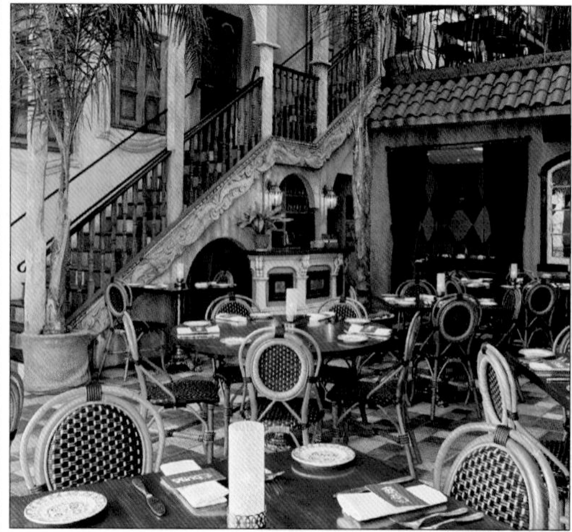

Cuba Libre in Old City recreates 1940s Havana *(see p146)*

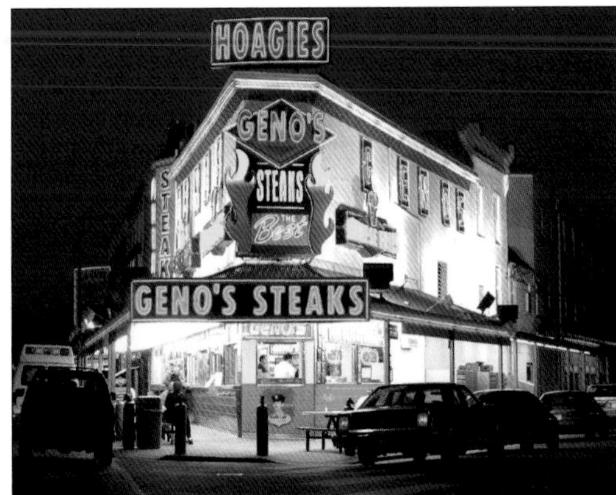

Geno's Steaks on Philadelphia's 9th Street *(see p150)*

HOURS AND PRICES

Luncheonettes and coffee shops open early for breakfast and may stay open through lunch only, catering to office workers. Finer restaurants open for lunch and dinner, with lunch served from 11:30am to 2:30pm or 3pm, and dinner from 5:30pm until 10pm or 10:30pm, and often later on weekends. Late-night restaurants that are also nightclubs stay open until 2am, but may stop serving food earlier.

Breakfast at diners and eateries can cost anywhere from $5 to $10 with a tip, while hotel buffet breakfasts can cost from $10 to $20. Full Sunday brunches at upscale restaurants and hotels can range from around $20 to $30 or more per person.

A typical lunch ranges from on-the-go sandwiches and sodas, from $5 to $9, to sit-down meals at restaurants that will cost $8 to $15 with a tip. Dinner is usually the big meal of the day. Starters and salads cost $5 to $10. Entrées can run $12 to $28, and up to $40 or more at high-end steakhouses and restaurants. Desserts and wine by the glass usually cost $5 to $12.

Some ethnic restaurants offer great quality food at less expensive costs. Greek, Chinese, Indian, Mexican, and Middle Eastern restaurants serve very generous portions at reasonable prices, with meals costing up to $15 or more per person.

EATERIES AND FAST FOOD

Good pizza, salads, and sandwiches abound in Philadelphia. Many pizza shops sell individual slices, as well as "hoagies" and cheesesteaks. *Taquerias* near the Italian Market in South Philly offer authentic Mexican dishes at low prices. The Reading Terminal Market, at 11th and Arch Streets, offers a wide variety of inexpensive food.

ALCOHOL AND SMOKING

Many restaurants serve wine by the glass or bottle. Simple eateries and fast-food restaurants generally do not serve alcohol. Philadelphia is known for its "BYOB" restaurants that do not sell alcohol but allow patrons to "Bring Your Own Bottle" at no extra charge. Few restaurants that sell liquor allow diners to bring their own wine. Most will impose daunting "corkage" fees for the privilege.

Restaurants and bars in Pennsylvania and New Jersey must stop serving alcohol by 2am. The legal drinking age is 21, and ID may be required when entering a bar. All restaurants and bars are non-smoking.

RESERVATIONS AND DRESS

Reservations for dining at upscale restaurants are recommended, and are often required on weekend nights. Nonetheless, some popular spots may not reserve tables, and use waiting lists. Even if you have reservations, you might have to wait for up to an hour on busy days.

Casual wear is accepted at most city restaurants, although there are some trendy and fine-dining establishments that expect patrons to wear smart-casual styles or business attire, so it is best to check when making reservations.

TIPPING

At most restaurants, your wait-person will bring you your bill. A 15 percent tip is considered a minimum, with up to 20 percent or more for excellent service.

CHILDREN

Well-behaved children are usually welcome in restaurants. It is not recommended, however, to bring young children to establishments that have late-night crowds and a large bar area, as patrons aged 21 or younger may not be allowed inside.

A waitress in period costume at the City Tavern restaurant *(see p146)*

Flavors of the Pennsylvania Dutch Country

Philadelphians savor the broad range of American and ethnic tastes from the many cultures that call the city home. Nearby Pennsylvania Dutch Country has its own unique flavors, comprising basic, hearty foods prepared from simple recipes. Amish and Mennonite cooks take advantage of the plentiful harvests to prepare dishes often characterized as good home cooking. To preserve the excess from the harvests, fresh country produce is both canned and jarred in homes and small shops, with much of it turned into tangy relishes and sweet jams. Such treats are available at various farmers' markets.

Corn-on-the-cob

Fresh produce at a farmer's market in Lancaster County

BOUNTIFUL HARVESTS

Amish and Mennonite food-stems from the cultural tastes that the settlers brought from their home countries of Germany and Switzerland – recipes later adapted to the available crops that could be cultivated in the New World. Throughout the generations, the Amish have continued to nurture their gardens and fields through traditional methods with horse-drawn farming equipment. They grow all manner of fresh vegetables including corn, string beans, carrots, beets, onions, tomatoes, peppers, lettuce, potatoes, sweet potatoes, cauliflower, and more. Fruits include apples, cherries, plums, peaches, and sweet watermelon, with many used as ingredients for the delicious desserts that have made the Pennsylvania Dutch Country famous.

MEATS AND DELIS

Amish delis and restaurants-feature a wide variety of cheeses, meats, and poultry, including fresh country sausages, sweet bologna, bacon, ham, dried beef and jerky, and smoked turkey. Cuts of fresh beef, pork, and chicken are favorites among the locals, who serve them up as part of tasty recipes such as scrapple, a dish that is made of pork, onions, cornmeal, and spices.

A selection of Pennsylvania Dutch Country cakes and desserts

LOCAL DISHES AND SPECIALITIES

Pennsylvania Dutch restaurants are known for their family-style buffets with meat dishes such as golden fried chicken, roast beef, chicken pot pie, and spicy sausage. Staples include mashed potatoes, home-made noodles and breads, and a choice of vegetables. Popular jellies and relishes include smooth apple butter, and Chow Chow, a mixture of sweet pickled vegetables. Amish recipes are handed down from mother to daughter to granddaughter, making for unique tastes. Dishes include Amish bean soup, corn fritters, spare ribs and sauerkraut, baking powder biscuits, cornmeal mush, and "Schnitz and Knepp," made with dried apples and ham. Popular desserts include Whoopie pie – chocolate cake surrounding white icing – and Shoofly pie, which has a coffeecake-like topping with a thick molasses bottom.

Fresh green apples

Chicken pot pie *comprises tender chicken pieces with vegetables and noodles, cooked in a pot of broth.*

Choosing a Restaurant

The restaurants in this guide have been selected for value, quality of food, atmosphere, and location. They are listed by area, starting with Philadelphia's Old City and moving on to restaurants farther away and beyond the city. All restaurants are non-smoking. For map references, *see pp194–97.*

PRICE CATEGORIES
The price ranges represent a three-course evening meal for one, a glass of house wine, tax, and service charges.

$ under $25
$$ $26–$35
$$$ $36–$50
$$$$ $51–$70
$$$$$ Over $70

OLD CITY

Ariana Restaurant — $

134 Chestnut St, Philadelphia, PA, 19106 ***Tel*** *(215) 922-1535* — **Map** 4 E3

This small and cozy restaurant serves authentic Afghan cuisine featuring Kabuli *pulao* (rice with vegetables and meat), marinated lamb kebabs, and dishes scented with spices such as cinnamon and cumin. The decor includes ethnic photographs, creating a unique atmosphere. There is bay window seating for groups in traditional Afghan style.

Aromatic House of Kebob — $

113 Chestnut St, Philadelphia, PA, 19106 ***Tel*** *(215) 923-4510* — **Map** 4 E3

A family-owned eatery in historic Old City, this restaurant features a comfortable café-like setting. It specializes in traditional Persian cooking, but also offers other popular fare such as *souvlaki* and *gyros* (Greek meat dishes) and kebabs. The restaurant usually stays open for patrons visiting the Old City in the late hours.

Franklin Fountain — $

116 Market St, Philadelphia, PA, 19106 ***Tel*** *(215) 627-1899* — **Map** 4 E3

This ice-cream parlor seems to have time-traveled from a hundred years ago. Home-made ice creams, sodas, and other desserts are treats from another era. Prices are high but so is the quality; brave the lines and lack of air-conditioning for excellent sundaes (especially hot fudge), unique beverages, and old-fashioned decor. Cash only.

Q BBQ & Tequila — $

207 Chestnut St, Philadelphia, PA, 19106 ***Tel*** *(215) 625-8605* — **Map** 4 E3

Credible versions of a variety of American barbecue cuisines are available here: Southern-style ribs, North Carolina pulled pork, Texas brisket. Also Tex-Mex specialties, good burgers, and a wide selection of tequilas. A small patio provides pleasant outdoor seating. Reasonable prices and a location near historical sights make this a popular spot.

The Bourse — $

111 S Independence Mall E, Philadelphia, PA, 19106 ***Tel*** *(215) 625-0300* — **Map** 4 D3

The lobby of the Bourse, a historic 19th-century commodities exchange building *(see p156)*, is home to a food court and several souvenir shops. Its many eateries offer Chinese food, pizzas, cheesesteaks, sandwiches, burgers, and more. The food court is an ideal lunch venue for sightseers in Independence National Historic Park.

Aqua Malaysian & Thai Restaurant — $$

705 Chestnut St, Philadelphia, PA, 19106 ***Tel*** *(215) 928-2838* — **Map** 4 D3

Malaysian and Thai cuisines are both represented here. The *Roti Canai*, a thin pancake-like bread served with a curry sauce for dipping, is a special treat. Classic Thai curries and noodle dishes are good choices as are the stew-like Malaysian Beef *Rendang* and (chicken) *Kari Ayam*. Plenty of options for vegetarians. BYOB.

Gigi Restaurant and Lounge — $$

319 Market St, Philadelphia, PA, 19106 ***Tel*** *(215) 574-8880* — **Map** 4 E3

Located in the heart of the historic Old City district, this hip restaurant has the largest outdoor seating space in the area. The menu features international cuisine, including American, French, Spanish, and Thai dishes, and delicious tapas. The Sunday brunch is recommended.

Han Dynasty — $$

108 Chestnut St, Philadelphia, PA, 19106 ***Tel*** *(215) 922-1888* — **Map** 4 E3

Traditional Sichuan Chinese food, featuring the famous combination of chili heat and numbing peppercorn tingle. A long way from westernized Chinese-style food, this is authentic cooking. Spicy Dan Dan Noodles with ground pork, wontons in chili oil, lamb with cumin, and "Fish in Dry Pot" stand out. Some tamer dishes are available too.

Kabul Afghan Cuisine Restaurant — $$

106 Chestnut St, Philadelphia, PA, 19106 ***Tel*** *(215) 922-3676* — **Map** 4 E3

This popular ethnic restaurant near the heart of Old City has traditional Afghan decor and a warm and welcoming atmosphere. The menu is replete with meat kebab and vegetarian specialties cooked with exotic Afghan spices. Call in advance to dine in traditional Afghan style on a platform with rugs and pillows. No lunch service.

Key to Symbols *see back cover flap*

The Continental Restaurant and Martini Bar $$

138 Market St, Philadelphia, PA, 19106 **Tel** *(215) 923-6069* **Map** *4 E3*

With its imaginative interior, the Continental is one of the hippest and most popular after-dark spots in the Old City's lively nightlife district. It serves contemporary cuisine with a pan-Asian flair, and has extensive martini, champagne, and wine lists. Latin and lounge music is played. Weekday lunch, weekend brunch, and daily dinner service.

Amada $$$

217 Chestnut St, Philadelphia, PA, 19106 **Tel** *(215) 625-2450* **Map** *4 E3*

A Spanish restaurant serving authentic tapas based on the earthy Mediterranean flavors that have long been the passion of founder and executive chef Jose Garces. The impressive menu of inspired creations gives guests the opportunity to mix and share multiple dishes. Signature tapas include octopus, garlic shrimps, and tortilla.

Chifa $$$

707 Chestnut St, Philadelphia, PA, 19106 **Tel** *(215) 925-5555* **Map** *4 D3*

This offering from Ecuadorian-American chef Jose Garces puts a unique spin on traditional favorites and modern Asian-Fusion trends, while emphasizing Chinese and Peruvian cuisines. Don't miss the excellent *ceviches*, pork belly buns, or crisp roast chicken, accompanied by a Pisco Sour from the bar.

City Tavern $$$

138 S 2nd St, Philadelphia, PA, 19106 **Tel** *(215) 413-1443* **Map** *4 E3*

Authentic colonial-style cuisine, such as West Indies pepperpot soup, is served at this historically accurate reconstruction of the original 1773 tavern. Colonial ales brewed according to George Washington's and Thomas Jefferson's original recipes are also served. Three floors with colonial decor and staff in period costume.

Cuba Libre Restaurant and Rum Bar $$$

10 S 2nd St, Philadelphia, PA, 19106 **Tel** *(215) 627-0666* **Map** *4 E3*

Trendy and happening, this restaurant's spacious atrium reaches out onto the sidewalk for alfresco dining in warmer months. Bright colors and balconies evoke memories of 1940s Havana. Two bars and four dining rooms serve up contemporary Cuban and inventive Latin cuisine. Brunch is on offer on the weekend.

DiNardo's Famous Crabs $$$

312 Race St, Philadelphia, PA, 19106 **Tel** *(215) 925-5115* **Map** *4 E2*

A favorite since 1976, this seafood restaurant serves up excellent crabs in a casual and friendly atmosphere. Specialties include steamed Louisiana crabs served "hot and dirty" Baltimore-style, jumbo shrimp, stuffed flounder, and more. Located one block from St. George's Church and Fireman's Hall. No lunch service on Sunday.

Eulogy Belgian Tavern $$$

136 Chestnut St, Philadelphia, PA, 19106 **Tel** *(215) 413-1918* **Map** *4 E3*

This cozy pub and restaurant features an enormous selection of 185 international and Belgian beers. Traditional Belgian fare, including fish, meatballs, fries, and mussels, is prepared in five different sauces. The restaurant has limited wheelchair access and does not allow children after 8pm.

Serrano-Tin Angel $$$

20 S 2nd St, Philadelphia, PA, 19106 **Tel** *(215) 928-0770* **Map** *4 E3*

This stylish restaurant sits in a 1820s townhouse-like building with the popular folk music café, Tin Angel, on the second level. It offers international cooking, with specialties such as Malaysian pork chop, vegetable *kung pao*, and calamari. No lunch service.

Spasso Italian Grille $$$

34 S Front St, Philadelphia, PA, 19106 **Tel** *(215) 592-7661* **Map** *4 E3*

This old world-style trattoria is located across from Penn's Landing and features traditional Italian cuisine with dishes from both southern and northern Italy. Popular dishes include home-made pastas, fresh seafood, veal, and chicken. The restaurant sports a warm and casual atmosphere. No lunch service on the weekend.

The Plough & The Stars $$$

207 Chestnut St, Philadelphia, PA, 19106 **Tel** *(215) 735-0300* **Map** *4 E3*

This trendy Irish pub is housed in the Corn Exchange Building. The restaurant plays traditional Irish music on Sundays and has plenty of Guinness on tap. The fare, however, is not necessarily traditional but instead gourmet and creative. The pub has some outdoor seating in the warmer months.

Buddakan $$$$

325 Chestnut St, Philadelphia, PA, 19106 **Tel** *(215) 574-9440* **Map** *4 E3*

An Asian-Fusion restaurant, Buddakan has a traditonal menu with some more contemporary items. The *edamame* (soy bean) ravioli, wasabi tuna pizza, and miso-glazed black cod are enduring classics. A giant Buddha statue gazes over a dramatically illuminated communal table. This persists as one of the most striking dining rooms in the city.

Fork $$$$

306 Market St, Philadelphia, PA, 19106 **Tel** *(215) 625-9425* **Map** *4 E3*

Located in the heart of the Old City nightlife district, Fork offers a mix of casual sophistication and an urban, upscale style. It serves new American, bistro-style cuisine with an international flavor. Decor includes delicately painted velvet curtains and chandeliers. It also has a unique center bar. No lunch service on Saturday.

Key to Price Guide *see p145* **Key to Symbols** *see back cover flap*

Jones

$$$$

700 Chestnut St, Philadelphia, PA, 19106 ***Tel*** *(215) 223-5663* **Map** 4 D3

Buffed-up versions of old-fashioned American comfort food served in a fun, retro setting and accompanied by goofy cocktails and a lively pop music soundtrack. Indulge your cravings for a Thanksgiving turkey dinner, mac and cheese, or chicken and waffles. Finish with a big piece of chocolate cake served with a glass of milk. Weekend brunch.

Ristorante Panorama and Il Bar

$$$$

14 N Front St, Philadelphia, PA, 19106 ***Tel*** *(215) 922-7800* **Map** 4 E3

This is an exquisite family-owned hotel *(see p134)* and restaurant near Penn's Landing. The bustling trattoria decorated with Florentine tiles and hand-painted murals features Italian food – home-made pastas and the finest cuts of veal. The unique "Il Bar" features the world's largest wine dispensing system and offers 120 wines by the glass.

Morimoto

$$$$$

723 Chestnut St, Philadelphia, PA, 19106 ***Tel*** *(215) 413-9070* **Map** 4 D3

This renowned restaurant's dining room is elegant and upscale with modern decor. One of the best fusion restaurants in Philadelphia, it brings contemporary Japanese cuisine to the table through Chef Morimoto's blending of traditional Japanese cooking with Western flair.

SOCIETY HILL AND PENN'S LANDING

Jim's Steaks

$

400 South St, Philadelphia, PA, 19147 ***Tel*** *(215) 928-1911* **Map** 4 D4

With its distinctive Art Deco storefront, Jim's is undoubtedly one of Philadelphia's busiest and most popular eateries. Long lines often stretch onto hip South Street as visitors and locals alike flock here for authentic Philly cheesesteaks with mounds of onions and dripping hot cheese. It also serves excellent hoagies.

South Street Souvlaki

$

509 S St, Philadelphia, PA, 19147 ***Tel*** *(215) 925-3026* **Map** 4 D4

One of the town's oldest and most popular Greek restaurants, this South Street icon recently celebrated its 25th anniversary. Specialties include classic Greek and Mediterranean cuisine, including lamb, seafood, and vegetarian dishes. Pleasant dining room and streetfront takeout window as well.

Marrakesh

$$

517 Leithgow St, Philadelphia, PA, 19147 ***Tel*** *(215) 925-5929* **Map** 4 D5

At Marrakesh you can sit on cushioned pillows and enjoy an authentic seven-course Moroccan feast beginning with a hand-washing ritual and ending with a tea ceremony. The restaurant has a number of private dining rooms for hire, and belly dancers are available upon request.

Percy Street Barbecue

$$

600 S 9th St, Philadelphia, PA, 19147 ***Tel*** *(215) 625-8510* **Map** 3 C5

A Texas-style barbecue joint right down to the red oak in the smokers, and the roadhouse feel of the room. The highlight is beef brisket: moist and tender with an assertive smoke flavor. Also on offer are pork ribs, chicken, and pork belly. Everything's served simply on butcher paper. Side dishes are good, and desserts are not to be missed.

Bridget Foy's

$$$

200 South St, Philadelphia, PA, 19147 ***Tel*** *(215) 922-1813* **Map** 4 E5

An American grill in the South Street district, it faces New Market and Head House Square. The menu offers American cuisine, with old standards such as steaks, fresh fish, burgers, and sandwiches. An outdoor café makes this great spot to break for lunch on bustling South Street.

Dark Horse Pub

$$$

421 S 2nd St, Philadelphia, PA, 19147 ***Tel*** *(215) 928-9307* **Map** 4 E4

A popular watering hole that doubles up as a restaurant. This colonial inn-style restaurant serves hearty pub fare, including steak and mushroom pie, as well as gourmet cuisine. It has five bars with a range of beers and wines. No lunch service on Monday.

Downey's

$$$

526 S Front St, Philadelphia, PA, 19147 ***Tel*** *(215) 625-9500* **Map** 4 E5

Blessed with its great location at South and Front Streets, Downey's – a "drinking house and dining saloon" – has been a neighborhood mainstay since 1976. Pub decor includes antiques and Irish memorabilia, while the menu features hearty Irish stews and American fare. It is also a vibrant night spot.

La Veranda Restaurant

$$$

Pier 3, 30 N Columbus Blvd, Philadelphia, PA, 19106 ***Tel*** *(215) 351-1898* **Map** 4 F4

Located on the waterfront at Penn's landing, this delightful restaurant features wide-ranging Italian and seafood dishes on its menu. Guests can enjoy breathtaking views of the Delaware River whilst dining on fresh fish and meats cut to order and cooked on a natural woodburning grill.

Pizzeria Stella $$$

420 S 2nd St, Philadelphia, PA, 19147 **Tel** *(215) 320-8000* **Map** *4 E4*

Neapolitan-style pizzas with creative toppings are the focus here. A traditional dome-shaped wood-burning oven is the centerpiece, and its high heat creates crisp pizza crusts in minutes. A few starters and salads balance the menu. Italian wine can be ordered by the glass. Save room for *gelato* (ice cream) for dessert.

Xochitl $$$

408 S 2nd St, Philadelphia, PA, 19147 **Map** *4 E4*

Contemporary Mexican cuisine, based on the traditions of the state of Puebla. Enticing snacks, vibrant *ceviches*, creative tacos and sandwiches, and a few fancier dishes show more sophistication than you'll find at the corner *taqueria*. The best margaritas in town are made from hand-squeezed limes and excellent tequila.

Southwark $$$$

701 S 4th St, Philadelphia, PA, 19147 **Tel** *(215) 238-1888* **Map** *4 D5*

The chef here has long-standing relationships with local farms, and serves only the freshest seasonal products. Vibrant flavors from the kitchen show the virtues of taking the farm-to-table movement seriously. At its handsome bar, housing a good selection of gin and rye whiskey, Southwark's bartenders concoct the best classic cocktails in town.

Zahav $$$$

237 St James Pl, Philadelphia, PA, 19106 **Tel** *(215) 625-8800* **Map** *4 E3*

Israeli street food given a gourmet spin. Modern techniques and excellent ingredients add extra gloss (and expense) to traditional snacks, salads, and kebabs. The chef's tasting menus offer an easy overview and good value. Don't miss the various types of hummus with freshly baked *laffa* bread, and lamb shoulder marinated in pomegranate juice.

Moshulu $$$$$

401 S Columbus Blvd, Philadelphia, PA, 19106 **Tel** *(215) 923-2500* **Map** *4 F4*

Lovely fine-dining restaurant aboard a restored, century-old sailing ship moored off Penn's Landing. The four-masted vessel is ablaze with lights at night, and offers excellent river and skyline views from indoor dining rooms and from atop the deck in warmer months. Bar and deck menu also available.

CENTER CITY

Penang $

117 N 10th St, Philadelphia, PA, 19107 **Tel** *(215) 413-2531, (215) 413-2531* **Map** *3 C2*

This trendy, storefront restaurant in the heart of Chinatown is always buzzing with activity. It has a predominantly Malaysian cuisine featuring spicy curry and seafood dishes, along with some Thai, Indian, and Indonesian specialties as well. Also serves beer and wine.

Reading Terminal Market $

12th and Arch Sts, Philadelphia, PA, 19107 **Tel** *(215) 922-2317* **Map** *3 C2*

Part farmers' market and part food court, the RTM offers everything from fresh produce to prepared meals. Highlights include DiNic's roast pork sandwich, Miller's Twist soft pretzels, Bassett's Ice Cream, and traditional Amish fare (Thu–Sat). Ethnic food stands are a good bet, or sample a classic "hoagie" (sandwich). Closes 5pm; some stands closed Sun.

Sakura Mandarin $

1038 Race St, Philadelphia, PA, 19107 **Tel** *(215) 873-8338* **Map** *3 C2*

Regional Chinese food that rises above the watered-down Chinatown cliches. Specialties of Shanghai, such as *xiao long bao* (soup dumplings) and "lion's head" (pork) meatballs are joined by spicy Szechuan dishes and crowd-pleasing Cantonese favorites. Try the unusual thin scallion pancake. Surprisingly good sushi and other Japanese dishes, too.

El Vez $$

121 S 13th St, Philadelphia, PA, 19103 **Tel** *(215) 928-9800* **Map** *2 F3*

Dine on delicious, modern versions of traditional Mexican classics at this fashionable Center City restaurant. The made-to-order guacamole and the Mahi-Mahi tacos are highly recommended. There is also an extensive selection of drinks, including wonderful pomegranate margaritas.

Zavino $$

112 S 13th St, Philadelphia, PA, 19107 **Tel** *(215) 732-2400* **Map** *3 B3*

A large portion of the menu at this tiny casual wine bar is taken up by pizza, and these Neapolitan-style creations are a highlight. The domed oven creates a charred, puffy crust minimally topped with high-quality ingredients. But don't miss the chef's other offerings including vibrant salads, pastas, and daily specials of hearty country-style Italian fare.

The Black Sheep Irish Pub $$$

247 S 17th St, Philadelphia, PA, 19103 **Tel** *(215) 545-9473* **Map** *2 E5*

Dine on hearty Irish stews and other favorites, including shepherd's pie, sandwiches, crab cakes, and more. Just one block from Rittenhouse Square, this pub and restaurant offers a relaxed atmosphere and has friendly staff. There are three floors with antique bars, and a drink selection from around the world. Wheelchair access limited to first level.

Key to Price Guide *see p145* **Key to Symbols** *see back cover flap*

Matyson
$$$

37 S 19th St, Philadelphia, PA, 19103 ***Tel*** *(215) 564-2925* ***Map*** *2 D4*

A consistent highlight of the Philly BYOB scene, this restaurant delivers interesting New American cuisine. Thematic, often whimsical, chef's tasting menus are available Mon–Thu at dinner and offer a wide variety of dishes and good value. The regular menu features fresh, high-quality, local ingredients. Open for lunch and dinner.

McCormick and Schmick's Seafood Restaurant
$$$

1 S Broad St, Philadelphia, PA, 19102 ***Tel*** *(215) 568-6888* ***Map*** *2 F4*

This upbeat and lively restaurant is an upscale fish house, located just across from historic City Hall. Features over 40 varieties of fresh fish that are flown in daily from both the Atlantic and Pacific Oceans. The two-story restaurant has a dark wood-paneled dining room accented by stained glass ceilings and mosaic floor.

Rouge
$$$

205 S 18th St, Philadelphia, PA, 19103 ***Tel*** *(215) 732-6622* ***Map*** *2 D5*

A hip bistro and popular late night spot in the swanky Rittenhouse Square area. They have wines of exquisite vintage and a trendsetting menu that is a cross between Continental, American, and French fare with contemporary seafood, poultry, and beef dishes. The biggest draw is the location, with outdoor seating facing the square.

Alma de Cuba
$$$$

1623 Walnut St, Philadelphia, PA, 19103 ***Tel*** *(215) 988-1799* ***Map*** *2 E5*

This cutting-edge restaurant, bar, and lounge brings modern Cuban cuisine to Philadelphia. Festive Cuban cocktails such as Mojitos and Daiquiris perfectly compliment the flavors, brilliant colors, and textures of the spectacular cuisine. Dishes include red bean soup with pumpkin and chorizo, and octopus *Escabeche* (pickled).

Amis
$$$$

412 S 13th St, Philadelphia, PA, 19147 ***Tel*** *(215) 732-2647* ***Map*** *3 B4*

A relaxed neighborhood *trattoria* from acclaimed chef Marc Vetri. House-cured meats and terrines are a highlight, as are the tender meatballs based on the chef's father's recipe. The pastas are not to be missed. Thoughtful Italian wine list and full bar. Prices are expensive considering the casual feel, but the high caliber of cooking makes it good value.

Devon Seafood Grill
$$$$

225 S 18th St, Philadelphia, PA, 19103 ***Tel*** *(215) 546-5940* ***Map*** *2 D5*

A much-visited and comfortable restaurant, the Devon Seafood Grill serves fresh fish specialties, including Maryland crab cakes, pan-roasted Alaskan halibut, live Maine lobsters, Block Island swordfish, and more. The dining room is elegant. It is particularly popular in the warmer months with sidewalk seating facing Rittenhouse Square.

Oyster House
$$$$

1516 Sansom St, Philadelphia, PA, 19102 ***Tel*** *(215) 567-7683* ***Map*** *3 A3*

A classic Philadelphia fish house, The Oyster House offers modern versions of old favorites like clam chowder, snapper (turtle) soup, lobster rolls, and crabcakes. But the main attraction is the broad selection of fresh oysters, expertly shucked to order. Try an innovative cocktail or an Oyster House Punch on the side. Closed Sun.

Parc
$$$$

227 S 18th St, Philadelphia, PA, 19103 ***Tel*** *(215) 545-2262* ***Map*** *2 D5*

This stylish addition to Rittenhouse Square pays tribute to French café culture. Ideal for a light snack or a more leisurely meal, this French bistro offers many classics such as onion soup and escargots, as well as meat and fish platters and a choice of baguettes. Inside are red leather banquettes backed with panels of frosted glass for privacy.

The Prime Rib
$$$$

1701 Locust St, Philadelphia, PA, 19103 ***Tel*** *(215) 772-1701* ***Map*** *2 E5*

This upscale steakhouse is one of Philadelphia's best. Housed in the prestigious Radisson-brand Warwick Hotel *(see p136)*, its decor is reminiscent of a 1940s Manhattan supper club. Its specialties include aged prime rib, blue-ribbon steaks, extra thick chops, and fresh seafood. Children are allowed only on request. Formal dress required. No lunch service.

Tinto
$$$$

116 S 20th St, Philadelphia, PA, 19103 ***Tel*** *(215) 665-9150* ***Map*** *2 D4*

Tapas-style dining with a Basque flavor from chef Jose Garces. More elegant (and expensive) than the *pintxos* (snacks) you'd find at bars in northern Spain, these flavors still have a rustic power. Village Whiskey, Garces' speakeasy bar next door, offers an unmatched selection of spirits, skilled bartenders, and the best hamburgers in town.

Lacroix at the Rittenhouse
$$$$$

210 W Rittenhouse Square, Philadelphia, PA, 19103 ***Tel*** *(215) 790-2533* ***Map*** *2 D5*

Elegant restaurant on the second floor of the Rittenhouse Hotel *(see p137)* with stunning views of Rittenhouse Square. Decorated with minimalist and Asian theme, it serves French-American cuisine with options of three, four, or five courses, and diners can also create their own menus. Dessert complimentary as a gift from the chef.

Smith & Wollensky
$$$$$

210 W Rittenhouse Square, Philadelphia, PA, 19103 ***Tel*** *(215) 545-1700* ***Map*** *2 D5*

One of the top steakhouses Philadelphia has to offer. *The New York Times* referred to this high-end restaurant chain as "a steakhouse to end all arguments." Patrons are treated to up to 18 and 28-ounce cuts, good chops, salads, seafood, and an excellent wine list too. Located in the posh Rittenhouse Hotel *(see p137)*.

LOGAN SQUARE AND PARKWAY MUSEUMS DISTRICT

Brigid's $$

726 N 24th St, Philadelphia, PA, 19130 ***Tel*** *(215) 232-3232* **Map** *1 C1*

A friendly neighborhood pub with a rotating selection of local beers on tap, and an amazing list of bottled Belgian ales. A small dining room in the back serves affordable, comforting food from many cuisines, posted on blackboard menus. Mussels are a long-time favorite, as is the half a crispy duck *Chambord*, drizzled with raspberry sauce.

The Bishop's Collar $$$

2349 Fairmount Ave, Philadelphia, PA, 19130 ***Tel*** *(215) 765-1616* **Map** *2 D1*

This friendly corner watering hole and restaurant serves creative pub fare, along with a wide-ranging selection of beers and ales. Tables are set up outdoors in the warmer months. Situated a couple of blocks from the Philadelphia Museum of Art and the Kelly Drive walking path along Boathouse Row.

Jack's Firehouse $$$

2130 Fairmount Ave, Philadelphia, PA, 19130 ***Tel*** *(215) 232-9000* **Map** *2 D1*

This unique restaurant sits within a former firehouse building that still retains its original interiors – complete with a firemen's sliding pole and an expansive arched doorway. Popular chef-owner Jack McDavid uses fresh local ingredients for "down home" American fare, often accenting Southern cooking styles. Live music on the first Friday of each month.

London Grill $$$

2301 Fairmount Ave, Philadelphia, PA, 19130 ***Tel*** *(215) 978-4545* **Map** *2 D1*

Trendy and comfortable, this corner restaurant combines the coziness of a neighborhood pub with the elegance of fine dining. The menu changes daily, and dishes such as roasted chicken with garlic mashed potato cake, broccoli rosemary jus, and honey glazed grilled salmon are on offer. No lunch service on Saturday.

Rembrandt's $$$

741 N 23rd St, Philadelphia, PA, 19130 ***Tel*** *(215) 763-2228, (800) 736-2726* **Map** *2 D1*

Located near the Philadelphia Museum of Art, this elegant restaurant is known for its fine dining, accented by fabulous views of the city skyline. Specialties include creative seafood, meat, pasta, and vegetarian dishes. It also has a full tavern menu and eight draught beers on tap.

Route 6 $$$

600 N Broad St, Philadelphia, PA, 19130 ***Tel*** *(215) 391-4600* **Map** *2 D1*

Named after the famous highway that begins from Provincetown in Massachusetts and runs through the heart of Cape Cod, this relaxed but sophisticated 150-seat restaurant offers a seasonal, sea-to-table menu, which features traditional coastal-town dishes, such as clam chowder, lobster rolls, and oysters, as well as whole fish selections.

Zorba's Tavern $$$

2230 Fairmount Ave, Philadelphia, PA, 19130 ***Tel*** *(215) 978-5990* **Map** *2 D1*

Discover sumptuous Greek food at this family-owned restaurant. Paintings depicting old-world Greece add a special ambience to the authentic cuisine. It offers a full menu with lamb and seafood specialties, and all the traditional dishes. Located within walking distance of the Philadelphia Museum of Art and Boathouse Row. Closed Monday.

Water Works Restaurant and Lounge $$$$

640 Water Works Dr, Philadelphia, PA, 19130 ***Tel*** *(215) 236-9000* **Map** *1 B1*

Built in 1812, the Fairmount Water Works building is now a national historic landmark overlooking the Schuylkill River. The restaurant's superb location and innovative American fusion cuisine makes for a fine dining experience and reservations are recommended. Wines are available by the glass.

Fountain Restaurant $$$$$

1 Logan Sq, Philadelphia, PA, 19103 ***Tel*** *(215) 963-1500* **Map** *2 E2*

Living up to the reputation of the posh Four Seasons Hotel *(see p137)*, this restaurant has been repeatedly rated as one of the city's best restaurants, serving Continental cuisine with delicate international influences. Elegant dining room with rich fabrics and warm woods. The restaurant offers splendid views of the Swann Fountain. Formal dress required.

FARTHER AFIELD

Geno's Steaks $

1219 S 9th St, Philadelphia, PA, 19147 ***Tel*** *(215) 389-0659*

Geno's is one of Philadelphia's cheesesteak giants on the outskirts of the Italian Market. Founded in 1966 opposite Pat's King of Steaks, it serves delicious, piping hot cheesesteak sandwiches 24 hours a day, 7 days a week from a bright, neon-lit corner storefront.

Key to Price Guide *see p145* **Key to Symbols** *see back cover flap*

Pat's King of Steaks $

1301 S 9th St, Philadelphia, PA, 19147 ***Tel*** *(215) 468-1547*

Founded in and family-owned since 1930, Pat's is known as the originator of the Philly cheesesteak with its sliced rib-eye steak, onions, cheese, and fresh Italian bread. In fact, locals will tell you it makes the city's best. Outside vendor windows and outside seating only. It is located at the Italian Market. Open 24 hours a day.

Chickie's and Pete's Café $$

1526 Packer Ave, Philadelphia, PA, 19145 ***Tel*** *(215) 218-0500*

This casual, south Philadelphia hotspot near the city's sports venues is always busy when the home teams play. Sightings of local personalities is common. The menu features crab fries, sandwiches, and cheesesteaks. Children have to be accompanied by adults after 10pm. A DJ plays recorded music.

Cantina Dos Segundos $$$

931 N 2nd St, Philadelphia, PA, 19123 ***Tel*** *(215) 629-0500*

"Dos" and its older sibling in South Philadelphia, Cantina Los Caballitos, have developed reputations as fun places for pitchers of affordable specialty margaritas, but don't overlook the well-prepared Mexican food. Some dishes serves include hearty goat tacos, vegan fajitas, and authentic *moles*. Kitchen open until 1am. Brunch daily.

Cochon BYOB $$$

801 E Passyunk Ave, Philadelphia, PA, 19147 ***Tel*** *(215) 923-7675* ***Map*** *4 D5*

Unsurprisingly Cochon, French for pig, focuses its menu around pork. Indeed you can find tender braised pork shoulder with lentils and brussels sprouts, a variety of home-made sausages, and bacon flavoring almost everything. Large portions and bold flavors prevail. It's BYOB, so bring a hearty red from the Rhone, or perhaps a bright white from Alsace.

Jake's and Cooper's Wine Bar $$$

4365-67 Main St, Manayunk, Philadelphia, PA, 19127 ***Tel*** *(215) 483-0444*

Choose from either the pioneering fine-dining restaurant Jake's or the casual and less expensive Cooper's Wine Bar to enjoy chef Bruce Cooper's creative cuisine. Pizzas covered with unconventional toppings, excellent burgers, and a thoughtful and affordable selection of wines by the glass make this a great place for a light dinner or a late-night bite.

Ralph's Italian Restaurant $$$

760 S 9th St, Philadelphia, PA, 19147 ***Tel*** *(215) 627-6011*

Cozy, comfortable, and classy restaurant at the Italian Market. Owned and operated by four generations of the same family since 1900, this neighborhood restaurant is one of the city's most popular Italian eateries. It serves up classic red sauce and pastas, veal, poultry, seafood, and meat dishes, including the likes of Pork Chops Pizzaiola.

Standard Tap $$$

901 N 2nd St, Philadelphia, PA, 19123 ***Tel*** *(215) 238-0630*

The original Philadelphia gastropub, this loud but cozy bar is great for sampling local beer on tap - it's the only kind they serve. Blackboard menus lack detail, but the food is artfully prepared. The burgers and pork sandwich are legendary. Their duck confit salad puts most French restaurants to shame. Finding a seat can be chaotic but it's worth the wait.

White Dog Café $$$

3420 Sansom St, Philadelphia, PA, 19104 ***Tel*** *(215) 386-9224*

An eclectic University City café housed in three adjacent Victorian brownstones. On the menu is an unusual blend of contemporary American cuisine that uses fresh ingredients from local, self-reliant farmers. Music is played in the smoke-free piano parlor. The bar offers happy hours from 10pm to midnight Sunday through Thursday.

Distrito $$$$

3945 Chestnut St, Philadelphia, PA, 19104 ***Tel*** *(215) 386-1072*

Mexican food is given the tapas treatment by chef Jose Garces. Meticulous preparation and quality ingredients, like Kobe beef, elevate even the humble taco to new heights. Be sure to try the intense *moles*, vibrant *ceviches*, and creative cocktails. Prices can be high but the amusing decor (wrestling masks) and friendly service lighten the mood.

Pod $$$$

3636 Sansom St, Philadelphia, PA, 19104 ***Tel*** *(215) 387-1803*

Asian-Fusion cuisine and reliably good sushi served in a fun, futuristic setting. Color-changing seating pods, and a screen projecting Japanese cartoons set the scene for modern food. Japanese, Thai, and Chinese flavors predominate, with elaborate sushi platters and favorites like wasabi-crusted filet mignon.

BEYOND PHILADELPHIA

ATLANTIC CITY White House Sub Shop $

2301 Arctic Ave, Atlantic City, NJ, 8401 ***Tel*** *(609) 345-1564*

An establishment in Atlantic City since 1946. Expect long lines, but it's worth the wait for classic submarine sandwiches. The "Special" (a large portion of various Italian cold cuts), tuna, and meatball subs are legendary. Some say their cheesesteak is better than those in Philadelphia. A half sandwich is huge, a whole sub could feed a family. Cash only.

ATLANTIC CITY Atlantic City Bar and Grill $$

1219 Pacific Ave, Atlantic City, NJ, 08401 ***Tel*** *(609) 348-8080, (609) 449-1991*

This family-owned restaurant opened more than 25 years ago and has become a favorite among locals, tourists, and even visiting celebrities and sports figures. Steaks, crabs, shrimp cocktail, lobsters, mussels, home-made pastas, pizzas, and sandwiches all feature on the menu. The spacious dining room has sports programming and is open until 4:30am.

ATLANTIC CITY Izakaya $$$$

1 Borgata Way, Atlantic City, NJ, 08401 ***Tel*** *(609) 317-1000*

An ornate restaurant inside the Borgata Hotel Casino & Spa, Izakaya's menu is inspired by the casual drinking and snacking culture of Japan. Chef Michael Shulson adds an elegant gloss to these simple foods. Try the gourmet dumplings, exotic meats cooked on a *robatayaki* grill, elaborate sushi rolls, and main dishes like Kobe sirloin or whole sea bass.

ATLANTIC CITY Primavera $$$$$

Caesars Casino, 2100 Pacific Ave, Atlantic City, NJ, 08401 ***Tel*** *(609) 348-4411, (800) 223-7272*

Fine dining with a range of northern Italian specialties and an extensive wine list in one of Atlantic City's best-known casino hotels, Caesars *(see p139)*. Try out the appetizer of oversized prawns with lemon-caper sauce. Intimate tables amidst artworks and murals of Venice enhance the ambience. Service is formal and reservations are required.

BRANDYWINE VALLEY Buckley's Tavern $$

5812 Kennett Pike, Centreville, DE, 19807 ***Tel*** *(302) 656-9776*

A favorite meeting place for locals in the Brandywine Valley, this tavern serves a variety of fine food, from the likes of Maryland crab cakes to Vietnamese shrimp salad. There is a popular outdoor dining patio. It is close to Longwood Gardens, Winterthur, and other attractions such as the Brandywine River Museum and Brandywine Battlefield.

BRANDYWINE VALLEY Chadds Ford Tavern and Restaurant $$$

US Rt 1 (1 mile south of Rt 202), Chadds Ford, PA, 19317 ***Tel*** *(610) 459-8453*

Family-owned and operated since 1968, this quaint country restaurant offers a menu ranging from home-made pub fare to fine food dishes. Housed in an 1830s tavern, the dining room is lit with hurricane candles and Tiffany lamps. Sample the crab cakes, a best-selling entrée. Reservations are recommended.

CAPE MAY The Black Duck $$$

1 Sunset Blvd, Cape May, NJ, 08204 ***Tel*** *(609) 898-0100*

Ask to dine on the patio if the weather's good. The sophisticated cooking here can feel a little dated, yet delicious. There's a wide array of seafood, much of it local, and plenty of other choices, including roast duck. Prices are high, but in line with comparable restaurants in the area. The BYO wine policy can save a few dollars.

CAPE MAY The Lobster House $$

Fisherman's Wharf, Cape May Harbor, Cape May, NJ, 08204 ***Tel*** *(609) 884-8296*

Feast on the region's freshest seafood in a picturesque dining room overlooking Cape May harbor, with many of the ingredients arriving in the kitchen via the restaurant's own boat. Cocktails can be enjoyed at dockside tables or on the deck of the 146-ft (50-m) *Schooner America*.

DOYLESTOWN Paganini Ristorante $$$

81 West State St, Doylestown, PA, 18901 ***Tel*** *(215) 348-5922*

A local favorite for fine Italian cuisine, this restaurant is in the heart of downtown Doylestown. It has several small dining rooms where patrons can ask for custom cooking such as fresh pastas and a variety of sauces. No dinner service on Saturday and no lunch service on Sunday.

GETTYSBURG Dobbin House Tavern $$$

89 Steinwehr Ave, Gettysburg, PA, 17325 ***Tel*** *(717) 334-2100*

This cozy and quaint colonial tavern and restaurant *(see p140)* date to 1776. Full of antiques, it has costumed servers and a historic ambience. The menu consists of old-fashioned hearty dishes such as charbroiled meats and fowl. It is located across from where Abraham Lincoln delivered the Gettysburg Address *(see p121)*.

GETTYSBURG Farnsworth House Inn $$$

401 Baltimore St, Gettysburg, PA, 17325 ***Tel*** *(717) 334-8838*

Quaint dining rooms housed in a historic 1810 Gettysburg inn *(see p140)*, where over 100 bullet holes from the Civil War can still be seen. Period specialties include game pie, pumpkin fritters, peanut soup, and sweet potato pudding. It features dinner theater every Friday and Saturday evening from December through February.

GETTYSBURG Herr Tavern and Publick House $$$$

900 Chambersburg Rd, Gettysburg, PA, 17325 ***Tel*** *(717) 334-4332*

Once used as the first Confederate hospital during the Battle of Gettysburg, this 1815 country inn is now a B&B with five elegantly decorated dining rooms. The menu offers carefully prepared meat and seafood entrées served with tasteful garnishes and sauces. Reservations are required on weekends. No lunch service on Sunday.

HARRISBURG Appalachian Brewing Company $$

50 N Cameron St, Harrisburg, PA, 17010 ***Tel*** *(717) 221-1080*

The first brewpub in Pennsylvania's state capital is located in an impressive, historic three-story brick-and-timber building. Along with a large selection of handcrafted ales and lagers there is also an innovative menu, with plenty of tasty choices to complement your drinks.

Key to Price Guide *see p145* **Key to Symbols** *see back cover flap*

HERSHEY Lebbie Lebkicher's at Hershey Lodge $$

West Chocolate Ave and University Dr, Hershey, PA, 17033 **Tel** *(717) 533-3311, (800) 437-7439*

This casual and friendly restaurant, located in the Hershey Lodge, offers full hot and cold buffets ranging from salads and soups to seafood and prime rib selections. A special buffet is set up for children with pizzas, chicken nuggets, macaroni and cheese, and other kid favorites. Near Hershey Park and other attractions.

KING OF PRUSSIA California Café Bar & Grill $$$

The Plaza at King of Prussia Mall, 160 N Gulph Road, King of Prussia, PA, 19406 **Tel** *(610) 354-8686*

Buttercup yellow walls and funky sea-green architectural details set the tone for this cool California-style restaurant, part of a countrywide dining chain. Eclectic and themed menu offering "savory" American fare, all of which is prepared with fresh, regional foods of the season. An upbeat dining experience while at the King of Prussia Mall.

NEW HOPE Havana $$$

105 S Main St, New Hope, PA, 18938 **Tel** *(215) 862-9897*

Casual, fun dining and drinking on the main street. The large patio is great for people-watching in good weather. Outdoor heaters, live bands, and DJs make it a vibrant spot all year long. The food is not the draw here, but simple nachos, sandwiches, and salads are good fillers. Everything's overpriced, but in New Hope, it's expected.

NEW HOPE The Landing $$$

22 N Main St, New Hope, PA, 18938 **Tel** *(215) 862-5711*

Elegant dining with dramatic views of the Delaware River. In the summer the deck is the place to be, but the dining room is also welcoming and comfortable. Simple snacks, salads, and sandwiches are given the same attention as the more sophisticated pastas, steaks, and seafood dishes. Kids' menu available. Open seven days a week.

NEW HOPE Logan Inn Restaurant $$$$

10 W Ferry St, New Hope, PA, 18938 **Tel** *(215) 862-2300*

A fine-dining restaurant in a historic inn dating back to 1727, Logan Inn is one of the five oldest in the US. Located in the heart of New Hope, it features a lovely dining room and a porch that offers views of the bustling town center. Carefully prepared duck, seafood, beef, and pasta specialties available.

PENNSYLVANIA DUTCH COUNTRY Plain and Fancy Farm Restaurant $

3121 Old Philadelphia Pike, Bird-In-Hand, PA, 17505 **Tel** *(717) 768-4400*

Everyday is like grandmother's home cooking at this popular family-style restaurant near the Amishview Inns *(see p141)* in the Pennsylvania Dutch Country. Friendly pass-the-platter dining features roast beef, golden fried chicken, baked Lancaster County sausage, mashed potatoes, shoofly pie, apple dumplings, and more.

PENNSYLVANIA DUTCH COUNTRY The Family Cupboard Restaurant $

3029 Old Philadelphia Pike, Bird-in-Hand, PA, 17534 **Tel** *(717) 768-4510*

Amish and Mennonite home cooking does not get much better than this. Daily specials and full lunch and dinner buffets feature made-from-scratch pies and dishes from fresh farm vegetables such as green beans and carrots, mashed potatoes, and ham, chicken, and beef. Great for family dining.

PENNSYLVANIA DUTCH COUNTRY Kling House Restaurant $$

Rt 340, Intercourse, PA, 17534 **Tel** *(717) 768-8261*

This popular restaurant offers unique Pennsylvania Dutch Country and American fare with home-made jellies and relishes made at the adjoining Kitchen Kettle Village. House specials include portabella mushroom focaccia and grilled pita-pizza, among others. Closed Sunday.

PENNSYLVANIA DUTCH COUNTRY Miller's Smorgasbord $$

2811 Lincoln Hwy E (Rt 30), Ronks, PA, 17572 **Tel** *(717) 687-6621*

Sample a wide range of Pennsylvania Dutch treats and eat as much as you want at this buffet-style eatery – a tradition since 1929. Chilled steamed shrimp and carved top sirloin, turkey, chicken pot pie, and fresh bakery desserts are favorites. No lunch service. Breakfast is served only on Sunday mornings starting at 8am. Located on busy Route 30.

PENNSYLVANIA DUTCH COUNTRY 1764 Restaurant $$$

14 E Main St, Lititz, PA, 17543 **Tel** *(717) 626-2115*

An elegant dining room with colonial decor adds to the charm of this restaurant within the landmark 18th-century General Sutter Inn. Black Angus beef, oversized chops, seafood, fowl, and pasta highlight the menu's fine food selections. Breakfast specialties include farm fresh eggs and grilled cinnamon buns.

PENNSYLVANIA DUTCH COUNTRY Historic Revere Tavern $$$

3063 Lincoln Hwy E, Paradise, PA, 17562 **Tel** *(717) 455-7663*

Built in 1740, this tavern was once owned by the 15th US president, James Buchanan. Casual dining in a colonial atmosphere with fireplaces. Seafood, steaks, and unique snapper turtle soup highlight the menu. Along busy Route 30 in the Pennsylvania Dutch Country. No lunch service on Sunday and Monday.

WASHINGTON CROSSING Washington Crossing Inn $$$$

1295 Washington Memorial Rd, Washington Crossing, PA, 18977 **Tel** *(215) 493-3634*

Dating to 1817, this restaurant sits near where General Washington crossed the Delaware River in 1776. New-style American cuisine is served in a colonial ambience. Chops, steaks, and seafood are very well prepared. Lunch menu includes radicchio and arugala salad, grilled rib-eye steak, and smoked turkey breast arugala.

SHOPS AND MARKETS

The Philadelphia area is a stronghold for shopping with stores and outlets ranging from specialty boutiques, grand shopping centers, and malls to discount retailers and factory stores. Key shopping areas mentioned on the following pages include Center City's boutiques and shops on Market and Walnut Streets, and the shops and galleries in Old City and in the chic district of South Street. Situated in downtown Philadelphia are Antique Row and Jewelers' Row, while a variety of upscale and trendy shops are the highlights on the main streets of Manayunk and Chestnut Hill. The King of Prussia Mall is one of the nation's largest retail shopping complexes, while the cities of Reading and Lancaster have perhaps the largest number of factory outlet stores in the country.

Precious gems at Jewelers' Row

SHOPPING HOURS

Most retailers in central Philadelphia are open seven days a week, from 10am to 6pm on Mondays through Saturdays with some varying hours, and from noon until 5pm or 6pm on Sundays. Many Center City stores are open for an extra hour or two on Wednesday nights and sometimes on Friday nights.

Outside the city, individual retail stores usually have similar hours from 10am to 6pm. Malls, however, are often open until 9pm or 9:30pm Monday through Saturday, and noon until 6pm or 7pm on Sundays. Some specialty stores have reduced hours on weekends, or may close one or two days during the week.

The popular VF Outlet Village in Reading, Pennsylvania

Storefronts on a street in Chestnut Hill, Philadelphia

TAXES

There is no sales tax on clothing and shoes in Pennsylvania. For all other items, there is a 6 percent state sales tax and an additional 1 percent tax within Philadelphia, adding up to a 7 percent sales tax when shopping in the city. However, no sales tax is levied if your purchases are shipped to an address outside Pennsylvania, but additional shipping fees may apply. Foreign visitors may have to pay duties on larger purchases they wish to take home.

SALES

Finding a sale in the US is as easy as picking up a local newspaper – especially on weekends. Most large retailers compete on a daily basis, with many regularly slashing prices. Smaller stores may have clearance racks with reduced items, while sales are often more limited in trendy shops and high-end boutiques. The nation's "biggest shopping day of the year" occurs on the day after Thanksgiving and is called "Black Friday," when prices are cut by 70 percent or more. Similar sales take place after Christmas.

PAYMENT

Except for the smallest stores, major credit cards are accepted at most shops, boutiques, and retail outlets. In fact, department stores usually issue their own credit cards for return shoppers, though these are often issued at higher interest rates. In the US, the major credit cards accepted are Visa, Master Card, American Express, Discover Card, and Diners Club.

Cash is always accepted, and identification is necessary when using traveler's checks. Personal checks are discouraged, unless drawn from a local or well-known US bank. Stores do not accept foreign currency.

RETURNING MERCHANDISE

Most shops and stores will-willingly issue refunds and credits for returns, providing the merchandise is in good condition and not used or damaged. Sales receipts must accompany goods. Time limits for returns vary from store to store, with most allowing between 10 to 30 days. Be aware, however, that certain items purchased during special sales or promotions are non-returnable, and that some stores will issue in-store-credit returns only and not cash.

A couple enjoying shopping

DEPARTMENT STORES

There is no shortage of world-class department stores in the Philadelphia area, with most concentrated in the **King of Prussia Mall** *(see p156)*, Center City, and a few other area malls.

The historic Wanamaker Building *(see p70)* at 13th and Market Streets was named after Pennsylvanian John Wanamaker, a businessman who is considered to be the father of the department store. This Italian Renaissance-style building has housed many of the best department stores since its completion in 1910.

Today, **Macy's** Center City occupies this impressive space. This flagship store features high-end designers and affordable brand names. It also has a full-service Visitors' Center where shoppers can make dinner reservations and get information on the city's attractions.

Another upmarket retail giant in Center City is **Barney's Co-op** and in the King of Prussia Mall, the high-end department store **Neiman Marcus** offers the ultimate shopping experience with some of the best names in fashion in women's apparel, accessories, shoes, and jewelry. The same is true for children's and men's clothing. The store also offers quality bed and bath items, novelty rugs, and furniture.

Nordstrom, another leading fashion specialty store, offers high-quality gifts, apparel, shoes, and beauty products from several hundred brand names. High fashion, stylish accessories, and the latest fragrances can be found at **Lord and Taylor** and at **Bloomingdale's**, which also stocks a wide range of house gifts, luggage, and more. **JCPenney** has a broad range of apparel, shoes, and gifts for men, women, and children. **Sears** is also one of the nation's best-known department stores, known for its large appliances, tools, lawn and garden gear, automobile repair services, and household services. The King of Prussia Mall also has another branch of Macy's.

Interior of King of Prussia Mall, a retail shopping complex

DIRECTORY

CENTER CITY

Barney's Co-op
10 Rittenhouse Sq.
Tel *(215) 563-5333.* **Map** 2 D5.
www.barneys.com

Macy's
1300 Market St.
Map 3 B2. ***Tel*** *(215) 214-9000.*
www.macys.com

KING OF PRUSSIA MALL

Bloomingdale's
Tel *(610) 337-6300.*
www.bloomingdales.com

JCPenney
Tel *(610) 992-1096.*
www.jcpenney.com

Lord and Taylor
Tel *(610) 992-0333.*
www.lordandtaylor.com

Macy's
Tel *(610) 337-9350.*
www.macys.com

Neiman Marcus
Tel *(610) 354-0500.*
www.neimanmarcus.com

Nordstrom
Tel *(610) 265-6111.*
www.nordstrom.com

Sears
Tel *(610) 962-6489.*
www.sears.com

Interior of Shops at Liberty Place, a shopping mall in Center City

MALLS

There are several indoor malls in and around Philadelphia, allowing people to enjoy and indulge in year-round shopping, dining, and entertainment.

The Gallery at Market East, the city's largest mall, is located in Center City along Market Street between 8th and 12th Streets. The four-level mall connects with both the Pennsylvania Convention Center and Market East Station. It houses another 130 shops and eateries, and more than 30 pushcarts stocked with merchandise ranging from sunglasses and artworks to household wares and all manner of eclectic items.

The **King of Prussia Mall**, located in a suburb to the northwest of the city, is accessible via the Schulykill Expressway and is a 30-minute drive from Center City. With seven department stores *(see p155)* and vast parking lots and garages, it is one of the nation's largest retail shopping complexes comprising two separate sections: The Plaza and The Court. Expansive buildings with elaborate glass-ceiling atriums house more than 360 specialty shops, and an array of 40 restaurants and eateries. Nearby, Mall Boulevard has a good selection of retail and wholesale stores, and a multi-screen movie complex. North of the city, along Route 1 in Bensalem, is the **Neshaminy Mall**, which includes 125 stores, restaurants, and a colossal 24-screen cinema complex.

Shop sign at Manayunk

SPECIALTY SHOPPING CENTERS

Groups of specialty shops are housed in large central Philadelphia buildings, offering visitors and office workers easy access to shopping – especially during the lunch hour or after work.

With offices and the luxury Park Hyatt hotel above it, the century-old **Bellevue Building** in Center City has a host of upscale boutiques, world-class restaurants, a spa, a food court with the classic American steakhouse, The Palm, and more to offer. Also in Center City, the **Shops at Liberty Place** features 60 shops that sell fine apparel, shoes, jewelry, specialty foods, and beauty products. An impressive glass dome sits atop a circular rotunda – all part of the complex that makes up Liberty Place *(see p79)*.

The Bourse Food Court and Specialty Shops is in the heart of Independence Mall, directly across from the Liberty Bell Center. The Bourse offers tourists in Old City a break from sightseeing itineraries with gift and souvenir shops and a food court.

SHOPPING DISTRICTS

Clusters of shops and restaurants in popular neighborhoods are known as shopping districts. One of Center City's most chic areas, **Rittenhouse Row**, includes upscale establishments along Walnut Street leading up to Rittenhouse Square *(see p78)*. Several restaurants have storefronts facing the square, with outdoor seating in summer.

Anchored by New Market and Head House Square, **South Street** *(see p67)* offers a diversity of stores, shops, restaurants, eateries, and bars. Many of these cater to the avant-garde and eclectic trends of the younger crowds that often cram the area along South Street from Front to 11th Streets.

Main Street Manayunk *(see p97)* is very popular on weekends for its many restaurants, pubs, and nightlife. Clothes and shoe shops, salons, antique shops, and a

Shops and boutique windows at Main Street Manayunk

host of boutiques and galleries also line Main Street.

In **Chestnut Hill** *(see p96)*, more than 100 boutiques, galleries, antiques stores, restaurants, and cafés take up nearly a dozen blocks along Germantown Avenue. **Jewelers' Row** and **Antique Row** span several blocks in Center City.

MARKETS

The city's central farmers' market is the popular **Reading Terminal Market** *(see p73)*, where vendors sell farm-fresh produce, meats, poultry and seafood, flowers, pastries, and baked goods. Amish specialties and ethnic dishes representing the city's diverse population are particularly popular.

The nation's oldest and largest outdoor market, the **Italian Market** *(see p99)*, features several blocks of vendors who sell seafood, fresh produce, meats, Italian specialties, and desserts. The area is home to some of the city's best Italian restaurants.

To savor some delicious, home-style cooking of the Pennsylvania Dutch Country, take some time to drive out to the small villages of Bird-In-Hand and Intercourse. **The Amish Barn Restaurant and Gift Shop**, for instance, offers authentic local food as well as handicrafts and souvenirs.

Vendors at the Italian Market, one of the city's oldest outdoor markets

DISCOUNT AND OUTLET MALLS

Located in an area northeast of Philadelphia is the **Franklin Mills Mall**, home to more than 200 retail and factory stores such as Last Call, Neiman Marcus, Ann Taylor, and Factory Store. Its outlets include those for Casual Corner, Saks Fifth Avenue, Polo Ralph Lauren, JCPenney, and many others.

A complex of restored old factory buildings, **VF Outlet Village** in Reading is one of the county's largest groupings of factory store outlets. Several multistory buildings house discounted clothing, shoes, and household wares from Vanity Fair, Wrangler, Lee, Liz Claiborne, London Fog, Tommy Hilfiger, and Reebok.

Atlantic City Outlets, The Walk, in New Jersey, has merchandise from manufacturers, including Van Heusen, Guess, Geoffrey Beene, Casual Corner, and Brooks Brothers, at reduced prices.

DIRECTORY

MALLS

The Gallery at Market East
Market St between 9th & 11th Sts. **Map** 3 C2.
Tel *(215) 625-4962.*

King of Prussia Mall
160 N Gulph Rd, King of Prussia.
Tel *(610) 245-5794.*

Neshaminy Mall
Route 1 & Bristol Rd, Bensalem. ***Tel*** *(215) 357-6100.*

SPECIALTY SHOPPING CENTERS

The Bourse Food Court and Specialty Shops
111 S. Independence Mall East. **Map** 4 D3.
Tel *(215) 625-0300.*

The Shops at the Bellevue
200 S Broad St. **Map** 2 F5.
Tel *(215) 875-8350.*

Shops at Liberty Place
16th & Chestnut Sts. **Map** 2 E4.
Tel *(215) 851-9055.*

SHOPPING DISTRICTS

Antique Row
Pine St between 9th & 17th Sts. **Map** 3 B4.

Chestnut Hill
7600–8700 Germantown Ave, Chestnut Hill.
Tel *(215) 247-6696.*

Jewelers' Row
Sansom St between 7th & 8th Sts; and 8th St from Chestnut to Walnut Sts. **Map** 3 C3.
Tel *(215) 278-2903.*

Main Street Manayunk
Main Street, Manayunk.
Tel *(215) 482-9565.*

Rittenhouse Row
Area around Rittenhouse Square. **Map** 2 D5.
Tel *(215) 972-0101.*

South Street
South St from Front to 11th Sts. **Map** 3 B4.
Tel *(215) 413-3713.*

MARKETS

The Amish Barn Restaurant and Gift Shop
3029, Old Philadelphia Pike, Rte 340, Bird-in-Hand, PA.
Tel *(717) 768-3220.*

Italian Market
9th St between Christian & Wharton Sts. **Map** 3 C5.
Tel *(215) 922-5557.*

Reading Terminal Market
12th & Arch Sts. **Map** 3 B2.
Tel *(215) 922-2317.*

DISCOUNT AND OUTLET MALLS

Atlantic City Outlets, The Walk
Michigan Ave between Pacific & Baltic Aves, Atlantic City, NJ.
Tel *(609) 872-7002.*

Franklin Mills Mall
1455 Franklin Mills Circle, PA.
Tel *(215) 262-4386.*

VF Outlet Village
801 Hill Avenue, Reading, PA.
Tel *(610) 378-0408.*

Fashion and Accessories

Center City is Philadelphia's main shopping district with more than 2,100 retail stores. Many offer the finest in clothes, shoes, accessories, and jewelry. Key fashion shops and boutiques are located along Walnut Street on Rittenhouse Row. Designer clothing stores are also found at the Gallery at Market East mall, as well as within the small shopping centers at the Bellevue Building and Liberty Place. When looking for the latest in high fashion, do not forget the department stores and specialty stores at the King of Prussia Mall.

WOMEN'S FASHION

With so many stores and boutiques to choose from, women will be delighted with a shopping spree in Center City. Located just one block from Rittenhouse Square on Walnut Street, **Jones New York** offers a range of fine apparel. Nearby, the **Knit Wit** boutique carries a variety of elegant black cocktail dresses as well as cruise-wear. **Ann Taylor**, on the same block, has upbeat and high-fashion designs for both business and pleasure. **Ann Taylor Loft**, **Express**, and lingerie store **Victoria's Secret** are also at Liberty Place.

The number of women's apparel stores in the King of Prussia Mall is extensive and you will need plenty of time to get round them all. In addition to Victoria's Secret and Ann Taylor, there are upscale stores from top international designers, the latest classic and trendy fashions from **New York and Company** and **Lane Bryant**, and the risqué designs of **Frederick's of Hollywood**.

Main Street Manayunk features several women's clothing boutiques. **Showing with Style** offers fashionable maternity clothes, while Nicole Miller and **Paula Hian Designs** stock upscale evening wear for women.

Window shopping at one of Center City's numerous upscale boutiques

MEN'S FASHION

Men looking for the perfect suit or designer clothing will not leave the city empty handed. **Boyds Philadelphia** has been around for over 60 years and is one of Center City's premier stores. One of the most elegant shops at the Bellevue, **Polo Ralph Lauren** has a full line of clothing from the world-renowned designer. Men will also find a variety of stores at the Shops at Liberty Place, including **Jos. A. Bank**, **Les Richard's Menswear**, and **Andrew's Ties**.

In the King of Prussia Mall, **Hugo Boss Store** features the label's clothing, sportswear, and accessories. Other popular men's stores include **Brooks Brothers**, a high-end business-wear retailer, and **Tommy Bahama**, which features casual clothing and sportswear inspired by coastal living.

Entrance to the upmarket shops in Liberty Place

MEN'S AND WOMEN'S FASHION

With shops in the Bellevue Building and Manayunk, **Nicole Miller** features men's and women's formalwear, as well as accessories. A line of both casual and dressy apparel can be found at **J. Crew** and **Express** at the Shops at Liberty Place, while casual wear is the highlight of **Old Navy. Finish Line**, at the Gallery at Market East, features athletic footwear. At King of Prussia, **7 For All Mankind** sells fine-quality couture denim. **Eddie Bauer** features winter clothes, while **Banana Republic** offers casual jeans and dressy jackets. Other popular outlets include **Abercrombie & Fitch**, and the hip styles of **Diesel**.

Casual sneakers

SHOES AND ACCESSORIES

Featuring a line of fur, shearling, leather, and cloth, **Jacques Ferber** on Walnut Street offers unique outerwear. **Fire & Ice**, located at the Shops at Liberty Place, specializes in hand crafted jewelry and accessories as well as unique items for the home.

For men's shoes, **Sherman Brothers** offers a wide selection of top brands and hard-to-find sizes. Both men's and women's choices for shoes abound in the King of Prussia Mall, with stores including **Bakers**, **Kenneth Cole, Rock-port**, **Timberland**, **Bostonian**, and **Johnston Murphy**.

JEWELRY

Philadelphia's Jewelers' Row was established in 1851, and is the nation's oldest and one of the largest diamond districts. Stores on the row include a seemingly unlimited selection of diamonds, rubies, sapphires, and emeralds. Owned by the same family for four generations, **Barsky Diamonds** specializes in diamonds. **Safian and Rudolph Jewelers**, in business for over 50 years, deals in precious stones, while **Tiffany & Co.**, in Center City, has offered the finest in jewelry, crystal, and accessories for more than 150 years. Other prominent Center City jewelers include **Govberg Jewelers** and **LAGOS The Store**.

DIRECTORY

WOMEN'S FASHION

Ann Taylor
1713 Walnut St.
Map 2 E5.
Tel *(215) 977-9336.*
King of Prussia Mall.
Tel *(610) 354-9380.*

Ann Taylor Loft
Liberty Place. **Map** 2 E4.
Tel *(215) 851-9055.*
King of Prussia Mall.
Tel *(610) 337-1550.*

Daffy's
1700 Chestnut St.
Map 2 E4.
Tel *(215) 963-9996.*

Frederick's of Hollywood
King of Prussia Mall.
Tel *(610) 265-1499.*

Jones New York
1711 Walnut St.
Map 2 E5.
Tel *(215) 864–0110.*

Knit Wit
1718 Walnut St.
Map 2 E5.
Tel *(215) 564-4760.*

Lane Bryant
King of Prussia Mall.
Tel *(610) 265-6106.*

New York and Company
King of Prussia Mall.
Tel *(610) 354-0560.*

Paula Hian Designs
106 Gay St, Manayunk.
Tel *(215) 487-2762.*

Showing with Style
4321 Main St, Manayunk.
Tel *(267) 297-7035.*

Victoria's Secret
Liberty Place. **Map** 2 E4.
Tel *(215) 564-1142.*
King of Prussia Mall.
Tel *(610) 337-0788.*

MEN'S FASHION

Andrew's Ties
1625 Chestnut St. **Map** 2 E4. ***Tel*** *(215) 988-1260.*

Boyds Philadelphia
1818 Chestnut St.
Map 2 D4.
Tel *(215) 564-9000.*

Brooks Brothers
1513 Walnut St. **Map** 2 E5. ***Tel*** *(215) 564-4100.*
King of Prussia Mall.
Tel *(610) 337-9888.*

Hugo Boss Store
King of Prussia Mall.
Tel *(610) 992-1400.*

Jos. A. Bank
Liberty Place. **Map** 2 E4.
Tel *(215) 563-5990.*
King of Prussia Mall.
Tel *(610) 337-2131.*

Les Richard's Menswear
1625 Chestnut St. **Map** 2 E4. ***Tel*** *(215) 751-1155.*

Polo Ralph Lauren
200 S Broad St. **Map** 2 F5.
Tel *(215) 985-2800.*

Senor
4390 Main St, Manayunk.
Tel *(215) 487-3667.*

Tommy Bahama
King of Prussia Mall.
Tel *(484) 688-8042.*

MEN'S AND WOMEN'S FASHION

7 For All Mankind
King of Prussia Mall.
Tel *(610) 265-1507.*

Abercrombie & Fitch
King of Prussia Mall.
Tel *(610) 265-5650.*

Banana Republic
1401 Walnut St. **Map** 2 F5. ***Tel*** *(215) 751-0292.*
King of Prussia Mall.
Tel *(610) 768-9007.*

Diesel
King of Prussia Mall.
Tel *(610) 768-5855.*

Eddie Bauer
King of Prussia Mall.
Tel *(610) 233-0086.*

Express
Liberty Place. **Map** 2 E4.
Tel *(215) 851-0699.*
King of Prussia Mall.
Tel *(610) 337-8912.*

Finish Line
9th & Market Sts.
Map 3 C2.
Tel *(215) 351-6202.*

J. Crew
Liberty Place. **Map** 2 E4.
Tel *(215) 977-7335.*

Nicole Miller
200 S Broad St. **Map** 2 F5.
Tel *(215) 546-5007.*
4249 Main Street, Manayunk.
Tel *(215) 930-0307.*

Old Navy
The Gallery at Market East, Market St between 9th & 11th Sts. **Map** 3 C2.
Tel *(215) 413-7012.*

SHOES AND ACCESSORIES

Bakers
King of Prussia Mall.
Tel *(610) 265-8948.*

Bostonian
King of Prussia Mall.
Tel *(610) 265-4323.*

Fire & Ice
1625 Chestnut St.
Map 3 A2.
Tel *(215) 564-2871.*

Jacques Ferber
1708 Walnut St.
Map 2 E5.
Tel *(215) 735-4173.*

Johnston Murphy
King of Prussia Mall.
Tel *(610) 265-0165.*

Kenneth Cole
1422 Walnut St. **Map** 2 E5. ***Tel*** *(215) 790-1690.*
King of Prussia Mall.
Tel *(610) 337-2650.*

Nine West
Liberty Place.
Map 2 E4.
Tel *(215) 851-8570.*

Rockport
King of Prussia Mall.
Tel *(610) 265-5800.*

Sherman Brothers Shoes
1520 Sansom St.
Map 2 E4.
Tel *(215) 561-4550.*

Timberland
King of Prussia Mall.
Tel *(610) 265-2193.*

JEWELRY

Barsky Diamonds
724 Sansom St.
Map 4 D3.
Tel *(215) 925-8639.*

Govberg Jewelers
1818 Chestnut St.
Map 2 E5.
Tel *(215) 546-6505.*

LAGOS The Store
1735 Walnut St.
Map 2 E4.
Tel *(215) 567-0770.*

Safian & Rudolph Jewelers
701 Sansom St.
Map 4 D3.
Tel *(215) 627-1834.*

Tiffany & Co.
1414 Walnut St.
Map 2 E5.
Tel *(215) 735-1919.*

Specialty Shops

With shopping districts, upscale shops, and one-of-a-kind stores, central Philadelphia has a wide range of merchandise that would satisfy even the hard-to-please shopper. Many specialty shops and gift stores specialize in finding the perfect gift or souvenir. Antique Row has numerous stores along an eight-block stretch in Center City, while in Old City sits a large cluster of art galleries. Other key shopping areas with unique crafts, books, and flower stores include Manayunk and Chestnut Hill. The colossal King of Prussia Mall has a seemingly unending choice of everything, from home furnishings and electronics to sporting goods.

Shops located in the Chestnut Hill market area

ANTIQUES

Spread over eight blocks on Pine Street between 7th and 11th Streets, Antique Row *(see p157)* features boutiques and shops offering a selection of fine furniture, period antiques, collectibles, estate jewelry, and vintage clothing. One such store is **M. Finkel & Daughter**, which sells period furniture, 17th- to 19th-century needlework, and decorative accessories. The nearby **Classic Antiques** offers a large selection of country French furniture, mirrors, and accessories as well as 18th- and 19th-century European antiques. The **South Street Antiques Market** is the city's only indoor antiques market with 27 dealers selling pieces from vintage Victorian to modern, including estate jewelry, furniture, pottery, and accessories.

ART GALLERIES

The Old City Arts Association has 50 members, including art galleries, which are open until 9pm on the first Friday of every month – an event that is appropriately called "First Friday." The **Moderne Gallery** features contemporary furniture, pottery, fine arts, and metalwork. The **Artists' House Gallery** offers works rendered by local artists and available for sale at affordable prices.

Located on Antique Row, **Seraphin Gallery** has art from international contemporary painters, sculptors, and photographers, including 18th- through 20th-century works by artists from America and Europe.

In Center City, **Newman Galleries** specializes in 19th-century American and European paintings, and early 20th-century American art from the New Hope School.

Established in 1974, **The Clay Studio** in Old City exhibits works by emerging and established artists and also offers a range of classes.

Gourmet cheese

BOOKS

An excellent choice for mainstream books and magazines is **Barnes & Noble** at Rittenhouse Square. Also in that square is the independent **Joseph Fox Bookshop**, while **Books a Million**, has a more commercial store in Gallery at Market East mall.

For hard-to-find books, the **Philadelphia Rare Books and Manuscript Company** features early printed books dating from the 16th century, and manuscripts, old bibles, and other books from around the world that cover a wide realm of topics. Opened in 1936, **Robin's Bookstore** is the oldest independent bookstore in the city with a vast collection of African-American books, literature, poetry, New Age, and children's books.

FOOD AND COOKERY

Within the Italian Market are specialty food stores. Family owned for more than 50 years, **DiBruno Bros. House of Cheese** sells more than 400 types of cheese and gourmet foods. **Termini Brothers Gold Medal Pastry Bakery** is a local favorite with handmade Italian confections made from recipes that date to the 1800s. Serving chefs and home cooks since 1906, **Fante's Kitchen Wares Shop** offers an extensive selection of cooking wares and utensils.

GIFTS, CRAFTS, AND SOUVENIRS

As a result of its varied traditions and its status as one of America's oldest cities, Philadelphia offers a range of gifts and mementos. **Xenos Candy'n Gifts** has classic souvenirs showcasing Old City sights, including replicas of Liberty Bell, flags, and other collectables. Similar items are found in **The Bourse** nearby, while the **Pennsylvania General Store** has locally-made foods and crafts. **Scarlett Alley** offers art, furnishings, jewelry, leather goods, books, and children's items. **Sweet Violet** features fine gifts for personal care as well as for homes. Fine-rolled, handmade cigars can be bought at the **Black Cat Cigar Company** and **Holt's Cigar Company** in Center City.

FLORISTS

A wide-ranging choice of flowers is available from Philadelphia's florists. Some, such as **Nature's Gallery Florist** in Center City, are also able to assist with the floral side of party planning. **Ten Pennies Florist**, a staple in Philadelphia for more than 30 years, offers exquisite arrangements for any occasion.

MUSIC

For the latest in music CDs and recordings, **f.y.e.** has extensive music selections featuring rock, pop, hip-hop, jazz, folk, classical, and more. Visit **Repo Records** on South Street to thumb through a wide range of import singles, and rows of used records and CDs. **Philadelphia Record Exchange** is the city's spot to find second-hand vinyl and CDs.

Music CDs

SPORTING GOODS

The nation's largest family-owned sports goods chain, **Modell's Sporting Goods**, has stores in Center City and King of Prussia Mall, and also sells home-team apparel and footwear. For camping gear, kayaks, and other outdoor items, shop at **Eastern Mountain Sports**, also at King of Prussia Mall.

DIRECTORY

ANTIQUES

Classic Antiques
922 Pine St. **Map** 3 C4.
Tel *(215) 629-0211.*

M. Finkel & Daughter
936 Pine St. **Map** 3 C4.
Tel *(215) 627-7797.*

South Street Antiques Market
600 Bainbridge St. **Map** 3 D5. ***Tel*** *(215) 592-0256.*

ART GALLERIES

Artists' House Gallery
57 N 2nd St. **Map** 4 E2.
Tel *(215) 923-8440.*

The Clay Studio
139 N Second St.
Map 4 E2.
Tel *(215) 925-3453.*

Moderne Gallery
111 N 3rd St. **Map** 4 E2.
Tel *(215) 923-8536.*

Newman Galleries
1425 Walnut St. **Map** 2 E5.
Tel *(215) 563-1779.*

Seraphin Gallery
1108 Pine St. **Map** 3 B4.
Tel *(215) 923-7000.*

BOOKS

Barnes & Noble
1805 Walnut St.
Map 2 D4.
Tel *(215) 665-0716.*

Books a Million
The Gallery at Market East, Market St. **Map** 3 C2.
Tel *(215) 923-1912.*

Joseph Fox Bookshop
1724 Sansom Street.
Map 3 A2.
Tel (215) 563-4184.

Philadelphia Rare Books and Manuscript Company
2375 Bridge St.
Tel *(215) 744-6734.*

Robin's Bookstore
110A S 13th St. **Map** 3 B3. ***Tel*** *(215) 567-2615.*

FOOD AND COOKERY

DiBruno Bros. House of Cheese
Italian Market, 930 S 9th St. **Map** 3 C5.
Tel *(215) 922-2876.*
109 S 18th St. **Map** 2 E4.
Tel *(215) 665-9220.*

Fante's Kitchen Wares Shop
Italian Market, 1006 S 9th St. **Map** 3 C5.
Tel *(215) 922-5557.*

Termini Brothers Gold Medal Pastry Bakery
1523 S 8th St.
Tel *(215) 334-1816.*

GIFTS, CRAFTS, AND SOUVENIRS

Black Cat Cigar Company
46 W Germantown Pike, East Norriton, PA.
Tel *(800) 220-9850.*

The Bourse
5th between Market & Chestnut Sts. **Map** 4 D3.
Tel *(215) 625-0300.*

Holt's Cigar Company
1522 Walnut St.
Map 2 E5.
Tel *(215) 732-8500.*

Pennsylvania General Store
Reading Terminal Market.
Map 3 C2.
Tel *(215) 592-0455.*

Scarlett Alley
241 Race St. **Map** 4E2.
Tel *(215) 592-7898.*

Sweet Violet
4361 Main St, Manayunk.
Tel *(215) 483-2826.*

Xenos Candy'n Gifts
231 Chestnut St. **Map** 4 E3. ***Tel*** *(215) 922-1445.*

FLORISTS

Nature's Gallery Florist
Map 2 D4.
Tel *(215) 563-5554.*

Ten Pennies Florist
1921 S Broad St. **Map** 3 C2. ***Tel*** *(215) 336-3557.*

MUSIC

f.y.e.
100 South Broad Street.
Map 3 B2.
Tel (215) 496-8338.

Philadelphia Record Exchange
618 South St. **Map** 4 D4.
Tel *(215) 922-2752.*

Repo Records
538 South St. **Map** 4 D4.
Tel *(215) 627-3775.*

SPORTING GOODS

Eastern Mountain Sports
King of Prussia Mall.
Tel *(610) 337-4210.*

Modell's Sporting Goods
934 Market St. **Map** 3 C2.
Tel *(215) 629-0900.*
King of Prussia Mall.
Tel *(610) 337-4522.*

ENTERTAINMENT IN PHILADELPHIA

Stretching along the "Avenue of the Arts," Broad Street is home to a plethora of renowned performing arts facilities. Heading the list are the Kimmel Center for the Performing Arts and the Academy of Music, home to the world-class Philly POPS, Philadelphia Orchestra, Opera Company of Philadelphia, and the Pennsylvania Ballet. Numerous other venues feature live chamber music, theater productions and musicals, rock, hip hop and jazz-fusion concerts, and varied programs of gospel. Universities also put on several music, theater, and dance shows. Nightclubs hosting live bands abound in Old City and South Street, while a drive or train ride of an hour or so brings you to Atlantic City's glittering casinos on the New Jersey shoreline.

Detail of façade at the Forrest Theater

Visitors wait for a show at Kimmel Center for the Performing Arts

INFORMATION

There are several websites and newspapers that carry the latest information on musical concerts, theatrical performances, nightlife, and other entertainment options in and around the city.

The *Weekend* section of the **Philadelphia Inquirer**, published every Friday, details the goings-on in town, from the latest movies to gallery exhibitions to extensive listings of live performances, including ballet, chamber and classical music, opera, theater, and jazz. The art district has its own website, **Avenue of the Arts**.

The **Philadelphia City Paper** and **Philadelphia Weekly** also showcase arts, music, and cinema listings. They also have extended information on daily nightclub acts and performances. These two publications are weeklies and are available free at many cafés, pubs, and bookstores throughout the city. They also have websites with up-to-date listings.

Philadelphia's most comprehensive news website is **www.phillyfunguide.com**. It has information on all types of activities in the city and also has a number of saver deals.

TICKETS

Seats for most of the major symphony, opera, chamber music, ballet, and pop performances in Philadelphia can be booked through **Ticket Philadelphia**. The main box office is in the **Kimmel Center for the Performing Arts**. Tickets can be bought in person, on the phone or online. Tickets for various events and theatrical performances can also be bought at the box office of each venue, or over the phone, online or in person via **Ticketmaster**. Be aware, however, that ticketing services often add a fee to the total cost. Ticketmaster is one of the world's largest e-commerce sites, in addition to having more than 3,300 retail outlets and 19 worldwide telephone call centers. It acts as the exclusive ticketing service for various performing arts venues and theaters.

Some hotels may also sell show tickets, especially those in Center City or near the theater district. Check with the concierge in your hotel for the best ticketing options.

The Philadelphia Orchestra at Verizon Hall in the Kimmel Center

"Avenue of the Arts" lights up for a night of theater and culture

ENTERTAINMENT DISTRICTS

The hub of Philadelphia's performing arts and theater district is the so-called **Avenue of the Arts**, which extends south of City Hall on South Broad Street. This two-block area is anchored by the Kimmel Center for the Performing Arts and the world-renowned **Academy of Music** *(see p76)*. Also located in this area is the Merriam Theater, hosting professional touring productions, as well as the 300-seat Wilma Theater *(see p164)*, whose productions address current political and social issues. Three blocks east of the area is the Forrest Theatre *(see p164)*, while the Prince Music Theater is on Chestnut Street.

Besides theater and cultural activities, Philadelphia has a thriving nightlife with scores of restaurants, nightclubs, smaller theater venues, and comedy clubs concentrated along South Street. A vibrant nightlife scene also abounds in the Old City area around Chestnut, Market, Front, and 2nd Streets with a wide variety of restaurants, cozy pubs, and martini bars.

Along the Delaware River, Columbus Avenue is home to some of Philadelphia's up-and-coming nightspots north and south of Penn's Landing – some are on piers stretching into the river, while others are seasonal outdoor clubs. Much of the city's lesbian and gay nightlife is centered in the neighborhood between Pine and Chestnut Streets north to south and Broad and 11th Streets west to east.

Across the Delaware, meanwhile, the Susquehanna Bank Center at the Camden Waterfront *(see p101)* hosts concerts through the year, drawing big-name musical acts, as does the Wells Fargo Complex in south Philadelphia *(see p166)*.

Going beyond Philadelphia, Atlantic City *(see p127)* is just a short drive or train ride from Center City, and an entertainment destination in itself, with more than a dozen sprawling casino hotels and resorts, most of which have popular nightclubs, concert venues, and pulsing and glitzy discos.

South Street – an entertainment hub for the younger crowd

DISABLED ACCESS

Most of the major concert halls and theaters in Philadelphia accommodate disabled patrons and wheelchairs. The **Kimmel Center for the Performing Arts and the Academy of Music** have accessible wheelchair seating locations for performances, captioning for the hearing impaired, and assisted listening devices available on a first-come, first-served basis. Call ahead for details.

Some smaller venues and clubs may be less than adequate in accommodating disabled patrons. Check with the venue or the **Mayor's Commission on People with Disabilities** for more information. The commission provides a forum for the disabled to express opinions on programs and services in Philadelphia.

DIRECTORY

TICKETING

Ticket Philadelphia
Tel *(215) 893-1999.*
www.ticketphiladelphia.org

Ticketmaster
Various Outlets.
Tel *(215) 574-3550.*
www.ticketmaster.com

DISABLED ACCESS

Kimmel Center for the Performing Arts & Academy of Music
Department of Audience & Visitor Services. **Map** 2 E5.
Tel *(215) 670-2327.*
www.kimmelcenter.org

Mayor's Commission on People with Disabilities
1401 JFK Blvd. **Map** 2 F4.
Tel *(215) 686-2798.*
www.phila.gov/mcpd

USEFUL WEBSITES

Avenue of the Arts
www.avenueofthearts.org

Philadelphia Citypaper.net
www.citypaper.net

Philadelphia Fun Guide
www.phillyfunguide.com

Philadelphia Weekly Online
www.philadelphiaweekly.com

Philly.com (Philadelphia Inquirer)
www.philly.com

The Arts in Philadelphia

A cultural Mecca for the performing arts, Philadelphia has world-class venues that host excellent chamber and symphony music, and some of the finest performances in opera, ballet, and theater. Topping the list are concerts by the renowned Philadelphia Orchestra and Philly POPS, which are performed in the city's premier venue, the multitheater Kimmel Center for the Performing Arts. Chamber music ensembles play before smaller crowds, while grand opera and ballet productions take the stage in the Victorian-era Academy of Music. Several theaters in and around Center City host performances that range from Broadway productions and musicals to African-American theater. Entertainment is also provided by choral groups and the area's top music schools, which hold classical concerts and dance performances by students.

Forrest Theater, host to touring dance and theater companies

CLASSICAL MUSIC AND SYMPHONY

One of the city's best, the **Philadelphia Orchestra** has shared the stage with some of the world's most influential classical musicians for more than 100 years. The orchestra's home was the **Academy of Music**, but it now performs at the Verizon Hall in the **Kimmel Center for the Performing Arts**.

Also performing at Verizon Hall is **The Philly POPS**, one of the nation's most-renowned POPS orchestras playing big band, classics, Broadway hits, and rock'n roll tunes. In summer, both orchestras perform at an outdoor venue, **The Mann Center**, also home to jazz, dance, opera, and musical theater programs.

Chamber music can be enjoyed on Sunday afternoons and Monday evenings at the Kimmel Center's Perelman Theater. The **Chamber Orchestra of Philadelphia** performs here, playing a musical repertoire from the 18th century to the present day. The **Philadelphia Chamber Music Society** presents more than 60 chamber music, piano, vocal, and choral concerts a year, which are performed by internationally known groups as well as emerging artists. Presenting a unique classical experience is the **Philomel Baroque Orchestra** – a small ensemble of accomplished musicians who play early classical and Baroque music on period instruments.

Academy of Music, oldest opera house in the US still used for its original purpose

THEATERS AND THEATER COMPANIES

Stage productions run the gamut from national touring shows to politically inspired acts produced locally. The **Philadelphia Theatre Company** is the city's leading producer of contemporary American theater, while the **Arden Theatre Company** brings to life dramatic and theatrical stories by the greatest storytellers of all time.

The **Forrest Theatre** hosts Broadway shows and is the city's premier theatrical arts venue. The **Walnut Street Theatre** – America's oldest – is home to musicals and plays.

The **Wilma Theater** has productions with contemporary themes, while the smaller **Society Hill Playhouse** features offbeat and "off-Broad Street" productions. The **Freedom Theatre**, located on the northern stretch of the Avenue of the Arts, is one of the country's leading venues for African-American performances.

Pennsylvania Ballet dancer performing *Swan Lake*

OPERA AND BALLET

Local lovers of grand opera have been enjoying performances by the **Opera Company of Philadelphia** since 1975. The **Pennylvania Ballet**, which has been thrilling audiences since it was established in 1963, performs at the Academy of Music and the Merriam Theater. Its season has six productions, including the old Yuletide favorite, The Nutcracker *(see p35)*, which has become an annual Philadelphia tradition.

VOCAL ARTS AND CHOIRS

There are several choral groups in the city such as the renowned **Philadelphia Boys Choir and Chorale**. The 100-member choir performs patriotic music and Broadway show tunes. The group holds more than 40 performances each year, and travels on international tours.

The **Philadelphia Singers**, an ensemble of 24 professional vocalists, performs with leading national and local orchestras and other performing arts organizations such as the Philadelphia Orchestra, the Pennsylvania Ballet, and the Curtis Institute of Music. A 100-voice symphonic chorus, the **Choral Arts Society of Philadelphia** also appears often with the Philadelphia Orchestra. The **Academy of Vocal Arts**, around since 1934, produces operas with the **Chamber Orchestra of Philadelphia**. The academy's resident artists also hold recitals and concerts.

MUSIC SCHOOLS' PERFORMANCES

Often considered one of the most prestigious conservatories, the **Curtis Institute of Music** trains some of the best young musicians from around the world. The students hold free public recitals and concerts in the institute's Field Concert Hall located opposite Rittenhouse Square, and play in various venues around the city when they are not touring.

Local musicians and students training in classical, jazz, dance, and theater arts also hold recitals and concerts at the **University of the Arts**, Temple University's **Esther Boyer College of Music and Dance**, and through **PENN Presents** at the University of Pennsylvania's Annenberg Center for the Performing Arts.

DIRECTORY

CLASSICAL MUSIC AND SYMPHONY

Academy of Music
1420 Locust St.
Map 2 E5.
Tel *(215) 790-5800; box office: (215) 893-1999.*

Chamber Orchestra of Philadelphia
Perelman Theater, Kimmel Center. **Map** 2 E5.
Tel *(215) 545-5451; box office: (215) 893-1709.*

Kimmel Center for the Performing Arts
260 S Broad St.
Map 3 A3.
Tel *(215) 790-5800; box office: (215) 893-1999.*

The Mann Center
52nd St & Parkside Ave.
Tel *(215) 546-7900; box office: (215) 893-1999.*

Philadelphia Chamber Music Society
Various venues.
Tel *(215) 569-8587; box office: (215) 569-8080.*

Philadelphia Orchestra
Verizon Hall, Kimmel Center. **Map** 2 E5.
Tel *(215) 893-1900; box office: (215) 893-1999.*

The Philly POPS
Verizon Hall, Kimmel Center.
Map 2 E5.
Tel *(215) 546-6400; box office: (215) 893-1999.*

Philomel Baroque Orchestra
Various venues.
Tel *(215) 487–2344; box office: (215) 569-9700.*

THEATERS AND THEATER COMPANIES

Arden Theatre Company
40 N 2nd St.
Map 4 E2.
Tel *(215) 922-8900.*

Forrest Theatre
1114 Walnut St.
Map 3 B3.
Tel *(215) 923-1515.*

Freedom Theatre
1346 N Broad St.
Tel *(215) 765-2793.*

Philadelphia Theatre Company
480 S Broad St.
Map 2 D5.
Tel *(215) 985-1400; box office: (215) 985-0420.*

Society Hill Playhouse
507 S 8th St. **Map** 3 C4.
Tel *(215) 923-0210.*

Walnut Street Theatre
825 Walnut St. **Map** 3 C3. ***Tel*** *(215) 574-3550.*

Wilma Theater
265 S Broad St.
Map 2 F5.
Tel *box office: (215) 546-7824.*

OPERA AND BALLET

Opera Company of Philadelphia
Academy of Music.
Map 2 E5.
Tel *(215) 893-3600; box office: (215) 732-8400.*

Pennsylvania Ballet
Merriam Theater, Academy of Music.
Map 2 E5.
Tel *(215) 551-7000.*

VOCAL ARTS AND CHOIRS

Academy of Vocal Arts
Various venues.
Tel *(215) 735-1685.*

Choral Arts Society of Philadelphia
Various venues.
Tel *box office: (215) 545-8634.*

Philadelphia Boys Choir and Chorale
225 N 32nd St.
Map 1 B2.
Tel *(215) 222-3500.*

Philadelphia Singers
Kimmel Center & various venues.
Map 2 E5.
Tel *(215) 751-9494.*

MUSIC SCHOOLS' PERFORMANCES

Curtis Institute of Music
Field Concert Hall & various venues.
1726 Locust St.
Map 2 E5.
Tel *(215) 893-7902; box office: (215) 893-1999.*

Esther Boyer College of Music and Dance
Temple University,
1715 N Broad St.
Tel *(215) 204-8301.*

PENN Presents
Annenberg Center for the Performing Arts, University of Pennsylvania.
Tel *(215) 898-6701; box office: (215) 898-3900.*

University of the Arts
Broad & Pine Sts.
Map 2 E5.
Tel *(215) 545-1664.*

Music and Nightlife

Philadelphia fills its after-dark hours with the latest sounds in rock, folk, pop, jazz-fusion, hip-hop, and salsa. These rhythms can be heard at venues offering live music, sometimes seven days a week. Many are clustered within the prominent entertainment districts of South Street, Old City, Main Street Manayunk, and the areas along the Delaware Avenue waterfront. Philadelphia is often a regular stop for major bands and musical acts on world tours, including top rock, jazz, hip-hop, and country and pop musicians. Those opting for a less energized night out can enjoy conversation and cocktails at friendly neighborhood taverns and bars located throughout the city.

ROCK AND FOLK MUSIC

For the top touring rock bands, check listings in local newspapers *(see p162)* for concerts at the **Wells Fargo Complex** and other major venues, including the **Tower Theater, Keswick Theatre**, and the **Susquehanna Bank Center**, located on the waterfront. Also check listings for concerts held in Atlantic City.

For a taste of local rock music, **Khyber PubPass** in Old City has shows several nights a week and is a mainstay for Philadelphia's rock scene. Live performances by local rock groups also take place at **The Legendary Dobbs** on South Street and the **Manayunk Brewing Company** in Manayunk.

Folk musicians and fans frequent the **Tin Angel** in Old City. One of the region's best venues for folk artists, gospel choirs, and alternative rock acts is **World Café Live**, located on the campus in University City.

BLUES, JAZZ, AND WORLD MUSIC

Blues and jazz clubs range from upbeat nightspots and restaurants, where top artists perform, to smaller and cozier lounges. **Warmdaddy's** is a popular southern blues club and restaurant offering live jazz. Its 100-seat dining room overlooks the main stage where artists perform nightly; Tuesdays are reserved for open jam sessions made up of local musicians. **Ortlieb's Lounge** is another hot venue that offers world-class jazz music seven nights a week. **Chris' Jazz Club**, on Samson Street, has become something of an institution amongst the city's jazz lovers. The line-up includes a good mix of up-and-coming and established talent. Some clubs offer a range of international music, such as salsa, flamenco, and more. For instance, musicians at **Alma de Cuba** belt out live Cuban music performances every week.

Alma de Cuba, famous for its Cuban cuisine and live music

Performers at the popular Chris' Jazz club

NIGHTCLUBS AND DISCOS

Philadelphia offers a wide range of late-night venues to suit all musical persuasions. The city's younger crowd parties late into the night with clubs churning out music until 2am. The cutting-edge dance club **Shampoo** features dance halls and lounges with multiple bars and DJs. On Delaware Avenue, restaurant and nightclub **Cavanaugh's River Deck** features concerts and DJs in an all-outdoors venue along the Delaware River, with views of the Benjamin Franklin Bridge.

A trendy nightspot for the city's chic elite is the **32° Luxe Lounge** in Old City. It includes two premium bars and a lush VIP lounge with European bottle service. The Polynesian-themed **Tiki Bob's Cantina** has a signature drink, the Tiki Nut. For classic funk to old-school hip-hop and reggae, to the latest DJ mixes, **Bleu Martini** in Old City is the place to be seen in Philadelphia.

BARS AND TAVERNS

Many Center City hotels and restaurants have comfortable bars that are ideal for relaxing and for conversation. Philadelphia also has a number of neighborhood bars and pubs that play live music. **Monk's Café** in south Philadelphia is a bistro with more than 200 beer brands from around the world and 20 Belgian draught ales. If you are not sure what to go for, their *Beer Bible* gives a description of each beer available.

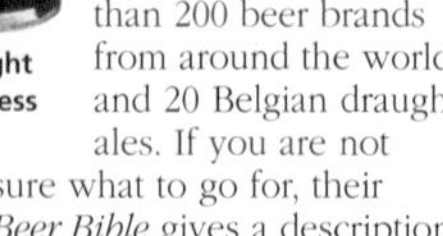

Draught Guinness

Irish pubs with great food and Guinness beer on tap include **Fergie's Pub**, which has live music most evenings and a traditional Irish menu, and the **Irish Pub** that serves Irish-American food in a casual dining ambience.

McGillin's Olde Ale House is the oldest operating tavern in the city, offering a great selection of beer. The **Bishop's Collar** has a friendly atmosphere with a selection of microbrews, and creative but inexpensive pub fare. It is a great place to unwind after visiting the Museum of Art or Boathouse Row.

GAY CLUBS AND BARS

Several nightclubs and bars are centered in the city's main gay and lesbian district, located between Broad and 11th Streets, and Chestnut to Pine Streets. **Woody's** is a popular gay lounge serving food and cocktails seven days a week. With three floors of energizing house music, disco, and hip-hop, **Voyeur Nightclub** has a bit of everything and is worth a visit. Nearby is **Sisters**, the city's largest lesbian bar with dining and dancing. For more information, visit the Greater Philadelphia Tourism and Marketing Corporation's website *(see p133)* or look at the Philadelphia Convention and Visitors Bureau's *Gay and Lesbian Travel Guide*, available at the Independence Visitors Center.

Voyeur Nightclub, a prominent gay nightspot

COMEDY CLUBS

Many clubs in town and across the river in New Jersey feature stand-up comedy acts. The city's "Original Comedy Club," the **Laff House** on South Street, brings in comedians from all over the country, with open mike nights, and main acts on Friday and Saturday nights. The **Helium Comedy Club** draws the nation's top acts to this 250-seat theater. Two lounges inside the club offer food and specialty drinks. Punters buying a drink before 7pm on Wednesdays can see that night's show for free.

DIRECTORY

ROCK AND FOLK MUSIC

Keswick Theatre
Easton Rd & Keswick Ave, Glenside, PA.
Tel *(215) 572-7650.*

Khyber PubPass
56 S 2nd St. **Map** 4 E3.
Tel *(215) 238-5888.*

The Legendary Dobbs
304 South St.
Map 4 D5.
Tel *(215) 501-7288.*

Manayunk Brewing Company
4120 Main St.
Tel *(215) 482-8220.*

Susquehanna Bank Center
1 Harbour Blvd, Camden Waterfront, New Jersey.
Tel *(856) 365-1300.*
www.susquehanna.net

Tin Angel
20 S 2nd St. **Map** 4 E3.
Tel *(215) 928-0978.*
www.tinangel.com

Tower Theater
69th & Ludlow Sts, Upper Darby, PA.
Tel *(215) 568-3222.*
www.tower-theater.com

Wells Fargo Complex
Broad St & Pattison Ave.
Tel *(215) 336-3600.*
www.comcast-spectator.com

World Café Live
3025 Walnut St.
Tel *(215) 222-1400.*
www.worldcafelive.com

BLUES, JAZZ, AND WORLD MUSIC

Alma de Cuba
1623 Walnut St.
Map 2 E4.
Tel *(215) 988-1799.*

Chris' Jazz Club
1421 Samson St.
Map 3 A3.
Tel *(215) 568-3131.*
www.chrisjazzcafe.com

Ortlieb's Lounge
847 N 3rd St.
Tel *(215) 922-1035.*
www.ortliebslounge.com

Warmdaddy's
1400 Colombus Blvd.
Map 4 E5.
Tel *(215) 462-2000.*
www.warmdaddys.com

NIGHTCLUBS AND DISCOS

32° Luxe Lounge
416 S 2nd St. **Map** 4 E4.
Tel *(215) 627-3132.*
www.32lounge.com

Bleu Martini
245 2nd St. **Map** 4 E2.
Tel *(215) 940-7900.*
www.bleumartini.com

Cavanaugh's River Deck
417 N Columbus Blvd.
Map 4 F1.
Tel *(215) 629-7400.*
www.theriverdeck.com

Shampoo
417 N 8th St. **Map** 4 D1.
Tel *(215) 922-7500.*

Tiki Bob's Cantina
461 N 3rd St. **Map** 4 E1.
Tel *(215) 928-9200.*

BARS AND TAVERNS

Bishop's Collar
2349 Fairmount Ave.
Map 2 D1.
Tel *(215) 765-1616.*

Fergie's Pub
Map 2 F5. ***Tel*** *(215) 928-8118.* **www**.fergies.com

Irish Pub
2222 Walnut St. **Map** 1 C4. ***Tel*** *(215) 568-5603.*

McGillins Olde Ale House
1310 Drury St. **Map** 3 B2.
Tel *(215) 735-5562.*

Monk's Café
264 S 16th St. **Map** 2 E5.
Tel *(215) 545-7005.*
www.monkscafe.com

GAY CLUBS AND BARS

Sisters
1320 Chancellor St. **Map** 3 A3. ***Tel*** *(215) 735-0735.*

Voyeur Nightclub
1221 St James Place. **Map** 2 F5. ***Tel*** *(215) 735-5772.*

Woody's
202 S 13th St. **Map** 2 F4.
Tel *(215) 545-1893.*

COMEDY CLUBS

Helium Comedy Club
2031 Sansom St. **Map** 2 D4. ***Tel*** *(215) 496-9001.*
www.heliumcomedy.com

Laff House
221 South St. **Map** 4 E5.
Tel *(215) 440-4242.*

Outdoor Activities and Sports

Whether you are an active participant or simply a spectator, there is no shortage of sporting activities in Philadelphia all year round. In the warmer months, the region's many recreational areas and parks are packed with hikers, bicyclists, joggers, and golfers. In the winter months, outdoor enthusiasts opt for ice-skating or head for the nearby ski slopes in the Pocono Mountains. Local sports fans are passionate about their many professional home teams that play throughout the year. They flock to the city's stadiums and arenas to watch baseball, football, basketball, and hockey. The area's colleges and universities compete in the above sports and others such as volleyball, swimming, and gymnastics.

Inline skater

BICYCLING, JOGGING, AND SKATING

Philadelphia has an extensive greenbelt running through it with miles of walking and biking trails, most of which are found in Fairmount Park *(see p97)*. On warmer days of the year, hundreds of enthusiasts take to the city's most popular trail, the 8.4-mile (13.5-km) paved inline skating, walking, and biking path that runs parallel to Kelly and Martin Luther King Jr Boulevard *(see p98)* along both sides of the Schuylkill River. The **Bicycle Club of Philadelphia** has information about the various bike paths within the area, and schedules bike rides each weekend for cyclists of all experience levels.

Other popular hiking and biking trails can be found along Wissahickon Gorge in Fairmount Park. There are also 6 miles (9.6 km) of trails within **Valley Forge National Historic Park** *(see p129)*. Valley Forge is a starting point for the 22-mile (35-km) bike path ending in Fairmount Park. The path runs on a former railroad track route along the Schuylkill River.

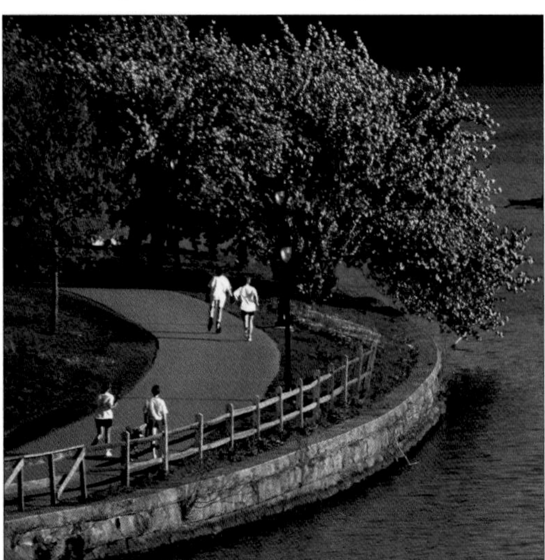

Paved walking and biking path in Fairmount Park *(see p97)*

GOLF AND TENNIS

The Philadelphia area has numerous 18-hole golf courses that challenge players at all levels. Courses situated in the city include the **Cobbs Creek Golf Club** and the **Walnut Lane Golf Club**, located within Wissahickon Valley Park. The professionally ranked **Broad Run Golfers Club** sits in scenic West Chester countryside, while **Makefield Highlands Golf Club** is the only true links-style golf course in the Tri-State area.

Public tennis courts in many parks are free on a first-come, first-served basis. Local tennis clubs that charge a fee include **Friends of Chamounix Tennis** situated in Fairmount Park and **Philadelphia Tennis Court**.

WINTER ACTIVITIES

As Christmas approaches, many outdoor enthusiasts bundle up and trade their inline blades for ice skates. Philadelphia and its surrounding areas have several ice-skating rinks, but the most popular is the **Blue Cross RiverRink** at Penn's Landing, where skaters enjoy an Olympic-sized rink with views of the Ben Franklin Bridge and the Delaware River.

Skiers head to the Pocono Mountains. This usually involves a day trip, and most ski slopes are within a two-hour drive. The **Pocono Mountains Vacation Bureau, Inc.** has information about ski slopes and snow conditions.

PROFESSIONAL SPECTATOR SPORTS

South Philadelphia's modern stadiums are the venue for most professional sports competitions held in the city. The **Philadelphia Phillies** play throughout the summer season at the Citizens Bank Park. The 43,000-seat stadium is one of the most fan-friendly ballparks to host major league baseball games. Rough-and-tumble football action kicks off in August as the

Philadelphia Eagles start their season with games at Lincoln Financial Field, a 68,000-seat stadium.

During the cold winter months, sports fans head back indoors to watch basketball played by the **Philadelphia 76ers** at the Wells Fargo Center, which seats 21,000. Hockey fans flock to the Wells Fargo Center as well for spirited games on ice with the **Philadelphia Flyers**. The area's minor league baseball team, the **Camden Riversharks**, plays ball at Campbell's Field at the Camden Waterfront. Other popular home teams play soccer and lacrosse.

For horse racing fans, the **Philadelphia Park Casino & Racetrack** has live thoroughbred racing all year round every Saturday through Tuesday. The racetrack is home to the GII Pennsylvania Derby on Labor Day.

Camden Riversharks in baseball action at Campbell's Field

COLLEGE SPORTS

Over a dozen colleges and universities in the Philadelphia area take part in intercollegiate sports programs and competitions, a tradition that dates back more than 200 years. Some of the nation's best college basketball is played by what is called the Big Five – **St. Joseph's University**, **University of Pennsylvania**, **Temple University**, **Villanova University**, and **LaSalle University**. Schools in the area have both men's and women's activities in a full range of other sports, and competitions in football, soccer, field hockey, volleyball, swimming, gymnastics, and more are held regularly.

DIRECTORY

BICYCLING, JOGGING, AND SKATING

Bicycle Club of Philadelphia
Tel *(215) 735-2453.*
www.phillybikeclub.org

Valley Forge National Historic Park
1400 N Outer Line Drive.
Tel *(610) 783-1099.*
www.nps.gov/vafo

GOLF AND TENNIS

Broad Run Golfer's Club
1520 Tattersall Way, West Chester, PA.
Tel *(610) 738-4410.*
www.broadrungc.com

Cobbs Creek Golf Club
72nd & Lansdowne Aves.
Tel *(215) 877-8707.*

Friends of Chamounix Tennis
50 Chamounix Dr, Fairmount Park.
Tel *(215) 877-6845.*

Makefield Highlands Golf Club
1418 Woodside Road, Yardly, PA.
Tel *(215) 321-7000.*
www.makefield highlands.com

Philadelphia Tennis Court
4700 Spruce St.
Tel *(215) 683-3639.*

Walnut Lane Golf Club
800 Walnut Lane.
Tel *(215) 482-3370.*
www.walnutlanegolf.com

WINTER ACTIVITIES

Blue Cross RiverRink
Penn's Landing. **Map** 4 F3. ***Tel*** *(215) 925-7465.*
www.riverrink.com

Pocono Mountains Vacation Bureau, Inc.
1004 Main St, Stroudsburg, PA 18360.
Tel *(800) 762-6667.*
www.800poconos.com

PROFESSIONAL SPECTATOR SPORTS

Camden Riversharks
Campbell's Field, 401 N Delaware Ave, Camden.
Tel *(856) 963-2600.*
www.riversharks.com

Philadelphia 76ers
Wells Fargo Center, 3601 S Broad St.
Tel *(215) 339-7600.*
www.nba.com/sixers

Philadelphia Eagles
Lincoln Financial Field, 1020 Pattison Ave.
Tel *(267) 570-4510.*
www.philadelphia eagles.com

Philadelphia Flyers
Wells Fargo Center, 3601 S Broad St.
Tel *(215) 465-4500.*
www.philadelphiaflyers.com

Philadelphia Park Casino & Racetrack
3001 Street Rd, Bensalem.
Tel *(215) 639-9000, (800) 523-6886.* **www**.philadelphiapark.com

Philadelphia Phillies
Citizens Bank Park, 1 Citizen Bank Way.
Tel *(215) 463-1000.*
www.phillies.com

COLLEGE SPORTS

LaSalle University
1900 W Olney Ave.
Tel *(215) 951-1000.*
www.lasalle.edu

St. Joseph's University
5600 City Ave.
Tel *(610) 660-1712.*
www.sju.edu

Temple University
801 N Broad St.
Map 2 F1.
Tel *(215) 204-8499.*
www.temple.edu

University of Pennsylvania
3451 Walnut St.
Map 1 A4.
Tel *(215) 898-6151.*
www.upenn.edu

Villanova University
Tel *(610) 519-4500.*
www.villanova.edu

CHILDREN'S PHILADELPHIA

Parents will find a plethora of activities that will keep their children amused when in Philadelphia and the surrounding area. Museums, such as The Franklin and the Academy of Natural Sciences, thrill kids with hands-on exhibits and workshops, while the Adventure Aquarium and the Philadelphia Zoo entertain with an array of sea creatures and animals. Educational tours can be taken at historic buildings, where actors dress up as colonial figures and perform skits. In the Dutch Country, kids can enjoy Amish-style buggy rides and much more at the Dutch Wonderland Family Amusement Park in Lancaster.

Actor dressed as George Washington

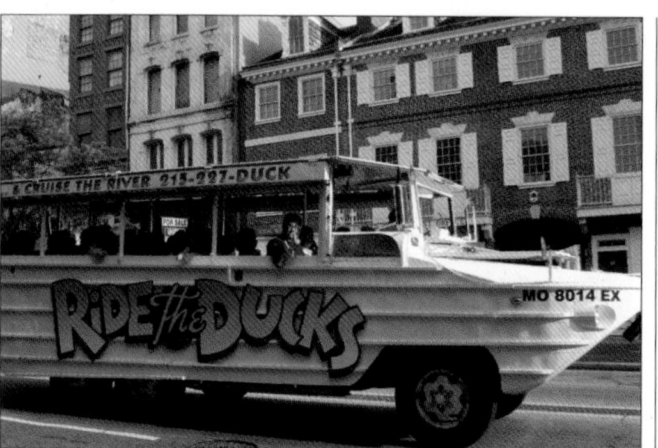

Ride the Ducks pleasure craft going around Philadelphia

HISTORIC SIGHTS AND TOURS

Tour guides at key historic buildings provide informative tours to young and old alike; however, some sights will interest children more than others. The **National Constitution Center** *(see pp48–9)* features interactive exhibits explaining the US Constitution, where children, for example, might try on a judge's robe at a replica of the Supreme Court bench, or cast their ballot for their all-time favorite president. Many tours cater to families, such as the popular **Ride the Ducks** *(see p175)*. Using amphibious vehicles, the tour whisks visitors through Old City and Society Hill and Penn's Landing before taking a dip in the Delaware River for an exhilarating cruise. Children and parents show their enthusiasm by raucously blowing colorful "duck whistles."

Kids also enjoy the multimedia **Lights of Liberty Show** *(see p175)*, a brisk walking tour through Old Town at dusk. Participants don headphones and watch images – which tell the story of the American Revolution – projected on historic buildings. For younger children, ask for a special version for ages 6 to 12.

Historic Lights of Liberty show at Independence Hall

MUSEUMS

Philadelphia's premier museum for children is the **Please Touch Museum**. Aimed at kids aged under eight, it has several exhibits that enhance a child's ability to learn discovery and play. For instance, the Alice's Adventures in Wonderland exhibit is based on the popular classic story and includes many settings from the book to encourage problem solving and language skills. The SuperMarket has checkouts, shopping carts, and toy food items, while Barnyard Babies teaches about life on a farm. Other activities include interactive theater performances with musicians, dancers, and storytellers. The museum is located in Memorial Hall in the Fairmount Park District.

Banner at the Academy of Natural Sciences

The Franklin Institute *(see p85)* has hands-on exhibits, with some such as Electricity Hall reflecting Benjamin Franklin's inventions. Children learn about the human heart and bioscience at the Giant Walk-Through Heart. Other exhibits include the Train Factory, which has an actual 350-ton (770,000-lb) locomotive, and the Franklin Air Show, which has a flight simulator. The Fels Planetarium features virtual tours through space. At the **Academy of Natural Sciences** *(see p85)*, children can see the fossils of a Tyrannosaurus rex and other species in Dinosaur Hall. Youngsters can also check out the Live Animal Center, which houses over 100 animals, and live butterflies stored in a tropical rainforest habitat that has been replicated at the museum. In addition to model boats and deep-sea diving apparatus, kids enjoy squeezing through the small hatches and passageways of the submarine *Becuna* at the **Independence Seaport Museum** *(see pp64–5)*. Boys, in particular, enjoy the old fire engines and pumpers at **Fireman's Hall Museum** *(see p51)*. At the **Fairmount Water Works** *(see p88)*, interactive exhibits challenge children to learn about city water resources. The center also has a virtual helicopter tour of the watershed.

The **National Liberty Museum** *(see p53)* takes a more serious approach to entertaining children by helping combat violence and bigotry through interactive exhibits, glass artworks, and more. One display is Kids Vote, which asks youngsters to take a stand on such issues as handgun law and the death penalty. Another exhibit, Jellybean People, features two life-sized models made of multicolored jellybeans to show that people are the same inside, regardless of skin color.

For children with an artistic flair, the **Philadelphia Museum of Art** *(see pp90–93)* offers drawing classes and gallery tours on Sundays. The **Pennsylvania Academy of the Fine Arts** *(see pp74–5)* has workshops on most Saturday mornings.

Beyond Philadelphia, in the Pennsylvania Dutch Country, Strasburg offers kids train displays, a train museum, and rides on the **Strasburg Railroad** *(see p119)*. In Hershey, children will love the simulated chocolate factory at **Chocolate World** *(see p124)*, and the roller coaster rides and attractions at Hershey Park.

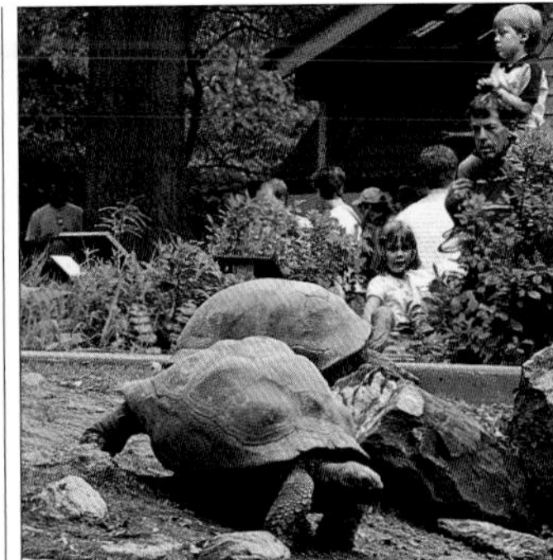

Philadelphia Zoo, home to many animal species

GARDENS, ZOOS, AND WATERFRONT ACTIVITIES

An instant hit with children is the **Philadelphia Zoo** *(see p98)*. While close-up views of wild animals such as lions and rare white tigers are a big draw, kids also enjoy the Tastykake Children's Zoo, where they can pet docile sheep, rabbits, and newly hatched chicks.

Tarantulas at the Insectarium

At the **Philadelphia Insectarium**, youngsters can safely observe the workings of a beehive from behind a glass partition, touch the likes of tarantulas and giant beetles, and see thousands of other live and mounted insects. Kids can also play in a man-made spider web.

The **Adventure Aquarium** at the Camden Waterfront *(see p101)* has a huge tank with hundreds of aquatic species, including sharks, sea turtles, and more than 1,000 kinds of fish. Kids can touch harmless species in the Touch-a-Shark exhibit and see seals frolic in outdoor pools. Also at the waterfront, the **Camden Children's Garden** is an interactive park with different areas, including the Butterfly Garden, Railroad Garden, Dinosaur Garden, and the Storybook Gardens. The **Sister Cities Park**, an outdoor oasis in the heart of the city, has a lovely children's garden with winding pathways, a stream, and a boat pond.

Interactive exhibits inside Fairmount Water Works

DIRECTORY

MUSEUMS

Please Touch Museum
4231 Avenue of the Republic.
Tel *(215) 963-0667.*
www.pleasetouchmuseum.org

GARDENS, ZOOS, AND WATERFRONT ACTIVITIES

Adventure Aquarium
1 Aquarium Dr, Camden, NJ.
Tel *(856) 365-3300.*
www.adventurequarium.com

Camden Children's Garden
3 Riverside Drive, Camden, NJ.
Tel *(856) 365-8733.*
www.camdenchildrensgarden.org

Philadelphia Insectarium
8046 Frankford Ave.
Tel *(215) 335-9500.*
www.myinsectarium.com

Sister Cities Park
200 N 18th St.
Tel *(800) 537-7676.*

Amtrak TRAIN

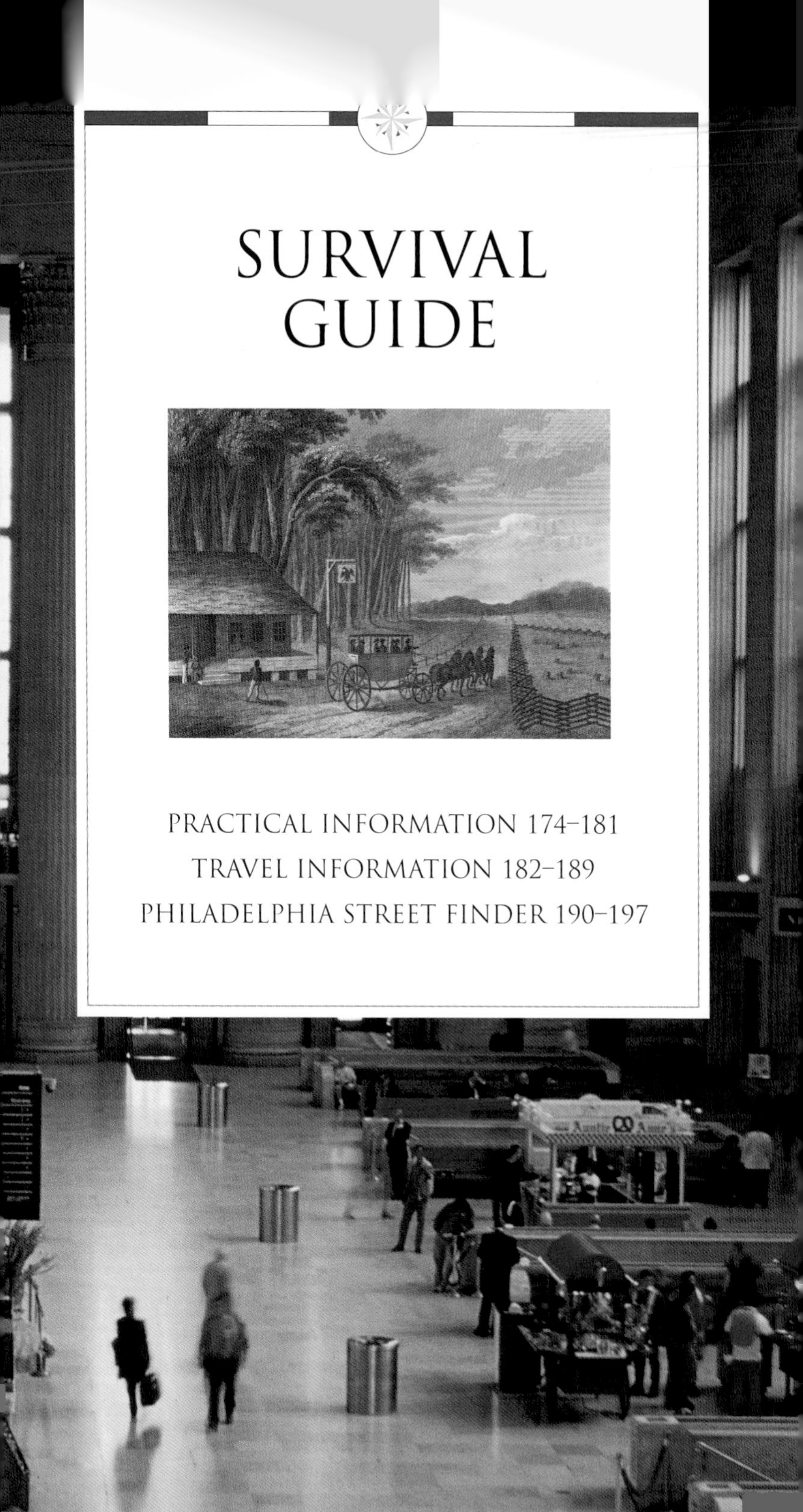

SURVIVAL GUIDE

PRACTICAL INFORMATION

Philadelphia thrives on tourism thanks to its rich colonial history and culture, and its world-class museums and restaurants. An efficient infrastructure – including clearly marked signs, a state-of-the-art visitor center, and a well-planned transit system – has been created by the city authorities and the National Park Service to give visitors a memorable vacation. Most of Philadelphia's central neighborhoods can be explored on foot and many areas in the city are safe, but visitors should take sensible precautions as in any major city. The following pages include tips on a wide range of practical matters to ensure a trouble-free stay.

Independence Visitor Center sign

VISAS AND PASSPORTS

All visitors to the US must have a valid passport and, in some cases, a visa. The US is 1 of 36 countries, including the UK, France and Australia, participating in the Visa Waiver Program (VWP), which permits those who qualify to enter without a visa and stay up to 90 days.

The US operates an Electronic System for Travel Authorization (ESTA) for VWP travelers. Visitors must register and pay online at https://esta.cbp.dhs.gov at least 72 hours in advance of departure; authorization will be valid for two years when issued. Alternatively, your national passport-issuing agency can provide information. VWP travelers who have not obtained approval through ESTA will be denied boarding any plane to the US.

It is always best to check the US State Department's website (www.state.gov/travel) before travel for the most up-to-date information and entry requirements.

TOURIST INFORMATION

The **Independence Visitor Center** *(see p45)*, located in the heart of Independence National Historical Park, is within walking distance of many sights in Philadelphia's central historic core. In addition to brochure racks and self-service information booths, visitor concierges assist with ticket sales and provide information on shopping, attractions, hotels, restaurants, and other visitor needs. The free, timed tickets which are required for entrance to Independence Hall are also available here.

Tour guide in colonial attire leading tourists in Old City

The **Greater Philadelphia Tourism Marketing Corporation** offers comprehensive information about the Philadelphia region on its website.

The **Philadelphia Convention & Visitors Bureau** provides information for tour groups, conventions, and international visitors on their website.

Smoking is prohibited in most buildings and stores, except in designated areas, and it is strictly banned from all restaurants, taverns, and pubs throughout the city.

ADMISSION PRICES

Attractions within Independence National Historical Park are free of charge, which makes Philadelphia a budget-friendly place to visit. A number of others, including the Rodin Museum, request nominal donations of $3–5. Admission fees for most major sights, such as the National Constitution Center and Franklin Institute, generally range between $10 and $16. Many offer discounts or free admission for children. The **Philadelphia CityPass** offers entry to six sights for $59 and is valid for nine consecutive days.

OPENING HOURS

Most museums and historic buildings open from 9 or 10am to 5pm daily, with extended summer hours. Business and banking hours are 9am–5pm Monday to Friday *(see p178)*. Central Philadelphia shops open 10am to 7pm *(see p154)*.

PUBLIC CONVENIENCES

Free public and wheelchair-accessible restrooms can be found at the Independence Visitor Center and in the Bourse at 5th Street between Market and Chestnut Streets. In other parts of Center City, the Reading Terminal Market, the Shops at the Bellevue, department stores, and malls have facilities.

TAXES AND TIPPING

Pennsylvania's state sales tax is 6 percent, with an extra 1 percent city tax in Philadelphia (7 percent total). There is no tax on clothing or shoes. Hotel taxes are 15.5 percent, and car rental taxes and fees can add 20 percent or more to the rental price.

It is usual to tip wait staff 15 percent of the final bill, and 20 percent or more for great service; for bar staff $1 per drink. Tip hotel or airport porters $1 per bag and at least as much for the room maid per night ($2 at upscale hotels), and up to $10 or more for a helpful concierge. Valet parking attendants expect $1–2, while cab drivers should be tipped 10–15 percent of the fare.

TRAVELERS WITH SPECIAL NEEDS

Most city buildings and sidewalks accommodate disabled persons as required by US law, but some historic colonial structures do not have adequate provisions. SEPTA buses *(see p186)* are equipped with lifts while **SEPTA CCT** and **ADA Paratransit** offer transportation for disabled passengers unable to use standard services. The **Mayor's Commission on People with Disabilities** provides information for disabled visitors to Philadelphia.

International Student Identity Card

STUDENTS AND SENIOR TRAVELERS

The Philadelphia area has numerous colleges and universities, so an **International Student Identification Card (ISIC)** or **Student Advantage Card** is recommended as these are accepted for discounts. Senior citizens also receive discounts, including reduced admission to many sights.

GAY AND LESBIAN TRAVELERS

Philadelphia is a gay-friendly destination known for its lively GLBT scene. Midtown Village (between 11th and Broad Streets and Chestnut and Pine Streets) is nicknamed "the Gayborhood" for its many gay-owned and gay-friendly shops, restaurants, accommodations, and clubs. The **William Way Community Center** hosts tours, activities, and programs geared toward the gay community. The weekly *Philadelphia Gay News* lists events, as does www.visitphilly.com.

RESPONSIBLE TOURISM

Greenworks Philadelphia, an initiative focusing on expanding environmentally friendly policies and programs, has had a major effect on the city's commitment to sustainability.

There are now several neighborhood farmers' markets from May through November. One of the most popular is the Saturday morning market at Head House Square in the Society Hill district. The **Clark Park Farmers' Market** in the University City area operates year-round (May–Oct: Thu and Sat, Dec–Apr: Sat). From Thursday to Saturday, Amish farmers bring their home-baked goods and produce to **Reading Terminal Market**, where other purveyors sell their foodstuffs all week long.

Many city restaurants, such as Matyson *(see p149)*, build their menus around locally sourced produce.

Several Philadelphia hotels, including Hotel Palomar *(see p136)*, have earned LEED status (Leadership in Energy and Environmental Design) for their energy-efficient design.

Locally grown, organic produce at a neighborhood farmers' market

DIRECTORY

CONSULATES

British Consulate
1818 Market St. **Map** 2 D4.
Tel *(215) 557 7665.*

Canadian Consulate
1650 Market St. **Map** 2 D4.
Tel *(267) 207-2721.*

TOURIST INFORMATION

Greater Philadelphia Tourism Marketing Corporation
www.visitphilly.com

Independence Visitor Center
6th & Market Sts. **Map** 4 D2.
Tel *(800) 537-7676.* **www**.independencevisitorcenter.com

Philadelphia CityPass
www.citypass.com/philadelphia

Philadelphia Convention & Visitors Bureau
1700 Market St. **Map** 2 E4.
Tel *(215) 636-3300.*
www.philadelphiausa.travel

TRAVELERS WITH SPECIAL NEEDS

ADA Paratransit
Tel *(215) 580-7145.*

Mayor's Commission on People with Disabilities
Tel *(215) 686-2798.*
www.phila.gov/mcpd

SEPTA CCT
1234 Market St. **Map** 2 F4.
Tel *(215) 580-7145.*

STUDENT TRAVELERS

International Student Identification Card
www.isic.org

Student Advantage Card
www.studentadvantage.com

GAY AND LESBIAN TRAVELERS

William Way Community Center
1315 Spruce St. **Map** 1 C5.
Tel *(215) 732-2220.*

RESPONSIBLE TOURISM

Clark Park Farmers' Market
43rd St & Baltimore Ave.

Reading Terminal Market
12th & Arch Sts. **Map** 3 C2.

Personal Security and Health

Philadelphia police insignia

For the most part, central Philadelphia is generally safe and the majority of visitors touring the sights do not have any problems with crime. Nonetheless, as in any big American city, taking common-sense precautions will ensure a trouble-free visit. Although major crime is rare in high-density tourist areas, it is advisable to be aware of your surroundings at all times. Public transportation and walking in much of the central area is usually safe during the day, but visitors should opt for a taxi at night or for staying in prominent nightlife areas such as those in Old City, Center City, and Society Hill and Penn's Landing.

Philadelphia police officers on bicycles

POLICE

The Philadelphia Police Department provides round-the-clock car patrols as well as bicycle, horseback, and foot patrols. Police presence is plentiful throughout Center City, and there is often 24-hour surveillance by police and National Park Service rangers around key sights in Independence National Historical Park. The city's public transportation service, SEPTA, has its own police force that patrols the underground transit systems. Traffic and parking enforcement officers also make rounds on foot. Most are friendly when approached and will offer directions. Park rangers are usually helpful with answering questions about city sights and attractions. In Center City, police stations are located at 8th and Race Streets (Map D2), 9th and South Streets (Map C4), and 1201 S. 20th Street.

IN AN EMERGENCY

Call 911 to report life-or-death emergency situations or matters requiring an immediate response from medical, police, or fire department personnel. Most hospital emergency rooms in and around the city are open 24 hours daily and take walk-in patients or those delivered by ambulance. Emergency rooms are busiest during week-end evenings so there might be a long wait. Hotel personnel can locate the nearest hospital, or arrange a doctor's appointment for non-life threatening medical conditions. To get specialized assistance for people with disabilities, call **Relay Services**. Philadelphia International has its own **Airport Medical Emergencies** center. The **University of Pennsylvania Dental School Clinic** is one of a number of city clinics offering emergency dental care services. Ask your hotel staff for assistance.

WHAT TO BE AWARE OF

The popular tourist areas in Center City and around Independence National Historical Park are generally safe, but it is wise to follow basic safety precautions. Watch out for purse-snatchers and pickpockets, and do not leave personal items such as handbags or cameras unattended. Avoid wandering into dark alleys and deserted streets, especially in West Philadelphia. Local police and park rangers can offer directions and answer questions.

Do not carry a large amount of cash or wear excessive jewelry. Carry just one credit card and enough cash for the day's activities; leave other cards, traveler's checks, and your passport locked in your hotel room safe. Passports should be carried only when exchanging currency or traveler's checks. It is wise to make copies of your passport and record your credit card numbers in case of theft.

You may see homeless people on the city streets. If approached, it is best to ignore requests for a cash handout.

A 24-hour CVS pharmacy in a Philadelphia neighborhood

Police car

Police SUV

Fire engine

The legal drinking age in Pennsylvania and New Jersey is 21. Young people need to show photo ID as proof of age when ordering alcohol. Liquor and wine can be bought only at state-run stores, while beer is sold at special distribution centers or by the six-pack in bars.

LOST AND STOLEN PROPERTY

If your property is lost or stolen, chances of recovery are slim. Nonetheless, contact local authorities through the **Philadelphia Police (Non-Emergency)** line to file a report and keep a copy of the same for insurance purposes. It may be helpful to contact the Lost and Found in department stores, the Independence Visitor Center *(see p174)*, or **Philadelphia International Airport**. Also, contact taxi companies or the public transit system in case missing items are turned in.

Call your debit or credit card company to report a lost or stolen credit card, and contact your currency exchange provider for lost traveler's checks *(see p179)*. If your passport is lost or stolen, contact your country's consulate or embassy immediately *(see p175)*.

HOSPITALS AND PHARMACIES

Philadelphia has excellent medical facilities should you become ill during your visit. There are a number of walk-in clinics that will treat minor ailments, while all main hospitals in the city offer accident and emergency care.

Visitors should be advised, however, that medical care can be expensive. Even if carrying medical insurance, you may still have to pay upfront and claim reimbursement from your insurance company later, so do not forget to ask for all necessary forms and receipts. Most medical facilities in the city accept credit cards.

Pack enough prescription drugs, and it is advisable to keep two sets of the same medicines in different travel bags, in the unlikely event that one is lost or stolen. There are several pharmacies open 24 hours daily in Central and Greater Philadelphia, including **CVS** and **Rite Aid**. Some pharmacies have medical personnel for minor, non-critical health issues (such as **Convenient Care Center**). Ask hotel personnel for directions.

TRAVEL AND HEALTH INSURANCE

Because the cost of medical care in the US is so high, it is essential to purchase travel insurance before you visit. Packages should include medical and dental coverage, as well as trip cancellation, flight delay, lost or stolen baggage, and even death and dismemberment insurance.

DIRECTORY

POLICE

All Emergencies
Tel *911* for police, fire, and emergency medical attention.

Philadelphia Police (Non-Emergency)
Tel *(215) 686-1776.*

IN AN EMERGENCY

Airport Medical Emergencies
Tel *(215) 937-3111.*

Dental Emergencies
Tel *(215) 925-6050.*

Relay Services (Special Assistance)
Tel *(800) 654-5984.*

University of Pennsylvania Dental School Clinic
240 South 40th St.
Tel *(215) 898-8965.*

LOST AND STOLEN PROPERTY

Philadelphia International Airport Lost and Found
Communications Center located between Terminals C and D.
Tel *(215) 937-6888.*

HOSPITALS AND PHARMACIES

Convenient Care Center
16th Street between Chestnut and Market Sts. **Map** 2 E4.
Tel *(215) 399-5890.*

CVS
1826 Chestnut St. **Map** 2 D4.
Tel *(215) 972-0909.*

Finding a Doctor (Non-Emergency)
Tel *(215) 563-5343.*

Rite Aid
2301 Walnut St. **Map** 1 C4.
Tel *(215) 636-9634.*
5040 City Line Ave.
Tel *(215) 877-2116.*

Thomas Jefferson University Hospital
111 S. 11th St. **Map** 3 C3.
Tel *(215) 966-6000.*

Banking and Currency

There is no shortage of local and international banks in Philadelphia, especially in Center City. Cash can be easily withdrawn through the city's numerous ATMs, which accept most major credit and debit cards. Foreign notes can be exchanged for American dollars in hotels and at currency exchange offices. However, be advised that most currency exchange offices and banks are closed on Sundays and hotels charge high commission. Also, it is prudent not to carry all your money and cards at the same time.

The lobby of a PNC Bank branch with multiple ATMs

BANKS AND CURRENCY EXCHANGE

Major banks found in Philadelphia include **PNC Bank**, **Citizens Bank**, **Citibank**, and **Wells Fargo Bank**, which are usually open from 9am to 5pm weekdays (later on Fridays), and 9am until noon on Saturdays. **TD Bank** is open daily and most branches are open until 8pm during the week. Currency exchange services are available at airport kiosks, **American Express Travel Services Office**, and several banks. Hours vary but most currency exchange offices are open from 9am to 5:30pm. Some hotels offer an exchange service but fees are higher. It is a good idea to bring around $100 into the US in case exchange services are not immediately available.

ATMS

Cash is easily accessible through the numerous ATMs in the Philadelphia area. They are found at bank entrances, in office complexes, at shopping malls, grocery stores, and restaurants, and even in convenience stores. Cash is distributed in $10 and $20 bills, and can be withdrawn with a debit or credit card, including VISA or MasterCard. ATMs often charge a fee for withdrawals by non-bank members, while the user's bank might also charge a fee. Generally, fees are significantly higher, sometimes up to $4, at free-standing ATMs not attached to a bank. One exception is

Automated teller machine (ATM) for convenient withdrawals

Wawa, a local convenience store chain, that offers ATMs with no service fees. Check with your bank which transaction fees apply. Also, notify your credit or debit card provider of your travel plans so your card does not get blocked while you are away.

CREDIT CARDS AND TRAVELER'S CHECKS

Most restaurants and shops accept major credit cards such as **Visa**, **MasterCard**, **American Express**, **Discover Card**, and **Diners Club**. Credit cards are not only safer than carrying lots of cash, some credit cards also offer insurance benefits on retail goods while providing reward points or airline miles. For travelers, credit cards are essential in the event of a medical emergency, as they are honored as payment at most US hospitals. A valid credit card is required for car rentals, and most hotels request credit card numbers to make a room reservation. Many businesses accept traveler's checks in US dollars as payment without charging a fee. You can cash them at local banks with identification such as a passport, driver's license, or student ID. Personal foreign currency checks are rarely accepted.

WIRING MONEY

Money can be wired internationally through **Western Union**, which has locations in supermarkets, convenience stores, travel agencies, business centers, and other locations including **Travelex Currency** in Center City. In addition to sending and receiving money within minutes, Western Union also offers overnight delivery of checks to private residences or offices as well as a three-day service whereby cash can be deposited directly into a designated bank account. The amount you may send and hours of operation vary by location. Fees generally start at about $40 and increase based on the amount being wired and expedited delivery options.

Coins

American coins (actual size shown) come in 1-, 5-, 10- and 25-cent, as well as $1 denominations; 50-cent pieces are minted but rarely used. Each coin has its own name: 1-cent coins are known as pennies; 5-cent coins as nickels; 10-cent coins as dimes; and 1-dollar coins (and bills) are sometimes called "bucks."

25-cent coin (a quarter)

10-cent coin (a dime)

5-cent coin (a nickel)

1-cent coin (a penny)

Bills (Bank Notes)

The units of currency in the United States are dollars and cents. There are 100 cents to the dollar. Bank notes come in the following denominations: $1, $5, $10, $20, $50, and $100. There is also a $2 bill, but it is rarely used and is more of a collector's item. Security features include subtle color hues and improved color-shifting ink in the lower right hand corner of the face of each note.

1-dollar bill ($1)

5-dollar bill ($5)

10-dollar bill ($10)

20-dollar bill ($20)

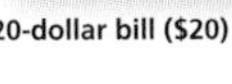

50-dollar bill ($50)

100-dollar bill ($100)

DIRECTORY

BANKS AND CURRENCY EXCHANGE

American Express Travel Services Office
16th St & JFK Blvd. **Map** 2 E4.

Citibank
1211 Walnut St. **Map** 1 A4.

Citizens Bank
1515 Market St. **Map** 2 D4.

PNC Bank
19th & Walnut Sts. **Map** 2 D4.

Wells Fargo Bank
123 S Broad St. **Map** 3 B3.

ATMS

Wawa
912-16 Walnut St. **Map** 3 C3.

CREDIT CARDS AND TRAVELER'S CHECKS

American Express
Tel *(800) 528-4800.*

Diners Club
Tel *(800) 847-2911.*

Discover Card
Tel *(800) 347-2683.*

MasterCard
Tel *(800) 307-7309.*

Visa
Tel *(800) 847-2911.*

WIRING MONEY

Travelex Currency
1800 JFK Blvd. **Map** 1 B3.
Tel *(215) 563-7348.*

Western Union
628 South Broad St. **Map** 2 F2.
Tel *(215) 735-5154.*

Communications and Media

A colorful US postage stamp

Like most major cities, Philadelphia has excellent communication systems. The US Postal Service is reliable and efficient, with regular pickups from mailboxes throughout the city. There are numerous local television and radio stations, as well as two major daily newspapers. Internet cafes and wireless hotspots are located throughout the city, and for those who need them, fax services are also available. With the advent of cell phones, card- or coin-operated pay phones are less common but can be found in hotels, malls, restaurants, and on some street corners.

CELL PHONES

The major cell phone services in Philadelphia are **Sprint**, **Verizon**, **AT&T**, and **T-Mobile**. The US uses a different frequency for cell services than that used overseas, so you need a quad-band phone to connect to the US network. Tri-band phones are usually compatible, too. You may also need to activate the "roaming" facility.

Alternatively, you can rent a cell phone, available at **AllCell Rental**, or buy a disposable phone at local pharmacies or convenience stores.

PUBLIC TELEPHONES

The increase in cell phone usage has resulted in fewer coin- and credit card-operated pay phones, but some are still available in hotel lobbies, shopping malls, restaurants, gas stations, bars, and some city streets. Pay phone rates vary by carrier but most local call charges start at about 50 cents for the first three minutes. Prices for long-distance or calls abroad can vary as different telephone companies set their own rates. Operator-assisted calls are more costly than calling direct. Prepare to have lots of dimes, nickels, and quarters on hand for coin-operated phones. Local and international phone cards can be bought from convenience stores.

INTERNET

Internet access is available at Internet cafés, public libraries, bookstores, and at some office supply and photocopy/fax centers, such as **FedEx Office**.

Most hotels have business centers where guests can check their emails. These services are often charged by the minute or by 15-minute blocks, which can become costly so check the hotel's prices before making a reservation.

Library Internet services are often free but may have time limits.

Many book stores and the **ING Direct Cafe** in Center City are free Wi-Fi hotspots, as are **Philadelphia Java Company** in the Society Hill neighborhood and **Old City Coffee** in the Old City arts district.

For connectivity on the go, many Amtrak trains offer Wi-Fi on some intercity routes out of Philadelphia.

One of many cafés offering Wi-Fi to its customers

USEFUL DIALLING CODES

- Philadelphia's area codes are **215**, **267**, and **445**. Western suburbs and surrounding areas use **610**, **484**, and **835**. The area code for the Pennsylvania Dutch Country and Gettysburg is **717**.
- For calls outside the local area but within the US and Canada, dial **1** followed by the area code and phone number.
- For local operator assistance, dial **0**.
- For local and national directory inquiries, dial **411**. Directory assistance for toll-free numbers is **1–800–555–1212**.
- Phone numbers with the codes **800**, **888**, **877**, or **866** indicate a toll-free number.
- For international direct-dial calls, dial **011** followed by the country code, city or area code, and number.
- To make an international call via the operator, dial **01** and then follow the same procedure as detailed above.
- For international directory inquiries, dial **00**.
- For more information about calling in Philadelphia, check the local *White Pages* directory, which also lists country codes for international calls.

POSTAL SERVICES

Philadelphia's **Main Post Office** at Market and 30th Streets, directly across from the 30th Street Station, is open 8am to 9pm Monday through Saturday and 11am to 7pm on Sunday. Most other branches are open weekdays from 9am to 5pm and Saturday from 9am to noon.

Letters and parcels weighing less than 16 ounces (454 g) require only stamps and can be mailed in the blue mailboxes on street corners, or in letter slots in hotels and office buildings.

Standard blue US mailbox

The cost of a stamp for first-class delivery of a standard letter is 44 cents. The US Postal Service, **FedEx**, and **DHL** offer a variety of overnight letter and parcel services, while **UPS** delivers large boxes and packages. FedEx offices are located in major office buildings in Center City and in Kinko's business services stores.

TELEVISION AND RADIO

Philadelphia carries the major US broadcast networks. Channel numbers vary depending on the service provider but generally you can find CBS on channel 3, ABC on channel 6, NBC on channel 10, PBS on channel 12, FOX on channel 29, CW on channel 57, and Telemundo on channel 62. Cable companies carry popular sports, news, entertainment, and movie networks, such as ESPN, HBO, and CNN.

Radio stations, on both the AM and FM frequencies, include a variety of music, talk, and news shows. Radio station KYW 1060 AM provides round-the-clock news, weather, sports, and finance reports. Some public radio stations offer commercial-free programming. WHYY-FM (90.9) focuses on call-in shows, political reports, and cultural news, while WXPN-FM (88.5) airs world, alternative, and new music. WRTI (90.1) focuses on jazz and blues as well as reporting on cultural events. Satellite radio is available through subscription and offers dozens of channels dedicated to a particular format.

NEWSPAPERS AND MAGAZINES

The city's two main daily newspapers are the *Philadelphia Inquirer* *(see p162)* and the *Philadelphia Daily News*. Both can be found in newsstands or in news boxes on street corners. Both weekday editions are 75 cents each. The *Inquirer*'s Sunday edition is $1.50; the *Daily News* does not publish a Sunday edition.

The *Philadelphia Business Journal* is published weekly and focuses on local business news as it relates to national trends. Other special-interest publications include the *Philadelphia Tribune* focusing on the African-American community, the *Philadelphia Gay News*, and *Al Dia*, the city's Latino newspaper. Two weekly alternative publications, *Philadelphia City Paper* and the *Philadelphia Weekly* provide political commentary and entertainment coverage. They are available for free and can be found in news boxes on street corners.

Monthly magazines *Philadelphia Magazine* and *Philadelphia Style* focus on trends, fashion, dining, and cultural activities.

DIRECTORY

CELL PHONES

AllCell Rental
1528 Walnut St, Suite 525.
Map 2 E5. ***Tel*** *(215) 985-2355.*

AT&T
110 S. 18th St.
Map 2 D5. ***Tel*** *(215) 587-9700.*

Sprint
1235 Chestnut St.
Map 3 A2. ***Tel*** *(215) 561 1853.*

T-Mobile
1506 Walnut St.
Map 3 A3. ***Tel*** *(215) 735 1770.*

Verizon
1700 Market St.
Map 3 A2. ***Tel*** *(215) 564-7800.*

INTERNET

FedEx Office
3535 Market St. **Map** 1 A3.

ING Direct Cafe
1636 Walnut St. **Map** 3 A3.

Old City Coffee
221 Church St. **Map** 4 E2.

Philadelphia Java Company
518 S. 4th St. **Map** 4 D4.

POSTAL SERVICES

DHL
Tel *(800) 225-5345.*

FedEx
Tel *(800) 463-3339.*

Main Post Office
3000 Chestnut St.
Map 1 B4. ***Tel*** *(215) 895-9012.*

UPS
Tel *(800) 742-5877.*

Selection of local Philadelphia newspapers at a newsstand

TRAVEL INFORMATION

Whether traveling from within or outside the country, Philadelphia is easily accessible by air, train, bus, and car. Philadelphia International Airport is served by many international and regional airlines. Amtrak's 30th Street Station is a busy rail hub on the Northeast Corridor line that runs between Washington, D.C. and Boston. The station is also a stop for trains arriving from other regions of the country. A number of interstate highways, that crisscross most of the Philadelphia metropolitan area, cater to motorists and long-distance bus services. The city also has a cruise ship terminal along the Delaware River that serves as a stop on some liners' itineraries.

US Airways plane

View of Terminal A at Philadelphia International Airport

ARRIVING BY AIR

Philadelphia is conveniently located in the middle of the US Northeast Corridor, situated about halfway between New York and Washington, D.C. Flying times are about 5 hours from the US West Coast, 1 to 3 hours from the Midwest, 3 to 5 hours from the Caribbean, and 7 to 10 hours from Europe.

Philadelphia is a hub for **US Airways** and **Southwest Airlines**. It is also served by many other airlines, including **Air Canada**, **Air Jamaica**, **British Airways**, **Delta Airlines**, **Frontier Airlines**, **Lufthansa**, and **United Airlines**.

PHILADELPHIA INTERNATIONAL AIRPORT

Philadelphia's airport is located 7 miles (11 km) south of Center City. Seven terminals accommodate more than 1,200 flights daily to and from 120 cities, with direct flights to 36 destinations in Europe, Canada, and the Caribbean, and connecting flights to Asia.

The International Terminal A-West has 13 gates and 60 ticket counters, over 20 retail shops and restaurants, and currency exchange centers.

Domestic service is located in Terminals A-East through F.

The airport also has more than 100 shops, restaurants, and fast food stands scattered throughout the terminals, with more than 30 contained in the Philadelphia Marketplace located between Terminals B and C.

Drivers who are picking up arriving passengers can wait in the nearby Cell Phone Lot. Located 1 minute from the passenger pick-up zone, the lot has space for 150 cars and monitors that provide real-time flight arrival information.

ON ARRIVAL

International flights arrive at Terminal A-West. The modern terminal has plenty of US immigration booths to ensure you get through security checks as soon as possible. There are also food halls, gift shops, and currency exchange desks in the terminal. A staff member fluent in the language of the plane's country of origin meets each plane to answer questions and direct visitors to the Immigration Hall (INS).

Upon arrival at INS, staff will check the customs and

Arrivals Hall at Philadelphia International Airport, featuring words from the Declaration of Independence

SEPTA bus ferrying passengers to Philadelphia

I-94 forms distributed during the flight. Both ask questions such as name, birth date, country of citizenship, passport number, and current address. The customs form asks further questions, including do you have any vegetables, fruit, or commercial merchandise in your baggage. The I-94 form consists of two parts; one part will be returned to you as you will need it on your return journey.

Non-US citizens are directed to CBP (Customs and Border Protection), where officers check passports, customs and I-94 forms, and will also fingerprint and photograph foreign visitors.

Passengers who warrant further inspection are directed to a secondary screening area.

Once cleared, everyone may collect their baggage in the Customs area; customs forms must be returned before exiting.

Upon exiting, passagers can proceed to the International Arrivals Hall.

TICKETS AND FARES

A little research can bring big savings on airfares. Generally, the lowest fares are available 14 to 21 days before the departure date, although reasonably priced tickets can still be bought 7 days in advance. Before booking, check the airlines' policies as changing travel arrangements can incur penalties.

While airlines and travel agents often offer good fares, it is worth examining popular travel Internet sites as well, such as **FareCompare**, **Expedia**, **Priceline**, **Travelocity**, **Kayak**, **Lowestfare**, and **lastminute.com**. These websites often sell consolidated tickets, which are also available through travel agents.

Several airlines offer special discounts through their websites, and while many of those offers require departures within a short time frame, the savings can be significant.

Other options include booking with smaller carriers and flying during the off-season, which can also reduce rates.

Philadelphia's high season peaks in the summer, then around Thanksgiving (late November), and the week before Christmas through New Year's Day. Book well in advance if you plan to travel during those times and don't expect to find any discounts.

TRANSPORT INTO THE CITY

SEPTA's Airport Regional Rail Line operates every 30 minutes and connects all terminals with Center City and Amtrak's 30th Street Station, which has rail connections to other points in the city and beyond. Train station for each terminal lie between the ticketing and baggage claim areas – visitors should look for the relevant signs. Tickets are $7.

SEPTA buses 37 and 108 also ferry passengers into the city for a $2 fare. Look for the red-white-and-blue SEPTA bus signs.

For shuttle van services, look for **Centralized Ground Transportation** counters in all baggage claim areas.

Taxis are plentiful at each terminal. They charge a flat rate of $28.50 for a trip into Center City, with an additional fee of $1 per passenger.

Major rental car companies also operate at the airport; they include **AVIS**, **Enterprise**, **Hertz**, and **National Car Rental**. Most have information phones at all baggage claim areas. There are limo companies specializing in airport transit, too.

ARRIVING BY CAR

Several major roadways and interstate highways lead to Philadelphia from surrounding states and major cities in the northeast. Driving times to Philadelphia from some of these cities are as follows: 6 hours from Boston, 2 hours from Baltimore and New York, and 3 hours from Washington, D.C. The resort beach towns of New Jersey are about 1 to 1 hour and 30 minutes away.

The major north–south highway is I-95, which leads into the city center as it parallels the Delaware River. From the east, motorists driving on the New Jersey Turnpike should take Exit 4 and then follow signs to the Benjamin Franklin Bridge or the Walt Whitman Bridge into Philadelphia.

An alternative from the New Jersey Turnpike is taking Exit 6 to connect with the Pennsylvania Turnpike that runs north of the city. This is the major highway leading into Philadelphia from the west. Take the Valley Forge exit and then proceed east on I-76, the Schuylkill Expressway.

Interstate 676 cuts through the middle of Center City, connecting I-95 with I-76.

It's a good idea to carry a road atlas map and a city street map for all trips by car.

The Benjamin Franklin Bridge across the Delaware River

Philadelphia's 30th Street Station on Amtrak's Northeast Corridor, the second busiest of the Amtrak system

ARRIVING BY TRAIN

Philadelphia is served by **Amtrak**, the country's passenger rail service, which links the city to the entire nation and to Canada. Most trains serving the city operate along the Northeast Corridor from Boston to Washington, D.C., with stops in Baltimore, New York, and a number of locations in New Jersey, Delaware, Connecticut, and Rhode Island. Amtrak's lines also provide express services such as the premium, high-speed Acela Express that runs from Boston to Washington, D.C.

Tickets can be booked online or by calling Amtrak. It is best to reserve well in advance and be as flexible as possible to ensure good seating and prices. Note that certain discounts may apply, including those for students and senior citizens. If booked in advance, tickets can be picked up on the day of travel at either an Amtrak service window or through kiosks at train stations.

Due to increased security measures, when conductors ask to see tickets, passengers from the US, Canada, and Mexico are required to show photo identification, which may be a driver's license or passport, while other foreign visitors must show a passport.

Passenger cars are comfortable and have snack bar services as well as dining cars on longer routes. Coach class seats for most journeys are reserved, except for shorter trips. Sleeping quarters are available on trains for long-distance destinations; some of the first class sleeping accommodations have showers and toilets in the compartments.

Philadelphia's main train hub is Amtrak's 30th Street Station – an impressive Beaux-Arts building with a columned façade and large atrium *(see p188–9)*. It is one of the busiest inter-city rail stations in the US. Inside are ticket booths for both Amtrak and SEPTA regional rail lines, restaurants, fast food eateries, gift shops, and newsstands. "Red cap" porters are available to help with luggage.

There are many taxis outside, and if you are carrying baggage, it is best to get a cab for the short hop to a central Philadelphia hotel.

An Amtrak train – backbone of America's passenger rail system

ARRIVING BY BUS

Greyhound Lines, which serves destinations across the US, operates a **bus terminal** in Center City on Filbert Street, between 10th and 11th Streets, one block north of Market Street. Buses arrive daily from New England, New York, and points south and southwest of Philadelphia. Transcontinental buses also arrive from routes through St. Louis and Chicago. Stops include Amtrak's 30th Street Station, and others in north and south Philadelphia.

Compared with other modes of transportation, such as trains or planes, Greyhound's fares are more economical. The company offers wide-ranging discounts, including those for students, senior citizens, children, military personnel, and veterans, as well as cheaper fares if tickets are bought online. While advance

Greyhound bus, an economical way to reach destinations across America

purchases might save you money, walk-up tickets are available at reasonable prices.

Greyhound's buses are modern and efficient. Much of its fleet is either equipped with lifts or other equipment to accommodate disabled passengers or those in need of help. Under certain conditions, personal care attendants may travel with disabled passengers at a reduced fare. For more information, call the **Greyhound Customers with Disabilities Travel Assistance Line** at least 48 hours before departure.

Two primary discount bus operators providing express bus services from around the East Coast and Midwest to and from Philadelphia are **BoltBus** and **Megabus**. Both companies run services to and from New York City and Washington, D.C., as well as other cities, and offer amenities such as free Wi-Fi access and plug-ins for electronic equipment. The fares start as low as $1 for a one-way ride. BoltBus stops across the street from the western entrance to 30th Street Station and tickets for the journey can be purchased in advance online, by phone, or on the bus at the time of departure. Cities that are served by BoltBus include Baltimore, Greenbelt, Boston, and Newark.

Megabus operates in the Northeast hub of Philadelphia and stops at both the Independence Visitor Center and 30th Street Station. In addition to New York City and Washington, D.C., the other major cities in the Northeast served by Megabus include Atlantic City, Boston, Baltimore, Harrisburg, Pittsburgh, Buffalo, Syracuse, and Toronto. Note that Megabus tickets are only available online. Also, be prepared to give the driver your reservation number or show a printout of the confirmation form.

DIRECTORY

ARRIVING BY AIR

Philadelphia International Airport
Tel *(215) 937-6937, (800) 745-4283.*
www.phl.org

Air Canada
Tel *(888) 247-2262.*

Air Jamaica
Tel *(800) 523-5585.*

British Airways
Tel *(800) 247-9297.*

Delta Airlines
Tel *(800) 221-1212.*

Frontier Airlines
Tel *(800) 452-2022.*

Lufthansa
Tel *(800) 645–3880.*

Southwest Airlines
Tel *(800) 435-9792.*

United Airlines
Tel *(800) 241-6522.*

US Airways
Tel *(800) 428-4322.*

TICKETS AND FARES

Expedia
www.expedia.com

FareCompare
www.farecompare.com

Kayak
www.kayak.com

lastminute.com
http://us.lastminute.com

Lowestfare.com
www.lowestfare.com

Priceline
www.priceline.com

Travelocity
www.travelocity.com

TRANSPORT INTO THE CITY

Airport Parking
Tel *(215) 683-9842, (215) 683-9825.*

AVIS
Tel *(800) 331-1212.*
www.avis.com

Centralized Ground Transportation
Tel *(215) 937-6958.*

Enterprise
Tel *(800)* RENT-A-CAR.
www.enterprise.com

Hertz
Tel *(800) 654-3131.*
www.hertz.com

National Car Rental
Tel *(800) 227-7368.*
www.nationalcar.com

ARRIVING BY CAR

Pennsylvania Department of Transportation
Travel information & interstate road conditions.
Tel *(717) 783-5186.*
www.dot.state.pa.us

Pennsylvania Turnpike Commission
Tel *(717) 939-9551.*
www.paturnpike.com

ARRIVING BY TRAIN

Amtrak
Tel *(800) 872-7245.*
www.amtrak.com

ARRIVING BY BUS

BoltBus
Tel *(877) 265-8287.*
www.boltbus.com

Greyhound Customers with Disabilities Travel Assistance Line
Tel *(800) 752-4841.*

Greyhound Lines
Tel *(800) 229-9424.*
www.greyhound.com

Greyhound Bus Terminal
1001 Filbert St.
Map 3 C2.
Tel *(215) 931-4000.*

Megabus
Tel *(877) 462-6342.*
www.megabus.com

Getting Around Philadelphia

Taxi sign

Most of Philadelphia's famous sights are in Independence National Historical Park, also known as "America's most historic square mile." These sights, including Independence Hall and the Liberty Bell, are within walking distance of each other in Old City, and just a short walk from attractions in Society Hill and Penn's Landing. A quick ride or stroll from the historic area brings visitors to Center City and Parkway Museums District. The Philly Phlash bus service runs through the heart of the city during the warmer months, while buses and subways, operated by the Southeastern Pennsylvania Transit Authority (SEPTA), run year-round. Taxis are also an easy and generally affordable option.

GREEN TRAVEL

Philadelphia is increasingly committed to eco-friendly initiatives as demonstrated by its Greenworks Philadelphia plan *(see p175)*. SEPTA has one of the largest hybrid bus fleets in the US and has been steadily replacing its diesel-powered buses with hybrid diesel/electric buses. Two car-sharing programs, **ZipCar** and **Philly CarShare**, have dozens of locations throughout Philadelphia that help alleviate traffic and emissions. There are also some designated bike lanes, and the core of the city is pedestrian-friendly.

FINDING YOUR WAY IN PHILADELPHIA

Thanks to the foresight of the city's founder William Penn, getting around central Philadelphia is easy with its simple grid pattern *(see p18)*.

Numbered streets begin at the city's easternmost boundary along the Delaware River at Front Street (technically "1st street") and progress westward in an ascending order. What would be "14th street" is called Broad Street (or Avenue of the Arts at its southern end).

These streets intersect Market Street, the demarcation for whether they're proceeded by "north" or "south" in the address. You'll notice that building numbers become larger the more distant they are from Market Street.

Many streets running east and west are named after trees, especially in Center City.

WALKING

With a compact, user-friendly downtown, the best way to explore Center City, Independence National Historical Park, and nearby sights is on foot.

Mounted on street poles throughout Center City are signs with colorful maps of the downtown area. Community service representatives in teal uniforms are also available throughout Center City to help visitors with directions.

TRAVELING BY SUBWAY

SEPTA operates subway routes throughout Philadelphia, making connections to regional rail lines at the Market East, Suburban, and 30th Street stations *(see transport map at back)*. Maps are also posted in each station.

There are two lines, the Market-Frankford Line (blue line) and the Broad Street Subway (orange line).

Subway fares are $2 and exact change is required. Transfers cost $1 for trips that necessitate more than one transit in the same direction. Independence passes, Family passes, and tokens are available at SEPTA sales offices, newsstands, or the Independence Visitor Center *(see p45)*. An Independence pass is a day ticket that allows travel on all forms of SEPTA transport in zone 1 and costs $11. A Family pass is similar to an Independence pass but is $28 and vaild for a family of up to five. Tokens are $1.55; they are cheaper than purchasing individual tickets.

TRAVELING BY BUS

SEPTA also operates bus routes throughout the city. Fares are the same as for subways *(see Traveling by Subway)*, and schedules are posted on the SEPTA website. Tickets and tokens can be bought on board, from newsstands or from SEPTA sales booths.

Useful routes include bus 38, which runs from Independence Mall to the Philadelphia Museum of Art and beyond. Bus 21 travels passed Penn's Landing to the University of Pennsylvania. Bus 42 circles neighborhoods in Society Hill along Spruce Street before heading west along Walnut Street to the University of Pennsylvania campus, returning via Chestnut Street.

Seats at the front are prioritized for elderly or disabled riders, who can board via lifts. Buses also have bike racks.

BICYCLES

Central Philadelphia has designated bike lanes on Spruce Street heading east and Pine Street heading west. Cycling is also permitted on Benjamin Franklin Parkway, which leads to the Philadelphia Museum of Art. This track continues onto the city's most popular cycling route that runs along Kelly Drive and West River Drive. Bicycles can be rented along here during the summer *(see p168)*.

Children under 12 years old must wear a helmet when

Bicycling – an enjoyable way to get out and see some sights

Colorful Philly Phlash tourist bus

riding a bike. Cyclists are required to obey all traffic signals and stay off sidewalks.

RIVERLINK FERRY

Operating from Memorial Day weekend in May through to the Labor Day weekend in September, **RiverLink Ferry** provides a scenic 12-minute ride across the Delaware River to the Adventure Aquarium and the *Battleship New Jersey*.

The ferry departs every 30 minutes from both the Camden Waterfront and Penn's Landing in Philadelphia. Visitors can purchase tickets at dockside terminals outside the Independence Seaport Museum for the outbound trip from Philadelphia.

Landlubbers can cross the river via the Waterfront Connection bus service ($2), which departs every 30 minutes from the Independence Visitor Center and stops at the same sights. Like the Riverlink Ferry, it operates only during the summer months.

GUIDED TOURS

Most city tours, ranging from guided walks to trips by horse-drawn carriage, are centered around the Independence National Historical Park district. The **Big Bus Company** offers tours on double-decker, open-roof buses with hop-ons and hop-offs at 20 sights. The **Constitutional Walking Tour of Philadelphia** provides several historic district guide options, including by MP3 player. **Ride the Ducks** is an excursion in an amphibious vehicle that ends with a big splash into the Delaware River. **Ghost Tours of Philadelphia** includes a candlelit walk with haunting tales through Old City and Society Hill. The night-time **Lights of Liberty Show** winds through Historic Philadelphia with narrators recounting America's struggle for independence. Between May and October, the **Philly Phlash** bus loops from Penn's Landing to Fairmount Park, making stops at more than 25 attractions.

TAXIS

Taxis can be hailed in the street, though the best place to find one is at a hotel. Several cab companies serve the city, and if you must reserve a taxi for a specific time, call at least 30 minutes in advance *(see Useful Numbers on Sheet map)*. Fares vary, with at least a $2.70 base fare and $2.30 for each additional mile. All taxis accept credit card payments.

DRIVING IN CENTRAL PHILADELPHIA

Except during rush hour, driving in town is not particularly difficult. The main Center City thoroughfares, Broad and Market Streets, have two-way traffic, while most other streets have one-way traffic. Vehicles are driven on the right side, and right-hand turns can be made at a red light after a full stop, unless a sign prohibits it. Seatbelts are required by law and using cell phones while driving is prohibited. Violators will be fined. With some exceptions, overseas visitors can drive with a valid driver's license issued by their home country. If the license is not in English, an international driving permit is required.

PARKING

Street parking is usually hard to find. It costs $2 per hour, payable by cash, credit card, or SmartCards (available from convenience stores) at green parking kiosks throughout Center City and Independence Mall. Put your receipt inside the windshield and keep track of the time; enforcement officers will write a ticket for expired receipts.

Parking on residential streets is often permitted for non-permit holders but read the signs carefully. Parking lots are numerous; rates can run from $15 to $30 plus per day.

DIRECTORY

GREEN TRAVEL

Philly CarShare
www.phillycarshare.org

ZipCar
www.zipcar.com

PUBLIC TRANSPORTATION

RiverLink Ferry
Penn's Landing. ***Tel*** *(215) 925-link*. **www**.riverlinkferry.org

SEPTA
Tel *(215) 580-7800.*
www.septa.org

GUIDED TOURS

Big Bus Company
2037 Colonial Drive, Croydon, PA (mailing address only).
Tel *(215) 788-6001.*
www.bigbustours.com

Constitutional Walking Tour of Philadelphia
Tel *(215) 525-1776.*
www.theconstitutional.com

Ghost Tours of Philadelphia
Tel *(215) 413-1997.*
www.ghosttour.com

Lights of Liberty Show
6th & Chestnut Sts. **Map** 4 D3.
Tel *(215) 629-4026.*
www.historicphiladelphia.org

Philly Phlash
www.phillyphlash.com

Ride the Ducks
Tel *(215) 227-3825, (877) 877-8225.* **www**.phillyducks.com

Traveling Outside Philadelphia

Philadelphia has an excellent regional rail service with SEPTA trains running from Center City to far western suburbs, parts of nearby New Jersey, and northern Delaware. Amtrak provides a daily train service to Lancaster, Harrisburg, and towns west of Philadelphia. New Jersey Transit takes passengers to Atlantic City and other areas along the Jersey shore. However, it is advisable and more practical to rent a car when traveling to remote sights in the Pennsylvania Dutch Country and Gettysburg.

SEPTA train – an ideal way to go beyond Philadelphia

MAIN TRAIN STATIONS

Amtrak's **30th Street Station** is a hub for train services along the East Coast with frequent transits to New York, Boston, and Washington, D.C. as well as daily departures to Lancaster, Harrisburg, and towns west of Philadelphia. "Red cap" staff offer free baggage assistance, but be sure to accept assistance only from uniformed staff, and request a claim ticket for each bag.

Interior of 30th Street Station, one of the biggest in Pennsylvania

Other facilities include free Wi-Fi and a selection of shops.

Suburban Station at 16th Street in Center City is a central point for regional rail service with connections to SEPTA's Market-Frankford Line. Here, dozens of underground shops offer a variety of wares.

Market East Station, at 11th Street, is adjacent to the Gallery at Market East mall and also intersects with the Market-Frankford Line.

REGIONAL RAIL SERVICE

SEPTA provides outstanding rail services to many of Philadelphia's outermost suburbs to the north, south, and west of the city. Trips to the outermost stops sometimes take over an hour.

SEPTA's Airport Line connects the city and outer suburbs with Philadelphia International Airport *(see p182)*. The Wilmington–Newark Line travels south, with a stop in Wilmington, Delaware. The Paoli–Throndale Line travels west and north from Center City, with Doylestown *(see p125)* as the last stop. The Manayunk–Norristown Line runs through Manayunk *(see p97)*, while the Chestnut Hill East and Chestnut Hill West Lines end their routes in Chestnut Hill, stopping along the way in Germantown *(see pp96–7)*.

Train are comfortable, air-conditioned, and have lots of seats. However, they fill up quickly during the morning and afternoon rush hour.

Tickets can be purchased at the three Center City stations, at suburban stations, and on board.

SERVICES TO NEW JERSEY

New Jersey is a short drive or train ride from Center City, Philadelphia. In summer the best way to reach the Camden Waterfront, just across the Delaware River from Penn's Landing, is by RiverLink Ferry *(see p187)*. You can also take the **PATCO** High Speedline over the Benjamin Franklin Bridge and get off at the Broadway stop for waterfront attractions. Collingswood and Westmont stops are also well placed for exploration on foot.

To reach New Jersey beach resort towns, you can take a 1 hour and 30 minute journey on **New Jersey Transit's Atlantic City Rail Line** departing from 30th Street Station.

SERVICES TO PENNSYLVANIA DUTCH COUNTRY AND GETTYSBURG

Renting a car is the best way to explore most of the towns and villages that lie beyond Philadelphia, but it is also possible to take organized bus tours or public transportation.

Amtrak provides train services from Philadelphia's bustling 30th Street Station to towns west of Philadelphia, including Lancaster and Harrisburg.

In Lancaster, the **Red Rose Transit Authority (RRTA)** operates bus schedules in the city and for surrounding towns, including Pennsylvania Dutch communities. These buses have busy timetables and tend to have limited services to the outlying smaller communities, including Paradise, Lititz, Intercourse, Bird-In-Hand,

Toll booths on Interstate 76, Philadelphia

and Ephrata. Buses to these areas usually stop after the afternoon rush hour. On weekends, service is reduced.

To reach Gettysburg, you will need to rent a car as no public transport travels there.

ROADS AND TOLLS

Turnpikes are interstate highways that charge tolls. The Pennsylvania Turnpike and the New Jersey Turnpike both require motorists to pick up a toll ticket before entering the highway, and then pay the toll when exiting.

The Pennsylvania Turnpike (I-76/276) is the fastest route from Philadelphia to Harrisburg, and a one-way toll costs approximately $5. Although not an interstate, the Atlantic City Expressway is also a toll road. Some expressways have both numbers and names, such as the Vine Street Expressway (I-676/30).

Some toll booths accept only cash or exact change while others use an electronic system known as "E-Z Pass" which scans vehicles and deducts the toll from the driver's account.

CAR RENTALS

To rent a car, US and Canadian residents must have a valid driver's license, while foreign visitors need an international driver's license and valid passport. The minimum rental age is usually 25, and a major credit card in your name is required.

Personal auto insurance often covers rental cars, but check the limitations of coverage with your insurance company. If you're not covered, it is a good idea to purchase liability and collision insurance.

ZipCar *(see p186)* offers by-the-hour car rental. Fees include a modest membership, and hourly rates can start from $7 per hour. A valid driver's license is required and, depending on country of origin, additional documentation might be requested.

GASOLINE

Most gas stations in Philadelphia have self-service pumps. However, in New Jersey, state law mandates that attendants pump the gas. Rented cars should be returned with a full tank to avoid extra charges.

RULES OF THE ROAD

The speed limit on interstates is usually 65 mph (105 km/h), and 55 mph (88 km/h) on highways in and around Philadelphia. City streets usually have a 25 to 35 mph (40 to 56 km/h) limit. It's wise to heed speed limits, since a speeding ticket can result in a hefty fine. In Philadelphia it is illegal to drive while talking on a cell phone.

Unless otherwise noted by a sign, making a right turn is permitted at a red light. Watch for pedestrians since they have the right of way.

Drive carefully during bad weather, as semi-trucks often spew mist during heavy rainstorms, resulting in poor visibility. Also, bridges and overpasses can become ice-slicked during winter.

Wearing a seatbelt is required by law. It is also a good idea to keep all doors locked, stay on main roads, avoid unfamiliar neighborhoods, and abstain from drinking alcohol. Be aware that drink-driving offenses are vigorously prosecuted in the US.

Members of affiliated international automobile clubs are entitled to take advantage of reciprocal benefits offered by the **American Automobile Association** (AAA).

DIRECTORY

MAIN TRAIN STATIONS

30th Street Station
2955 Market St.
Map 1 B3. ***Tel*** *(800) 872-7433.*
www.amtrak.com

Market East Station
1170 Market St. & 12th Sts.
Map 1 B3. ***Tel*** *(215) 580-6500, (215) 580-7428.*

Suburban Station
34 N 16th St & JFK Blvd.
Map 2 E4. ***Tel*** *(215) 580-5739.*

SERVICES TO NEW JERSEY

Atlantic City Rail Line
Tel *(800) 772-2287.*

New Jersey Transit
Tel *(800) 772-2287.*
www.njtransit.com

PATCO
Tel *(856) 772-6900.*
www.ridepatco.org

SERVICES TO PENNSYLVANIA DUTCH COUNTRY AND GETTYSBURG

Red Rose Transit Authority (RRTA)
45 Erick Rd., Lancaster (Lancaster County). ***Tel*** *(717) 397-4246.*
www.redrosetransit.com

RULES OF THE ROAD

American Automobile Association
24-hour emergency road service.
Tel *(800) 763-9900.*
www.aaa.com

PHILADELPHIA STREET FINDER

Map references given in this guide for sights, hotels, restaurants, shops, and entertainment venues refer to the Street Finder maps on the following pages *(see* How the Map References Work). Map references are also given for Philadelphia's hotels *(see pp134–41)* and restaurants *(see pp145–53)*. A complete index of the street names and places of interest marked on the maps can be found on the following pages. The map below shows the area of Philadelphia covered by the four Street Finder maps. This includes the sightseeing areas (which are color-coded) as well as the rest of central Philadelphia. The symbols used to represent sights and useful information on the Street Finder maps are listed in the key below.

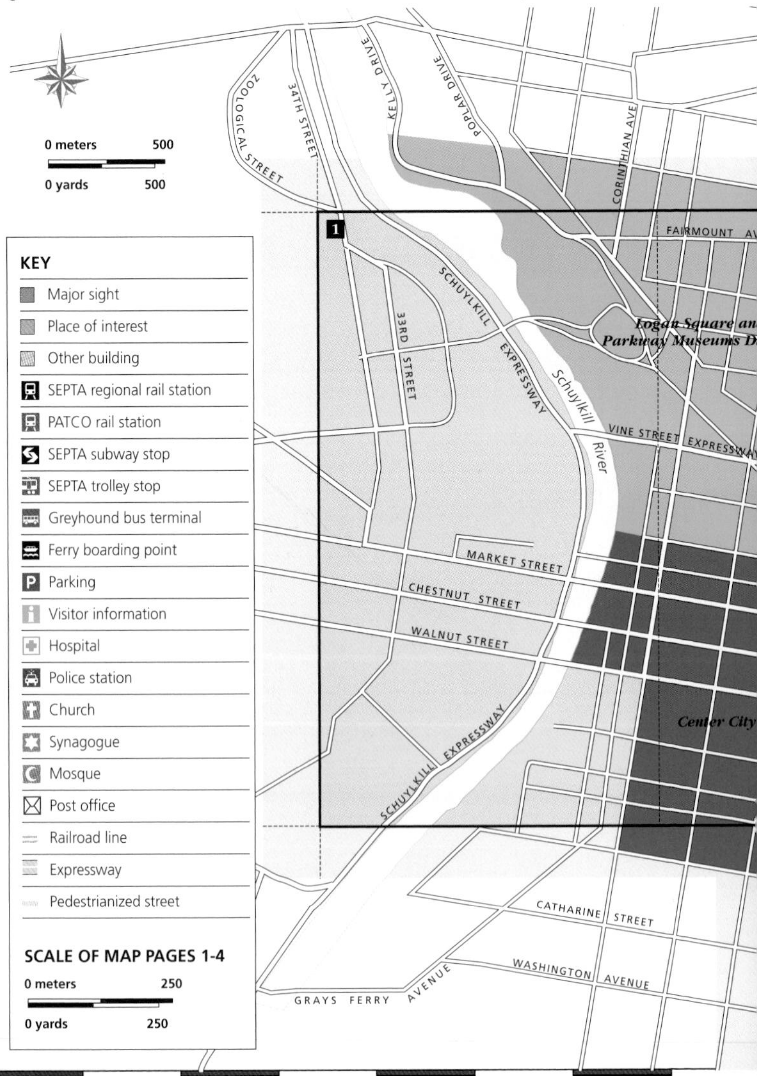

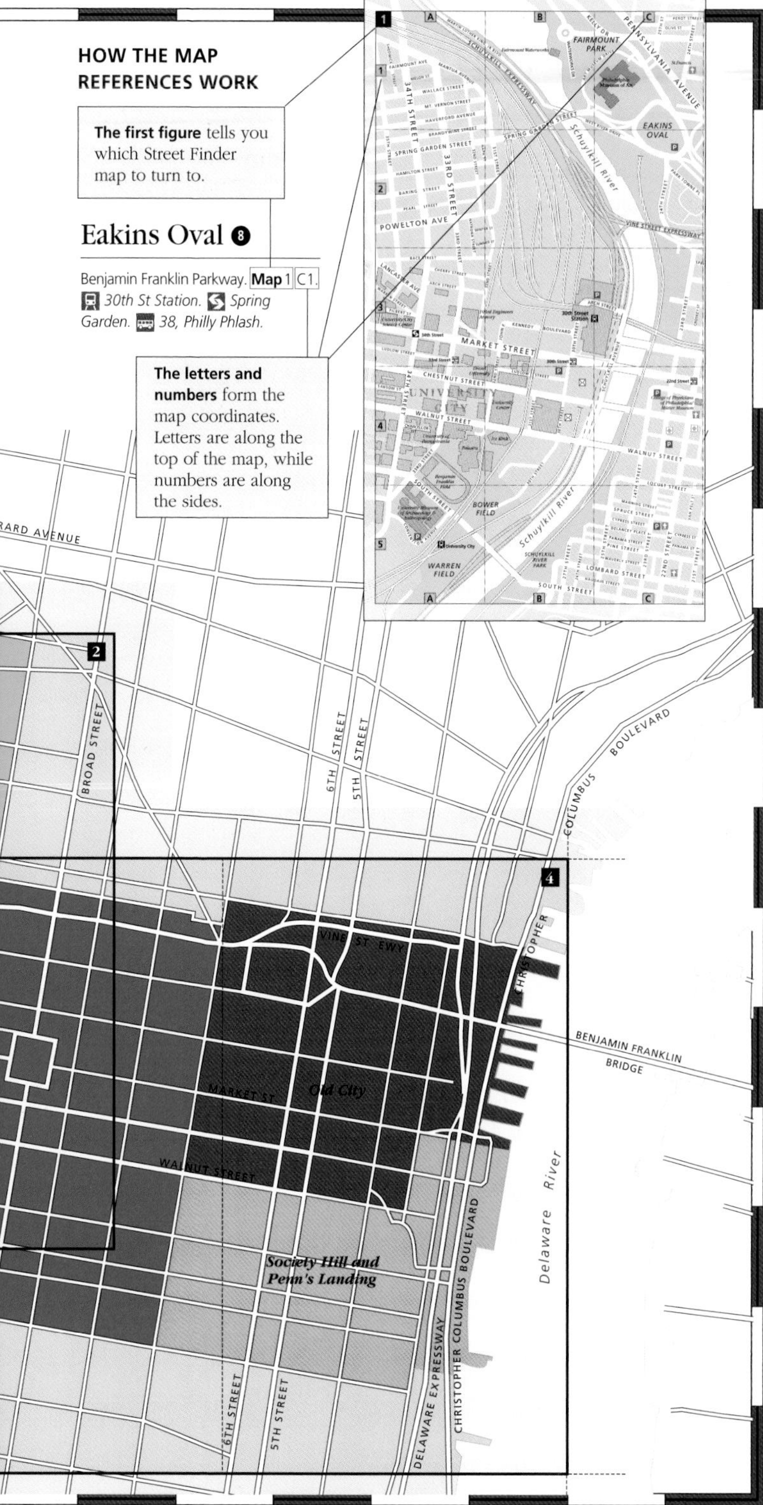
HOW THE MAP REFERENCES WORK
The first figure tells you which Street Finder map to turn to.
Eakins Oval 8
Benjamin Franklin Parkway. Map 1 C1.
30th St Station. Spring Garden. 38, Philly Phlash.
The letters and numbers form the map coordinates. Letters are along the top of the map, while numbers are along the sides.
FAIRMOUNT PARK
PENNSYLVANIA AVENUE
EAKINS OVAL
SCHUYLKILL EXPRESSWAY
Schuylkill River
34TH STREET
33RD STREET
SPRING GARDEN STREET
POWELTON AVE
VINE STREET EXPRESSWAY
MARKET STREET
UNIVERSITY CITY
WALNUT STREET
BOWER FIELD
WARREN FIELD
SOUTH STREET
LOMBARD STREET
RARD AVENUE
BROAD STREET
6TH STREET
5TH STREET
COLUMBUS BOULEVARD
VINE ST EWY
CHRISTOPHER
BENJAMIN FRANKLIN BRIDGE
MARKET ST
Old City
WALNUT STREET
Society Hill and Penn's Landing
Delaware River
DELAWARE EXPRESSWAY
CHRISTOPHER COLUMBUS BOULEVARD

Street Finder Index

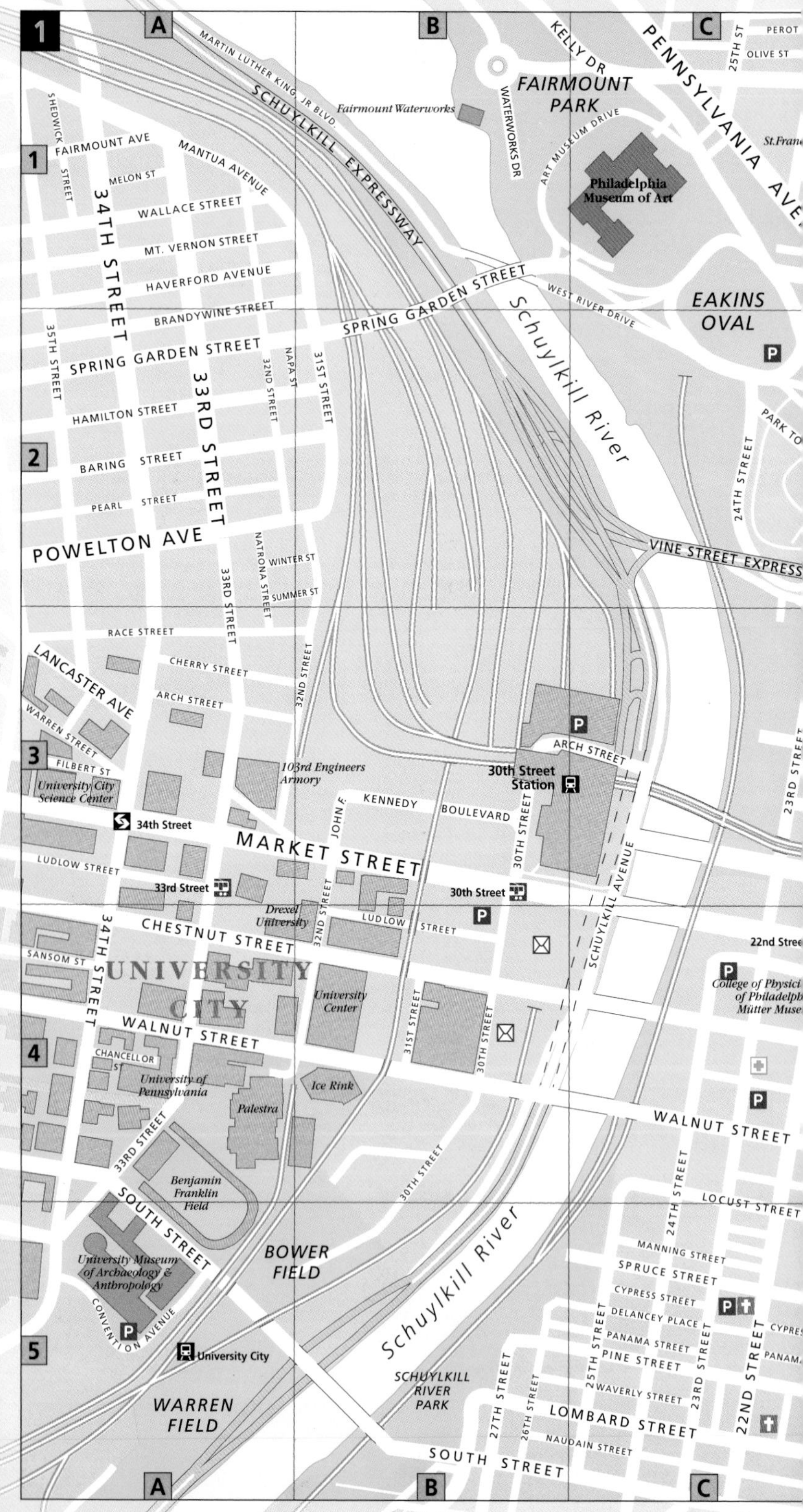

1
A
B
C
1
2
3
4
5
MARTIN LUTHER KING, JR BLVD.
SCHUYLKILL EXPRESSWAY
Fairmount Waterworks
KELLY DR
FAIRMOUNT PARK
WATERWORKS DR
ART MUSEUM DRIVE
PENNSYLVANIA AVE
PEROT
OLIVE ST
25TH ST
St.Franc
Philadelphia Museum of Art
SHEDWICK STREET
FAIRMOUNT AVE
MANTUA AVENUE
MELON ST
34TH STREET
WALLACE STREET
MT. VERNON STREET
HAVERFORD AVENUE
BRANDYWINE STREET
SPRING GARDEN STREET
WEST RIVER DRIVE
Schuylkill River
EAKINS OVAL
35TH STREET
32ND STREET
NAPA ST
31ST STREET
33RD STREET
HAMILTON STREET
BARING STREET
PEARL STREET
POWELTON AVE
PARK TO
24TH STREET
VINE STREET EXPRESS
NATRONA STREET
WINTER ST
SUMMER ST
RACE STREET
LANCASTER AVE
CHERRY STREET
ARCH STREET
32ND STREET
WARREN STREET
FILBERT ST
University City Science Center
103rd Engineers Armory
30th Street Station
23RD STREET
JOHN F. KENNEDY BOULEVARD
30TH STREET
34th Street
MARKET STREET
LUDLOW STREET
SCHUYLKILL AVENUE
33rd Street
30th Street
Drexel University
LUDLOW STREET
CHESTNUT STREET
SANSOM ST
UNIVERSITY CITY
22nd Stree
College of Physici of Philadelph Mütter Muse
University Center
31ST STREET
WALNUT STREET
CHANCELLOR ST
University of Pennsylvania
Ice Rink
Palestra
WALNUT STREET
33RD STREET
30TH STREET
24TH STREET
Benjamin Franklin Field
SOUTH STREET
LOCUST STREET
MANNING STREET
SPRUCE STREET
BOWER FIELD
University Museum of Archaeology & Anthropology
CYPRESS STREET
DELANCEY PLACE
CONVENTION AVENUE
PANAMA STREET
CYPRE
PANAM
University City
PINE STREET
25TH STREET
23RD STREET
22ND STREET
SCHUYLKILL RIVER PARK
27TH STREET
26TH STREET
WAVERLY STREET
WARREN FIELD
LOMBARD STREET
NAUDAIN STREET
SOUTH STREET

D
E
F
2
Eastern State Penitentiary
CORINTHIAN AVENUE
CAPITAL ST
UBER ST
OLIVE ST
BROWN ST
SWAIN STREET
RIDGE AVENUE
Fairmount
FAIRMOUNT AVENUE
MELON STREET
NORTH STREET
WALLACE ST
WALLACE STREET
SPRING GARDEN
MOUNT VERNON STREET
GREEN STREET
BRANDYWINE STREET
Thomas Eakins House
22ND STREET
20TH STREET
19TH STREET
18TH STREET
17TH STREET
16TH STREET
1
WATTS ST
LEMON ST
SPRING GARDEN STREET
NECTARINE ST
BUTTONWOOD STREET
HAMILTON STREET
Community College of Philadelphia
Spring Garden
BROAD STREET
Rodin Museum
21ST STREET
PARKWAY MUSEUMS DISTRICT
15TH STREET
2
BUTTONWOOD ST
PENNSYLVANIA AVENUE
FRANKLINTOWN PARK
Barnes Foundation
CALLOWHILL STREET
FRANKLIN TOWN BLVD
BENJAMIN FRANKLIN PARKWAY
WOOD STREET
Free Library of Philadelphia
WINTER STREET
VINE STREET
The Franklin Institute
LOGAN CIRCLE
VINE STREET EXPRESSWAY
Hahnemann University & Hospital
RACE STREET
VAN PELT STREET
LAMBERT ST
WOODSTOCK STREET
Cathedral of Sts. Peter & Paul
Magee Rehabilitation Hospital
Race Vine
JUNIPER STREET
CLARION STREET
13TH STREET
CAMAC ST
3
Academy of Natural Sciences
Moore College of Art & Design
APPLETREE STREET
CHERRY ST
BENJAMIN FRANKLIN PKWY
MOLE ST
CARLISLE ST
ARCH STREET
LOGAN SQUARE
18TH STREET
CHERRY STREET
APPLETREE ST
Pennsylvania Academy of the Fine Arts
Pennsylvania Convention Center
CUTHBERT STREET
JOHN F. KENNEDY BOULEVARD
Suburban Station
JOHN F. KENNEDY PLAZA
Arch Street United Methodist Church
Masonic Temple
MARKET STREET
UDLOW STREET
19th Street
FILBERT STREET
RANSTEAD ST
City Hall
COMMERCE STREET
Juniper
15th Street
CENTER CITY
The Shops at Liberty Place
13th Street
4
CHESTNUT STREET
RANSTEAD ST
CLOVER ST
20TH STREET
19TH STREET
SANSOM STREET
16TH STREET
15TH STREET
WALNUT STREET
RITTENHOUSE SQ W
RITTENHOUSE SQUARE
CHANCELLOR STREET
SYDENHAM ST
St MarkAs Episcopal Church
LOCUST STREET
RITTENHOUSE SQ
Walnut-Locust
15th-16th Street
LATIMER STREET
Academy of Music
12th-13th Street
12TH STREET
RITTENHOUSE SQUARE
BACH PL
Library Company of Philadelphia
5
DELANCEY PLACE
17TH STREET
CHADWICK ST
SMEDLEY ST
SYDENHAM ST
Kimmel Center for the Performing Arts
SPRUCE STREET
QUINCE STREET
CAMAC STREET
DELANCEY PL
CYPRESS ST
11TH STREET
UBER ST
WAVERLY STREET
PINE STREET

3
A
B
C
2
NOB
17TH STREET
WOOD STREET
VINE STREET
VINE STREET
VINE STREET
VINE STREET
13TH STREET
12TH STREET
RIDGE AVENUE
WOOD STREET
Habnemann University & Hospital
1
Cathedral of Sts. Peter & Paul
BENJAMIN FRANKLIN PKWY
Magee Rehabilitation Hospital
Race Vine
BROAD ST
WATTS STREET
JUNIPER STREET
CLARION STREET
SUMMER ST
EXPRESSWAY
VINE STREET
WINTER STREET
RACE STREET
16TH STREET
MOLE ST
15TH STREET
CARLISLE ST
CAMAC ST
SPRING STREET
CHERRY STREET
RACE STREET
CHINATOW
ARCH STREET
Pennsylvania Academy of the Fine Arts
Pennsylvania Convention Center
11TH STREET
10TH STREET
CHERRY ST
9TH STREET
CUTHBERT ST
Suburban Station
JOHN F. KENNEDY PLAZA
JOHN F. KENNEDY BLVD
Arch Street United Methodist Church
Masonic Temple
FILBERT STREET
CUTHBERT STREET
Reading Terminal Market
Greyhound Bus Terminal
MARKET ST
15th Street
City Hall
Juniper
COMMERCE STREET
FILBERT STREET
LUDLOW ST
The Shops at Liberty Place
City Hall
13th Street
Market East Station
COMMERCE STREET
RANSTEAD ST
8th a
Mar
11th Street
MARKET STREET
CHESTNUT STREET
CLOVER ST
LUDLOW STREET
8th Street
CENTER CITY
SANSOM STREET
WALNUT STREET
JUNIPER STREET
13TH STREET
12TH STREET
11TH STREET
CHESTNUT STREET
CHANCELLOR ST
St Mark's Episcopal Church
SYDENHAM ST
15TH STREET
BROAD STREET
Thomas Jefferson University Hospital
SANSOM STREET
17TH STREET
15th-16th Street
Walnut-Locust
3
LATIMER STREET
Academy of Music
Thomas Jefferson University
WALNUT STRE
12th-13th Street
BACH PL
Library Company of Philadelphia
LOCUST STREET
9th-10th Street
STREET
SMEDLEY ST
Kimmel Center for the Performing Arts
HUTCHINSON ST
DARIEN
SPRUCE STREET
DELANCEY PL
CYPRESS STREET
SPRUCE STREET
MIKVEH ISRAEL CEMETERY
MANN
16TH STREET
PINE STREET
JUNIPER STREET
CAMAC STREET
CYPRESS STREET
WAVERLY ST
University of the Arts
QUINCE STREET
CLINTON STREET
9TH STREET
Pennsylva Hospital
LOMBARD STREET
Lombard-South
Antique Row
PINE STREET
Suzanne Roberts Theatre
NAUDAIN STREET
WAVERLY STREET
RODMAN ST
SOUTH STREET
RODMAN STREET
LOMBARD STREET
4
WASHINGTO
SEGER PLAYGROUND
SQUARE WES
KATER STREET
Philadelphia Arts Bank
BAINBRIDGE STREET
JUNIPER ST
13TH STREET
SOUTH STREET
RODMAN STR
12TH STREET
DELHI ST
PERCY ST
STREET
16TH STREET
MOLE ST
HICKS ST
15TH STREET
FITZWATER STREET
BAINBRIDGE STREET
KATER STR
ALDER
SCHELL
ROSEWOOD ST
BROAD STREET
SARTAIN STREET
MARVINE STREET
JESSUP STREET
11TH STREET
CLIFTON STREET
WARNOCK STREET
PALUMBO PLAYGROUND
FITZWATER STREET
PEMBERTON STR
WEBSTER STREET
CATHARINE STREET
CHRISTIAN STREET
WEBSTER STREET
DELHI STREET
HUTCHINSON ST
PERCY STREET
MILDRED STREET
8TH STREET
CLYMER ST
MONTROSE STREET
10TH STREET
9TH STREET
7TH STREET
CITY PARK
5
CARPENTER STREET
MONTROSE STREET
CHRISTIAN STREET
KIMBALL STREET
HALL ST
WASHINGTON AVENUE
CARPENTER STREET
MONTROSE STREET
KIMBELL STREET
ELLSWORTH ST
ALTER STREET
PASSYUN

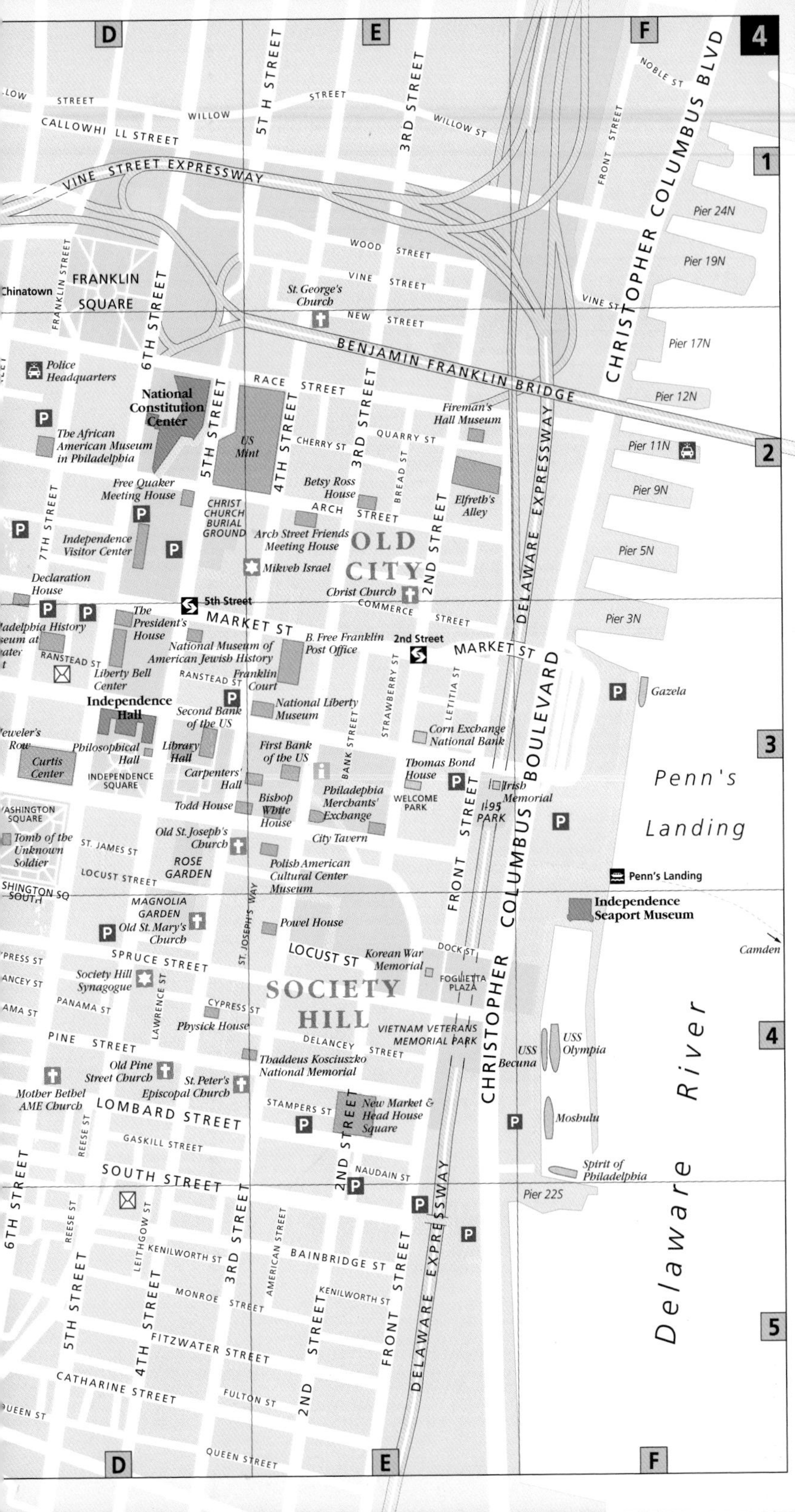

D
E
F
4
1
2
3
4
5
CALLOWHILL STREET
WILLOW STREET
VINE STREET EXPRESSWAY
5TH STREET
3RD STREET
WILLOW ST
NOBLE ST
FRONT STREET
CHRISTOPHER COLUMBUS BLVD
Pier 24N
Pier 19N
Pier 17N
Pier 12N
Pier 11N
Pier 9N
Pier 5N
Pier 3N
WOOD STREET
VINE STREET
VINE ST
NEW STREET
St. George's Church
Chinatown
FRANKLIN SQUARE
FRANKLIN STREET
6TH STREET
BENJAMIN FRANKLIN BRIDGE
Police Headquarters
National Constitution Center
RACE STREET
The African American Museum in Philadelphia
US Mint
CHERRY ST
QUARRY ST
Fireman's Hall Museum
4TH STREET
BREAD ST
DELAWARE EXPRESSWAY
Free Quaker Meeting House
CHRIST CHURCH BURIAL GROUND
Betsy Ross House
ARCH STREET
Elfreth's Alley
7TH STREET
Independence Visitor Center
Arch Street Friends Meeting House
OLD CITY
2ND STREET
Mikveh Israel
Declaration House
Christ Church
COMMERCE STREET
5th Street
The President's House
MARKET ST
B. Free Franklin Post Office
2nd Street
National Museum of American Jewish History
RANSTEAD ST
Liberty Bell Center
Franklin Court
STRAWBERRY ST
LETITIA ST
BOULEVARD
Gazela
Independence Hall
Second Bank of the US
National Liberty Museum
BANK STREET
Corn Exchange National Bank
Philosophical Hall
Library Hall
First Bank of the US
Curtis Center
INDEPENDENCE SQUARE
Carpenters' Hall
Thomas Bond House
Irish Memorial
Penn's Landing
Todd House
Bishop White House
Philadelphia Merchants' Exchange
WELCOME PARK
I-95 PARK
Tomb of the Unknown Soldier
ST. JAMES ST
Old St. Joseph's Church
City Tavern
ROSE GARDEN
Polish American Cultural Center Museum
LOCUST STREET
COLUMBUS
Penn's Landing
Independence Seaport Museum
MAGNOLIA GARDEN
Old St. Mary's Church
ST. JOSEPH'S WAY
Powel House
SPRUCE STREET
LOCUST ST
Korean War Memorial
DOCK ST
Camden
Society Hill Synagogue
LAWRENCE ST
SOCIETY HILL
FOGLIETTA PLAZA
PANAMA ST
CYPRESS ST
Physick House
VIETNAM VETERANS MEMORIAL PARK
CHRISTOPHER
PINE STREET
DELANCEY STREET
USS Becuna
USS Olympia
Old Pine Street Church
Thaddeus Kosciuszko National Memorial
Delaware River
Mother Bethel AME Church
St. Peter's Episcopal Church
LOMBARD STREET
STAMPERS ST
New Market & Head House Square
Moshulu
REESE ST
GASKILL STREET
SOUTH STREET
NAUDAIN ST
Spirit of Philadelphia
Pier 22S
DELAWARE EXPRESSWAY
LEITHGOW ST
KENILWORTH ST
AMERICAN STREET
BAINBRIDGE ST
MONROE STREET
KENILWORTH ST
FRONT STREET
FITZWATER STREET
CATHARINE STREET
FULTON ST
QUEEN STREET
QUEEN ST

General Index

Page numbers in **bold type** refer to main entries.

N

Q

R

S

Acknowledgments

Main Contributor

Richard Varr spent a part of his childhood in Philadelphia and returned to the area in 1999. A former television and newspaper reporter, he now writes for newspapers, magazines, and websites, including Porthole Cruise Magazine and onboard publications of several cruise lines.

Factchecker

Scott Walker

Proofreader

Word-by-Word

Indexer

Jyoti Dhar

DK London

Publisher Douglas Amrine
Publishing Manager Lucinda Cooke
Managing Art Editor Kate Poole
Senior Designer Tessa Bindloss
Senior Cartographic Editor Casper Morris
Senior DTP Designer Jason Little
Dk Picture Library Martin Copeland, Romaine Werblow
Production Controller Louise Daly
Revisions Team Beverley Ager, Emma Anacootee, Shruti Bahl, Julie Bond, Andi Coyle, Emer FitzGerald, Anna Freiberger, Rhiannon Furbear, Camilla Gersh, Vinod Harish, Phil Hunt, Sumita Khatwani, Hayley Maher, Sonal Modha, Helen Peters, Marianne Petrou, Jeanette Pierce, Arun Pottirayil, Rada Radojicic, Ellen Root, Azeem A. Siddiqui, Beverly Smart, Jeanette Tallant, Jeffrey Towne, Helen Townsend, Ajay Verma, Ros Walford.

Additional Photography

Shaen Adey, Paul Bricknell, Geoff Dann, Steve Gorton, Dave King, Andrew Leyerle, Tim Mann, Ray Moller, Stephen Oliver, Ian O'Leary, Tim Ridley, Clive Streeter, Scott Suchman, Matthew Ward, Jerry Young.

Dorling Kindersley would like to thank the following people whose contributions and assistance have made the preparation of this book possible.

Cartography

Back Endpaper reproduced with permission from SEPTA.

Special Assistance

The Barnes Foundation: Henry Butler; Independence National Historical Park: Superintendent; Gettysburg Convention & Visitors Bureau: Stacey Fox; Greater Philadelphia Tourism Marketing Corporation: Paula Butler, Kristen Ciappa, Meryl Levitz, Cara Schneider, Donna Schorr; National Liberty Museum: Amanda Hall; Pennsylvania Convention Center Authority: Patti Spaniak; Pennsylvania Dutch Convention & Visitors Bureau: Cara O'Donnell; Philadelphia Academy of the Fine Arts: Laura Blumenthal, Gene Castellano, Robert Cozzolino, Barbara Katus, Michelle McCaffrey; Philadelphia Convention & Visitors Bureau: Ellen Kornfield, Marissa Phillip; Philadelphia Museum of Art: Holly Frisbee, Rachel Udell; Philadelphia Water Department: Ed Grusheski; Rodin Museum: John Zarobell.

Photography Permissions

Dorling Kindersley would like to thank the following for their assistance and permission to photograph at their establishments:

Academy of Natural Sciences, Atwater Kent Museum, Bishop White House, City Tavern, College of Physicians of Philadelphia/Mütter Museum, Civil War & Underground Railroad Museum of Philadelphia, Eastern State Penitentiary, Ebenezer Maxwell House, Confederate Memorial Hall, New Orleans, Gettysburg National Military Park Visitor Center and Cyclorama Center, Independence Hall, Independence Seaport Museum, Landis Valley Museum, National Constitutional Center, Pennyslvania Academy of the Fine Arts, People's Place Quilt Museum, Reading Terminal Market as well as all the state and national parks, churches, hotels, restaurants, shops, museums, galleries, and other sights too numerous to thank individually.

Picture Credits

a – above; b – below/bottom; c – center; f – far; l – left; r – right; t – top

Works of art have been reproduced with the permission of the following copyright holders:

© ARS, NY and DACS, London 2011 84b, *Irish Memorial* by Glenna Goodacre 104cr, *Frank Rizzo* by Diane Keller 99br, *Horticulture Mural* by David McShane 89bc, *L'Ouverture* by Ulrick Jean Pierre 51tc, Cover of *The Saturday Evening Post* (June 28, 1958) by Norman Rockwell 27ca.

The publishers would like to thank the following individuals, companies, and picture libraries for their kind permission to reproduce their photographs:

ALAMY IMAGES: Bernie Epstein 115t; Jeff Greenberg 115bl; Andre Jenny 42tl, 100b; Dennis MacDonald 144cla; Mira 183br; vario images GmbH & Co. KG/ Hady Khandani 177cl.
Photograph ©2010 reproduced with the Permisson of THE BARNES FOUNDATION: 25cra, Tom Crane 26cb, 86bc, 86tr, 87bl, 87tl. BRIDGEMAN ART LIBRARY: © The Barnes Foundation, Merion, Pennsylvania, USA *Postman* 1889 (oil on canvas) by Vincent van Gogh (1853–90) 86tr; *Gardanne* 1885–86 (oil on canvas) by Paul Cezanne (1839–1906) 86cl; *After the Concert* 1877 (oil on canvas) by Pierre-Auguste Renoir (1841–1919) 87cra; *Card Players and Girl* 1890–92 (oil on canvas) by Paul Cezanne (1839–1906) 87crb.
CENTER CITY DISTRICT: 187tl; CLIVEDEN (A NATIONAL TRUST PROPERTY): 21cra, 107br. CHRIS'S JAZZ CAFÉ: 166BL; CITY TAVERN RESTAURANT: 143br; CORBIS: 9 (inset), 13tl, 18t, 20tr, 21cr, 22crb, 23t, 33bc, 37 (inset), 38, 83cra, 111(inset), 173(inset), 185b, 189tl; The Barnes Foundation, Merion Station, Pennsylvania 83c; Dave

Bartuff 39t, 40tr; Bettmann 8–9, 17ca, 17bl, 19ca, 19crb, 19bc, 21tl, 21br, 22t, 22bl, 22br, 23bc, 40cla, 53br, 131(inset); Kevin Fleming 94; Rose Hartman 61br; Robert Holmes 36–37; Kelly-Mooney Photography 127b; Bob Krist 2tr, 80; 68, 172-3, 188bl; Francis G. Mayer 16, 20-21c, 63br, Mary Ann McDonald 115crb; Charles O'Rear 46b; Philadelphia Museum of Art: *Peaceable Kingdom* by Edward Hicks (1780–1849) 18crb, 90tr, *Sunflowers* by Vincent van Gogh (1853–90) 90cl, 91cla, *Dormition of the Virgin* (1427) by Fra Angelico (1387-1455) 92cl, *Jester Vase* (1894) by Marc-Louis-Emmanuel Solon (1835-1913) Joseph E. Temple Fund 92bc, *The Staircase Group* (1795) by Charles Willson Peale (1741-1827) The George W. Elkins Collection 92br; 93tl, *Bird Tree* (1800–1830) Bequest of Lisa Norris Elkins (Mrs. William M. Elkins) 93c, *Gala Ensemble* Italy (late 19th to early 20th century) Bequest of Helen P. McMullen 93b; PictureNet 113 tr; Poodles-Rock 20cl, 20br; Bill Ross 2–3, 127t; Joseph Sohm: Visions of America 21crb, 42bl, 48c; Joseph Sohm- ChromoSohm Inc. 43cla; David H. Wells 83br, 102. CORBIS SABA: Erik Freeland 23crb; CVS/PHARMACY: 176br.
DREAMSTIME.COM: Richard Guinon 123br.
FAIRMOUNT WATERWORKS & INTERPRETIVE CENTER: 171bl
FLEISCHMAN GERBER AND ASSOCIATES: Esto/Peter Aaron 77br; THE FOOD TRUST: 175bc; FREE LIBRARY OF PHILADELPHIA: 18bl, 19br, 21bc.
GETTYSBURG CONVENTION & VISITORS BUREAU: Paul Witt 123cl. GREATER PHILADELPHIA TOURISM MARKETING CORPORATION: 133bl, 174tc; R.Kennedy 44cra; C. Ridgeway 25ca; GREYHOUND LINES, INC.: 185tl.
ING DIRECT – PHILADELPHIA CAFÉ: 180bl.
LEONARDO MEDIA LTD.: 133tl
MASTERFILE: David Zimmerman 110–111.
NATIONAL CONSTITUTION CENTER: 48tr. NATIONAL MUSEUM OF AMERICAN JEWISH HISTORY: 27cr, 41t.
PENNSYLVANIA ACADEMY OF THE FINE ARTS: 27tl, 74tr, 75cra, 75crb, *The Cello Player* (1896) by Thomas Eakins Oil on canvas. 64 1/4 x 48 1/8 inches. Accession no:1897.3. Joseph E. Temple Fund 74cl, *The Fox Hunt* by Winslow Homer Oil on canvas. 38 x 68 1/2 inches. Accession no: 1894.4. Joseph E. Temple Fund 74br, *Pantocrator* (2002) Oil on linen (triptych) 87 7/8 x 193 3/4 inches. Accession no: 2033.7.a-c by Vincent Desiderio 75tl. PENNYSLAVANIA DUTCH CONVENTION & VISITORS BUREAU: 11br, 34cla, 112b, 118b; K. Baum 113b; THE PENNSYLVANIA TURNPIKE COMMISSION: 189tl; PHILADELPHIA CONVENTION & VISITORS BUREAU: ©Alma de Cuba PR 166c; ©Barnes Foundation 25cra; ©Bob Krist 14tr; ©Camden Riversharks Baseball/David Brady 169t; ©Cuba Libre Restaurant & Rum Bar/Mimi Janosy 142br; Melvin Epps 58cl; © Independence Seaport Museum/Rusty Kennedy 65cra; ©The Inn at the Union League of Philadelphia 70tr; ©National Constitution Center/Scott Frances Ltd. 25cb, 40cl, 48bl, 49tl, 49cr; Jim McWilliams 32cla, 34br, 168b, 170b, 184t; ©Pennyslavania Academy of the Fine Arts/Rick Echelmeyer 24; ©Pennyslavania Ballet/Steve Belkowitz 164c; ©Pennyslavania Horticultural Society/Rob Ikeler 32br; Jon Perlmutter 30cla; ©Philadelphia International Airport/ Richard McMullin 182b; ©Philadelphia Office of the City Representative 33cra; ©Philadelphia Orchestra/Eric Sellen 162b; ©The Plaza and The Court at King of Prussia 155b; ©Ritz Carlton, Philadelphia 132b; Edward Savaria Jr. 10tc, 25bl, 35cla, 35br, 46c, 70cl, 70b, 71crb, 101b, 142cl, 143tl, 158tr, 160cla, 163tl, 170cla; 190tc Anthony Sinagoga 41crb, 44cl, 158bl ©Valley Forge Convention & Visitors Bureau 170t; ©Westin Philadelphia 132t; PHILADELPHIA MUSEUM OF ART, PENNSYLVANIA: 91cra, Portrait of Dr. Samuel D. Gross (The Gross Clinic) (1875) by Thomas Eakins. Gift of the Alumni Association to Jefferson Medical College in 1878 and purchased by the Pennsylvania Academy of the Fine Arts and The Philadelphia Museum of Art in 2007 with the generous support of some 3,600 donors 91bl; Noah's Ark (1846) by Edward Hicks, Bequest of Lisa Norris Elkins, 1950 91crb; PHILADELPHIA POLICE DEPARTMENT OFFICE OF MEDIA RELATIONS: 177cla, 177tl; PHILLIES: 32tc; PHOTOLIBRARY: Mark & Audrey Gibson 186br; PNC FINANCIAL SERVICES GROUP: 178cla; PURE: 167tr.
STA TRAVEL GROUP: 175clb.
U.S. AIRWAYS: 182tc.
RICHARD VARR: 43cr.
WYK HOUSE AND GARDEN: 106t.

Front endpaper: All special photography except CORBIS : cr, Kevin Fleming tr, Bob Krist tl; MASTERFILE: David Zimmerman cl.

JACKET:
Front - PHOTOLIBRARY: JTB Photo.
Back - ALAMY IMAGES: Mike Booth bl; Lee Foster cl; Andre Jenny cla; CORBIS: Bob Krist tl.
Spine - PHOTOLIBRARY: JTB Photo t.

SEPTA Regional Rail & Rail Transit

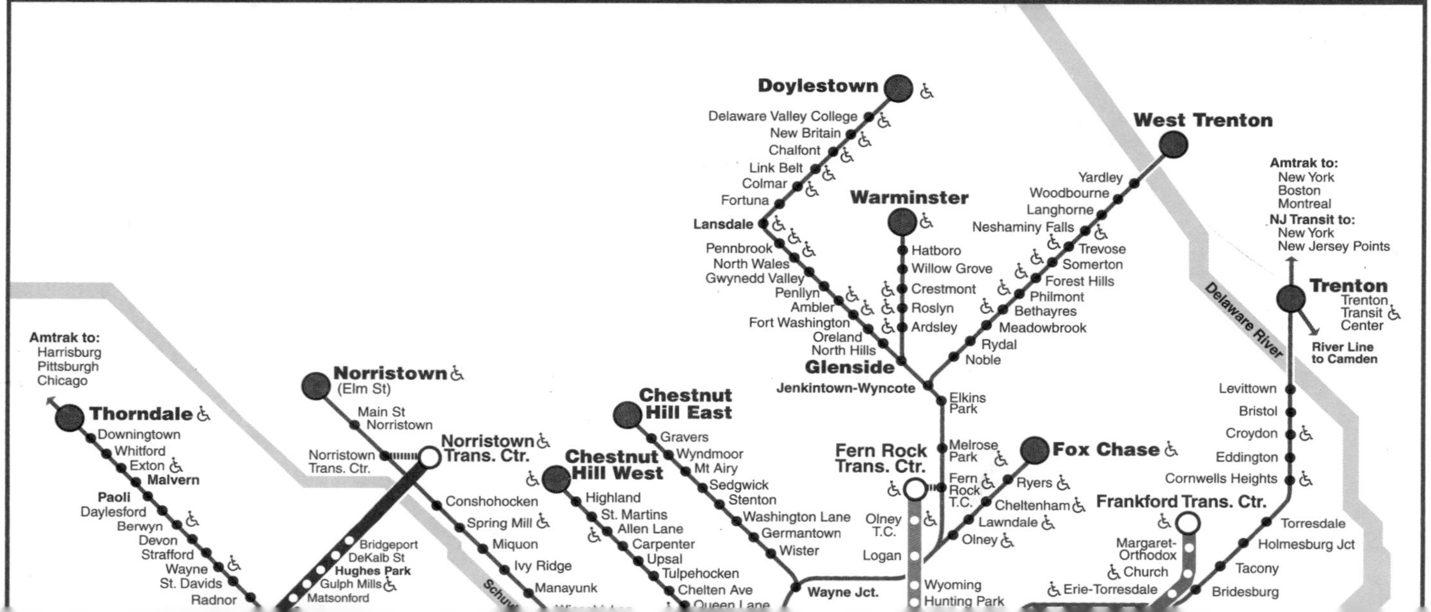

Doylestown
Delaware Valley College
New Britain
Chalfont
Link Belt
Colmar
Fortuna
Lansdale
Pennbrook
North Wales
Gwynedd Valley
Penllyn
Ambler
Fort Washington
Oreland
North Hills
Glenside
Jenkintown-Wyncote

Warminster
Hatboro
Willow Grove
Crestmont
Roslyn
Ardsley

West Trenton
Yardley
Woodbourne
Langhorne
Neshaminy Falls
Trevose
Somerton
Forest Hills
Philmont
Bethayres
Meadowbrook
Rydal
Noble
Elkins Park
Melrose Park
Fern Rock T.C.

Amtrak to:
New York
Boston
Montreal
NJ Transit to:
New York
New Jersey Points

Trenton
Trenton Transit Center
River Line to Camden
Delaware River
Levittown
Bristol
Croydon
Eddington
Cornwells Heights
Torresdale
Holmesburg Jct
Tacony
Bridesburg

Fox Chase
Ryers
Cheltenham
Lawndale
Olney

Fern Rock Trans. Ctr.
Olney T.C.
Logan
Wyoming
Hunting Park

Frankford Trans. Ctr.
Margaret-Orthodox
Church
Erie-Torresdale

Amtrak to:
Harrisburg
Pittsburgh
Chicago

Thorndale
Downingtown
Whitford
Exton
Malvern
Paoli
Daylesford
Berwyn
Devon
Strafford
Wayne
St. Davids
Radnor

Norristown (Elm St)
Main St Norristown
Norristown Trans. Ctr.
Norristown Trans. Ctr.
Bridgeport
DeKalb St
Hughes Park
Gulph Mills
Matsonford

Conshohocken
Spring Mill
Miquon
Ivy Ridge
Manayunk

Chestnut Hill East
Gravers
Wyndmoor
Mt Airy
Sedgwick
Stenton
Washington Lane
Germantown
Wister
Wayne Jct.

Chestnut Hill West
Highland
St. Martins
Allen Lane
Carpenter
Upsal
Tulpehocken
Chelten Ave
Queen Lane